WORKING AMERICANS
1880–2012

Volume I: The Working Class
Second Edition

WORKING AMERICANS
1880–2012

Volume I: The Working Class
Second Edition

by Scott Derks

Grey House
Publishing

PUBLISHER: Leslie Mackenzie
EDITORIAL DIRECTOR: Laura Mars
ASSOCIATE EDITOR: Diana Delgado
PRODUCTION MANAGER: Kristen Thatcher
MARKETING DIRECTOR: Jessica Moody
AUTHOR: Scott Derks
CONTRIBUTORS: Jael Bridgemahon, Marshall Derks, Ellen Hanckel
COPYEDITOR: Elaine Alibrandi

Grey House Publishing, Inc.
4919 Route 22
Amenia, NY 12501
518.789.8700 FAX 845.373.6390
www.greyhouse.com
e-mail: books@greyhouse.com

Publisher's Cataloging-In-Publication Data
(Prepared by The Donohue Group, Inc.)

Derks, Scott.
    Working Americans ... / by Scott Derks. -- 2nd ed.

    v. : ill. ; cm.

    Date range in the title varies.
    1st ed. published in 2000.
    Content: V. 1. The working class [1880-2012]
    Includes bibliographical references and indexes.
    ISBN: 978-1-59237-564-6 (v. 1)

    1. Working class--United States--History. 2. Labor--United States--History. 3. Occupations--United States--History. 4. Social classes--United States--History. 5. Immigrants--Employment--United States--History.

HD8066 .D47 2012
305.5/0973/0904

TABLE OF CONTENTS

INTRODUCTION

The first edition of *Working Americans 1880-1999 Volume I: The Working Class* marked the beginning of a widely acclaimed series that now includes 12 volumes. Each volume portrays, decade by decade, a different group of working Americans -- middle and upper classes, children, women, activists, athletes, armed forces, entrepreneurs, and most recently, musicians. These volumes show, through historical documents and personal stories, how Americans worked, where they lived, what they bought, and how they kicked backed. Each profile is supported by material covering the society and history that shaped their choices and decisions.

This second edition of volume I takes another look at America's working class, bringing the story into the 21st century. In the 12 years since the first edition, America has gone through a number of historic events, including the 9.11 terrorist attack, the 2008 economic crisis, America's first African American President, and $4.00/gallon gasoline. *Working Americans 1880-2012 Volume I: The Working Class, Second Edition* follows the survival of America's working class through such major events, into 2012.

New Content

With six brand **new chapters** that cover 2000-2012, **new currency conversion charts** for all chapters that show, for example, that a comic book that cost .10 in 1939 would cost about $1.57 in 2010, and a **new comprehensive index** (that was sorely missed in the first edition) this is truly a second edition whose time has come.

Over the years, the *Working American* series has become a favorite supplement to school curricula around the country, used in social studies, history, economic and mathematics classrooms. All the chapters in these reference books have been carefully designed to enhance understanding of the growth and development of the working class over 132 years. This volume begins in the late 1800s, at a time when jobs were shifting from the agrarian to the industrial sector. The late nineteenth century also saw more records kept and more statistics gathered, which provided a wealth of archives from which to draw original material. From the many government surveys, social worker histories, economic data, family diaries and letters, newspaper and magazine features and many, many first hand interviews, this unique reference assembles a remarkably personal and realistic look at the lives of ordinary working Americans.

Personal Profiles

Chapters in *Working Americans* each cover a decade, except those that open and close the work.

Each chapter begins with a detailed overview that anchors the profiles with a historical summary; the overview is also where you will find the currency conversion charts. Following the overview are three different family profiles that are arranged by Life at Home, Life at Work, and Life in the Community sections. This material is bulleted for easy reading. Lots of images break up the text and bring the subject alive.

This second edition includes 40 personal profiles. Although these are all based on actual, documented families, real names are not used in most cases. The profiles comprise 28 different occupations, represent 16 ethnic groups, and travel over 22 states. These pages take you:

■ Into the home of thrifty Portuguese 1882 potato farmers;
■ To dinner with a worried Detroit auto worker in 1930, who lived through the 1929 stock market;
■ On a climb to the top of telephone lineman's payscale at $3,880 in 1950;
■ With a Mexican immigrant to his English lessons in 1981, necessary to keep his factory job;
■ Into the restaurant of a waitress whose excellent tips dried up after 9.11.01;
■ On the phone with a young telemarketer in 2005 as she sells diabetic supplies;
■ Next to a 50-year-old Virginian who lost her job as a box maker in 2012.

Economic Profiles

Following the personal profiles are economic profiles. This section includes statistical comparisons designed to put each family's lifestyle and key decisions into perspective. You will find charts that include the average wages of various professions during a specific year, a selection of prices for typical goods and services, and significant events and inventions of the time. Chapters also examine important issues faced by the family, such as how they coped with war, the depression, outsourced jobs, or a bad housing market.

Current Events and Images

In addition to personal and economic data, each profile is further enriched by a Historical Snapshot, listing significant cultural, political and social events of the profiled year, and actual magazine and newspaper articles of the day.

Plus, readers will find more than 15 images per profile – more than 600 total – ranging from original photographs, advertisements, campaign buttons, war posters, postcards, etc. The many sources that were used to compile this detailed reference work are detailed at the back of the book.

This second edition of *Working Americans 1880-2012 Volume I: The Working Class* is also available as an ebook. Visit www.greyhouse.com for more information.

Preface

This book grew out of a myth. Every generation provides a certain level of romance to the time gone by, gilding those bygone eras with a gentleness they often did not deserve. Several years ago, I heard a man on the radio ruminating about the good old days of yesterday. He chuckled about the pleasures of turn of the century life, recalling picnics and crimeless streets and his family's first outing in an automobile in 1905. He was, of course, remembering the vanished good old days of the rich, and a romanticized history at that. Few of us—at least statistically—can lay claim to a background of Rockefeller wealth and privilege. These chapters are the stories of ordinary people, determined to get through the day.

For most of us, our journey to America began in the bottom—not the top—of the ship. Our legacy was written by people who calculated their income in pennies or, at best, dollars, not thousands of dollars. This book is about these people.

History is often framed in the words of politicians or a vision of big events. For all of us who learned about wars and elections and heroic flights across the Atlantic, dozens are left to wonder about the role our families played in the building of the United States—both economically and socially.

For me, preparing the second edition of Working Americas has been like visiting an old friend. Originally authored a dozen years ago, this new volume retains the intimate examination of working class lives, while spreading a little soothing medicine on some aging muscles. This time, an index has been added to aid researchers, financial conversion charts allow the reader put pricing decisions into a modern day perspective and six new chapters capture the economic turbulence of the first twelve years of the new century. The new material clearly documents the traumas and joys experienced by Americans struggling to find a job or to keep the one they've got. *Working Americans 1880–2012 Volume 1: The Working Class*, second edition, examines the economic and social lives of 40 families.

Each profile details the earnings of a working class family, how they spent their money and what they did with their time both at work and at home. It is economics and social history at its most revealing. We see families from the country work through the complex issues of whether to buy a car, shoes for the children or take a vacation—a concept virtually unknown during most of the first half of the twentieth century.

Using the real dollar expenditures of actual families, this book captures single snapshots of time: the willingness of a Russian steelworker in 1910 to work beyond the normal 12hour-a-day shift to earn enough money to bring his intended bride to America; the decision of a 1892

Georgia couple between steady textile paychecks and the freedom of farming; or the pathos of a Tennessee man's church prayer in the early 1940s, "Brothers and sisters, I want to tell you this. The greatest thing on earth is to have the love of God in your heart, and the next greatest thing is to have electricity in your house."

Each profile is different, just as each family is different. None of us are average and neither were our ancestors. Some profiles intensely study the family's economic life at home, detailing nearly every expenditure during the year, including, as in our 1930 profile, every piece of clothing purchased by every member of the family. Other profiles focus on life at work such as pressures faced by the African-American family living in Harlem during the depths of the depression. Fascinating portraits appear: the Polish tailor in 1907 who buys the cheaper "loose milk" rather than the coming rage of bottled milk; the "club life" of Cuban cigar makers in Ybor City, Florida in 1912; or the desire of a Chicago candy maker to leave work early on Wednesday evenings as a break from a 92 1/2-hour work week.

Working Americans is about the issues that would have been discussed at the end of a long, long day. That's why money, what folks made, and how people spent their cash is emphasized. It's part of that dinner conversation: more potatoes meant things were not going well; meat said they were. New clothes for school sometimes required that lunches consist of soup and bread. Buying a radio was a big deal that was discussed for months and then purchased through an installment plan.

Beyond simply describing economic life, *Working Americans* opens a window onto families experiencing change: the Virginia farm family in the 1920s who, with the invention of affordable automobiles, could choose a church not based on distance; or the life of a woman supporting her family in 1923 while her husband looked for work; or the Norwegian family in the 1880s who were finding the weather of Iowa severe and daunting. *Working Americans* looks at the lives of Portuguese sweet potato farmers, new Mexican immigrants to California in the last two decades of the 20th century, and the struggles of a 60-year old South Carolina printer who must choose between his job and caring for his invalid wife.

Many of the families' day to day lives were touched by traumatic events. For instance, the Filipino family who worked at Hickam Air Base, Hawaii, in the months following the Japanese bombing in 1941, and were forced to endure a life full of blackouts, restrictions on fishing. and the question of Japanese loyalty—an ethnic group that composed one third of the island's population. Or consider the story of an African American family who lived and worked in Memphis in 1968, the same year Martin Luther King, Jr. was shot and killed in that city.

You will find, I believe, that the good old days were not as good as some memories recall, nor as different as we would like to think. The newspapers and magazines were full of tragedies and wide-ranging discussions of issues that seem as fresh as today: smoking, immigration, dating, and concerns about children and the marrying age. We find that in the 1920s, educators were concerned that children no longer knew how to play children's games without instruction, so they issued a booklet designed to teach children how to play schoolyard games.

I hope, ultimately, this is the story of each of us. Most of our ancestors arrived in this country crowded into steerage class. A ten and twelve hour day was our legacy. What we have today was built upon the ideas, energy, and efforts of millions. By necessity, the history books only recognize those who made millions, not about the millions who made it happen. This is their story—not the story of the little people—the story of *Working Americans*.

Scott Derks

The Value of a Dollar, 1860-2010

Over time, historians and economists have studied the value of money and how it relates to human events. This allows us to comprehend how changing monetary values influence economic and cultural events, not just on the national level, but also on the individual level. Economic information offers insights into economic trends, allowing economists to anticipate events that may occur in the future, especially as they relate to financial markets. Historians utilize this data to gain insights on political and cultural trends.

By employing indexes based upon consumer expenditures, economists and historians can look back and compare monetary trends over periods of time. If we know that a comic book was worth 10 cents in 1939, for example, we can use the 2010 Consumer Price Index on the following page to calculate that this comic book would have cost approximately $1.57 in 2010.

The 13 conversion tables in this edition use this method. There is one for each decade discussed, and they are located directly before the decade introductions. These conversion tables focus on the material presented in the "Family Profile" sections of this edition, so not all years are included.

The United States government did not focus on actual inflation rates and indexing consumer pricing until the twentieth century. During World War I, prices were rising rapidly, especially in shipbuilding centers in the United States. It was during this period that the federal government started compiling an index essential for calculating cost-of-living adjustments in wages. This work began in earnest around 1917, but the government developed estimated indexes as early as 1913. This information is compiled today by the U.S. Department of Labor under the Bureau of Labor Statistics.

Since limited information was available prior to 1913, this edition uses an alternative index, based upon John J. McCusker's principal of determining the value of money, for the pre-1913 tables and dollar information. Therefore, tables in this book expressing values prior to 1913 are approximations, and comparison 2010 dollars should be rounded up to the nearest tenth. For example, if a solid oak high-back chair cost $1.00 in 1880, and the conversion table shows the value in 2010 dollars to be $21.28, it is conservative to say that this chair would have cost approximately $30.00 in 2010.

Charts with data close to 1913 used the Consumer Price Index developed by the United States Federal Reserve and provide a more accurate comparison of actual dollars in 2010. Government indexes for the year 2011 were unavailable for estimated forecasts at press time.

Composite Consumer Price Index 2010=1

Year	Amount	Year	Amount	Year	Amount	Year	Amount
1860	$26.32	1898	$26.32	1936	$15.69	1974	$4.42
1861	$25.00	1899	$26.32	1937	$15.15	1975	$4.05
1862	$21.74	1900	$25.64	1938	$15.47	1976	$3.83
1863	$17.24	1901	$25.64	1939	$15.69	1977	$3.60
1864	$13.89	1902	$25.64	1940	$15.58	1978	$3.35
1865	$13.33	1903	$25.00	1941	$14.84	1979	$3.00
1866	$13.70	1904	$24.39	1942	$13.38	1980	$2.65
1867	$14.71	1905	$25.00	1943	$12.61	1981	$2.40
1868	$15.38	1906	$24.39	1944	$12.39	1982	$2.26
1869	$16.13	1907	$23.26	1945	$12.12	1983	$2.19
1870	$16.67	1908	$23.81	1946	$11.18	1984	$2.10
1871	$17.86	1909	$23.81	1947	$9.78	1985	$2.03
1872	$17.86	1910	$22.73	1948	$9.09	1986	$1.99
1873	$18.18	1911	$22.73	1949	$9.16	1987	$1.92
1874	$19.23	1912	$22.73	1950	$9.05	1988	$1.84
1875	$20.00	1913	$22.03	1951	$8.39	1989	$1.76
1876	$20.41	1914	$21.81	1952	$8.20	1990	$1.67
1877	$20.83	1915	$21.59	1953	$8.14	1991	$1.60
1878	$21.74	1916	$20.01	1954	$8.11	1992	$1.55
1879	$21.74	1917	$17.04	1955	$8.14	1993	$1.51
1880	$21.28	1918	$14.54	1956	$8.02	1994	$1.47
1881	$21.28	1919	$12.61	1957	$7.76	1995	$1.43
1882	$21.28	1920	$10.91	1958	$7.55	1996	$1.39
1883	$21.74	1921	$12.18	1959	$7.47	1997	$1.36
1884	$22.22	1922	$12.98	1960	$7.37	1998	$1.34
1885	$22.73	1923	$12.75	1961	$7.29	1999	$1.31
1886	$23.26	1924	$12.75	1962	$7.20	2000	$1.27
1887	$22.73	1925	$12.46	1963	$7.13	2001	$1.23
1888	$22.73	1926	$12.32	1964	$7.04	2002	$1.21
1889	$23.81	1927	$12.53	1965	$6.92	2003	$1.19
1890	$23.81	1928	$12.68	1966	$6.71	2004	$1.15
1891	$23.81	1929	$12.68	1967	$6.53	2005	$1.12
1892	$23.81	1930	$13.06	1968	$6.27	2006	$1.08
1893	$24.39	1931	$14.35	1969	$5.94	2007	$1.05
1894	$25.64	1932	$16.04	1970	$5.62	2008	$1.01
1895	$25.64	1933	$16.91	1971	$5.39	2009	$1.02
1896	$25.64	1934	$16.28	1972	$5.22	2010	$1.00
1897	$26.32	1935	$15.92	1973	$4.91		

For Ellen and her friend Merlin

The author wishes to thank Cheryl Quick for her editorial assistance and insight. Edna Horning provided critical research that was invaluable, and Marshall Derks added depth and energy to the process, gathering and substantially writing material for three chapters: 1930, 1935, and 1974. Ellen Hanckel also deserves thanks for tolerating the constant clicking of the keys and arcane revelations about life in times past. This work would have been poorer without the assistance of many friends who provided photographs, insight and information: Jim Nash, Jim McColl, Robert and Nancy Wirsing, Bill Marion, Sonny Howell, Maureen Boler, Sally Gaillard, Jan Brown, Rick Layman, Patricia Hankins and Ben and Adam Pace.

Value of One Dollar	
Year	Value in 2010 USD
1880	$21.28
1890	$23.81
1892	$23.81
1895	$25.64
1898	$26.32

Values are approximate based upon economic historical data and 2010 U. S. Dollar

1880–1899

The 20 years leading to the twentieth century were shaped by major change—the movement of people from farm to factory, the rapid expansion of wage labor, the explosive growth of cities and massive immigration. Nearly everywhere the economic and social life of the working class was changing rapidly. Farmers, merchants, and small-town artisans found themselves increasingly dependent on market forces and huge concentrations of power unprecedented in American history. The new emerging capitalist order was fast producing a continent where only a few were very rich and many were very poor. It was an economy on a roll with few rudders or regulations.

The most visible shift throughout America was the movement away from the land. Before the Civil War, the United States was overwhelmingly an agricultural nation. By the end of the century, nonagricultural occupations employed nearly two-thirds of the work force. As important, two of every three Americans came to rely on wages instead of self-employment as farmers or artisans. At the same time, industrial growth began to center around cities. Once manufacturers could use steam power instead of water power, they no longer had to locate their factories alongside rivers. Instead they built in urban areas where they had better access to railroads, raw materials, consumer markets, and a good supply of labor. The people followed factories into the cities, which grew at twice the rate as the nation as a whole. A modern, industrially-based work force emerged from the traditional farmlands of America, reshaping the U.S. economy and economic lives of its people. In 1890 newspaper editor Horace Greeley remarked, "We cannot all live in cities, yet nearly all seem determined to do so."

The new cities of America were home to great wealth and poverty; both produced by the massive migrations and influx of immigrants willing to work at any price. It was a time symbolized by Andrew Carnegie's steel mills, John D. Rockefeller's organization of the Standard Oil Monopoly and the manufacture of Alexander Graham Bell's wonderful invention, the telephone. By 1894 the United States had become the world's leading industrial power, producing more than England, France, and Germany, its three largest competitors, combined. For much of this period the nation's industrial energy focused on the need for railroads, requiring large quantities of labor, iron, steel, stone, and lumber. In 1883 nine-tenths of the nation's entire production of steel went into rails. The most important invention of the period—in an era of tremendous change and innovation—may have been the Bessemer converter, which transformed pig iron into steel at a relatively low cost—increasing steel output 10 times from 1877 to 1892.

The greatest economic event during the first two decades of the Nineteenth Century was the great wave of immigration that swept America. It is now believed to be the largest worldwide population movement in human history, bringing more than 10 million people to the United States to fill the expanding need for workers. In the 1880s alone, 5.25 million immigrants arrived, more than in the first six decades of the Nineteenth Century. This wave was dominated by Irish, German, and English workers. Scandinavia, Italy, and China sent scores of eager workers, normally men, to fill the expanding labor needs of the United States. To attract this much-needed labor force, railroad and steamship companies advertised throughout Europe and China the glories of American life. To an economically depressed world, it was a welcome call.

The national wealth in 1890 was $65 billion; nearly $40 billion was invested in land and buildings, $9 billion in railroads, and $4 billion in manufacturing and mining. By 1890, 25 percent of the world's output of coal was mined in the United States. Annual production of crude petroleum went from 500,000 barrels in 1860 to 63.6 million in 1900. This was more than the wealth of Great Britain, Russia, and Germany put together.

Despite all the signs of economic growth and prosperity, America's late-Nineteenth Century economy was profoundly unstable. Industrial expansion was undercut by a depression from 1882 to 1885, followed in 1893 by a five-year-long economic collapse that devastated rural and urban communities across America. As a result, job security for workers just climbing onto the industrial stage, was often fleeting. Few wage-earners found full-time work for the entire year. The unevenness in the economy was caused both by the level of change under way and irresponsible speculation, but more generally to the stubborn adherence of the federal government to a highly inflexible gold standard as the basis of value for currency.

Between the very wealthy and the very poor emerged a new middle stratum, whose appearance was one of the distinctive features of late-Nineteenth Century America. This new middle class fueled the purchase of one million light bulbs a year by 1890, even though the first electric light was only 11 years old. It was the middle class also that flocked to buy Royal Baking Powder, (which was easier to use and faster than yeast) and supported the emergence and spread of department stores that were sprouting up across the nation.

This group was largely composed of people of old American stock or immigrants from the British Isles who worked as either self-employed businessmen or at professional jobs. Merchant tailors, who once labored alongside their employees, began to dress more elegantly, received their customers in well-appointed shops, and hid the actual manufacturing process in a back room.

In the midst of these changes, working men and women began to embrace the idea of collectivity and the power of mutual, rather than individual, action to blunt the dramatic impact of industrial capitalism on their daily lives. Unions in a variety of forms emerged, along with energetic reform movements designed to blunt the social changes imposed by the capitalist fervor of the Age of Endeavor. Labor unions protested the abuse of workers. Factory workers, often treated as expendable extensions of the machines they operated, experienced long, 60-hour work weeks. Working conditions were often deplorable. Between 1880 and 1900 unions organized 23,000 strikes, sometimes violent, involving 6.5 million workers.

1880 Family Profile

This family of first-generation Norwegians—the Lundens—immigrated to Iowa to grow wheat and corn. They live in a close-knit community of fellow Norwegians who depend upon each other for support, labor and friendship. The father in this family of ten helps his neighbors read letters from home and also preaches in the community.

Life at Home

- The Lunden family leaves Norway in 1870 on a ship carrying 284 emigrants to North America. Their journey takes 49 days, or seven weeks. One immigrant child dies during the journey.
- The passengers bring a total of $6,300 with them when they arrive in Quebec, Canada.
- The Lundens include 11 persons: a 53-year-old grandmother, the father at age 30, wife at a similar age, two of his brothers, and two of his aunts and children. None speaks English.
- The trip to the farm requires a train ride to Detroit, Michigan. ("The speed of the train proved quite disturbing") and a boat trip to Milwaukee.
- The boat they use to reach Milwaukee had just arrived with a cargo of cattle. No effort is made to clean the boat before loading the human passengers for the return trip. "For a boatload of immigrants one could not be expected to provide first-class accommodations; at any rate none such were provided."
- The family moves into their new house, their third in Iowa in 1880. For the first time since they arrived in the United States in 1870, the family enjoy a wood-frame, two-story house, not a log home. The family has eight children at the time, seven of whom survive to maturity.
- Family responsibility is clearly divided. The cows and the hens, the milk, the butter, and the eggs lie within the mother's province. The farming of wheat is the father's.
- "She recognized the man as the head of the house, but only on the rarest instances did he oppose her will."
- She's described as being of "average build, though a little taller than most women." Her labor is hard and her days are long, "for the household was numerous and the duties to home and farm were becoming increasingly more insistent."

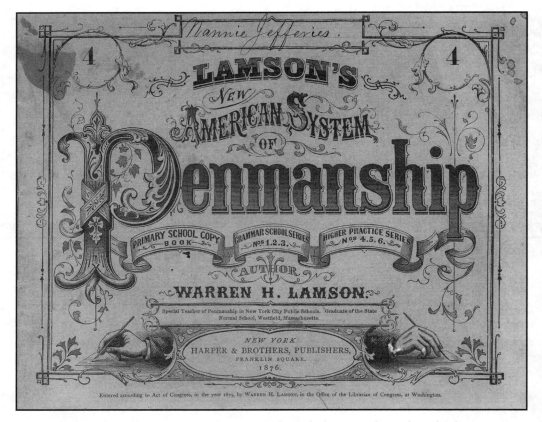

The mark of an educated person was quality penmanship, which was emphasized at school.

- The most important meal of the day is at noon. "In the evening the women of the farm had so many duties that they were able to serve only a simple supper."
- Meals often include potato mash and "something resembling American hasty pudding."
- Sunday afternoons include a gathering where very strong, Norwegian-strength coffee is served.
- In the fall, the family makes trips into the surrounding countryside to pick grapes, plums, cherries, and occasionally walnuts.
- Dried fruits can be purchased throughout the year including apples, peaches, currants, and raisins. Currants are occasionally served as a dessert but raisins are too expensive to be eaten often.
- Christmas is celebrated from December 23 to January 6 in Norwegian tradition; gifts are never exchanged, although the food served is the best the family can afford.
- The father often assists his neighbors in writing letters. "Most of our neighbors were industrious readers, but they did not trust themselves to write letters."
- He also serves as the unofficial notary for the settlement, especially when letters come from Norway. Latin and German are both still used in Norway and the father knows them both.
- Many of the homes have books, but they are nearly always religious in nature. Bunyan's *Pilgrim's Progress* is popular, along with German Pietists Philipp Jakob Spener and Hermann Francke.

- Almanacs published free by patent medicine makers such as Ayer's, Green's, or Hostetter's are popular reading material.
- Hostetter's contain amusing pictures; the medicine itself, Hostetter's Stomach Bitters, contains large amounts of alcohol and is widely sold, especially in prohibition territory.
- The family occasionally read a Chicago-based Norwegian newspaper; the older children who have learned to read English occasionally get their news from the *Chicago Tribune*.
- Norwegian is spoken within the family and throughout the community, but English is taught at school.
- Schools emphasize the ability to read and write, but the mark of an educated person is quality penmanship. Some schools use the Lamson's American System of Penmanship to teach penmanship.
- The family had become Lutheran after immigration, drawn by the faith's doctrine that the evidence of "conversion must and will appear in the daily conduct of a living Christian."

Demorest's Monthly Magazine, April 1873, "Domestic Warfare," by Molly Dolittle:

"Don't like roaches: do you? They took possession of our kitchen, because the Croton was handy, and they are thirsty little wretches, and I never could go in there of an evening without elevating my skirts, and treading about as gingerly as if there were eggs underfoot. Their patent-leather backs would crack as they scampered before my intruding feet, and yet I couldn't believe they were half as annoyed by my presence as I was by theirs. How to get rid of them, was a question more momentous to the Doolittle household than that of 'equal rights' or the 'Alabama Claims.' We baited them with ailanthus leaves and cucumber skins; had Mr. Knowles himself blown his non-explosive powder into their very citadels, and tried other and various experiments, but the results, though promising at first, did not answer our sanguinary expectations. The few carcasses we swept up were but a handful to the tribes that swarmed in pantries, fireplaces, and convenient corners. A few of the ambitious ones actually haunted our bed-rooms, and 'how they got there, we wondered.' Loose poisons we were afraid of, but finally the case became so alarming as to demand a desperate remedy, and having a small quantity of Paris green in the house, we put that in the bellows and blew it carefully into all the places where roaches most did congregate. The bellows, I suppose you are aware, has a tin box at the nozzle, with a slender pope through which the powder is blown in the direction required. Once doing encouraged us to continue this mode of assault, and now it is only necessary to repeat the dose twice a year, in the Spring and Fall, to escape a repeat of the dose twice a year."

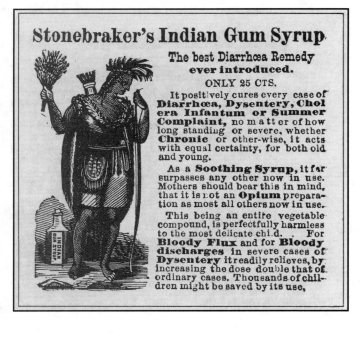

- The father does not believe in drinking, dancing, or card playing. Social relaxation is permitted on the Sabbath; unnecessary labor and noisy activities, such as baseball games, are not allowed. The mother is not as strict.
- The man also serves as a lay preacher in the community, as formalized services conducted by ordained ministers are rare in rural communities.
- The Lundens avoid visits to the doctor's office because of the language barrier; they prefer to visit the druggist who employs a Norwegian clerk so symptoms can be described to him and a solution prescribed.
- Recognizing the language problem, druggists in the community begin stocking and suggesting products Norwegians want such as oil of spike to help "morbid conditions" or Hoffman's Anodyne, a plaster designed to help rheumatism.
- The father votes Republican, as do most Scandinavians.

Life at Work: Farming

- The principle crops are corn and wheat, both of which are planted by hand using a mule and steel plow. Small children often follow the plow with the seed.
- The family also raise cows for milk and the making of butter.
- Tough strains of wheat, resistant to cold and drought, are imported from Russia for the western farmers.
- When the Norwegian newspaper out of Chicago advertises the Walter A. Wood self-binder machine for binding grain, it causes much excitement; binding with twine is an important advancement.
- Newspaper reports indicate that haying went well in 1880 with a heavy crop with a lower-than-usual proportion of clover. "The excessive rains of the past three or four weeks have overflowed some marshes and low meadows, which may prevent cutting upon them for some time yet."
- The speed of harvesting wheat is immensely increased in the 1880s by the combination reaper-thresher, known as a combine, which is drawn by 20 to 40 horses.
- Wild grass fires are an ever-present danger to the farmers on the plains. This usually means building a counter fire to control the danger.
- Farmers are also plagued with locusts, which form in huge swarms. "On clear days one could see them passing before the sun in darkening clouds. Where they alighted to feed nothing was left to harvest. The farmers tried to trap them in large pans of tin coated in tar."
- During periodic national depressions, the family experiences little change. "The country had no banks and no

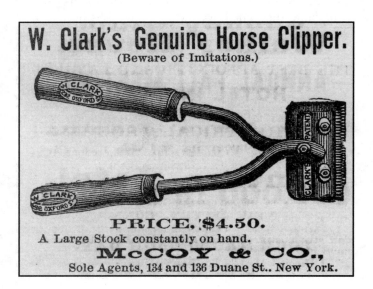

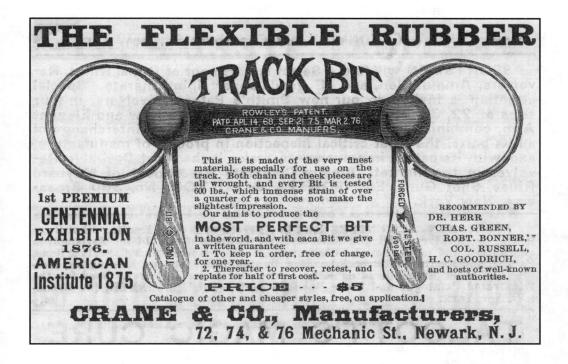
business establishments larger than small stores. There could be no failures where there was nothing to fail."

- When prices drop and money is hard to get, some men steal away from their debt-burdened farms by night, taking their mortgage chattels with them. "The Minnesota border was not more than a dozen or fifteen miles away, and when the line was crossed the fugitives were reasonably safe from the agents of the law."

Wheat farming dominated the economy of the community.

- The 1880 census shows that 24 percent of Iowa farmers are tenants; by the turn of the century 35 percent of all farmers are tenants.
- Barbed wire, the invention of Joseph F. Glidden, is a boon to homesteaders by reducing the expense of fencing in an almost timberless country; in 1883 Glidden's company is producing 600 miles of new barbed wire per day.

Life in the Community: Winnebago County, Iowa

- Winnebago County is in the northeastern corner of Iowa near the Mississippi River.
- Studies of immigrants suggest that early immigrants play a key role in attracting relatives and friends to the new country.
- Between 1877 and 1890, the new U.S. Postal money order system transfers an average of $2.3 million to Europe annually. Approximately 44 percent of the money is used for prepaid passage tickets to America.
- Most of the settlers to Winnebago County come across the ocean on steamers, which carry as many as 300 passengers in the cabin class and 1,500 in steerage, the level most immigrants can afford.
- Immigration is encouraged by steamship lines that employ agents in the major European cities to promote travel to the United States; the agents are paid on the number of tickets sold, not truth told.
- Many Norwegians find Winnebago County, Iowa, cold and trying, even though most had come came from farms in Norway that were 1,200 miles closer to the North Pole; the severity of the winters in Iowa is a disappointment to some.

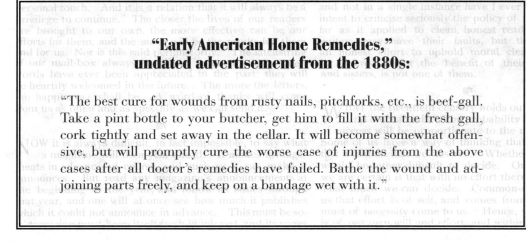

"Early American Home Remedies," undated advertisement from the 1880s:

"The best cure for wounds from rusty nails, pitchforks, etc., is beef-gall. Take a pint bottle to your butcher, get him to fill it with the fresh gall, cork tightly and set away in the cellar. It will become somewhat offensive, but will promptly cure the worse case of injuries from the above cases after all doctor's remedies have failed. Bathe the wound and adjoining parts freely, and keep on a bandage wet with it."

13220 "DRY GROWN" WHEAT

- In the 1870s the assurances of the real estate agents, officers of land-grant railroads, state officials, and immigration agents are right when they say that "rain will follow the plow"; this statement is less true in the 1880s as the cruel variability of the grassland climate shows itself.
- Norwegians who quickly take on American ways are often called "Norwegian Yankees."
- Most of the immigrant farmers are desperately poor and their daughters often find work as domestic helpers in nearby towns.

10417   A MISSISSIPPI RIVER LANDING.

Donnelly's Studio, PALMYRA, MO.

- American parents frown on any union with young men or women "of the invading race"; Norse farmers regarded marriage into an American family treason.
- Railways helped open the agricultural West by making it profitable to market crops across the country; immigrant farmers were also a source of railway revenue when they needed to ship their crops to market.
- In 1880, the Minneapolis and St. Louis Railroad has just completed track to Forest City, the closest town, bringing great relief to the farmers who no longer have to haul their grain long distances.
- In the United States, the Western states and railroads are eager for immigrants to fill the land; they want buyers of the 500,000 acres of land that the federal government has granted them along their right-a-ways.
- As early as 1852 Wisconsin employed a commissioner of emigration to tout the jobs of that state.
- An 1880 story by the *New York Times* on "Opportunities for Settlers upon the Public Lands" said, "There is very little public land in this state unoccupied, and the character of what there is left may be learned through the United States Land-Offices at Des Moines and Sioux City. Nearly 1,000,000 acres are held by various railroads in the middle part of the western section of the state, however, these are purchasable at from $2.50 to $10 and more per acre."
- New Norwegian immigrants are very afraid of being cheated on land deals or in purchasing supplies because most do not speak English well; some immigrants have been charged excessive interest, up to 55 percent, in crooked land deals.
- All farmers, regardless of nationality, take July 4th off to celebrate Independence Day; most Norwegians do not understand the Declaration of Independence, but love the band music.
- Labor unions are showing phenomenal growth in the West following the Great Strike of 1877, when railroad employee wages are cut 10 percent, the third salary reduction in three years. Cities across the nation are affected in what becomes the bloodiest labor disturbance the United States has ever experienced.
- In all, 57 strikers, soldiers, and rioters die during the strike, and $3 million in railroad property and 126 locomotives are destroyed.
- The Noble Order of the Knights of Labor, which seeks to gather all American workers into one big union, is moving toward 700,000 members. Better pay and the eight-hour day are rallying cries.
- Demonstrations in cities such as Denver, Colorado, and San Francisco, California, break out that year against Chinese labor; mobs smash Chinese homes, cut the pigtails off Chinese men, and lynch victims.

HISTORICAL SNAPSHOT
1880–1881

- The U.S. population was 50 million; 65 percent of the people lived in the country
- 539,000 Singer sewing machines were sold, up from 250,000 in 1875
- The United States boasted 100 millionaires
- A&P grocery stores operated 95 stores from Boston to Milwaukee
- The plush Del Monte Hotel in Monterey, California, opened
- The country claimed 93,000 miles of railroad
- Halftone photographic illustrations appeared in newspapers for the first time
- Midwest farmers burned their corn for fuel; prices were too low to warrant shipping
- President James A. Garfield was assassinated
- The Diamond Match Company was created
- Marquette University was founded in Milwaukee
- Barnum & Bailey's Circus was created through the merger of two companies
- Chicago meatpacker Gustavus F. Swift perfected the refrigeration car to take Chicago-dressed meat to the East Coast markets
- Josephine Cockrane of Illinois invented the first mechanical dishwasher
- For the first time, a U.S. Constitutional amendment to grant full suffrage to women was introduced in Congress; it was introduced every year until its passage in 1920
- Economic unrest swept California, including its Chinese laborers, who numbered 75,000 and represented nine percent of the population
- Thanks to high tariffs, the U.S. Treasury was running an annual surplus of $145 million
- The U.S. had 2,400 magazines and daily newspapers, plus 7,500 weekly newspapers
- The typewriter and the telephone were both novelties at the 1876 Centennial in Philadelphia; by 1880, approximately 50,000 telephones existed nationwide, a number that would triple to 1.5 million by the turn of the twentieth century
- The camera was increasing in importance as an instrument of communications among all people; George Eastman's famous slogan was "You Push the Button, We Do the Rest" helped make Kodak a part of many American homes
- Most magazines carried little advertising in 1880; *Harper's Monthly* refused all advertising but those of its publisher until 1882
- Only 367 hospitals had been founded nationwide in 1880

1880 ECONOMIC PROFILE

Income, Standard Jobs

Bricklayers	$2.68/day/60 hrs. per week
Carpenters	$2.15/day/61 hrs. per week
Engineers	$2.48/day/65 hrs. per week
Farm Laborers	$1.25/day/63 hrs. per week
Firemen.	$1.37/day/60 hrs. per week
Hod Carriers.	$1.82/day/60 hrs. per week
Marble Cutters	$2.40/day/60 hrs. per week
Plumbers.	$3.37/day/54 hrs. per week
Stonemasons.	$2.58/day/60 hrs. per week

Selected Prices

Boraxine Detergent, Large Package	$0.10
Button Boat Shoes	$0.60
Colgate's Harness Soap, per Cake	$0.35
Demorest's Illustrated Monthly Magazine, per Year.	$3.00
Dental Fees, Silver Fillings	$0.50
Dr. Rose's Obesity Powders	$0.10
Horsfords Acid Phosphate, for Mental Exhaustion	$0.50

A Midwestern family wearing their matching shirts, all made from a bolt of Montgomery Ward calico cloth.

patterns, wrought in designs like guipure lace, to be worn over plain batiste.

In wash-goods we have the same designs, polka dots, stripes, and gray sprigs on dark ground. French percale will be popular for blouses and box-plaited waists. The newest percales have white polka dots on a ground of deep blue, brown, plum-color, gray, or black. *Broché* linen is a name given to heavy batiste on which are palm, oak, or fern leaves embroidered in white by machinery. It is used for overdresses.

SPRING BONNETS.

THE "turquoise" silk, so-called, reappears with admixtures of straw or crêpe for spring bonnets. A pretty gray, with blue, is trimmed with a black lace scarf, a bouquet of blue flowers with jet centres, and ruche of black lace inside.

Another is of pale pink silk and light drab *crêpe de Chine*. This bonnet is ornamented with pale pink ribbons, white lace, and a bunch of shaded carnations.

A very stylish bonnet has a high coronet set up from the crown, which is rather flat. It is composed of a mixture of blue turquoise silk and *crêpe*, the crown being formed of the silk, the coronet of *crêpe* bound with silk, and edged with blonde. The coronet is covered with pale, pretty forget-me-nots, and round the crown there is a standing plaiting of blue *tulle*, which shows a delicate wreath, partly hidden, of the same flowers.

Black lace bonnets are revived, with coronets of fine jet and lace, or brims inside, in which are ruches of white or colored tulle. Strings and lappets of wide black lace accompany the all-black bonnets, but colored flowers, combined with lace or trails of grasses or smilax, are sometimes used in conjunction with colored ruches.

Black and white straw is in great favor for the sailor style of hat, simply trimmed with black or dark blue *gros grain* ribbon and jet buckles.

Sailor hats of white chip have also appeared, trimmed with dark blue.

High, square-crowned hats of black and white straw are rather singularly ornamented for spring wear with a foulard scarf, polka-dotted. These, of course, are intended to match costumes. To the scarf is added a wing, mounted as an aigrette.

Dressy costumes no longer re-quire that the bonnet should be *en suite*. Contrasts in color are now required, and considerable latitude permitted. Uniformity in street-dress and traveling toilettes is still desirable, and harmony of tone is preserved throughout costumes of every description, which have any pretensions to fashion; but fine straw, chip, and other fabrics of the same kind having taken the place, to a great extent, of lace, *crêpe*, and other frail materials, a great many bonnets are not needed; and the trimming of a costly Italian straw or chip is generally arranged to meet the exigencies of different colored dresses.

"Costume bonnets," as they are called, are therefore usually made in silk, or silk and *crêpe*, and simply ornamented; black and black and white straws are used for traveling and morning wear, and fine chips and straws for more dressy occasions.

SPRING BONNETS AND HATS.

HATS and bonnets are still so intimately connected as in many cases to require only a pair of strings to designate them. A leading style is a perfectly round shape without tabs at the sides, with the brim turned up all around and variously indented.

The crown is of medium height, either flat, in sailor shape, or a soft puff, according to the material. This usually has much drapery at the back to replace the chignon, and may be worn with or without strings at pleasure. It is placed rather far back on the head, and is a becoming style to fresh, youthful faces. The one illustrated is made in silk, and would appropriately complete a costume matching in color. When of straw very little trimming is required for this shape.

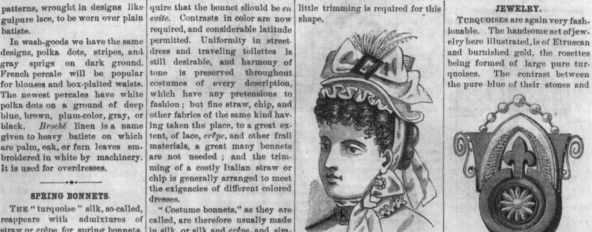

In bonnets proper, most of the shapes have rolled coronet fronts, and the crowns, while rather high, are placed more upright than formerly, so that although worn pretty well back on the head, they will not have the effect of falling off. Short capes also form a distinct feature, but are close to the

head. One of the neatest shapes somewhat resembles the gipsey, with the brim fitting close to the hair all around, but has a higher crown, with the trimming disposed around it so as to add to the apparent height. The one shown illustrating this style is made in white chip, trimmed with black velvet, black lace, and white Marguerites. It makes a very lady-like and becoming bonnet, which can be worn with any costume.

BERTHES.—The *berthe* is frequently the chief ornament of an evening dress, and is continued into a drapery of lace and ribbon over the skirt.

JEWELRY.

TURQUOISES are again very fashionable. The handsome set of jewelry here illustrated, is of Etruscan and burnished gold, the rosettes being formed of large pure turquoises. The contrast between the pure blue of their stones and the deep color of the Etruscan gold is especially beautiful. The illustrations are given the natural size, and the set is valued at $66. They come from the well-known establishment of Ball, Black & Co., which is a sure guarantee of the style, quality, and workmanship.

THE subjoined illustrations represent a set of solid gold jewelry, ornamented with the colored

Chicago Tribune, June 19, 1880, "Female Suffrage, It Should Be Based on Education":

"We have had a Woman Suffrage Convention here (Milwaukee). I attended all the meetings. I cannot understand myself, my own feelings, whether it is my early education, public opinion, or if it really does jar on my sense of what should be. Some way, I do not feel much satisfaction in regard to the meetings. I do not think it unwomanly for women to speak in public. I agreed mostly in all they said; still it seemed to me that they have not got hold of the right end of the thread to untangle the knots. I cannot see any good they have accomplished, but I suppose they have, as good always comes from earnest, true hearts, even if it cannot be seen immediately. If women could vote I would want to, but I fail to see how voting is going to help matters much. The leaders of the Woman Suffrage say it will help the cause of temperance, the fallen, and all others in distress. I have not such great faith in women. Earnest women are but a handful of the multitude of thoughtless, ignorant, careless, or 'afraid of Mrs. Grundy' kind. Then there are many more good women who would vote but would not dare or would not care to feel the censure their husbands would heap upon them, especially should their ideas differ in regard to the one to be voted for. I hope to see the time when voting will only be tolerated where intelligence and sobriety are. In no other way can we have an intellectual, grand Government . . . My idea is that woman should, first, help herself more, and not wait for some man to come along and do the little things that she can do for herself. Woman makes herself helpless and inefficient in the eyes of men, even if she is not so. By helping themselves I do not mean the doing of those things best done by a man. Second, women should educate their boys to a true appreciation of womankind, young and old. Third, let every girl be educated to do something well, whereby she can make an honest living for herself. With such a foundation to build upon, in a few generations there will be a higher, truer, nobler Government than the sun ever shone upon, and there will be no need for woman suffrage meetings. Suffrage would come as a right and justice would be done."

Chicago Tribune, March 1, 1880:

"The American Union made two new flank-movements on the Western Union to-day. At 9 a.m. the wires of the Catskill, Cairo & Windham Telegraph company were taken out of the offices of the Western Union at Catskill, N.Y. and transferred to the offices of the rival company, who have just completed a line on the west side of the Hudson from this city to Albany. Notice was given that the rates to Philadelphia would be 15 cents, a reduction of 1 cent on the rate charged by the Western Union."

Knickerbocker Hoof Ointment for Horses,
    per Jar $1.00
Ladies' Pentagraph Tracing Wheel $0.25
Ladies' Pocket Watch $29.00
Ladies' Trimmed Hat $2.50
Lovejoy's Weather House, Indicates Change
    in the Weather $2.00
Magic Inkstand, 10 Quarts of Fine Ink $2.00
Man's Cassimere Pants $2.00
Marvin's Boudoir Safe, Highly Ornamental $100.00
Milson's Patent Ozone Disinfectant,
    Small Size $8.00
Raisin Grape Vines, by Mail $0.35
Silver-Plated Dinner Knives, per Dozen $3.00
Solid Oak High-Back Chair $1.00
Stud Fee, Trotter Named Alamo $50.00
University Piano $180.00
Working Shoes $0.98

MME DEMOREST'S MIRROR OF FASHIONS.

838 BROADWAY N. Y.

R.H.MACY & CO
14TH ST. 6TH AV.
NEW YORK.

C. B. WEBSTER.   J. B. WHEELER.

February 1st, 1881.

Dear Madam: We beg to call your attention to the extensive additions made to our buildings, greatly increasing the facilities in every department.

Owing to the growing demands upon our Mail Order Department, we have thoroughly reorganized and enlarged it making it one of the principal features of our business.

We are now prepared to execute all orders by mail, to any part of the United States or Canadas.

Our Spring and Summer Catalogue, descriptive of our stock of goods, with prices, will be issued about March 15th. In the meantime, we will cheerfully furnish any information relative to our stocks, and should you favor us with any orders, you may rely upon our judgment in their execution, at the lowest market prices.

Our Catalogue is now being carefully compiled, with the object of placing before our patrons and the public, a comprehensive list of goods at prices that cannot be equalled by any other house in this city.

LADIES' LUNCH.

For the convenience of ladies while shopping, we have fitted up one large section of our second floor as a Ladies' first-class Restaurant, under the management of one of the best caterers in this city. Almost anything desired in the way of a cold lunch, with hot tea, coffee and chocolate, can be obtained. Ladies will find, near Superintendent's desk, Telegraph Office, Telephone, and conveniences for writing; also the leading daily papers.

HOW TO REACH US.

The Sixth Avenue Metropolitan Elevated Road lands passengers at our door. The Sixth Avenue Surface Line, the Christopher and Twenty-third Street Ferry Lines, and the Fourteenth Street and Union Square Lines, pass the door, connecting with all lines of Stages and Surface Lines in New York.

The Fifth Avenue Stages pass within one block, the Broadway Surface Road, Madison and Ninth Avenue Stages within two blocks, making the location one of the most central in New York, accessible to all Ferries and Hudson River Railroads.

Spring Catalogue and Samples forwarded FREE upon application.

Very respectfully,

R. H. MACY & CO.,
14th Street, 6th Ave., and 13th Street, N. Y.

Mail Order Shopping

- Montgomery Ward and R.H. Macy & Company provided dream books in the form of mail order catalogs to the women of rural America, who wished for elegant dresses and bought practical dishes.
- The original concept of the principal catalog company in the West, Montgomery Ward of Chicago, was to create a mail order store that would stock every possible product a farmer needed, plus many more he would want when he read about them in the catalog.
- Equipment sold through mail order changed farmers' lives; pumps, feed cutters, cane mills, corn shellers, threshers, saws, and grinders were now available. In addition, farmers could buy steam engines and windmills by mail order to provide power for farm machinery.
- Montgomery Ward worked with the National Grange of the Patrons of Husbandry to organize farmers into buying clubs to reduce freight costs.
- Both Montgomery Ward and the Grange were interested in cutting out the middleman to keep costs to the farmers low.
- Ward offered its customers a money-back guarantee on merchandise, including shipping costs; it was the first mail order company to use the concept.
- Montgomery Ward catalogs gave ordering instructions in twelve languages, reflecting the diverse nature of the United States in the 1880s.
- The growth of the company and its catalog paralleled the gradual, if sometimes halting, advance of living and working standards in the Midwest and the Great Plains.

The Grolier Club, a New York Society of Book Lovers, declared in 1946 that the Montgomery Ward catalog was one of the 100 most influential American books in history:

"The mail order catalog has been perhaps the greatest single influence in increasing the standard of American middle-class living. It brought the benefit of wholesale prices to city and hamlet, to the crossroads and the prairies; it inculcated cash payment as against crippling credit; it urged millions of housewives to bring into their homes and place upon their backs and in their shelves and on their floors creature comforts which otherwise they could never have hoped for; and, above all, it substituted sound quality for shoddy."

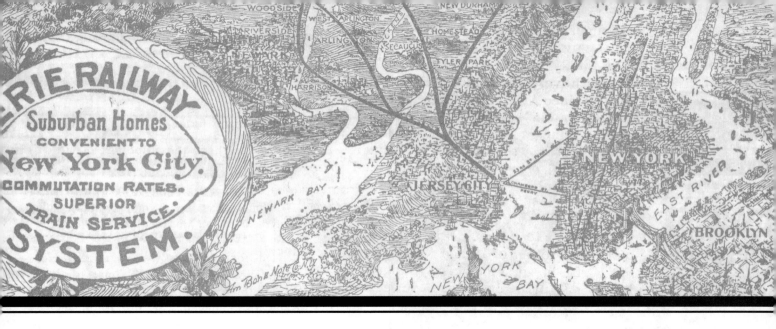

1890 Family Profile

The McGloin family of three is led by a third-generation Scotch-Irishman who lives in Atlanta, Georgia, with his wife and young son. He is a 54-year-old card grinder in a textile mill and a Confederate War veteran. His wife, age 25, works at home sewing and knitting for her neighbors. They have a four-year-old child. The family also takes in a boarder in their two-room apartment to make ends meet.

Annual Income

Husband's Income	$312.00
Wife's Income	$40.00
Boarder Rent	$10.00
Total	$362.00

Annual Budget

Food	$249.70
Other	$121.70
Rent	$21.00
Total	$392.40

This family spent $30.40 more than it made in 1890, using installment credit available at the mill store.

Life at Home

- The McGloin family rents a two-room apartment, paying $21.00 annually, or $1.75 a month; the boarder (probably a relative of the woman) pays $10.00 a year or about $0.93 per month.
- All heat is provided with wood, which costs $35.00 a year.

A Confederate War veteran and his wife of half his age.

- Lighting is by oil and oil lamps. The family uses 13 gallons of oil during the year at a cost of $1.95.
- The home is comfortably furnished: "They have a sewing machine," a government survey says. It does not mention rugs which are commented upon in the survey's review of other homes in the community.
- The man is a Civil War veteran; the 29-year difference in their ages is common because of the number of men killed in the war and the low birthrate in the South during reconstruction.
- He is descended from the Scots-Irish, who began immigrating to the United States in the 1840s; many settled in the American South.
- The Protestant Irish immigrants begin to call themselves Scots-Irish to distinguish themselves from the predominantly Catholic newcomers. Many have no skills except farming, but most lack the financial resources to become homesteaders.
- During the past year, the man spent $20.00 on clothing; the wife spent $20.00 on herself and $6.00 was used for the young child.
- Most of the family's clothing is sewn at home, probably with cloth purchased in bulk, and Clark's Spool Cotton, the most popular thread of the time.
- Clark's not only provide a quality product; they allow isolated women to tour the world with elegant color pictures of faraway places.
- The McGloins spent $26.90 in 1890 for furniture, listed under Other. In that year, a five-drawer drop head sewing machine in an oak cabinet costs $9.85, a chifforobe in solid oak is $11.00, and a washstand is $4.85.

The couple's child at four years old.

To market its thread, Clark's Spool Cotton provided colorful pictures of the world with each purchase.

- The family spends $2.60 annually with the Woodsmen of the World for burial insurance, $3.00 to the Baptist Church, and $0.50 to other charities.
- The man, like many his age, is proud of his association with the Woodsmen and other fraternal organizations.
- The man grew up on a farm in southern Georgia and was enticed by promises of higher pay to begin mill work. Recruiters distributed fliers known as "dodgers" that offered social events such as fairs and circuses in addition to train fare and company housing to attract workers.
- The recruiters often focus on large rural families, which can supply three or four additional workers, in addition to the man of the house.
- The McGloins raise vegetables and chickens beside their home to supplement their diet and cash flow.
- The woman also sews for her neighbors, creating shirts and dresses. In addition, she does crocheting similar to the "four-in-hand scarves" that are popular.
- Roundworms are a problem that year throughout the South; many families find relief with Dill's Worm Syrup, advertised as "an elegant preparation for Round and Pin worms. It is pleasant to take—the Children like it."

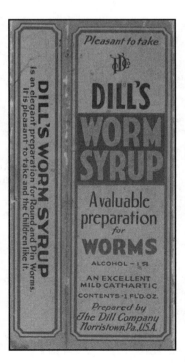

Life at Work: Textiles

- To attract an adequate labor force, mills build houses, schools, churches, and stores, and provide water, sanitation, doctors, teachers, and other services.
- The monthly rental for cottages within a typical mill range from $2.50 to $4.00 per month; the Atlanta Fulton Cotton Spinning Company charges only $1.50 monthly.
- Mills quickly learn that the "best operatives will not go where the tenements are bad."
- Most manufacturers view the company town as an extension of the factory itself.
- Placing the houses near mills reduces travel time and tardiness; in many communities it is a status symbol to live in the shadow of the factory walls.
- The factory refuses to hire Black workers, who are available and capable.
- Labor costs consume about 55 percent of a textile mill's expense in 1890. Daily wages are $1.00 a day for laborers and vary between $1.25 and $3.50 a day for skilled workers.

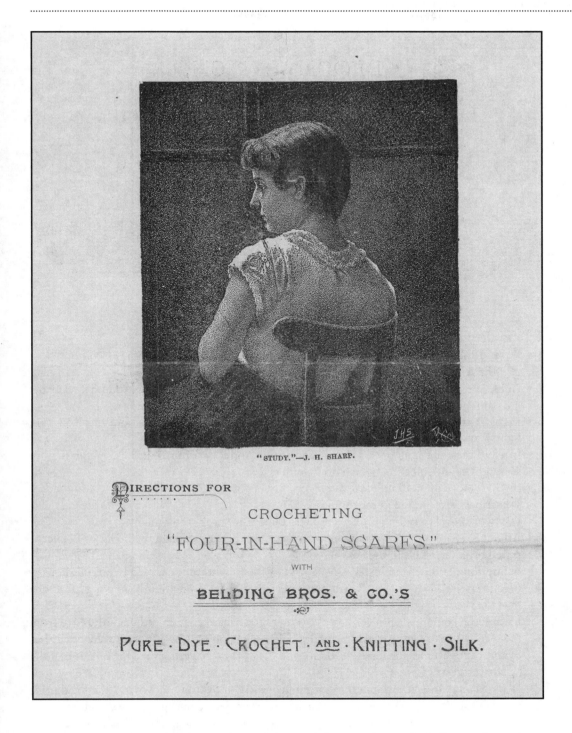

"STUDY."—J. H. SHARP.

DIRECTIONS FOR

CROCHETING

"FOUR-IN-HAND SCARFS."

WITH

BELDING BROS. & CO.'S

PURE · DYE · CROCHET · AND · KNITTING · SILK.

- Women, who comprise the majority of the work force at the textile mill, earn from about $1.50 to $6.00 per week, which runs six days and averages 11 hours per day.
- Like many textile workers, the McGloins are newly arrived from the farm and maintain close connections to farming, agricultural prices, and farm equipment.

Life in the Community: Atlanta, Georgia

- From 1860 to 1890, Atlanta has grown from 9,554 people to 65,533, composed of 37,000 Whites and 28,000 Blacks.
- Unlike the impact of immigration on Northern cities, 90 percent of Atlanta's residents are from the South; only 3.8 percent are foreign-born.
- In 1887 the city begins converting from gas to electric streetlamps and has 167 "arc lights" and 436 "series lights" in use three years later.
- In 1890 the chief sanitary inspector reports that about two-thirds of the city's privies are served by night-soil carts, which now number 12.
- In 1890 more than 40 miles of water pipe are laid and 3,759 residential and commercial subscribers are entered in the tap book.
- Few working class Whites and even fewer Blacks live near water mains.
- Atlanta's desire to become a manufacturing center is handicapped by the lack of concentrated urban markets in the South.
- In addition, Southern industry is penalized by the freight rates charged to Southern manufacturers; rail rates going North are higher than rates going South, making all goods made in the South more expensive.
- During the late nineteenth century the centers for urban growth in the South move from the seacoast to the industrial interior. In 1860 the region's 10 largest cities were ports, but by the 1890s two inland cities—Atlanta and Nashville—have assumed the position of the South's largest.
- Department stores in Atlanta have begun using an innovation known as "the fixed price method" so housewives know what each item costs before they go to the counter.
- Department stores have begun using the telephone and pneumatic tubes to move cash and receipts about the store.
- Department stores provide housewives with a new freedom, the right to look around the store without the obligation to make a purchase.
- This freedom means that the humblest wife of a mill hand can rub shoulders with the city's elite while shopping for handkerchiefs.

The Ladies' Home Journal,
December 1893,
"Side Talks with Girls,"
by Ruth Ashmore:

- "In signing a letter to a young man I would not put just my Christian name, but, instead, would write my name out in full."
- "It is not necessary to put on the deepest mourning for a mother-in-law; a nun's veiling would be in perfectly good taste."
- "Massage given with olive oil will tend to develop the bust, neck, and arms, but if one has a tendency toward superfluous hair the oil will be apt to increase its growth."

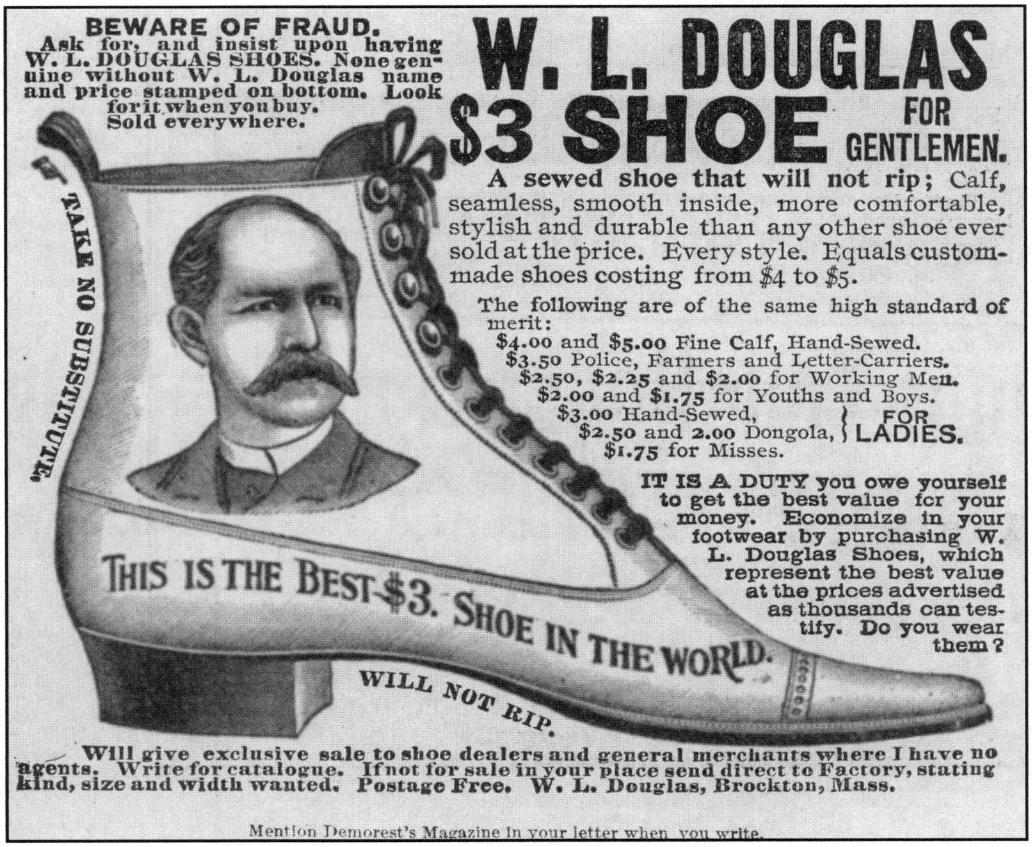

HISTORICAL SNAPSHOT
1890–1891

- The massive immigration that was transforming the nation left the rural South largely unaffected

- Two-thirds of the nation's 62.9 million people still lived in rural areas; 32.7 percent were immigrants or the children of at least one immigrant parent

- New Irish women immigrants to America outnumbered the men in 1890; Irish women were in demand as servants

- The census showed that 53.5 percent of the farms in the United States were fewer than 100 acres

- The first commercial dry cell battery was invented

- Three percent of Americans, age 18 to 21, now attended college

- *Literary Digest* began publication

- The population of Los Angeles reached 50,000, up 40,000 in 10 years

- Restrictive anti-Black "Jim Crow" laws were enacted throughout the South

- The first full-service advertising agency was established in New York City

- Thousands of Kansas farmers were bankrupted by the tight money conditions

- The $3 million Tampa Bay Hotel was completed in Florida

- American Express Traveler's Cheque was copyrighted

- Ceresota flour was introduced by the Northwest Consolidated Milling Company

1890 Economic Profile

Annual Food Expenditures

Beef	$0.00
Butter	$5.00
Cheese	$1.00
Coffee	$4.50
Eggs	$5.20
Fish	$1.50
Flour/Meal	$25.00
Fruit	$4.00
Hog Products	$17.00
Lard	$6.50
Milk	$3.60
Molasses	$2.00
Other	$3.50
Other Meat	$13.00
Potatoes	$6.40
Poultry	$2.00
Rice	$0.50
Sugar	$4.00
Tea	$0.00
Vegetables	$13.00
Vinegar/Pickles	$2.00
Total	$119.70

"The Irish American Family Album, Arrival," by Rosalie B. Hart Prior, an Irish immigrant who arrived in 1834 at age 10:

"None of us had ever seen a Negro before, and children were nearly frightened to death. They were a great curiosity, even for the grown people. We arrived at a time when the cholera was raging in New Orleans; people were dying so fast that it was impossible to dig graves, and the dead were buried in trenches. The immigrants were forbidden to eat vegetables or fruit, as it was supposed that they were dangerous. The majority obeyed orders, but others disregarded the rules . . . and were the only ones who escaped."

Atlanta Constitution, May 2, 1890, "Where the Pistol Toters Live":

"A close reading of the new columns of the Northern dailies convinced us long ago that, despite the talk about the hip pocket in the South, there is a much larger percentage of pistol toters in the North than in this region. If the newspapers tell the truth, young men, boys, and even women in the North carry pistols much more generally than was ever the custom in the South. In this section our laws against carrying concealed weapons are very strict, and they are rigidly enforced. Up North, whatever the laws may be on the subject, they do not appear to be respected. _The New York Tribune_ ought to be a good authority on this matter. It says that a very fair percentage of the men one meets on the streets of New York have revolvers stored away somewhere about their persons. It thinks that this percentage is larger on Broadway than on the less pretentious streets, and says that if a mad dog should take a turn around Union Square the spectator would be astonished to see the number of men who would draw pistols."

Amusements

Alcohol	$3.25
Books/Newspapers	$0.00
Medical	$65.00
Tobacco	$13.00
Vacations	$0.50
Total	$81.75

Income, Standard Jobs

Bricklayers	$3.55/day/55 hrs. per week
Farm Labor	$1.49/day/63 hrs. per week
Glassblowers	$3.80/day/51 hrs. per week
Hod Carriers	$1.80/day/57 hrs. per week
Marble Cutters	$3.21/day/54 hrs. per week
Painters	$2.61/day/55 hrs. per week
Plasterers	$3.50/day/54 hrs. per week
Plumbers	$2.94/day/48 hrs. per week
Stonemasons	$3.39/day/50 hrs. per week

Selected Prices

Bicycle Skirt	$2.50
Castoria Medicine for Infants	$0.35
Cigar	$0.05
Coffee, 11 Pounds Parched	$1.00
Cupid Snap Waist For Children	$1.00
Dominola Card Game	$0.20
Gillespies' Patent Horse Muzzle	$2.50
Grapevines, Three Sample Vines	$0.15
Hall Typewriter	$40.00
Henderson Flexo Girdle	$1.25
J. Bride & Co. Pocket Watch	$12.00
Lemonoide Furniture Polish	$0.50
Linene Collars or Cuffs	$0.25
Lowney's Chocolate Bon-Bons	$0.60
Music Box, Self Playing, Eight Tunes	$15.00
Oil Heater, No Coal, No Ashes,	$12.00
Printing Press, Self Inker	$5.00
Rice, Fancy White Rice, 240-Pound Sack	$0.04
Standard Shirt	$1.50
Twilled Lace Thread, 500 Yards	$0.10
White Label Soup, Two Dozen Pint Cans	$2.00

Demorest's Family Magazine, April 1890, "Diseases Incident to the Season":

"During the winter and spring months, the fat babies—with more adipose than muscle, more loose, flabby tissue than good vital development—will be having the croup. A little exposure will bring it on. The 'depurators' are not all doing faithful work: the liver is sluggish and skin is torpid, and very little chilling on the surface will send the debris of the system into the wrong direction. Instead of being carried off through the natural outlets, and the system purified from day to day, it will remain in the blood; and the first check that is given to the skin depuration will turn all this waste in on the mucous surfaces. If the bowels should chance to be the weakest part, we shall have a case of diarrhea or dysentery; if the lungs should incline to be weak, then beware of an attack of pneumonia: though with the general conditions before referred to, it will be in all probability the croup.

The child may have had these croupy attacks before. If so, the mother will at once understand the situation: the wheezy breathing will give her a note of warning, and the doctor will be immediately summoned, for this is a disease which you cannot afford to trifle with. Often a few hours will develop symptoms and conditions that are necessarily fatal. But supposing it to be a first attack: the mother may not be made aware of the fact that the child is seriously ailing, and when at last she concludes to send for the physician, he will know, the moment he enters the room, that it will be a struggle between life and death. The sharp 'crowing' sound that is made as the child tries to get his breath tells that the 'false membrane' is already formed or forming, and that the chances are already against the patient."

By 1890, the cloakmakers of New York were beginning to organize in response to the dismal working conditions. This report, written in 1908 by William Leiserson, detailed the struggles of the Jewish labor movement in New York in the 1890s:

"In February 1890, the cloakmakers began to rebel against the reduction in wages and the bad treatment to which they were subjected at the hands of the contractors. Shop after shop went on strike, and they called upon the United Hebrew Trades to conduct the strikes for them. That body sent a committee of three, among them Joseph Barondess, a delegate from the Knee Pants Makers, to 92 Hester Street, where most of the strikers were assembled. The committee found the men from each shop conducting separate meetings in different rooms. To each of the meetings they repeated their plan of uniting all the strikers in one strong union. It was hailed with joy, and Barondess was elected to lead the united strikers.

The strike lasted six weeks, and ended with a complete victory for the union. Even Meyer Jonasson, the most prominent cloak manufacturer in New York, was forced to come to the basement at 92 Hester Street, the striker's headquarters, to sign the union agreement. All together, 3,500 cloakmakers had been out, but many went back to work within three weeks when some employers began to concede to the demands.

As a result of the victory the Cloakmakers' Union became very strong. Immediately after the settlement it had 2,800 members divided into nine branches, one for each cloak manufacturing house. This form of organization was found unsatisfactory and the executive committee decided to divide the union into branches of 300 members each. By May 1, 1890, the union had grown to eleven branches with over 3,000 members. It had good control of the trade, and the employers were afraid of it. For a short time there was peace. Toward the end of May, however, ten manufacturers suddenly locked out all their cloakmakers. They refused to employ any more union men.

The struggle was most bitter. At first it seems as if the union would be defeated, but Barondess got the cutters and the contractors to join the operators against the manufacturers. On June 16, 1890, Operators and Cloakmakers Union No. 1, Cloak and Suit Cutters' Union, and the Contractors' Union, entered into an agreement to combine their strength against the manufacturers' association until the unions were recognized. The united force held a mass meeting in Cooper Union, where addresses were delivered in Yiddish and English. Six thousand people were present at the meeting.

The sympathy of the press during this strike was with the strikers. Many New York papers opened subscription lists to help them. The suffering of starving cloakmakers fighting for a chance to live they described in great headlines. When, after striking for two months some of the men became violent and attacked the scabs, the papers said they had been driven to desperation by hunger.

The public helped the strikers in many ways. A Jewish congregation offered dinners at 5 cents a piece to cloakmakers with union cards. Collections for their benefit were taken up in churches, department stores, and bank houses. A certain Professor Garside, of whom very little was known except that he was an eloquent speaker, became prominent in this strike as a friend of the cloakmakers. He brought to the union every day sacks full of money which he had gathered by collections throughout the city.

The lockout had lasted nine weeks when the manufacturers asked the union to send a committee to settle all offences. The joy of the strikers was unbounded. A monster mass meeting was held in Cooper Union to celebrate the victory. The large auditorium was packed and many were turned away.

Cloakmakers . . . *(continued)*

The negotiations of the committee with the manufacturers lasted three days. Then an agreement was brought to the Union, signed by the manufacturers. It was written in English. Since few cloakmakers could understand the language, the strike committee decided to take the agreement to Abraham Cahan to find out whether it was a good settlement or not. Cahan read it and was astounded. 'It was the worse settlement that could have been made,' he declared, and advised them to call a mass meeting immediately, and there he read the agreement to the audience in their own language.

That mass meeting will be remembered by those who attended it as long as they live. Cahan read the agreement point by point and there arose cries of 'Treachery! Villainy! Let us continue the strike!'

A vote was taken by ballot on the question of remaining on strike. The affirmative received 1,536 votes, while 20 voted against striking. Then came the question of getting funds. All the old sources were exhausted. But hundreds of men and women took off their rings, watches, and earrings. With tears in their eyes they took them to the chairman on the platform and told him to sell or pawn their jewelry, only that they may have money to continue the strike. In a quarter of an hour there was thrown on the chairman's table over $10,000 worth of jewelry.

This meeting was fully described in the newspapers the next day. The manufacturers saw that the strikers were bound to hold out for a long time. In two weeks an agreement was signed granting all the demands of the union. The important difference between the agreements was that the first one submitted made no mention of a price list. It had left the employers free to lower wages."

1892 FAMILY PROFILE

This second-generation Portuguese farm family—the Soares family—lives in northern California, where they grow sweet potatoes. They live in a community of Portuguese immigrants
whose sweet potatoes are well-known; he is a tenant farmer. They have three children, two
boys and one girl. Like many farm families, little is known about their economic lives; the
woman takes great pride in her thriftiness.

Life at Home
- The Soares family lives in a three-room house and spends little on clothing. They are sav-
  ing their money to buy a neighboring farm, which includes a farmhouse.
- Surveys of these families remark on the "cleanliness and neatness of the homes, along
  with a tradition of thrift."
- The family is Catholic; the church is a link to the past and the old country.
- Meals center around fish stew, fava beans cooked in tomato sauce with onions, and ba-
  calau.
- Another study comments that drunkenness is least common among "the Portuguese, Italians, Germans, and Jews."
- The Soares family is able to read *Uniao Portuguesa*, a foreign-language newspaper published in San Francisco.

Life at Work: Farming
- The first Portuguese farmers arrive in 1883.
- Farmers can purchase small tracks of land, approximately 20 acres, which are selling for
  $100.00 an acre, plus water rights of $1.00 a year, per acre.
- The Portuguese farmers are credited with making the sweet potato a major commercial
  crop.
- The sweet potato plants are started in hotbeds and then planted in the fields.
- Most of the crop is shipped to San Francisco.

Portuguese farmers were known for the neatness of their homes and a tradition of thrift.

- In the beginning, many food brokers are skeptical that sweet potatoes will sell and farmers are forced to sell on consignment.
- Shipping sweet potatoes to market is made more difficult because the train schedule is unpredictable.
- Farmers are forced to spend hours waiting by the tracks to flag down the train so their produce can be taken to market.
- Freight rates from Atwater to San Francisco are $0.44 per hundred pounds.
- To be competitive the Portuguese farmers form cooperatives and partnerships that allow them to ship cheaper and buy supplies less expensively.
- By 1892, sweet potatoes from the area are called "Atwaters" and command a higher price than sweet potatoes grown in the Sacramento delta area.
- Irrigation is critical to the production of sweet potatoes; in 1889 California irrigates one million acres of land.

Life in the Community: Northern California
- Prior to 1888 the area of Atwater and Buhach is used for dry grain farming.
- The Crocker-Huffman irrigation system allows the area to be opened to irrigated crops such as sweet potatoes.
- The Portuguese farmers of Atwater tend to come from other parts of California, not directly from the Azores.
- Nearly all arrive "poor in circumstances albeit rich in enterprise and they acquired land on installment payments."
- Prior to 1890 census records show that 36,342 Portuguese immigrated to the United States, locating primarily in Massachusetts or California.

Uniao Portuguesa, "The Celebration of the 350th Anniversary of Portuguese Explorer Juan R. Cabrilho's Landing in California in 1542," September 4, 1892:

"On the 29th all business places closed as hundreds poured into the city . . . at 10:00 the representative of Governor Markham arrived . . . anchored offshore was the reproduction of the 'San Salvador,' built by the commission . . . and flying the Spanish flag. All the crew, a total of nine, was composed of Portuguese in honor of the great navigator . . . Carrying a Spanish flag and cross 'Cabrilho disembarked while local Indians (taking part in the drama) knelt. Cabrilho then lifted his sword high reenacting the first claim to California. . . . It is difficult to describe the solemn feeling of that moment.'"

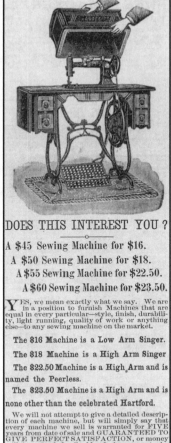
- In 1892 Oakland is the unofficial Portuguese capital of California with 4,000 Portuguese residents.
- The farmers form fraternal societies to provide insurance and assistance to members who become sick or widows who lose their husbands.
- At the death of a member the surviving members are assessed the sum of $1.00; the money is given to the widow and children of the deceased.
- These societies also raise money to assist other countries, especially Latin or Catholic, which have suffered tragedies such as hurricanes or earthquakes.

The Oakland Tribune, February 23, 1892:

"On Sunday morning the new Catholic church on Chestnut Street, north of Seventh, recently built for the Portuguese members of that denomination, was dedicated to St. Joseph with appropriate ceremonies by His Grace the Right Reverend Patrick W. Riordan, Archbishop of the Diocese. The opening of the new edifice ends a long struggle for the natives of Portugal in Oakland, who have worked earnestly for a great many years to secure for themselves a place of worship where they can perform their religious duties in their native tongue. There are many hundreds of these Portuguese families in this city, and very few of them know much of the English language. In fact much difficulty was experienced at the confessional and during church ceremonies because of this fact, which ultimately led to the establishment of a Portuguese church in St. Mary's parish."

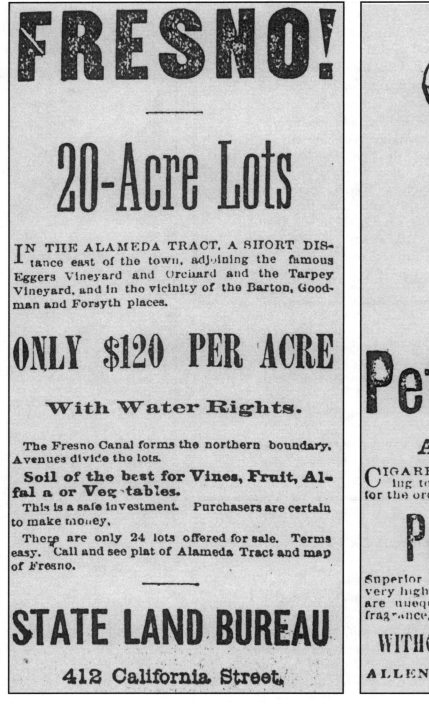

- In California the Portuguese are also involved in salmon fishing, sheep herding, growing asparagus, the dairy industry, and canning factory work.
- Festivals are important to the Portuguese workers to include mountains of food; the Portuguese immigrant believes that he will lose face if he cannot provide a "good table" or runs out of food during a party.
- As with most foreign-speaking groups in America, a short-lived newspaper in the language of the old country is created.
- Considerable anti-Catholic feeling is growing nationwide, causing problems and tension in the community.
- Most of the public land disposal in California occurs between 1870 and 1918; during this time more than 30 million acres pass from public to private hands; the Soares family, and the Portuguese community of Atwater, do not appear to benefit from that program.
- Recently more newcomers from the East have been coming to the area; in a rate war between the Southern Pacific and the Santa Fe railroad, the Southern Pacific is offering passenger rates of $1.00 for persons travelling from Kansas City to Los Angeles.
- Wheat cultivation dominates many parts of California because of the climate and ease of transportation of dry grains to the East Coast.
- Many California growers are dependent on markets outside the state, requiring cooperation and sophisticated marketing programs to sell their product.
- California growers adopt trade names as a marketing ploy in the 1880s to sell more of their produce.

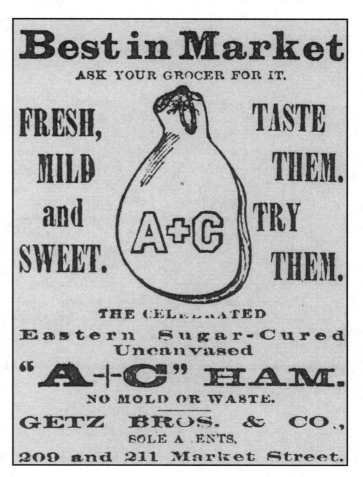

- It is estimated that the cost of planting and bringing to bearing a 10-acre citrus orchard in Los Angeles County in 1885 is $230.00 per acre.
- In 1890, California produces 1.5 million cases of canned goods, valued at $6 million.
- The dried fruit and canning industry is growing in California to make sure that "seasonal glut" does not drive prices down.
- The introduction of the refrigerated railway car, which appears in 1889, has a revolutionary impact on the marketing of fresh fruits to the East Coast.
- Southern Pacific Railroad is offering special rates to farmers if the growers supply 15 cars of produce daily.
- Cheap labor, provided by Chinese workers, is critical to the success of Northern California fruit growers.
- "At the present prices of fruit, we could not grow it without Chinese labor," the Reverend William Brier, a fruit grower, tells a U.S. Senate Committee investigating Chinese immigration.
- Smaller farmers typically hire Chinese labor, paying them less than non-Chinese workers; the average agricultural wage for non-Chinese is $1.90 per day.
- The Chinese are prohibited from owning land in California after 1886.

The Advantage of Chinese Labor:

"It is a fact, however, that they do a great deal of work white men will not do out here; they do not stand idle, but take the first job that is offered them. And the result is that they are used all over the State, more and more, because they chiefly, of the laboring population, will work steadily and keep their engagement. Moreover, the admirable organization of the Chinese labor is an irresistible convenience to the farmer. 'How do you arrange to get your Chinese?' I asked a man in the country who was employing more than a hundred in several gangs. He replied, 'I have only to send to a Chinese employment office in San Francisco, and say that I need so many men for such work and at such pay. Directly up come the men, with a foreman of their own, with whom alone I have to deal. I tell only him what I want done; I settle with him alone; I complain to him, and hold him alone responsible. He understands English; and this system simplifies things amazingly. If I employed white men I should have to instruct, reprove, watch, and pay each one separately; and of a hundred, a quarter, at least, would be dropping out day after day for one cause or another. Moreover, with my Chinese comes up a cook for every twenty men, whom I pay, and provisions of their own which they buy. Thus I have nobody to feed and care for. They do it themselves.'"

1893 News Profile

To attract additional farmers to the West, newspapers created publications entirely composed of letters from successful farmers and information about the area. This article signed by Jacob Bauer, appeared in a publication called, *Letters from Washington Farmers, Information Concerning the Pacific Northwest, January 16, 1893*. His article was entitled "Adams and Lincoln Counties: A German Who Can Farm More Acres Here Than in Any Other Place He Knows of."

Ritzville, Adams County, Washington, June 16, 1892. "I am a German and emigrated from Russia in 1879 to Hitchcock County, Nebraska, where I lived for three years, but did not succeed in raising a crop while I lived there. I had to work on the railroad to get money to support my family of six persons. From Nebraska I moved to Walla Walla, Washington. In 1882 I bought four horses, two cayuses, three cows, a wagon and plow and came to Adams County in the Big Bend Country. I entered a homestead, 160 acres of free government land, three miles west of Ritzville and put up a small cabin. I had no money left and was dependent upon what I could earn. I now have a deeded homestead of 160 acres of free government land, also 160 acres of railroad land which cost me $4.50 per acre, and 160 acres of railroad land which I bought secondhand at $8.00 per acre, making 480 acres in all, and all my land is under cultivation. I now have a good new house, barn, granary, sheds, wagons, buggy gang plow, grain drills, header, a one-third interest in a thresher, and all necessary machinery to farm 500 acres of land. I have 12 workhorses and 13 cattle. I have in crop this year 240 acres bidding fair for a large yield. Last year being dry I raised but 1,200 bushels of wheat from 130 acres, which I sold at $0.80 per bushel. The year before I had in crop 160 acres and my wheat on summer fallow land averaged four bushes per acre, and that on sod 27 bushes. My oats averaged nearly 75 bushes per acre. I have a fine orchard, trees one to six years old doing nicely and bearing fruit, including some of the one-year-old trees. The older trees are mostly apple, while the younger are prune, plum, cherry, and pear. I have a good well 90 feet deep of pure soft water. My potatoes yield large crops, are dry and mealy, and require no cultivation as we are not troubled with weeds and do not have any potato bugs. Carrots, beets, onions, cabbage, watermelons, pumpkins, and all garden vegetables do well and are of fine quality. I have helped my friends in Russia a good deal by sending them money. I wish my

Russian countrymen would come here as they can make independent homes for their families. I can farm more acres here than anywhere else I know of as the weather is always nice and we can work out in the field most of the time. We commence seeding about February 1st to 20th. The winters are mild so we need but little feed or shelter for stock. We have a good market for our farm and dairy products and poultry at Ritzville, a town on the Northern Pacific Railroad of 400 inhabitants, the county seat of Adams County and the trade center for this portion of the Big Bend Country. I am well pleased with this country and would not sell my property that I have made here for any reasonable price. There is room in this district of the county for many families to secure comfortable homes. I will be glad to answer inquiries relative to this region."

1898 FAMILY PROFILE

The Pattersons, a Virginia Black family of five, live in a community marked by tobacco and an emerging Black middle class that plays a key economic role in the life of the community. The man is a wood turner creating plow handles; his wife works as a stemmer in the tobacco factory, along with one child. They have three children under the age of 16.

Annual Family Income

Husband's Income	$144.00
Wife's Income	$120.00
Child's Income	$30.00
Total	$284.00

Annual Budget

Clothing	$60.00
Food	$117.00
Fuel	$30.00
Miscellaneous	$30.00
Rent	$36.00
Total	$273.00

Life at Home

- The Pattersons rent a two-room home; the living room is on the first floor, the kitchen on the second. The staircase is open. The monthly rent is $3.00.
- They hope to buy a lot near their home for $50.00 and build a three-room house, which will cost $300.00 to $500.00, depending upon how much work the family do themselves.
- A building association in Farmville composed of White and Black shareholders will assist the family with the financing of the home.

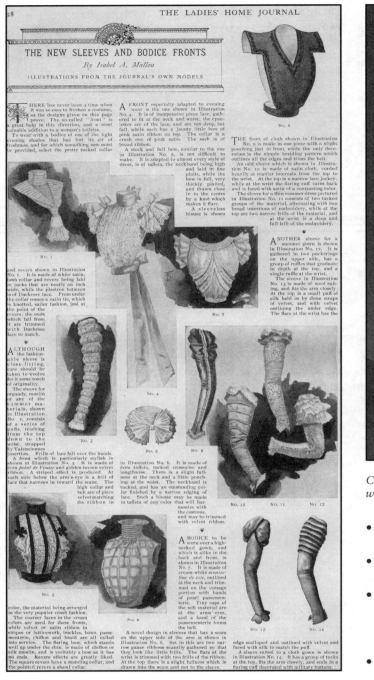

Color prints from Demorest's Family Magazine *were mounted on the walls of the family home.*

- The family maintains a small vegetable garden to supplement their diet; they keep chickens for eggs and meat.
- The woman's mother died when she was two so her father raised her "and I had to work."
- "I learnt how to cook when I wasn't big enough to reach the stove. When I was little, my father used to carry me to the field with him and put me in a basket and sit me under a tree while he worked."
- The children, like all children in the community, grow up working with their parents or on a neighboring farm, especially at planting and harvest time.
- The surveyor of Farmville finds that many residents, including the Pattersons, cannot answer the question, "age at nearest birthday," because few records had been kept.
- The children attend school approximately 109 days a year, or approximately six months.
- None of the children, all under the age of 16, have married, breaking a pattern of early marriages or cohabitation set during slavery days and the first generation of freemen.

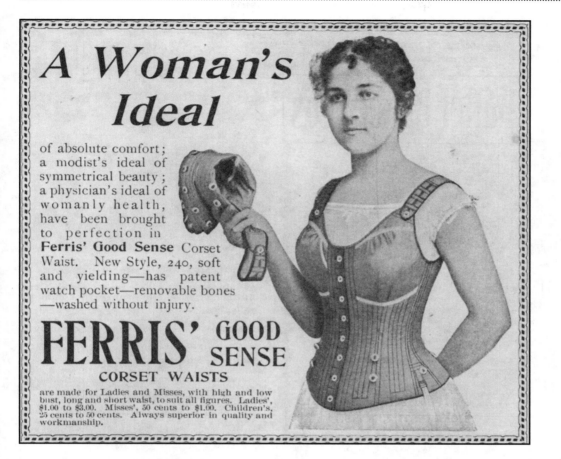

- Within the community, 42 percent of the people can read and write, 17.5 percent can read but not write, and 40 percent are "wholly illiterate."
- The Pattersons enjoy reading *Demorest's Family Magazine*; many of the color prints have been removed from the magazine and mounted on the walls of their home.

How American Buying Habits Change, Achievement of Status:

"One of the major advantages of a shorter workday cited by the Industrial Commission established by Congress in 1898 was the time thus afforded the development of citizenship. Conscious, perhaps, of the larger proportion of foreign-born in the labor force, it argued in its report: 'On the side of the working population . . . they gain not only in health, but also in intelligence, morality, temperance, and preparation for citizenship . . . Lessening of hours leaves more opportunity and more vigor for the betterment of character, the improvement of the home, and for studying the problems of citizenship. For these reasons the short workday for working people brings an advantage to the entire community.'"

FIGURE NO. 268 R.—LADIES' LOUIS XIV. COSTUME.—This illustrates Pattern No. 8299 (copyright), price 1s. 8d. or 40 cents.

(For Description see Page 380.)

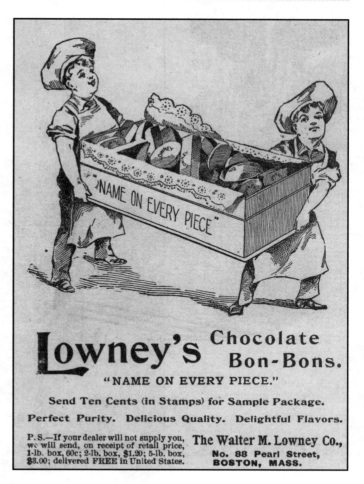
Labor Review of Benefits, 1896:

"The Lehigh Coal and Navigation Company of Pennsylvania and their 5,000 employees have since 1883 maintained a fund to which the company contributes the interest on an investment of $20,000, and a fixed amount for each ton of coal mined. The men contribute a portion of their earnings, normally one-half of one percent for inside workmen and one-fourth of one percent for outside workmen. The death benefits of this fund are $30.00 for funeral expenses and half-pay for 18 months to the family. Those disabled by accidents receive half-pay for a period not exceeding six months."

- *The Ladies' Home Journal* is also very popular in the community for its sewing and fashion tips.
- Black dolls for children have been manufactured in Germany since the 1890s, but are more widely available through advertisements in *Youth's Companion Magazine*.

Life at Work: The Wood Foundry and Tobacco Shed

- The foundry where the man works is engaged in woodworking, chiefly the turning of plow handles.
- The plow handles are turned on a mechanical lathe that requires that he stand all day.
- The foundry employs 10 Black and four White mechanics, and pays them from $0.75 to $1.00 a day "without discrimination."
- The company operates only when orders are available; this man works 32 weeks a year; he hunts, fishes, and gardens while laid off the other 20 weeks each year.

Women working as stemmers in the tobacco shed, removing stems from the tobacco leaf.

- He occasionally can sell some of the produce from his garden during the summertime.
- The woman works as a stemmer in the tobacco sheds.
- The manufacture of tobacco strips requires ridding the dry tobacco leaf of the woody stem.
- Loose tobacco is taken to the factory and placed on the floor according to grade, style, and quality.
- Once enough of a certain grade or style has been gathered into a "hogshead of strips" it is taken to another room and sprinkled and steamed, a little at a time.
- The bundles are stemmed once the leaves are supple and pliant.
- Women and young men then draw out the stems and children then tie the strips of tobacco into uniform bundles.
- These bundles are weighed, stretched on sticks and hung up in the drying room for eight to ten hours.
- When thoroughly dried and cooled the tobacco is again steamed as it hangs, then cooled for two days. Finally, it is steamed a third time in a steam box, straightened, and packed into a container known as a hogsheads.
- Women who stem the tobacco get $0.50 for every hundred pounds of stemmed tobacco and can, with the aid of children, stem from 100 to 300 pounds a day.
- This woman makes $6.00 a week or about 200 pounds per day during a six-day week.
- Children are often kept from school for all or part of the harvest time to help with the factory work.
- Other women laborers receive $0.35 to $0.40 a day.
- Men who prize, steam, and pack tobacco receive from $0.75 to $1.00 a day.

The father worked in the wood foundry as a wood turner making plow handles.

"Rural Free Delivery," by Max Bennet Thrasher:

"The reasons given for the opposition (to rural free delivery of mail) were generally that small local offices at a distance from the railroads would be discontinued, and the patrons did not believe they would be so satisfactorily served by the new arrangement. I think this feeling arose in the main from the rather common distrust of any innovation, especially when it has to do with an institution so old and respected as the post office. Moreover, the local office is usually located in a country store. The merchant, fearing that the doing away with the office will injure this trade, argues that it ought to be retained, and arrays on his side all those who are attached to him by friendship or by accounts of more or less longstanding on the store's ledger."

Life in the Community: Farmville, Virginia

- Farmville, Virginia, is located within Prince Edward County, which is near the center of Virginia. It produces seven-eighths of the tobacco crop of the state.
- Farmville is the county seat and a market town of 2,500 inhabitants on the upper waters of the Appomattox.
- Agriculture dominates the economy of the county, tobacco being the leading crop followed by corn, wheat, oats, and potatoes.

Insurance through the Trade Unions:

"Insurance, an important part of a worker's life and expenditures, was often provided by associates or craft guilds. The International Wood Carvers' Association of North America, for example, was organized in 1883 and boasted a membership of 1,800 on April 30, 1898. A benefit of $50 is paid on the death of a member. The total death benefits paid from January 1, 1897, to January 11, 1898, amounted to $1,850. Tool insurance, not to exceed $30.00 was also provided for. Only a national convention vote of all the locals can authorize the spending of the funds of the national body for strikes. The strike benefit is $6 a week for single men and $8.00 a week for married men. The union numbered only 700 members in 1897. In a similar fashion, the Sailors' Union of the Pacific was founded March 6, 1885. The membership on January 1, 1898, was 1,471. In 1897, $750 was spent for shipwreck benefit and $310.45 for the relief of the sick and burial of the dead."

- More than 70 percent of the farms in the county are cultivated by their owners; 31 percent of the farms are fewer than 50 acres in size.
- The county's population is 14,000, of which 9,000 are Black, 5,000 are White. At the time of the Civil War, the slave property of the county was valued at $2.5 million.
- The town is three-fifths Black and has been growing since 1850. Since 1890, however, the Black population has declined because of the large emigration to the cities, principally Richmond, Norfolk, Baltimore, and New York.
- As a result of emigration Farmville's population shows fewer persons aged 20 to 30 than might be expected.
- Public buildings in the town include an opera house, a normal school for White girls, a courthouse and a jail, a bank, and a depot.
- The only school for Black children is a large, frame building with five rooms. The school term is six months, from September 15 to April 1.
- The teacher's salary averages $30.00 a month, which restricts the competition for this job to residents of the town. Between the ages of five and 15 years, the boys and girls attend school in the same proportion. After that the boys largely drop out and go to work.
- Of the 205 children who attend the school in 1896–97, only 52 percent attend the full term of six months. Thirty-three percent attend half the term and 11 percent less than three months.
- Boys generally drop out once they turn 16 to work; girls tend to stay in school longer.
- The air is described as "good" with an "abundance of lithia and sulphur waters, which now and then attract visitors."
- Farmville is the trading center for six counties; on Saturday, the regular market day, the town population swells to nearly twice its normal size "from the influx of county people—mostly Negroes—some in carriages, wagons, and ox carts, and some on foot."

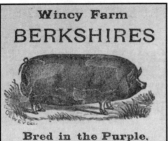
- Of the 459 Black working men in Farmville, 128 work in the tobacco factory, 58 are laborers, 17 are porters, 14 work for the canning factory, 10 in wood turning, 6 are coopers (make barrels), five are barbers and three peddle candy.
- The women are largely confined to jobs as domestic servants, teachers, day laborers, or employees of the tobacco and canning factory.
- Servants ordinarily receive $4.00 per month; a cook makes $5.00 per month.
- The business enterprises in which Farmville African-Americans are engaged on their own are brick-making, the grocery trade, barbering, restaurant keeping, wood selling, whip-making, steam laundering, hotel keeping, and farming.
- The brick-making business of Farmville is owned by a former slave who bought his own and his family's freedom, then purchased his former master's estate and eventually hired his former master to work for him. He owns 1,000 acres of land in the county and a considerable number of buildings.
- In his brickyard he hires about 15 hands, mostly boys from 16 to 20 years of age. The brickyard runs five or six months a year, making 200,000 to 300,000 bricks. His men receive $12.00 a month and extra pay for extra work.
- Over half of the brick homes in the area are made with bricks from his establishment. He has repeatedly driven White competitors out of business.
- The wealthiest African-American in the town is the barber, who is reportedly worth about $10,000. There are five barbershops in the community—three for Whites and two for Blacks—and all are run by African-Americans.
- Many former slaves who have been house servants turned to barbering and restaurant management. The income of a barber varies from $5.00 to $15.00 a week.
- The position of preacher is the most influential of all positions in the community; of the two leading preachers in town, one is paid $480.00 a year and house rent; the other, $600.00 a year.

The Land of the Dollar,
by George W. Steevens:

"The American is a highly electric Anglo-Saxon. His temperament is of quicksilver. There is as much difference in vivacity and emotion between him and an Englishman as there is between an Englishman and an Italian. Yet curiously there is just as much difference between him and the Italian. His emotion is not the least like that of the Southern European. For behind the flash of his passion there shines always the steady light of dry, hard, practical reason. Shrewd yet excitable, hot-hearted and cool-headed, he combined the Northern and the Southern temperaments, and yet is utterly distinct from either."

- The economic importance of the Black population of Farmville has brought many White men to say "mister" to the preacher and teacher and raise their hats to their wives.
- The Black town jailer, is also a wood merchant, a whip-maker, and a farmer. He is currently educating his younger daughters at the seminary in Lynchburg.
- Many in the community are sharecroppers, a system that grew out of the post-Civil War period. Sharecropping makes it possible for planters to obtain labor without paying wages and for landless farmers to get soil without buying it or paying cash rent.
- The lack of capital still impacts growth in Farmville and much of the South.
- Only 47 national banks exist in the 10 cotton states of the South, and many counties in Virginia have no banking facilities at all; the highly risky business of agriculture has to compete for what little money is available.
- The unique credit institution that grows up to meet this need is the country store. The merchant performs the functions of the banker for large and small farm owners. The landlord of croppers had to furnish teams, tools, food, clothing, and shelter, while his tenants produced the crops.

Southern Christian Advocate, 1897, "Did She Pay?" by Kathleen Mcp. L. Willson:

"Since there are still some skeptics as to the value of the education of women, let me help them to the truth by a brief story. It tells of the education of a girl and some results which followed. There is nothing unusual about it. The circumstances are so common that every observer must have met a similar case. The girl's home was a plain little cottage in a quiet neighborhood. Her father and mother were pious, sensible people whose school advantage had been meager, but while they were not well educated, they coveted for their children greater blessing than they had enjoyed. The oldest child was this daughter who was sent to the neighborhood school, until she had learned all her teacher could give her. Then came the question, which is puzzling many a parent's heart today: 'Can we afford to send her to college?' The matter was anxiously discussed for months and father and mother spent many sleepless nights trying to decide it. Sometimes, too, the daughter was admitted to the consultation, but although a thirst for learning was already fixed in her, and she was ambitious for further development, she hardly dared hope for such as great a luxury as a college course. At last a catalogue was sent for and the rates were carefully studied. All in the home were surprised that the expense could be so small. It seemed within reach, provided the strictest economy should be practiced at home . . . Our girl—did go to college, and went determined to get the most out of the advantages there. She was not an ideal girl, yet one with good sense and keen observation . . . When she went home for vacation she fell into her old place in the household, and was a helper, not 'a summer-boarder.' During the second and third vacation she taught at a little school, thus making some money to help pay the bills for next term. At the end of the fourth year, she was graduated, not at the top of her class, but with credit, and she went home to a proud and happy family. Soon she took a school and was regularly at work. All these years many changes were going on in the home. There were improvements everywhere. The father and mother became more interested in current affairs. Several newspapers were subscribed for and read with interest. The whole house took on a different air. In the rooms could be seen the touches of a cultured woman's hand. While the furniture was the same, it was tastefully arranged; and the few pictures were hung with better effect . . . Our friends are no longer hesitant over the question which once puzzled them, but ask another, 'Can we afford not to send our children to college?' This they have settled once and forever. Father, has the same question been presented to you?"

- The landowner seldom has sufficient cash, which is provided by the merchant, normally using the planter's share of the crop as a security pledge.
- Merchants often demand that the sharecroppers grow "cash crops" such as cotton or tobacco, not vegetables, to improve their chances of getting paid back.

HISTORICAL SNAPSHOT
1898-1899

- The "grandfather" clause marched across the South, restricting most Blacks from voting, and ushering in discriminatory "Jim Crow" laws

- Union Carbide Company was founded

- Motorcar production reached 1,000 per year

- Goodyear Tire and Rubber Company was founded

- The *New York Times* dropped its price from $0.03 to $0.01; circulation tripled

- Pepsi-Cola was introduced by a New Bern, North Carolina, pharmacist

- Uneeda Biscuits was created

- J.P. Stevens & Company was founded in New York

- The trolley replaced horse cars in Boston

- Wesson Oil was developed

- United Mine Workers of America was founded

- The boll weevil began spreading across cotton-growing Southern states

- Virginia continued to experience an influx of Scots-Irish farmers

1898 Economic Profile

Annual Food Expenditures

Food expenses are typically $2.00 to $2.50 per week

Butter	$0.10
Coffee	$0.15
Flour	$0.30
Lard	$0.16
Meal	$0.12
Meat	$0.50
Miscellaneous	$0.50
Soap	$0.05
Sugar	$0.12

Income, Standard Jobs

Bricklayers	$3.41/day/48 hrs. per week
Engineers	$3.17/day/60 hrs. per week
Glassblowers	$3.97/day/54 hrs. per week
Hod Carriers	$1.97/day/48 hrs. per week
Marble Cutters	$4.22/day/48 hrs. per week
Painters	$2.47/day/50 hrs. per week
Plumbers	$3.74/day/48 hrs. per week
Stonemasons	$3.67/day/48 hrs. per week

Selected Prices

Ayers Cherry Pectoral, for Coughs	$1.00
Boy's Knee Pants	$0.50
Bucklen's Arivica Salve for All Skin Eruptions	$0.25
Canfield Baby Diaper	$0.65
Cleveland Baking Powder	$0.15
Cookie and Biscuit Cutter	$0.15
Crackers, Baby Educator, Six in a Box	$0.20
Dongola Button Shoes for Women	$1.50
Gossamer Powder	$0.25
Insecticide, Tough on Flies, per Quart	$1.00

Self Culture, A Magazine of Knowledge, April 1897, "The Science of Wholesome Living":

"A common mistake in our diet is that it contains an excessive amount of sweetmeats. Indeed, we use far too much sugar nowadays. Not merely is our diet badly adjusted, but as a rule we use a needless quantity of food. Excess of one-sided foods should be avoided. Such foods are butter and pork (fatty foods) and rice (starchy foods). Cod-fish, which may be cited as a one-sided food, contains only flesh-formers. It may be generally said that most of the staple foods are not one-sided. This is the case, for example, with milk and oatmeal. It is a fortunate circumstance that the promptings of Nature do much to rectify the tendency we have to indulge in one-sided foods. The custom of eating rice or potatoes with fish, or meat pulse with rice (Hindoos) and skimmed milk with potatoes (Irish), is based on sound physiological principles. Another example of how, under Nature's cravings, a proper adjustment of nutrients in food is effected, is afforded by the food of lumbermen of the American forest, where work is of a most arduous kind. The staple articles of their diet are beans and fat pork, the former rich in flesh-formers, and the latter a most concentrated fuel food."

Madonna Yarn, 25-Gram Ball $0.15

Man's Keep's Collar, Four-Ply Linen $0.15

Modene Hair Remover, for Face,
Neck, Arms $1.00

Paper Dolls, Set of Three, Two Girls,
One Boy $0.15

Perfection Flour, Half Barrel $2.50

Salada Ceylon Tea, per Pound $0.50

Sewing Needles, Package of Four $0.25

Shingles, per Thousand $2.00

Stereoscopic Pictures, See the World,
One Dozen $1.50

Vegetable Seeds, Six Varieties $0.25

Typical Prices Paid for Commodities

Boys' Suits, Each $3.50

Canned Goods $0.10

Chickens, Each $0.15

Coal, Bituminous, Ton $4.50

Corn Meal, Peck $0.12

Eggs, Dozen $0.12

Fresh Pork, Pound $0.06

Green Corn, Ear $0.01

Ham and Bacon, Pound $0.10

Lard, Pound $0.08

Men's Suits, Each $10.00

Milk, Quart $0.06

Starch, Pound $0.05

Sugar, Pound $0.06

Tea, Pound $0.40

Watermelon, Each $0.10

Wheat Flour, 12-Pound Bag $0.35

Women's Dresses $5.00

Wood, Uncut, Cord $2.00

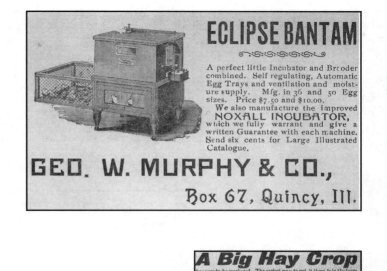

Value of One Dollar	
Year	Value in 2010 USD
1900	$25.64
1902	$25.64
1905	$25.00
1907	$23.26
1909	$23.81

Values are approximate based upon economic historical data and 2010 U. S. Dollar

1900–1909

The dawning of the new century gave every evidence that America was the fulfillment of the New World's promise of economic freedom blended with political freedom. In the eyes of the world, America was the land of opportunity. Millions of immigrants flooded to the United States; incumbent President William McKinley campaigned in 1900 on the slogan, "The dinner pail is full." Theodore Roosevelt proudly proclaimed in 1902, "The typical American is accumulating money more rapidly than any other man on earth." The United States had become a full participant in the world economy.

At the beginning of the century, the 1900 U.S. population, comprising 45 states, stood at 76 million, an increase of 21 percent since 1890; 10.6 million residents were foreign-born and more were coming every day. The number of immigrants in the first decade of the twentieth century was double the number for the previous decade, exceeding 1 million annually in four of the 10 years, the highest level in U.S. history. Business and industry were convinced that unrestricted immigration was the fuel that drove the growth of American industry. Labor was equally certain that the influx of foreigners continually undermined the economic status of native workers and kept wages low.

The first decade was marked by the widespread and expanded use of electricity and the technological changes it spawned. Both altered the ways factories operated and the types of skills their workers needed. A bottle-making machine patented in 1903 virtually eliminated the hand-blowing of glass bottles; another invention mechanized the production of window glass. A rotating kiln first manufactured in 1899 supplied large quantities of cheap, standardized cement, just in time for a nation ready to leave behind the fad of bicycles and fall madly in love with the automobile. Thanks to innovation, the United States led the world in productivity, exceeding the vast empires of France and Britain combined.

The change in productivity and consumerism came with a price: the character of American life. Manufacturing plants drew people from the country into the cities. The traditional farm patterns were disrupted by the lure of urban life. Ministers complained that life-long church-goers who moved to the city often found less time and fewer social pressures to attend worship regularly. Between 1900 and 1920 urban population increased by 80 percent compared to just over 12 percent for rural areas. During the same time the non-farm work force went from 783,000 to 2.2 million. Unlike farmers, these workers drew a regular paycheck, and spent it.

With this movement of people, technology and ideas, nationalism took on a new meaning in America. Railroad expansion in the middle of the nineteenth century had made it possible to move goods quickly and efficiently throughout the country. As a result, commerce, which had been based largely on local production of goods for local consumption, found new markets. Ambitious merchants expanded their businesses by appealing to broader markets.

In 1900, America claimed 58 businesses with more than one retail outlet called "chain stores"; by 1910, that number had more than tripled, and by 1920 the total had risen to 808. The number of clothing chains alone rose from seven to 125 during the period. Department stores such as R.H. Macy in New York and Marshall Field in Chicago offered vast arrays of merchandise along with free services and the opportunity to "shop" without purchasing. Ready-made clothing drove down prices, but also promoted fashion booms that reduced the class distinctions of dress. In rural America the mail order catalogs of Sears Roebuck and Company reached deep into the pocket of the common man and made dreaming and consuming more feasible.

All was not well. A brew of labor struggles, political unrest, and tragic factory accidents demonstrated the excesses of industrial capitalism so worshiped in the Gilded Age. The labor-reform movements of the 1880s and 1890s culminated in the newly formed American Federation of Labor as the chief labor advocate. By 1904, 18 years after it was founded, the AFL claimed 1.676 million of 2.07 million total union members nationwide. The reforms of the labor movement called for an eight-hour workday, child-labor regulation, and cooperatives of owners and workers. The progressive bent of the times also focused attention on factory safety, tainted food and drugs, political corruption, and unchecked economic monopolies. At the same time, progress was not being made by all. For Black Americans, many of the gains of reconstruction were being wiped away by regressive Jim Crow laws, particularly in the South. Cherished voting privileges were being systematically taken away. When President Roosevelt asked renowned Black educator Booker T. Washington to dine at the White House, the invitation sparked deadly riots. Although less visible, the systematic repression of the Chinese was well under way on the West Coast.

The decade ushered in the opening of the first movie theater located in Pittsburgh in 1905. Vaudeville prospered, traveling circuses seemed to be everywhere, and America was crazy for any type of contests whether it was "cute baby" judging or hootchy-kootchy belly dancing. The decade marked the first baseball World Series, Scholastic Aptitude Tests, the subway, and Albert Einstein's new theories concerning the cosmos. At the same time, the $1.00 Brownie Box camera from Eastman Kodak made photography available to the masses.

Working women flocked to the newly available sewing machines and the new paper patterns available for fashionable dressing at home. The most popular women's magazines of the day were not complete without a pattern or two to sew. And none-too-soon elastic rubber began to replace whalebone and lace in women's undergarments, providing greater comfort. By 1905 the consumer was able to enjoy such marvels as Ovaltine and non-shatter safety glass.

1902 Family Profile

Mary Kennealy, a single Irish woman, works as a clerk in a downtown department store in Boston, Massachusetts. Like many young working women, she is a boarder in a home that consists of a man and his wife and their three children, two girls and a boy. They rent a five-room furnished home. The man is a loom fixer and one of his children is also employed.

Annual Woman's Income: $364.00

Annual Budget

Clothing	$55.00
Food	$78.00
Miscellaneous	$23.00
Room and Board	$208.00
Total	$364.00

Life at Home

- Mary makes approximately $7.00 per week, depending upon sales commissions and the time of the year. Her room and board is approximately $16.00 a month, or $4.00 a week, more than half of her regular pay. She eats most of her meals with the family with whom she lives, who may be relatives, reducing her food costs.
- The family of seven, plus boarder, lives in a five-room house that has no bathroom. According to the survey, the house is well-furnished. The family can also boast some savings. The head of the household makes $12.37 per week.
- This woman shares a bedroom with one of the family's children.

"The Irish American Family Album." Encouraged by his brother Frank, who had immigrated to New York City, Paul O'Dwyer decided to leave his home in County Mayo, Ireland:

"There was a custom, which must have grown up in the famine of 1848, that was known as the 'American Wake.' It occurred on the eve of an Irish emigrant's departure for the United States. In those days most emigrants never returned, hence the term 'wake.' My relatives and neighbors gathered in the house, stood around, and encouraged me. They said such things as, 'Well, you're going to be with your brothers, so it will be just like home.' I knew that was not true, but I smiled just the same. The older people were saddened, and I had mixed emotions. I feared going to America, but I knew there was nothing for me in Mayo. The neighbors left about midnight.

Each one pressed a coin into my hand. The sum came to $7.00 in all, a tremendous amount for the poor of our parish to part with. My mother had purchased a new suit for me, tightly fitted and in keeping with the latest Irish style. It was a blue serge suit and the bottom of the jacket barely came to my hips. The next morning my mother and sisters accompanied me on the trip to the railroad station by pony and trap (cart). There were periods of silence when we faltered in making the best of it. At the station my sisters cried, and my mother didn't. It wasn't manly to cry, so I didn't either until the train left the station. Then I did. I felt bereft and terrified."

- The house has no electricity, no running water, and no indoor toilet facilities.
- Mary is unmarried and is probably a first-generation Irish immigrant.

The Family Finances

Annual income for the family with whom Mary stays is $1,071. This family of seven is a second-generation Irish family. The father earns $612.00 a year, or $12.37 a week. His 16-year-old son earns $258.00 annually. The woman, as a boarder, pays the family $195.00 a year, which includes meals. The family is composed of three adults, three children under the age of 14, and one child over the age of 16. The father is employed as a loom fixer in a textile mill.

Annual Family Budget

Amusements and Travel	$20.00
Clothing	$115.00
Education	$15.00
Fuel and Light	$57.00
Furniture	$20.00
Groceries	$286.00
Insurance	$9.00
Meat, Fish, and Ice	$182.00
Milk	$44.00
Newspaper	$12.00
Personal Expenditures	$52.00

DIAMOND HAND-BOOK SERIES No. 3 — 10 CENTS

WOMEN'S SECRETS OR HOW TO BE BEAUTIFUL

Religion and Charity	$18.00
Sickness and Funeral	$30.00
Societies and Unions	$15.00
Total	$875.00

Life at Work: Retail

- Mary works as a department store clerk.
- She starts work at 8 a.m. Business starts to build at 11 a.m. and she works until 6:30 p.m.; she is allowed 30 minutes for supper during her 10-hour day.
- Sitting while at work or "unnecessary conversations" can lead to dismissal.
- In some stores, sales clerks earning $7.00 per week are routinely fined $0.30 for 10 minutes' tardiness.
- Typically, department store employment pays $2.00 a week during the two-week Christmas rush, plus five percent commission. The woman is often asked to work 12 to 16 hours a day during the holiday season.
- Supper costs $0.15. She reports, "We were fed in droves and hurried away before the last mouthful was swallowed. The meal oyster stew, which was left over from the previous day, consisting of hot milk and three oysters."
- Generally, room and board provided to working women under the age of 30 years costs $2.50 a week, if they are willing to occupy a single bed in a dormitory.
- The dorms accommodate 10 to 15 women each, most of whom are saleswomen. Our family's tenant once lived in a boarding house and prefers living with a family.
- From the beginning of department stores, female clerks dominate the sales force, but not management; some stores boast 80 percent female clerks at the turn of the century.
- One manager reports, "I've been a manager for 13 years, and we never had but four dishonest girls, and we've had to discharge over 40 boys in the same time. Boys smoke and

"The Irish American Family Album," by Dorothy and Thomas Hoobler:

Michael Donohue, the son of immigrant parents who settled in New York around 1905, describes how he decided to take a civil service test for city employment: "I wanted to be an artist, but I didn't feel that it was in the cards right then. It was too insecure for someone from my background. I was concerned about finding a gainful occupation. The only great desire I had was to become a civil servant and I zeroed in on that. It was the only idea I got encouragement for. And essentially, for the typical Irishman, it required very little in the way of education." (Donohue passed the civil service test for a fireman's job.)

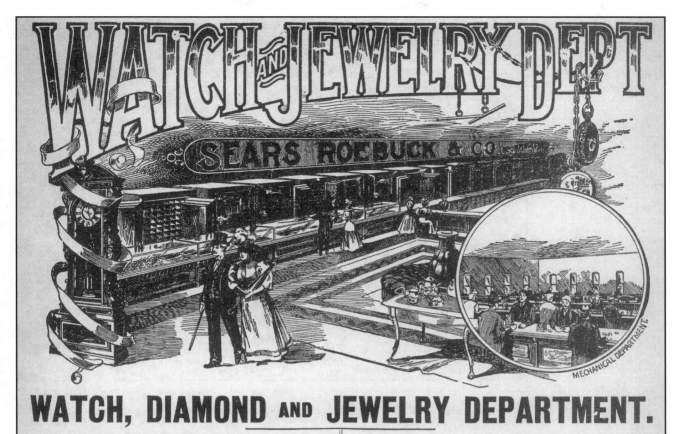

MECHANICAL DEPARTMENT.

WATCH, DIAMOND AND JEWELRY DEPARTMENT.

WE CALL SPECIAL ATTENTION to our very complete lines of Watches, Diamonds and Jewelry, goods that will appeal to the most refined taste. There is perhaps no other merchandise in which so much reliance must be placed upon the dealer. Confidence must be had when buying watches and jewelry, and to inspire that degree of confidence in us we guarantee every item as represented or we will cheerfully refund your money.

IN WATCHES ESPECIALLY we acknowledge no competition. Our watch department is the largest and most complete in the world, and our prices by reason of our purchasing power are the lowest of any, quality considered.

SEARS, ROEBUCK & CO.'S Special Watch Movements are the perfection of mechanical skill, made especially for us after our own original design and in such large quantities that we get them at a price which enables us to sell them to you at what other dealers very often ask for cheap and unreliable watches.

WE WANT YOUR ORDERS FOR EVERYTHING IN THE WATCH, DIAMOND AND JEWELRY LINE.

 OUR GUARANTEE With every gold filled, silver or solid gold watch we give a certificate of guarantee. With gold filled watches the certificate guarantees the case to wear and keep its color for two, five, twenty or twenty-five years, and the movement to be an accurate timekeeper for five years. This guarantee is given in addition to the guarantee which is fitted in the back of the watch case. As to the value of our guaranty, we will refer you to the first page of this book under the head of OUR RELIABILITY.

TERMS Our only terms are cash with the order. While in the interests of economical business methods we require the full amount of cash with the order, as explained in the introductory pages of this catalogue, we stand ready to immediately refund the money including transportation charges for anything that does not prove entirely satisfactory and fully as represented. You run no risk whatever in sending cash with your order.

OUR PRICES In Watches and Jewelry we buy EVERYTHING direct from the manufacturers in large quantities for spot cash. As we sell for cash, having no bad debts, we are satisfied to sell at prices which the retailer pays, and, on a large per cent of goods, for much less money.

 **MAIL SHIPMENTS** We recommend sending Jewelry, Watches, etc., by mail, as it is perfectly safe and far the cheapest. Postage is 1 cent per ounce. A watch packed for shipment weighs from 6 to 8 ounces; chains, rings and other small articles of jewelry about 2 ounces. Packages amounting to $1.00 or over should be registered, which costs 8 cents extra. We guarantee the safe delivery of all registered mail packages. Be sure to send enough for postage, and if any balance remains we will return it to you.

ENGRAVING We charge for engraving in script on jewelry, watches, etc., 2½ cents per letter; in old English, small, 5 cents per letter; small script monograms on jewelry, etc., from 25 to 75 cents. In writing orders when goods are to be engraved, write or draw plain letters, so as to avoid mistakes. We cannot exchange goods after they have been engraved.

REGARDING ENGRAVINGS ON WATCH CASES It sometimes happens that we are out of the exact engraving on watch case ordered, but we aim to carry exact designs. When the exact engraving cannot be had, we always have a very similar one, which we will take the liberty of sending rather than delay your order. It being understood, you can return same if not perfectly satisfied.

WATCH REPAIRING We have a thoroughly equipped mechanical department, which is fitted with all of the latest tools and appliances for the repairing of all kinds of watches. We have a large force of thoroughly skilled watchmakers under the supervision of a very competent foreman, and any watch sent to us for repairs will receive very careful and prompt attention. We do not solicit for watch repair work, but are willing to accommodate our customers who wish to have work done in a thoroughly first class manner. Our charges are about one-half what is usually charged by the retail dealers, but the work will be done in a very superior manner. We cannot give an accurate estimate of the cost of repairs without a thorough examination. Our charges are merely enough to cover cost of manufacture and labor. None but a thoroughly competent watchmaker should ever take a watch to pieces, for the chances are that he will ruin it.

YOU CAN MAKE MONEY SELLING WATCHES, ETC.

For when you can buy them for the same, or less money than the retail dealer who sells on from 30 to 100 per cent profit and has large expenses in the way of rent, clerk hire, fuel, light, etc., you can readily see that you could undersell him and still make a handsome profit for yourself.

lose at cards, and do a hundred things that women don't and they get worse instead of better. I go in for women."

- Other stores like women because of their sales skills, their ability to be "a queen behind her throne," and others simply liked the fact that women are willing to work cheaper.
- Of the 153 families in this survey, 32 show women working. Their income contributions equal five percent of the family total.
- Women typically leave the work force after marriage; 85 percent of all working women are unmarried.
- In Massachusetts at this time, only six percent of all saleswomen are married although approximately one-third are living independently of their parents, similar to Mary Kennealy.

Labor Department Testimony before a Congressional Commission, 1901:

"The front doorbell and the bay window have become boons to the social condition of the tenement dweller. The early tenements never had private entrances. When the individual began to build his own house, he had a doorbell and a private entrance, even though a family lived on the floor above him. He also has a bay window on his house, and everything also has to be in keeping with that bay window – better furnishing and belongings of all types."

Life in the Community: Boston, Massachusetts

- Boston is experiencing heavy immigration and competition for jobs. The principal immigrants now include Slavs, Greeks, and Sicilians. Many American workers believe these immigrants are keeping wages low and hampering union efforts.

- Over the next 10 years immigration increases, but many of the men come without families, intent on earning their fortune and returning to their homeland.

- Among Italian immigrants 78 percent are male and among Greeks, 95 percent. Many migrate to America in spring, stay until autumn, and return to their home country during winter.

- The North and West ends of Boston become predominantly areas of tenements and lodging houses by the turn of the century to include Mary and the family she lives with.

- Millions of immigrants flood the city after the cost of steerage passage from Bremen, Germany, is lowered to $33.50 in the 1890s.

- Most transportation within Boston is provided by electric trolley cars.

- The country's first subway opens in Boston in 1898, and an estimated 50 million people use the line in its first 11 months. By 1901 Boston is operating a unified streetcar and rapid transit system servicing most of the Boston metropolitan area on 300 miles of track. For a nickel fare, more than 222 million passengers annually ride its rails.

- Boston is taking a leadership role nationally in the development of city parks for all its citizens. Since 1898, the city has spent more than $200,000 a year to develop parks. By 1915, the city would boast 26 playgrounds for full-time operation. Nationwide, in 1903 only 18 cities have public playgrounds of any description. By 1923 there are 6,601 playgrounds in 680 cities.

- The new concept of newspaper comic strips is expanding rapidly. Richard Outcault, who in 1894 invented the popular strip, "The Yellow Kid," introduced "Buster Brown" in 1902, based on members of his family.

- Sports become popular and newspapers are starting to carry sports scores, reflecting the popularity of professional sports nationwide.

- A group of aggressive $0.10 and $0.15 popular magazines are gaining widespread popularity, notably *McClure's*, *Cosmopolitan*, and *Collier's* with "muckraking" stories of the poor and corruption in the big cities of America.

- Quality bicycles sell for $100 each, although cheaper models are available; however, the cycling craze is coming to an end.

- The typical phone connection across the city takes a minimum of 40 seconds; the installation of the home phone is

WHAT THEY DID TO THE DOG-CATCHER IN HOGAN'S ALLEY.

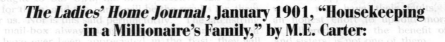

The Ladies' Home Journal, January 1901, "Housekeeping in a Millionaire's Family," by M.E. Carter:

"The laundry department is an interesting quarter. Here again only skilled hands can find employment. Three or four women are busy from early in the morning until evening. Sometimes nine o'clock finds them hard at work. Fortunately they have Sunday to themselves or they would soon give out, the tension is so continuous."

considered a luxury. Most people go to the nearest hotel or neighborhood store at the invitation of the proprietor to use the phone.

- Most brownstones are illuminated by gas. The wealthy use electricity to operate revolving electric fans. It is predicted that cooking can be done with gas in the future.
- A musical sensation at the turn of the century is the autoharp, which becomes widely available thanks to the *Sears and Roebuck Catalogue*. It can be played "without instruction."
- Minstrel shows are going strong, highly stylized with black-faced men, white-voiced tenors, ballad-singing baritones, clog-dancing, banjos, and trumpets. The Eagle Minstrels Show costs $0.25, $0.50, or $0.75 depending on the seat.

Roxy Theatre violinist.

Boston Daily Advertiser, "Well-to-Do Farmer Seeks Divorce," July 14, 1902:

"John Haskins, a well-to-do farmer of Secaucus, is seeking separation from his wife Marthat because she is a 'new woman.' Haskins says she spends nearly all her time 'attending club meetings and reading trashy literature on the enfranchisement of her sex.' He married her 18 months ago as a help mate, he says, but she proved to be an incumbrance too expensive for a farmer, refusing to milk cows, feed chickens, make butter or perform 'any of the duties normally expected of one of her station.'"

HISTORICAL SNAPSHOT
1902–1903

- The Brownie Box camera was introduced by Eastman Kodak Company with a sales price of $1.00
- The hamburger was introduced by Louis Lassen in New Haven, Connecticut
- Firestone Tire and Rubber Company began operations based on a patent for attaching tires to rims
- 30,000 trolley cars operated on 15,000 miles of track in American cities
- U.S. railroads now charged an average $0.75 per ton-mile, down from $1.22 in 1883
- The first modern submarine, the *Holland,* was purchased by the navy
- Uneeda Biscuits achieved sales of more than 10 million packages per month
- Life expectancy nationwide in 1900 was estimated to be 47 years
- The census determined that the U.S. population was 76 million; over the next 20 years it would grow 40 percent to 106 million, pushed by a steady influx of immigrants
- Membership in the American Federation of Labor reached the million-person mark
- The National Association of Manufacturers launched an anti-union campaign that promoted the right of Americans to work when and where they pleased, depicting labor organizers as agitators and socialists
- The price of coal in New York went from $5.00 to $30.00 a ton during a five-month strike of anthracite coal workers
- Rayon was patented by U.S. Chemist A.D. Little
- Russian American Morris Michtom and his wife introduced the teddy bear with movable arms, legs, and head
- Philip Morris Corporation was founded
- Charles Lewis Tiffany, founder of Tiffany and Co., died, leaving an estate of $35 million
- The first automat restaurant was opened by Horn & Hardart Baking company in Philadelphia
- The Wright Brothers made the first sustained manned flights in a controlled gasoline-powered aircraft
- The 24-horsepower Chadwick motorcar was introduced; it was capable of going 60 mph. Price: $4,000
- Massachusetts created the first automobile license plate
- Bottle-blowing machines cut the cost of manufacturing electric light bulbs
- The Harley-Davidson motorcycle was introduced
- An automatic machine to clean a salmon and remove its head and tail was devised by A.K. Smith, speeding processing and cutting costs
- Sanka Coffee was introduced by German coffee importer Ludwig Roselius

1902 ECONOMIC PROFILE

Income, Standard Jobs

Average for All Industries,
   Including Farm Labor $489.00
Clerical Workers in Manufacturing . . $1,025.00
Domestic $264.00
Farm Labor $264.00
Finance and Insurance Executive $1,067.00
Gas and Electricity Worker $605.00
Ministers $737.00
Public School Teacher $346.00
Telephone Industry Worker $397.00
Wholesale and Retail Worker $521.00

Selected Prices

Alarm Clock, No Battery Necessary $2.50
Botanic Blood Balm, Cures Eczema,
   Bottle $1.00
Coffee, 10-Pound Tin $2.10
Dance Lessons, Waltz, Two-Step,
   Polka $5.00
Delmar Camera, Folding $3.75
Gild-Filled Glasses $1.90
Graphophone Grand Talking
   Machine $25.00
Ladies' Home Journal, per Copy $0.10
Minnesota Sewing Machine $23.20
Petroleum Jelly, Jar $0.04
Princess Bust Developer, Bottle $1.50
Rocking Chair, High Back, Carved $2.85

A PRETTY EVENING GOWN

Strangle Food Pesticide, Can $0.25
Talcum Baby Powder, Box $0.08
Thimble, Solid Silver $0.15
Woman's Suit, Three-Piece $2.98

Department Stores

- In 1890 a new world of retailing was created by rapid urban development, changing patterns of consumption, women's evolving roles, and rapid industrialization.
- Stores began focusing on large assortments rather than specialization, the historic pattern of stores.
- Cheap but stylish clothing was reducing the obvious differences in class appearance, and the introduction and availability of canned goods was starting to reduce differences in regional cooking.
- In Mary's store, seven-foot-tall shelving is being scrapped for display cabinets five to five and one half feet in height to allow customers "to take in the entire store at a glance."
- Custom-made displays that allowed the customers easy access to merchandise are also emerging.
- Establishing a fixed price or "one price" system on merchandise only evolved in 1875. Prior to that every price on every item was negotiated.
- As department stores developed, fixed pricing became necessary; the salespeople of Macy's or Wanamaker department stores could not be expected to negotiate prices the same way an owner might.
- Department stores also pioneered the concept of "sales." The past practice had been to hold stock indefinitely until sold; slow-moving goods could grow dusty for more than a decade.
- The economics of moving products quickly propelled the stores. A dozen pairs of stockings bought in January and sold in February could result in additional sales if re-invested in stockings and sold again in March—reaping higher profits than one-time or two-time sales during the year.
- Department stores pioneered changes in newspaper advertising. John Wanamaker pioneered the full-page ad in 1879 and then introduced drawings, and later photographs, into newspaper advertising. By 1902 most major department stores followed this practice.
- Many of the stores were huge. In 1900 Jordan Marsh had a work force of 3,000–5,000, making it the fourth largest employer in New England.
- One of the first actions of the National Women's Trade Union League, created at the Boston convention of the American Federation of Labor in 1903, was a resolution requesting that the federal government make an investigation of women in industry.

FOR BUSINESS OR TRAVELING

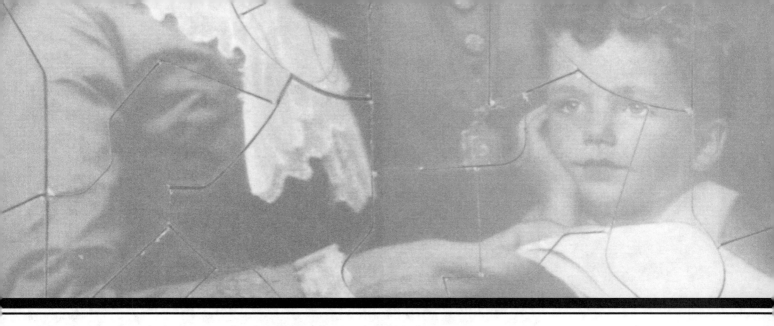

1905 Family Profile

The Stella family of nine Italian Catholics lives in a tenement house in one of the most over-crowded and poverty-ridden sections of New York City. The man, a first-generation American, is an oyster selector, working long hours on the docks. The woman works as a "washerwoman." Three of the seven children work with their father on the docks.

Annual Income
Husband $744.00
Wife $410.00
Three Children $346.00
   Total $1,500.00

Annual Budget
Clothing. $560.00
Food $520.00
Insurance, Dues $56.60
Light and Fuel $55.00
Rent $168.00
Sundries $169.40
   Total $1,529.00

Life at Home
- Rent is $14.00 a month for four rooms for nine people. The Stella family has no bath, and only one family in 10 has a toilet in their apartment.
- They do have a window and access to outer air; the apartments in the back of the building have no windows.
- The children older than 14 are considered boarders; it is the custom for older children to pay approximately $5.00 a week board to their mother, according to their ability to work, clothe themselves, and save toward getting married.
- Breakfast consists of rolls and coffee, occasionally eggs or oatmeal.

An English coal-heaver home on West 28 Street.

- Lunch is usually yesterday's leftovers or simply bread and milk.
- Supper will include macaroni, fish or meat, lentils, and beans.
- On Sundays, the family allows itself greater latitude for dinner and enjoys a roast, once a month.
- Most food is bought daily in small quantities; dry food such as potatoes, flour, tea, coffee, and sugar are generally bought in quantities to last a week.
- Since food is often scarce, guests are rarely invited for meals; on holidays relatives join together for celebrations.
- Eight percent of the total disbursement for food is for liquor used in the home, chiefly beer at meals.
- Coal is purchased by the bag only when needed. Three of the four rooms are usually heated by one stove in the kitchen.
- Gas, which is used for cooking, is burned by the "quarter-meter," a system by which a quarter dropped in the meter supplies 250 cubic feet of gas and requires another quarter when it runs out.
- The woman of this house knows how every clothing dollar is spent. Her family enjoys a large clothing budget; she loves cheap, gay, stylish clothing.
- To dress in this manner, they live on a poor street and spend less for food than similar families with nine people in the house.
- The family budget permits $11.00 for sickness, mostly for doctors and medicines in cases of acute and chronic illness.
- No money is spent on dentists that year.
- The Stellas carry workman's insurance which costs $0.10 for each member of the family and is paid weekly to a collector who comes through the neighborhood. The family carries the insurance for burial expenses. They fear a pauper's burial.

- They contribute $8.00 to the Catholic Church in 1905.
- Little money is available for recreation or excursions. The family has been to Coney Island once; often Sundays are spent at the city park.
- Newspaper comic strips are becoming more widely popular, many of which play off the changing scenes of New York, often poking fun at one ethnic group or another.

- The girls in our families love to read *Life Magazine,* which features the Gibson girl every month. With her pompadour, wasp waist, and aloof beauty, many girls try to dress and look like her.
- It is a common practice to buy clothing on the installment plan, the credit card system of its day.

Life at Work: Oyster Fishing

- Oyster cultivation began in the 1820s and by the time of the Civil War, oyster plats had been mastered.
- By the 1880s, New York City had become the center of the northern oyster industry, leading the country in overseas and transcontinental oyster shipments.
- At the turn of the century, the oyster is king in New York and New England; New York is shipping 100,000 barrels of oysters to England alone.
- Oystering is a major employer throughout New England, employing oystermen, deck hands, openers, and vendors.
- An oyster selector is considered an important job, requiring a man of experience and integrity to grade the loads.
- Unlike Chesapeake Bay oystering, which works largely public oyster grounds, in New York the oysters come from privately operated and controlled land.
- Northern oysters are considered superior by many because they are cultivated and grown in robust waters where only the best survive.
- New York becomes known for its Blue Point Oysters, originally harvested near the town of Blue Point, near Patchogue.
- In 1908 the New York legislature attempts to prevent other regions from selling oysters under the Blue Point name, as they had become so popular.
- Pollution reduces the local crop by the turn of the century; New York and its oystermen depend upon oysters from Connecticut, and by 1927 the New York oyster beds are closed because of pollution.

The Fishing Gazette, 1891:

"The best season for planting (oysters), it is thought, extends from the middle of March to the middle of April, although this industry is frequently continued until June. The oystermen begin shipping their produce to market on September 1, continuing until December, when they cease their weekly trips to New York until March. Some of them who sell to speculators do not go to market at all, but in these instances, which are rare, half the job of the oysterman's life is lost. The pleasant sense of ownership which attaches to a smart sloop well laden with valuable produce and skimming merrily over the smooth water to the markets of New York, is perhaps as great a compensation to the oysterman whose heart is in his work as the substantial rewards with which he returns a few hours later."

- Other than man, the starfish is the most destructive enemy of oysters, particularly in Long Island Sound.
- As early as 1679 New York State was regulating oyster gathering to prevent their extinction, the natural result of over-harvesting.

Life in the Community: New York City

- The subway system, opened in 1904, is replacing the city's elevated line. By 1907, 84 miles of underground track have been completed. That same year the last horse cars are removed from Fifth Avenue, in part because of pressure from the Fifth Avenue Association.
- The tobacco industry, particularly cigar making, is leaving New York City for sunnier climates, particularly Florida.

- Newcomers continue to flood into the city from Russia, central Europe, and Italy, but in numbers Jews are dominant. In 1905 the East Side's elementary school population is 95 percent Jewish. By 1910 more than 1.1 million Jews are living in New York.
- In the crowded tenements of the Lower East Side of New York, the population density is estimated at 330,000 people per square mile.
- As impressive as the Jewish arrivals is the influx of southern Italians, a migration that is labeled the "greatest and most sustained" population movement from one country to another.
- In the 1880s Italians, who are flooding into the city, face ridicule because of their religion, customs, and willingness to act as strikebreakers.
- Most of the first arrivals are males; many of the "birds of passage" intend to return to their homeland.

New York Herald, April 7, 1905, "The Immigration Problem":

"Restrictive legislation has had little effect, apparently, in checking the tide of immigration. More rigid exclusion tests have rid us of certain undesirables. Our doors are closed to defectives, criminals, paupers and contract laborers, but though we have succeeded in raising the level of qualification we have not materially reduced in bulk the raw material which we must assimilate each year and try to fit for citizenship. According to a recent report issued by the Commissioner General of Immigration, the rush of aliens to our ports is steadily increasing. In the six months ended February 28, 405,569 immigrants were admitted, against 306,428 for the same period in the preceding year. One unsatisfactory feature of this year's record is the disproportionate increase of immigration from Southern Europe. In February last the arrivals from Austria-Hungary numbered 30,088; 23,254 more than were recorded from the dual monarchy in February, 1904. Gains were also shown in the arrivals from Italy and Russia. These three countries furnished last year practically two-thirds of the applicants knocking at our gates. Russia sent 145,141, Austria-Hungary 177,155 and Italy 193,296. Together they sent 515,592, against 297,277 applicants from the rest of the world."

- In 1885 the United States Congress had passed a law aimed at Italians, making it unlawful to import laborers specifically for use as strikebreakers.
- The statute also strikes at the padrone system, which enables resident leaders to contract out the labor of the immigrants and arrange the lives of newcomers.
- The average size of the 200 families in the study is 5.6 people; the average income for the families is $851.00, or an average weekly income of $16.38, assuming that the family does not suffer any layoffs during the year.
- The United Hebrew Charities calculates that an average family needs $0.225 to spend for food a day per man, less for children.
- For most families rent and insurance are the obligations met first; food and clothing are considered less important.
- When a new pair of shoes is purchased for a child, food is cut down for that week.
- To supplement their clothing budget, a third of the families receive gifts of clothing from relatives, employers, churches, and charitable organizations.
- Women usually make their own dresses from patterns in the *Ladies' Home Journal*.
- In most cases coal is bought by the pail, bushel, or 100-pound bag.
- The ten-hour day is the working rule; most laborers rise at 5 a.m. to be at work on time with their lunch pails by 7 a.m.
- A favorite nostrum, or patent medicine of the day, Lydia Pinkham's Vegetable Compound, is sold through ingenious advertising methods which include newspaper advertisements and enticements such as free puzzles.

The Ladies' Home Journal, May 1904, "Article, the Patent Medicine Curse," by Edward Bok:

"Instead of paying one or two dollars for honest, intelligent medical advice they invest from twenty-five to seventy-five cents for a bottle or this, or a box of that."

The Alcohol in Patent Medicines:

	% of Alcohol
Ayer's Sarsaparilla	26.2%
Carter's Physical Extract	22.0%
Faith Whitcomb's Nerve Bitters	20.3%
Hooker's Wigwam Tonic	20.7%
Hostetter's Stomach Bitters	44.3%
Lydia Pinkham's Vegetable Compound	20.6%

The Cost of Living in New York, by Lee K. Frankel, Manager of Hebrew Charities, 1906:

"The furniture was a menagerie. If there are three rooms, the so-called parlor is a combined parlor, sitting room and bedroom. As a rule it contains a table, bed and a few chairs. Occasionally a rocking chair or a sofa is found. In the corner there is a sewing machine; on the walls a few cheap pictures, family portraits and the like. Cheap ornaments are found here and there and in some instances a cheap carpet. The second room, which is a combination dining room and kitchen, has a table covered with oilcloth, a few chairs, a stove, and kitchen utensils which hang on the walls, owing to the lack of a cupboard. Frequently an icebox is found. The third room, which is a bedroom, contains an iron folding bed, chair and trunk. Clothes hang on the wall. At times there is a bureau. The washing of the family is done at the sink in the kitchen, there being no wash stands or bowls in the bedroom. In one family only was a piano found."

The purchase of Lydia Pinkham's tablets was promoted with puzzles and gifts.

- In those pre-drug regulation days, Lydia Pinkham's Vegetable Compound is 20 percent alcohol, a formula that makes even the strictest teetotaler feel better at night.
- Nestlé Food for children offers a free sample (sufficient for six meals) to any mother "who is not acquainted with Nestlé's Food and who is anxious to try it."
- The quality of a man's pocket watch often defines his station in life: the rich carry a time-piece of heavy gold; the working man cherishes a silver Ingersoll costing $1.00.
- Most professional workers wear derby hats to work; laborers and boys wear caps.

The number of immigrants flooding the city was attracting criticism.

- The Fifth Avenue Coach Company of New York City offers an electric autostage to customers. It seats eight inside, four out and the fare is $0.05.
- Storefront penny arcades featuring a movie for a nickel are proliferating throughout the city. Immigrant entrepreneurs create Nicolets, Nickeldromes, and nickelodeons attracting thousands of working class people for a few minutes of fun.
- The short 15- to 20-minute feature is just right for a housewife to leave a carriage in the vestibule and carry her baby inside, for children to drop in after school, or factory workers to see on the way home from work.
- The silent presentations are enlivened with piano music; the rate of movement changes constantly because the cameras are operated by hand.
- Pyrography, the delicate art of burning designs into leather cushions, is popular in magazine articles that year.
- Sports are rapidly growing in popularity. Unfortunately, refinement of the rules is still needed. In 1905, 18 young football players are killed and 150 are injured on the football field, creating enough of a public uproar that President Theodore Roosevelt demands more humane rules.
- The second Vanderbilt Cup auto race of 1905 draws 100,000 paying fans to see Mercedes and Locomobiles run over 284 miles.

HISTORICAL SNAPSHOT
1905–1906

- The newly formed Industrial Workers of the World (IWW) attacked the American Federation of Labor for accepting the capitalist system

- A New York law limiting hours of work in the baking industry to 60 per week was ruled unconstitutional by the Supreme Court

- U.S. auto production reached 15,000 cars per year, up from 2,500 in 1899

- William Randolph Hearst acquired *Cosmopolitan* magazine for $400,000

- Royal Typewriter Company was founded by New York financier Thomas Fortune Ryan

- Sales of Jell-O reached $1 million

- Oklahoma was admitted to the Union

- Planters Nut and Chocolate Company was created

- A-1 Sauce was introduced in the United States by Hartford's G.F. Heublein & Brothers

- Samuel Hopkins Adams' *The Great American Fraud* exposed the fraudulent claims of many patent medicines

- The Temperance movement was gaining momentum; New York had one saloon for every 200 people

- Anti-liquor campaigners received powerful support from the Woman's Christian Temperance Union, lead by Frances E. Willard, who often fell to her knees and prayed on saloon floors

- Former U.S. President Grover Cleveland wrote in *The Ladies' Home Journal* that women of sense did not wish to vote: "The relative positions to be assumed by men and women in the working out of our civilizations were assigned long ago by a higher intelligence than ours."

- Current President Theodore Roosevelt admonished well-born white women who were using birth control for participating in willful sterilization, a practice becoming known as racial suicide

- As early as 1891 recent Irish immigrants dominated police work in cities such as Boston, New York, and Chicago, prompting a cartoon showing "The Wonder of the Age. An American Policeman; The Only Policeman Ever Born in America."

1905 Economic Profile

Income, Standard Jobs

Average for All Industries, Including Farm Labor	$510.00
Clerical Workers in Manufacturing	$1,076.00
Domestic	$278.00
Farm Labor	$302.00
Finance and Insurance Executive	$1,115.00
Gas and Electricity Worker	$543.00
Minister	$773.00
Public School Teacher	$392.00
Telephone Industry Worker	$401.00
Wholesale and Retail Worker	$393.00

Selected Prices

Aercel Washcloth, Cleans Itself	$0.05
Bishop's Hat	$3.00
Bissell Carpet Sweeper	$4.00
Blondine Hair Bleach, Large Bottle	$0.70
Boy's Shoes	$1.75
Cabbage Plants	$1.50/1,000

THE WONDER OF THE AGE AN AMERICAN POLICEMAN

PLEASE DON'T HANDLE

THE FAT GIRL AGE 17

THE ONLY POLICEMAN EVER BORN IN AMERICA

"Immigration and Race Elements," by James B. Connally,
American History Told by Contemporaries, Volume V.
Twentieth Century United States, 1900–1924:

"It is a common observation on workers where Italians are employed in numbers that with their dollar and a quarter a day they draw more cash at the end of the month than highly paid engineers. The reason is simple; they save rigidly. Sale bread and flour are cheap; they make their macaroni as often as they buy it ready-made; the woods for a mile around furnish their fuel; field, meadow and swamp contribute to their larder in a way truly amazing to one used to civilized city life."

Card Game. $0.50
The Convert Automobile $750.00
Fancy Percale Cloth for
    Dresses, per Yard. $0.10
Jell-O, Four Kinds . . . . $0.25/Two Pkgs.
Masury's Railroad Lead Paint,
    White, per Gallon $0.98
Men's French Tan Blucher Oxfords $3.50
Palmolive Soap, per Bar. $0.05
Popular Mechanics Magazine, per
    Year $1.00
S.R. & Co. Handmade Baseball $0.90
Sears and Roebuck Alarm Clock,
    Oxidized $2.50
Tailor-Made Suit for Women. $35.00
Utility Pompadour Comb $0.25
Vudor Porch Shades. $2.00
Women's American Lady Shoes. $3.00

How the Other Half Lives, by Jacob A. Riis:

"The Italian comes in at the bottom, and in the generation that came over the sea he stays there. In the slums he is welcomed as a tenant who 'makes less trouble' than the contentious Irishman or the order-loving German, that is to say: is content to live in a pig-sty and submits to robbery at the hands of the rent-collector without murmur. Yet this very tractability makes of him in good hands, when firmly and intelligently managed, a really desirable tenant. But it is not his good fortune often to fall in with other hospitality upon his coming than that which brought him here for its own profit, and has no idea of letting go its grip upon him as long as there is a cent to be made out of him."

1907 FAMILY PROFILE

This second-generation Polish Czorpa family of six lives in Buffalo, New York, where the father works up to 12 hours a day out of his home as a tailor, stitching together cloth brought to him each day by a jobber. To make a living and have enough to eat, two of his four children must work.

Annual Income

Husband	$422.00
Children	$181.00
Total	$603.00

Annual Budget

Transportation	$19.81
Clothing	$114.91
Education and Reading	$8.58
Food	$335.23
Fuel and Light	$38.66
Furniture	$5.10
Insurance	$26.94
Health	$15.70
Miscellaneous	$7.87
Recreation	$4.90
Rent	$90.24
Taxes, Contributions	$9.30
Total	$677.24

Life at Home

- The rent of $8.00 a month provides the Czorpa family with four rooms with 1½ windows to a room, within a two-story frame house in an overcrowded tenement area on the east side of Buffalo. It has a grass plot in front and a yard behind.

2 SEARS, ROEBUCK & CO., CHICAGO, ILL. CATALOGUE No. 117. 385

$4.45 ECONOMY REFRIGERATORS AND ICE CHESTS $17.95

At $4.45 to $17.95 we offer wonderful values in this line of Economy Refrigerators and Ice Chests. Solid cast brass trimmings, galvanized steel inside linings and shelves, removable drain pipe, patented drip cup and swinging front baseboard. Convenient in arrangement, they are excellent preservers of food with an economical consumption of ice. Constructed on the best scientific principles, with a perfect insulation and circulation, they combine utility, cleanliness, solidity and durability.

THIS ICE CHEST we furnish in five different sizes, all built with a thick outer case of thoroughly seasoned northern elm, high gloss golden finish. The inner walls are built in the same perfect manner as the refrigerators and are economical in the use of ice. They are lined with a good quality galvanized steel and have galvanized steel shelves and ice rack. They are equipped with drain pipe, drip cup and finished first class throughout. While an ice chest does not have the cold dry air circulation like our refrigerators, yet they are excellent preservers of food and will give satisfaction. We recommend the purchase of one of our high grade refrigerators because of the greater convenience in handling the food and ice, the cold dry air circulation which keeps the provision chambers perfectly dry, always cold and will preserve the food better with less consumption of ice. Securely crated and shipped direct from factory in Southern Michigan.

Catalogue No.	Width	Depth	Height	Shipping Weight	Price
1K551	24⅞ inches	16¾ inches	24½ inches	70 pounds	$ 4.45
1K553	31¾ inches	21⅛ inches	25¾ inches	93 pounds	6.75
1K555	36¾ inches	24¾ inches	30⅞ inches	130 pounds	9.45
1K556	40¾ inches	26¾ inches	33⅛ inches	185 pounds	11.25

THIS IS A CONVENIENT, attractive and desirable refrigerator, substantially built and has our perfect insulated walls by which the ice is protected and the food preserved. The ice chamber is lined with galvanized steel and the bottom protected by a corrugated ice rack.

THE FOOD CHAMBER is lined with a good quality of galvanized steel and has double paneled door with heavy cast brass hinges and patent lock, with adjustable strike which allows the door to close with a slam, making an airtight joint; fitted with patent drain pipe and drip cup.

THE OUTER CASE is made of thoroughly seasoned northern elm, high gloss golden finish and having a swinging front baseboard. We use better material, the galvanized steel linings are heavier, the hardwood case better constructed, and the insulation and circulation of the cold dry air more perfect than the ordinary refrigerators sold by other dealers. The preservation of the food and the saving of ice will almost equal the value of the refrigerator in a single season.

SELECT ANY REFRIGERATOR from this line and send us your order, subject to ten days' trial, and we will guarantee the refrigerator which we will send you to give splendid satisfaction.

Catalogue No.	Width	Depth	Height	Ice Capacity	Shipping Weight	Price
1K560	24¾ inches	16⅛ inches	39¼ inches	35 pounds	100 pounds	$6.85
1K561	26⅞ inches	17⅞ inches	41¼ inches	45 pounds	110 pounds	8.75
1K562	27⅞ inches	18½ inches	43⅛ inches	60 pounds	125 pounds	9.65

We furnish No. 1K562 refrigerator with a porcelain lined water cooler, faucet and glass holder as shown in the illustration at $2.50 extra. The water cooler reduces the capacity of the ice chamber.

ACCESSIBLE, CLEANABLE, DURABLE.

THIS REGRIGERATOR requires but a small floor space, yet has roomy ice and provision chambers. An ice saver, a food saver and a space saver. The outer case is made of thoroughly seasoned northern elm, high gloss golden finish. Note the massive double paneled doors fitted with heavy cast brass hinges and our patent locks and strike. The doors can be closed with a slam and the joints are airtight. The ice chamber door opens from the front, a convenience in filling and chopping the ice. The floor of the food chamber is on a level with the bottom of the door, making it easy to clean. The ice and food chambers are lined with galvanized steel and fitted with drain pipe and drip cup. Has swing front baseboard.

THE INSULATED inner walls, the perfect system of dry air circulation, keep the provision chamber cold, dry and wholesome. An excellent preserver of the food with an economical consumption of ice; built to give superiority in general construction, convenience and refrigeration; securely crated and shipped from factory in Southern Michigan.

Catalogue No.	Width	Depth	Height	Ice Capacity	Shipping Weight	Price
1K571	24⅛ inches	18 inches	49¾ inches	50 pounds	120 pounds	$10.25
1K572	28 inches	19 inches	55½ inches	75 pounds	160 pounds	12.75

ECONOMY REFRIGERATOR $14.35

ECONOMY LARGE DOUBLE DOOR FAMILY REFRIGERATOR

COLD, DRY AND ROOMY. PERFECT INSULATION, PERFECT CIRCULATION AND PERFECT PRESERVATION OF THE FOOD.

THE REFRIGERATOR has an ice capacity of 100 pounds and is a splendid size for large families. It has beautifully carved northern elm case, in high gloss golden finish. Solid brass hinges and locks, and the best quality galvanized steel linings, galvanized ice rack and provision shelves. It has a removable waste pipe and our improved trap to prevent the entrance of warm air. A swinging front baseboard.

IT HAS OUR PERFECT SCIENTIFIC INSULATION, which makes it wonderfully economical for natural or artificial ice. The ice chamber is of ample capacity. The double doors to the provision chamber assist in maintaining a low temperature, as well as saving in ice, as when but one door is open at a time less warm air enters the refrigerators. Built with a view to convenience, economy and satisfactory service and every inch of space carefully utilized.

THIS REFRIGERATOR IS SURE TO PLEASE YOU.

No. 1K581

It is solid and substantial in appearance and elegant in finish and the decorations add greatly to its appearance.

Catalogue No.	Width	Depth	Height	Ice Capacity	Shipping Weight	Price
1K581	35¾ inches	21⅛ inches	45¾ inches	100 pounds	165 pounds	$14.35

ECONOMY REFRIGERATOR $17.95

LARGE DOUBLE DOORS. CONVENIENCE, CLEANLINESS, COLDNESS.

No. 1K575

DO NOT BUY A REFRIGERATOR TOO SMALL. It should be large enough to hold several days' supply of provisions and an ample supply of ice. This refrigerator has an ice capacity of 125 pounds and will readily hold a 100-pound piece of average dimensions with room to spare. The food chamber is large, roomy and convenient. The ice chamber doors in front make it easy of access. The perfectly insulated walls and galvanized steel linings, the perfect duplex circulation of the cold dry air from the ice chamber downward through the food chamber, passing and repassing in a constant flow, will keep provisions and milk fresh, sweet and pure. The outer case is made of thoroughly seasoned northern elm, high gloss golden finish. Doors have thick raised moulded panels and fitted with heavy cast brass hinges and patent adjustable locks and strikes. Has swing front baseboard, removable drainpipe and hinged drip cup. Shipped direct from factory in Southern Michigan.

Catalogue No.	Width	Depth	Height	Ice Capacity	Shipping Weight	Price
1K575	36¾ inches	19⅞ inches	50¾ inches	125 pounds	195 pounds	$17.95

Russell Sage Foundation, "The Households of a Mill Town," by Margaret F. Byington, 1908:

"Expenses incurred for health count as a luxury to be indulged in only with increasing income. When, for instance, a child is ill, the state of the pocketbook, no less than the seriousness of the disease, determine whether the doctor shall be called. Tonics for the rundown in springtime are dispensed within a laborer's home. Perhaps the tendency in this direction that is most serious in its results is the custom of relying upon midwives in confinement. While it is more frequent among the foreigners, many English-speaking women call in midwives because their fees are much smaller and because they help in housework. There are no visiting nurses whose assistance can be secured for an hour or so."

- The family budget includes $4.64 for ice, which comes in blocks and is kept in the tub. Several of their neighbors have iceboxes and even refrigerators. A recession is under way creating an uneven flow of income.
- The family has decided to forgo the purchase of an icebox costing $8.75 because of uncertainty. It would have to be purchased on the installment plan.
- The fuel and light expenditures include coal, usually bought by the 100-pound bag for $0.35 to $0.40, by the 75-pound bushel for $0.25, or by the 25-pound pail for $0.10.
- A family with an income of $600.00 occupying four rooms needs three bushels a week for two months in the fall, two bushels a week for four months in winter, and a total of six bushels for the six months of spring and summer.
- Electricity is unavailable; gas and kerosene are used for illumination in this home.
- The cost of fuel and light is kept to $38.66 by gathering free wood for burning, often boxes thrown out by the merchants or waste materials from building operations.
- The Czorpa family suffers from inadequate water and sewer facilities in the neighborhood; dry closet vaults or outhouses are shared and extremely difficult to keep clean.
- Only 14 percent of families making approximately $600.00 a year have bathrooms in their homes; only 26 percent have a toilet, so it is unlikely this family of six has bathroom facilities.
- Only one in 20 workers own bathtubs; running water is often available only at the outside spigot.
- Milk is sold either "loose" at the grocery store for $0.05 to $0.06 a quart or bottled, in compliance with sanitary requirements, available for $0.08 a quart bottle. Condensed milk at $0.10 a can is frequently used to the exclusion of fresh milk.
- The use of bottled milk increases as family income grows. It is likely the Czorpas use "loose" milk, which they would have to carry in their own pail from the store.
- The cost of buying tobacco products including cigarettes, pipes, and cigars is $9.40 annually for many families.
- The father uses a barber for haircuts that cost $0.10; the children's hair is cut at home.
- The meals of the Polish family are similar to others in Buffalo except that a breakfast of coffee and bread is more common, meat is more often served at lunch, and a chicken for

Sunday dinner is frequent. The Italian families tend to have macaroni once or twice a day and beer every day.

- The nutrition investigation included in the study of Polish Buffalo workers attempts to determine the level of "sufficient nourishment" necessary for a person. The standard used states that "a person at moderate muscular work consumes 100 to 125 grams protein, 50 to 70 grams fat, 350 to 600 grams carbohydrate, with fuel ranging from 3,000 to 7,000 calories per day."

- It costs approximately $0.21 a day per person to feed the family, which includes liquor used at table. This level is considered the lowest possible expenditure to be sufficiently nourished.

- Using the standard measure of spending $0.21 or more per day, per man, 86 percent of the Polish families are well nourished.

- The family spends $8.58 yearly on education and reading, which includes the parochial-school tax. Newspapers generally cost $0.01 each daily and $0.05 on Sunday.

- As second-generation immigrants, this family probably purchases a foreign-language newspaper such as the *Slovak American*, published in New York.

- The Czorpas have some books in their home and have made use of the public library during the year.

- Nearly all Polish families purchase life insurance, frequently used for burial expenses; only a quarter of the Italian families in Buffalo buy insurance.

- The cost of a funeral ranges from $30.00 to $50.00 for a child to $130.00 for the funeral of an adult.

- It is rare for any of this family or their neighbors to visit a dentist. A dentist normally charges $0.50 for pulling a tooth.

- An illness can easily cost a family three to four weeks of wages. Typical diseases of the time, as reported by the survey in order of the number of cases, include pneumonia, accidents, measles, tuberculosis, diphtheria, typhoid fever, nervous prostration, female disorders, and rheumatism.

Buster Brown Vacation
Days Carnival.

- The typical cost of travelling to and from work is $19.00 a year, $8.00 more than for a similar working person in New York City because of the greater distances the Buffalo workers travel to work.
- The family enjoys their recreation taking a trip, using parks, and going to the theater, most likely the "five-cent theater" or moving picture exhibition.
- Paid vacations are extremely uncommon in 1907; weekend visits by the whole family to Coney Island in New York are reported in the survey.

Life at Work: Tailoring

- The man works out of his home as a tailor or sewing machine worker.
- Each day he makes coats, vests, knee-pants, and trousers based on the orders provided by the jobber, who works for a factory.
- Generally the needlework is done by machine with the finishing work done by hand.
- His children assist him by cutting out patterns and sometimes running simple seams, speeding up the work.

McClure's Magazine, December 1904, "Plight of the Tailors," by Ray Stannard Baker:

"Each year crowds of foreign immigrants poured into the East Side. They were poor, ignorant, and they had been oppressed; they knew nothing of American life, though they expected much; they found at once that living here, rent, food, and fuel were far more expensive than in their old homes. The first necessity, therefore, was work, no matter what, to furnish them with the necessaries of life. There are not many things which an unskilled foreigner, knowing no English, can do; but almost any man or woman can sew. And thus flourished the sweatshop, the home of the 'task system,' where men, women and children worked together in unhealthful, often diseased and sometimes immoral surroundings. Nowhere in the world at any time, probably, were men and women worked as they were in the sweatshop, the lowest paid, most degrading of American employment. The sweatshop employer ground all the work he could from every man, woman and child under him. It was no uncommon thing in these sweatshops for men to sit bent over a sewing machine continuously from eleven to fifteen hours a day in July weather operating a sewing machine by foot-power, and often so driven that they could not stop for lunch. The seasonal character of the work meant demoralizing toil for a few months in the year and a not less demoralizing idleness for the remainder of the year."

- To make ends meet, his work week averages 60 or more hours.
- Many other Polish immigrants in Buffalo take similar jobs to support their families.
- Workers making a similar amount include carpenters, paper-hangers, molders, painters, watchmen, hackmen, delivery men, and gardeners.

Life in the Community: Buffalo, New York

- Buffalo's population includes 95,000 Poles and 20,000 Italians.
- Buffalo is considered a "smoky city" at this time.
- The city of Buffalo serves as the hub of the largest manufacturing centers in upstate New York.
- Eighty percent of the working class families give money to religious organizations, labor unions, and lodges. About 25 percent of the men in the economic class of this Polish tailor are union members.
- Employment in mills, factories, and railroad yards is extremely hazardous and life-threatening. In 1907, at least half a million Americans are killed, crippled, or seriously injured while on the job.
- In a survey of the community, *The Ladies' Home Journal* is widely purchased, even among individuals who cannot read English, because of all the fashion illustrations.

The Ladies' Home Journal, May 1904,
"The Court of Last Resort," and "Department of Authoritative Answers to Questions":

"Question: Is it a fact that young men and young women are marrying at later ages than formerly?

"Answer: Statistics do not support the belief that men and women marry later in life now than formerly. The percentages of women marrying before they are 20, 25, 30, 35, and 45 years old are almost unchanged from those of ten years and more ago. The figures for men show a different distribution: 22 percent (as against 19 percent in 1890) are married before they are 25; 55 percent (43 percent in 1890) before they are 30; 72 percent before they are 35 (as compared with 63 percent in 1890) and 83 percent (no change from 1890) before they are 45."

HISTORICAL SNAPSHOT
1907–1908

- In 1908, the *New York Times* inaugurated the custom of dropping an illuminated ball to greet the new year in what everyone now calls Times Square

- Sales of Jell-O reached nearly $1 million nationally

- Sears Roebuck distributed 3 million copies of its spring catalogue

- Cadillac was advertised at $800.00, a Ford Model K at $2,800.00

- Horses were sold for $150.00 to $300.00

- The first self-contained electric clothes washer was developed in Chicago

- The American Society for Keeping Woman in Her Proper Sphere was formed

- The first Christmas "stamps" were sold to raise money for tuberculosis research

- The first Mother's Day is celebrated in Philadelphia, Pennsylvania

- New York City passed the Sullivan Ordinance prohibiting women from smoking in public places

- Publication of the *Christian Science Monitor* began

- Wealthy American Reformer Maud Younger founded the Waitresses' Union in San Francisco after waitressing in order to learn about the life of working women

- The first canned tuna fish was packed in California

- Westinghouse Electric went bankrupt

- Two subway tunnels were opened to traffic in New York City

- The "Rich Man's Panic," or Panic of 1907, resulted in financial reforms that increased the flexibility of the money supply and eventually led to the Federal Reserve Act of 1913

- Industrial production levels peaked in 1906 before the depression of 1907–09. The employment levels in 1906 were not equaled again until the outbreak of the First World War

- In 1908, the U.S. Supreme Court issued a unanimous ruling holding that laws limiting the maximum number of hours that women can work to 10 hours a day are constitutional

1907 Economic Profile

Annual Food Expenditures

Alcoholic Drinks at Home $12.01
Cereals $60.31
Eggs, Butter, Milk, etc. $80.23
Meat and Fish $105.56
Sugar, Tea, Coffee, etc. $21.63
Vegetables and Fruit $55.49
   Total $335.23

Weekly Food Expenditures

Meat and Fish

Four Pounds Fresh Beef $0.48
Four Pounds Salt Beef $0.28
One-Pound Chicken $0.14
One-Pound Fish $0.05
One-Pound Ham $0.16

Eggs, Dairy Products

One Pound Butter $0.27
14 Eggs $0.25
One Can Condensed Milk $0.10
Seven Quarts Milk $0.70

Cereals

One Package Breakfast Food $0.10
12 Loaves Bread $0.60
One Package Crackers $0.10
Flour $0.05
Three Dozen Rolls $0.35

Vegetables and Fruits

One Pound Dried Peas $0.05
Fresh Fruit $0.05
Two Quarts Potatoes $0.16
One Can Tomatoes $0.08
Turnips, Onions, etc. $0.10

Sugar, Tea, etc.

Molasses (One Pint Monthly) $0.03
One Bottle Pickles $0.10
Three Pounds Sugar $0.17
One Pound Tea $0.18

Alcoholic Drinks

Two Pints Beer $0.20

Families dreamed all year of spending a day on the beach at Coney Island.

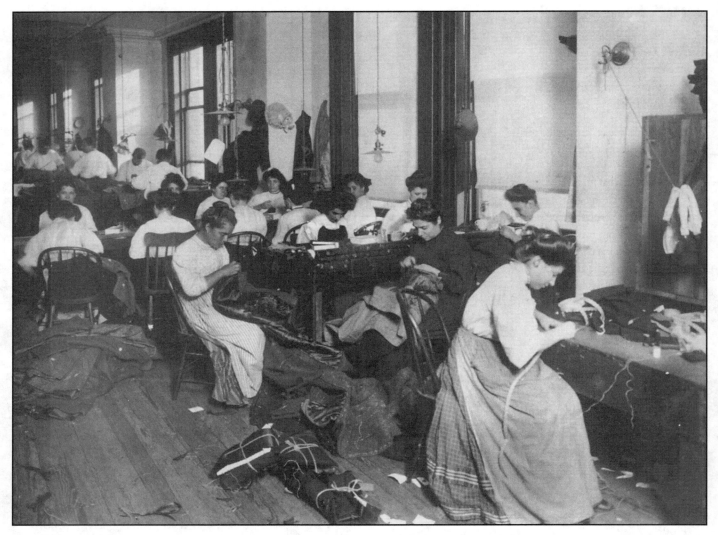

Sweatshops, devoted to the manufacture of cheap, ready-to-wear clothing, hired thousands of unskilled immigrants.

According to a study of working class families, the clothing included all needs for a normal family of four making approximately $600.00. The family would not be expected to make all these purchases in a single year.

For the Man: Total $43.00

Two Hats or Caps $2.00
Six Collars $0.60
Gloves or Mittens $0.50
Four Handkerchiefs. $0.30
Six Pairs Hose $0.60
Two Pairs Overalls $1.50
One Overcoat $15.00
One Pair Pantaloons $2.00
One Suit. $10.00
Four Ties $0.50

Three Work Shirts. $1.00
Two White Shirts. $1.00
Two Pairs Shoes. $4.00
Repair of Shoes $1.50
Summer Underwear $1.00
Winter Underwear. $1.50

For the Woman: Total $25.50
Three Aprons. $0.50
One Cloak $5.00
Two Dresses of Wash Goods. $2.50
Gloves or Mittens $0.50
Six Handkerchiefs $0.45
One Hat. $1.50
Linen, etc. $0.70
One Petticoat. $0.50
Six Pairs Stockings. $0.60
Two Pairs Shoes. $3.00
Repair of Shoes $1.25
Sundries. $1.00
Summer Underwear $0.50
Winter Underwear. $1.00
Three Waists $1.50
One Woolen Dress $5.00

For Each Boy: Total $10.00
Two Hats. $0.50
Mittens $0.25
One Overcoat $2.50
Six Pairs Stockings. $0.50
One Pairs Shoes. $1.25
One Suit. $2.50
One Pair Trousers $0.50
Summer Underwear. $0.50
Winter Underwear. $1.00
Two Waists $0.50

For Each Girl: Total $15.00
One Cloak $2.00
Four Dresses of Wash Goods $2.00
Gloves or Mittens $0.25
Six Handkerchiefs $0.25
One Hat $1.25
Two Petticoats. $0.50
Repair of Shoes $1.25
Ribbons, etc. $0.50
Two Pairs Shoes. $2.50
Six Pairs Stockings. $0.50
Summer Underwear. $0.50
Winter Underwear. $1.00

The average worker made $542.00 in 1907.

Four Waists $1.00
One Woolen Dress $1.50

For Washing
Laundry ($0.05 a week) $2.50
Soap ($0.15 a week) $7.50

Income, Standard Jobs

Average of All Industries,
  Including Farm Labor $542.00
Domestic $316.00
Farm Labor $319.00
Gas and Electricity Worker $623.00
Medical/Health Services Worker $306.00
Public School Teacher $431.00
State and Local Government Worker . . $694.00
Street Railway Worker $658.00
Wholesale and Retail Trade Worker . . . $593.00

Selected Prices

Arrow Cuffs, per Pair $0.25
Blackberry Balsam, Remedy for Dysentery, Diarrhea $0.20
Boyden's Famous Shoes, per Pair $4.75
Cheviot Pajamas, Military Colors $1.15
Cigarettes $0.15/10
Cotton Shirt $5.50
Derby Hat $2.75
Grandfather Clock, 79 Inches High $30.00
Ideal Motor Oil, "No Gum, No Carbon," per Gallon $0.60
Man's Roadster Model Bicycle $14.95
Pocket Watch, 21-Jewel, 14-K Gold, ... $32.50
Razac Ready Razor $3.50
Sears and Roebuck Walking Plow $8.62
Socks, Three Pairs $1.00
Suspenders, Pair $0.50
The Financial Forum Magazine $1.00/Year
Tie $0.27
Typewriter Rental, per Month $2.00
Uneeda Biscuit Cracker, Dust Tight Package $0.05
Waltham Orient; Two-Passenger $400.00
Whitfield Carbon Paper, "No Smudge, No Blur," 25 Sheets $0.50

1909 Family Profile

Rosi Knaust, a 23-year-old single, German woman, is employed as a chocolate dipper, where she works a 92½-hour week during the busy Christmas season. She lives by herself in Chicago, Illinois, a city coping with the crush of immigration during the past two decades. She is considered lucky to be such a skilled worker.

Annual Income: $738.00

Annual Budget

The Chicago study provides no personal information about this worker. As a reference, the average per capita consumer expenditure in 1909 of all workers nationwide is:

Auto Parts	$0.59
Auto Purchases	$1.85
Clothing	$30.00
Dentists	$0.91
Food	$81.43
Furniture	$3.25
Gas and Oil	$1.36
Health Insurance	NR
Housing	$61.48
Intercity Transport	$2.97
Local Transportation	$5.12
Personal Business	$9.61
Personal Care	$2.88
Physicians	$3.24
Private Education and Research	$4.59
Recreation	$9.49
Religion/Welfare Activities	$9.05

Telephone and Telegraph $1.00
Tobacco $6.33
Utilities $4.00
Average Per Capita Consumption $318.42

Life at Home

- Rosi lives by herself in a tenement and shares a bathroom with four others.
- Groceries she is likely to purchase include the following:

Bread, Homemade, per Loaf $0.04
Columbia Family Soap, 10 Bars $0.40
Crystal Domino Sugar, Two-Pound Box . . . $0.18
Fancy Dry Picked Turkeys, per Pound $0.19
Fancy Soft Shell Almonds, One Pound $0.21
Florida Head Lettuce, Three for $0.25
Granulated Yellow Cornmeal, 10 Pounds . . $0.19
Hawaii Sliced Pineapple, 2½-Pound Can . . $0.23
Honey Washed Figs, One-Pound Box $0.25
Jersey Sweet Potatoes, 10 Pounds $0.23
Large Black Cherries, in Syrup, per Can . . . $0.23
Oranges, per Dozen $0.18
Old-Fashioned Japan Tea, per Pound $0.37
Wilbur's Breakfast Cocoa, One-Pound Can. $0.35
Wisconsin June Pears, per Can $0.12

Life at Work: The Chocolate Factory

- A general depression nationwide exists in 1907–1908 that disappears by 1909, increasing the demand for candy production during the Christmas season.
- During the Christmas rush, normally from October 15 to December 15, Rosi works 92½ hours per week dipping cherries into chocolate.
- According to her foreman, "The 1909 rush season began October 15 and from that time until Christmas it was necessary to make 40 days, or 360 hours, extra time."
- During the rush season, the factory opens at 6:30 a.m., with an unpaid half-hour for lunch at noon and one half-hour for supper, closing at 9:00 p.m. for a work day of 13½ hours.
- When the foreman is asked if it is difficult to get the girls to begin work at 6:30 a.m., he says, "No, they like it; but it is hard to keep them at work Wednesday and Saturday nights."
- On Wednesday nights, this working woman often brings her own lunch and then works through the supper half-hour so she can stop work early—by 8:30 p.m. rather than

9:00 p.m. Wednesday is the traditional night for workers to seek entertainment.

- The remainder of the year she works a 68- to 72-hour week, normally working six days a week. Unlike many workers of her day, she works year-round. She receives no paid vacations or paid sick leave.
- During the Christmas season, she makes $23.12 a week, or approximately $0.25 per hour. During the remainder of the year, she makes an average of $14.21 a week. Her pay is near the top of the scale among fellow workers; chocolate dipping is a prestigious position.
- Her wages are based on her piece rate production, not hours. At the time of the survey, she has worked in the candy factory for approximately eight years, since she was 15 years old.

The elevated rail system linked the factory worker to the factory.

- In 1909, 944 women work in eight Chicago candy factories, concentrated on the west side of the city. Approximately 194 of the women are younger than 16 years old.
- The candy factories operate year-round, six days a week, during the normal season. Workers average a 68-hour work week.
- The largest of the factories employs 293 women, including 83 women under the age of 16. The smallest of the factories employs 35 women.
- The prevailing system of payment is a piece-rate basis which encourages long hours. "During the summer months business is very dull," the foreman says. "The girls work at times only three or four days a week. They have always counted upon making up this summer's loss during the Christmas rush."
- Rosi's factory is sanitary, although it only has two toilets for 200 female workers. It is not recorded how often the bathrooms are cleaned. The majority of the chocolate dipper's work can be done while sitting and sometimes standing.
- The per capita consumption of candy in 1880 was 2.2 pounds; by 1914 the per capita consumption is 5.6 pounds.
- Types of candy produced in the candy factories include stick and hard candies, cough drops, lozenges, licorice, gumdrops, caramels, popcorn, and fancy novelties.
- Other jobs in the candy making industry and representative average weekly pay during the normal season are: packer, $7.00; bonbon roller, $5.50; lozenge cutter, $8.00; cornball maker, $4.50.
- The candy industry started on the East Coast but quickly fans out across the country. Since the basic ingredients are dairy products, Chicago becomes a natural hub for candy making and candy bars in particular.
- Chicago has 1,000 Greek-owned candy stores in 1906. The candy industry is a mainstay of the large Greek community. From 1904 to 1909 the number of Greeks in Chicago doubles from 7,500 to 15,000—"12,000 of whom came and went according to their work in the city or on the railroad lines in states further west. As the Greeks became more numerous on the West Side, they invaded the Italian section, gradually displacing Italians from the area."
- The factories are primarily located on the West Side of Chicago. According to an early observer of Greek immigration to the United States, the district becomes more typically Greek than some sections of Athens. "Practically all stores bear signs in both Greek and English, cook houses flourish on every corner, in the dark little grocery stores one sees

black olives, dried ink-fish, tomato paste, and all the queer, nameless roots and condiments which are so familiar in Greece."

- Rigid tradition forbids Greek women from entrance into the labor market, especially after marriage. If they work it is usually in industries which also employ Polish, Bohemian, Russian, and Italian women. To be a domestic is frowned upon. Greek men consider it a disgrace to have a wife or a sister working outside the home.

- In 1908, the Russell Sage Foundation surveys the confectionery manufacturing industry in Pittsburgh to determine the conditions for workers. They find that candy must be protected from the smoke which makes the city picturesque to a non-resident.

- Yet the means adopted to protect the product from outside impurities involve serious harm to the workers. The atmosphere is cloudy from boiling kettles and cooling candies; the need for fresh air is urgent. Some of the small workrooms are well kept and well

"Conversation with German Workers in Chicago," by Alfred Kolb, 1909:

"Whoever isn't just a bag of rags will make something of himself here. That's why I came over (from Germany). You say that wages are better here. You might just be right. But what're you worrying about wages for: you've got to become your own boss if you want to get on. But those days are over in America. I tried it myself a couple of times. The last time as an innkeeper. Me and my late wife, we'd saved ourselves a nice little sum. Within a year everything was gone. No, you can forget it nowadays; for everyone who gets rich, there are ten who go broke. And it's getting worse every year. For the Yankees who were present, this sort of thing was grist for their mills. 'And whose fault is it, anyway that it's getting worse and worse?' They shouted, 'Who else if not the quarter million European starvelings who come over every year and take up all the jobs. High time for some sort of law against this rabble. Stay home, why don't you, we don't need you. You work like snails anyway.'"

aired, it is true, but the type of room most in evidence is steamy, dark, and narrow, with windows tightly closed.

- The survey says, "It has long been declared that men make the best cooks. In recurring instances, when cooking is for a critical public, and not for an indulgent home, some rule of survival selects the undomestic sex to do the work." The wholesale making of candy is no exception. Men are the cooks, the makers.

- Men preside over the open furnaces where the chocolate is melted and the caramel is prepared. They are responsible for baking the peanuts; they have entire charge of the hard candy making, with all its wonderful possible variations of peppermint canes, round kisses with red stars in the middle, suckers, and chips in green, white, and red.

- The wrappers twine waxed paper around the peppermint canes, and twist the peanut kisses with a little rosette at each end. There are nine girls to handle the output of three furnaces; they work here by the week, because the kinds of candy change so frequently that at piece rates they would not be able to make anything. Half of them are laid off in February, but in March the sudden popularity of peanut kisses brings in so many orders that the wrappers have to work overtime every night for three weeks.

- Separated by piles of boxes and cases of stock are six chocolate dippers, two of them experts. Their work is more nearly a trade than that of the other girls, and they are respected accordingly.

- One woman, who has been employed at teaching new girls in factories from Boston to Denver, says, "You can't just teach a dipper. A girl's got to have a natural talent for it or she'll never succeed. It's like millinery, an art that you're born with."

- The chocolate dippers sit at a table with pans of hot melted stuff in front of them. Each girl has a mixing board, beside her a square of waxed paper, indicating where the chips are to be put, and how many each paper is to hold. Taking the chip in her left hand, she dips first the top and then the bottom of the chocolate, and with her right hand puts it on the waxed paper and finishes by a ridge or other decoration. She is paid by the hundred pounds.

- The packer takes the waxed sheets of chips from the table, and puts up the candy in half-pound boxes, crediting each dipper with her amount. The two expert dippers can usually turn out 100 pounds a day, which means a total pay of $9.00 a week.

- Cleanliness in candy factories is recognized as axiomatic. But sufficient air, pure air, circulation of air, are essentials to health which are not axiomatic, and the absence of which is met with at every hand.

- In the dipping department the air is changed at frequent intervals and artificially cooled to about 60 degrees, so the chocolate will be kept at the right heat.

- The emphasis is on quality of output. There are neither fines for bad work, nor rate cutting if the girls make too much. Instead, the rates are in many cases a little better than those of the other factories, the attitude of the managers is a little more liberal, and the result is the retention of the best candy makers in the Pittsburgh trade.

- Concerning wages in the candy industry, the Pittsburgh study finds "The wage basis for both the packers and the miscellaneous hands is on the whole the same, and that same is extremely low. Of the 526 girls in the two departments, only 21 are earning $7.00 a week; the majority earn about $4.00 to $5.00."

> **"Pessimism and the Labor Movement," 1908:**
>
> "Complaints concerning the human resources at our disposal are, when considered reasonably, completely unfounded. Whoever shares our view of the world must know that the people living today, coming out of society utterly consumed by egoism and ground up, as it were, between the grindstones of master and slave, have no choice but to be the way they are."

> ### *Chicago Tribune*, December 1, 1909:
>
> "More than 100 additional women tailors yesterday joined the strikers of that craft making a total of 500 men and women involved. At a meeting of strikers at 10 South Clark Street, officers of the Union charged the employers with breaking contracts made with the employees six weeks ago. The contracts called for an eight-hour day and pay at the rate of time and a half of overtime. A joint committee of the Chicago Federation of Labor, including billposters, stage employees, scene painters, and musicians, will deliver an ultimatum to Chicago theater managers on Thursday unless a favorable answer is received by the time relative to the demands of the striking billposters."

- Among the dippers, however, we may expect to find a different situation. Here, we have seen that real skill is needed, or if not skill, a knack that everyone does not possess. Sometimes a girl can learn to dip in two weeks; for others, it will take six months, and there are some who never learn. The chocolate curls, hearts, and bands on top of creams are marks of hand-dipped work, and it is the prize of a good dipper to make exact decorations on piece after piece, gauging each time the right amount of chocolate.
- If the chocolate itself is either too hot or too cold, it cannot be used, and if when dipped, one hot streak will be left on the outside of the chocolate, it will not dry and the piece will be worthless. The dipper must keep adding hot chocolate to her board from the steam-heated pan on the table to keep it at the right working temperature; moreover, she must see to it that the air in the workroom is dry, or the chocolate will be sticky and cannot be worked easily. The responsibility is on the dippers themselves to keep their windows closed most of the time.

Life in the Community: Chicago, Illinois

- The population of Chicago stands at three million people in 1910, over 70 percent of whom are foreign-born or the children of foreign-born parents. "It is a veritable babel of languages," a Frenchman observes. "It would seem as if all the millions of human beings disembarking year by year upon the shores of the United States are unconsciously drawn to make this place their headquarters."
- Chicago attracts worldwide attention as the nation's leading railroad center. The elevated rail system efficiently links the working class to factories in different parts of the city.
- The commercial center buildings are particularly remarkable because they are all brick, stone, and concrete, the consequence of a city ordinance passed in the wake of the great Chicago fire of 1871.
- The rise of activity—professional and recreational—among women drives the demand in 1909 for simplified clothes. Working women, particularly in cities, are a prominent part of the consumer culture fostered by women's magazines and those who advertise in them. This growing work force hopes to use their earnings to create lives for themselves that resemble those they read about in magazines and books.

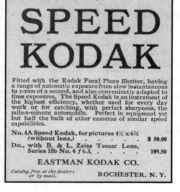

• In the nineteenth century there was a marked difference between the dress of working class women and that of women in the upper class. By the 1910s, however, the key difference between the clothing of the well off and that of the working class was quality, not design. Mass-produced versions of the latest styles in clothing and dress are increasingly available and affordable. Where a middle-class woman could wear a fancy dress made of white linen

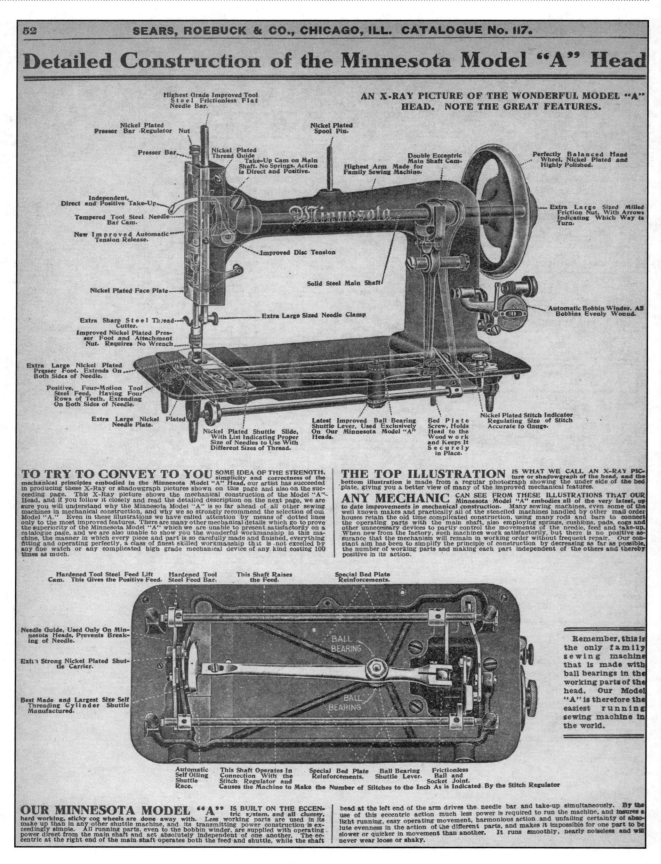

with lace inserts, a working class woman could afford a simpler cotton version that, to the casual observer, looked much the same.

- The empire line is incorporated into the S-curve silhouette in women's dresses, which are still one piece but now have slightly raised waistlines and long, sweeping trains.

- The American Ladies Tailors Association exhibition in New York highlights the "suffragette suit," designed in protest against heavy, impractical skirts. It features a jacket with many pockets and a separated skirt with creases and cuffs like those of men's trousers.

- Marshall Fields, Chicago's leading department store, encourages workers of all ethnic and economic stations to visit the store. Store rules distributed to the store's salespeople stipulate that they be "polite and attentive to rich and poor alike."

- Despite this egalitarian attitude, department stores reinforce the notions of bourgeois good taste and propriety, emphasizing the correct clothes for each occasion.

- By 1909, silent movies become a mass medium and exhibition sites spring up everywhere. There are 10,000 "nickelodeon" or moving picture theatres in America this year, most of which are basically converted street-front stores.

- Early movie houses display an atmosphere of warm informality. Audiences often take part in the show, applauding and making comments about the actions or characters on-screen. Most films are often less than 10 minutes and often accompanied by music or sound effects, and sometimes a running commentary to help explain the lots.

- Among working class workers, activities such as amusement parks, movie theatres, dance halls, fraternal orders, skating rinks, and spectator sports become popular in the first decade of the 1900s.

HISTORICAL SNAPSHOT
1909

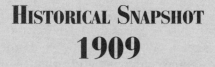

- D.W. Griffith featured 16-year-old Mary Pickford in his films; the former Gladys Smith made $40.00 a week starring in silent movies

- 20,000 members of Ladies Waist Maker's Union staged a three-month strike; they won most of their demands

- A tobacconist convention that year protested the automobile; they were concerned that it would lure people away from homes and clubs and smoking would be diminished

- The Sixteenth Amendment to the Constitution, authorizing income taxes, was passed by Congress

- More than 25 miners were killed in an explosion at the Saint Paul Mine in Cherry, Illinois

- Chicago's Jane Addams, founder of Hull House, ended her term as appointed member of the Chicago Board of Education, where she had lobbied for compulsory education and laws to end child labor

- By 1911, Milton Hershey, the father of the modern candy industry, had sales of $5 million a year making almond bars, kisses, and chocolate cigars

- The National Association for the Advancement of Colored People was founded by W.E.B. DuBois, Chicago reformer Jane Addams, Mary W. Ovington, and others

- The International Ladies' Garment Worker's Union called a strike to protest poor working conditions and low wages

- The Kansas attorney general rules that women may wear trousers

- Western women began to wear V-neck shirts, which some condemned as immoral

- The U.S. Congress passed the Mann White Slave Traffic Act to prohibit interstate and foreign transport of females for immoral purposes

- The U.S. Senate heard a resolution to abolish sex discrimination in the Constitution

1909 ECONOMIC PROFILE

**A sampling of "Room for Rent" advertisements
appearing in the *Chicago Tribune* in 1909 included:**
- "New Washington Hotel, Washington Blvd., neatly furn. rooms, $8 up."
- "Kenwood, nicely furnished, heated 3 to 5 room flats, light housekeeping; $18 up."
- "2333 Michigan Ave. In Private Home. High class 2 and 3 room suites, location and transportation the very best; people of refinement only."

Income, Standard Jobs
Average of All Industries,
    Including Farm Labor $544.00

Clerical Workers in Manufacturing. . $1,136.00
Domestics $420.00
Farm Labor $328.00
Gas and Electricity Workers $618.00
Medical/Health Services Workers $326.00
Ministers $831.00
Public School Teachers $476.00
State and Local Government
    Workers $696.00
Steam Railroads, Wage Earners $644.00
Street Railway Workers. $671.00
Telegraph Industry Workers $622.00
Wholesale and Retail Trade
    Workers. $561.00

Selected Prices

Arnica Jelly Sunburn Remedy, Tube $0.25
Baking Powder, Good Luck Brand,
    per Pound $0.10
Bed, Iron with Corner Posts Made
    of Steel Tubing. $1.89
Caster Oil Tablets, per Box $0.10
Cleaner, Old Dutch, per Can. $0.10
Coca-Cola Drink by Glass $0.05
Cold Cream, per Tube. $0.10
Corset, Has High Bust Effect $1.00
Face Powder, Lablache, per Box $0.50
Home Lessons in Spanish, French,
    Italian, German, per Language $5.00
Mantel Clock, Case Imitates
    Black Italian Marble $5.05
Nestor Cigarettes, Pack of 10,
    Imported $0.40
Night Dresses, Handmade $7.25
Records, Wax-Cylinder,
    Standard Size. $0.18
Sewing Basket, to Include Scissors,
    Bodkins, Pen Knife, Knitting
    and Crocheting Needles . . . . . $7.50–$35.00
Sewing Machine with Seven
    Drawers. $16.45
Silk Stockings, French, per Pair. $4.50
Stereoscopic Views, 100 Views
    of St. Louis World's Fair $0.85
Washing Machine $5.15
Woman's Coat, for Fall and
    Winter, Broadcloth $40.00
Woman's Shoes, of Conora
    Coltskin. $1.39

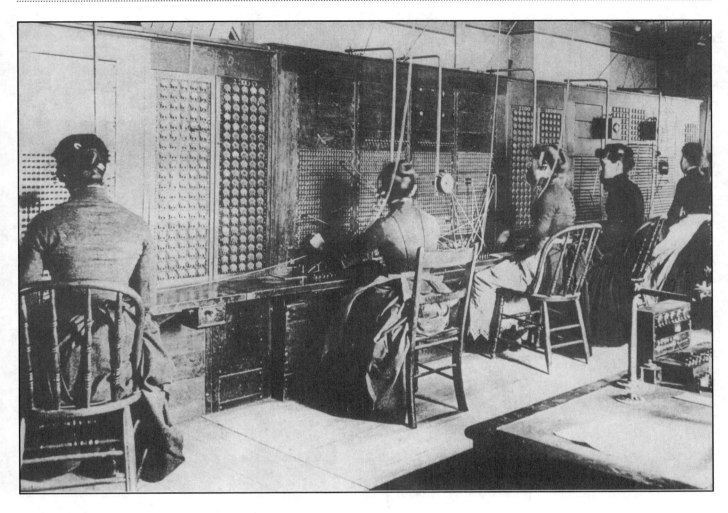

Chicago's Work Force

- No laws restricted the number of hours women could work. Illinois instituted 10-hour-day restrictions in 1910. The law restricted the hours of work to 10 per day, but not the number of days. Many factories began operating seven days a week, 10 hours a day to get around the 10-hour-a-day limitation rule.

- The number of women in Chicago's manufacturing work force rose steadily, if slowly, from 15.3 percent in 1880 to 19.5 percent in 1910. Typically, they were in their teens and 20s, earning money to supplement their families' incomes before they married.

- In 1909, the city was teeming with newcomers from southern and eastern Europe, especially Greece, Italy, and Poland. These immigrants competed with earlier immigrants from northern and western Europe, particularly from Germany, Ireland, and Scandinavia.

- Illinois workers under the age of 16 were restricted to eight hours a day and 48 hours a week. Despite this limitation, 25 percent of the work force in the box making industry in Chicago was under age 16. One manager of a large factory said this large portion of children in the box industry was due to the greater adaptability of young girls. "Their fingers are nimble and small so they are able to more readily manipulate the small boxes, some of which, particularly the baby-ring boxes, are less than an inch in any dimension."

Thousands of women were hired as telephone operators as the popularity of the telephone grew.

- Women ticket agents of the elevated railway companies of Chicago employed 284 women in 1909. The regular 84-hour work schedule ran from 7 a.m. to 7 p.m.—12 hours a day, for seven days a week. No allowance was made for an occasional afternoon off or for a Sunday or legal holiday. "If a girl desires such leave she makes a request and an 'extra' is sent to relieve her; the 'extra' receiving the full rate of pay which is deducted from the regular agent's wage."
- Despite the long hours these positions (on the elevated railway line) are in great demand. In the office of one of the roads there are about 2,000 applications on the waiting list. One of the attractions of the position to a girl of ability is the independent nature of the work, each agent being responsible for the conduct of her station. Then, too, the pay, which ranges from $1.70 (a day) on one road to $2.00 (a day) on another, is rather higher than the earnings possible in other work of the same character.

- There has been some consideration of three eight-hour shifts, instead of two 12-hour shifts. The president of one of the five elevated railroads said "the direct effect of such a demand would be the discharge of all woman agents and the continuation of the two 12-hour shifts, composed entirely of men."

- Within the small retail store industry, work hours were customarily from 8 a.m. until 6 p.m., with 45 minutes for a lunch. During the four weeks before Christmas, when overtime work was required, workers often stayed until 11 p.m.—requiring that they stand from 11 to 14 hours a day. More than one woman reported in the survey "spending all of Christmas day in bed as a result." Supper money, ranging from $0.25 to $0.50, was the usual compensation for overtime work.

- At neighborhood stores, which supplied every item from groceries to furniture to evening dresses, saleswomen spoke not only English, but at least one other language. Girls were found during the survey who spoke Bohemian, Polish, Russian, German, and English. "The Lithuanian girls are especially in demand because in addition to Lithuanian they usually speak Polish, Bohemian, and German."

- The women who shopped in these stores belonged to wage-earning families and were occupied with household duties during the day. It was their custom to shop in the evening when husbands could stay at home and take care of the children or go with the wife "to approve or disapprove of the purchases."

Short Talks about Working Women, U.S. Department of Labor, 1927:

"With the development of the factory system women were transformed from breadwinner taken for granted in the home to the paid breadwinner outside the home. The factory system has had its largest development within the nineteenth century, and the greatest number of women entered industrial pursuits in the decade from 1900 to 1910, this being due largely to the rapid expansion of industry in that period."

Chicago Tribune, September 2, 1909:

"No more peach basket hats; no more scoop shovels nor wide expanse of Merry Widows. This is the decree as set forth at the opening meeting of the convention of the National Association of Retail Milliners in the assembly room in the Fine Arts building last evening. The milliners declare that the extreme styles in millinery have gone to stay because they have meant only the loss of business and money. The whole attitude and experience of the milliners was summed by Mme. Maerie, the president of the Association. She said, 'The last season provided disastrous, short and unprofitable owing to the launching of extreme styles such as the fruit basket hat.'"

Value of One Dollar	
Year	Value in 2010 USD
1910	$22.73
1912	$22.73
1915	$21.59
1917	$17.04
1919	$12.61

Values are approximate based upon economic historical data and 2010 U. S. Dollar

1910–1919

As the second decade of the century began, the economy was strong and optimism was high especially among the newly emerging middle class, who had benefited from technology, a stable economy, and the unregulated, often unsafe labor of the working class. Jobs were readily available to everyone; America enjoyed full employment, yet hours remained long and jobs were often very dangerous. Child and female exploitation were rampant, and violent, company-led opposition to unions was common.

Yet in the midst of blazing prosperity, the nation was changing too rapidly for many, both demographically, economically, and morally. Divorce was on the rise. One in 12 marriages ended in divorce in 1911, compared with one in 85 only six years earlier. The discovery of "salvarsan 606," the miracle treatment for syphilis was hailed as both a miracle and an enticement to sin. As the technology and sophistication of silent movies improved yearly, the Missouri Christian Endeavor Society tried to ban films that included any kissing. At the same time, the rapidly expanded economy, largely without government regulation, began producing marked inequities of wealth; affluence for too few and hardship for too many. The average salary of $750.00 was rising, but not fast enough for many. And on the political front, a Democrat controlled the White House for the first time since 1892 after Teddy Roosevelt's Bull Moose Party, Howard Taft's Republicans, and Eugene Debs' Socialists split the vote sufficiently to allow Woodrow Wilson to slip into the presidency.

Immigration continued at a pace of one million annually in the first four years of this decade. Between 1910 and 1913 some 11 million immigrants—an all-time record—entered the United States. The wages of unskilled workers fell, but the number of jobs expanded dramatically. Manufacturing employment rose by 3.3 million or close to six percent in a year during the period. At the same time, earnings of skilled workers rose substantially accompanied by a backlash focused on ways to protect American workers' jobs. This resulted in a series of anti-immigrant laws that culminated in 1917 with Congress passing a literacy requirement—over President Woodrow Wilson's veto. Other permanent bars to the free flow of migrants into the United States were soon erected. From the beginning of World War I until 1919, the number of new immigrants fell sharply at the same time the war effort was demanding more and more workers. Wages for low-skilled work rose rapidly. By 1919, the American Federation of Labor boasted an army of four million workers, or 80 percent of all union members nationwide. Of the union workers not represented by the AFL, the most important were the four railroad brotherhoods, which were highly cooperative.

The Progressive Movement, largely a product of the rising middle class, also helped shape the decade, raising questions about work safety, the rights of individuals, the need for clean air and shorter work hours. It was a people's movement that grasped the immediate impact of linking the media campaign to the their cause. The results were widespread: South Carolina prohibited the employment of children under 12 in mines, factories, and textile mills; Delaware began to frame employer's liability laws; the direct election of senators was begun; and nationwide communities argued loudly over both the right and the ability of all women to vote and the need and lawfulness of alcohol consumption.

During the decade, motorized tractors changed the lives of farmers; electricity extended the day of urban dwellers, powered trolley cars, and made vacuum cleaners, hair dryers, and electric ranges a reality. Wireless communications bridged San Francisco to New York and New York to Paris; the Bell system alone operated six million telephones in 1915 and was considered essential in middle class homes. As the sale of parlor pianos hit a new high, more than two billion copies of sheet music were sold as ragtime neared its peak. Thousands of Bibles were placed in hotel bedrooms by the Gideon Organization of Christian Commercial Travelers, reflecting both the emerging role of the travelling "drummer" or salesman and the evangelical nature of the Progressive Movement.

But one of the biggest stories was America's unabashed love affair with the automobile. By 1916 the Model T cost less than half its 1908 price and nearly everyone dreamed of owning a car. Movies were also maturing during the period, growing rapidly as an essential entertainment for the poor. Some 35 percent of the population—including many newly arrived immigrants—went weekly to the nickelodeon to marvel at the exploits of Charlie Chaplin, Mary Pickford, and Douglas Fairbanks, Sr.—each drawing big salaries in the silent days of movies.

The second half the decade was marked by the Great War, later to be known as the First World War. Worldwide it cost more than nine million lives and swept away four empires—the German, the Austro-Hungarian, the Russian, and the Ottoman—and with them the traditional aristocratic style of leadership in Europe. It bled the treasuries of Europe dry, and brought the United States forward as the richest country in the world.

When the war broke out in Europe, American exports were required to support the Allied war effort, driving the well-oiled American industrial engine into high gear. Then, when America's intervention in 1917 required the drafting of two million men, women were given their first taste of economic independence. Millions stepped forward to produce the materials needed by a nation. As a result, when the men came back from Europe, America was a changed place for both the well-traveled soldier and the newly trained female worker. Each had acquired an expanded view of the world. Women possessed full suffrage in only Wyoming, Colorado, Utah, and Idaho.

The war forced Americans to confront one more important transformation. The United States had become a full participant in the world economy; tariffs on imported goods were reduced and exports reached all-time highs in 1919, further stimulating the American economy.

1910 Family Profile

Velimir Rzhevsky, a 28-year-old Russian worker, works beyond his normal 12-hour, seven-day-a-week shift to earn enough money to bring his 20-year-old sweetheart to America so they can get married. He is employed by U.S. Steel in Pittsburgh, Pennsylvania, where he works a regular 72-hour week manning the blast furnace.

Annual Income: He makes approximately $654.00 a year.

Annual Budget

Clothing.	$50.00
Food	$253.00
Furniture	$29.00
Insurance, Dues	$25.00
Light and Fuel	$44.00
Rent	$149.00
Savings	$20.00
Sundries	$84.00
Total	$654.00

Life at Home

- He has been in the United States for three years and saving money for the past two.
- During the past year, Velimir was married in a Greek Orthodox wedding. His wife Vera is approximately 20 years old, from Kiev, Russia.
- They got married as soon as he could save enough to bring her to the United States.
- For two years he has worked an average 80 hours per week, often asking for overtime beyond his normal 72 hours; now he wants to work less.
- Overtime hours are paid at the regular rate, not an increased rate.
- They live in a three-room tenement house in the McKees Rocks section of Pittsburgh.

How Long are We Going to Tolerate This?

Some Pictures of Actual Examples of the Extent to Which the Silly Girl and the
Masculine Fool are Carrying Their Vulgar Horseplay at Weddings

ILLUSTRATIONS BY C. M. RELYEA

A NEWLY wedded couple in New Hampshire upon their return from a six months' wedding trip found a painted stork holding this inscription on the front steps of their own home. It was thought to be a splendid joke. But the bride went into hysterics and a few days afterward lost her unborn child, and narrowly escaped losing her own life.

T HROWN at a departing couple in New York in an automobile a shoe struck the glass, broke it, and a piece of the glass entered the eye of the bridegroom. The wedding journey was postponed, the bridegroom was taken to the hospital where it was found that he would permanently lose the sight of the injured eye. He has to go through the rest of his life with one eye, thanks to the joke of his friends.

S OME jokers tied a tin wash-boiler to the back of a bridal carriage in Missouri. The noise frightened the horses and they ran away, throwing out the bride and bridegroom. The bridegroom was thrown on his head against the curb, and although months have now passed he has not yet regained his reason.

F OR trunks, carriages, etc., at weddings a favorite decoration is just a representation of the stork as is here illustrated, this one having been tacked on a bridal carriage in Ohio. Perhaps vulgarity reaches its limit with such representations, and yet they form a large part of the idea of fun of the vulgarians at weddings.

- They have no electricity or indoor toilet.
- They recently purchased a bed, made of iron and painted white, a table, and a rug as part of their wedding celebration from his savings.
- When he came to the United States he planned to work, save his money, and return to the motherland. He has decided to stay in America.
- Now he is saving money to bring his younger brother to Pittsburgh; his brother makes the equivalent of $0.50 a day in Russia.
- Like most immigrants (78 percent), this family has burial insurance.
- Velimir will occasionally purchase a "penny-paper" to look at the pictures and practice reading English.
- Physically he is very strong as are most steel men.
- They attend the Greek Orthodox Church, which is well funded and well attended, particularly by men.

Life at Work: The Steel Industry

- This man works for U.S. Steel as an unskilled laborer in the blast furnace section. In 1910 he works 46 weeks during the year, seven days a week, 12 hours per day.
- The average work week in non-farm industries this year is 51 hours.
- The blast furnish is known for its low hourly rates, but does offer relatively steady work throughout the year.
- Approximately 45 percent of the blast furnace workers earn between $0.16 and $0.18 per hour; 39 percent make between $0.19 and $0.25 per hour.
- From 1900 to 1910 the cost of retail prices for food rose 33 percent while wages in the steel industry went up 17.5 percent.
- His job is to unload the oar cars by running the cars on high trestles and then, by opening the hoppers, allowing the ore to run down into the piles below.
- When he first came to work, the old-style furnace was filled by hand; the temperatures from the furnace could run as high as 118 degrees; now machinery allows workers less exposure to the heat.
- The workers must still be cautious of the toxic fumes produced by the furnace and "flame ups" from the furnace that can burn a man severely.
- The labor force consists of relatively unskilled laborers, recruited from the ranks of the recent immigrants, most of whom come from rural areas and are more accustomed to farm work.

- The skilled positions within the mills are generally held by workers who are English, Scotch, German, Irish, and Welch. Many learn the trade abroad before they come to the United States.
- The skilled workmen are machinists, millwrights, electricians, bricklayers, and locomotive and stationary engineers.
- A handful of companies nationwide control all of the steel and iron work.
- Nationwide, the industry employs approximately 275,000 people; approximately 6,000 belong to either the Sons of Vulcan union or the Amalgamated Association.
- The Amalgamated Association of Iron, Steel and Tin Workers is very weak after major battles with both Carnegie Steel Company and United States Steel Corporation.
- The majority of steel workers are employed 12 hours per day and 30 percent work seven days a week.
- Some companies, notably United Steel Corporation in Pittsburgh, have moved to reduce the work week for its employees from seven to six days.
- Many workers object to the reduction in the work week because it reduces their pay.
- Others object because the day off is during the week, not a Sunday, and thus they have "nothing to do" with friends at the mills, their children at school, and wives busy with their regular household duties.
- The hardest part of the schedule, the workmen report, is not working seven days but working 12 hours at a stretch.

- After a 12-hour shift, workers are often asked to fill in for workers who fail to show, adding overtime and creating an 18-hour day.
- Some discussion of three eight-hour shifts, rather than two 12-hour shifts, has begun, recognizing that the steel mill must run continuously.
- Reformers are urging the industry to adopt the shorter hours and keep worker's pay constant, arguing that in the production of steel, labor constitutes only 17 percent of the total cost of production.
- This survey shows that 30 percent of the employees work some overtime each week, normally six hours per week on top of a regular 72-hour week.
- Steel mills often stop production entirely; 60 percent of all steelworkers are laid off up to four weeks each year.
- In 1910 the largest use of steel is for the rails in railroads, followed by structural shapes, steel plates, and rods for reinforced concrete work.
- The increasing use of machinery within the industry is displacing the need for some unskilled jobs, which comprise about half of the work force.
- Although many ethnic groups are represented at the mill, the company likes to hire Poles and Slovaks because they are "strong, steady and capable of being trained rapidly."
- The duties of the unskilled laborer include handling the materials produced in the steel process or cleaning up the site, mostly slag and scrap.
- The semiskilled workers, the fastest growing job category, are normally machine operators.

Wage-Earning Pittsburgh, by Peter Roberts, 1914:

"Religious ceremonies and observations have the strongest hold upon Poles, Lithuanians, Croatians, and Servians. We have seen that the number of men, all in the prime of life, so intent upon the religious exercises that the least movement of the priest at the altar found immediate response in every member of the audience. The ritual of the church has a deep hold upon Slav and Lithuanian; often the men go to confession at six in the morning in order that they may go to communion the day following. When men are so employed that they cannot attend mass on Sundays, they will attend one on Saturdays. The home must be consecrated once a year; and hundreds take their baskets laden with provisions to church on Easter morning that the priest may bless the feast they hope to enjoy that day."

Wage-Earning Pittsburgh, 1914:

"The day laborer of a generation ago is gone—a change which has been swifter and more complete in Pittsburgh than in many other of our industrial centers. 'Where are your Irish, your Welsh? Your Germans? Your Americans?' I asked an old mill hand. 'Go to the city hall and the police station,' he said. 'Some of them are still in the better paid jobs in the mills but mostly you'll have to look for them among the doctors and lawyers, office holders, clerks, accounts, salesmen. You'll find them there.'"

The day laborer in the mills today is a Slav. The foreign-born of the steel district include, it is true, representatives of every European nation, but I shall deal here only with the races from Southeastern Europe, which for twenty-five years have been steadily displacing the Teutonic and Keltic peoples in the rough work of the industries. The tendency of the Italians is to go into construction, railroad work, and the mines, rather than into the plant and yards; my group narrows itself down to the dominate Magyar, Slav and Lithuan-

ian . . . Roughly speaking, one-quarter of the population of Pittsburgh is foreign-born. The foreign is nowhere more at home than here, and nowhere has he been more actively welcomed by employers. The conflict of customers and habits, varying standards of living, prejudices, antipathies, all due to the confluence of representatives of different races of men, may be witnessed here. The whole territory is thrown into a stern struggle for subsistence and wage standards by the displacements due to these resistless accretions to the ranks of the workers. The moral and religious life of the city is equally affected by this inflow of peoples.

The most backward of them are superstitious and ignorant, victims of cunning knaves and unscrupulous parasites. Their religious training differs widely from that of peoples of Protestant antecedents, and institutions that were dear to the founders of the city are fast being undermined by the customs of immigrants from southeastern Europe."

- No female or child labor is used within the industry; most companies insist that employees must be at least 16 years old and at least one company will only hire individuals 18 and older.
- Steel work is considered too physically challenging for women.
- A bonus fund, based on production, has been established at the steel mill for supervisory and professional employees, but it is not available to the work force, causing discontent.
- U.S. Steel has made efforts to "make partners, practically, of its workers," through a stock purchase plan.
- The majority of workers are 20 to 44 years old; only 13 percent of the work force is over 45 years old.
- The foreman does all hiring of unskilled workers and few records are kept other than a worker's name, nature of his work, and rate to be paid.
- For the employment of the skilled workers, the steel mills have a centralized employment department, where extensive records are kept.
- Steelworkers are paid semimonthly; most industries at the time pay weekly.
- Some steel mills operate company stores. One competitor in New Jersey "owns every dwelling in the community, and also owns every acre of land in the immediate vicinity upon which a dwelling could be constructed. It also owns the only railroad entering the community."

Conditions of Employment in the Iron and Steel Industry, 1913:

"The general lack of effort for the improvement of the communities in which the employees of the steel industry live may in part be attributed to the fact that practically all the employees are adult males. No women are employed in the mills, and very few children. Since the workmen are so largely grown men, the steel manufacturers have felt no responsibility beyond that of paying the established scale of wages. Furthermore, since the manufacturer or managers are brought into contact with the women and children of the community only indirectly, if at all, it is not surprising that very little notice has been taken of the conditions under which they live.

Another reason which may have a bearing on the general indifference of the managers of steel plants toward the communities in which they are situated is that the labor force is not generally recruited from among the native population but from the more recently arrived immigrants.

Finally, the apparent cause of the failure of most of the plans for education, recreation, or general improvement of the adult employees is the schedule of the working hours. Libraries and night schools are at best unattractive at the end of a 12-hour day, and all forms of amusement, except those stimulating, are likely to be passed by. Good libraries exist in many of the towns, but in all cases, the steel workers' patronage is extremely limited. In many cases cards are issued in the name of the steel workers, but the books are drawn by their wives and children."

- The steel mill also owns the only store in the community, as well as a bakery, a dairy, a truck farm, and an abattoir.
- A voluntary retirement program starts at age 60 after 20 years of service; a man who worked 25 years and averaged $60.00 a month for the last 10 years of his service would receive $15.00 a month in retirement.

Life in the Community: Pittsburgh, Pennsylvania

- Allegheny County, Pennsylvania, produces 19 percent of the pig iron and 27 percent of the nation's steel.
- Other prominent steel-producing communities include Allentown, Pennsylvania; Ironton, Ohio; Birmingham, Alabama; St. Louis, Missouri; and Pueblo, Colorado.
- New arrivals dominated the bottom ranks of the steel industry; in 1907, 11,694 of the 14,359 common laborers working in the Carnegie plants of Allegheny County are Eastern Europeans.
- Approximately 32 percent cannot speak English.
- In 1880 Slavs, Lithuanians, Hungarians, and Italians formed less than 1 percent of the population of Pittsburgh; by 1910 they represent 13 percent.
- The U.S. Immigration Commission classifies all workers who earn less than $1.50 a day as unskilled; under that

rule 50 percent of Italians and Slavs are unskilled; 70 percent of Croatians are unskilled, and 85 percent of Serbs and Bulgarians are classified that way.

- Hungry immigrants are often accused of undermining American workers; "These guys have no pride," a craftsman said, "they are not ruled by custom. When the foreman demands it they throw down the saw and the hammer and take up the wheelbarrow."

- When determining whether the worker is paid by the piece or the hour, the rule is, "If the machine depends upon the man for speed, we put on piece work; if the machine drives the man, we pay him by the day."

- Of 500 industrial fatalities in Allegheny County in one year, 293 of the victims are foreign-born.

- Both U.S. Steel and Pittsburgh Steel Company now have accident prevention programs; no state or local regulations govern deaths on the job.

- The geographical contour of the region has an influence on keeping the foreign population within certain limited districts.

- The two rivers, the Allegheny and the Monongahela, have cut their bed into the Allegheny range, leaving a narrow strip of land on either side of their banks which offers limited sites for dwellings, mills, and factories.

- Clustering the worker's homes near the factory is considered an advantage to the employer so that the "crude labor force within easy call, and night work and the cost of carfare help keep the mass of men employed in common labor near the mills and on the congested low lands."

- The Croatian, Servian, Romanian, and Greek populations are 95 percent male; hence the men use boarding houses.

- Each man pays $0.75 to $1.00 a week for a place to sleep and the little cooking and washing that care to be done.

- The boarding houses keep food accounts based on what everyone eats and every two weeks the sum is divided equally among the boarders. The bill for two weeks will normally amount to $3.00 a man, so the average boarder will spend only $10 a month on room and maintenance.

- A number of Russians pay $3.00 a month for room rent; they buy bread made by Russian Jews, get a herring and a pot of beer and live—not always—in peace.

The Greek Orthodox Church grew rapidly due to immigration.

- Alcohol consumption, especially among immigrant men without wives, is very high; drunk and disorderly charges are common.

- It is not unusual, the report says, for a boarding boss to rent but one room; he and his wife put their bed in one corner, the stove in another, and the boarders take the remaining corners.

- Sometimes the rooms are so crowded that the boss and his wife sleep on the floor; and cases are repeatedly to be found where a bed is being worked on a "double shift—day and night."

Learning English was a priority for many steel workers.

- A strike in 1909 at McKees Rock, where our couple lives, is continuing to attract media attention. *The Wall Street Journal* calls the company's methods "sordid and inhuman."
- *The New York Evening Post* accuses the Pressed Steel Car company, against whom the strike is held, of "grinding out" profits "at the expense of the laborers."

Abstracts of Reports of the Immigration Commission, 1911:

"While social conditions affect the situation in some countries, the present immigration from Europe to the United States is in the largest measure due to economic causes. It should be stated, however, that emigration from Europe is not now an absolute economic necessity, and as a rule those who emigrate to the United States are impelled by a desire for betterment rather than by the necessity for escaping intolerable conditions."

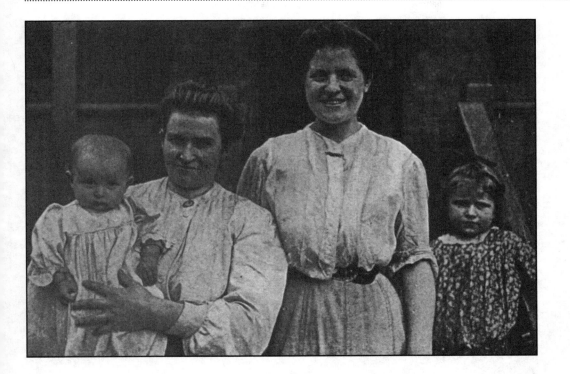

The Ladies' Home Journal, April 15, 1911, "What Girls Ask":

"Dear Mrs. Hathaway: I should like to know what a girl is going to do who is situated as I am. My sister is engaged to a drummer. And he comes to see her every Sunday night. We live in a little flat and there is only one parlor. When he comes the family all sit in the dining-room, so as to let them have the parlor. I am not engaged, but I have a friend who is very attentive. He sells goods for a whole-sale grocery house and only returns to his home-town once a week, for Sunday. We don't want to push in where we are not wanted, so we go walk-ing. We walk until we almost drop. The magazines say a girl shouldn't meet a person on the street and walk around with him so much, but what can a person do? He is strictly all right and has a fine position, and my folks like him; but we can't ever seem to get on, the ways things are. Bessie K.

It pinches my heart to think of a girl having no place but the street in which to entertain a friend, one who she has every reason to feel means to make the relationship more than a mere friendship. If the magazines say you shouldn't have the comfort of a Sunday walk then the magazines are wrong.

The first practical thing I will suggest is that your sister should be asked to take her turn at Sunday walks and let you have the parlor once in a while. Turn about is fair play. Take it up with her and see if she will be reasonable.

If she is selfish, as some sisters are, then I will ask a friend to allow you the use of her room once in a while. You must know someone who would be glad to do it if she knew you wanted it. I wouldn't in the least mind asking. Some great writer said that 'All mankind loves a lover,' which was his way of saying that most people are interested in seeing young people happy. You might find help and sympathy where you least expect them."

- As a result a government investigation is launched. *The American Federationist* in September, 1910, says, "Public opinion at the present moment is arrayed against the working conditions in the steel industry."
- Reformers in Pittsburgh have opened schools for immigrant children and clubs have been formed to teach the workers English.
- The National Slovak Society has 50,000 members; the Polish National Alliance boasts 75,000.
- The Italian organizations have concentrated on citizenship; four-fifths of all Italians in Pittsburgh who have been in the country five years are now nationalized; many quickly become voters, giving the Italians a powerful voice in city business.
- Pittsburgh banks, discovering that immigrants are savers, create foreign exchange departments, headed by men who can speak the language of the immigrants.
- A banker doing business with the Servians says that each pay day he sends back between $20,000 and $25,000 to the old country.
- The fraternal organizations among the Slavs, Lithuanians, and Italians promote thrift, provide insurance, and help those who are sick or in need.

HISTORICAL SNAPSHOT
1910–1911

- Nationwide only 43 percent of the 16-year-olds were still in school

- Western Union abolished the $0.40 to $0.50 charge for placing telegraph messages by telephone

- *Women's Wear Daily* began publication in New York

- U.S. cigarette sales reached 8.6 billion cigarettes, with 62 percent controlled by the American Tobacco Trust

- Florida orange shipments rebounded to their 1894 level

- 70 percent of bread was baked at home, down from 80 percent in 1890

- *The Flexner Report* showed most North American medical schools were inferior to those in Europe

- The return of Halley's Comet stirred fear and excitement, as many hid in shelters or took 'comet' pills for protection

- The average man made $15.00 for a 58-hour work week; the family spent 42 percent of its income on food

- A movement began to restrict the sale of morphine except by prescription

- More than 10,000 nickelodeons were now operating nationwide

- Supported by increasing sales of parlor pianos, over two billion copies of sheet music were sold

- Father's Day and the Boy Scouts of America made their first appearances

- The concept of the "weekend" as a time of rest gained popularity

- New York's Ellis Island had a record one-day influx of 11,745 immigrants in 1911

- The 1910 census recorded that 2,200 communities nationwide had between 2,500 and 50,000 people; in 1860 the number was 400 communities

THE GREATEST PERIOD IN A GIRL'S LIFE

By Harrison Fisher

A Series of Six Pictures, of Which This is the Second

The Trousseau

The Next Picture of This Series Will Appear in an Early Number

1910 ECONOMIC PROFILE

Income, Standard Jobs

Average for All Industries,
    Including Farm Labor $574.00
Clerical Workers $1,156.00
Domestics $337.00
Farm Labor $336.00
Federal Civilian $1,096.00
Gas and Electricity Workers $622.00
Medical and Health Workers $338.00
Public School Teachers $492.00
Telegraph Workers $649.00
Wholesale and Retail
    Trade Workers. $630.00

Selected Prices

Airplane Fare over Columbia, SC $5.00
Baseball $1.15
Bedspread, Crocheted, 68 x 79 . . . . $0.68
Bicycle $15.95
Chiffonier Mirror, 14 x 22 . . . . $14.90
Cloth, Black Taffeta . . . . $0.67 per Yard
Coca-Cola Drink by Glass $0.05
Diamond Ring, Man's Solitaire $100.00
Dress, Silk $10.95
Exterior Ready Mixed
    Paints. . . . . $0.98 per Gallon
Handkerchief. $0.14
Lawn Mower, 16-Inch. $5.89
Poke Bonnet Hat $27.89
Porch Rocking Chair. $2.25
Sanitol Toothpaste. $0.25
Shovel $0.48
Soap Dispenser $5.00
Umbrella $2.74
Uneeda Biscuit Crackers $0.05
Violin, Student. $3.75

1912 Family Profile

This Cuban Rodenas family of four is supported by the booming cigar making industry in the Ybor City section of Tampa, Florida. Both the man and the woman work in the cigar industry, although the woman often works shorter hours so she can care for their two children, both under the age of 14.

Annual Income

Husband	$1,035.00
Wife	$580.00
Total	$1,615.00

The father of the Rodenas family of four works as a hand cigar maker, making $0.45 per hour working about 46 hours weekly; the average worker receives $0.29 per hour. Since cigar makers are paid on a piece rate, not hourly, the man makes more than 1,000 cigars each week.

The woman works as a bander, making $0.18 per hour, or about $11.50 per week, the average wage for that type of worker in the industry. She frequently works fewer hours, about 40, so that she can tend the children. Cigar workers throughout the country set their own hours and protect that privilege vociferously.

Annual Budget

The study of Cuban cigar makers does not provide a detailed listing of home expenses. A national consumer expenditure from that time period, adjusted for a family of four would be as follows:

Auto Parts	$4.36
Auto Purchases	$16.84
Clothing	$118.08
Dentists	$3.80
Food	$361.36
Furniture	$13.88
Gas and Oil	$9.40

Housing. $251.12
Intercity Transport $13.28
Local Transport. $24.52
Personal Business $39.44
Personal Care $12.32
Physicians $11.96
Private Education $19.88
Recreation $40.24
Religion/Welfare $33.76
Telephone $4.52
Tobacco $29.56
Utilities $18.56
Per Capita Consumption $1,347.80

Life at Home

- The Rodenas family lives in a one-story house which is very close to its neighbor's.
- Although the houses are close together, common areas are set aside for gardens to grow vegetables, cutting the family's food bill by 30 percent.
- Italian vegetable vendors also tour the neighborhood with additional fruits and vegetables.
- In these pre-air conditioning days of Florida, windows are left open. None of the homes is heated because of the climate of Florida.

More than 10,000 nickelodeons entertained workers nationwide.

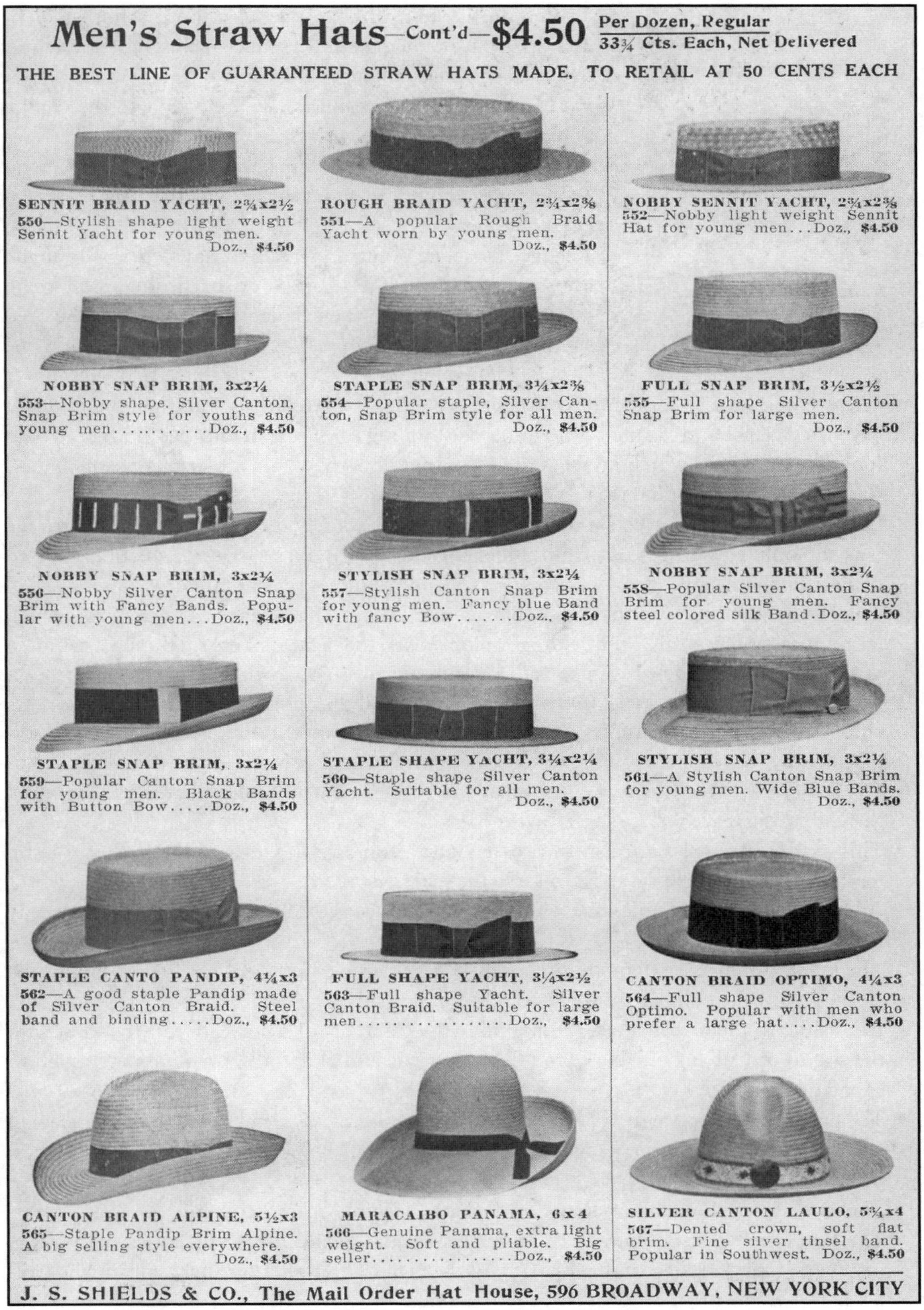
Men's Straw Hats—Cont'd—$4.50 Per Dozen, Regular 33¾ Cts. Each, Net Delivered
THE BEST LINE OF GUARANTEED STRAW HATS MADE, TO RETAIL AT 50 CENTS EACH
SENNIT BRAID YACHT, 2¾x2½
550—Stylish shape light weight Sennit Yacht for young men. Doz., $4.50
ROUGH BRAID YACHT, 2¾x2⅜
551—A popular Rough Braid Yacht worn by young men. Doz., $4.50
NOBBY SENNIT YACHT, 2¾x2⅜
552—Nobby light weight Sennit Hat for young men...Doz., $4.50
NOBBY SNAP BRIM, 3x2¼
553—Nobby shape. Silver Canton, Snap Brim style for youths and young men...........Doz., $4.50
STAPLE SNAP BRIM, 3¼x2⅜
554—Popular staple, Silver Canton, Snap Brim style for all men. Doz., $4.50
FULL SNAP BRIM, 3½x2½
555—Full shape Silver Canton Snap Brim for large men. Doz., $4.50
NOBBY SNAP BRIM, 3x2¼
556—Nobby Silver Canton Snap Brim with Fancy Bands. Popular with young men...Doz., $4.50
STYLISH SNAP BRIM, 3x2¼
557—Stylish Canton Snap Brim for young men. Fancy blue Band with fancy Bow.......Doz., $4.50
NOBBY SNAP BRIM, 3x2¼
558—Popular Silver Canton Snap Brim for young men. Fancy steel colored silk Band. Doz., $4.50
STAPLE SNAP BRIM, 3x2¼
559—Popular Canton Snap Brim for young men. Black Bands with Button Bow.....Doz., $4.50
STAPLE SHAPE YACHT, 3¼x2¼
560—Staple shape Silver Canton Yacht. Suitable for all men. Doz., $4.50
STYLISH SNAP BRIM, 3x2¼
561—A Stylish Canton Snap Brim for young men. Wide Blue Bands. Doz., $4.50
STAPLE CANTO PANDIP, 4¼x3
562—A good staple Pandip made of Silver Canton Braid. Steel band and binding.....Doz., $4.50
FULL SHAPE YACHT, 3¼x2½
563—Full shape Yacht. Silver Canton Braid. Suitable for large men.................Doz., $4.50
CANTON BRAID OPTIMO, 4¼x3
564—Full shape Silver Canton Optimo. Popular with men who prefer a large hat....Doz., $4.50
CANTON BRAID ALPINE, 5½x3
565—Staple Pandip Brim Alpine. A big selling style everywhere. Doz., $4.50
MARACAIBO PANAMA, 6x4
566—Genuine Panama, extra light weight. Soft and pliable. Big seller................Doz., $4.50
SILVER CANTON LAULO, 5¾x4
567—Dented crown, soft flat brim. Fine silver tinsel band. Popular in Southwest. Doz., $4.50
J. S. SHIELDS & CO., The Mail Order Hat House, 596 BROADWAY, NEW YORK CITY

- Conversations between neighbors often take place from window to window, rather than yard to yard; secrets are whispered from neighbor to neighbor to prevent all from hearing.
- One resident reveals that a friend boils and stirs hot water in the kitchen during hard times so that more affluent neighbors will think that stew is cooking.

- The ethnic make-up of the neighborhood is both Cuban and Spanish; no single ethnic group exclusively dominates any area of ever-changing Ybor City.
- Parades, picnics, and festivals are important to the energy and social action of the society and take place often.
- Seventh Avenue is a social magnet for the family, who promenade down the street on a Saturday night where everyone speaks and visits.
- The weekly social events include the chavateros, who invite housewives to bring their knives for sharpening; mondongo men, who sell kidneys; the heladeros who sell fruit-flavored sherbets; and the maniseros, who sell peanuts along the crowded thoroughfare.
- The evening is often a time for courtship: "Mother would take us walking up and down Seventh Avenue and all the boys would be standing on the curb and the mothers would look like little hens watching their chicks so that nobody would look at us or touch us—the boys would go wild trying to get a word with us."
- One girl says, "If you even sat on the porch outside, somebody had to be there. Marriage was the only way to get out from under the skirts of the mothers—so the first male to come along and smile at us, we would marry him. And there is not divorce."
- The family is struggling from the debts acquired during the Cigar Strike of 1910, which lasts for several months. Although no union exists, the cigar makers of Tampa are united in their demands and are even considered militant by union leaders.
- The 1910 strike involves 12,000 workers after a number of selectors are fired. Workers charge that the manufacturers have violated the unofficial wage agreement. The strike is defeated by the importation of strikebreakers from Havana in 1911.
- The social life of the family is centered around the El Centro Asturiano, the social club of the Cuban cigar workers, especially the men.
- This club, like most Latin clubs, protects and promotes the idea of the supreme Latin male; women's auxiliaries exist to serve the male members.
- A Latin writer says that anyone who does stay home is considered "hen-pecked and only half a man."
- The men normally see their children only during the evening meal before heading to the club to enjoy the company of men and the gaming tables.
- According to the newspapers, "On Sunday the Cantinas of Ybor City reverberated with the sound of Cubans playing dominoes and cards and club halls are commonly filled to capacity."
- The club includes more than 5,000 books, a staircase of Mexican onyx, and a dance hall with a marble floor and magnificent chandeliers. It boasts approximately 3,000 members.
- The club also includes a bowling alley and gymnasium for its members.
- The family also looks forward to the club's annual picnics. In 1911, more than 6,000 members, their families, and guests attend the picnic at Sulphur Springs, causing the trolley company to press all of its cars into service. "Every nationality is represented," reports the *Tampa Morning Tribune*.
- El Centro Asturiano burns in June, 1912, and all of its members are granted full membership privileges to the rival club, El Centro Español, operated by the Italian cigar makers.
- The Rodenas family, like many in the community, pays $1.50 per month for social benefits and total medical protection through La Benefica Española; through the efforts of Cuban cigar workers a hospital described as the first "electric ambulance" is built.

- Yellow fever is a constant threat to the family, along with typhoid, dengue fever, malaria, and tuberculosis, similar to other communities which see large numbers of immigrants.
- When cigar workers contract tuberculosis, requiring a long convalescence, the medical package offered through the club, provides for $415.00 and transportation to a Havana, Cuba, sanatorium.
- Church attendance among Cuban cigar makers is poor, and donations to the Catholic Church are low, even while large social clubs are being constructed.
- Of the approximately "10,000 souls" identified by the Catholic church as potential communicants, only 160 come to mass on Easter, a traditional high holy day of the Catholic Church.

Life at Work: The Cigar Industry
- The family lives within walking distance of the cigar factory.
- Among the total population of Tampa, 82 percent of Cuban males work in the cigar industry compared with 45 percent of the Italians and 78 percent of the Spanish men.
- Of the 11,541 total employees within the factory, 64.6 percent are females; 35.4 percent are males.
- Although many women work at the factory, it is unusual for a married woman to work there; only 20 percent of the working Cuban women are married.
- Women are often employed in support roles and are given little encouragement to become cigar makers.
- A study of women cigar workers show more irregular hours; many married women arrive early and work quickly so they can leave work in time to meet their children when they come home from school.

Women worked in supportive roles in the cigar industry.

- Nationally, female membership in the Cigar Makers International Union is 10 percent; when the CMIU organizes the Jacob A. Mayer Company in 1907, 30 women are fired because the union does not allow "this kind of work."
- The 1910 census lists 58,725 male cigar makers nationwide, of whom 18,032 are born of native parents. Among union cigar makers in New York City, separate union locals are created for the Bohemians, Jewish, and Spanish-speaking cigar makers.
- Cigar workers become educated thanks to the traditions of lectors, one of the most prestigious professions in the cigar industry.
- Lectors, or readers, are hired to entertain the cigar roller. They are paid by the cigar worker and the more popular the lector, the higher the salary he can demand.
- Lectors are usually seated in a chair elevated above the cigar roller tables so their voices can be easily heard throughout the room.
- They begin the day by reading excepts from a local newspaper and a newspaper from Spain or Cuba, followed by a reading from a novel or the works of a political philosopher.
- Cigar workers, many of whom are unable to read and write, are able to quote Shakespeare, Voltaire, Zola, and Dumas.
- The lector custom is not widespread outside Tampa, except in the Jewish cigar making shops in New York.
- Future labor leader Samuel Gompers serves as a reader before heading the American Federation of Labor.
- Ventilation is extremely controversial in cigar factories. Usually the windows remain closed despite the heat. Open windows cause a draft for the men who sit in virtually the same position all day, but more important, the fresh air dries out the tobacco and makes it harder to work, resulting in lower production.
- Cigar makers want to make cigars with tobacco that is dry and pliable.

- The smell of a cigar factory is intense and overpowering; recalling their first days on the job workers often mention the nausea and intoxication of the thick, penetrating smell, which makes it "difficult for them to walk in a straight line."
- The tobacco produces a fine brown dust that settles everywhere, contributing to the fact that cigar workers' mortality rate from tuberculosis is second only to stonecutters.
- Cigar makers change their clothing in the morning and don an apron to begin work. The tobacco stains everything that is not covered.
- Cigar making is considered a craft, performed by artists; the apprenticeship of an aspiring cigar maker often lasts three years with a pay of only $5.00 a week.
- Young cigar makers are expected to smoke their own cigars to test the quality of the product they produce.
- All wages are paid weekly on Saturdays. The pay, in cash, is based on how many cigars the worker produces, measured per thousand. All pay is based on piece work, not by the hour.
- For Spanish hand work, where all tobacco is Clear Havana, a cigar maker who makes 1,000 cigars 4½ inches long will be paid $17.00 for straight work, $18.00 for shaped cigars, and $21.00 for perfectos, the hardest to make.
- The Ybor City factory clearly has a class system with packers and selectors at the top, who look down upon cigar makers, who are over strippers and banders.
- Other job types in the cigar industry are bunch makers, rollers, and steamers.
- It is customary within the industry that cigar makers take home three cigars at the end of the day and six on Saturday; each cigar maker creates "smokers" for his own personal use as part of his or her pay. Female cigar makers take the freebies home to husbands and boyfriends.
- Women and some men often refuse to work during high Christian holidays such as Holy Week, the week before Easter, or Ascension Thursday.
- The cigar making industry is considered a travelling fraternity. Like carpenters, hatters, and printers, many cigar makers travelled from factory to factory, knowing a good cigar maker can get a job almost anywhere in the country.

Decorative, distinctive labels helped to identify and sell cigars.

- The cigar makers of Ybor City shun the national union, distrusting the German influences. The unions themselves exclude some nationalities, including "Chinese coolies" and often women, who they believe will be disloyal and capable of undermining the solidarity of the union.
- Cigars produced in Ybor City are considered "high end" or more expensive; however, since 1907 they have faced increasing competition from cigar makers who are pushing $0.05 and $0.10 cigars. Several "cheap cigar" manufacturers relocate from New York City to Tampa in 1910 and 1911.

- American cigar employee workers by city according to the 1910 census: New York, 22,416; Tampa, 8,061; Philadelphia, 6,216; Detroit, 4,354; Chicago, 4,161; Pittsburgh, 3,061; Baltimore, 2,648; Cincinnati, 2,437; other cities, 86,224; total cigar workers, 139,578.
- Unlike the diversified ethnic populations of the industrial cities of the North, Florida's late 19th-century cigar communities are founded by Spanish-speaking immigrants. They produce one item, handmade cigars made from Cuban tobacco.
- The pressure to produce cigars is so high many workers do not take the time to go to the bathroom fearing "you are going to lose 10 minutes and you are going to lose 10 to 15 cigars or 20. Many times you waited until you got home."

Cigar workers became educated thanks to a paid lector who read to the workers all day.

Life in the Community: Tampa and Ybor City, Florida

- The first cigars are made in Tampa in 1886 in Ybor City after Vicente Marinez Ybor, Edward Manrara, and Serafin Sanchez, all originally from Spain, move their cigar factories from Key West, Florida, to avoid labor problems.
- The climate of Tampa, on the west coast of Florida, possesses a high humidity that is well-suited for the making of cigars.
- Tampa is celebrated as the "Smokeless City of Smokes," attracting thousands of immigrants, particularly Italians, Spaniards, and Cubans to the trade. Its skilled industrial work force is composed almost exclusively of immigrants, who do not have to compete with entrenched ethnic groups from earlier migrations such as the Irish and the Germans.
- Cigar manufacturing expands even further in the 1890s when many factories relocate from New York and Key West. The great fire of 1886 in Key West contributes to this move to Tampa. Many in Key West fear a repeat of the devastation. Eleven Key West factories move to Tampa following the fire; 13 from New York are also located in the city.
- By 1895 approximately 10,000 Cubans reside in Florida, approximately 2.3 percent of the state's population.
- By 1900 Tampa has become the leading manufacturing city in Florida, thanks largely to its production of millions of pure Havana cigars.
- By 1909 Florida's cigar industry gives employment to 12,280 wage earners, manufacturing products valued at $21.5 million and representing 29.6 percent of the total value of the manufactured products of the state.
- In 1910 approximately 38,000 people live in Tampa, up from 15,800 in 1900. The West Tampa sections, where the Rodenas family lives, boasts 10 cigar factories, a $20,000 opera house, and streetcar service. "West Tampa is just like the wild west, a frontier town. There are cock fights, boxing matches, horses tied to hitching posts in front of cantinas. West Tampa is called La Caimareri'a or 'place of gators.'"
- At the start of the 1910 cigar maker's strike in Tampa, nearly 1,000 unionized construction workers, printers, machinists, and longshoremen march with more than 2,000 cigar workers to a rally in Ybor City that attracts 5,000.

Working-Class Life, The 'American Standard' in Comparative Perspective, 1899–1913, by Peter R. Shergold:

"One of the most common complaints against the city's (Pittsburgh) stogie-manufacturing workshops was that male and female employees worked in close proximity. William Matthews visited one cellar in 1905 where 'huddled at least fifteen people, men and young girls making stogies. The Laws of God and the laws of men (were) violated every day.'"

The Ladies' Home Journal, April 1911, "Girls' Affairs," an attempt to unravel some of the perplexities that come to girls in their relation to the other sex:

"I have a friend whom I have known a long time. We are very sympathetic, and like the same books and people. He comes often to see me and seems to enjoy himself. He takes me out, too, and we always have good times together. The other young folks in our set seem to think we are engaged. The girls talk to him as if he belonged to me, and the rest of the fellows have stopped coming to see me. But really there isn't anything to it yet. He has never said a word and I don't know what to make of it. My sister says perhaps he is waiting for me to say something. What would you do?

"Answer: This is a difficult situation. The first question for you to ask yourself is whether you really have a right to think your friend means to come to more serious purposes. It may be that he enjoys your society in a frank way and has no idea that anything more can be expected. If so I do not think much of his cleverness. It is certainly quite natural that your other friends

should consider the matter settled, and this is why it is either ungenerous or stupid of him to let such a situation continue. Sometimes a man does this out of pure thoughtlessness. He forgets that while he is monopolizing a girl she may lose other friends and other chances. The girl is rather helpless under it too. She cannot say to him: Are you in earnest? What do you mean to do? All the best sentiment and tradition are against such a course. If she were to take things into her own hands in this way she would never feel happy or at rest about it. No, there is nothing direct that can be done. But you might try a little judicious discipline. Do not be at home one of the usual times he calls. Try absent treatment for a while. Don't sit in the parlor waiting for him every night, like a ripe plum ready to drop into his mouth when he says the word. He will value your society more when he finds it is not easy to get and that you have other friends who want to see you."

The Immigrant World of Ybor City:

"People date their lives from various strikes in Tampa. Older residents of Ybor City measure their family and generational histories by the yardstick of the great strikes of 1899, 1901, 1910, 1920, and 1931." José Yglesias, a native of Ybor city and noted author.

- The integrated audience hears speakers in English, Spanish, and Italian encourage the men and women to strike.
- Latin cigar makers who leave Ybor City often encounter social boundaries; "A Latin can't cross Twenty-second street," one writer says.
- Signs reading "No Dogs or Latins Allowed" or "No Dagoes" are posted in Tampa by the Anglo population.

HISTORICAL SNAPSHOT
1912–1913

- Congress extended the eight-hour day to all federal employees

- Women composed a quarter of all workers employed in nonagricultural jobs

- L.L. Bean was founded by merchant Leon Leonwood Bean

- Although medical schools had opened their doors to women in the 1890s, they still restricted admissions to five percent of the class by 1912

- One-third of American households employed servants, who worked 11 to 12 hours a day, with only one afternoon off a week; domestic service was the largest single category of female employment nationwide, often filled by immigrants

- Women who married seldom stayed at work; women were forced to choose between marriage and career; of the women graduating from college before 1910, only a quarter ever married

- Nationwide approximately 57 percent of the 16- and 17-year-olds no longer attended school

- The electric self-starter for motorcars was perfected and was now being used by Cadillac, an innovation designed to eliminate the hand crank

- A fire at the Triangle Shirtwaist Company in New York City incinerated 146 women workers, mostly girls, leading to increased regulations on the hours and conditions of labor in factories

- Direct telephone links were now available between New York and Denver

- Ford produced more than 22 percent of all U.S. motorcars

- Oreo biscuits were introduced by National Biscuit Company to compete with biscuit bon-bons

- A merger of U.S. film producers created Universal Pictures Corporation

- A&P began rapid expansion featuring stores that operated on a cash-and-carry basis

- Brillo Manufacturing Corporation was founded

- Camel cigarettes were introduced by R.J. Reynolds, creating the first branded cigarette

- Congress strengthened the Pure Food and Drug Law of 1906

- Peppermint Life Savers were introduced as a summer seller when chocolate sales were down

1912 ECONOMIC PROFILE

Income, Standard Jobs

Average for All Industries
Including Farm Labor $592.00
Clerical Workers in
Manufacturing $1,209.00
Domestics $350.00
Farm Labor $348.00
Gas and Electricity Workers $641.00
Medical Health Workers $352.00
Public School Teachers $529.00
State and Local Government
Workers $724.00
Telephone Workers $438.00
Wholesale and Retail
Trade Workers $666.00

Selected Prices

Abraham and Straus Baby
Dress $0.98
Baseball $1.15
Cotton Petticoat $1.48
Crayons, 28 Colors $0.04
Eureka Vacuum Cleaner $35.00
Fulton Special Hammer $0.66
Gingham Cloth, per Yard $0.09
Grandma Soap, Borax
Powdered $0.05
Hotel Room, Tampa, Florida,
per Night $2.00
J.F. Oxford Talking Machine $14.95

John M. Smyth Suit,
   Blue Serge $7.98
Man's Wedding Ring, 14-Karat $2.59
Marshmallows, 200 to a Box $0.42
Mead Bicycle $10.00
Porch Rocking Chair $2.25
Sanitol Toothpaste $0.25
Silk Dress, Pongees $10.95
Sweater Blouse, Turndown Collar $1.19
Toilet Paper, 1,000 Sheets, Six Rolls $0.27
Wilson Hose Supports $0.25

The Golden Age of Lithography

- The Golden Age of Lithography in the United States ran from 1880 to 1914, an era when the work was produced by commercial brand names with Spanish titles, advertising Florida cigars made with Cuban tobacco.
- Unscrupulous cigar manufacturers used Spanish brand names and claimed cigars were Cuban, even when they were not.
- While banding of cigars was common, it was not universal. Banding consists of putting a small, decorative paper band around each cigar, indicating by word or design the brand of the cigar. It was a hand operation. The bander received the cigars from the packer.

- A high-grade cigar was made by hand and usually was the work of one person.
- In the stripping department, the large stem running through the middle of the leaf was removed. The cigar was made in the rolling department. After the cigars were made, they were sorted by color and packed in boxes, which were labeled and stamped.
- No cigar factory visited kept records of the time worked; the wages paid were determined by the quantity produced and the size, shape, and quality of the cigar made.
- The average pay for male bunch makers, hand was $0.26 per hour; females, $0.22 per hour; male cigar makers, hand, was $0.29 per hour; $0.24 for females.

A CHANCE FOR OUR BABIES

By Della MacLeod

1915 NEWS PROFILE
WORKING CHILDREN STUDY

In 1915, a study was conducted on the working children of Chelsea, Massachusetts, a suburb of Boston, who took out work permits when they were 14 years of age. The study attempted to survey children who quit school to work, and why. The researcher then followed the progress of each worker over a four-year period to measure the relationships of their goals to reality.

Study Number One

Peter is native-born of English parents. He became 14 years old on May 18, 1914. He left school June 16, 1914. Education: completed eighth grade; additional school training included an electrical course for 13 months. In addition, after going to work, he completed at Evening High School a commercial course, which took nine months, and a chemistry course that took four months. His first job, acquired through the Free Employment Bureau, was at a manufacturing facility that made dental plates; his occupation: running errands. According to the survey he worked eight hours per day, 49 hours per week and was employed for seven months. He started at $4.00 a week and moved to $4.50 a week.

His second job, as an office boy in a law firm, was acquired through a friend. He stayed employed seven months at $5.00 a week.

Comments: Has always intended to be electric wireman; when 16 will get a place in electrical shop. Is studying chemistry now and when 16 will enter Franklin Institute for a four-year course. Considers jobs so far as only temporary; has no special preference in either.

Four years later Peter is in the United States Navy with a rating of electrician.

Study Number Two

Joseph is native-born of Italian parents. He became 14 years old on December 20, 1913, and left school March 12, 1914. He took his first regular position March 13, 1914. Education: completed first year of high school; continuation school training—printing six months; other school after going to work—Technical High School, printing, and woodworking for five months. He got his first job through his brother in the leather industry. He worked nine hours per day, or 49 hours per week. He worked for six months at $4.50 to $5.00 a week, which was more than allowed by law. The inspector required him to stop working more than eight hours per day; he did not want to accept a position in the cutting room, where he could work legal hours.

His second position was as a baker in his father's business. He stayed two months and earned home support. At the same time he managed a Sunday newspaper route, from which he made $2.20 per week.

His third job was in the printing industry running errands, where he was employed three months. He preferred the first position because it was in the line of business which he wanted to follow. He was angry when he had to leave because of the illegal hours. In the third position he became dissatisfied with running errands, so he asked for a change of work and was made an apprentice. He did not like printing because he thought it was bad for his eyes, which were weak, and the pay was poor.

After he is 16 he wishes to enter the shipping department of a leather concern and work up, later going into the business with his father and brother. "I'm that kind of boy; I have to work every minute or I'm sick."

In a 1918 follow-up, he was employed as a salesman and chemist at a weekly wage of $25.00, working 50 hours per week.

Study Number Three

Anna is native-born of Russian-Jewish parents. She became 14 on October 22, 1914, and left school on October 22, 1914. She took her first regular position on November 23, 1914. Education: Completed eighth grade, continuation of school training—bookkeeping, 14 months. Her first job was offered to her by her father, who was a custom tailor. Her job was office work. She worked only five hours per day, which was illegal; (the law required a minimum of six hours daily if a child left school to go to work). At the time of the survey she had been employed one year and three months. Her pay was described as "support."

Her comments: Undecided as to future but likes bookkeeping and office work. Is about to go to work in a hosiery mill as a topper, but does not know what her chances are. Does not care to learn tailoring, her father's trade.

In December, 1918, she was employed as a clerk in a hospital office at a weekly wage of $10.00, working 48 hours per week.

Study Number Four

Maria is native-born of German parents. She became 14 years old on December 13, 1913, and left school June 21, 1914. Ed-

ucation: She completed the seventh grade; continuation of school training—bookkeeping, three months. Before leaving school she was employed for about 2½ years as nursemaid for her sister-in-law, working two hours a day after school and receiving $0.50 cents per week.

Her first job, which she got through a friend, was in garter and suspender manufacturing. Her job was putting buttonhole slips on suspenders. She made a weekly wage of $3.50. She quit because the wages were too low.

Her second job was in shoe manufacturing, a job she got through her sister. Her job varied from tagger, trimming pumper, stripper, and stayer. Her weekly wage ranged from $4.00 to $5.50.

Her comments: Knows relation of her occupation to other occupations in the factory where she is employed at present, but does not know opportunities for advancement or how long she will stay at the work. The survey said she was "fairly indifferent to work." She said, "My interest is taking care of children. It has always been my longing."

In December, 1918, she was employed as a stayer in the shoe factory at a weekly wage of $10.00, working 50 hours per week.

Findings of the Study

- Approximately one-third of the children of Chelsea took out employment certificates when they became 14 years old, a step required if they were to work before they were 16 years old.
- Among foreign-born children, nearly 60 percent went to work before they were 16 years old. Girls became regular workers at twice the rate of boys.
- Italians were more likely than children of other nationality groups to leave school to go to work.
- In Cambridge, 36 percent of the children born in Portugal took out work certificates, a larger proportion than of any other foreign-born group.
- Only one-fifth of the working children were foreign-born, while 72 percent had foreign-born fathers.

> ## *Our New Immigration Policy,*
> ## by Professor Robert De Courcy Ward:
>
> "It is significant that in the period 1871–1880 the 'old' immigration from northern and western Europe amounted to slightly over two million persons, while the new immigration from southern and eastern Europe and near Asia, numbered only 180,000. In the years 1874–1914, the period immediately preceding the war, the 'old' contributed about three million while the 'new' contributed over 10 million."

- Where the fathers were native, girls furnished only 37 percent of the working children. In families where the father was foreign-born, the proportion of girl workers rose to 45 percent.
- Many of the foreign-born children had barely completely the fourth grade when they went to work.
- Approximately 70 percent of the children who went to work came from families with both parents in the house; three percent of the children did not live with either parent.
- Of the children who went to work, 12 percent of their fathers were unemployed, 19 percent were laborers, and about 20 percent were skilled or semiskilled mechanics. Approximately 14 percent were factory workers; eight percent teamsters, drivers, and expressmen, and eight percent merchants and peddlers. Only two percent of the children had fathers who were clerical workers.
- Approximately 16 percent of the children came from families in which the mother also worked outside the home.
- Forty percent of the children left school and went to work because their earnings were needed at home.
- The economic need for child labor decreased as the family's length of residency in the United States increased.
- Girls were more likely than boys to take their first positions during a summer vacation.

> ## *Today's Housewife Magazine,* June 1917, featured a story
> ## about the Association for the Study and
> ## Prevention of Infant Mortality:
>
> "It has had to deal with the fact that a newborn child has, in this country, less chance of living a week than a man of ninety; less of living a year than a man of eighty. Actually, it had to realize that the mere business of being a baby must be classified as an extra hazardous occupation, and one not nearly as adequately protected as most factory labor."

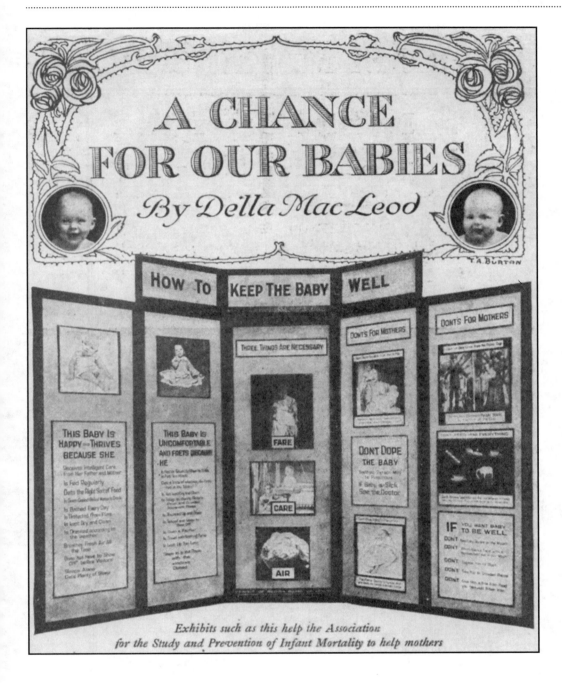

Exhibits such as this help the Association
for the Study and Prevention of Infant Mortality to help mothers

Occupations of the Nation's 41 Million Workers in 1916

Coal Miners	750,000	Longshoremen	250,000
Electric Light and Power	100,000	Lumbermen	200,000
Farmers and Farm Workers	11,000,000	Private Servants	3,500,000
Factory Workers	7,000,000	Professional Men	2,000,000
Laundry Workers	175,000	Telephone and Telegraph Operators	290,000

HISTORICAL SNAPSHOT
1915–1916

- The United States population passed 100 million

- The cost of laying 1,000 bricks in 1916 was $5.77 at an hourly rate of $0.65 per hour, or $5.20 a day; in comparison the cost of laying 1,000 bricks in 1909 was $4.00, in 1918, $10.42, and by 1920, $18.50

- Nearby Boston had constructed 26 playgrounds by 1915 with every section of the city enjoying more and more playgrounds

- An attempt by Congress to exclude illiterates from immigrating, a bill promoted by the unions to protect jobs, was vetoed by President Howard Taft in 1913, reasoning that illiteracy, which was often due to lack of opportunity, was no test of character

- U.S. Pullman-car porters pay reached $27.50 per month, prompting U.S. Commission on Industrial Relations to ask if wages were too high

- Kraft processed cheese was introduced by Chicago-based J.L. Kraft and Brothers

- Pyrex glass was developed by Corning Glass researchers

- IWW organizer Joe Hill was executed by firing squad

- The Woman's Peace Party was founded with social worker Jane Addams, the founder of Hull House in Chicago, as its first president

- The Victor Talking Machine Company introduced a phonograph called the Victrola; by 1919 Americans spent more on phonographs and recordings than on musical instruments, books and periodicals, or sporting goods

- An easy divorce law requiring only six months of residence was passed in Nevada

- D.W. Griffith's controversial three-hour film epic, *The Birth of a Nation*, opened in New York; tickets cost an astronomical $2.00

- A Chicago law restricted liquor sales on Sunday

- American Tobacco Company selected salesmen by psychological tests

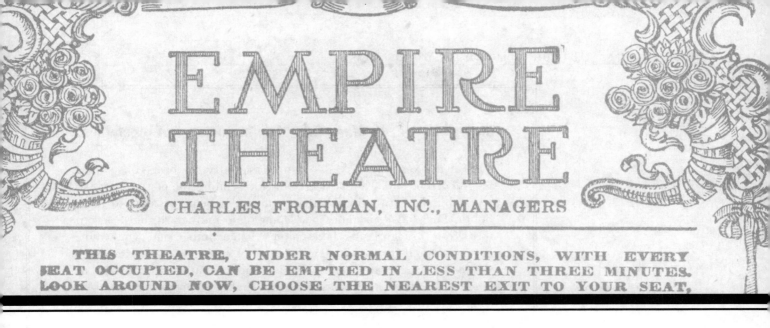

EMPIRE THEATRE

CHARLES FROHMAN, INC., MANAGERS

THIS THEATRE, UNDER NORMAL CONDITIONS, WITH EVERY SEAT OCCUPIED, CAN BE EMPTIED IN LESS THAN THREE MINUTES. LOOK AROUND NOW, CHOOSE THE NEAREST EXIT TO YOUR SEAT.

1919 FAMILY PROFILE

The Perova family, a first-generation Russian family of five, lives in Lawrence, Massachusetts, which feeds the clothing industry of New York and makes America a leading nation in the ready-made clothing industry. The woman is second-generation Lithuanian and they have three children.

Annual Income: $1,385

Our family's father is the sole wage earner, so the mother is able to do all the housework, including sewing and laundry.

Annual Budget

Clothing	$265.61
Food	$600.00
Fuel, Heat, and Light	$71.34
Rent	$182.00
Sundries	$266.24
Total	$1,385.19

Life at Home

- They rent a tenement that consists of four rooms, which are unheated but do have gas and indoor toilet. No bathtub is available.
- Families living at a minimum standard like the Perovas usually burn about three tons of coal a year. The average cost of chestnut and stove coal is $14.00 a ton.
- Some families do not buy coal in ton or half-ton lots, but by the more expensive method of purchasing it in bags from the neighborhood stores.
- Gas, which is generally used for lighting and cooking, costs $1.25 per thousand cubic feet. Our family spends an average of $2.00 a month.
- Our family prefers to burn cordwood in the spring and autumn instead of coal.
- About 15 percent of the Lawrence mills employees ride to and from work. Streetcar fares are $0.10 a trip and jitney fares are $0.07.

Today's Housewife Magazine, "The Importance of Vegetables":

"The list of vegetables available in this country has been considerably lengthened of late. The dasheen, which resembles the potato in consistency, but has an entirely different flavor, is being introduced in the South. The chayote is another welcome plant immigrant that has come to us from foreign lands. It resembles the cucumber somewhat, but is better adapted for cooking. Sorrel is a neglected vegetable that might well be more generally used. There is a variety that can be grown in the garden. It can be eaten as greens and makes a most delicious cream soup. It is among the very few really acid vegetables and for that reason adds novelty."

- Fashion still requires hair be worn long. Short-haired women, like long-haired men, are associated with radicalism and possibly free love.
- At mealtime the concept of counting calories is well understood, but the idea of vitamins is still unknown.

- Cigarette smoking is increasing in popularity; the number of cigarettes sold during the next decade will double. Fatima cigarettes cost $0.23 for a pack of 20.

Life at Work: Textiles

- The textile mills in Lawrence feed the clothing industry of New York City, making the United States a world leader in ready-made clothing.
- Of 35,750 mill workers in Lawrence, 23,034 are foreign-born and of these only 5,100 are naturalized. About 1,800 have taken out their first papers, but over 16,000, or nearly 70 percent, are aliens.
- English is a second language to more than 70 percent of the work force; about half of the workers speak English "fairly well."
- The general appearance of the mill workers indicates that "American customs are exercising a considerable influence on their standard of living," one survey says.
- The New England mill system utilizes the "family system" in which immigrant men, women, and children all work.
- The mills of Lawrence are beginning to use the "scientific management" concepts developed in the 1880s, including the introduction of cost accounting systems, a time clock for workers, more managerial control and regimentation, production and inventory controls, and incentive wage plans to stimulate production.

- In 1912 the radical labor group Industrial Workers of the World (IWW) leads a large and violent strike in Lawrence, Massachusetts. The strike attempts to publicize the fact that the woolen industry, which enjoys the highest protection under the Payne-Aldrich tariff, is paying starvation wages. Male operatives earn a maximum of $10.00 for a 54-hour week.
- It is the first major American strike in which foreign workers are organized and in which women and children play a vital role. The strike lasts two months.
- A second major strike takes place in 1919.
- A political cartoon in the *Chicago Tribune* shows the Statute of Liberty walking off the job and tossing away her torch, while saying "Everyone else in the country is doing it. I think I'll strike for an 8 hour day."

Life in the Community: Lawrence, Massachusetts

- The population in 1915 is 90,259, of whom only 12,034 are native-born of native parents.
- The city's 41,347 foreign-born include 8,587 Italians, 5,443 French Canadians, 5,154 English, 5,084 Irish, 3,022 Poles, and 3,603 of Russian birth, including Lithuanians, Finns, and Jews.
- The leading industry in Lawrence is the manufacturing of woolens, although cotton goods are made at several plants.
- Nearly all the people of Lawrence live within a mile and a half of the city hall.
- The city is arranged on the hills rising from the Merrimac Valley, which work against the development of ethnic neighborhood groupings.
- On the flat land in the center of the city is a crowded and undesirable tenement district. The more prosperous people of all races live on the higher land.
- The downtown stores and markets share the meat and grocery business of Lawrence with a large number of stores situated in the separate neighborhoods. Clothing stores are confined to the downtown district.
- Motion picture houses in Lawrence cost $0.10 in the afternoon and normally $0.20 in the evening; the daily newspaper costs $0.02; the Boston Sunday paper is $0.07.
- Doctors charge $2.00 for an office call and $3.00 for a house visit.
- Nearly 100 clubs and societies are available in the community. A considerable part of the social life is carried on through these organizations. Some of the lodges also offer their members sick or death benefit privileges.
- Approximately 70 percent of the wage earners and their families have burial insurance.
- Lawrence is predominantly Roman Catholic and the church is well supported. About one-third of the children attend parochial schools. The church charges $0.60 a month per child.
- In addition to Roman Catholic churches, there are five churches of the Greek or other Eastern rites, and Protestant churches for Italians, Germans, Armenians, Syrians, and Swedes.
- Automobiles are still a luxury of the affluent; most are open, since the sedan, or closed car, has not gained popularity.

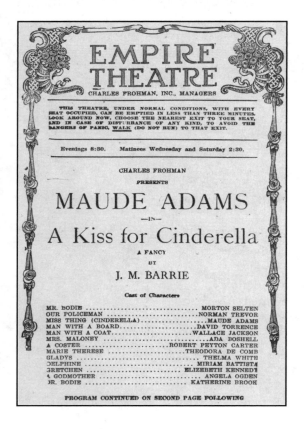

- The number of cars on the road would more than triple in the next decade, from seven million in 1919 to 23 million in 1929; the average speed limit in most states is 15 miles an hour in residential areas and six miles an hour on curves.
- Automatic traffic lights would not appear until the 1920s.

HISTORICAL SNAPSHOT
1919–1920

- Boston police struck against pay scales of $0.21 to $0.23 per hour for 83- to 98-hour weeks.

- The cost of living in New York City was up 79 percent from 1914

- The dial telephone was introduced in Norfolk, Virginia

- Wheat prices soared to $3.50 per bushel as famine swept Europe

- Kellogg's All-Bran was introduced by the Battle Creek Toasted Corn Flakes Company

- U.S. ice cream sales reached 150 million gallons, up from 30 million in 1909

- *The New York Daily News* became the first tabloid newspaper, or small-sized picture-oriented newspaper

- Boston Red Sox pitcher and outfielder Babe Ruth hit 29 home runs for the year; the New York Yankees purchased his contract for $125,000

- More than four million American workers struck for the right to belong to unions during 1919, including 365,000 steelworkers who struck against the United Steel Workers, which still maintained a 12-hour day. The Federation of Churches backed the strikers, declaring that their average work week of 68.7 hours was inhuman. Big Steel used its $2 billion in war profits and military force to break the strike.

- The Bureau of Labor Statistics reported that 1.4 million women had joined the American work force since 1911

- Following the 1918 strike by the Union Streetcar Conductors protesting the employment of female conductors, the War Labor Board ruled in favor of the continued employment of women

- The southern leaders of the National Association of Colored Women protested the conditions of domestic service workers, including the expectation of White male employers of the right to take sexual liberties with their servants

"Open your mouth and shut your eyes,
And I'll give you something to make you wise."

Painted by Edward V. Brewer for Cream of Wheat Co.   Copyright 1917 by Cream of Wheat Co.

***Ethnic Chicago*, Edited by Peter d'A Jones and Melvin G. Holli, 1981:**

"The most important employers of Italians in the pre-1920 period were Inland Steel Company, the National Brick Company and Canedy-Otto Machine Works (in Chicago). As one observer wrote, 'They worked under brutalizing conditions. Chicago Heights had steel mills, chemical factories, foundries, dye factories, very dusty wood-working factories, etc. Every place was a place of heat, grime, dirt, dust, stench, harsh glares, overtime, piece work, pollution, no safety gadgets, sweat, etc. The workers were, as the Italians called them, 'Bestie da Soma,' beasts of burden."

1919 ECONOMIC PROFILE

Examples of Weekly Expenditures

Candy, Tobacco, etc. $0.45
Medical Care $0.60
Movies and Other Entertainment $0.67
Organizations $0.20
Reading Material. $0.20

***Short Talks about Working Women*, United States Department of Labor, Bulletin of the Women's Bureau, No. 59:**

"The significance of women's employment lies chiefly in its trend, and from 1910 to 1920 there was considerable change in the number of women in the various occupations. We find that domestic and personal service lost women at a slightly higher rate than 2 from every 15 and that agricultural pursuits lost them at the rate of 2 from every 5. There was a striking increase among women in the professional ranks, and in clerical service they more than doubled. The trend of women's employment within the decade is particularly significant in view of the popular belief during the war, when women were the second line of defense, that the number of women in industry was increasing tremendously, a belief not sustained by the census figures of 1920."

Examples of Weekly Food Expenditures

Two Pounds Chuck	$0.48
One Pound Dried Cod	$0.30
Two Pounds Flank	$0.30
One Can Salmon	$0.23
One Pound Butter	$0.68
One Pound Cheese	$0.43
One Dozen Eggs	$0.62
14 Quarts Milk	$2.38
Three Pounds Cabbage	$0.12
Three Pounds Carrots	$0.14
Two Pounds Dried Beans	$0.21
Two Pounds Onions	$0.12
One Can Tomatoes	$0.17
Three Quarts Apples	$0.34
Four Bananas	$0.12
Three Oranges	$0.11
½ Pound Raisins	$0.14
12 Pounds Bread	$1.24
One Pound Corn Meal	$0.07
One Pint Molasses	$0.15
One Pound Rice	$0.18
Three Pounds Rolled Oats	$0.21
Three Pounds Sugar	$0.33
½ Pound Cocoa	$0.22
½ Pound Coffee	$0.22
¼ Pound Tea	$0.12
Total	$11.75

Examples of Yearly Clothing Purchases

For the Man: Total $51.05

One Cap	$1.00
One Pair Heavy Trousers	$3.50
Two Pairs Shoes	$11.00
Two Shirts	$2.80
One Straw Hat	$1.75
One Suit	$26.00
One Sweater	$5.00

For the Woman: Total $49.40

Three Apron Material	$1.40
One Coat	$25.00
One Cotton Skirt	$1.00
One Dress Material	$8.00
Gloves	$2.75
Two House Dresses (Material)	$3.00
Three Night Gowns (Material)	$2.90

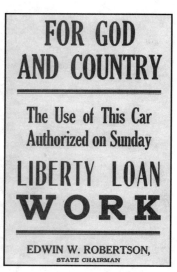

Six Pairs Stockings. $1.45
Four Union Suits $3.90

For the Boy, 13: Total $24.30
Two Caps. $1.75
Mackinaw $7.50
Three Shirts (Material) $1.60
Two Pairs Shoes. $7.50
Eight Pairs Stockings. $3.20
Three Ties $1.25
One Pair Trousers $1.50

For the Girl, 9: Total $27.44
One Coat $9.00
One Wool Dress (Material). $6.00
Three Union Suits $2.50
Three Blouses (Material). $1.31
Two Night Gowns (Material) $1.28
Two Pairs Shoes. $6.50
One Pair Mittens. $0.40
One Windsor Tie. $0.45

Income, Standard Jobs

Average for All Industries
   Including Farm Labor $1,201.00
Clerical Workers in
   Manufacturing. $1,999.00
Domestic $539.00
Farm Labor $706.00
Gas and Electricity Workers $556.00
Medical Health Workers. $606.00
Public School Teachers $377.00
State and Local Government
   Workers. $640.00
Telephone Workers $392.00
Wholesale and Retail
   Trade Workers. $508.00

Selected Prices

Bacardi Rum. $3.20/Fifth
Camel Cigarettes . . . . $0.18 per Pack
Cigars. $0.10
Corset Cover $1.50
Golf Bag. $3.45
Hat, Easter Style $5.00
Imperial Gin $2.15/Fifth
Overcoat $30.00
Phonograph Record $1.50
Rug, 6' x 9' $43.50

SUBSCRIBER

HONOR EMBLEM

4th LIBERTY LOAN

Single Room for Rent . . . . $4.00 per Week
Soap $0.07
Tobacco . . . . $0.15 per Package
Underwear $1.25
Washing Machine $15.75
Work Shirt, Coat Style. $0.75

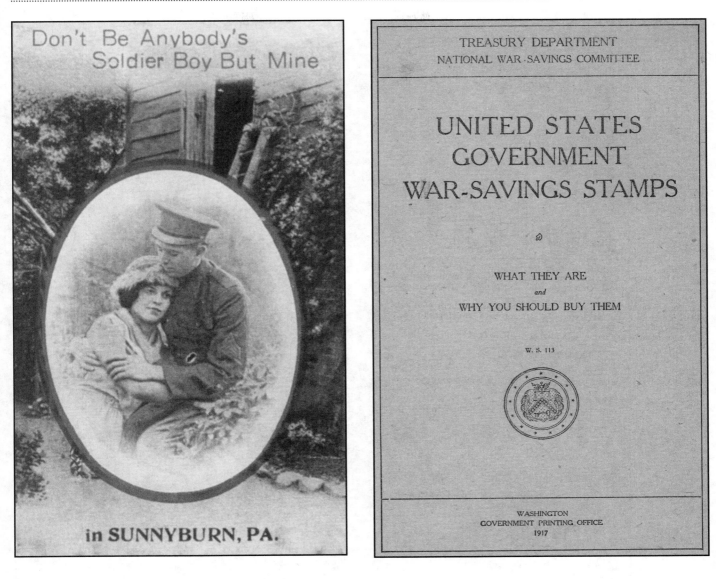

Don't Be Anybody's Soldier Boy But Mine

in SUNNYBURN, PA.

TREASURY DEPARTMENT
NATIONAL WAR-SAVINGS COMMITTEE

UNITED STATES
GOVERNMENT
WAR-SAVINGS STAMPS

WHAT THEY ARE
and
WHY YOU SHOULD BUY THEM

W. S. 113

WASHINGTON
GOVERNMENT PRINTING OFFICE
1917

The Impact of World War I

- During the war, fuel savings were accomplished with campaigns such as "heatless Mondays" and "lightless nights." To save petroleum, voluntary "gasless Sundays" were introduced.
- Daylight saving time, conceived first by Benjamin Franklin, was introduced to conserve power. Head of the Food Administration, Quaker-humanitarian Herbert C. Hoover mobilized the nation for less waste and more production. Children were urged to be "patriotic to the core" when eating apples. And meatless Tuesdays and Victory Gardens became a part of the culture. To Hooverize became a synonym for "to economize."

Maxwell

$655

No Extras To Buy

Everyone about to buy an automobile is interested in cost—both first cost and after cost. Unless the car you buy really is completely equipped, its price does not at all represent the first cost.

The following is a list of equipment on the Maxwell Car with its approximate retail cost:

	Approximate Retail Cost
1—Electric Starting and Lighting System, Lamps, etc.	$95.00
2—High-Tension Magneto	50.00
3—Demountable Rims	25.00
4—Speedometer	15.00
5—Clear Vision, Double Ventilating Rainproof Windshield	12.00
6—Linoleum Covering for Running and Floor Boards	8.00
7—Anti-skid Rear Tires (cost difference over smooth treads)	5.00
8—Electric Horn and adjuncts	3.50
9—Spare Tire Carrier	3.50
10—Oil Gauge	1.50
11—Robe Rail	1.50
12—Front and Rear License Brackets	1.50
	Total, $221.50

If you purchase an automobile which lacks these features, you must add their cost to the price of the car if you want real automobile comfort. Deduct this amount ($221.50) from the price of the Maxwell ($655) and then you will realize what wonderful value is represented by the Maxwell Car.

Think of it—a beautiful stream-line car, built of special heat-treated steel, with a powerful four-cylinder motor; thoroughly cooled by a gracefully rounded radiator of improved design and a fan—sliding gear transmission—semi-elliptic front and three-quarter elliptic rear springs, making shock absorbers unnecessary—one-man mohair top—high quality upholstery, and ample seating capacity for 5 adults, really fully equipped for $655.

The high-priced car features mentioned, as well as the light weight of the Maxwell Car, account for the wonderfully low after-cost records of the Maxwell. The Maxwell is lowering all economy records for

1st—Miles per set of tires
2nd—Miles per gallon of gasoline
3rd—Miles per quart of lubricating oil
4th—Lowest year-in-and-year-out repair bills

See the new 1916 "Wonder Car" at the nearest Maxwell dealer's, and you will realize that it is the greatest automobile value ever offered.

Every feature and every refinement of cars of twice its price

Write for beautifully illustrated catalogue. Address Department A. L.

MAXWELL MOTOR COMPANY, Incorporated   - - - - - - DETROIT, MICHIGAN

- Hang-the-Kaiser movies carrying titles such as "The Kaiser, the Beast of Berlin" and "To Hell with the Kaiser" attacked the "Hun" in the bloodiest way.

- To raise the army required during the Great War, increasing enrollment from 200,000 to four million in a few months, women were admitted to the armed forces; some 11,000 to the navy and 269 to the marine corps.

- Recruits were supposed to receive six months of training in America and two more months overseas. So great was the urgency that many American soldiers, known as doughboys, were swept into battle scarcely knowing how to handle a rifle and bayonet.

- Even though Prohibition was not yet the law of the land, nearly half of the population nationwide lived in "dry" territory which controlled, restricted, or abolished alcohol sales. Lawrence, Massachusetts, is "wet."

- During the war with Germany, orchestras in Boston found it unsafe to present German-composed music, including Wagner and Beethoven; banks with German names changed their names; the teaching of the German language was discontinued in many schools. Sauerkraut became "liberty cabbage" and hamburger became "liberty steaks."

- In Oklahoma, the Germans of that state were looked upon suspiciously even though many were Mennonites or Brethren congregations with pacifist leanings. To reduce conflicts, the German-Russian-Mennonite settlement of Korn, west of Oklahoma City, changed its name to Corn.

First Generation, In the Words of Twentieth-Century American Immigrants, Theresa Bonacorsi, Italian Immigrant:

"I was sixteen when I started work (in the woolen mills of Lawrence, Massachusetts). I was born in 1905. We started at $15.55 for 48 hours. We used to work Saturday for four hours, then they stopped that. At American Woolen I used to do spooling. It's when the threads come out. They've been twisted; they've been spun; they've been wound on another spool. Then we used to get them and used to put them on spikes like in forty threads. We had to watch them; it was like an inspection to see that the yarn was all right. While the threads were coming down, if there was any bad yarn, you had to take that out. Then they used to take it to the dressing room. All these threads used to be made into cloth. Worked there right through 'til they shut down."

- The death rate nationwide decreased between 1900 and 1920 from 17 to 12.6 persons per thousand for whites and from 25 to 17.7 per thousand for non-Whites. This improvement was largely possible through a sharp decline in deaths from typhoid fever, tuberculosis, and the near elimination of smallpox and malaria.
- On average the cost of living increased 84 percent from 1914 to 1919.
- Adjusted for inflation, national income increased from $480.00 per capita in 1900 to $567.00 in 1920.
- During the war period, food prices increased 99 percent; rent rose 35 percent; clothing costs rose 105 percent; yard goods rose 165 percent.
- During this period, coal costs increased 72 percent and gas rose 39 percent, resulting in an average increase of the five-year period of 59 percent. The price of a motion picture doubled from $0.05 to $0.10, and the cost of daily newspapers also doubled.

Dr. B. M. Anderson, Economist of the Chase National Bank, said:

"The physical condition of our capital equipment deteriorated very substantially in 1919. The condition of the railroads grew worse; public utilities, including traction lines, deteriorated. The housing shortage increased and grew acute. Building costs were so high, and capital so scarce, that it was virtually impossible to get mortgage money in anything like adequate volume . . . Agricultural capital in terms of fences, barns and the like appears to have deteriorated during 1919, and soil fertility was inadequately maintained. We are living on capital, using up past accumulations instead of increasing our long-time wealth and resources."

Peace-Time World of the Army, by Secretary John W. Weeks:

"During the Civil War, smallpox claimed over 7,000 victims, during the World War only 14. In the Civil War malaria claimed 15,000—in the World War 25. In the Spanish-American War, 20,000 men suffered from typhoid—in the World War we had 2,000 cases—a contrast between twenty percent and one-twentieth of one percent, of the total engaged in these wars. We are shocked to discover that approximately half of our young men, who were examined for service, had physical disabilities of some sort. We should be pleased to realize that after a comparatively short time in service, under the supervision of our physical trainers and our medical men, the recruits were generally developed into fine specimens of American manhood."

Value of One Dollar	
Year	Value in 2010 USD
1921	$12.18
1923	$12.75
1925	$12.46
1926	$12.32
1927	$12.53

Values are approximate based upon economic historical data and 2010 U. S. Dollar

1920–1929

Following the Great War, America enjoyed a period of great expansion and expectation. The attitude of many Americans was expressed in President Calvin Coolidge's famous remark, "the chief business of the American people is business." The role of the federal government remained small during the period and federal expenditures actually declined following the war effort. Harry Donaldson's song, "How Ya Gonna Keep Em Down on the Farm After They've Seen Paree?" described another basic shift in American society. The 1920 census reported that more than 50 percent of the population—54 million people—lived in urban areas. The move to the cities was the result of changed expectations, increased industrialization, and the migration of millions of Southern Blacks to the urban North.

The years following the Great War were marked by a new nationalism symbolized by frenzied consumerism. By 1920 urban Americans had begun to define themselves—for their neighbors and for the world—in terms of what they consumed. The car was becoming universal—at least in its appeal. At the dawn of the century, only 4,192 automobiles were registered nationwide; in 1920 the number of cars had reached 1.9 million. Simultaneously, aggressive new advertising methods began appearing, designed to fuel the new consumer needs of the buying public. And buy they did. From 1921 to 1929 Americans bought and America boomed. With expanded wages and buying power came increased leisure time for recreation, travel, or even self-improvement. And the advertising reenforced the idea that the conveniences and status symbols of the wealthy were attainable to everyone. The well-to-do and the wage earner began to look a lot more alike.

The availability of electricity expanded the universe of goods that could be manufactured and sold. Radios, electric lights, telephones, and powered vacuum cleaners were possible for the first time; they quickly became essential household items. Construction boomed as—for the first time—half of all America now lived in urban areas. Industry, too, benefited from the expanded use of electrical power. At the turn of the century, electricity ran only five percent of all machinery; by 1925, 73 percent. Large scale electric power also made possible electrolytic processes in the rapidly developing heavy chemical industry. With increasing sophistication came higher costs; wages for skilled workers continued to rise during the 1920s, putting further distance between the blue collar worker and the emerging middle class.

Following the war years, women who had worked men's jobs in the late teens usually remained in the work force, although at lower wages. Women, now allowed to vote nationally, were also encouraged to consider college and options other than marriage. Average family earnings increased slightly during the first half of the period while prices and hours worked actually declined. The 48-hour week became standard, providing more leisure time. At least 40 million people went to the movies each week; college football became a national obsession.

Unlike previous decades, national prosperity was not fueled by the cheap labor of new immigrants but by increased factory efficiencies, innovation, and more sophisticated methods of managing time and materials. Starting in the teens, the flow of new immigrants began to slow, culminating in the restrictive immigration legislation of 1924 when new workers from Europe were reduced to a trickle. The efforts were largely designed to protect the wages of American workers—many of whom were only one generation from their native land. As a result, wages for unskilled labor remained stable; union membership declined and strikes, on average, decreased. American exports more than doubled during the decade; heavy imports of European goods virtually halted, a reversal of the progressive movement's flirtation with free trade.

These national shifts were not without powerful resistance. A bill was proposed in Utah to imprison any woman who wore her skirt higher than three inches above the ankle. Cigarette consumption reached 43 billion annually, despite smoking being illegal in 14 states and the threat of expulsion from college if caught with a cigarette. A film code limiting sexual material in silent films was created to prevent "loose" morals, and the membership of the KKK expanded to repress Catholics, Jews, open immigration, make-up on women, and the prospect of unrelenting change.

The decade ushered in Trojan contraceptives, the Pitney Bowes postage meter, the Baby Ruth candy bar, Wise potato chips, Drano, self-winding watches, State Farm Mutual auto insurance, Kleenex, and the Macy's Thanksgiving Day Parade down Central Park West in New York. Despite a growing middle class, the share of disposable income going to the top five percent of the population continued to increase. Fifty percent of the people, by one estimate, still lived in poverty. Coal and textile workers, Southern farmers, unorganized labor, the elderly, single women, and most Blacks were excluded from the economic giddiness of the period.

In 1929 America appeared to be in an era of unending prosperity. U.S. goods and services reached all time highs. Industrial production rose 50 percent during the decade as the concepts of mass production were refined and broadly applied. The sale of electrical appliances from radios to refrigerators skyrocketed. Consumers were able to purchase newly produced goods through the extended use of credit. Debt accumulated. By 1930 personal debt had increased to one-third of personal wealth. The nightmare on Wall Street in October, 1929, brought an end to the economic festivities, setting the stage for a more proactive government and an increasingly cautious worker.

1923 FAMILY PROFILE

The Gaskell family of four lives in Tulsa, Oklahoma, supported by the woman, who works in a printing plant as both a packer and proofer. The husband is an unemployed coal miner; the woman, age 30, is Welch. They have two children under the age of 12, one of whom is still in diapers.

Annual Income: $631.80

She makes $12.15 a week at a printing plant located outside Tulsa, Oklahoma. Her husband is unemployed. He made about $800.00 in 1922, the last year he was employed at the coal mines.

Annual Budget

The survey does not provide detailed expenditures for the family. The National Consumer Expenditures in 1923, per capita are:

Auto Parts	$4.97
Auto Purchases	$20.45
City Transport	$5.22
Clothing	$64.52
Dentists	$2.72
Food	$128.14
Furniture	$8.78
Gas and Oil	$12.38
Housing	$94.80
Per Capita Consumption	$594.87
Personal Business	$22.17

```
Personal Care. . . . . . . . . . . . . . . . . . . . . . . . $7.79
Physicians . . . . . . . . . . . . . . . . . . . . . . . . $7.15
Private Education . . . . . . . . . . . . . . . . . . $7.26
Recreation . . . . . . . . . . . . . . . . . . . . . . . $23.44
Religion, Welfare. . . . . . . . . . . . . . . . . . . $11.57
Telephone . . . . . . . . . . . . . . . . . . . . . . . . $2.71
Tobacco . . . . . . . . . . . . . . . . . . . . . . . . . $11.46
Utilities. . . . . . . . . . . . . . . . . . . . . . . . . . $8.97
    Total . . . . . . . . . . . . . . . . . . . . . . $1,039.37
```

Life at Home

- The man has fought in World War I, returning home to work in the coal mines. He saw little action, but loved travelling across country on a train and enjoyed seeing France.
- He has now grown angry that the government that asked him to fight doesn't care that he has lost his job.
- In 1922 the coal industry fell on hard times, laying off more than half of its workers.
- Anti-Catholic newspapers are gaining wide circulation; much of the anger of bad times is directed at Catholics and many see the Ku Klux Klan as the answer to their problems.
- Recently, he lost the War Risk Insurance he earned because the family budget cannot meet the payments.
- He continues to look for work, travelling as far as Oklahoma City for opportunities.
- It is likely that he operates an illegal liquor still, as do many unemployed miners. Prohibition has begun in 1920.

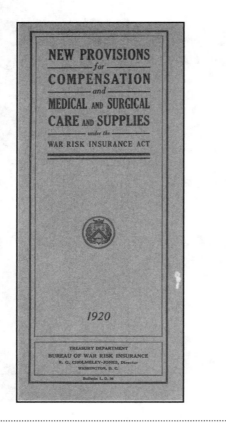

Life at Work: Printing

- She is hired to package and ship print jobs after they are completed. Recently, because she has an 11th grade education, she serves as a proofreader of copy to catch spelling and grammatical errors.
- Occasionally, she also handsets type, especially for the headlines of short-run fliers that must be produced quickly. She is a valuable employee, who works hard to make sure all the work does not pile up or come at once.
- Even though her husband is currently unemployed, she is still responsible for cooking all meals and caring for the children.
- She recently saves enough money, by skipping lunch, to purchase a new stove, replacing the coal stove that is hard to regulate. A likely choice is a Kalamazoo gas range that can be purchased on the installment plan. The cash price is $47.90; the credit price is $52.70.
- Although the state limits a working woman's hours to nine, an eight-hour day is standard and the six-day week is more common than a 5½ day week. This 48-hour week is less than the state mandate of no more than 54 hours per week.
- Most of the printing plants in the state use an eight-hour schedule rather than nine-hour days.
- Most of the women in laundries and food manufacturing work a full nine-hour day.
- She is allowed an hour for lunch, a practice common in the manufacturing industry.
- Lighting is good at the printing plant, a necessity of the printing facility.
- State law requires that "establishments employing females shall provide suitable seats," which takes place at the printing facility.
- She has previously worked in a factory that makes overalls, where she was paid on a piece-meal basis. Nearly all of Oklahoma's shirt and overall workers are female. Even though she made $14.50 a week stitching overalls, she likes working in a printing plant better because she is paid on a time-work basis and knows what she will make every week.
- In addition, the conditions at the overall plant are less favorable. A survey shows that the factory has no lunchroom, no cloakroom or restroom; light bulbs are unshaded and cause glare; a common drinking cup and common towel are shared by all workers and no seats are provided for most workers, who stand throughout the day.
- No outside windows or exhaust fans are available at the plant, despite the heat.
- The printing plant does not have air conditioning despite the heat, although an exhaust fan is available.

Copyrighted by the Chicago "Tribune"

"EVERYTHING BUT THE KITCHEN STOVE"

Is what Will Rogers says we promised the soldiers, when they went away, but now: "You didn't tell him he had to come home on a stretcher before you would give him anything, did you?"

Life in the Community: Tulsa, Oklahoma

- Between 1910 and 1920, the nation's urban population increases 29 percent; in Oklahoma the growth is 69 percent.
- The Oklahoma coal industry, which pays operators $6.00 a day during World War I, peaks in 1920.
- The discovery of rich oil and gas fields in the mid-1920s transforms the economy of the state and reduces the competitiveness of coal; many coal miners lose their jobs.

- In 1870, unemployment in the Eastern part of the U.S. caused many miners to accept the railroad's offer of free transportation to Indian Territory. Scores of skilled immigrants from the British Isles came to the Oklahoma mines.
- A generation later Irish, Scottish, and Welch surnames are common in the state.
- In 1903 an Oklahoma miner's base wage is $2.45 per day; little machinery is used because labor is so plentiful.
- Workers often work in knee-deep water or crawl on all fours during their 12-hour shifts.
- Once the coal mines are unionized in 1903, hours are reduced to eight per day.
- Oil is drilled in Oklahoma in 1897; by 1905, 255 producing wells are in Indian Territory.
- Oklahoma is the Southwest's leading producer of crude oil, a lead the state maintains until 1928 when surpassed by Texas.
- The oil wells produce fabulous wealth for a few.
- The state's oil- and gas-producing fields increase from 39 in 1908 to 110 in 1915; the flood of crude into the market over the same period drives prices from $1.05 per barrel to $0.35 a barrel.

- The outbreak of war in Europe and the rising sales of automobiles drives prices back up. In addition, farmers anxious to take advantage of wartime agricultural prices purchase large numbers of gasoline-driven equipment.
- By the mid-1920s, the Greater Seminole Field, which encompasses five counties and seven major pools of oil, pumps 10 percent of all the oil produced in America.
- Although many of the discoveries are made on Indian Territory property, by the time of the great oil booms, many Indian allotments have passed to white owners through embezzlement, forgery, or deliberate mismanagement of the probate courts.

- Only among the Osage are mineral rights reserved to the tribe as a group; the discovery of the Burbank field in the 1920s makes the tribe the richest Indians in the world.
- Social change sweeps the country in the 1920s, raising issues about morality and ethics.
- Many of the women begin to wear their hair short or "bobbed," and the new fashion of Dutch collars under their sweaters and flat shoes is gaining popularity.
- The Women's Auxiliary of the Episcopal Church centers upon a nationwide morality campaign, conducts a series of meetings for girls to discuss the problem of "upholding standards." The Catholic Archbishop of the Ohio diocese issues a warning against the "toddle" and "shimmy" and "bare female shoulders."
- Utah considers a statute providing for fine and imprisonment for women who wear skirts higher than three inches above the ankle; in Ohio a bill is drafted that no garment composed of any transparent material shall be sold, nor any "garment which unduly displays or accentuates the lines of the female figure."
- Even a deck of "Old Maid" playing cards reflects the changing times, featuring Rudolf Sheik, Mandy Lou, Sailor Al K. Hall, Hiram Squash, and Doughboy Dolph.

HISTORICAL SNAPSHOT
1923–1924

- The Popsicle was patented under the name Epsicle

- The Butterfinger candy bar was created and marketed by dropping parachuted bars from an airplane

- Commercially canned tomato juice was marketed by Libby McNeill & Libby

- The first practical electric shaver was patented by Schick

- A.C. Nielson Company was founded

- Zenith Radio Corporation was founded

- 10 automakers accounted for 90 percent of sales; a total of 108 different companies were now producing cars

- Hertz Drive Ur Self System was founded, creating the world's first auto rental concern

- 30 percent of all bread was now baked in the home, down from 70 in 1910

- The first effective chemical pesticides were introduced

- *American Mercury* magazine began publication

- Radio set ownership reached three million

- Ford produced two million Model T motorcars; the price of the touring car fell to $290.00

- Dean Witter and Company was founded

- Microbiologists isolated the cause of scarlet fever

- Emily Post published *Etiquette*, which made her the arbiter of American manners

1923 ECONOMIC PROFILE

Income, Standard Jobs

    Average for All Industries
        Including Farm Labor $1,299.00
    Clerical Workers in Manufacturing . . $2,126.00
    Domestics $711.00
    Farm Labor $572.00
    Gas and Electricity Workers $1,339.00
    Medical Health Workers $845.00
    Public School Teachers $1,239.00
    State and Local Government
        Workers $1,336.00

Hiram Wesley Evans, "The Klan's Fight for Americanism," *The North American Review*, 1926:

"The greatest achievement so far has been to formulate, focus, and gain recognition for an idea, the idea of preserving and developing America first and chiefly for the benefit of the children of the pioneers who made America, and only and definitely along the lines and purpose and spirit of those pioneers. The Klan cannot claim to have created this idea: it has long been a vague stirring in the souls of the plain people. But the Klan can fairly claim to have given it purpose, method and direction and a vehicle. When the Klan first appeared the nation was in the confusion of sudden awakening, from the lovely dream of the melting pot, disorganized and helpless before the invasion of aliens and alien ideas. After ten years of the Klan it is in arms for defense. This is our greatest achievement. The second is more selfish; we have won the leadership in the movement for Americanism. Except for a few lonesome voices, almost drowned by the clamor of the alien and the alien-minded 'liberal,' the Klan has alone faced the invader. This is not to say that the Klan has gathered into its membership all who are ready to fight for America. It is an idea, a faith, a purpose, an organized crusade."

Telephone Workers $1,069.00
Wholesale and Retail Trade
    Workers $1,272.00

Selected Prices

All-Wool Blankets, 60"x 84" Pair $14.50
American Kampkook Gas Grill $15.00
Armstrong Waffle Iron $4.00
Baby's Portable Bathtub, Rubber $5.75
Bloomers, Mercerized Cotton. $1.10
Brassiere, in Camisole Style. $0.79
Crosley Radio $14.50
Electric Percolator $7.15
Floor Paint, per Gallon $1.95
Frock, Cotton Voile. $13.25
Hamilton Wristwatch, Man's $38.00
Kodak No. 1 Camera $50.00
Lablashe Face Powder. $0.50
Licecil Insecticide, per Bottle. $1.00
Listerine Mouthwash $0.79
Milk of Magnesia Laxative, Bottle $0.39
Montague Montamower, Lawn
    Mower. $18.00
S.C. Red Pullet, Sired by a 296-Egg
    Cock $5.00
Underwood Typewriter. $50.00

Walnut Dresser, Louis XVI Style $98.00
Wilbur Buds' Chocolate, per Pound $1.00
Woman's Kitchen Apron $0.98

The Twenties:

"America was experiencing a sports boom. The family car made beaches, golf courses, stadiums and parks accessible. In 1923 almost 150,000 automobile racing enthusiasts watched the Memorial Day Races at Indianapolis, and more than 300,000 saw the World Series. That same year, three boxing matches drew 200,000 fans and superstars Babe Ruth, Helen Wills, Bobby Jones, and Babe Didrikson were becoming familiar names to millions."

Working Women of Oklahoma

- In 1920, 94,594 women weare gainfully employed in Oklahoma, 13.2 percent of the total female population 10 years of age or over. In only four states was the proportion of women gainfully employed smaller.

- Of all working women in Oklahoma, 25 percent engaged in domestic and personal service, 25 percent worked in agriculture, 30 percent in clerical or professional occupations, and 20 percent in trade, transportation, and manufacturing, including retail store workers, telephone operators, and women who worked in laundries and hotels.

Married Women in Industry, Women's Bureau, 1924:

"In 1920 there were 1,920,281 married women who were gainfully employed. The bureau wanted to find how these mothers managed to take care of the children and do other work at the same time, so the census records were looked at again to see whether any light on the subject could be discovered. It was found that half of these mothers of young children earned money at home by taking in boarders or doing laundry or some other form of work which did not obligate them to leave home, so they could look out for the children and work at the same time. But the other half went out to work and spent their days in mills making woolen and worsted cloth, and in factories making handkerchiefs and other manufactured articles. Wonder arose as to what became of these little children while their mothers were away from home all day, and, because there was no other way to find out, agents were sent to visit as many of these families as they could.

During these visits, among every five women one was found who was working at night and looking out for her children during the daytime, and one who just left the children alone at home to look out for each other. Sometimes, the father worked at night and cared for the children in the daytime while their mothers were away, and sometimes the neighbors or the landlady or the relatives kept an eye on the children. Only one woman in twenty had someone who was paid especially to care for her young children while she was away at work.

Does this give you a picture of the pressure under which women are working in industry? Can you see all these mothers leaving home at 6:30 or 7 in the morning after they have washed and dressed the children and fixed their breakfast and lunches? Can you see these mothers working all day, and can you imagine their thoughts as they wonder whether the children are all right and whether some one has seen to all the many little things little children need? And at the end of the day's work in factory or mill can you picture the homecoming of these mothers and the tasks which await them?"

- Black women, who dominated the domestic and personal service jobs, averaged $8.70 per week, or $3.45 a week less than White women workers in Oklahoma.
- Of 2,586 women surveyed, only 12 were foreign-born.
- The women typically worked 54 hours per week, or an average of nine hours per day. Those employed by the 17 different telephone exchanges throughout 25 communities in Oklahoma, worked a scheduled eight hours per day, or 48 hours a week.
- Oklahoma manufacturing ranked 30th nationally in the value of manufactured products.

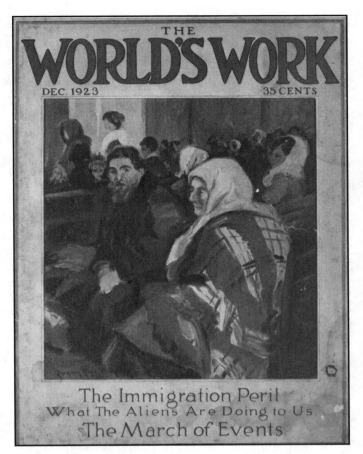

THE WORLD'S WORK

DEC. 1923   35 CENTS

The Immigration Peril
What The Aliens Are Doing to Us
The March of Events

Speech by Meyer London, Socialist Party—New York in 1921, regarding federal legislation to limit immigration, Congressional Record, 67th Congress, 1st Session, 1921:

"At whom are striking in this bill? Why, at the very people whom a short while ago you announced you were going to emancipate. We sent two million men abroad to make the world 'safe for democracy' to liberate these very people. Now you shut the door to them. So far, we have made the world safe for hypocrisy and the United States incidentally unsafe for the Democratic Party, temporarily at least (laughter). The supporters of the bill claim that the law will keep out radicals. The idea that by restricting immigration you will prevent the influx of radical thought is altogether untenable. You cannot confine an idea behind prison bars. You cannot exclude it by the most drastic legislation. The field of thought recognizes no barriers. The fact that there was almost no immigration during the war did not prevent us from importing every abominable idea from Europe. We brought over the idea of deportation of radicals from France, not from the France of Rousseau, Jaurès, and Victor Hugo but from the France of the Bourbons. We imported the idea of censorship of the press and the passport system from the Russia of Nicholas II. We imported the idea of universal military service from Germany, not from the Germany of Heine, Boerne, and Freiligrath but from the Germany of the Kaiser."

"The Immigration Peril, New Mexico an Example," by Gino Speranza, *The World's Work*, December 1923:

"It cost the New Mexican House $7,287.50 for the salaries of its employees during its 60 days of life last year—a modest sum as those things go, but over one-fifth of this amount was for 'translators and interpreters.' That item in terms of life means that there were members, duly elected to the Lower House of New Mexico, who to-day cannot transact their legislative business in English.

There is a specific provision in the Compact between the people of New Mexico and the United States, to the effect that the 'ability to read, write, speak, and understand the English language sufficiently well to conduct the duties of the office without aid of an interpreter, shall be a necessary qualification for all members of state legislature.' It was under that Compact that New Mexico was admitted to the Union 'on an equal footing with the original states.' It is easy to say that all is unfair and illegal. It is. But we must search for the causes of an evil if we wish to right

it. You do not right it by simply distributing the offices more equably between the two races in New Mexico, as so many of the 'natives' demand. You would not get American self-government by that method; you would simply extend that mongrel tribal government of some of our big cities wherein the various racial constituencies are 'recognized.' The root of the evil and of the social tragedy in New Mexico lies in the historical fact, therefore, that two different and separate civilizations, distinct in antecedents, ideals, history, standards, habits, and political life, are trying to live side by side as one family. With the best intentions we have legalized an impossibility and have constitutionally equalized unequals. Under the law these 'natives' are 'Americans' and 'fellow citizens': actually, under the stress of historic and natural laws, they have a 'common consciousness' and a 'general will' so different from those of the American people that they are not and cannot be in any real sense, 'Americans.'"

The Wizardry of the Automobile, by Allen D. Albert:

"There are absorbing stories in the rusty little car parked these days before the high school in the county seat. This one brings two brothers 11 miles from a farm where neither parent had more than four months of schooling in any year or passed beyond the sixth grade. This one bears the daughter of a dairyman who tells you with a steady look into our eyes that she has never learned to milk and never intended to learn. This one picks up the high school students of three

families from Wintergreen Bottoms, a community hopelessly sullen and lawless unless its children save it. Farm men rode to town meetings of the farm bureau; farm women to meetings of the domestic science club; all of them to the circus or the movies; or the winter concert season. In our youth such expeditions would have required half a day in travel. In our motoring middle life they require less than half an hour each way."

*Stearns-Knight-type
Six Cylinder Coupe*

Built with the Deliberation of Old World Craftsmanship

YEARS ago Knight-type Motor Cars became the choice of European Royalty because old-world craftsmen built this famous engine so perfectly that trouble was seldom if ever experienced.

When The F. B. Stearns Company became the first organization in America to adopt the Knight Sleeve-valve Engine, this Company determined to hold production to a minimum until such time when it could develop men and machinery to manufacture Knight-type Motor Cars in large numbers and still maintain the extreme precision which has given the Sleeve-valve Engine its world-wide reputation for silence, power, and unequalled durability.

After twelve years of unparalleled success in the pioneering and building of Knight-type automobiles The F. B. Stearns Company has now reached the point where it is able to produce these remarkable cars in quantities and at a price that cannot purchase elsewhere an equal amount of style, comfort, and economical motor car transportation.

We invite you to visit the nearest Stearns Dealer at your earliest convenience and ask that one of the beautiful new Stearns Sixes or Fours be demonstrated to you. Or, write direct to the factory for descriptive catalog and name of the nearest dealer.

THE F. B. STEARNS COMPANY, CLEVELAND, OHIO

Stearns Sleeve Valve MOTOR CARS

FOUR AND SIX CYLINDER MODELS

Changing styles and morality contributed to the rise of the KKK, which opposed change.

1925 Family Profile

The Urbig family lives in a mill village created by the company in Spartanburg, South Carolina. They join thousands of others who migrate from failed farms to the emerging textile industry, trading freedom for a regular paycheck. Like many textile families, the man, his wife, and two of their three children work at the Saxon Mill.

Annual Income
Husband	$950.00
Wife	$600.00
Children	$350.00
Total	$1,950.00

National Consumer Expenditures
Auto Parts	$6.96
Auto Purchases	$20.82
Clothing	$62.04
Dentists	$3.26
Food	$160.59
Furniture	$9.49
Gas and Oil	$15.70
Housing	$98.89
Intercity Transport	$4.95
Local Transport	$9.13
Per Capita Consumption	$619.45
Personal Business	$27.33
Personal Care	$7.79
Physicians	$7.68
Private Education	$7.72

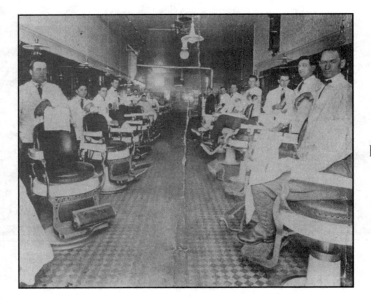

Recreation. $24.52
Religion/Welfare. $11.31
Telephone and Telegraph $5.88
Tobacco. $13.13
Utilities $9.82
   Total $1,126.46

Life at Home

- The Urbigs live in a community that includes 168 homes, 23 of which are the latest thing in bungalows.
- They have savings of more than $201.00, saved week to week. The mill runs its own bank to assist the workers in saving. Many who will not open an account at a regular bank will make regular deposits here. The mill pays interest on funds undisturbed for six months.
- Our family also keeps a Christmas Savings Club account, like most of their neighbors, and also carries $500.00 in life insurance. Every member of the family, except the youngest, is insured.
- Running water is in every house and is not metered, measured, or restricted as to use. Its cost is included in the mill-controlled rent.
- Three wet-wash laundries compete for the dirty clothing of Saxon Mill residents, freeing the women for other duties.
- This family's mother sews most of the children's clothing. Work dresses are made by a village seamstress and dress-up, or Sunday clothes, are bought "ready-made."
- Our family has electricity, as do all the houses in Saxon Mill. They have a percolator to make coffee and a curling iron, but no other electrical appliances. They also have a bathtub, although many houses do not. One neighbor uses his tub for scalding a hog at butchering time. The rest of the year he stores wood there.
- Radio set ownership has now reached three million nationwide; our family is saving for a set. Several neighbors already have one.
- This family takes the daily newspaper. Reading consumes a good share of the leisure. Reportedly 65 percent of the families take a newspaper during the week.
- The Urbig family has a Bible, but few other books of their own. Most are borrowed from the mill library. Light fiction is a favorite. The teenage daughter saves her money to buy confession magazines available at the bookstore.
- The youngest child, a girl still attending school, works part-time at the mill, and dreams of getting a "city" job like her brother.
- The son distinguished himself during the Great War. When he returns from the war, a local bank has been stripped of all its clerks. He takes a minor job and is

recognized for his hard work. Even though he only has a seventh-grade education, he now works for a local bank as a bookkeeper.

Life at Work: Textiles

- The mill is built at the turn of the century with $200,000. The city of Spartanburg supplies half of the capital needed to build the plant. The new factory comprised 10,000 spindles, a measure used in mills to determine size.
- The original mill village built includes 40 houses of four different styles, all built near the mill; it also includes several churches, a barbershop, and a general store.
- Saxon Mills becomes a voting precinct almost as soon as the mill is built. In 1904 88 votes are cast out of a male population numbering 150.
- For more than two decades, entire families have continued to migrate between the mill and the farm, an indication that for some, agriculture is often being supplemented rather than supplanted by the textile industry.
- The American Cotton Manufacturer's Association reports that the low cost of mill house rents, free light and water, and coal and wood at cost add the equivalent of $4.36 to the weekly wage of each worker. "Where there are three or four workers in a family, as is often the case, this mounts up."
- The mill is built with local money and management of the mill is by local men.

Annual Report of Commission of Agriculture, Commerce, and Industry of State of South Carolina, 1925:

"The magnitude of the economic importance of the textile industry in the South is illustrated by the figures for South Carolina, where, in 1925, the produce of the cotton mills was 74 percent of the value of all the industrial products of the State, 70 percent of the wages paid were to textiles employees, 70 percent of all wage earners in the State were textile operatives, 65 percent of the total number were localized in the mills of the Piedmont with 27 percent of these centers in Spartanburg County, which since 1920 has been the premier manufacturing district of the State."

The Textile Community, by Alexander Ramsay Batchelor:

"Before this work was started an article upon the subject of the mill people was read ('The South Buries Its Anglo-Saxons,' *The Century Magazine*). It was a dark picture of the living and working conditions of these people. Although I had mingled with them and thought that I knew something of their lives and their attitude toward their work, perhaps I had been mistaken. I committed myself to an honest survey and placed in the questionnaire several questions on working conditions, grievances, etc. If these people are buried, they do not know it. With few exceptions, no evidence was found of anything other than petty grievances that could be found in any shop, office or school. All answers were relative to some other mill, to the farm, or former conditions at this mill. Invariably, those who had recently left the farm were satisfied. They all said that conditions were better at the mill. There is a fellowship at the mill, a community of interest that is not found on the farm. In the mill, the people helped each other in time of need, whereas the isolated farmer could not afford to do so."

- The builders of the cotton mills are not primarily manufacturers; they see themselves as the builders of a new state.
- At this time only 13 cities in South Carolina exceed a population of 10,000.
- In 1906, of the 53 houses in the village, five are overseers' houses of six rooms each, six are six-room, two-story houses, and two are six-room houses for the executives. Each has a front and back porch. There is neither plumbing nor running water in any of them. Wells are placed equal-distance in the blocks.
- A sewerage system is started in 1910 and all the houses have bathrooms in which toilets have been installed. Sixty of the 168 homes now have bathtubs.
- The Urbigs pay $0.25 a week per room, or $1.50 a week in rent.
- The daughter dreams of getting married and moving into one of the bungalettes costing $1.25 a week. The houses are built along an attractive street known as Honeymoon Lane. Her 16-year-old boyfriend works in the mill and also serves as swimming instructor at the community pool.

Life in the Community: Spartanburg, South Carolina

- Spartanburg County includes two colleges and 37 textile mills. During a typical month, the county bookstore sells 25 copies of *Harpers* and 750 copies of confession and adventure magazines—from under the counter where they are concealed.
- In 1923 the *Spartanburg Herald* announces construction of the city's first major office building with a headline that reads "Ten-Story Skyscraper Will Cost Over Million Dollars."

***Linthead, Growing Up in a Carolina Cotton Mill Village*, by Wilt Browning, "Everything had its own ritual, so when a new family moved to the cotton mill and spoke the first day, everyone was surprised":**

"New neighbors normally didn't speak to the old-timers for a day or two. It was a ritualistic checking out period for both the neighborhood and the newly arrived. Check out the kids, check to see whether the man of the house seems friendly or grumpy, check to see if they arrived with animals or not, check to see what kind of car and if they had a car at all. Besides, the migration to the mill hills of the South had long ago been dominated by farmhands leaving the red clay fields in search of a more stable livelihood. And they brought with them a quietness, an aloofness that was still not uncommon on the mill hills of the 1940s and 1950s. They were a people with a strong work ethic and with the understanding of an unspoken code that tolerated personal intrusions not at all."

- A small headline that same day announces that President Warren G. Harding has died.
- While in other parts of the United States men roll over Niagara Falls in barrels or walk across the falls on tightrope, a daredevil human fly scales the outside of the eight-story Chapman Building as hundreds of spectators gawk on the sidewalk below.
- No house is more than a five-minute walk from the mill.
- Fifty more homes are under construction in the village in 1925.
- In 1925 the mill village includes streetlights, streetcar service to town, and a Piedmont & Northern Railway station in the village.

- That same year the Interstate Commerce Commission grants Spartanburg the same preferential freight rates already in effect in Atlanta and Norfolk, Virginia, adding to its importance as a trade center.
- Spartanburg is the only city in South Carolina with a commercial airport, the principal reason that Col. Charles A. Lindbergh's only stop in the state, following his famous flight, is in that city.
- Improvements encompass the building of a community educational and social center and playground, including the transformation of one millpond into a lake for swimming and recreation purposes.
- Closely identified with village life is the vacation camp of the Saxon Mills, located on Lake Summit, 40 miles away in the Blue Ridge Mountains.
- Among the families in Saxon Mills, five percent have pianos, 16 percent have a Victrola or phonograph machine, one percent have radios and 31 percent have automobiles. The children of 18 of the 168 families are attending college.
- Furniture is bought on the installment plan. When one article is paid for another is purchased.
- Ninety percent of the families carry life insurance, which is paid weekly, normally $0.10 to $0.25. The purpose is invariably to provide for "a good burying."
- Typhoid fever and measles often drain a family of all savings, establishing debt at the mill store. Several children in the mill die of measles during the 1922 and 1923 epidemic.
- Although prohibition is under way in 1925 and many Southern counties have been "dry" prior to the constitutional change, illegal liquor traffic continues mostly in the form of

moonshine whiskey. "A touring car brings it in from the country and sells it on the quiet at the picture show."

- Use of snuff is common among mill village women.
- Hobbies in Saxon Mills include raising White Leghorn roosters which are shown in Madison Square Garden in New York in 1925; "Bill's library of 1,024 books with a review written in the back of each"; a weaver who makes doll's furniture; and a girl who tints photographs.
- The first regularly licensed radio broadcasts in America begin on August 20, 1920, but radio does not become a reality in Saxon Mill until almost a decade later. By then fairly inexpensive radio sets are flooding the market, but by 1930 not a single commercial radio station operates in South Carolina.
- The average wage paid to textile workers in four Southern states is $644.00 a year.
- "The individual wage is small but a father and mother with six children, two of whom are of working age, can earn about $25.00 to $30.00 a month," reports Richard Woods Edmunds in *Cotton Mill Labor Conditions in the South and New England.*
- Ninety-nine percent of the workers are from the Southern states of South Carolina, North Carolina, Virginia, Georgia, or Tennessee.
- Approximately 90 percent of the mill workers are formerly farmers, 64 percent leaving jobs as farm tenants and 26 percent former owners of the farmland.
- Textile mill recruiters, who visit farms seeking employees, favor large families where father, mother, and children can all be employed.
- Small children in the home are cared for by older children one-third of the time, a nurse one-third, and grandparents 23 percent of the time.
- Black nurses are hired to care for children when the mother can negotiate a wage low enough to allow a margin of profit for the mother working in the mill. Widowed mothers with young children often attempt this form of child care.
- On average, two children in every home work in the mill. Often the mother leaves mill work when her children are old enough to take her place.
- The average mill family has 3.5 children in the home. They are encouraged to attend school until 14 so they can learn more than their parents, most of whom cannot read.
- Most children attend school until they are 14 before beginning mill work
- Some parents move from mill to mill to obtain a better education for their children.
- Night school is also available in the community for adults, most providing elementary schoolwork. For advanced work, the International Correspondence School Textile Courses are used.

Cotton Mill People of the Piedmont, by Marjorie A. Potwin:

"Real Southerners, they stress the personal equation and hold individual sovereignty and the freedom of contract supreme. They have fine independence, yet they seem to lack studied self direction. Group consciousness among them is more from external pressure than internal motivation. They desire being treated as a mass. Their group action is collective individualism, unless led to abnormality in the heat of religious or patriotic fervor. They are sympathetic with each other in trouble; yet, notwithstanding a pronounced clannishness among families, when it comes to matters of common endeavor, 'every tub must set on its own bottom,' as their own homey words express it. However, is this a local or sectional or national characteristic? Perhaps the least American thing about these contemporary ancestors of ours is that they do not envy wealth. Life close to the soil does not breed socialistic covetousness and those who think about wealth at all have seen it created by the ability and sustained endeavor of their neighbors. Moreover, most of the mill people are accumulating in proportion to the evolution of their wants, and they feel prosperity in terms of improvement, not exploitation. Also, too, they live in a section where a prevalent idea is to get the maximum of comfort with the minimum of exertion."

- Approximately 25 percent of mill workers farm on the side, leave mill work occasionally to work on a farm, or talk about returning to the farm.
- Textile mill workers are known as a "moving population," often moving from job to job and town to town every few years. One man says he always keeps "moving money" on hand. When he takes a job at a new mill, the first money he makes is put away for a rainy day, and a rainy day for him is moving day.
- Some of the workers cannot resist the call of the land and every spring return to the farm, where they tend cotton and then return to the mill in the fall. Many put their children, restricted from mill work by child labor regulations, to work on the farm. The children are routinely taken out of school several weeks before the session ends and returned weeks after the fall session has begun.
- About 30 percent of the workers are Baptist, 16 percent Methodist, and slightly less than half claim no organized religion or faith. Approximately 50 percent of the children attend Sunday School.
- A local religious leader commands his followers not to work on the night shift because in the Bible it is written that Christ said, "the night cometh, when no man can work." (John 9:4) Little came of the edict.
- Many families still discuss the six-week-long revival held by the Rev. William Ashley "Billy" Sunday, the world's most widely known evangelist in 1922. Services are held in a huge, frame "tabernacle" built to the evangelist's specifications, seating 7,000 people. It is by far the largest auditorium in South Carolina at the time.

Letter to the Editor, *Rhode Island Red Journal*:

" 'I have raised poultry for over 30 years, but when I first started I had very little luck; most of the bad luck was my own, in that I did not feed right and did not understand how to mate the birds for best results. But after years of experience and reading the best poultry papers and following the advice of the best poultry men, I can now say I have good luck, and I have some of the finest birds one wants to see. Well, in all the years of poultry I was like lots of others today. Almost every year I tried a different kind, think-

ing the other fellow had a better kind. About fifteen years ago I took to the Reds and will say that if anyone has Reds and feeds them the way they should be fed, they will pay no question about it. But no one can expect hens to lay with half enough to eat and in winter with a shed where rain, snow and sleet goes throughout the birds. No matter how good a hen is, she can't lay without feed. Just so with a cow. One will not get any milk from the best cow by feeding it straw.'
Mr. Hillie Borg, Nokomis, Illinois"

- In 1925 cotton prices are severely depressed, following the war. Many South Carolina-based banks, which are agriculturally-oriented, will fail in 1926 and 1927, long before the more famous crash of 1929.
- After cotton prices drop from the World War I levels of $0.50 or more per pound to $0.05 per pound by the mid-1920s, the farmer is also harmed by the invasion of the boll weevil, a highly destructive pest that makes cotton farming a highly speculative venture, at best.

How do you like him? First Cock and Color Special at Both Kansas City and Chicago Coliseum.

Dixie Red Farm.

EUREKA

We would breed 'em redder if we could. You could breed 'em better if you would avail yourself of this opportunity.

Special Stock Sale

We are offering as an introductory stock offer several carefully selected trios at $25.00, on approval. These trios are priced at about 40 per cent of their actual worth. Blood tells and these birds are out of our great line of Chicago and Heart of America winners.

RAWNSLEY-BACH

Route 22, LOUISVILLE, KY.

HISTORICAL SNAPSHOT
1925–1926

- Refrigerator sales reached 75,000, up 10,000 from 1920

- Florida land prices collapsed as investors discovered that many lots they had purchased are under water

- The $10 million Boca Raton Hotel in Florida was completed

- Al Capone took control of Chicago bootlegging

- Chesterfield cigarettes were marketed to women for the first time

- The Book-of-the-Month Club was founded

- Aunt Jemima Mills was acquired by Quaker Oats Company for $4 million

- Machine-made ice production topped 56 million pounds; up 1.5 million from 1894

- The first ham in a can was introduced by Hormel

- The first blue jeans with slide fasteners were introduced by J.D. Lee Company

- Synthetic rubber was pioneered by B.F. Goodrich Rubber Company chemist Waldo Lonsburg Serman

- Cars appeared for the first time in such colors as "Florentine Cream" and "Versailles Violet"

- As prosperity continued, 40 percent of Americans earned at least $2,000 a year

- "Yellow-Drive-It-Yourself-Systems" became popular; $0.12 a mile for a Ford and $0.22 a mile for a 6-cylinder car

- Earl Wise's potato chips were so successful he moved his business from a remodeled garage to a concrete plant

- Wesson Oil, National Spelling Bees, and the *New Yorker* magazine all made their first appearances

what a whale of a difference
just a few cents make

1925 ECONOMIC PROFILE

Income, Standard Jobs

Average for All Industries
   Including Farm Labor $1,434.00
Clerical Workers in Manufacturing $2,239.00
Domestic $741.00
Farm Labor $382.00
Gas and Electricity Workers............... $1,552.00
Medical Health Workers.................... $916.00
Public School Teachers.................... $1,299.00
State and Local Government Workers........ $1,377.00
Telephone Workers........................ $1,108.00
Wholesale and Retail Trade Workers $1,416.00

Selected Prices

Armstrong Waffle Iron...................... $4.00
Arts and Crafts Misson
   Oak Set, Seven Pieces $28.50
B. Altonman & Co. Handkerchiefs,
   Hemstitched $1.80/Dozen
Barn Paint $1.54/Gallon
Colgate Ribbon Dental Cream............. $0.25/Tube
Condo Typrocraft Typewriter
   Ribbon........................... $3.00/Dozen
Durant Four Automobile,
   Five Passenger $890.00
Forham's for the Gums $0.60
Hamilton Strap Watch..................... $38.00
Kalamazoo Stove Company
   Oil Heater $4.95
Licecil Insecticide Lice Poison
   for Chickens $1.00/Bottle
Life Magazine, Weekly $5.00/Year
Lily White Columbia River
   Salmon......................... $0.44/per Can
Marvex Women's Gloves,
   Suede and Kidskin $5.50
Pall Mall Cigarettes, per 20................. $0.30
Shinola Shoe Polish $0.08
Starr Best Boy's Suit, Blue Denim $2.95
Steinway & Sons Piano, Upright............. $875.00
Victrola Talking Machine,
   Mahogany Cabinet $125.00
Wrigley Juicy Fruit Gum .... $0.39/10 Packs

1926 FAMILY PROFILE

Jean Williams teaches elementary school children in Syracuse, New York, where she lives by herself, but shares a bathroom with three other women boarders. She teaches her children from the *McGuffey Readers* which glorify the rural past and are cautious of city life.

Annual Income: $1,539.00

Annual Expenditures

Amusements	$22.50
Car Fare	$27.00
Clothing	$240.00
Food	$437.11
Forhan's Toothpaste	$9.00
Incidentals	$22.50
Medical Services	$36.00
Newspapers	$9.00
Rent	$390.00
Total	$1,193.11

Life at Home

- Miss Williams pays $7.50 a week for a room in a large boarding house. She shares a bathroom down the hall with three other tenants—all female. Rooms in Syracuse for single women range from $6.00 per week to $11.00 a week.
- A study of clerical workers in Washington, D.C., in 1919 finds that most clerical workers save money by having two women to one room. This is rarely found among the teachers.

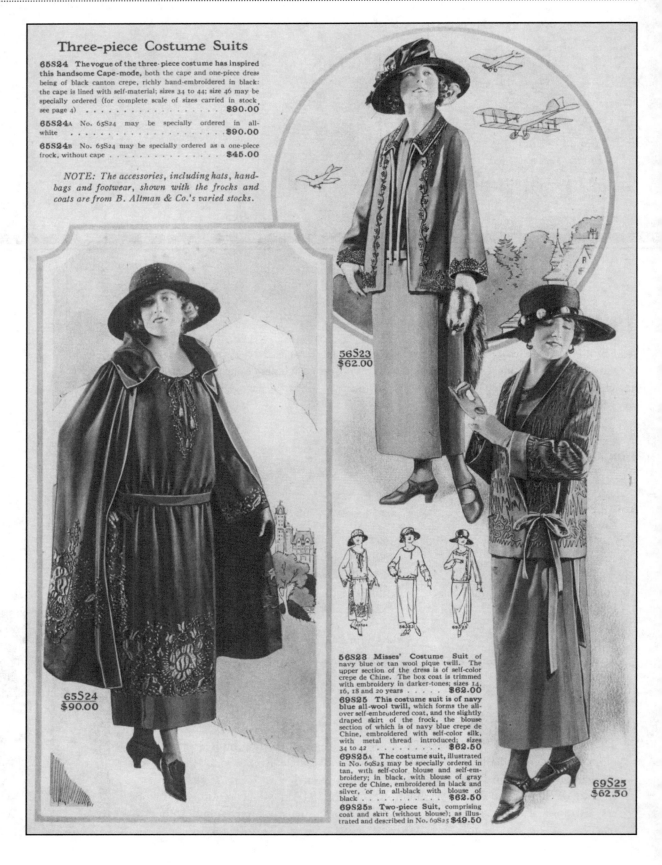

Three-piece Costume Suits

65S24 The vogue of the three-piece costume has inspired this handsome Cape-mode, both the cape and one-piece dress being of black canton crepe, richly hand-embroidered in black; the cape is lined with self-material; sizes 34 to 44; size 46 may be specially ordered (for complete scale of sizes carried in stock, see page 4) **$90.00**

65S24A No. 65S24 may be specially ordered in all-white **$90.00**

65S24B No. 65S24 may be specially ordered as a one-piece frock, without cape **$45.00**

NOTE: The accessories, including hats, handbags and footwear, shown with the frocks and coats are from B. Altman & Co.'s varied stocks.

56S23
$62.00

65S24
$90.00

56S23 Misses' Costume Suit of navy blue or tan wool pique twill. The upper section of the dress is of self-color crepe de Chine. The box coat is trimmed with embroidery in darker-tones; sizes 14, 16, 18 and 20 years **$62.00**

69S25 This costume suit is of navy blue all-wool twill, which forms the all-over self-embroidered coat, and the slightly draped skirt of the frock, the blouse section of which is of navy blue crepe de Chine, embroidered with self-color silk, with metal thread introduced; sizes 34 to 42 . . . . **$62.50**

69S25A The costume suit, illustrated in No. 69S25 may be specially ordered in tan, with self-color blouse and self-embroidery; in black, with blouse of gray crepe de Chine, embroidered in black and silver, or in all-black with blouse of black **$62.50**

69S25B Two-piece Suit, comprising coat and skirt (without blouse); as illustrated and described in No. 69S25 **$49.50**

69S25
$62.50

- The rents in New York City range from $3.00 to $15.00 a week and in Schenectady, $4.00 to $6.00 weekly.
- Our teacher saves money by being her own washwoman whenever possible.
- She spends money for both a local newspaper and an out-of-town newspaper, probably from New York, on Sundays.
- Brand name food items commonly purchased by a majority of the teachers include Borden's Evaporated Milk, Maxwell House Coffee, Lipton's Tea, Kellogg's Cornflakes, Quaker Rolled Oats, Pillsbury Best Flour, Good Luck Oleomargarine, Del Monte Red Alaskan Salmon.

The Young Women's Christian Association publishes the following set of standards for teachers who are living away from home:

"In general the house that habitually receives transient roomers without character references should not be considered.

There should be good provision for natural as well as artificial lighting.

There should be an indoor bathroom—completely equipped with superior sanitary equipment (toilet, porcelain bowl, porcelain or enameled iron tub, hot and cold water, mirror). The bathroom should not be located on a hall to which the general public has access.

No more than six people should be expected to use one bathroom.

There should be a room in the building, other than a bedroom, in which the roomer may receive men guests. The common name for this room is parlor, living room, office, reception room."

Short Talks about Working Women:

"In general it may be said that many manufacturers have recognized the futility of the long, fatiguing day, and have gradually come to realize that an eight-hour day is just as productive as a longer shift."

Sample of Food Prices

	Average Price	Cost per Year
Bananas	$0.34	$3.76
Canned Tomatoes	$0.22	$2.29
Chuck Roast	$0.24	$7.14
Coffee	$0.58	$19.14
Cornflakes	$0.10	$1.21
Cornmeal	$0.07	$2.23
Cream of Wheat	$0.25	$1.00
Hens	$0.44	$10.97
Lard	$0.20	$5.45
Macaroni	$0.13	$5.77
Onions	$0.07	$4.89
Pork Chops	$0.37	$10.70
Potatoes	$0.06	$42.52
Raisins	$0.15	$1.38
Rice	$0.12	$3.84
Salmon	$0.39	$3.52
Sirloin Steak	$0.42	$11.37
Sugar	$0.32	$8.98

- Teachers' salaries comprise about 75 percent of the total expenses of the schools in the state.

Sample of Clothing Prices

- New York City wholesalers control the retail prices of clothing and trademark articles by not selling to dealers who cut the standard price of the article.

Dress Coat	$81.50
Dry Cleaning	$8.50
Hat	$5.10
Shoes	$24.00
Shoe Repair	$4.68
Silk Dress	$25.50
Sport Coat	$49.50
Stockings, Lingerie, Misc.	$41.65
Wool Dress	$26.30

Life in the Community: Syracuse, New York

- Located near the center of the state, in the Great Lakes Plain, Syracuse gets its start from salt manufacturing, especially after the construction of the Erie Canal. Irish immigrants settle early in the area and promote the manufacture of plows, shoes, hardware, and other farm products.

- At the time, it is the fourth largest city in the state and is well-known for the manufacture of high-grade steel and automobile parts. The Franklin automobile, which boasts an air-cooled rather than a water-cooled engine, establishes the region as an automobile manufacturer.
- The city also manufactures church and ornamental candles, following a tradition started by German immigrant Anthony Will in 1855.
- Teachers use a variety of books, or "readers," to instruct their children, such as the *McGuffey Reader,* which worships the rural lifestyle of the past and views urbanization with caution.

1927 Family Profile

The Rutherfords, a farm family of five from Culpeper County, Virginia, now have an automobile and the freedom to travel, visit nearby towns, and even attend a church that is more than a buggy ride away. The couple has been married 22 years, is blessed with both electricity—a rarity in rural America—and four children, ages three, 16, 19, and 21.

Annual Income: The family makes approximately $1359.

Annual Budget

Advancement and Recreation	$81.00
Automobile	$176.00
Clothing	$235.00
Food	$277.00
Fuel and Light	$89.00
Health	$59.00
Household Furnishings	$25.00
Life and Health Insurance	$25.00
Other	$70.00
Personal	$53.00
Rent	$269.00
Total	$1,359.00

Life at Home

- This family owns a wood frame house with seven rooms, no running water or baths, and some electrical lights. Heat is produced entirely by burning wood in two fireplaces.

The children attended school near the farm.

- The farm consists of 200 acres, half of which are under cultivation.
- Both the man and woman graduated from elementary school.
- Two of the four children (both girls) finish eighth grade—which is average for the community.
- The 19-year-old girl is already married and moves out of home to land given to her by her parents.
- The oldest son graduates from high school and goes to college. He attends one year and returns home.
- The Virginia compulsory school law requires that children from ages eight to 16 attend school, although in many rural areas school does not start until September 15 and ends April 15 to accommodate harvest and planting seasons.
- The average farmer works between 12 and 13 hours per day during the summer and about 10 hours per day during the remainder of the year. The number of hours recorded for the homemaker and farmer are similar.
- The family eats mostly in the kitchen where the cooking is done, and during the winter confines itself to living in the three rooms that can be heated—living room, kitchen, and one bedroom.

John Martin Magazine for Boys and Girls, December 1926:

"The Honest-to-Goodness Woman: Very early in the morning the Honest-to-Goodness-Woman did arise. She said to herself: 'I will not waste a minute.' She did not forget to take her bath, to clean her teeth, and to brush her hair; she did all these things in order, and neatly dressed herself besides helping the children. Then she went downstairs. She did not waste a minute. As usual she put on the steam for the porridge, and let the oatmeal cook while she busied herself at other things. There were the draughts of the stove to open; the ashes to shake down, to take out and empty; there was the bread to set for rising; the dishes to place on the table; the toast to make; the apple sauce to serve, and the cocoa to prepare."

- This family has electricity. Only one in six neighbors has electricity or gas. Even among the wealthiest farm families in the county, only 25 percent have electricity.
- The father has promised to buy a washing machine, now that electricity is available and used for some lights. Oil lamps are still used in all bedrooms.
- The family has seen a Minnesota washing machine with console advertised in the Sears Roebuck Catalog for $33.95. In Richmond they have seen a Cork Wall, Top-Icer "Alaska" Refrigerator for $16.95 that can be purchased with "deferred payments."
- The Rutherford family is cautious about the spreading use of "installment credit," advertised as "exercising your credit." An estimated 15 percent of all retail purchases are now made on deferred payments.

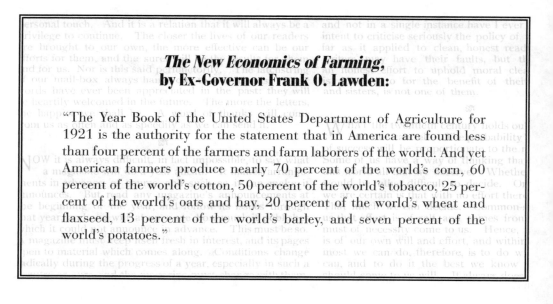

The New Economics of Farming, by Ex-Governor Frank O. Lawden:

"The Year Book of the United States Department of Agriculture for 1921 is the authority for the statement that in America are found less than four percent of the farmers and farm laborers of the world. And yet American farmers produce nearly 70 percent of the world's corn, 60 percent of the world's cotton, 50 percent of the world's tobacco, 25 percent of the world's oats and hay, 20 percent of the world's wheat and flaxseed, 13 percent of the world's barley, and seven percent of the world's potatoes."

- They have seen more than one family go bankrupt following the war when prices fell and farm equipment purchased on credit to meet the increased war demand and is still unpaid for.
- The temptation to buy is great, from the Sears Catalog or the advertisements in popular magazines. More than $1.5 billion is spent on advertising to stimulate purchases. Photographs in advertisements become more realistic and more frank. Products such as Odoro-no and Kotex are advertised openly in popular magazines.
- The $277.00 food bill would be higher if most food were not grown on the farm; only 15 percent is purchased.
- The family contributes about four percent of their income, or $68.00, a year to the church.

- Our family spends $60.00 on doctors and dentists. A county health unit is available and emphasizes preventive medicine, reducing the opportunity for communicable diseases to spread.

- They spend $25.00 annually for insurance; 38 percent of neighbors in a similar financial situation have insurance, mostly life insurance on the head of household. Most families have little savings for this type of tragedy and most of the insurance is used to cover burial costs, not to provide future income for the family.

- The average cost of a funeral for families that carry insurance is $432.00. Among the Irish, the average bill is $452.00, among Italians $421.00, and among Jews, because of simpler ceremonies, $247.00.

- The average hospital bill, including the physician's fee and special nurse, is $300.00. The average per capita cost per day of a hospital stay is $6.65, up 135 percent from 1913 when the average per capita cost per day is $2.83. During that same time period, the average length of stay per patient is reduced from 15 days in 1913 to 12 days in 1926.

- The Rutherfords got a telephone this year by selling more cattle than originally planned. Half of the neighbors now have telephones. Six families share a single party line and our family must wait to use the phone if any of the other families are using it first.

- Reading material is available in this home, including monthly periodicals, such as *The Ladies' Home Journal*, newspapers and books, many of which are described as short stories "of an emotional nature."

- This family spends $21.00 a year on recreation and entertainment, including newspapers and magazines: *Time*, the weekly news magazine, costs $0.15 per issue.

- Our family normally goes into town six times a month, frequently on Saturday nights. Movies they may see include *The Enemy*, a great love story; *Alias the Deacon*; *Smile Awhile*, "a Kaleidoscopic Knock-out"; and *Secrets of the Soul*, "a drama of man and his psychological problems with technical assistance provided by Dr. Sigmund Freud."

Canning Calls for the New Kind of Sink.

Fruit and Vegetable Acids Cannot Roughen or Discolor This Sink

"Standard" PLUMBING FIXTURES

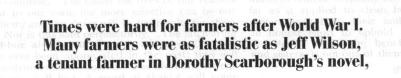

Times were hard for farmers after World War I. Many farmers were as fatalistic as Jeff Wilson, a tenant farmer in Dorothy Scarborough's novel,

In the Land of Cotton, when he said, "If I was to start to hell with a load of ice, there'd be a freeze before I got there."

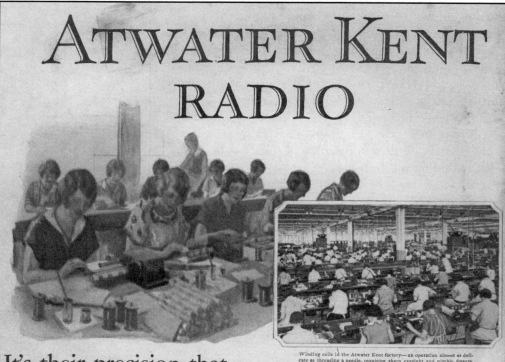

ATWATER KENT RADIO

Winding coils in the Atwater Kent factory—an operation almost as delicate as threading a needle, requiring sharp eyesight and nimble fingers.

It's their precision that makes your set work and keep on working

THE SECRET of Atwater Kent reliability is not alone in expert designing nor in the exacting factory and laboratory tests, but in the extreme care given to every phase of manufacturing. As we make all the parts ourselves, we are able to attain standards of precision otherwise impossible.

For instance, coil winding. As no radio set is better than its coils, we wind our own. At first, we employed men at this task. But the accurate winding of wire only 3/1000th of an inch in diameter happens to be an almost incredibly delicate operation.

A hair's breadth difference in spacing might affect, if ever so little, the perfect reception you demand in your home.

So now all Atwater Kent coils are wound by women (with the help, of course, of wonderful automatic machines). Their sharper eyes, nimbler fingers, quicker reflexes, assure the rightness which every coil must have. For the same reason, you will find hundreds of women working in many other parts of this clean, bright, airy, wide-spaced modern factory. They contribute *precision*—with speed.

This is one of the ways we get that uniform accuracy which so delights the experts when they study Atwater Kent Radio—accuracy which makes the set we send to the Cook Islands in the South Seas work just as efficiently as the set in your home.

You may not *see* the difference that all our extra care makes in a radio instrument. But you *hear* it—and you feel it in freedom from service troubles.

ATWATER KENT MANUFACTURING CO.
A. Atwater Kent, President
4704 Wissahickon Avenue   Philadelphia, Pa.

MODEL E RADIO SPEAKER. New method of cone suspension, found in no other speaker, makes certain the faithful reproduction of the entire range of musical tones. $24

Atwater Kent Radio Hour every Sunday night on 23 associated stations

ONE Dial Receivers licensed under U. S. Patent 1,014,002

Prices slightly higher from the Rockies West

MODEL 30, a powerful ONE Dial, six-tube Receiver. The mahogany cabinet of unobtrusive beauty is the type that many people prefer. Without accessories. $65

MODEL 35, a powerful ONE Dial, six-tube Receiver with shielded cabinet, finished in two tones of brown crystalline. Ideal for a small table, window sill or bookshelf. Without accessories. $49

MODEL 33, a very powerful ONE Dial, six-tube Receiver with solid mahogany cabinet. Unusually effective where distance-getting is essential or inside antenna is necessary. Simple antenna adjustment device assures remarkable selectivity. Without accessories. $75

- The newspaper carries the news that the first "synchronized sound" movie, *The Jazz Singer,* featuring Al Jolson, has opened in New York that year, but it would not arrive in Richmond until 1928. The movie is to revolutionize the motion picture industry.
- Magazines feature the Atwater Kent Radio: "It's their precision that makes your set work and keep on working."
- During the past five years the family has left Culpeper County on a pleasure trip three times, once to go to Richmond, once to Washington, D.C., once for a funeral.

"The Flapper: A National Institution," by Samuel Crowther,
American History Told by Contemporaries, Volume V,
Twentieth Century United States, 1900–1929:

"During the past several months I have traveled from coast to coast and from Fargo, North Dakota, to El Paso, Texas; through all the states and in all the cities and many of the towns, I did not find a town over two thousand—and I doubt if there is one—where Jeanette or Lucille or Marie is not running a 'beauty parlor' or a 'beauty shoppe' and doing fairly well. It means that we today are rich enough to go in for luxuries not just in the big cities but everywhere in our land . . . We cannot comprehend that to America has come a new order of things—that dire poverty is as rare as smallpox is obsolete; that we are in the midst of a great experiment the like of which the world has never even dreamed of, and thus it lies with us to carry on or to flunk."

A comparison of Virginia urban families with a similar income showed the following average expenditures:

Advancement and Recreation	$128.00
Clothing	$275.00
Food	$554.00
Health	$90.00
Household Furnishing	$56.00
Household Operating	$363.00
Life and Health Insurance	$78.00
Personal	$70.00
Rent	$331.00

Life at Work: Farming

- Many in the community still grow tobacco and cotton because transportation hurdles restrict the use of perishable crops in favor of products which can stand rough handling and the crudest form of processing for marketing and storing. Cotton and tobacco are cash crops with established markets.
- Dependency on a single crop also means that as prices drop cotton liens increase, and often crop liens can be obtained only by continuing to grow the products such as cotton, on which merchants are willing to make advances.
- Cotton does not ripen all at once, requiring three pickings to harvest the crop. International Harvester Company introduces cotton picking machines in 1924. They fail to become popular in the cash-poor and sometimes labor-rich South because mechanically picked cotton contains trash and unripe cotton, which many cotton gins cannot handle.
- The farms of America, particularly in the South, are becoming depopulated as young workers rush to the cities for manufacturing jobs.

- The Great War has drawn a half million Blacks out of the rural South and into the factories of the North. By the end of the decade another million African-Americans have left the deep South to take up employment in the Northeast and Midwest.
- The severe depression that follows World War I fosters the idea that sinister economic forces are deliberately conspiring to harm the farmer. Farm prices drop dramatically in 1921 and still have not returned to the inflated prices of 1914 to 1919.
- By 1927 the producers of stable crops in Virginia are feeling the competition of the lower cost producing areas farther west.

Your Money's Worth, by Stuart Chase and F.J. Schlink:

"Listerine advertising has gone through at least four successive stages. First it was promoted as a more or less general remedy. Secondly came the brilliant halitosis offense. Thirdly came the deodorant appeal. Fourthly appeared the dandruff copy. 'Listerine,' says the American Medical Association in its July 4, 1925 report, 'is not a deodorant but merely covers one smell with another.' A true deodorant, on the other hand, abolishes the original smell."

> ### George E. Roberts, Vice-President, National City Bank, Richmond, Virginia:
>
> "The population of the world is steadily increasing and the best and most available lands of this continent and of all continents are occupied. We have come nowhere near the limits of food production in this country, but have come to the end of the cheap and easy increase. The free lands are gone, the cheap lands are gone, and the increase of the future must come from lands that require considerable investment of capital for irrigation, for drainage, for clearing, and by more scientific methods of culture."

Life in the Community: Culpeper County and Richmond, Virginia

- Culpeper County is close to the Blue Ridge Mountains in the Piedmont region of Virginia. It is located in the northern part of the state. The land area is 384 square miles and has a population of 13,292 in 1920.
- The topography is less rugged than many Piedmont counties, but several detached spurs or mountains give the southwestern portion of the county a more broken and picturesque appearance.
- The soil is red clay, chocolate, and black silk, sometimes sandy, and is well adapted to white corn, rye, oats, hay, and legumes. The leading crops are wheat, corn, and legumes.
- The region is suitable for fruit growing, and apples do well, especially along the mountainsides.
- Cattle, hogs, and the dairy industry are also important. Forest products include railroad ties, tan bark, and pulpwood.
- Culpeper, the county seat, is incorporated and in 1920 has a population of 1,118. Organization among the farmers has grown in recent years.

> ### Games and Equipment; Small Rural Schools, Department of the Interior, Bureau of Education, 1927:
>
> "Time was, and not long ago, when the activities of the school playground developed spontaneously. Their significance in life was necessary. We live, however, in a day when the instinct for play and the knowledge of games, both in rural and urban communities, have strangely diminished; and this change has not only made this importance evident, but has likewise made it needful for the educator to stimulate and instruct in these activities."

Where cleanliness is most considered, paint and varnish are indispensable

"Save the surface and you save all" — Paint & Varnish

PAINT makes dirt noticeable and easier to remove. Paint brings light into dark places. And where are cleanliness and light more needed than where milk starts its journey from cow to cup?

In cow barns, milk house, testing laboratory—paint and varnish assist in the business of making milk safe for infants and adults. Walker-Gordon plants are models of what surface protection means to all who produce or use milk. Painting is as regular a part of the program as milking.

The magic of paint and varnish is to give the user what he needs, be it sanitation, light, better appearance, preservation, alone or in combination. "Save the surface and you save all" states a very practical truth. The benefits are great—and open to everyone.

SAVE THE SURFACE CAMPAIGN
18 East 41st Street, New York

A cooperative movement by Paint, Varnish and Allied Interests whose products and services conserve, protect and beautify practically every kind of property.

- The services of a farm demonstration agent are available to the people of the county. It may very accurately be stated that in progressive agricultural development, Culpeper takes rank among the leading counties of Virginia.
- Chosen as the site of the Fifth Federal Reserve Bank in 1914, Richmond is becoming a financial center with strong banks and a strong manufacturing base. The city boasts the world's largest cigarette factory, baking powder factory, and furniture company.
- The city builds its first free library in 1924, the last city of its size to do so.
- The U.S. Customs' receipts at Richmond pass $2 million in 1926, up from $20,000 in 1897.
- Richmond, the "big city" where our family occasionally travels for supplies and entertainment has increased in population from 1910 to 1920 by 35 percent, topping 171,000 people.
- The South in the 1920s is the nation's most rural region. Not a single Southern state meets the superintendent of the census's modest definition of "urban" in 1920, having a majority of its population in cities of 2,500 or more souls.
- The percentage of Blacks in the city's population has declined from 45 percent in 1870 to 29 percent in 1927 as the emigration to Northern cities accelerates after World War I.
- The average weekly pay rate for White workers in the paper products industry is $18.54; in the tobacco industry the pay is $12.87 weekly.
- Blacks are largely confined to lower paying jobs; the average wage of domestics in one-servant homes is $8.00 per week and in two-servant homes, $12.00 a week. Most are furnished with meals and uniforms.
- A survey of single women living in Richmond shows that clerical workers make an average $1,082 per year; female factory workers average $667.00.
- For clerical workers the cost of board, room, food, fuel, light, and laundry comprises 42 percent of the women's total expenditures, or $460.00. They also spend $306.00 on clothing, $28.96 on health issues, $57.22 on recreation and amusement, education and advancement $51.98, miscellaneous $205.53.
- In those days before radio broadcasts of baseball games, fans can gather at the *Richmond Times-Dispatch* and "watch" the game on a baseball diamond rigged up on the wall of the newspaper. As events take place, the reporter telephones his editor, who uses movable figures representing the players, to move around the bases. When the batter makes a base hit, a bell rings and the figure at bat moves to the proper base. Excited crowds jam the street to follow the heroic feats of Roger Hornsby or Walter Johnson.

"CRAYOLA" in Eskimo Land

WHEN David Binney Putnam, the 13-year old explorer, went to Greenland last summer, he took some "CRAYOLA" Crayons with him.

In the picture above you see Kakutia, the Eskimo artist, with two happy little Eskimos. Kakutia used the "CRAYOLA" Crayons to draw pictures for David's book, which is called "David Goes to Greenland."

It will be fun for you to get some "CRAYOLA" Crayons, and after you have read David's book, to see whether you can draw a polar bear the way Kakutia did.

BINNEY & SMITH CO.
41 East 42nd Street   New York, N.Y.

HISTORICAL SNAPSHOT
1927–1928

- 20 million cars were on the road, up from 13,824 in 1900

- Transatlantic telephone service between London and New York began; calls cost $75.00 for three minutes

- J.C. Penney opened its 500th store, and sold stock to the public

- Wonder Bread was introduced

- Broccoli became more widely marketed in the United States

- Rice Krispies were introduced by W.K. Kellogg

- Peanut butter cracker sandwiches, sold under the name NAB, which stands for National Biscuit Company, were sold for $0.05 each

- U.S. per capita consumption of crude oil reached 7.62 barrels

- Presidential candidate Herbert Hoover calls for "a chicken in every pot and two cars in every garage"

- The Ford Model A appeared in four colors including "Arabian Sand"

- The Hayes list of dos and don'ts for Hollywood films included licentious or suggestive nudity, ridicule of clergy, and inference of sexual perversion

- The Al Capone gang netted $100 million in the illegal liquor trade as Prohibition continued

- President Calvin Coolidge urged the nation to pray more

- The post-war education obsession included a wide variety of "how-to" courses and books

- A phonograph with an automatic record changer was introduced

- Volvo, Lender Bagels, and Movietone News all made their first appearances

Every farm woman can have extra washing help!

Nowadays, tractors, mechanical milkers, and other machines help to make things a bit easier for the men on the farm. And today, as for over a quarter of a century past, Fels-Naptha is still giving extra help to the women-folks.

Thousands upon thousands of farm women rely upon the extra help of Fels-Naptha wherever and whenever there's a "soap-and-water" job to be done. From washing clothes to keeping the dairy things sweet and wholesome.

The extra help of Fels-Naptha makes clothes cleaner more quickly, more easily, for unusually good soap and plenty of dirt-loosening naptha work together. Women appreciate that! They save time in all their cleaning, for Fels-Naptha gives extra help they'd hardly expect from any other soap. And of equal importance is the service of Fels-Naptha in saving their strength—in helping to guard good health, so needful for the many duties in a farm home!

You really can't put a money value on this extra help. But get a Golden Bar; and, using it in your own way, you'll soon see that it is worth at least many times a penny or so more a week. Try it and see!

FELS-NAPTHA
THE GOLDEN BAR WITH THE CLEAN NAPTHA ODOR.

1927 ECONOMIC PROFILE

Income, Standard Jobs

Average for All Industries,
   Including Farm Labor $1,380.00
Building Trades $1,719.00
Domestics $756.00
Farm Labor $387.00
Federal Civilian $1,907.00
Gas and Electricity Workers $1,558.00
Medical and Health Workers $931.00
School Teachers $1,393.00
Telegraph Workers $1,215.00
Wholesale and Retail Trade
   Workers $1,573.00

Selected Prices

Atwater Kent Model Radio $65.00
Book, *Winnie the Pooh* $2.00
Boy's Romper Suit $0.59
Brassiere Corset $3.50
Chicken Medicine, Stops Sorehead $0.35
Corn Cake Pans, Makes 11 . . . . $0.85
Corn Popper $1.75
Cotton Plaid Blanket $1.72
Faultless Wagon $1.00
Hershey's Milk Chocolate, Box of 24 . . . . $0.97
Kelly Falls City Ax, Four Pounds $1.20
Man's Wristwatch, 14-K White Gold . . . $38.50
Mill Falls Hacksaw $2.00
Squibbs Dental Cream $0.40
Tangee Lipstick $1.00

This Smoking World, by A.E. Hamilton, The Century Company, New York, 1927:

"As to why women have taken up the practice of smoking, opinion is diverse, of course. Some lay the cause to the war, when women smoked to keep doughboys company. Others attribute it to the inferred slump of moral standards following the war. One theory has it that knitting, crocheting, tatting, and their like having gone the way of spinning and weaving; women's hands are again idle and have welcomed the cigarette as a relief for nervous tension in their fingers."

The New Happy Baby Doll. $6.48
Universal Toaster, Electric. $4.95
Victor Mousetrap $1.80
Wheelbarrow, 43 Pounds $6.25
Winchester Model 94 Rifle $31.98
Wrigley's Spearmint Gum, 10-Pack $0.39

The Development of the Automobile

- Thanks to the development of the automobile and improving roads, farmers emerged from a position of comparative isolation. As a result, they often drove to nearby cities to watch silent moving pictures.
- The automobile allowed the family to select a church that was farther from the farm and attended social activities in neighboring communities. When an ordinary horse team was the only transportation available, the family was restricted to events no more than six or seven miles from their home.

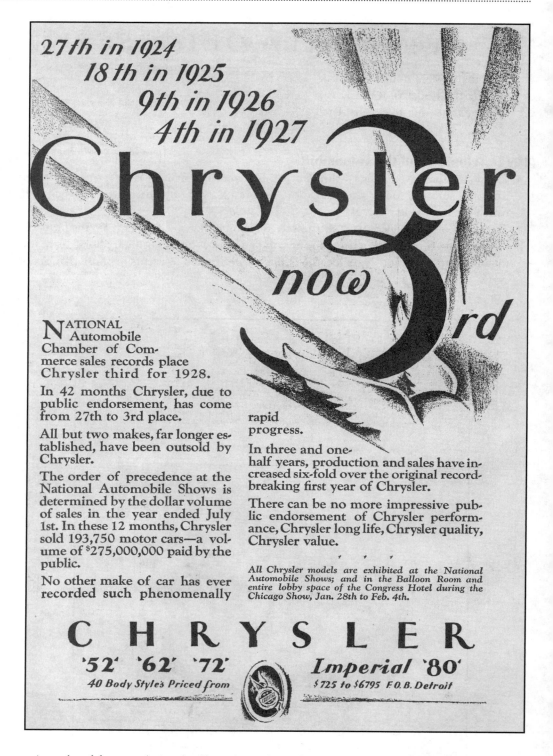

- A study of farm and city dwellers showed similar amounts paid for clothing, about 14 percent of total expenditures.
- The automobile was a high priority among farmers. Among the poorer farmers' homes of Culpeper County only five percent had running water, baths in none, modern lighting in less than two percent, and no modern heating devices. Yet 40 percent of the farm families owned and operated cars for business and pleasure.

"Confessions of a Ford Dealer," *Harper's Monthly Magazine*, June 1927, The Twenties:

"Like I say, when I first took the agency I was my own boss like any other businessman, selling as many cars as I could and buying more when I needed them. I didn't have to make many sales on installments, because people who wanted cars usually saved up in advance and had the cash in hand when they got ready to buy. Occasionally some man that I knew would want a little time, in which case I just charged it the same as if it were a bill of dry goods or groceries, and when the account fell due he paid me. There was no such thing then as putting a mortgage on the car and taking it away from him if he didn't pay up. If I didn't believe a man I simply didn't give him credit. I did a pretty good business this way and by 1916 was selling an average of about 10 cars a month. Then one day a representative of the Company came to see me. He said my quota had been fixed at 20 cars a month, and from then on that number would be shipped to me. I sure got it in the neck when the slump of 1920 came on. If anyone wants to know what hard times are he ought to try to do business in a Western farming community during a panic. Almost overnight half of our sheep men went bankrupt when wool dropped from $0.60 a pound to $0.20, and hardly any buyers at that price. The potato growers couldn't get enough of their stuff to pay freight to the Chicago market, and most of them let the crop rot in the ground. Of our four banks in town two went into the hands of receivers and the other two had to call in every possible loan in order to save their own necks. A lot of our Main Street retailers fell into the hands of their creditors that year, too. I was in about as bad a fix as anyone else. By then I had agreed to take 30 Fords a month. From September to January that year I sold exactly four cars."

Sample Prices of Used Automobiles in Richmond

1923 Studebaker Sedan, Refinished . . . $375.00
1923 Essex Touring Car, Best $200.00
1923 Deluxe Nash Sedan $475.00
Ford 10-Ton Truck Chassis, Tires
   Good $100.00
1926 Overland "6" Coupe $550.00

- At the high end of the scale, the New Seven-Passenger Sport Touring Lincoln was selling for $4,600 to $7,300 depending on options.
- Chrysler was boasting that they had moved from 27th in sales nationally to third place since 1924. "In these 12 months, Chrysler sold 193,750 motor cars, a volume of $275 million paid by the public."

Value of One Dollar	
Year	Value in 2010 USD
1930	$13.06
1932	$16.04
1935	$15.92
1937	$15.15
1939	$15.69

Values are approximate based upon economic historical data and 2010 U. S. Dollar

1930–1939

The decade of the 1930s was tragically marked by the longest, most severe depression in the nation's history. Economic paralysis gripped the nation as banks failed, railways became insolvent, unemployment rose, factories closed, and foreign trade declined. By 1932 one in four Americans was jobless. One of every four farms was sold for taxes. Five thousand banks closed their doors. In urban areas, apple sellers appeared on street corners, breadlines at soup kitchens lengthened, and people slept on park benches. The homeless wandered from city to city seeking work only to rediscover the pervasive nature of the economic collapse. In some circles the American Depression was viewed to be the fulfillment of Marxist prophecy—the inevitable demise of capitalism.

In the midst of the Depression entered Franklin D. Roosevelt, the New Deal, and his focus on the "forgotten man," giving rise to a swirl of government programs designed to lift the country out of its paralytic gloom. Despite its haphazard, often disconnected nature, the New Deal brought electricity to the farmer, Social Security checks to the elderly, work for the struggling arts, and hope for a nation that had lost hope. "This generation of Americans," Roosevelt said, "has a rendezvous with destiny."

Roosevelt's early social experiments were characterized by relief, recovery, and reform. Believing that the expansion of the United States economy was temporarily over, Roosevelt paid attention to better distribution of resources and planned production. The Civilian Conservation Corps (CCC), for example, put 250,000 jobless young men to work in the forests for $1.00 a day. By 1935 government deficit spending was spurring economic change. By 1937 total manufacturing output exceeded that of 1929; unfortunately, prices and wages rose too quickly and the economy dipped again in 1937, driven by inflation fears and restrictions on bank lending. Nonetheless, many roads, bridges, public buildings, dams, and trees became a part of the landscape thanks to federally employed workers. The Federal Theatre Project, for example, employed 1,300 during the period, reaching 25 million people with more than 1,200 productions. Despite progress, 10 million workers were still unemployed in 1938; farm prices lagged manufacturing progress. Full recovery would not occur until the United States mobilized for World War II.

While the nation suffered from economic blows, the West was being whipped by nature. Gigantic billowing clouds of dust up to 10,000 feet high swept across the parched Western Plains throughout the thirties. Sometimes the blows came with lightning and booming thunder, but often they were described as being "eerily slight, blackening everything in their path." All human activity halted. Planes were grounded. Buses and trains stalled, unable to race clouds that could move at speeds of more than 100 miles per hour. On the morning of May 9, 1934, the wind began to blow up the topsoil of Montana and Wyoming, and soon some 350 million tons were sweeping eastward. By late afternoon, 12 million tons had been deposited in Chicago. By noon the next day Buffalo, New York, was dark with dust. Even the Atlantic Ocean was no barrier. Ships 300 miles out to sea found dust on their decks. During the remainder of 1935 there were more than 40 dust storms that reduced visibility to less than one mile. There were 68 more storms in 1936, 72 in 1937, and 61 in 1938. On the High Plains, 10,000 houses were simply abandoned, and 9 million acres of farm turned back to nature. Banks offered mortgaged properties for as little as $25.00 for 160 acres and found no takers.

The people of the 1930s excelled in escape. Radio matured as a mass medium, creating stars such as Jack Benny, Bob Hope, and Fibber McGee and Molly. For a time it seemed that every child was copying the catch phrase of radio's Walter Winchell, "Good evening, Mr. and Mrs. America, and all the ships at sea," or pretending to be Jack Benny when shouting "Now, cut that out!" Soap operas captured large followings and sales of magazines like *Screenland* and *True Story* skyrocketed. Each edition of *True Confessions* sold 7.5 million copies. Nationwide movie theaters prospered as 90 million Americans attended the "talkies" every week, finding comfort in the uplifting excitement of movies and movie stars. Big bands made swing the king of the decade; jazz came into its own. And the social experiment known as Prohibition died in December, 1933, when the 21st Amendment swept away the restrictions against alcohol ushered in more than a decade earlier.

Attendance at professional athletic events declined during the decade, but softball became more popular than ever and golf began its drive to become a national passion as private courses went public. Millions listened to boxing on radio, especially the exploits of the "Brown Bomber," Joe Louis. As average people coped with the difficult times, they married later, had fewer children, and divorced less. Extended families often lived under one roof; opportunities for women and minorities were particularly limited. Survival, not affluence, was often the practical goal of the family. A disillusioned nation, which worshiped the power of business, looked instead toward a more caring government.

During the decade United Airlines hired its first airline stewardess to allay passengers' fears of flying. The circulation of *Reader's Digest* climbed from 250,000 to eight million before the decade ended and *Esquire*, the first magazine for men, was launched. The early days of the decade gave birth to Hostess Twinkies, Bird's Eye frozen vegetables, windshield wipers, photoflash bulbs, and pinball machines. By the time the Depression and the 1930s drew to a close, Zippo lighters, Frito corn chips, talking books for the blind, beer in cans, and the Richter scale for measuring earthquakes had all been introduced. Despite the ever-increasing role of the automobile, in the mid-1930s, Americans still spent $1,000 a day on buggy whips.

1930 FAMILY PROFILE

The Broos family of four lives in Detroit, Michigan, where the man works for Ford Motor Company, which is undergoing major shock waves in the early days of the Depression. Wages have held steady since the 1929 stock market crash, but most workers are fearful of layoffs and their future. This couple has two daughters, 15 and 10 years old.

Annual Income: $1,712.24
The man makes approximately $1,695.00 annually; the woman does not work outside the home. The daughters have a small farm and sell produce that nets $17.24.

Annual Budget

Barber	$12.37
Cleaning Supplies	$16.64
Clothing	$145.63
Food	$556.12
Fuel	$109.42
Furniture and House Furnishings	$271.29
Housing	$415.40
Life Insurance	$75.00
Medical Expenses	$102.36
Miscellaneous	$90.82
School Expenses	$6.41
Transportation	$37.40
Total	$1,838.86

Life at Home

- The family lives in a five-room flat with three bedrooms, two common rooms, and a bathroom. Rent is $415.40 annually, or $35.40 a month.

MIXING CAKE BATTER

Use your Mixmaster for every beating occasion because you will find that the finished cake is more satisfactory as electrical mixing does a much more EVEN and THOROUGH job than can be done by hand. In cakes you will notice how much finer the grain, how much further the same ingredients go, how much lighter and fluffier the cake, and how you will do the entire job in one-third the time. One reason women sometimes do not have success with their cakes in beating by hand is that they whip one part of the batter too long while another part of the batter may be underbeaten. With the Sunbeam Mixmaster, the bowl revolving automatically, and the even electrical mixing, each part of the batter is thoroughly beaten automatically.

BUTTER COOKIES

1 pound sugar	1 pound butter 4 eggs	4 cups flour

Allow butter to be soft. Cream butter and sugar in large bowl of Mixmaster. Add 1 egg at a time and lastly flour. This may be divided into parts. Different flavorings, spices, chocolate or coloring may be added.

Put through a cookie press or roll out, place in ice box to chill, then slice and bake.

You can mix and juice at the same time in MIXMASTER

DROP GINGER COOKIES

1½ cups brown sugar	1 cup molasses	1 teaspoon ginger
1 cup lard or half butter and lard	5 cups flour (bread flour)	1 teaspoon salt
2 eggs	1 teaspoon soda	1 cup boiling water

Cream shortening and sugar. Add eggs one at a time. Add molasses. Beat 3 minutes on medium speed. Sift flour, measure, add soda, ginger and salt. Sift. Then add 1 cup boiling water. Beat five minutes. Drop from spoon on greased cookie sheet. Yield 6 doz. Temperature 375°. 10 to 12 minutes.

MIXMASTER helps with every kitchen task

PARTY COOKIES

½ cup butter	3 tablespoons milk	½ teaspoon baking powder
½ cup sugar	1½ cups flour	
1 egg	⅛ teaspoon salt	

Put butter and sugar in large bowl of Mixmaster. Cream thoroughly, add egg, then sifted dry ingredients alternately with milk. When all mixed, remove from Mixmaster. Divide into two parts. Add melted chocolate to one part or tint with a food coloring. Roll both parts out to about ¼ inch thickness. Place one on top of the other and roll until thin. Then roll up (jelly roll like) and place in ice box for several hours. Slice and bake in quick oven about 400 degrees.

Each bowl turns itself on the ball-bearing platform

ALMOND PRETZELS

¼ pound almonds (blanched)	6 tablespoons confectioners' sugar	2 cups flour
½ pound butter		

Place Food Grinder attachment on Mixmaster, and put through ¼ pound almonds. Then place large bowl on Mixmaster platform and put into it the butter and confectioners' sugar. Turn on Mixmaster and cream well; then add flour and almonds which were ground. Mix in Mixmaster until all is a creamy mass. Roll out into tiny rolls pencil shape and cross. Bake at 400° until golden brown and roll in sugar while still hot.

"I want to tell you the MIXMASTER is the perfect beater, and think from my praises of it there will be more sales among my friends. I knew I had seen the perfect mixer, so went and purchased it the next day. It has saved me many an arm-ache in just the short time I have had it. So perfectly lovely to operate and take care of. Saves a great deal of time, and above all, it beats and whips perfectly. I'm a very much satisfied MIXMASTER owner." —E. K. B., Mears, Mich.

[8]

- At their flat, hot water is available from the tap in both the kitchen and bathroom, and running water is available in the yard.
- The flat also includes a sink and a sewer connection.
- They want to purchase a home but are now afraid to make the commitment of buying a house with its increased costs, such as taxes, upkeep, and water; these expenses would add $100.00 to their yearly housing costs.
- Also, most mortgage lenders require a 30 percent down payment on a house, and most mortgage loans are for a term of 10 years, which can include a balloon payment, putting the payments out of reach.
- The couple, both of whom are third-generation Dutch, pride themselves on controlling their expenses and living within their means.
- The income of this household is essentially unchanged since 1923; when the Depression begins Ford actually increases hourly wages; rumors of layoffs are everywhere. This family is trying to make due until the "recession" disappears. His income will fall dramatically as Ford Motor Company struggles with the multi-year Depression.
- The income of an automobile factory worker throughout the 1920s provides an above-average standard of living to include single-family dwellings, nutritional diets, washing machines, electric irons, radios, and even an automobile.
- Food represents the family's greatest expenditure at $556.12, or 32.3 percent of the income.

Economic Problems of the Family, by Hazel Kyrk, 1933:

"In her book, *Successful Family Life on a Moderate Income,* Mrs. Abel lays down as her first principle for success—the money income of the family tolerably certain and earned wholly or chiefly by the man. Is the latter one of the requirements that should be set up? There is no doubt that the ideal home as many would picture it is one in which the whole of the money income is furnished by the husband and father. The reasons presented for taking this position would, it is believed, be of very diverse character.

There are those who view with complacence the gainful employment of working class wives and mothers but object to it in the case of women in their own family or class. No concern may be felt over the wide-spread practice of employment outside the home by Negro women but a similar condition among White women, especially the native-born, may be considered most alarming. This dual standard suggests the basis for certain of the objections to the wife as a contributor to the money income."

Annual Food Expenditures

Bread	$54.20
Coffee	$12.82
Dried and Canned Fruit	$6.99
Dried and Canned Vegetables	$14.59
Eggs	$36.57
Flour and Meal	$10.37
Fresh Fruits	$32.90
Fresh Vegetables	$36.59
Ice	$6.94
Lunches and Meals Eaten Out	$19.68
Meat	$104.37
Milk and Milk Products	$120.83
Other	$79.61
Poultry	$10.16
Seafood	$9.50
Total	$556.12

- Eating out is too expensive for this family; the father is the only member of the family who eats lunches out.
- Ice is used by the family only in the summer for the icebox; in the winter the cellar is used for refrigeration.

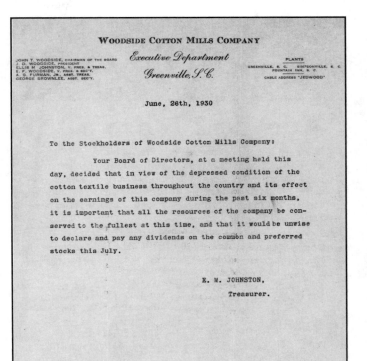

- Meat is the second greatest expenditure. Beef roast is the family's favorite dish; they consume 49 pounds annually.
- Of the fresh fruit, apples are the family favorite. The father normally takes one to work with him inside his lunchbox. Florida oranges are also very popular, when in season.
- Potatoes are the most eaten vegetable; tomatoes and cabbage are the two other most popular vegetables; broccoli is not mentioned in the survey although it is making a nationwide comeback.
- The food budget includes an undeterminable amount of liquor and beer which cannot be counted due to its illegal nature at the time.
- The father's work shirts cause his clothing costs to be slightly more than the mother's.
- The woman begins to buy skirts that are knee high, the fashion of the day; she is able to wear them only in the summer and even then only a little due to her husband's dislike of them.
- Some laundry is sent out. The father has two suits and the mother three dresses that have to be dry-cleaned on occasion. These clothes are brought out of the closet only on special occasions due to the high cost of having them cleaned.
- The Broos family has central heating, which is not uncommon, but still a luxury for a majority of families who work in the factory.
- The washing machine was a family gift in 1929, purchased on the installment plan.
- Labor-saving appliances such as the washing machine are paving the way for the woman's liberation from the house and giving her the ability to do more for the community in the form of church groups, which she readily joins.
- The family buys a radio at the urging of their daughters who listen to the extremely popular *Amos and Andy*

Blondie made her first comic strip appearance in 1930.

Three Sheets in the Wind Show the Sensational Bargains for You in Ward's

60TH ANNIVERSARY SALE of SHEETS and CASES

OUR BEST SELLING BRAND... *Reduced!*

64 by 64 Threads to the Inch

OUR famous Longwear Bleached Sheets and Cases at the lowest prices in years. Same standard quality, free of starch—same sturdy spun, selected stocky cottons that give such unusual wear and fine appearance. Beautifully bleached, hand torn, well finished. Ward's laboratory has tested them for washability, for wear, for thread count. Despite the claims of others there are no sheets or cases made that give you better value at the price. We Pay Postage on orders of $2.00 or more—See Page 115. For Easy Payments see Budget Plan Page 169.

Longwear — Cut From 84¢ Each — 69¢ EACH 81 by 90-In.

Hemmed Sheets—Bleached

Size Before Hemming	Length Less 5 in. for Hems	Price 90 Days Ago	NOW Ea.	NOW 6 for
72 by 90	18 U 9831—For single or three quarter beds. Postage each 9¢.	78¢	65¢	$3.80
81 by 90	18 U 9832—For Double beds. Postage each 9¢.	84¢	69¢	$4.04

Extra Long Hemmed Sheets—Bleached.
Length less 5 in. for Hems.

Size	Description	Price 90 Days Ago	NOW Ea.	NOW 6 for
81 by 99	18 U 9837—For Double beds. Postage each 9¢.	92¢	77¢	$4.52
81 by 108	18 U 9834—Extra large. Postage each 9¢.	$1.00	85¢	$5.00

Hemmed Pillow Cases—Bleached.

Size	Description	Price 90 Days Ago	NOW Ea.	NOW 6 for
42 by 36	18 U 9840—Hemmed 20½ by 32 in. Postage each 2¢; Six 9¢.	21¢	18¢	$1.03
45 by 36	18 U 9841—Hemmed 22 by 32 in. Postage each 2¢; Six 9¢.	22¢	19¢	$1.09

OUR FINEST QUALITY BRAND... *Reduced!*

Fine Count 72 by 68 Threads to the Inch

Sensational low prices on Treasure Chest, our finest cotton Sheets and Cases! To be compared only with higher priced nationally advertised brands. Amazingly strong—we tested and found them ready for more use after 364 washings in a commercial laundry.

Treasure Chest — Reduced From $1.09 Each — 89¢ EACH 81 by 90-In.

Hemmed Sheets—Bleached.

Size before Hemming	Length less 5 in. for hems.	Price 90 Days Ago	NOW Ea.	NOW 4 for
81 by 90	18 U 9853—For Double beds. Postage each 9¢.	$1.09	89¢	$3.46
72 by 99	18 U 9854—For single or three quarter bed. Postage each 9¢.	$1.09	89¢	$3.46
81 by 99	18 U 9856—For double beds. Postage each 9¢.	$1.14	$1.00	$3.90
81 by 108	18 U 9869—For double bed. Extra long. Postage each 10¢.	$1.25	$1.09	$4.26

Hemmed Pillow Cases—Bleached.

Size	Description	Price 90 Days Ago	NOW Ea.	NOW 4 for
42 by 36	18 U 9859—Hemmed 20½ by 32 in. Postage each 2¢; four 9¢.	26¢	23¢	87¢
45 by 36	18 U 9861—Hemmed 22 by 32 in. Postage each 2¢; four 9¢.	28¢	25¢	95¢

OUR LOWEST PRICED GRADE... *Reduced!*

Star Bargain—Bleached Sheets and Cases

When they sold for considerably more, these Star Bargain Sheets and Cases were Big Bargains. Today they're some of the very best buys we know, for those who want serviceable quality at lowest prices. Neatly hemmed cotton sheets; muslin cases are hemmed, hemstitched. You'll consider the values as startling as we do—for we were determined to make this Anniversary offer something the whole family would talk about for years to come. For easy Payments see Budget Plan Page 169.

STAR BARGAIN — Cut From 59¢ Each — 54¢ EACH 81 by 90-In.

Hemmed Sheets—Bleached.

Size before Hemming	Length less 5 in. for hems.	Price 90 Days Ago	NOW Ea.	NOW 6 for
81 by 90	18 U 9811—For double beds. Postage each 9¢.	59¢	54¢	$3.14
54 by 90	18 U 9812—For single beds. Postage each 7¢.	49¢	44¢	$2.54
81 by 99	18 U 9849—For double beds. Postage each 9¢.		59¢	$3.44

Muslin Pillow Cases—Bleached.

Size	Description	Price 90 Days Ago	NOW Ea.	NOW 6 for
42 by 36	18 U 9850—Hemmed 20½ by 32 in. Postage each 2¢; Six 9¢.	14¢	11¢	61¢
42 by 36	18 U 9852—Hemstitched 20½ by 32 in. Postage each 2¢; Six 9¢.	15¢	13¢	73¢

Order Now—Prices May Never Be So Low Again

CBA KS *Montgomery Ward & Co* 33

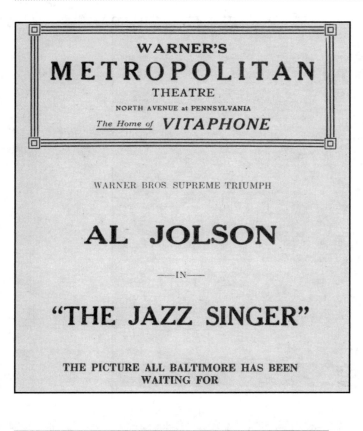

show; it is 15 minutes long and is broadcast throughout the country as one of the first nationally syndicated radio shows.

- The father also listens to the radio messages of Father Charles Coughlin on Sundays; the radio priest preaches a message that strikes a cord with Detroit's auto workers; his topics include attacks on communism, President Herbert Hoover, international bankers, and the gold standard.
- The family's 16-year-old daughter catches the flu and the parents, with memories of the Spanish Flu epidemic in 1918, rush her to the hospital; the doctor assures them it is not serious and gives them a prescription.
- Medical expenses also include general checkups for the family and eyeglasses for the father and one of the daughters.
- The children go to public school, which requires that children pay for their schoolbooks.
- The family contributes $15.00 to the Dutch Congregationalist Church annually.
- They love motion pictures, and they spend $6.45 annually to see about 30 movies that year. They mostly go in the afternoon when the tickets are cheaper.
- The Broos family enjoys Charlie Chaplin in his guise as the little Tramp, and have heard that a talkie, *The Jazz Singer* with Al Jolson, exists, but have never seen it.
- The technology of talkies make state and local censorship of the movies more difficult; self-censorship through a new production code is created in 1930 that includes script reviews.
- In addition to movies, the children enjoy clipping the cartoons each day from the newspaper and are compiling the story of "Why Mothers Get Gray" into scrapbooks covering years of cartoons.
- The "family telephone" is located at the corner down the street and costs $0.05 per call. It is used exclusively for calling the doctor or relatives on special occasions.
- The family in 1930 spends more money than it makes, allowed by the spread of installment buying, which becomes more popular in the 1920s; this brings about a standard of living hike in material terms but also brings a wave of bankruptcies.
- For this family, installment credit is used to buy furniture. During the decade they buy many things on installment such as a bicycle and a radio. This year they are $102.39 in debt.

Life at Work: Ford Motor Company

- This worker makes $7.00 a day, thanks to a raise given by owner Henry Ford in 1930 despite signs of a recession; layoffs begin late in 1930 reducing the number of hours, thus he averages $6.91 a day working 245 days.
- Ford Motor Company, unlike most of the other automobile companies, does not pay for piecework, but hourly.
- Many manufacturers believe that the more money a worker can earn, the harder he will work.
- This pay philosophy gives employees an incentive to work but also saves the company money when machinery breaks and the workers are unable to produce.
- Ford institutes an eight-hour day in 1914, although a worker is expected to get to work 15 to 20 minutes early to gather his tools and set up, and is not paid for his 15- to 20-minute lunch break, or the time it takes at the end of each day to put his tools up.
- The factory is now producing the Model A, which is selling very well; the manufacture of the Model T is phased out in May, 1927, as the 15 millionth Model T rolls off the assembly line.
- This family experiences some loss of employment after the Model T is eliminated and the factory is being retooled for the Model A; 60,000 men in Detroit are laid off during the changeover.
- When Ford introduces the Model A in December, 1927, 25 million people nationwide take the trouble to visit a showroom to see the new car during the first week—8.5 percent of the entire country's population.
- The Model A manufactured in 1930 has four cylinders, balloon tires, and a reliable electrical system, including a self-starter; it has a cruising speed of 55 miles per hour.

- The Model A costs $495.00, approximately $100.00 less than the equivalent Chevrolet, Ford's primary competitor.

Life in the Community: Detroit, Michigan

- Historically, Detroit is a Great Lakes' center for food processing, copper smelting, and iron making.
- The coming of the automobile industry, especially the construction of Henry Ford's huge plants at the satellite industrial centers of Highland Park and River Rouge, allows Detroit to grow from being the nation's 18th largest city in 1880 to the fourth largest in 1920 with a population just shy of one million.
- The urban transformation is driven by European immigrants and rural American immigrants, both seeking a better life.
- During the twenties the Model T is not only a part of American material life but also a large part of its cultural life; vaudeville is especially happy to jump on the Ford bandwagon. The Temple Theater Building, Detroit's largest vaudeville theatre, has the city's first electric sign—a car with spinning wheels in lights that carry the slogan, "Watch the Fords Go By."

- Nationwide the American people have improved their per capita income from $480.00 in 1900 to $681.00 in 1930, adjusted for inflation, and Detroit has prospered more than most.
- Automobile production has increased 255 percent from 1919 to 1929; no other major industry has seen a similar improvement; chemical production, for example, improves 94 percent.
- During the same timeframe corporate profits rise 62 percent; workers are rewarded with an increase of 11 percent.
- Nationwide the 36,000 wealthiest families receive an aggregate income in 1929 nearly equal to the total income received by more than 11.6 million families receiving less than $1,500 a year.
- As the Depression begins the 200 biggest corporations in America own almost one-half of the total corporate wealth and about one-fifth of the total national wealth.
- Concentration of wealth is strongest in industries devoted to manufacturing and mining.

American Automobile Workers, 1900–1933, Stan Coulthard, a Chrysler worker talks about getting a job:

"I didn't know what a milling machine was; in fact I'd never worked in a machine shop before. I was taken on in the morning and told to report for the night shift the same day. As soon as I got in I was asked where were my tools? I lied by saying that I'd had no time to go home to get them. I got to the milling machine and didn't even know how to switch it on. I mucked about for a while pretending to be busy until the foreman had gone. Then I told the feller next to me that I'd just got in from Boston, that I didn't know one end of the machine from the other, that I needed a job and could he help me? He said he came from Boston, too, and showed me what to do. After a while he said that the stock I was making was scrap, that there was some good stuff in a pan behind me and to let on that I'd produced it. When the foreman came round to check and he passed it all right! I went on like that for two or three days until I'd got the hang of things. They got it out of my hide before I'd finished so I had no qualms whatever about cheating them."

- By the 1930s, even retailing, long thought to be a refuge for the small entrepreneur, gives way to big corporations establishing chains of retail outlets. Americans now buy more than one-fourth of their food and clothing and about one-third of their tobacco from "chain stores."
- In October 1929, Detroit's Department of Public Welfare carries 156,000 persons on the rolls; in April 1930 the number has risen to 728,000.
- By 1930 when the Depression begins, 750,000 men are unemployed in Michigan; those who are still employed see their wages cut by 40 percent.
- Lines for the soup kitchens extend for blocks; approximately 4,000 children are said to be standing in the bread lines each day.
- By 1932, 18 percent of the city's children are suffering from severe undernourishment; 15 banks fail, taking the savings of 30,000 depositors.
- One in nine married women is a wage earner; 42 percent come from families who live at or below the subsistence level and are working for bread and butter.
- The mayor of Detroit creates the "Homeless Men's Bureau" to find shelter and food for the many unemployed and unattached men who roam the streets.
- Hundreds of people are sleeping nightly in Detroit's Grand Circus Park.

OUT OUR WAY.   —By Willia[m]

— WHY MOTHERS GET GRAY —
THE TIMER

J.R.WILLIAMS

REG. U.S. PAT. OFF.   ©1930 BY NEA SERVICE, INC.

The children enjoyed clipping the daily cartoon from the newspaper, especially "Why Mothers Get Gray."

- In the winter of 1930 the city's municipal lodging homes shelter 5,000 persons each night and feed 10,000 each day.
- The urbanization of America is continuing; a third of the population now lives in places with 100,000 inhabitants and an eighth in places with one million or more.

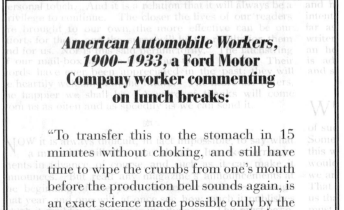

American Automobile Workers, 1900–1933, a Ford Motor Company worker commenting on lunch breaks:

"To transfer this to the stomach in 15 minutes without choking, and still have time to wipe the crumbs from one's mouth before the production bell sounds again, is an exact science made possible only by the application of Ford production principles."

HISTORICAL SNAPSHOT
1930–1931

- Unemployment passed four million

- More than 1,352 banks closed in 1930; 2,294 followed in 1931

- The first analog computer was placed in operation by Vannevar Bush

- U.S. had one passenger car per 5.5 persons; the car boom collapsed in the wake of the Depression and one million auto workers were laid off in 1931

- Gasoline consumption rose to nearly 16 billion gallons

- Trousers became acceptable attire for women who played golf and rode horses

- Radio set sales increased to 13.5 million

- Advertisers spent $60 million on radio commercials

- Boeing hired eight nurses to act as flight attendants

- *Fortune Magazine* was launched by Henry R. Luce; the cost was $1.00 per issue

- The University of Southern California polo team refused to play against the University of California at Los Angeles until its one female member was replaced by a male

- Laurette Schimmoler of Ohio became the first woman airport manager, earning a salary of $510 a year

- The fledgling movie industry now employed 100,000 people

- Alka-Seltzer was introduced by Miles Laboratories

- Clairol hair products were introduced by U.S. chemists

- Bird's Eye Frosted Foods were sold nationally for the first time

1930 Economic Profile

Clothing Expenses

Man's Clothing Costs: Total $58.99

Belts	$0.37
Cleaning, Pressing, and Repairing	$1.46
Collars	$0.10
Footwear	$14.40
Garters	$0.33
Gloves and Mittens	$3.03
Handkerchiefs	$0.60
Head Gear	$3.72
Mufflers and Scarfs	$0.33
Other Clothing	$0.23
Pocketbooks	$0.06
Shirts	$5.45
Suits and Coats	$11.34
Suspenders	$0.11
Ties	$1.52
Trousers	$10.45
Umbrellas	$0.05
Underwear	$4.56
Watches	$0.88

Woman's Clothing Costs: Total $60.17

Belts	$0.01
Bloomers, Step-Ins and Drawers	$3.02
Brassieres	$0.27
Chemises	$0.25
Cleaning, Pressing, and Repairing	$0.52
Coats	$11.93
Collar and Cuff Sets	$0.01
Corsets	$1.34
Dresses	$13.52
Footwear	$16.27
Gloves and Mittens	$0.80
Hairpins, Fancy Comb, Ornaments, Etc.	$0.20
Hand Bags and Purses	$0.93
Handkerchiefs	$0.50
Head Gear	$3.30
Kimonos and Bathrobes	$0.29
Night Gowns	$0.04
Other	$0.01
Petticoats and Slips	$3.35
Sanitary Supplies	$0.71
Scarfs	$0.23
Shirts and Vests	$0.93
Sweaters	$0.64

What control means to an airplane *self-control* means to a human Life!

SELF CONTROL (25)   THE HOPE OF A NATION POSTER SERIES   MARCH
COPYRIGHTED 1930 By ROACH-FOWLER CO, K. C.

Umbrellas. $0.18
Union Suits $0.74
Waists and Blouses $0.05
Watches and Jewelry $0.13

Fuel Expenses

Anthracite Coal $14.81
Bituminous Coal $34.98
Coke $10.41
Electricity. $20.43
Gas. $22.69
Kerosene $2.90
Matches and Candles $1.61
Wood $1.59
    Total $109.42

Furniture Expenses

Bed Springs $9.01
Blankets. $6.39
Brooms and Brushes $1.29
Curtains, Draperies, Portieres,
    and Sofa Pillows $5.27
Electrical Appliances, Toasters $1.06
Lamps, Electric Bulbs,
    and Lamp Shades $2.19
Mattresses $14.58
Mops $0.95
Musical Instruments, Cost $5.00
Musical Instruments,
    Upkeep. $3.43
Napkins, Cotton $1.69
Other Furniture and
    Furnishings $3.22
Phonographs, Cost $17.00
Phonographs, Upkeep $2.34
Pillows $3.50
Pillowcases. $2.02
Pressure Cookers $8.25
Quilts and Comforters $5.31
Radio, Upkeep. $8.37
Sheets. $4.48
Spreads $3.17
Table Oilcloth $0.98
Tablecloths, Cotton. $1.82
Towels, Cotton $1.77
Towels, Linen $1.65
Trunks, Travelling Bags,
    and Suitcases $12.00

Washing Machine $51.90
Window Shades $4.99
    Total $183.63

Medical Expenses

Dentist $17.32
Eyeglasses $9.41
Medicine $9.08
Nurse $20.00
Physician and Surgeon $46.55
    Total $102.36

School Expenses

Books $6.01
Other $3.34
    Total $9.35

Miscellaneous

Charity $2.43
Church $15.00
Dances $3.70
Excursions $2.86
Gifts Outside the House $14.15
Laundry Work Sent Out $19.23
Magazines and Periodicals $3.04
Motion Pictures $6.45
Music Lessons $28.97
Newspapers $14.59
Other Amusements $3.63
Other Miscellaneous Expenses $5.26
Plays and Concerts $1.50
Postage $1.65
Telephone $3.90
Tobacco $22.72
Toilet Articles $4.75
Toilet Preparation $9.11
Tools $6.15
    Total $169.09

Income, Standard Jobs

Average for All Industries,
    Including Farm Labor $1,388.00
Bituminous Coal Mining $909.00
Building Trades $1,233.00
Domestics $676.00
Farm Labor $444.00

Federal Civilian $1,768.00
Gas and Electricity Workers $1,603.00
Manufacturing, Durable Goods $1,391.00
Manufacturing, Nondurable
    Goods. $1,425.00
Medical/Health Services
    Workers. $933.00
Motion Picture Services $2,179.00
Nonprofit Organization
    Workers $1,698.00
Passenger Transportation
    Workers $1,587.00
Personal Services $1,200.00
Public School Teachers. $1,455.00
Radio Broadcasting Workers $2,624.00
Railroads $1,717.00
State and Government Workers. $1,517.00
Telephone and Telegraph
    Workers $1,410.00
Wholesale and Retail
    Trade Workers $1,569.00

Selected Prices

A.C. Spark Plug. $0.60
Airway Lightfood Shoes $0.75
Cheviot Trousers $2.89
Dunlap Hat for Men $5.00
Gasoline Iron. $3.98
Golden Crest Hosier $0.89
Goodyear Firestone Goodrich Tire $2.95
J.C. Higgins Baseball $0.95
Juniper Windsor Cook Stove $21.50
Kool Mild Menthol Cigarettes,
    per Pack $0.15

This Smoking World,
by A.E. Hamilton, The Century Company, New York, 1927:

"The fact remains that a businessman or a physician cannot always stop to rest when he feels weary and oppressed. Nor can a soldier in the trench turn on the warm water faucet for a calming neutral bath. Tobacco, a mild sedative, put up in inexpensive, convenient form and ever on hand, affords a constant temptation toward artificial rest."

Kraft Marshmallows, Box of 200 . . . . . . $0.65
Lady Elgin Wristwatch $25.00
Lakeside Lawnmower $5.49
Light Bulbs, 40-Watt, Package
    of Eight $1.00
Pepperell Blanket. $0.31
Petroleum Vaseline Jelly,
    Four Ounce Size $0.13
Rogers Brothers Silver Plate
    Flatware, 26-Piece. $28.45
Tobrin Screwdriver, per Dozen $10.00
Underwood Typewriter. $49.50
Winnerset Microscope Outfit,
    Complete $6.00

Ford Motor Company

- Ford was one of the leading names in automobile manufacturing during most of the 1920s, but failed to upgrade its Model T until the late 1920s and began losing favor with the public; during 1927 and 1928 Ford lost $280 million during the conversion from a Model T to a Model A.
- By 1929 the popularity of the Model A was tremendous; Ford produced $1.5 million in automobile sales, a market share of 34 percent and profits of $90 million.

Henry Ford (right) and son, Edsel, introduced the Model A in 1927.

Ford Motor Company worker, November 12, 1929:

"After 14 years and three months of best endeavor for the Ford Motor Company, I, with thousands of others, have been sent home. By economy I have a comfortable home nearly paid for. The rental of a few rooms supply most of our needed necessities. I don't think we shall need any help from the Community Fund but unless the factories open up before long there will be dire suffering in Detroit."

- Owner Henry Ford despised systematic organization and believed in keeping his executives, including his son, constantly in conflict with each other; this often led to mismanagement of production and sales.
- Generally, the auto industry's anti-unionism was a model for United States industrial leaders.
- Company spies, blacklists, private disciplinary forces, and the simple refusal to talk to collective bodies of workers was part of the industry.
- Ford Motor Company had a department to oversee the behavior of its workers; their office periodically would speak to relatives, visit workers' homes, oversee their living conditions and habits, and offer advice as to how money should be spent. Many of those activities were justified by Ford as a way to teach immigrants how to adapt to American ways.
- Some workers disliked the practices but others found them merely to be some of Ford's eccentricities that in some ways were beneficial; Ford's justification for these practices was simple: "a well-regulated home life makes for a well-regulated work life."
- Ford Motor Company's Detroit employment of 128,000 in 1929 would fall to 37,000 workers in the summer of 1931.
- Between 1929 and 1932 the annual production of cars declined 75 percent but motor vehicle registrations dropped only 10 percent; Americans, no matter the state of the economy, were unwilling to give up the luxury afforded by an automobile.

1931 NEWS PROFILE
BUILDING HOOVER DAM

Massive public works projects like the Hoover Dam were an important part of the New Deal's response to the Great Depression. Hoover Dam was the first of the great multipurpose dams, providing flood control, water for irrigation, and hydroelectric power to the Southwest. The 60-story-high dam across the Colorado River was built by The Six Companies, a consortium mainly of little-known Western construction contractors. This is the story of one family that worked on "one of the monumental engineering achievements of the twentieth century."

Erma Godbey, 1931: "We had heard a lot about the Boulder Canyon Project while we lived in Colorado and took the Denver Post, because the regional offices of the Bureau of Reclamation were in Colorado . . . so we thought what we'd do is come over here. My mother and stepfather came down from Colorado to visit us. They were driving an old seven-passenger Dodge touring car. We had no car, so we had them drive us over here. We put a mattress and two baby cribs and two baby mattresses on the top of the car and tied them on. Then all of us got in the car. We brought a few cooking utensils and very few clothes and some bedding with us—and that's all. We had four children and my baby was only five months old. . . . It was terrifically hot. My God it was terribly hot and dusty. None of the roads were paved in those days. It was just ungodly, it was so hot.

We got into where Boulder City is now, down from where the airport used to be; that's where the Six Company camp was. It was all tents. We stopped there and asked about a job. They said we just have a tent mess hall here, and we have tents for the men that are working, and you'll have to go down into the river bottom. We still had to keep on driving. . . .

It was called Ragtown, but was officially Williamsville, after Claude Williams, who was in charge of it. It looked like anyplace that is just built out of pasteboard cartons or anything else. Everyone had come just in a car, with no furniture or anything. My mother looked around. They got to go back to Colorado. She said, 'Well, I'll never see you again, I'll never see you again.' I said, 'Oh Mom, we're tough. Remember, we're from pioneer stock.' After all, my mother had driven cattle from Texas on horseback to Colorado when she was 14 years old. I said, 'We're pioneer stock; we'll last.' But she cried, and she left us. . . .

We were right in among all these other people that were already camped there. Some had tents, but a lot them just had canvas or blankets or anything they could have for shelter. There was one little fellow that they called 'Johnny behind the Rock.' There was a great big boulder as you came down Hemenway, Washington, to go to into Ragtown. He just kind of moved around where the shade was. He didn't have any tent or anything. He just kept moving wherever the shade was that the rock made.

What I had to do—I had blankets made out of pure wool that I had had made up at Utah Woolen Mills. They had cost me $32.00 a pair, which was a lot of money in those days, when men were only making four bucks a day wage. We got a hold of some clothesline, and we had some safety pins. We put some poles in the ground and pinned those beautiful wool blankets with safety pins to those poles to try to make a little bit of shade from the terrible heat. It would get to be 120 by nine in the morning, and it wouldn't be below 120 before nine at night. It just seemed like the river just drew the heat right down there. You could just see the heat dancing off the mountains, the black cliffs down there. I would wrap my babies in wet sheets so they could sleep. But for my littlest baby, the one that was only five months old, Ila, I would put the wet sheet around her crib so the air would blow through it. But it wasn't enough.

It was about four days that we were like that, just with the blankets for shade. There was a little camp real close to us. The man who lived in that tent worked in drilling the diversion tunnels. He wasn't a miner; he just was somebody who needed to have a job. When they would blast in the tunnels, they would just set the blast off as the men came off the shift. Then the next shift would muck out, but the blast would go off between shifts. This man was so anxious to get in to work to earn his wages that he went in a little ahead of some of the other men, and the blast hadn't finished going off. Just as he put his shovel down to muck out, a delayed blast went off and made the handle of the shovel go like this and it disemboweled him. His wife—the only thing she could do was to have the body sent back home to her relatives or it would be buried in Las Vegas in the old cemetery—that was the Woodlawn Cemetery at the time. Then she'd just have to move on, since she had no way of making a living or anything. So we bought her tent. That way we had a small tent, but it still wasn't big enough for anything but maybe to do a little cooking in it. . . .

We had to haul drinking water from the river. They had dug a couple of holes a little bit in from the river, and when the river would seep through the sand it would be pretty good. But, of course, when people would dip a lot into these wells, it would get riley again, so you'd have to let it settle. My husband didn't want to drink that water, and I didn't either. I had brought over my copper boiler, so I had something to put water in. He would just take the boiler and swipe water from the mess hall when the cooks were busy feeding the men. I didn't give my nursing baby enough water to drink. I gave her about the same amount of water that I had given my other babies that I had raised up in Colorado. She pretty near dehydrated. So one night when all my other children woke up and wanted a drink of water, I picked up the baby to nurse her and she just knocked the cup I was drinking from right out of my hand. It was a 10-ounce white granite cup. It spilled on her. My husband said, 'Mama, I think the baby's thirsty.' We gave her a drink, and she drank 10 ounces of water. She drank it from the cup, and she never did take water out of a bottle after that.

They did have outside toilets that the government furnished. The rangers would put slaked lime in them about twice a week. The only thing you could do with garbage was to burn it. There was no garbage removal or anything. Everybody just had to burn their garbage on their own premises, as best they could.

They would go to work at 7:00 in the morning. It was so terrible hot by noon that men were passing out with the heat. So they decided that they would go to work at 4:00 in the morning and work until noon. Another shift would come on at 4:00 in the afternoon and work until midnight. But nobody would work during the very bad heat of the day between noon and 4:00. So then my husband had to be at work at 4:00 in the morning. That meant I had to get up at 2:30 in the morning and get some breakfast going for him and get his lunch packed. I was still using the campfire. The very first money we got, we got somebody to go into Las Vegas and we got a Coleman camp stove. We had a carbide lamp—that's what miners use, you know. And we had the carbide crystals. So what I would use at night was the carbide lamp.

The reason I left Ragtown was not only the heat. Four people died—four women died in one day. That was the 26th of July, 1931, and it was terribly hot. There was a woman that was 60 years old and a girl 16, and another woman that I don't know how old she was or anything much about her, and then there was a woman that was 28 that was only three tents from me. Her husband was working the swing shift in the diversion tunnels. They had come out from New York State. She was sick. He had done the best he could. He left her with a thermos bottle with ice. We could get ice once a day where they brought the ice in. They had a big dog, a big police dog. She just got to feeling terribly bad, so she tied a note to her dog's collar and told him to get the ranger. He knew what she'd told him, but where was the ranger? Mr. Williams was anywhere. He probably wasn't in his office when the dog went hunting for him. In the note she had asked Mr. Williams to come and get her and take her to the river so she could get in the water to get cooled off. By the time Mr. Williams got to her after the dog got to him, she was just lying across of folding cot and she was dead. They told us women that were close. There were three of us that went over into her tent. We kind of straightened her up on the bed.

They sent for the other ranger or somebody to get her husband out of the tunnels. The woman had been dead for probably an hour by the time he got there. He immediately tried to give her artificial respiration. Then her looked at we three women, and he said, 'Anybody going to Alaska? Anybody want to buy a fur coat?' We all just batted our eyes, hearing this in over 120-degree heat. Who in the heck would want a fur coat? But we got to thinking later that what the poor man was trying to do was get enough money out of the fur coat to bury his wife. They couldn't even move her into Vegas right away, because there wasn't any transportation. They had taken the other three people earlier in the day into Las Vegas. I went back to my tent, and I told my husband, 'We've got to get out of here. We've just absolutely got to get out of here. I've got to get somewhere I can get the babies to a doctor if need be, and also myself.'"

1935 FAMILY PROFILE

Sam and Edna Whitley, an African-American couple, live in crowded Harlem, New York. Like thousands of other Southern Blacks, they move to the urban North from the rural South to escape the poverty of the sharecropper system. He now works as a Pullman Porter; she works as a domestic, when employment is available. They have no children.

Annual Income: $955.85
The man makes $716.75 working 47 weeks.
The woman makes $239.10 working 30 weeks.

Annual Budget
Clothing and Personal Care $86.98
Food $403.37
Home Maintenance. $416.75
Medical Care. $26.76
Other $53.53
Taxes and Contributions. $8.60
Transportation $32.50
   Total $1,028.49

Life at Home
- The family emigrates from South Carolina to Harlem in 1926; they are sharecroppers who lose hope of ever being free from constant debt to buy their own land.
- When the Whitleys first arrive in New York and are eligible, they do not request any relief; the husband has too much pride to consider taking charity from the government.
- They were each 18 when they married eight years ago. Sam has little formal education though his mother had taught him the rudiments of reading and writing using the family Bible.

It's Our Anniversary Treat!

Regular $1.69 Seller
For This Sale, Only $1.29

Lovely RAYON and COTTON Bedspread

COLORS
Blue
Rose
Gold
Orchid
Green

We bought them all, thousands of them! We had to get them at a sensationally low price for our Anniversary Sale. They're new, rich looking Bedspreads; cotton for good weight and wear . . . gleaming Rayon for beauty.
18 U 2863—Size 80 by 105 inches. Extra long double bed size. Colors as listed at left. State color. Postage 9¢. Each........... $1.29
18 U 2864—Size 80 by 90 inches. Double bed size, does not cover pillows. Colors as listed at left. State color. Postage 9¢. Each........... $1.00

Usual Value $1.39
NOW $1.00

COLORS
Blue
Rose
Gold
Orchid
Green

GUARANTEED WASHABLE!
Sold Only by Ward's at This Special Price
The mightiest cotton Bedspread Value we've ever seen! Beauty that WASHES . . . sturdy weight, long wearing Indanthrene Dyed Cotton yarns. Launder it . . . . . . let the sun pour on it . . the colors will always be lovely.
18 U 2629—Size 80 by 105 inches. Extra long double bed size. Colors listed in panel at right. State color. Postage 9¢. Each........ $1.00

Usual Value $2.50
NOW $1.94

COLORS
Blue
Rose
Gold
Orchid
Green

ATTRACTIVE RAYON AND COTTON SPREAD
This beautiful Spread is superior to any we've found to date selling up to $2.50 and $2.95! Heavy and long-wearing, the lovely pattern and colors will do more to take that "tired look" away from your bedroom, than all the scrubbing and polishing you can do! It's larger, and that silky looking Rayon pattern is lovelier than most spreads of this quality. "Rayon-and-cotton" is ideal for wear and style!
18 U 2865—Size 84 by 105 inches. Extra double bed size. Colors listed in panel above. State color. Postage 10¢.............. $1.94

Usual Value $1.95
NOW $1.58

COLORS
Blue
Rose
Gold
Green
Orchid

AUTHENTIC COPY!
COLONIAL ROSEWOOD DESIGN
Quite the most fashionable Cotton Bedspread you could choose! The inspiration for this spread was a beautiful Colonial woven Rosewood design. We had this fine copy made, of high grade cotton in a quality that will last for years. In all our merchandising experience we've never seen a more beautiful cotton Bedspread.
18 U 2645—Size 84 by 105 inches. Extra large double bed size. Colors listed in panel at right. State color. Postage 10¢. Each................ $1.58

PATCHWORK DESIGN COLONIAL QUILTS
$1.69 $1.98 Value

We believe it is the best Quilt value in the country today! Unbleached muslin back. Filled with good clean cotton. Scalloped and taped all around. Use it as a light weight quilt or a bedspread.
Predominating colors of Blue; Rose; Gold; Orchid and Green. State color.
18 U 3313—Size 67 by 78 inches finished. Postage 12¢. Each..... $1.69

36 Montgomery Ward & Co CBA

Parcel Post Orders of Less Than $2.00 Must

- He dropped out of school in the third grade to support his mother; he does not remember ever meeting his father.
- Edna is a preacher's daughter; she can both read and write. Her education went through the sixth grade, before she was forced to work in the cotton fields full-time.
- The couple wants children, but are uncertain about their jobs; throughout America the birth rate has dramatically fallen since the Depression began and financial uncertainty increases.
- The family lives in a three-room tenement house that includes one bedroom; because of its age the ceilings are high and airy, but the plaster, plumbing, and wiring are old and often fail.
- Even though the tenement is in need of repairs, the landlord is unresponsive; the demand for housing is so high in Harlem the family cannot find a more responsive landlord or a better apartment; requests for repairs are often ignored for months.
- The family recently decides to improve the looks of their home, making several purchases through Montgomery Ward. One of the buys is a new rayon and cotton bedspread for $1.94.
- They have electricity and running water but no refrigerator.
- Black families who rent apartments in Harlem often pay higher rent for comparative housing than White families in other parts of New York; because of discrimination, African-Americans are limited in the places they can rent.

The tales of Little Orphan Annie, a poor, orphan child, were popular.

- Because of the Depression, nationwide housing standards are deteriorating; new construction is down dramatically.
- The Department of Markets receives a large number of complaints from Harlem about high prices and "short weighting" (when a dishonest store clerk uses hollow weights to cheat the customer).
- Food costs in Harlem are higher than in other parts of the city; a dozen eggs costs $0.40 in most neighborhoods but costs $0.42 in Harlem.
- Despite the Depression, food prices rise 11 percent between 1934 and 1935.
- The percentage of income spent on the "Other" category for Whites and Blacks in New York is comparable. They both spend about two percent of their income on tobacco, though half as much on books and magazines.
- Medical care costs are generally those of emergencies, such as when the husband deeply cut his leg on a nail that was jutting out of the stairs.
- The Depression has caused the closure of many movie picture theaters across the city, but the price of regular admission has dropped from $0.30 to $0.20 per person.
- This couple often listens to Roosevelt's reassuring messages on radio; Edna writes Roosevelt—along with 450,000 other Americans—a note of congratulations in 1933 during his first week in office.
- The tales of *Little Orphan Annie*, a poor, orphan child who finds a rich sugar daddy to help her, is particularly popular in the Depression-torn 1930s.

Life at Work: The Pullman Company

- Sam works as a Pullman porter, serving the first class passengers who travel with a sleeper; he often takes long trips from New York to Miami working up to 18 hours at a stretch.
- Sleeping car porters become an American institution, once the first sleeping car on a train is introduced shortly after the Civil War.
- When he gets his job, he goes through a short training program, then works for six months on probation before being hired.
- Pullmans are known for their courteous, efficient service, and for doing whatever it takes to make their first class travelers comfortable.
- Most Pullman porters are recruited from the friends and relatives of men already in the service.
- He makes up berths, keeps the cars in order, sees that the washrooms are clean and adequately supplied with towels, handles baggage, and tends to the customers' well-being.
- In addition to coping with the long hours of being on call—to meet every whim of the passenger—porters are subject to the abuse of passengers with very little recourse.
- Pullman porters are subject to firing for slight infractions; one platform agent habitually accuses porters of drinking on the job—including some who don't drink.
- He now has enough experience to bid for a "port-in-charge" position, but does not have the reading and writing skills to complete the paperwork and keep appropriate records.
- This man is worried about rumors that the declining first class traffic will reduce the number of weeks he works yearly.
- A lot of a porter's income comes from customers' tips; the base living salary is often not adequate, further encouraging porters to be especially courteous.
- The Pullman Company pioneers in providing comfortable sleeping cars, quality service, and an enjoyable ride, all innovations for the time.
- The Pullman Company begins during the Civil War and gains prominence after its much-publicized trek across the United States carrying the assassinated President Abraham Lincoln's body to burial.

Miss Phoebe Snow
Has stopped to show
Her ticket at
The Gate, you know.
The Guard, polite,
Declares it right.
Of course—
It's Road of
Anthracite.

Lackawanna Railroad

- After the Civil War, former slaves with few employment opportunities outside fieldwork are quickly seen by Pullman as the perfect employees for its sleeping cars.
- In addition to their skills, the recently freed slaves can be paid much less than their White counterparts.
- Many Americans still preserve their antebellum attitudes toward the former slaves, giving Pullman a ready market for their services; even the common man, for the price of a Pullman ticket, can be waited upon in all the comfort of a Southern gentleman.
- Because of the size of Pullman cars, which are both taller and wider than most other railroad cars, many bridges and tracks have to be redesigned to accommodate them.
- By 1869 Pullman is extending its routes to include every major city and many small towns across the United States.
- Pullman cars are added to regular railway runs based on schedules and number of tickets sold.

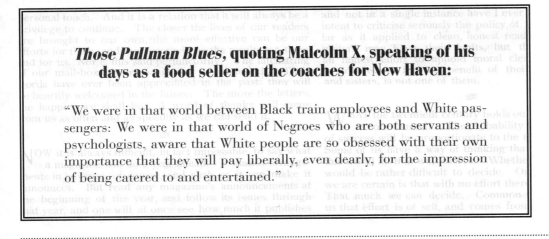

Those Pullman Blues, quoting Malcolm X, speaking of his days as a food seller on the coaches for New Haven:

"We were in that world between Black train employees and White passengers: We were in that world of Negroes who are both servants and psychologists, aware that White people are so obsessed with their own importance that they will pay liberally, even dearly, for the impression of being catered to and entertained."

Those Pullman Blues, quoting Norman Bookman:

"One time a man was riding with us on the Lark. He was talking and they were discussing politics, and they were saying, 'Well, there's so many niggers in San Francisco and so many niggers in L.A.,' and so on. The woman with him looked up at me—I didn't say anything till the next morning. [The train] came in, and she was with him. They were not together. And I said, 'Pardon me, I'd like to ask a question if I may. What did I do wrong last night? I've been up all night wondering what was done wrong. I thought I was giving fair service.'

Then he started apologizing for having made the mistake in saying those words, and he wanted to give me a little piece of change for it. I said, 'Oh, no, you don't owe me nothing.'

But now, you see, I could have put it another way or jumped in that night. They're all drinking, and it could have been an embarrassing thing, or he could have gotten angry, or maybe I got angry and cussed him out, or something else. So you learn how to handle these things this way."

Life in the Community: Harlem, New York

- Harlem begins as one of the first suburbs of New York after its founding in 1657. It is eight miles from City Hall and holds the country homes of the gentry.
- In 1878–81 it becomes home to downtowners fleeing Italian and Jewish immigrants; many of the buildings become known for their posh elegance.
- "Little Italy" and "Little Russia" grow up on the outskirts of Harlem, but Harlem is for the elite.
- By 1905 a housing glut, caused by overspeculation, permits the less affluent, including Blacks, to come in droves.
- By 1920 Harlem has become a Black mecca; 109,000 Blacks live in Manhattan and it is becoming clear that the influx is overwhelming the already meager resources of Harlem.
- Harlem in the mid-1920s very quickly becomes known as a slum.
- Real estate is still in White hands, so even though people in Harlem pay higher rent, very few repairs are made.
- Rent parties are a common sight among residents of Harlem. As the name suggests, they are primarily used to raise enough money to pay the rent. The typical entrance fee is $0.25, and inside one finds live music and the opportunity to buy refreshments (including liquor much of the time), dance, etc.
- Bandleader Count Basie is creating a revolution in jazz; the Basie piano style de-emphasizes the left hand while promoting the use of the high-hat cymbal and the relaxed style of the saxophone.
- The density of people in Harlem in 1935 is 336 per acre, while the density of people in Manhattan is 223 per acre; many Black families take in borders to supplement their incomes.
- The Afro-American Realty Company tells clients that it doesn't matter how many people live in the house as long as the rent is paid up.
- Between 1918 and 1935, food prices fall 24 percent, clothing 15 percent, rent one percent, and house furnishings four percent; meanwhile fuel and light prices rise 29 percent.

Poverty was a constant companion under the sharecropper system.

- Coal that fetched $4.00 a ton in the mid-1920s sells for $1.31 in 1932; miners pay goes from $7.00 a day to $1.00 a day.
- Unemployment has gone from 1.4 percent in 1918 to 20.3 percent.
- Unemployment during the Depression falls heaviest on the very young, the elderly, the least educated, the unskilled, and rural Americans.
- By the 1930s as jobs grow scarce and African-American migration increases, many workers in Harlem are grossly over-qualified for the positions they hold; a doctor of medicine might be a janitor in a hospital or a man with a master's in business might work in a factory with no hope of ever being promoted to management.
- One-fifth of all the people on the federal relief rolls are Black, a proportion double the African-American presence in the population.
- To keep as many people working as possible, many industries restrict the number of hours each employee can work. Some 100,000 American workers in 1931 apply for jobs in what appears to be the new promised land: Soviet Russia.
- The passage of the National Labor Relations Act, also known as the Wagner Act, in 1935 establishes a mandate for industry to bargain with unions—the first time in American history the national government has placed its weight behind the principle of unionism.

New York Times, June 7, 1935:

"Supreme Court Justice Charles C. Lockwood, who was born in the Williamsburg section of Brooklyn, upheld yesterday the city's action in acquiring, over property owners' objections, 12 square blocks of land for the Williamsburg low-cost housing project.

He ruled that the condemnation proceeding whereby the city took the land from the former owners was legal in every respect. He also observed that in days past minority groups in Williamsburg had opposed the substitution of trolley cars for horse cars, and the building of the Williamsburg Bridge.

The housing project is intended to provide homes for persons of small means and is to be financed by federal funds. One of the objections to the city's method of taking the land through its right of eminent domain was that the project was to benefit only a single class of persons and not the public as a whole."

- In 1935 the community is still in an uproar over the Harlem riots, starting when a young African-American boy is caught stealing and word spreads that the boy has been beaten and killed by the shop owner; the Young Liberators and the Young Communist League fan the flames of the riot with fliers that allege brutality.
- Following the riots, New York Mayor La Guardia creates a committee to investigate conditions in Harlem that led to the riot; topics to investigate include housing, playgrounds, discrimination in employment, education, and relief agencies.
- Despite the Depression, a nationwide government study of working class families which compared 1918 with 1935 shows some improvement in living conditions is being made.
- Basic food needs are met more fully 1935 than in 1918; the study says it is because food is available year-round.
- Milk consumption has increased one-fourth nationally, reducing the widespread calcium deficiencies of 1918.
- Housing is more comfortable; modern plumbing and electricity are the norm rather than the exception. According to census reports, only one in four dwellings had electrical service in 1917; four in five do in 1930.
- Radios, which were unknown in 1918, are commonplace in 1935.
- During this same time period most working class homes switch from cooking with coal or wood to gas.
- The use of machines to wash clothes is becoming universal.

HISTORICAL SNAPSHOT
1935–1936

- The Social Security Act passed Congress

- The Emergency Relief Appropriation Act gave $5 billion to create jobs

- Fort Knox became the United States Repository of gold bullion

- One-tenth of one percent of U.S. corporations made 50 percent of earnings

- Sulfa-drug chemotherapy was introduced to relieve veneral disease sufferers everywhere

- Nylon was developed by Du Pont

- Beer cans were introduced

- One-third of farmers received U.S. treasury allotment checks for not growing food or crops

- New York State law allowed women to serve as jurors

- Polystyrene became commercially available in the United States for use in products such as kitchen utensils and toys

- An eight-hour day was passed in Illinois

- Seven million women paid more than $2 billion for 35 million permanents

- Margaret Mitchell's *Gone with the Wind* sold a record one million copies in six months

- A *Fortune* poll indicated that 67 percent favored birth control

- Trailer sales peaked; tourist camps for vacationing motorists gained popularity

Willson Whitman's *God's Valley*, 1939:

"A lot has been said about the sharecropping system and you could say a lot more without explaining just how bad it is. You have to see it, and you have to think about it. A lot of Southerners see it without thinking, because the people it produces are such sorry-looking folks that it is taken for granted that such people would be in trouble anyhow. But there are more of these people than there used to be. Just in the last few years it's got so that more than half the farmers work for other men, and in the cotton country 60 out of a hundred do."

1935 ECONOMIC PROFILE

Income, Standard Jobs

Average of All Industries, Including Farm Labor	$1,115.00
Bituminous Coal Mining	$957.00
Building Trades	$1,027.00
Domestics	$485.00
Farm Labor	$324.00
Federal Civilian	$1,759.00
Federal Military	$1,154.00
Gas and Electricity Workers	$1,589.00
Manufacturing, Durable Goods	$1,264.00
Manufacturing, Nondurable Goods	$1,178.00
Medical/Health Services Workers	$829.00
Motion Picture Services	$1,892.00
Passenger Transportation Workers	$1,361.00
Personal Services	$915.00
Public School Teachers	$1,293.00
Radio Broadcasting	$2,089.00
Railroads	$1,645.00
State and Local Government Workers	$1,361.00
Telephone and Telegraph Workers	$1,378.00
Wholesale and Retail Trade Workers	$1,279.00

Selected Prices

Baby Seat, Loom Woven Lined with Cotton	$12.98
Birdbath, Sandstone	$50.00
Broiler Pan, Oval Aluminum	$0.75
Charcoal Grill	$1.95
China Cabinet, Pine, Extra Width	$32.50
Dinnerware, Semi-Porcelain, for Six	$4.98
Fishing Reel	$8.25
Flashlight	$1.39
Garden Tractor, Handiman, Four Hp Motor	$242.00
Gun Case, Custom Made with Lambskin	$3.00
Jergens Lotion	$0.69
Olive Oil	$0.39
Paper Pattern for Dress	$0.15
Pocket Radio	$2.90
Pressure Cooker, Eight-Quart	$7.45
Razor Blade	$1.00
Shotgun, Double Barrel	$30.00
Sportman's Encyclopedia	$1.00
Tire, Goodyear All Weather	$15.55
Waterhose, 25' Green ⅝"	$3.00

The Sharecropper System

- By moving to New York, the couple broke the cycle of poverty inherent in the sharecropper system.
- In general, the tenant farmer borrowed everything he needed to work with—seed, plow, mule, etc.—from the landowner, who was paid back with a portion of the crops.
- This system came into play after the Civil War, according to some "so that plantation owners could pretend that the Emancipation Proclamation had never occurred."
- This system normally imprisoned the tenant farmer; rarely could enough "good years" equal the cost of the goods "borrowed" so the sharecropper could purchase land.
- Their decision was reenforced by the boll weevil invasion of 1923, which wiped out entire cotton fields, and caused a general depression in the South. They moved North to see if what they had heard about freedom was true.
- They were not alone; in 1920, 85 percent of all Blacks lived south of the Mason-Dixon line compared with 92 percent at the time of the Civil War; by 1940 the percentage would drop to 76 percent.
- The couple did not engage in any practices such as illegal liquor distilling to supplement their income, despite the temptation; they needed the money but after a neighbor was taken to jail for manipulating the gas meter, the husband decided that it was better for him not to engage in those activities.

Today, Sherwood Anderson, "I Want to Work," April 1934:

"The New Deal has cracked something open. In the South and pretty much all over the United States there was, before Roosevelt came, a feeling that to have anything to do with a union meant a certain social blight . . . in reality, half of it is resistance to change, any kind of change. The President's job isn't just to get people back to work, get higher prices for farm products. There is a higher job he has already begun, a kind of striking down into men's imaginations. It has already gone pretty far.

I went to a meeting of Negro workers. Even the illiterate ones can listen to the radio. Just because a man can't read or write doesn't necessarily mean that he hasn't a mind. I have found that out myself, living these last five years among mountain men in southwest Virginia . . . the Negroes were at their meeting discussing the same things I had heard discussed in a Sunday school class . . . labor, the yellow dog contract, the lockout, advisability of labor getting itself intelligently organized . . . 'If a man like President Roosevelt thinks labor should organize, why shouldn't I think so?' That is the notion.

At the meeting of Negroes a Black man got up and proposed that at the next meeting to be held, he bring his preacher.

There were objections, apologetic but determined objections. 'I believe in God and His son, Jesus Christ, but there is the carnal and the uncarnal. We have come here to talk about the carnal. We have to talk among ourselves.'"

Augusta Swanson, *Telling Memories among Southern Women*:

"I had two sisters and one brother, all half-sisters and a half-brother. Everyone had different fathers. My mother, she was not married. My father was White and brother's father was White, but the others were Colored. Because, see in the country, they didn't have no money, and the only way you could get it was to go with these White men to get a little change. And that's why so many of them had these babies with White men. Because they'd offer them a little change where Colored didn't have nothing to give them. Nothing to help them get along—no money, nothing.

And when she'd tell me my daddy was White and was coming to see me, if I had listened to her, I probably would have had money. But I couldn't stand him. It made me mad when she told me that. He owned a grocery store. And when she'd tell me he was coming over and wanted to talk to me, I wouldn't even come out to see him. I didn't want to see no White man.

The other thing they could do on the planta-tion to get by was to put the children out to work. And so when I was eight years old, my mother sent me to live with a lady. Her name was Miz May. She wanted someone to keep her company.

At first, I wasn't big enough to do anything, but she taught me how to read and write, cro-chet, knit, cook, and how to housekeep. She used to fool me to death. She'd come tell me that the fairy had hid a present, a big surprise, and she'd say, 'Augusta, the only way you can find that surprise, you have to move everything, and make sure you general clean, because if you don't, you'll never find that surprise.' And so, here I am working myself to death, just moving and dusting, moving trying to find it. And I never did find it. But I sat right by her and slept right in her room on a cot, right by her just like I was her daughter. And all I learned was through her, 'cause she would teach me everything right there. That's why I never did go to school."

Roosevelt's Depression Policies

- Roosevelt's Depression policies were designed to address what he viewed as harmful and unfair imbalances in the American economy.
- He also sought some measure of economic security and predictability of life's material circumstances.
- The owners of industry, he said, had failed to pass on a fair share of the productivity and profit gains to labor in the form of higher wages or to the consumer in lower prices.
- This produced a vicious cycle in which the worker's wages failed to keep pace with the capacity—and seductive nature—of a booming industrial economy.
- A better-balanced American economy was a critical concept in New Deal conversations.
- Nationwide 2.54 percent of the population was headed by a father employed in the "professional service," 4.7 percent in business and managerial employment, 14 percent in small retail or were highly skilled workmen, 40.7 percent were workmen, and 18.7 percent were farmers.

1936 News Profile
The Migratory-Casual Worker

Throughout American history, temporary, transient workers have been an important, although invisible part of the work force. This is the story of two men whose lives have been lived on the road, job to job. They were interviewed as part of a Works Progress Administration report on "The Migratory-Casual Worker" published in 1937.

John McClosky

"Born in Missouri in 1889. Went to Illinois in covered wagon along with father, mother, three sisters, two brothers. Father ran hoist at coal mine, traded horses, peddled fish, crockery, and did jobs of work around Peoria, Illinois. About 1893 my mother and one sister died of typhoid fever. Dad came to Seattle. Built and lived in one-room shack at the foot of Kinnear Park. Moved to six miles north of Bellingham. On this place I begin to do hard labor, helped saw stove wood. I hauled wood to Bellingham and peddled it. Then I got a job as bellboy in Byron Hotel (was awfully green) then went to work for Western Union, messenger boy.

Ran away from home. Went to Seattle and got a job as deck boy on steamship that went to San Francisco. I got paid off there, got taken by sights of the big city. Came to my senses, my boat had sailed. I had $0.05 left in my pocket. I spent it for a newspaper and looked through the ads. Porter wanted, restaurant. Convinced the boss I could do the work, $5.00 a week and board. Stayed there 10 days, had fight with cook, got fired. Got a job on a steamer to San Diego. Worked three months then quit. Got a job in a family hotel in San Francisco as bellboy, stayed there three weeks and got fired for pulling a boner. Went back to San Diego. Left after short time. Got job in Hotel San Rafael, San Francisco, bellboy, $15.00 per month.

About this time I began to think of home for the first time. After four weeks I wrote home. Dad had moved to near Blaine, Washington, on 40 acres of unimproved land. Headed for home. Went to Aberdeen on a lumber schooner, Seattle on train, to Blaine on a boat. Stayed awhile. Struck out for Seattle. Got job as flunkey in logging camp. Never stayed long in one place. Get few dollars, got to Seattle, go broke—then go back and work some more. After a while I would get sick. Go home. Stay a short time. Gone again.

I finally got work in a new shingle mill nearby father's ranch. I worked there in the woods cutting shingle bolts, and learning to saw and pack shingles. Then I went to Everett, Washington, and lived around there cutting shingle bolts, sawing, and packing. Worked in shingle mills up and down Puget Sound. Never stayed long in one place. I put in three years on Vancouver Island sawing shingles. Spent most of my winters on a trap line in Whatcom County, near my father's ranch.

In 1918 I married. Wife and I came to Seattle and I longshored up to the general strike of 1919. Drove a car for my brother-in-law for 18 months. Went east of the mountains logging. Back to Seattle. Peddled handbills from house to house. Worked for junk company. Cut wood on the beach. Worked on a paving job, wheeling sand and gravel to the concrete mixer.

My wife's health was poorly, and they said the mountain air would help her. I went up to Lake Wenatchee to cut shingle bolts and took my wife. Stayed there two years while my wife's health greatly improved. Picked apples in Wenatchee Valley for the first time. Wife wanted divorce. Started same then changed mind. After another year took notion for divorce. I went to San Joan Island and cut cordwood from January to August. When I came out to Bellingham I found I was divorced.

I worked two months mucking on the Cascade Tunnel. Sawed shingles at Quilcene, Washington. Worked one winter for a coal company in Seattle. Made cedar shakes one summer at Kerriston, Washington. Was married while there. Wife and I parted same year. Since then I have been knocking around Washington working here and there on odd jobs, mostly in the Wenatchee Valley but I have only averaged four months work per year since 1928."

Tony Slonig

"I was born in Ohio. My folks took me back to the old country (Austria) when I was a baby and I don't know why. My father worked in the vineyards, and I did also. I kept running away from home and working. My uncle wrote me about how fine everything was in America, and I came over here and found it wasn't so fine. (Oh yes, I did make good money, but that's all gone now.)

I went to work in an iron foundry in Verona, Pennsylvania, for $1.75 a day. Then I got a big job with an insulator company doing piece work, trimming insulators. I was making as high as $10.00 a day. I was young and full of hell and went into the city every night and got drunk, stayed out all night, and would come back to work in the morning too sleepy to see. The inspector would come along, take a look at an insulator and throw it into the scrap heap. I told him not to do it and got mad and hit him over the head with one. He chased me and I ran and when we passed the cashier's window my check was already waiting for me.

The papers came out all about the big wages Henry Ford was paying, and I got hungry for that. Packed up and went to Detroit. Found that everyone there was a mechanic. Worked at common labor until I could buy some tools, then worked for Ford for 13 months for $5.60 a day during the war. I quit him because there wasn't enough money in it. Went back to Detroit and worked as a machinist.

In 1924 I met my wife and got married to her. I worked at piece work in the Fisher Body Plant, getting as high as $20.00 a day. In 1926 I went to work for the U.S. Radio Corporation or $1.50 an hour. In 1929 I got my arm caught and tore up the muscles in it. I was sick four or five months. My wife was in the family way and we had one hell of a time. I signed a petition I was OK and went back to work for two months in 1930, then they laid me off because there wasn't enough work. I had slowed down because my hand got numb when I tried to use it and I couldn't grasp a lathe like I used to. I had the case reopened twice trying to get more damages, but the company had smarter fellows than I had.

Well, my wife went back to her folks. They foreclosed the mortgage on our house. My wife's brother-in-law and sister had to move in with the old folks too, making nine of us in the little house. Her folks didn't like me and said I was a foreigner and a Catholic and didn't have an education. I packed up and left. They had me arrested for deserting my family, and made me work for the relief and report to the judge every week. I couldn't stand it, so I came out West in 1933.

I hitchhiked through the Dakotas, inquired in a pool hall for a job, and found one on a farm plowing for $0.50 a day. Worked there for eight weeks and never got but $4.00. Was walking around the street hungry when I met a fellow half drunk who told me about a job he was supposed to go to that I could have if I wanted. I was so lucky he was drunk. I harvested there and made about $60.00. Then I went to Colorado to work in the sugar beets, but nothing

there but Mexicans. I got a job cutting grapes for Filipino contractors. They hire more men than they need so they can collect for boarding them. We had rice three times a day and slept on the floor like hogs. I think I owed them board when I left. It was terrible there and if the government doesn't believe it, I've got the man's name here on a card and you can go see for yourself.

I started to pick cotton but heard that there was a big strike on and two people killed so I got cold feet and left the country. Had a dishwashing job for a fellow who got sick, but he was only sick a week. Then I hit the freight and got in a good job harvesting at Colfax, Washington. I tried to pick apples, but couldn't find anything. Went to Moxie, Washington, and picked hops and sure made it good—about $25.00 in two weeks, slipped in lots of leaves in the bottom of the sack. I found a farm job where I have been ever since. They expected me to milk six cows and kept piling on more work, all for just tobacco money, so I quit. I'll do most anything I can find, though. Think I'll stay in Washington, because if you go to California, you can't get nothing to do unless you are a Filipino or a native son."

1937 FAMILY PROFILE

Timothy Danielson, a Tennessee farmer-turned-welder, works for the Tennessee Valley Authority (TVA) building dams. During the past four years, his income has risen almost five times. As a farmer he rarely made more than $350.00 a year, electricity was unavailable, he did not own a radio or an icebox refrigerator. Now that he and his wife, Martha, live in the TVA-created community of Norris, they have three children, electricity, a radio, refrigerator, and are saving for a car.

Annual Income: $1,700

The man works as a welder 33 hours a week, making approximately $1.25 a hour, or $41.25 a week. He works 46 weeks in 1937, spending the other six on his brother-in-law's farm during spring planting and fall harvesting.

Annual Budget

This survey does not include any personal information on the Danielsons; instead it focuses on the development of the Norris Community, constructed by TVA as part of the Norris Dam Project on the Clinch River, near Knoxville, Tennessee. A sample of consumer expenditures nationally, on a per capita basis, shows the following:

Auto Parts	$3.10
Auto Usage	$41.87
Clothing	$42.65
Dentists	$3.10
Furniture	$6.98
Gas and Oil	$16.28
Health Insurance	$0.78
Housing	$68.24
Intercity Transport	$3.10
Local Transport	$6.98
New Auto Purchase	$15.51

The Tennessee Valley Project improved the lives of poor tenant farmers and their families.

Personal Business $25.59
Personal Care. $7.75
Physicians $6.16
Private Education $4.65
Recreation $26.36
Religion/Welfare Activities $6.98
Telephone and Telegraph $3.88
Tobacco $13.18
Utilities $23.26
Per Capita Consumption. $517.21

Life at Home

- The town of Norris is created by the Tennessee Valley Authority to construct the Norris Dam.
- The construction town of Norris is designed as a permanent community of small houses, electrically equipped, which are rented to workmen.
- Unlike many "textile towns," which stack row after row of houses together on a street, Norris' neighborhoods follow the undulating grade of the natural land; thousands of trees are left standing to beautify the homes.

- The houses built in Norris use the traditional Southern "dog-trot" or "shotgun" house design, with a hall or breezeway right the middle with rooms on each side. (The term "shotgun house" is used to indicate that a shotgun blast can pass through the house from one end to the other without hitting a thing.)
- When first completed, Norris includes 291 single-family homes, 10 duplexes, and five apartment houses.
- The planners add a park, a playground, and a town common; also, the town eventually finds itself on the edge of a lake.
- Beer is not sold in Norris; most TVA projects are dry.
- Because Norris is set up more like a technical college than a construction site, the man can take woodworking classes and mathematics.
- His math class includes 30 other men, all his age, who sign up voluntarily.
- Other classes include technical subjects for dam builders and even a "discussion group" on the history of public ownership and labor problems in America.
- TVA's concept of rebuilding the Tennessee Valley includes helping the entire family; one employee qualification that is brought up critically during a congressional investigation is the TVA qualifier, "Is his wife an asset?"
- Cooking and decorating classes are available for the woman, which she uses to improve the look of the house.
- The Authority makes free educational movies available in Norris; at the commercial theater, curly-headed moppet Shirley Temple is the town's top box office draw.
- Farm users find they can have electrical appliances for the first time; the TVA reports in 1937 that in the four states covered by the Authority, TVA customers bought 8,680 electric refrigerators, 4,288 electric ranges, 1,547 electric water heaters, and 4,949 electric washers.
- During the past two years, $5.2 million worth of appliances have been sold to TVA customers.
- The Norris Dam's construction requires that the entire graveyard be moved, including the remains of Martha's grandparents, where they have been buried near Hogskin Creek; 100 cemeteries with 5,219 graves are removed.
- At Caryville, where Timothy's family originates, with a population of 1,000, 73 houses, along with a nine-room brick school and the Baptist church, are moved to make way for the lake.
- The family's diet and cash flow is supplemented by work on a farm owned by the wife's brother; the TVA's 33-hour work week leaves time for outside activities.
- The family plans to buy a car when they can afford it; used cars in 1937 cost $485.00 for a 1936 Willys DeLuxe sedan; $395.00 for a 1935 Chevrolet Coach "with new radio and tires"; $245.00 for a 1933 Ford V-8 Coach; and $145.00 for a 1930 Chevrolet Coupe.

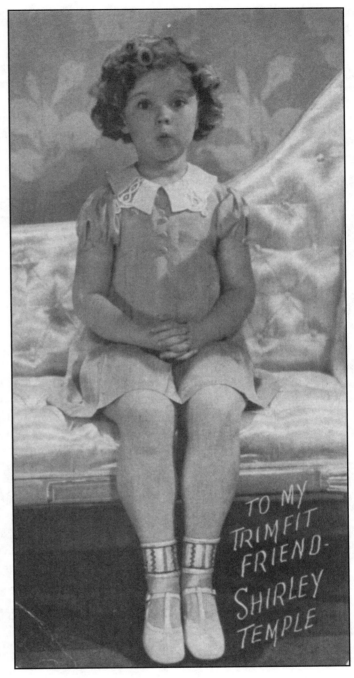

TO MY TRIMFIT FRIEND- SHIRLEY TEMPLE

Life at Work: The TVA

- When the project begins in 1933, 40,000 people take the civil service examination to get jobs.
- This man begins working for the TVA doing construction and graduates to welder, a job he enjoys. He also keeps a small farm with his brother-in-law.
- In 1933, when Timothy begins work for the TVA, it is estimated that the dam will take four years to complete; the dam is completed 18 months ahead of schedule.
- To provide the maximum number of jobs, the project has four shifts and a 33-hour week to spread work, leaving time for additional study and raising vegetables.
- In 1935, 3,263 employees work on the Norris Dam out of 15,807 employed by the TVA that year.
- The Norris Dam at completion is 265 feet high, 1,872 feet in length, and 204 feet thick at its base. The reservoir area covers 34,200 acres.
- After gaining experience in construction and welding, Timothy is allowed to rotate jobs every five weeks to gain experience in different kinds of jobs, including foreman.
- At construction camps meals cost $0.35 for all you can eat, $0.30 if you are a regular boarder. In Norris the standard price is lower, $0.25 per meal.
- Meals include fruit, cereals, and salads, "with so much to eat you can be a Yankee and have dinner at night, or a Southerner and have supper in the evening."
- Nearly all dam-builders are craft unionists; the office worker's union has CIO affiliation.
- Sample wages paid by the TVA in 1937 include: carpenter, $1.10 per hour; rigger, $1.25 per hour; accounting clerk, $1.50 per hour; rigger foreman, $1.50 per hour; shovel operator, $1.50 per hour.
- In comparison, in 1934 the per capita income of farm households is less than $167.00; only one farmhouse in 10 has an indoor toilet; only one in five has electricity.
- Illiteracy is twice as common in rural areas as in cities.
- Sample wages of employees who receive annual incomes include: geologist, $2,900; millwright, $1,800; secretary, $2,300; forester, $2,100; erosion engineer, $2,400; purchasing agent, $3,000; carpenter foreman, $3,200.
- In 1938, the Knoxville paper says, "It is no news that the number of employees in the Authority who are unhappy over the conditions of their work is increasing. To a large extent this fact merely results from the growing maturity of the Authority and it's a reaction from the possibly excessive enthusiasm of the organization days."

Writer Norman Cousins' panacea to unemployment, "Will Women Lose Their Jobs?" 1939:

"There are approximately 10 million people out of work in the United States today; there are also 10 million or more women, married and single, who are jobholders. Simply fire the women, who shouldn't be working anyway, and hire the men. Presto! No unemployment. No relief rolls. No Depression."

- Wages are set by the government's definition of "prevailing" wages with "due regard" for rates secured through collective agreement.
- The TVA introduces fertilizers, and new farming methods are bringing back the soil of the region; terracing, contour farming, strip cropping, and soil surveys improve yields.
- Many farmers do not wish to change.
- In exchange for free fertilizer, Martha's brother agrees to follow the advice of the agricultural experts, keep records of yields, and conduct tours for their own crops and for their neighbors'.
- Eventually, 15,000 demonstration farms similar to this family's are established throughout the TVA.
- A nursery set up at Norris provides tree seedlings for wind breaks, erosion control, and fruit to the family for the farm.
- The TVA electrical rates are below the prevailing rates in the area; one man sees his bill drop from $2.30 a month to $0.75; the *Tupelo Journal* (Mississippi) reports that its bill fell to $18.94 from $41.38 a month.
- Many homeowners report increased use of electricity because of its affordability.
- Farmers, long without electricity because it had been unprofitable to string lines into the mountains, gain electricity for the first time in the 20th Century.
- In Georgia, Tennessee, Alabama, and Mississippi, the number of electrified farms grows 185 percent from 29,370 in 1932 to 83,150 at the end of 1937.
- The minimum rate is $0.75 per month, assuming there are five to 10 users a mile; for two to five users the minimum rate goes to $1.20.

Life in the Community: Norris, Tennessee

- Norris is a totally planned community, conceived by the Tennessee Valley Authority as a modern, almost Utopian town.
- Many of the most modern concepts concerning education, socialization, and adult education are incorporated in the town's design.
- The houses are of board-and-batten construction, built by local carpenters and masons who are paid a union wage.
- Insulation is included because these houses are to be heated with electricity, not fires.
- The road from Knoxville, called the freeway, is designed as a "wide rural road," but enough land is purchased on each side of the road to prevent "hot dog stands and Coca-Cola signs."
- Norris includes a tract of woodland, "a green belt they called it," of community forest.
- Land is provided for community gardens and the new residents are given plants for their yards if they are willing to put them out.

CINEGRAPHS EIGHT

STARS OF HOLLYWOOD
On Your Own Home Movie Screen

- The school is placed in the center of town; the building is two stories high and "they backed it up against a hill so the children on the second floor could walk out without having to use stairs."
- The school's technology includes a "trick electric eye" to turn on the lights in cloudy weather.
- The school is different from anything the community has ever experienced.
- The children do not carry books home; instead, they study in the library from an array of books; the library is also made available to "grown people in the town" who are also permitted to use the school auditorium and woodworking shop at the school.
- Instead of report cards, teachers write letters to the parents concerning their child's progress; "they put down grades only in case some child might be transferred."
- And instead of keeping up the attendance record, if a child comes to school with a cold they send him home with a note saying, "please keep him there." It seems unusual to most people, but the children do well with their work.
- Prior to the TVA, teachers are paid according to the attendance records of the children.
- The classroom "wasn't like ordinary schooling;" the science class uses the weather-station readings to make forecasts about the river, for example.
- In addition, the school creates a business to deliver the town's news bulletins; in return the town contributes a five-acre plot of ground. "So they organized the Norris School Produce company to raise vegetables. When they needed capital, they raised $50.00 by selling 500 $0.10 bonds, paying three percent interest. Stock in the company, though, was obtainable only by work—eight hours for one share."
- Instead of building three or four churches, the community decides by a 99 percent vote to have a "Religious Fellowship" to include all denominations and meet in the school auditorium.

Freedom from Fear, by David M. Kennedy

"At the instructions of the Roosevelt administration, Lorena Hickok drove to the country to get a firsthand view of the economic conditions in the early days of the Depression. One of her stops was the company coal mines of West Virginia. In her report she wrote, "Some of them have been starving for eight years. I was told there are children in West Virginia who never tasted milk! I visited one group of 45 blacklisted miners and their families, who have been living in tents two years . . . Most of the women you see in the camps are going without shoes or stockings . . . It's fairly common to see children entirely naked . . . some of the families had been living for days on green corn and string beans—and precious little of that. And some had nothing at all, actually hadn't eaten for a couple of days. At the Continental Hotel in Pineville (Kentucky) I was told that five babies up one of those creeks had died of starvation in the last 10 days . . . Dysentery is so common that nobody says much about it . . . ."

TVA Director David Lilienthal's speech to the Kiwanis Club, Madison, Wisconsin, October 1, 1934, on the creation of the TVA:

"There are thousands of families in those hills that have never seen as much as $100.00 in cash in a year. This great area with six or seven million people has yet to get a decent economy. During the heyday of prosperity, they went north—to Detroit, Pontiac, Cleveland, Cincinnati, Columbus, and to other cities. They went by the hundreds of thousands. Then the Depression came. From 1929 through 1930, 1931, and 1932, prosperity was "just around the corner." And they waited in Detroit, Cleveland, Columbia, and Pontiac for prosperity, until they had spent everything they had. Then the folks back home had to send money from their meager incomes to bring their boys home. They are back in the hills now with their cabins overcrowded with no work to do. That mountain region is a relief station for our great industrial centers. It is supporting the people who were sent home when there was no further work for them in industry. Today the government is helping them. Otherwise there would be starvation on a large scale.

The mountain country has been exploited. I have been making a study to show you the final fruits of rugged American initiative. Here is a country that years ago had the finest hardwood forest in America. If there had been a plan—if they had cut the right timber and had foresters to take care of the rest and had established little mills and manufacturing places—the area could have had prosperity for centuries. Instead of that, lumber companies bought the land for $0.25 to $1.00 an acre, more or less, and hired men for $0.75 a day, stripped the timber, and left the blackened stumps and the people behind. They had no sense of responsibility and made no effort to put these people on their feet. You have the same story in northern Wisconsin, where people sit in poverty after the stripping of the land.

In some places they found oil and built pipelines. They hired some of the people for a few years, paying them perhaps $1.00 or $2.00 a day in flush times. After the oil was flowing they no longer needed workers, so the people were left 'broke' again. The same thing happened when gas was discovered. Last fall, while the oil and gas were being piped out for use in Northern cities, two-thirds of the people in the counties that produced it were on relief. Trachoma, tuberculosis, and pellagra exist everywhere. Schools and local governments are breaking down financially. A man seldom sees conditions as bad in city slums that exist in that country.

I could give example after example from that area where the same thing has happened. Rugged individualism has abandoned these areas, and we must see what we can do to help them. We must, if possible, get these people off of government relief and help them to be self-supporting, self-respecting citizens. We hired 100 men and put them on one of our construction jobs. They had been sitting in idleness for years. They were young fellows who did not want their lives to rust. They have made excellent workmen. In Chicago, Detroit, and Cleveland, the problem is to get prosperity back; in many communities down here there has never been prosperity."

- This decision later leads to rumors that the TVA town of Norris is "churchless," even though services are held each Sunday.
- The house cannot be purchased, only rented; "Uncle Sam owns the place in perpetuity."
- Author Willson Whitman comments about Norris, "while building houses and a good school for Knoxville people wasn't what they started to do, it's a nice town, and they've

Construction crew in the cafeteria at Cherokee Dam.

never had a crime there, unless you agree with the Republicans who say it was a crime to build it in the first place."

- The spring lecture on "modern problems" at the Norris Religious Fellowship Hall is the "employability of women." The series, according to Pastor Jack Anderson, is to broaden the field of religion to include all of life.

- In 1937 the city of Knoxville increases the minimum city water rate to consumers outside the city, to include Norris; the rate goes from $1.50 to $2.00 per month for 3,750 gallons.

- That same year, in nearby Alcoa, Tennessee, the Aluminum Workers Union goes out on strike seeking an hourly wage increase from $0.45 to $0.60 per hour to bring local workers in parity with New Kensington, Pennsylvania, workers, who make $0.63 per hour.

- On April 23, the *Knoxville News* reports "Geneva Hamby, child-bride of the Great Smoky Mountains was a 'crying and a 'carryin' on today because 'thuh law' had taken away her 32-year-old husband, raw-boned Homer Peel. The 11-year-old girl protested that 'ah love mah man' but Sheriff S.B. Latimore rapped on the door of the honeymoon cabin high in the hills and arrested the gangling bridegroom on a charge of violating Tennessee's recently enacted 'child-bride' law. 'Ah'd ruther have thuh girl in an orphanage than a gettin' married at her age,' said the girl's 32-year-old mother, who has six children. 'Hit ain't decent, ah tell ye.'"

HISTORICAL SNAPSHOT
1937-1938

- The United Automobile Workers were recognized by General Motors as sole bargaining agent for employees

- The principle of the minimum wage for women was upheld by the Supreme Court

- Packard Motor Car Company sold a record 109,000 cars

- General Motors introduced automatic transmission

- Icemen continued to make regular deliveries to more than 50 percent of middle class households

- Spam was introduced by George A. Hormel & Company

- *Popular Photography* magazine began publication

- Congress's wage-and-hour law limited the work week to 44 hours

- Recovery stumbled, *Wall Street's Dow Jones Industrial Average* fell

- Eastern Airlines was created

- Owens-Corning Fiberglass Corporation was incorporated to produce products utilizing newly developed fiberglass

- The first high-definition color television was demonstrated

- The ballpoint pen was patented

- Consumption of beef and dairy products increased by three percent

- The first nylon stockings went on sale

- From September 1, 1936, to June 1, 1937, 484,711 workers were involved in sitdown strikes

- A study showed that people spent 4.5 hours daily listening to the radio

- Spinach growers erected a statue to cartoon character Popeye in Wisconsin

1937 ECONOMIC PROFILE

Income, Standard Jobs

Average of All Industries,
Including Farm Labor $1,259.00
Bituminous Coal Mining $1,170.00
Building Trades $1,278.00
Domestics $588.00
Farm Labor $407.00
Federal Civilian $1,797.00
Federal Military $1,132.00
Gas and Electricity Workers $1,705.00
Manufacturing, Durable Goods $1,491.00
Manufacturing, Nondurable
Goods $1,267.00
Medical/Health Services Workers $876.00
Motion Picture Services $1,972.00
Passenger Transportation Workers . . $1,505.00
Personal Services $978.00
Public School Teachers $1,367.00
Radio Broadcasting $2,361.00
Railroads $1,774.00
State and Local Government
Workers $1,505.00
Telephone and Telegraph Workers . . $1,481.00
Wholesale and Retail Trade
Workers $1,352.00

Selected Prices

Chesterfield Pipe, 5" Size $0.39
Cold Wave Fan, Oscillating. $5.50
Eileen Drury Women's Frock $1.98
Florsheim Men's Shoes $8.75
Goodyear Double Eagle Car Battery . . . $16.95
Goodyear Wings Deluxe-8 Radio. $38.50
Hercules Pitchfork. $1.35
J.C. Higgins Basketball $3.59
Kenmore Deluxe Vacuum Cleaner $31.45
Kodak Bantam Camera. $22.50
Lifetime Steel Bed, Complete $16.50
Lysol Disinfectant, Large Size $0.83
Maternity Corset $2.98
Merit Ax $0.98
Morninglow Bath Towels, Four $0.79
Nestlé's Baby Hair Treatment $0.83
Polar Air Refrigerator $22.98
Sir Walter Raleigh Smoking Tobacco $0.15
Supertone Gene Autry Guitar $8.45
Velflor Rug, 9' x 12' $8.75
Wildroot Hair Tonic $0.47
Windex Window Cleaner $0.39

THE CREATION OF THE TVA

- In 1933, when Roosevelt came to office, 13 million people were out of work, a third of the work force, and a third more people than the year before.
- The sum of all goods and services produced by the country had fallen by half since 1929.
- Farm prices, marriages, and birth rates were all down.
- No matter how desperate conditions were nationally, they were worse in the Tennessee Valley.
- In 1933 the annual per capita income in the Valley was $168.00.
- Malaria affected up to 30 percent of the population of some areas.
- More than half the region's three million people lived on farms; half of those lived on farms they did not own.
- Only three farms in 100 had electricity.
- Unchecked fires burned 10 percent of the region's woodlands yearly.
- The answer, President Franklin Roosevelt declared, was the Tennessee Valley Authority, a development envisioned to help flood control, prevent soil erosion, improve soil, and promote better economic diversification through industry.
- The bill creating the TVA was signed May 18, 1933.
- Less than three months after the TVA Act was signed, construction began on the first hydroelectric dam located on the Clinch River in northeast Tennessee.

Installation of a rotor in the Norris Dam powerhouse.

Knoxville News, "TVA Head's Wife Leads WCTU-like Campaign," April 23, 1937:

"NORRIS—This is the modern, up-to-date—some call it Utopian—town of the modern, farthest reaching arm of the New Deal. People have come from all over the world to see it and the scientific, esthetic, and social developments it represents.

Yet on Tuesday the people here will go to the polls like those of any other American country town to vote on whether they want beer sold in the town and if so, how.

The pre-referendum campaign is much like the old-fashioned temperance rows that have split less modern American villages for 100 years. Norris, child of the New Deal though it may be, is uninfluenced by the fact that it was the New Deal that brought prohibition repeal to America as the very first of its accomplishments. It seems to be anybody's guess as to the outcome of the beer fight.

The pre-election campaign so far has been featured by the circulation of a petition opposing the sale of beer in Norris. It was signed by 128 persons, mostly women. The importance of the petition lies not so much in the number of persons who signed it as the fact that it was circulated by Mrs. A.E. Morgan, wife of the TVA Chairman . . ."

- This required the digging of a 650-mile navigable waterway from Knoxville, to the upper reaches of the Tennessee River system, to Paducah on the Ohio to promote conservation and the development of recreational facilities, and to attract new industries to the region.
- When Roosevelt was asked, "What are you going to say when they ask you the political philosophy behind the TVA?"

  "I'll tell them it's neither fish nor fowl," Roosevelt answered, "but, whatever it is, it will taste awfully good to the people of the Tennessee Valley."

A History of the Tennessee Valley Authority:

"One day in the early 1940s a TVA land buyer was driving on a country road at dusk when he saw the farmer of a newly electrified farm, sitting on a little knoll overlooking his farm. Below him the house, the barn, and smokehouse were ablaze with light. And on the hill sat this farmer enthralled by a special wonder.

About a week later the TVA man attended a church to which this farmer belongs. During the service, the farmer got up to express his spiritual condition: 'Brothers and sisters, I want to tell you this. The greatest thing on earth is to have the love of God in your heart, and the next greatest thing is to have electricity in your house.'"

- By 1939 five hydroelectric facilities were in operation and five others were under construction.
- The TVA and electricity became synonymous to the farmers of the Tennessee Valley; a roadside sign in rural Tennessee read, "Farm for Sale. Have TVA."
- Electricity supplied farmers with pumps, washing machines, and other labor-saving devices; one Mississippi farmer reported that his ability to own a refrigerator in 1936 allowed him to sell butter, cream, and milk, providing an extra $30.00 a month in income.
- Seven of 12 million acres needed erosion control in 1933, and one million acres were eroded to the point of abandonment.
- During the war effort, TVA power was used by the Aluminum Company of America to manufacture aluminum for airplanes and by the secret "Manhattan Project" in Oak Ridge, Tennessee, where the atomic bomb was being developed.

Value of One Dollar	
Year	Value in 2010 USD
1940	$15.58
1942	$13.38
1943	$12.61
1945	$12.12
1947	$9.78

Values are approximate based upon economic historical data and 2010 U. S. Dollar

1940–1949

During the turbulent World War II years, Americans were consumed with the national war effort and recovery. Slow at first to mobilize around the growing threat of war from Germany, Italy, and Japan, America responded forcefully following the bombing of Pearl Harbor in December, 1941. People from every social stratum either signed up for the military or went to work supplying the military machine. Even children, doing their share, collected scrap and helped plant the victory gardens that symbolized America's willingness to do anything to defeat the "bullies." In addition, large amounts of money and food were sent abroad as Americans observed meatless Tuesdays, gas rationing, and other shortages to help the starving children of Europe.

Business worked in partnership with government; strikes were reduced, but key New Deal labor concessions were expanded, including a 40-hour week and time and a half for overtime. As manufacturing demands increased, the labor pool shrank, and wages and union membership rose. Unemployment, which stood as high as 14 percent in 1940, all but disappeared. By 1944 the U.S. was producing twice the total war output of the Axis powers combined. The wartime demand for production workers rose more rapidly than for skilled workers, reducing the wage gap between the two to the lowest level in the twentieth century.

From 1940 to 1945 the gross national product more than doubled, from $100 billion to $211 billion, despite rationing and the unavailability of many consumer goods such as cars, gasoline, and washing machines. Interest rates remained low, and the upward pressure on prices remained high, yet from 1943 to the end of the war the cost of living rose less than 1.5 percent. Following the war, as controls were removed, inflation peaked in 1948; union demands for high wages accelerated. Between 1945 and 1952 confident Americans, and their growing families, increased consumer credit by 800 percent.

To fight inflation, government agencies regulated wages, prices, and the kind of jobs people could take. The Office of Price Administration was entrusted with the complicated task of setting price ceilings for almost all consumer goods and distributing ration books for items in short supply. The Selective Service and the War Manpower Commission largely determined who would serve in the military, whose work was vital to the war effort, and when a worker could transfer from one job to another. When the war ended and regulations were lifted, workers demanded higher wages; the relations between labor and management became strained. Massive strikes and inflation followed in the closing days of the decade and many consumer goods were easier to find on the black market than on the store shelves until America retooled for a peacetime economy.

The decade of the 1940s made America a world power and Americans became worldly. Millions served overseas; millions more listened to broadcasts concerning the war in London, Rome, and Tokyo. Newsreels brought the war home to the moviegoers who numbered in the millions. The war effort also redistributed the population and the demand for labor; the Pacific Coast gained wealth and power, the South was able to supply its people with much-needed war jobs and provide Blacks with opportunities previously closed to them. Women entered the work force in unprecedented numbers, reaching 18 million. The net cash income of the American farmer soared 400 percent.

But the Second World War extracted a price. Those who experienced combat entered a nightmarish world. Both sides possessed far greater firepower than ever before, and within those units actually fighting the enemy, the incidence of death was high, sometimes one in three. In all, the United States lost 405,000 men and women to combat deaths; many suffered in the war's final year, when the American army spearheaded the assault against Germany and Japan. The cost in dollars was $350 billion. But the cost was not only in American lives. Following Germany's unconditional surrender on May 4, 1945, Japan continued fighting. To prevent the loss of thousands of American lives defeating the Japanese, President Truman dropped atomic bombs on the Japanese cities of Hiroshima and Nagasaki, ending the war and ushering in the threat of "the bomb" as a key element of the Cold War during the 1950s and 1960s.

Throughout the war, soldiers from all corners of the nation fought side by side and refined nationalism and what it meant to America through this government-imposed mixing process. This newfound identify of American GIs was further cemented by the vivid descriptions of war correspondent Ernie Pyle, who spent a considerable time talking and living with the average soldier to present a "worm's eye view" of war. Yet, despite the closeness many men and women developed toward their fellow soldiers, spawning a wider view of the world, discrimination continued. African-American servicemen were excluded from the marines, the Coast Guard, and the Army Air Corps. The regular army accepted Blacks into the military—700,000 in all—only on a segregated basis. Only in the closing years of the decade would President Harry Truman lead the way toward a more integrated America by integrating the military.

Sports attendance in the 1940s soared beyond the record levels of the 1920s; in football the T-formation moved in prominence; Joe DiMaggio, Ted Williams, and Stan Musial dominated baseball before and after the war and Jackie Robinson became the first Black in organized baseball. In 1946, Dr. Benjamin Spock's work *The Common Sense Baby and Child Care* book was published to guide newcomers in the booming business of raising babies. The decade also discovered the joys of fully air-conditioned stores for the first time, cellophane wrap, Morton salt, daylight savings time, Dannon yogurt, Everglades National Park, the Cannes Film Festival, Michelin radial tires, Dial soap, and Nikon 35mm film.

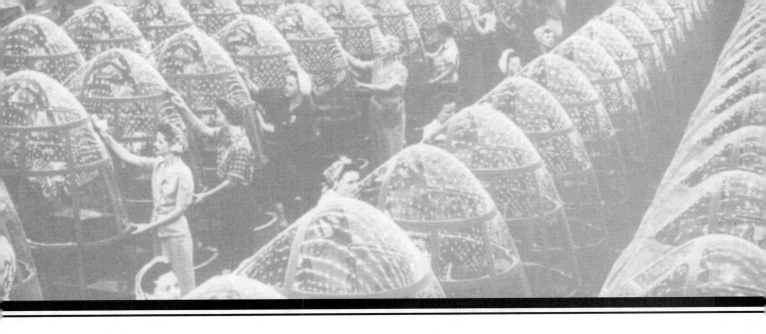

1942 Family Profile

The Fagans, a Wichita Falls, Texas, family of seven, is struggling with the changes brought by the Second World War and the reality that the three boys are now teenagers and eligible for the draft shortly. The man and woman operate a small store which sells groceries, hardware, and soft drinks to the local community. They have five children, three boys and two girls. The children often assist with stocking and manning the counter.

Annual Income: $2,300.00
The couple works together in the store to produce its annual income; this family also have the luxury of using various goods within the store to supplement their diet and lifestyle.

Annual Expenditures

Automobile	$248.00
Clothing	$262.00
Received in Kind	$30.00
Education	$18.00
Food, Direct Expense	$593.00
Food, Received in Kind	$149.00
Furnishings	$142.00
Household Operations	$92.00
Housing, Including Fuel, Light, and Refrigeration	$522.00
Medical Care	$102.00
Other	$26.00
Other Transportation	$43.00
Personal Care	$47.00
Reading	$22.00
Recreation	$85.00
Tobacco	$47.00

Cost of Meals at Home $526.00
Beer $12.15
Food Purchased away from Home $100.00
Whiskey, Gin, Rum $9.92
Coal $17.05
Electricity $38.23
Fuel Oil $9.49
Ice $2.58
Kerosene, Gasoline $3.35
Wood, Kindling $1.76

Life at Home

- Rent is $21.00 a month for the Fagan family, comparatively low for the nation. Elsewhere monthly rent averages $25.86 in Asheville, North Carolina; $31.95 in Boston, Massachusetts; $28.24 in Indianapolis, Indiana; $21.67 in New Orleans, Louisiana; $32.70 in Worcester, Massachusetts.
- Meat is rationed to 28 ounces per person, per week, butter is rationed at four ounces per week, the sale of sliced bread is banned, and flour and canned goods are rationed.
- Shoes are rationed to three pairs a year; new sneakers are not available because of the rubber shortage.
- The family is having its best year since 1928 thanks to a booming economy; a few customers even pay back old debts accumulated during the rough days of the Depression.
- They give $27.00 to the church, $2.50 to the Red Cross, and $5.00 to the Community Chest.
- This family pays $97.45 for life insurance during the year; $28.00 is spent on U.S. Savings Bonds to support the war effort.
- Their federal income tax that year is $6.65; the poll tax, giving them the right to vote in Texas, is $1.00.
- This family does not own any stock and does not receive any dividend income in 1942, similar to 83 percent of the families in the survey.
- The family is concerned about the Revenue Act of 1942, which provides for $7 billion in new individual income taxes, a near doubling of the federal tax burden; by lowering the personal exemption to $624.00, 13 million families will pay taxes for the first time in 1943.
- The demands of the war require that every man from 18 to 65 be registered for the Selective Service; the military prefer men 18 to 26 years old; the boys in the family are 14, 15, and 17 years old.
- The oldest son is already talking about enlisting on his 18th birthday; the 15-year-old has always dreamed about being the first person in his family to go to college and is unsure of how the war will affect his plans.
- Like 20 million American families, the Fagans plant a "victory garden" which accounts for 40 percent of this family's—and the country's—vegetable needs.
- *House and Garden Magazine* devoted its entire January, 1942, issue to "Planning a Defense Garden, how to grow and preserve necessary fruits and vegetables."
- The girls in the family like to read about the Bobby Sox phenomenon in the glamour magazines, but have not gotten the courage to try the turned-down anklet and pleated skirt look.

- Movie theaters often devoted entirely to newsreels of the war are now available in Dallas; in Wichita Falls moviegoers keep abreast of the war through Fox's *MovieTone News,* featuring the resonant voice of Lowell Thomas.
- Movies are extremely popular; weekly attendance nationwide is 80 million, but it is difficult for the family to see a movie and leave the store unattended.
- The boom in movie attendance, *Fortune Magazine* says, is sparked by "more people with more money to spend, and fewer things to spend it on. In addition, the strains and pressures of war are goads that drive millions into movie theaters, where for a little while they can escape reality and relax in comfortable darkness."
- Movie theaters are pioneers in the use of air-conditioning, so they can show movies five times a day, year-round—an important consideration in Texas.
- The family is concerned about a measles epidemic sweeping Texas, and whether the younger children will be infected; in 1941 the nation suffered through a very bad measles outbreak.

Life at Work: The Grocery Store

- The Fagan family operates a small corner grocery that sells vegetables, milk, canned goods, tobacco, and other necessities to the neighborhood. No alcohol is available at the store.
- The couple works the store together, often putting in hours from 7 a.m. to 9 p.m.; the store is often the social gathering point of the community.
- The children often study while standing by the cash register.
- For many years the store has been a gathering place for teenagers and adults who buy "sodas" and candy and talk; the teenagers gather around the Coca-Cola machine, the men around the stove near the back—winter or summer.
- The store also has a radio that plays constantly, attracting customers and keeping the family informed of war news.
- Many radio programs are tied to product promotions such as Pepsi's Radio Thriller, *Counter-Spy;* signs promoting radio programs, tobacco, and medicines cover the walls of the store.

- The night that Joe Louis, the "Brown Bomber," defends his heavyweight boxing title against Buddy Baer, a huge crowd gathers at the store to listen to the fight; although Baer has a weight advantage and nearly 10 inches more in reach, Louis floors him twice before ending the fight two minutes and 56 seconds in the first round.
- The store also sells comic books, including *Archie* and his friends, Walt Disney's *Donald Duck* and *Superman; Captain America* and *Wonder Woman,* both started in 1941, are selling well as American patriotism surges.
- The family once sold pairs of silk stockings to the women of the neighborhood; now that silk is unavailable only rayon stockings are sold.
- Some customers have expressed anger at the couple because of rising prices, saying, "you're getting rich off me"; since the outbreak of fighting in Europe in September, 1939, prices have been rising; in 1942, driven by inflation, prices increase monthly on some items.
- The shortage of stateside cigarettes produces a new joke in Texas, "Give me a pack of stoopies." It is a jab at the practice of storeowners who "stooped" under the counter to retrieve a pack of cigarettes for a favored customer.
- Borden's milk is a popular item thanks to "Elsie the Cow" advertising; in addition to milk, Elsie mugs, cigar bands, jigsaw puzzles, soap, and neckties are available.
- Late in 1942 the Office of Economic Stabilization freezes wages between $5,000 and $25,000, along with food, transportation fares on street cars, trains, and utilities.
- The family owns an automobile for business and pleasure; its use is not yet restricted by war rationing of gasoline which has begun on the East Coast but not in Texas where gasoline is readily available.
- In 1942, Americans own nearly 34 million cars, approximately three-fourths of all cars in the world, an average of one per family.
- Europeans often express surprise that families without homes or jobs own cars.

- To Americans, cars—besides being utilitarian—stand for mobility, individualism, freedom, and prestige, and represent a symbol of themselves they can take everywhere they go.
- The family is still adjusting to "war savings time," the start of daylight savings time, designed to save energy.

Life in the Community: Wichita Falls, Texas

- Wichita Falls has a population of 45,000; 88 percent are White located in northern Texas near the panhandle.
- The people most affected by economic life from the war in 1942 are farmers who are receiving better prices for their goods and the people who live near where military goods are produced.
- Wichita Falls' farm economy almost immediately sees new life thanks to the war effort.
- Only 25 percent of rural people between the ages of 25 and 29 have finished high school, and more than a third of farm people have failed to complete grammar school; in South Carolina 14 percent of Whites and 27 percent of young Blacks have to sign their Selective Service registration forms with a mark.
- The Works Progress Administration determines in 1940 that the "maintenance income for a family of four, which would permit simple food, rather meager clothing, and no telephone" is approximately $1,350.00 a year; nearly 50 percent of all families earn less than $1,500.00 "cash" income in 1941.

"I had quite a time persuading the Smithsonian to give it back to me, as you may imagine."

DRAWING BY CHAS. ADDAMS; © 1970 THE NEW YORKER MAGAZINE, INC.

HISTORICAL SNAPSHOT
1942–1943

- Unemployment nationwide fell to 4.7 percent from its 1933 high of 25.2 percent
- Office of Price Administration was formed to control prices
- A tire-rationing plan commenced; gas rationing began
- Paine, Webber, Jackson, & Curtis was created
- Zinc-coated pennies were issued by the U.S. Mint
- Florida passed California as the leading U.S. producer of oranges
- Kellogg introduced Raisin Bran cereal
- Sunbeam bread was introduced
- Maxwell House instant coffee was included in military K rations
- Dannon yogurt was introduced
- U.S. automobile production was halted until 1945
- Congress approved income-tax withholding from paychecks
- Zenith Radio Corporation introduced a $40.00 hearing aid
- Shoes were rationed to three pairs per year, per person
- The sale of sliced bread was banned
- Sales of Bibles increased 25 percent; religious books grew in popularity
- The sale of women's trousers increased 10 times over the previous year
- Of the vegetables consumed in the United States, 40 percent came from victory gardens; two-thirds of the crop was grown by Japanese-Americans detained in camps
- The motion picture industry produced 80 war movies
- Enrico Fermi secretly accomplished a controlled nuclear fission reaction at the University of Chicago; in a coded message he informed President Franklin D. Roosevelt, "The Italian navigator has entered the new world."
- Reports of the deportation of Jews from Occupied Western Europe reached the United States

1942 Economic Profile

Furnishings

Cleaning Equipment	$6.72
Floor Covering	$16.43
Furniture	$28.62
Glass, China, Silverware	$2.91
Household Linens, Bedding	$19.89
Kitchen Equipment	$37.38
Laundry Equipment	$6.88
Miscellaneous	$16.78
Radio Purchase	$8.03

Annual Clothing Purchases

Men and Boys over 16 Years of Age

Coats, Jackets, Sweaters	$7.57
Dress Shoes	$5.72
Gloves, Handkerchiefs	$6.97
Headwear	$3.20
Hose, Dress Socks	$3.55
Jewelry, Watches	$2.01
Shirts	$6.86
Shoe Shines, Repairs	$1.99
Suits, Trousers, Overalls	$25.56
Underwear, Nightwear, Robes	$5.37
Upkeep, Cleaning, Pressing	$5.64
Work Shoes, Leather Sole	$3.16

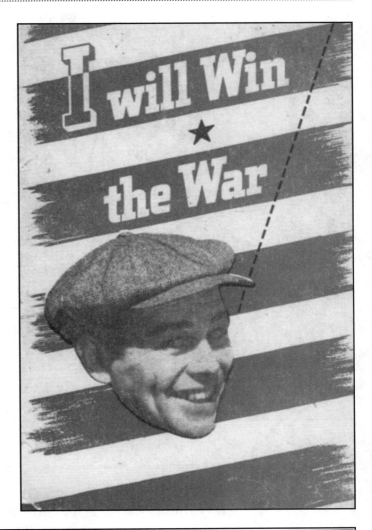

Pamphlet, "I Will Win the War":

"I'm not a soldier, sailor, or marine, but I can do my share toward winning the war. And I'm going to do it, too. I may never get near a battleship or carry a gun into battle, but I can make stuff soldiers need. The government tells me that I'm more important right at my machine than anywhere else.

Believe me, fella, I'm hitting the ball these days. Never knew I could turn out so much work. It's fun, too, for every time my machine turns over, I say to myself, 'Well, there's one more nail in Hitler's coffin and one more piece of bad news for the Nips . . .'

My wife is right on the job doing her share, too. She tells me she used to use paper to start fires in the fireplace, and a lot of paper she just burned up. Well, she saves it all now— every piece of it—newspapers, magazines, boxes, wrapping paper. She bundles it up and about once a month she sells it to the junk man. Buys Defense Stamps with the money. You'd be surprised how quickly you can fill up a book of Defense Stamps when you put your mind to it. We used to waste grease. Now we save it. We figure saving waste means less tax to pay."

Take him to the zoo. Increasing his general interests will make him alert and ready for reading.

Women and Girls over 16 Years of Age

Accessories	$5.34
Bloomers, Panties	$1.23
Coats, Sweaters, Furs	$21.62
Corsets, Girdles	$2.49
Dresses, Suits, Aprons	$22.58
Headwear	$4.70
Home Sewing	$2.54
Hosiery	$10.60
Shoe Shines, Repairs	$0.86
Shoes	$11.27
Slips, Rayon, Silk	$2.54
Underwear, Nightwear	$10.93
Upkeep, Cleanings	$3.95

Income, Standard Jobs

Average of All Industries, Including Farm Labor	$1,778.00
Bituminous Coal Mining	$1,715.00
Building Trades	$2,191.00
Domestics	$706.00
Farm Labor	$769.00
Federal Civilian	$2,265.00

Everywoman's Magazine, "How to Make Your Child Want to Read," by Irma Dovey, May 1945:

"Don't try to make Johnnie a Quiz Kid. But take him to the farm, to the zoo, and to see the trains come in. There must be dozens of interesting things to see within walking distance of your house. And a bus ride is, in itself, an education—besides taking you to the library, to a big department store, to watch workers repairing the pavement, to a building under construction, or to the airport. Certainly, it's hard work, but you wanted to know how to get him ready to read! It isn't all sitting home in the rocking chair, although that is part of it.

You must, of course, read to him. You are doing one of the best things you can to smooth his school-day path. Choose from different fields.

Don't limit yourself to "Uncle Wiggly" and "Dagwood" just because they are convenient. Or to the "Three Pigs" and "Three Bears" because you heard them when you were his age . . . .

Got down to the library and get some new books. You are sick of the old ones and know them by heart, so this will be worth almost as much to you as to him. Try *Wait for William*, or *Angus and the Ducks*, or *The Little Woman Wanted Noise*. Find the fun in *Cinder*, or laugh over the plight of *Mike Mulligan and his Steam Shovel*. There is no use in reading from *Peter Rabbit* every night, when you can read *Ezra, the Elephant* or *Millions of Cats* for a change."

Federal Military $1,485.00
Finance, Insurance, Real Estate $1,885.00
Gas and Electricity Workers $2,040.00
Manufacturing, Durable Goods $2,292.00
Manufacturing, Nondurable
    Goods $1,654.00
Medical/Health Services Workers . . . $1,036.00
Miscellaneous Manufacturing $1,540.00
Motion Picture Services $2,124.00
Nonprofit Organization Workers . . . $1,482.00
Passenger Transportation Workers . . $1,990.00
Personal Services $1,199.00
Public School Teachers $1,512.00
Radio Broadcasting and Television . . $2,667.00
Railroads $2,303.00
State and Local Government
    Workers $1,574.00
Telephone and Telegraph Workers . . $1,715.00
Wholesale and Retail Trade $1,608.00

Selected Prices

Allstate Tractor Tires $35.15
Armours Peanut Butter, 24 Ounce Jar . . . $0.41
Crosley Recording Disks,
    Carton of Five $1.50
Dulux Paint, Enamel, Quart $2.00
Edgewood Handbag $5.00
Jackson and Perkins Rose,
    Climbing $1.50
Kitchen-Aid Mixer $29.95
Man's Winthrop Shoes $9.50
Marshall Fields & Co. Globe, 10 Inch . . . $2.95
Pyrex Casserole Pie Plate,
    One Quart Size $0.50
Randolph Tall Chest $175.00
Russels Prints' Dress,
    Rayon Jersey $21.00
Seagram's King Arthur Gin, Fifth $1.70
Sears Tea Kettle $3.49
Shinola Shoe Polish $0.09
Simmons Beautyrest Mattress $39.50
St. Joseph's Aspirin,
    100 Count Bottle $0.35
The Majestic Home Incinerator $29.95
Theatre Ticket, *Porgy & Bess,*
    New York $2.75
Time Magazine, Weekly $0.10
Underwood New Deluxe
    Typewriter $29.75

A NATION AT WAR

- A poll taken by *Fortune Magazine* a few months before Pearl Harbor indicated that 70 percent were opposed to entering the war, but 67 percent were ready to follow Roosevelt's lead; following the attack on Pearl Harbor, a public opinion poll found that only two percent of Americans disapproved of the declaration of war against Japan.
- Following the December, 1941, attack on Pearl Harbor, fear gripped the nation: in Georgia, convicts were put to work round-the-clock in an effort to improve shoreline approaches and bridges; in Los Angeles, California, an anti-aircraft battery-fired at imaginary warplanes, injuring dozens; in Wisconsin an effort was made to create a guerilla army composed of the state's 25,000 deer hunters.
- In early 1942, Americans tacked black cloth to their windows and waited, expecting an invasion from the air by the Japanese, similar to Pearl Harbor.
- The army placed machine gun emplacements on the roof of the White House; they also proposed painting the White House black to make it less visible from the air; President Roosevelt blocked the plan.

- After the Pearl Harbor bombing, rubber instantly became the most critical strategic material of war; nine-tenths of the nation's rubber came from the Far East.
- Four days after Pearl Harbor a freeze was put on the sale of new passenger car tires, and on December 27 tire rationing was authorized.
- Gas rationing quickly followed; to drive alone and ignore carpooling became unpatriotic.
- Long-distance telephone calls were limited to five minutes because of the war emergency.
- Married men enjoyed a military exemption from the first draft calls, a provision that by one estimate prompted 40 percent of the 21-year-olds caught in the first registration to marry within six weeks.
- During the war, large numbers of women went to work in factories, changing attitudes about women and work; in the mid-1930s, 80 percent of Americans objected to wives working outside the home; by 1942 only 40 percent still disapproved.
- When war was declared, four million Americans were unemployed and 7.5 million others were earning less than the legal minimum wage of $0.40 per hour.
- Nothing short of production marvels swept U.S. industry; Henry J. Kaiser turned out 600 "Liberty Ships" in 1942 using a new section-by-section manufacturing technique.
- That year in Dallas 38,000 fans gathered for the sixth annual Cotton Bowl to watch the Crimson Tide of Alabama roll over the Aggies of Texas A&M; however, the Rose Bowl between Oregon and the Duke Blue Devils was moved from the West Coast to the East Coast out of war fears.

Life Magazine, "Smith Girls, Job Market Opens Wide for College Graduates as War Reduces Manpower," September 28, 1942:

"The employment boom that is sweeping old-sters, youngsters, and mothers of families into jobs left vacant as men go off to war, last spring invaded the nation's colleges, precipitating many a young girl graduate into a juicy job for which she once would have had to labor long and hard. At Smith College, which is known for its excellent placement bureau, the number of jobs available to the class of '42 jumped from 1941's total of 642 to a new high of 1,420. Every girl in the class could have chosen between three or four good openings. And those who did not prefer volunteer war work, marriage, or idleness walked straight from college to job, minus experience or training, bearing only the fruits of their academic years. Whereas $1,200 a year was considered a good starting salary in 1941, this year's candidates av-eraged $1,600 with the promise of speedy raises after a brief training program. Most were hired to replace men who had gone or were about to go to war, and many entered traditionally masculine fields—banking, engineering, accounting, statis-tical, and technical work . . .Smith is now offer-ing a series of 'war minors' to prepare students for fields in which women do the work of men . . . Life then profiled six women; one of the women was Suzanne Cook Vroom (Mrs. William Vroom) of Worchester, Massachusetts. . . .

Mrs. Vroom became a war bride last Febru-ary when she flew to California to marry her fi-ancé just before he sailed for Australia with his company. She became a war widow last month when she received word that her husband had been killed in action. In this personal disaster, the job which she took in July with the Liberty Mutual Insurance Company in Boston served as a bulwark to her courage. She went right on working. Having first enrolled in a training class for claims adjusters at a yearly salary of $1,300 plus a bonus of about $150, she is now working in the field, investigating accidents, and deter-mining where claims for damages are justified."

1942 NEWS PROFILE

Maki Nakano, an American-born woman of Japanese parents, was living in California when the Second World War broke out. She was treated as a foreign enemy and placed in camps during the war along with 40,000 persons of Japanese descent. As Lt. Gen. John L. DeWitt, commander of Western Defense said, "A Jap is a Jap." Under Executive Order 9066, 119,803 Japanese-Americans were removed to temporary camps in barren and isolated areas of six western states and Arkansas. Most were held for at least three years.

"We were living in rural areas of California when war broke out. The summer of '42—that was my summer. That was the year I graduated. But we went to camp in April. Graduation was supposed to be the following June. Pearl Harbor was 1941, and we were evacuated the spring of '42. We didn't finish up the end there.

A storefront in Little Tokyo, Los Angeles. The owners—like thousands of others—had to sell and get out.

Living on the coast you'd have blackout curtains on your windows and all this stuff. And the Japanese had curfews. We had to be off the streets by 9 o'clock, in our houses. The Chinese wore pins, 'I am Chinese.'

It was like a Sunday morning, and it must have been 11 o'-clock when we heard the news. I just dreaded going back to school that Monday. Of course, it was worst the first day, the Monday after Pearl Harbor, 'cause every class you went to discussed it and kids acted just like it was your fault. It wasn't inferred. It was, 'Those damn Japs.' It was all of this, and you were part of it. There were those who included you, that you were responsible, too, because you're Japanese descent, was the feeling we got. It was, 'Oh God, I'm going through the floor.' And there were those that said, 'I'm not speaking to you anymore.' You know, I began to feel so guilty—that I had to take the blame, too, because it was Japan and my parents are from Japan. But there was a tension in the house about Japan too; there was an embargo placed on Japan and there were things happening there politically.

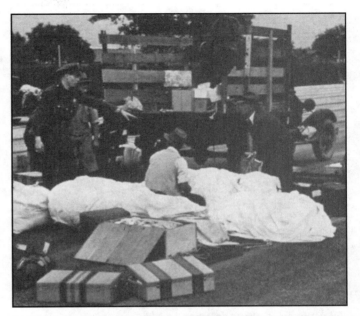

My parents didn't know what was going to hit. Then my father, as an alien, had to get permits to go, I forget what the distance was. He was having trouble making money. My brothers were commuting to this high school and junior high school. Absolute strangers would yell, 'Get the hell to Yokohama! Get the hell off the streets.'

My father had the worst experience. I don't know where he had been, but he was walking. I don't know how far he was from home. A group of people started following him and yelling epithets at him. I don't know what provoked it. He just didn't say a thing and just ignored that mob. I'm sure if he had started yelling at them or said something, they would have attacked him. Maybe it was just some kids, I don't know. So at that time, it was kind of a relief to be sent to camp.

My family didn't sell. They just gave things away. Certain things we stored with the next-door neighbor—this Black family.

My mother had two big kotos, the Japanese instrument that's six feet long. We used to play that very well. She taught us to play it. It's the only thing we wanted, and we never got it back.

The Japanese associations were basically like merchants' associations. They disseminated information about leaving. First, you had to report to get your typhoid shots and all your other shots. And then families were assigned numbers, and we all wore the tag with the family number, and our luggage would have the tag on. That's when we left . . . When you first arrived, you were assigned your barracks. The barracks, the horse stalls, are in rows and you're given numbers . . . They had metal army cots. You all had to report to a certain place where they gave you muslin-like mattress covers and you filled

The Santa Anita Racetrack served as one of the Assembly Centers. Evacuees were ordered to open their baggage for inspection, then were processed by a registrar.

The final destination for evacuees was a camp of crude barracks like this one in Tule Lake, California.

it with straw for your bed. Since we had a large family, we had two stalls. And the stalls were divided because the horse stayed in the back, and there was a front area. So what they did was whitewash the walls and put the linoleum on the floor. My father, mother, and the younger ones were on one side, and my older sister and I and the two older boys on the other.

They were able to build more permanent camps away from the coast, and those of us in that particular area were sent to Utah. I remember leaving in January. We went to the more permanent camp in Topaz, Utah. That was on a desert. The dust storms were awful. There was nothing you could do except get inside, because all that sand would be swirling around and it would filter through the windows. Everything was just covered. And the winters were cold. I worked in Utah as a nurse's aid . . .

My youngest brother was two. He stayed in till he must have been five or six. When he came to Minneapolis, he spoke with the Isseis, who spoke Japanese all the time, so he spoke English with a Japanese accent . . .

When I think of how the whole thing was done—I guess it could happen again, with an executive order, and never mind about taking any rights. There are many people in different parts of the country who are not aware of that whole evacuation, and those who are aware, they thought we were just like our parents who were born in Japan."

1943 FAMILY PROFILE

This Filipino family of four, the Hidalgos, came to Hawaii in the 1930s, a territory of the United States to find work. He works in maintenance helping to rebuild Hickam Field, destroyed during the second wave of the Japanese attack on Pearl Harbor on December 7, 1941. His wife works part-time. They have two children, who are still attending school.

Annual Income

Husband's Income	$450.00
Wife's Income	$148.00
Total	$598.00

Annual Budget

Clothing	$37.90
Food	$124.75
Fuel, Light	$8.89
Furniture and Equipment	$34.50
Housing	$19.32
Liquor	$5.34
Miscellaneous	$8.53
Personal Care	$18.38
Reading	$3.16
Recreation	$21.56
Tobacco	$4.30
Transportation	$18.57
Total	$305.20

Life at Home

- The Hidalgo family, as are all families on Hawaii at this time, is seriously crowded; an average of 1.7 persons per room in the tenant-occupied units in wartime Hawaii is common.

Thousands of sailors on Liberty in Honolulu changed the island forever.

- The average rent is $24.00 a year; only 10 percent of the families pay $40.00 or more. Since most of the families in the survey are full-time residents and have not moved since the war started, their rent is not much higher than in prewar days.
- Of 100 families in the study, over half have five or more members working; two-thirds are 14 years or older.
- Because of labor shortages, employment opportunities have improved for everyone, even persons of Asian extraction.
- Annual income for all families that year is $414.68; Caucasians average $409.37; Hawaiians or part-Hawaiians average $412.10.
- Personal taxes include $96.00, including income taxes of $80.00 and victory tax deductions of $16.00.
- Annual take-home earnings average nearly $20.00 less than total earnings per worker after payroll deductions of approximately $9.00 for war bonds, $6.50 for the victory tax, and additional amounts for social insurance benefits.
- Fifty percent of workers receive less than $150.00 per month in pay after deductions.
- Filipino families average six members as do native Hawaiian families.
- Like many families on the island, the family purchases a radio that year to listen to war developments.
- Due to censorship, the radio broadcasts no longer include the weather report.
- Half of the families on the island, including this one, have telephones in their homes; they share a party-line with four other families.

"The Year in Retrospective," *Paradise of the Pacific* Magazine, December 1942, by LaSelle Gilman:

"The population of the Territory has expanded amazingly; any casual observer on the streets of Honolulu could see that uncounted thousands of soldiers and sailors have arrived. No one expects the Territory ever to return exactly to the conditions that prevailed here before the war."

Large numbers of Japanese-American volunteers became the core of the 442nd Infantry battalion.

- Individual purchases of war bonds and stamps by wage earning and clerical workers is generous, comprising eight percent of their income.
- The price controls created by the OPA (Office of Price Administration) on apparel and shoes are making them more affordable, particularly shoes.
- Ninety percent of meals are eaten at home; only 18 percent of total food costs come from outside the home.

- After 18 months of war, curfews and blackouts are accepted and commonplace.
- War-inflated incomes and larger expenditures, despite higher prices, are resulting in more satisfactory diets and more luxuries.

	Monthly	Yearly
Charcoal	$0.16	$1.92
Gas	$2.07	$24.84
Electricity	$3.50	$42.00
Ice	$0.31	$3.72
Kerosene	$0.52	$6.24
Wood	$0.70	$8.40

	Monthly	Yearly
Domestic Service	$1.54	$18.48
Laundry Sent out	$2.23	$26.76
Other	$0.37	$4.44
Other Cleaning and Kitchen Supplies	$0.75	$9.00
Soap for Household Use	$1.58	$18.96
Stationery, Postage	$0.48	$5.76
Telephone	$1.72	$20.64
Toilet Paper, Paper Towels	$0.74	$8.88
Water Rent	$1.55	$18.60
Total	$10.96	$131.52

- Food rationing is not present at the time of the survey in June, 1943.
- Fresh fish, an important part of the diet in Hawaii, is very scarce in 1943 because of wartime restrictions on fishing.
- Chickens cost $3.00 each; fish, $1.90.
- Rice is often purchased in 100-pound quantities.
- More money is spent on whole milk than any other food item. The usual price is $0.20 per quart; the $1.45 spent each month on milk averages one quart per family, per day.
- Poi, the native Hawaiian substitute for bread and potatoes, is hard to find in 1943, but the family consumes 12 pounds a week, spending $1.50.
- California eggs are $0.15 less per dozen than local eggs because they often have been in cold storage for months or in transit for 10 to 14 days without refrigeration. Local eggs are typically $0.79 per dozen.

- Oranges shipped from California are the most important fruits purchased; they account for half the total expense for fresh fruits. The average purchase is 2.5 dozen per week.
- Other fruits include local papaya and watermelon, mainland plums, pears, lemons, grapefruits, and grapes.
- Canned vegetables and fruits account for 3.5 percent of food expenditures.

Life at Work: Military Support

- The Japanese sneak attack on Pearl Harbor is the worst military disaster in U.S. history; five battleships sunk, three others damaged, 10 smaller warships knocked out, some 2,400 American soldiers killed.
- Hickam Field is bombed by the Japanese during the second wave of the attack on Pearl Harbor; 121 people are killed during the attack, 274 wounded, and 37 missing; the Japanese destroy a total of four B-17s, 12 B-18s, and two A-20 bombers during the raid; all still on the ground.
- The bombers are parked on the apron of the runway with their wingtips just ten feet apart, guarded by soldiers armed with revolvers to repel saboteurs; they are an easy target for an aerial attack.
- When the Japanese attack the island in 1941, 40 percent of the population of Hawaii is the same nationality as the pilots.
- Hickam Field experiences a rapid buildup following the Japanese bombing in December, 1941.
- When the Japanese attack Pearl Harbor, the Army Air Force has 292,000 soldiers and 9,000 planes nationally; when the Japanese surrender in August, 1945, the AFF has enlisted 2.3 million men and women and has 72,000 planes in service.
- Including all services, the United States' war machine goes from producing 5,865 airplanes in 1939 to 96,369 a year in 1944.
- Altogether, 44 percent of all families in Honolulu are gainfully employed during the war in 1943.

Life in the Community: Honolulu, Hawaii

- After the attack on Pearl Harbor, the beaches are ringed with barbed wire.
- The Second World War brings shortages, prosperity, and full employment to Hawaii as many Hawaiians go to work to support the military.
- With the war on, tourism disappears; the Royal Hawaiian Hotel becomes the Rest and Relaxation Annex for Pearl Harbor Submarine-Based Personnel; they pay $0.25 a night for what had been $50.00 suites.
- Home sewing increases during the war, sparking increased sewing machine expenditures and yard goods. Three-quarters of the Honolulu families report purchases of yard goods during the year. Women of Japanese ancestry have a sewing tradition. Also, their small size often makes off-the-shelf purchases difficult.
- Two out of five wage earning and clerical workers in Honolulu have hot and cold running water; the remainder have cold running water. All have electric lights and about three out of four have gas or electric cooking stoves.

- Entertainment during the war includes La Hula Rhumba featuring Bill Lincoln, "a true son of Hawaii" costing $3.50 per person to dine and dance.
- Electricity costs are lower than normal because of blackout restrictions; in semitropical Honolulu artificial heat is not necessary in any season.
- Wood and charcoal are purchased by the Japanese families primarily for use in heating water for their outdoor baths.
- Food supplements such as vitamin and mineral concentrates and cod-liver oil represent $0.22 of the budget.
- Meals eaten at restaurants, cafeterias, and fountains cost an average of $0.56 per person.

La Hula Rhumba

"The Smartest Club in Town"

GOOD FUN, Hawaiian style, that the Islands knew before the war, has been recaptured at LA HULA RHUMBA. . . . The need for such fun was recognized by the management, who had the courage to pioneer, and establish Hawaii's first wartime night club. Here you will find distinctive atmosphere, excellent food and the superb music of Ray Andrade and his orchestra. We must work to win . . . but relaxation is essential, too . . . and at La Hula Rhumba you can have the kind of good time that builds up the morale!

744 LUNALILO STREET
PHONE 2788
For Reservations

- Food prepared in the home costs an average of $0.27 per person.
- Sport clothes are more popular in Honolulu than in most mainland cities.
- Furniture shipments to Hawaii have been severely limited to conserve shipping space. The rattan furniture that was so popular in pre-war days has been off the market since the fall of the Philippines.
- Since the turn of the century, island plantations need additional labor, importing Japanese to the island, making them the biggest single group of plantation workers.
- During the early part of the century Portuguese workers arrived, as well as African-American labor.

Shoal of Time, by Gavan Daws:

"As if to rub salt in the racial wound, Commanding General Delos C. Emmons of the Hawaiian War Department approved the formation of a Businessmen's Military Training Corps, a whole- and part-Hawaiian group organized to 'watch the local Japanese.' Once again the loyalty of the heart had to be shown in day-to-day life. A hundred and fifty of the dismissed (Japanese) guardsmen, almost all of them university students or graduates, went to work as laborers for the United States Army Corps of Engineers. They called themselves the Varsity Victory Volunteers, and for $90.00 a month they helped to dig ditches, lay roads, and string barbed wire. In peacetime this work would have been beneath a nisei university graduate; it was exactly the sort of thing the Japanese wanted to leave behind on the plantations but the volunteers had to make their own racial point, that race and loyalty were separate things. They and other young Japanese began talking of themselves not as nisei, but as Americans of Japanese Ancestry, AJAs."

- Filipino workers arrived in the 1920s and by 1932, more than 100,000 Filipinos had been brought to the island.
- The Filipinos, like many ethnic groups, divide themselves into divisions known as Tagalog, Visayan, and Ilocano.
- The Chinese immigrants have two major groups, the Punti and the Hakka, who often do not speak to the other.
- The first statehood bill for Hawaii was introduced in 1919 by Prince Jonah Kuhio Kalanianaole, the island's delegate to Congress; it failed to pass.
- Another attempt was made in the 1930s, but a sensational murder trial obscured the statehood debate and it, too, failed.
- The presence of a large number of Japanese workers on the island was considered a roadblock to statehood in 1935.
- Following the bombing of Pearl Harbor by the Japanese in 1941, intense debate rages concerning the loyalty of the 160,000 Japanese civilians, 40 percent of the population of the territory.
- During the course of the war, almost 1,500 Japanese Hawaiians are interned; about 37 percent are already U.S. citizens.
- Twelve Japanese newspapers and three magazines are shut down; loyalty boards exist on every island to observe and question Japanese residents.
- Japanese aliens living near military bases are required to move to other locations; most Japanese are required to turn in cameras, guns, and anything else the government judges useful for espionage or sabotage.
- Persons accused of crimes who are brought to the military provost court get swift action, normally in 30 minutes—often an order to buy war bonds or donate a pint of blood to the blood bank.

Population of Honolulu in the 1940 census. 179,326

Japanese	34 percent
Caucasians	28 percent
Hawaiians or part-Hawaiians	17 percent
Chinese	12 percent
Filipinos	8 percent

HISTORICAL SNAPSHOT
1943–1944

- President Roosevelt's $109 billion federal budget earmarked $100 billion for the war effort

- Rent controls were imposed nationwide

- The American Broadcasting Company (ABC) was created by Lifesavers millionaire Edward Noble

- Meat rationing was set at 28 ounces per week; meat production rose 50 percent

- The sale of sliced bread was banned

- Russell Marker pioneered the oral contraceptive, Syntex S.A.

- The first automatic, general purpose digital computer was completed at Harvard

- The Federal Highway Act established the interstate highway system

- War was costing the U.S. $250 million per day

- The GI Bill of Rights was enacted to finance college education for veterans; four percent home loans were available with no down payment

- U.S. soybean production rose as new uses were found for beans

- U.S. grocers tested self-service meat markets

- Gasoline averaged $0.21 per gallon

- The American Jewish Congress reported that over three million Jews had been killed by the Nazis

- The paper shortage limited Christmas cards; women recycled their brown grocery bags

- *Amos 'n' Andy* was canceled after 15 years and 4,000 consecutive radio shows

- During a War Bond rally at Gimbels' basement in New York City, Jack Benny's $75.00 violin was bought for $1 million by Julius Klorten, president of Garcia Grande cigars

- Uncle Ben's converted rice appeared

1943 ECONOMIC PROFILE

Examples of Annual Clothing Purchases

Woman: Total $29.71

Bathing Suit $0.75
Brassieres $1.94
Cotton Dress $4.81
Jewelry and Watches $12.20
Kimonos or Holokus $0.24
Rayon Hose $6.24
Silk Blouse $2.76
Sunsuits and Shorts $0.77

Income, Standard Jobs

Average of All Industries,
    Including Farm Labor $2,181.00
Bituminous Coal Mining $2,115.00
Building Trades $2,503.00
Domestics $919.00
Farm Labor $1,002.00
Federal Civilian $2,628.00
Federal Military $1,565.00
Gas and Electricity Workers $2,284.00
Manufacturing, Durable Goods $2,619.00
Manufacturing, Nondurable
    Goods $1,895.00
Medical/Health Services Workers . . . $1,127.00
Motion Picture Services $2,250.00
Nonprofit Organization Workers . . . $1,679.00
Passenger Transportation
    Workers $2,280.00
Personal Services $1,386.00
Public School Teachers $1,608.00
Radio Broadcasting Workers $2,929.00
Railroads $2,585.00
State and Local Government
    Workers $1,687.00
Telephone and Telegraph
    Workers $1,878.00
Wholesale and Retail Trade
    Workers $1,781.00

U.S. Battleship Pennsylvania.

Selected Prices

Arrow White Man's Shirt $2.75
Bayer Aspirin, Bottle $0.59
Berleley Razor Blades, 18 to a Box $0.25
Carole Brassiere $0.59
Carson, Pirie Scott & Co. Dress $7.95

Dulux Paint, Quart $2.00
Eastman Brownie Camera. $2.56
Fleece Diapers $1.79
Fleet's Lip Balm $0.25
Iron Jack Plane $3.98
Milk of Magnesia, Gallon. $0.61
Oldsmobile Custom Convertible. . . . $1,450.00
Pillsbury Flour, 24-Pound Bag $1.09
Seagram's Blended Whiskey, Fifth. $2.70
Towncraft Shoes $4.79
Underwood Deluxe Typewriter $29.75
Vims Vitamins, 24 Tablets $1.69
Sunbeam MixMaster,
   West of Denver $24.50
Westclox Country Club Alarm Clock. . . . $3.45
Whitman's Sampler Chocolates $1.00

Wartime Events

- The Office of Price Administration set up at Lihue, Kauai, the territory's first local war price and rationing board.
- The territorial office of food control asked Hawaii's cooperation in observing a "roastless and steakless" two weeks in order to equalize the territory's civilian meat supply.
- Because of Honolulu's acute housing shortage, the 85 duplex houses of the Palolo evacuation center were turned over to the Hawaii Housing Authority for rent to Oahu families.

Frank Platt was working for an elevator company in Louisville, Kentucky, when the war started. It immediately went out of business so he went to work for the America Air Filter Company, which was building carburetor filters for aircraft:

"Building carburetor filters suddenly became a booming business, particularly after we got involved in desert areas, where aircraft just didn't last any time because of the sand and grit. There was a big demand for filters. The major problem in our plant was the manpower, or lack of manpower. As a result, in my plant we converted about 90 percent to women. That did create some problems, because the plant wasn't designed to cope with it facility-wise, and certainly the men working there were not used to working with women. We ran a 24-hour, seven-day-a-week operation, and as superintendent, I would try to cover at least a part of all three shifts and would spend a good many Saturday nights bailing someone out of jail. We took a lot of young fellows in there who were just below the draft age, and a lot of them came out of the hills of Kentucky, had never been in a big city before. As a result, they kind of went wild. They made money that they had never had, and they were on the loose. From time to time we had some troubles in the plant, too, with the girls, but nothing of a real serious nature."

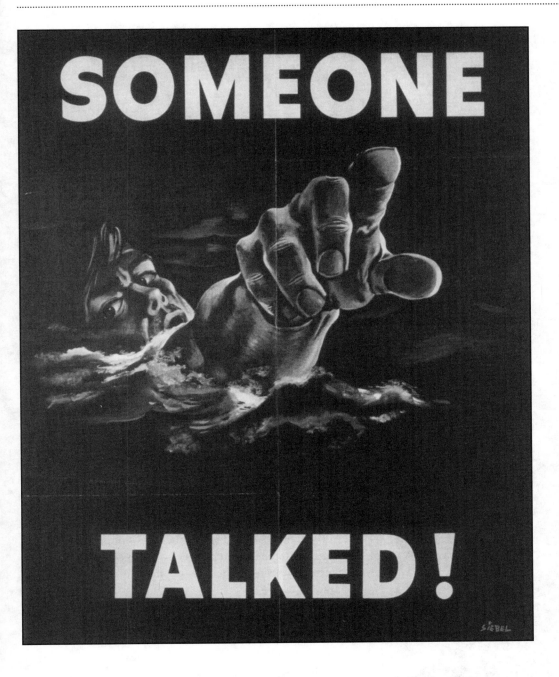

- The territory instituted "pay as you go" income tax under which all residents started paying a "withholding tax" of two percent of all personal income and dividends.
- About 2,400 persons of Japanese descent in the Hawaiian territory filed petitions to ask permission to Anglicize their names. The record number of decrees in 1942 totaled more than all name changes in the past eight years combined.
- A petition on behalf of 5,000 Koreans in Hawaii seeking to have their status changed from "enemy" to "friendly alien" was filed.
- More than 1,700 Hawaiian residents of Japanese ancestry presented a check to the United States government with the request that the money be used for "bombs on Tokyo" as an expression of their horror and condemnation of Japan's recent cold-blooded murder of American fliers who were prisoners of war.

USS Pennsylvania.

- Blackout schedule in 1943, Honolulu: 8 p.m. to 6 p.m.; drug stores, food stores, and barber shops in Honolulu, approved to remain open until 10 p.m., provided dim-out lighting was used.
- Blackout regulations were relaxed to allow lights in homes up to 10 p.m. nightly, except in rooms from which the sea could be seen.
- The Royal Hawaiian Band started giving evening public concerts with controlled lights in Honolulu's parks, the first evening programs since the war began.
- 2,500 pounds of Hawaiian rubber was shipped to the mainland, the first shipment of locally produced and processed rubber, thanks to experimental processing developed on Oahu.
- Honolulu businessman John A. Balch distributed a pamphlet proposing that "at least 100,000 Japanese be removed from Hawaii to the mainland." The pamphlet was entitled "Shall the Japanese Be Allowed to Dominate Hawaii?"
- The White House restored certain government functions to Hawaii in 1943, which had been controlled by the army since the bombing of Pearl Harbor in December, 1941.

1945 FAMILY PROFILE

This sergeant in the Army Air Corps, Stanley Howze, had been in the military three years when he was assigned to Kirtland Field, Albuquerque, New Mexico. He had recently married a woman, Carolyn Wells, from Mount Holly, North Carolina, where she returned following their honeymoon and lives with her parents. They met prior to the war and his enlistment.

Annual Income: $1,368

As a first sergeant, Stanley is paid $114.00 per month; his food, most of his clothing, and all housing are furnished by the military. No information is available concerning his expenditures except that he sends $40.00 a month to his new bride.

National Consumer Expenditures

Auto Parts	$5.00
Auto Usage	$29.30
Clothing	$93.62
Dentists	$4.29
Food	$290.15
Furniture	$10.72
Gas and Oil	$12.86
Health Insurance	$2.86
Housing	$91.48
Intercity Transport	$7.86
Local Transport	$12.15
Personal Business	$29.30
Personal Care	$14.29
Physicians	$10.01
Private Education and Research	$7.15
Recreation	$43.59

Relation/Welfare Activities $12.86
Telephone and Telegraph $8.58
Tobacco $20.72
Utilities $32.16
Per Capita Consumer $854.73

Life at Home

- The couple has known each other for several years before they are married in 1944 on Pearl Harbor Day, December 7.
- They met in Charlotte, North Carolina, when she worked as a clerk for the Pacific and Northern Railway and he was attending King's Business College in Charlotte, probably in 1941.
- He enlists in 1942 in the newly formed Army Air Corps.
- They write often while he is away; they are married at Mount Holly Presbyterian Church, Mount Holly, North Carolina.
- He has been stationed at Kirtland Field, Albuquerque, New Mexico, since 1943 and she visits several times.
- Now married, she still works for the Pacific and Northern Railroad and lives with her parents, planning to return out West.

Mabel Wiggins in St. Paul, Minnesota, recalls:

"The fellows were so nice. Whenever anyone came back on leave to be transferred someplace else, they'd put in long-distance calls to all the wives. I was awakened so many times at three o'clock in the morning—my 'W' was down on the list—and someone would say, 'I had dinner with Russell two nights ago, and he's just fine.'

One day the telephone rang, and the operator was so gay. She said, 'Mrs. Wiggins, where are you,' and I said, 'What do you mean, where am I?' She said, 'Are you sitting down?' She wanted to tell me my husband was calling from the East Coast, that he'd arrived; they had such times, she said, with people who'd faint. And they used to have an older man who had such understanding and sensitivity deliver the death notices, the telegrams. They couldn't do it over the telephone, because people just fell apart."

- Movies they attend "together" while living apart include *God Is My Co-Pilot* and *They Were Expendable,* the tale of a PT boat squadron in the Philippines, outnumbered and outgunned, starring John Wayne and Robert Montgomery.
- Because of war shortages, the wedding presents do not include a toaster, which along with refrigerators and cars, is unavailable because all manufacturing resources are devoted to war materials.
- The couple is excited by the benefits of the GI Bill, which encourages veterans to go out and get a mortgage and an education—both of which will spawn the post-war suburban boom.
- Carolyn is saving money for another train trip to New Mexico; airline travel is considered too expensive and too experimental; all pilots, including airline pilots, are still considered "daredevils."
- The railroads dominate transportation and carry nearly a half-billion passengers.
- She is still finding some food shortages such as sugar and oils, but generally prices are stable in the closing days of the war.
- Rationing still exists for many products.
- Fresh fruits such as apples and oranges are too expensive to buy; bananas are not available at all, and most meat is high, as are eggs.
- Carolyn's parents own a small farm so she has created a vegetable-laden victory garden full of tomatoes, corn, squash, and okra; the farm's chickens also provide sufficient eggs and meat.
- Coffee is available sporadically in North Carolina, but is often expensive; returning to New Mexico is more important than a morning cup of coffee to this woman.
- She is learning to drive on roads outside the farm; rural North Carolina has only two-lane roads, no four-lane highways exist and the speed limit on most roads is between 35 and 45 miles per hour.
- Thirty percent of all cigarette production is set aside for the armed forces, making smokes scarce; gasoline rationing permits only three gallons of gas a week per family.
- In the first five months after Pearl Harbor an estimated 1,000 women a day marry servicemen; the old taboos of class, family consent, and lengthy courtship are swept aside.
- Most courtships and marriages are carried on long distance; many spend their entire $21.00 a month in private's pay on long-distance calls.
- Marriage alone does not warrant deferment from the military, though many young men assume it will; J.R. Woods and Sons, one of the largest manufacturers of wedding rings, reports a 250 percent increase in sales after the Selective Service Act is approved.
- An advertisement for Wrigley's Spearmint chewing gum reads, "Millions working for Victory have found chewing gum is a real help on the job. The makers of Wrigley's Spearmint Gum are trying hard to supply everybody. So please buy only what you need . . . and chew each stick longer. The flavor lasts!"

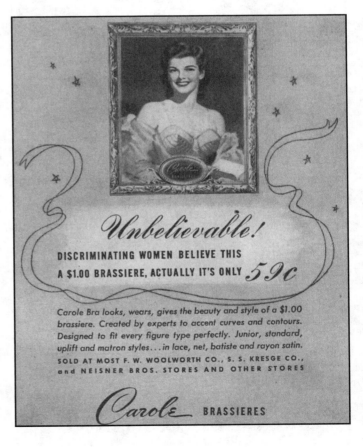

"I need a couple guys what don't owe me no money fer a little routine patrol."

Life at Work: Military

- Once Stanley reaches Kirtland Field he is told that a pre-existing medical condition prevents him from being shipped overseas; he is given desk duty as a clerk.
- In his new world, chow means food, on the double means hurry, and SOS is the acronym for chipped beef and gravy served to him on toast at six every morning. (The "O" and "S" stood for " . . . on a shingle.")
- This soldier feels right at home among the country music and raucous barracks language; the only reading material permitted during the first six weeks of training is the Bible, but novels and comics are now permitted.
- Among this soldier's prized possessions is a deck of Venga Girl playing cards, cellulose-coated and moisture-resistant decks of playing cards depicting long-legged women in tight clothing. The deck costs $1.00.
- Soldiers overseas or at Kirtland Field love the work of America's 23-year-old soldier-cartoonist Bill Mauldin, which features the life of a pair of grizzled grunts named Willie and Joe.
- The base regularly stages dinner-dances for the soldiers; this soldier and his soon-to-be wife attend a dance at the Alvarado Hotel starting at 7:30; the invitation says, "Brother! We ain't a' whistlin' Dixie when we say you'll be sorry if you miss this one."
- Movies are an important form of entertainment; nationally the motion-picture attendance will reach an all-time high in 1945–46; a double feature with cartoons costs $0.30 off base, free on base.
- During the day, the soldier from North Carolina often passes his spare time bowling, an activity of little note in his native North Carolina.
- In training camp, this man—like all soldiers—gives up his civilian identity for a rank and a serial number and focuses on marching in cadence of 128 steps per minute, memorizing the manual of arms, and enduring the drudgery of kitchen police.
- Recruits no longer train with make-believe guns and tanks, as they had early in the war; the highly efficient war machine is producing enough weapons for combat and training.
- In all, 10 million men are ordered to report for induction during the Second World War.
- The minimum height for draftees is five feet and the minimum weight 105 pounds; selectees have to have correctable vision and at least half of their natural teeth.

Life in the Community: Kirtland Field, Albuquerque, New Mexico

- Kirtland Field is activated in 1941 with the arrival of approximately 500 officers and enlisted men comprising the

Third Air Base Squadron, the Seventh Materiel Squadron, and the Headquarters and Headquarters Squadron.

- These united squadrons make up the Fourth Air Base Group and are supplemented by the 19th Bombardment Group.
- The 19th Bombardment Group leaves Kirtland on September 27, 1941, and arrives in the Hawaiian Islands on the morning of the Japanese attack on Pearl Harbor.
- Kirtland becomes the first permanent bombardier training school on December 15, 1941, eight days after the bombing of Pearl Harbor.
- Kirtland Field's primary advantage as a bombardier training sight is the ability to carry on flight missions throughout the year.
- Graduates of Kirtland Field's first few classes are assigned to newly activated bombardier schools as instructors.
- Church services available on the base include Catholic mass from 9 a.m. to 1 p.m.; Protestant services on Thursdays at 7:30 p.m., Sundays at 10 a.m. and Sundays at 6 p.m. for evening vesper service; Jewish reform services are held on Fridays at 7:45 p.m. at Temple Albert, downtown; Jewish Conservative services are held at 8 p.m. Fridays at Congregation B'nai Israel, downtown, or Orthodox services at 8 p.m. Fridays by Rabbi Spiro, of Congregation B'nai Israel, who "may be reached at the Elks Club or through the chaplain's office."
- Stanley was raised a Southern Baptist and attends the Protestant church on Sundays, but often finds the services confusing because Presbyterian, Episcopalian, and Baptist ministers rotate performing Sunday morning services.

Country Gentleman Magazine, "The Kilowatts Take Over," by Hickman Powell, April 1946:

"Our electric rate is so cheap that my wife never complains about paying the entire bill out of her house money, even though we hooked the barn, pumped water for more and more cattle, put in the milker, the cooler, and lot of other things. So I never paid much attention to just how much juice we were using, until last night, I asked her to get out the back bills for a checkup.

Nine years ago, when she was putting the oil lamps away in the attic and I was still complaining about the company's minimum rate, we would just have laughed at anyone who predicted that this year we would be averaging more than 500 kilowatt hours a month. But that was the fantastic tale the bills told. The quiet little kWh had just sneaked up on us...Out of all the reports, plans, prognostications, and statistics, one simple, violent fact stands out: American farmers are using four times as much REA (Rural Electric Authority) power as they did in 1941. REA consumers used as many kilowatt hours in the last three months as they did in a year before Pearl Harbor."

Home Front, by Robert Heide, a second-generation German living in Irvington, New Jersey, during the war:

"My brother Walter, who turned 18 during the war, joined the Army Air Force to become a tail-gunner on a bomber that flew many dangerous missions over Italy and Germany. Cousin Sonny became an army paratrooper and later joined the navy full-time and another cousin, Teddy, went into the infantry.

For the war's duration we kept a small banner in our front window for my brother. A blue star against a white satin background framed in a red felt border showed the world and passersby that our house like many houses had a son—or daughter for that matter—on active duty in the service. Some banners had more than one blue star on a field of white; and if a serviceman lost his life in battle, a banner with a gold star was hung in the window, a symbol of the utmost sacrifice.

During the war my father, who had previously been a tool-and-dye-maker, contracted to do defense work for the Singer Company (manufacturers of sewing machines) in Elizabeth, New Jersey. My sister Evelyn worked part-time after high school at Uncle Fred's new stainless steel diner situated next to a gas station in the Vailsburg section of Newark. Following her job as a part-time diner-girl-waitress and after graduating from Frank Morell High School, Evelyn decided to accept an office position at the Prudential Insurance Company in downtown Newark. There she purchased savings bonds and a hope chest, and began making her own suits and dresses on her Singer sewing machine from send-away fashion magazine patterns."

Service stars were displayed representing each family member who had joined the military. A gold star replaced the blue star when someone in the family was killed in action.

- The May Act of 1941 allows local communities to shut down brothels near military installations; by 1944 some 700 municipalities have closed their red-light districts.
- At the same time 3,000 USO—United Service Organization—centers are opened so a GI can enjoy a clublike atmosphere and find a date for the Saturday-night dance.
- On Broadway, Richard Rodgers and Oscar Hammerstein II's play, *Oklahoma!*, opens in 1943, and is still going strong; considered one of the most sought-after tickets in New York, seats cost as much as $12.00 each.

HISTORICAL SNAPSHOT
1945

- President Franklin Delano Roosevelt died in office; Harry Truman became president
- World War II ended
- Penicillin was introduced commercially
- Approximately 98 million Americans went to the movies each week
- The Beechcraft Bonanza two-engine private plane was introduced
- The U.S. Gross National Product was $211 billion, double the GNP of 1928
- Ballpoint pens, costing $12.50 each, went on sale
- Weed killer, 2,4-D was patented
- About one million Americans suffered from malaria
- Tupperware Corporation was formed
- Strikes idled 4.6 million workers, the worst stoppage since 1919
- The Dow Jones Industrial Average peaked at a post-1929 high of 212.50
- Wage and price controls ended on all areas except rents, sugar, and rice
- U.S. college enrollments reached an all-time high of more than 2 million
- Ektachrome color film was introduced by Kodak Company
- Tide Detergent was introduced; by 1949 one in four laundry detergent consumers would use it
- Timex watches were introduced at $6.95 and up
- Hunt Foods established "price at time of shipment" contracts with customers
- The U.S. birth rate soared to 3.4 million, up from 2.9 million in the previous year
- Superglue and coats for lapdogs were introduced
- New York State forbade discrimination by employers, employment agencies and labor unions on the basis of race, the first time in American history a legislative body enacted a bill outlawing discrimination based on race, creed, or color.
- President Harry Truman declared May 13, 1945, Mother's Day
- The Boy Scouts collected 10 million pounds of rubber and more than 370 million pounds of scrap metal during the war; the children of Chicago collected 18,000 tons of newspapers in just five months
- War shortages forced book printers to use thin, poor-quality paper for books in the closing days of the war; Ernie Pyle's *Brave Men*, a celebration of military heroism, sold more than a million copies; Richard Wright's *Black Boy*, a memoir of Black life, sold 540,000 copies
- An RCA 10-inch television set sold for $374.00

1945 ECONOMIC PROFILE

Income, Standard Jobs

Average of All Industries,
    Including Farm Labor $2,364.00
Bituminous Coal Mining. $2,629.00
Building Trades $2,600.00
Domestics $1,312.00
Farm Labor $1,307.00
Federal Civilian $2,646.00
Federal Military. $1,931.00
Gas and Electricity Workers $2,596.00
Manufacturing, Durable Goods $2,732.00
Manufacturing, Nondurable goods $2,211.00
Motion Picture Services. $2,567.00
Nonprofit Organization Workers $1,876.00
Personal Services $1,725.00
Public School Teachers $1,822.00
Radio Broadcasting and Television. $3,515.00
Railroads. $2,711.00
State and Local Government Workers $1,938.00
Telephone and Telegraph Workers $2,246.00
Wholesale and Retail Trade Workers $2,114.00

***Democracy in Jonesville*, by W. Lloyd Warner, describing a typical send-off of recruits in a small town:**

"At 6:30 a crowd of people gathered outside a local café where the selectees were having their breakfast and receiving final instructions. Outside, the high school band would fall into position and next a color guard from the American Legion. As the boys came to the door of the café, they lined up and the head of the draft board called 'Forward march.' They marched down Liberty Street to the railroad station where a large crowd had gathered. Everywhere little groups of people surrounded the individuals about to leave.

As the train would come around the curve from the west the conversation would pick up tensely and the band begin to play. Hurried kisses, embraces, and handshakes from relatives and friends. One by one the boys shook hands with the draft board and climbed onto the train. The train pulled out and the buzz of excitement in the crowd was drowned out by the band playing the "Marine Hymn." Within a minute or two the station became deserted except for the two men loading mail onto a truck. Jonesville had made another contribution to the war."

Selected Prices

Airline Ticket, California to
Chicago $75.00
Burpee Marigold Seeds, Package $0.10
Child's Honeysuckle Dress $1.80
Dixie Belle Gin, Fifth $3.12
English Antique Grandfather
Clock $375.00
Falcon Magni Vue Camera $9.95
Faucet Queen $0.39
Food Chopper, Double Action $2.98
Harvel Wristwatch $47.50
Johnson's Electric Floor Polisher $44.50
Kenmore A. Washer $119.95
Men's Goldblatt's Shorts,
Boxer Style $1.94
Nabisco Honey Grahams Cereal,
Large Box $0.27
Nash Ambassador Custom
Cariolet Car $2,345.00
Noxema Night Cream, Big Jar $0.59
Ouija Board Game $1.59
Pepsi-Cola Bottled Drink $0.05
Ronay Calf Purse $11.00
Silvertone Commentator Radio $11.75
Silvertone Harmonica $1.79
Sunbabe Doll, Drinks and Wets $1.98
Toni Home Permanent Kit $1.40
Walgreen's Mineral Oil, Pint. $0.05
Women's Calderon Belt. $4.00

I'LL - B - C - N - U

Military men collected postcards depicting the elimination of the enemy, as well as of everyday life.

U. S. Sailors Life "Washday"

The War

- By 1945 the war was drawing to a close, but the price of victory was high: 253,573 dead, 651,042 wounded, 114,204 prisoners, 65,834 missing.
- After Pearl Harbor the United States Army grew from 300,000 men to 1.5 million in two years; Chief of Staff General George Marshall described the 1941 army as having "the status of that of a third-rate power."
- The army reflected America's changes in the past 25 years following severe restrictions on European immigration; 91 percent of Americans were native-born according to the 1940 census.
- The 961,000 Black men who entered the service faced strict racial segregation throughout most of the war; in training camps African-Americans had separate eating and recreational facilities; army units were segregated by race, and no Black officer could outrank a White one.
- The army, with the support of the American Red Cross, segregated the blood plasma donated by Blacks and Whites; ironically the man who perfected the method of preserving plasma, Dr. Charles R. Drew, was himself Black.
- Since the start of the war, five million women found jobs in areas previously closed to them or once held by men now in the military; at the height of war production, 3.5 million women worked on assembly lines alongside six million men.

1944 Christmas Menu

General Mess

Kirtland Field   Albuquerque, N. M.

- To meet the labor shortage, the federal government lowered the age limit for the employment of women from 18 to 16 years.
- Within weeks after V-J Day, in 1945, most of the women were released from their wartime jobs; a United Auto Workers Women's Bureau survey of one shipyard showed 98 percent wanted to keep working.

WORKING AMERICANS 1880–2012 VOLUME I: THE WORKING CLASS

"In Gottes Eigenem Land" (In God's Own Country), Nazi propaganda article describing life in the United States:

"The American woman is a disaster. While the European woman complements the man, the American woman wants to be equal, or even superior, to him—both being unnatural and senseless. She plays fast and loose with her married life; on the average, gets two to seven divorces and . . . at age 40, her nerves are shot and she winds up in a bridge club or a religious group."

- A 1945 survey found that 57 percent of American women and 63 percent of men believed that if the man of the house could support his family, his wife should not be allowed to work, regardless of her wishes.
- Prisoners of war held in America in 1945 included 378,898 Germans, 51,455 Italians, and 5,435 Japanese.
- By war's end, Americans had purchased $150 billion in war bonds.
- American soldiers purchased three million bottles of perfume in France as gifts to loved ones, double the number of total bottles imported from France to the United States prior to the war.

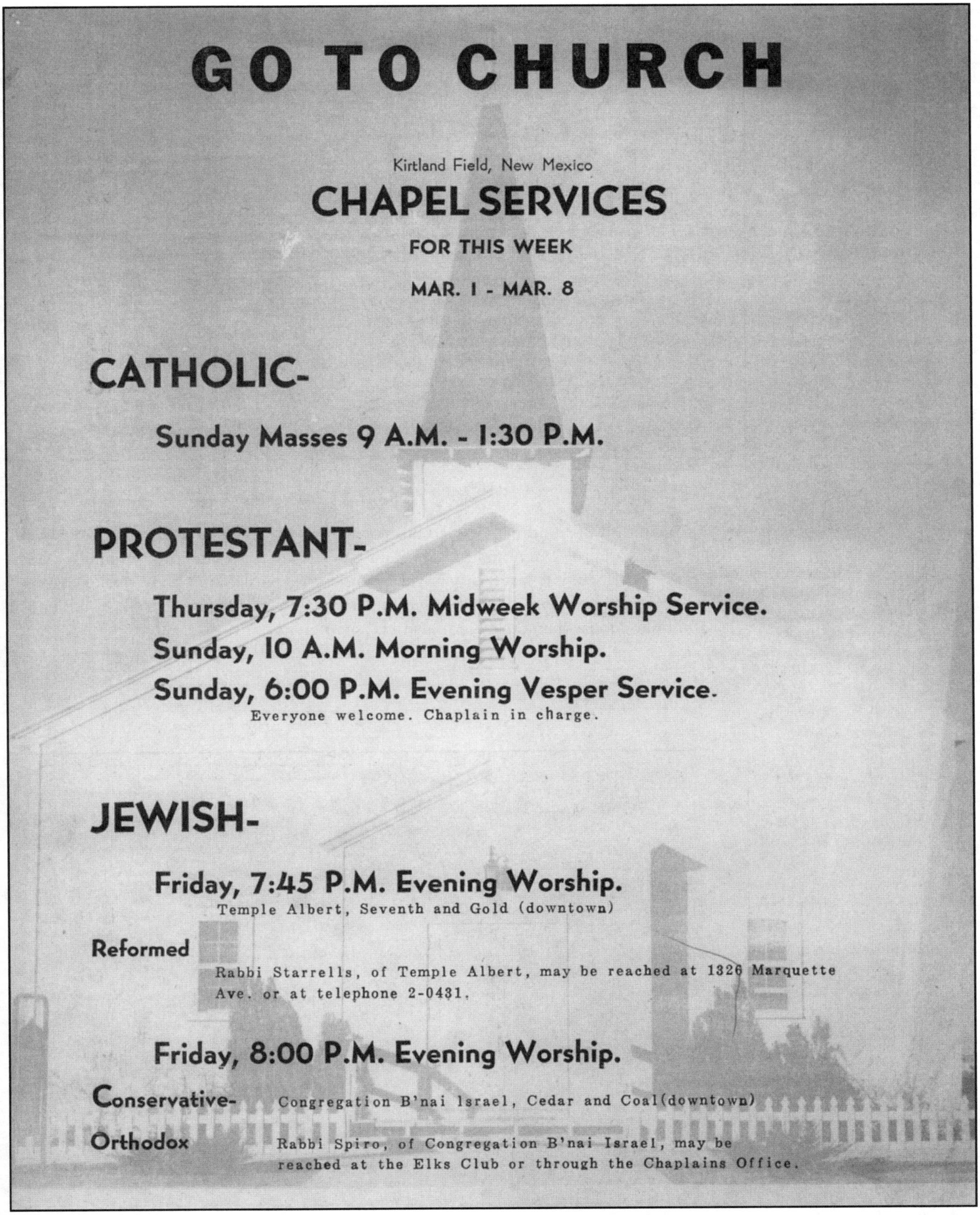

GO TO CHURCH

Kirtland Field, New Mexico

CHAPEL SERVICES

FOR THIS WEEK

MAR. 1 - MAR. 8

CATHOLIC-

Sunday Masses 9 A.M. - 1:30 P.M.

PROTESTANT-

Thursday, 7:30 P.M. Midweek Worship Service.

Sunday, 10 A.M. Morning Worship.

Sunday, 6:00 P.M. Evening Vesper Service.

Everyone welcome. Chaplain in charge.

JEWISH-

Friday, 7:45 P.M. Evening Worship.

Temple Albert, Seventh and Gold (downtown)

Reformed

Rabbi Starrells, of Temple Albert, may be reached at 1326 Marquette Ave. or at telephone 2-0431.

Friday, 8:00 P.M. Evening Worship.

Conservative- Congregation B'nai Israel, Cedar and Coal (downtown)

Orthodox Rabbi Spiro, of Congregation B'nai Israel, may be reached at the Elks Club or through the Chaplains Office.

- The liberation of hundreds of German concentration camps in 1945 exposed Hitler's war-time work: the extermination of six million Jews and five million communists, democrats, clergymen, intellectuals, Jehovah's Witnesses, Gypsies, and homosexuals.
- The American war expenditures from mid-1940 to V-E day came to $276 billion, or $104 billion more than the government had spent in its entire history.

1947 NEWS PROFILE

In 1945, this 17-year-old woman became a switchboard operator in Dublin, Georgia, where she joined the Communications Workers of America (CWA). Here she describes her life and first labor strike in 1947 as post-war America began to turn its attention to working conditions and workers at home. In the 1950s and 1960s, Selina Burch became a top official of the CWA, an administrative assistant to one of the union's 12 district vice-presidents.

"I grew up in Dublin, Georgia. My father was a farmer and my mother was a homemaker. My mother died when I was 13 and I moved in with my grandmother and four old-maid aunts—three of them were schoolteachers. There was no labor background in my family at all.

I began work for Southern Bell on August 7, 1945, as an operator. I had graduated from Dublin High School and had worked in a coffee shop for about a year—there's no labor market in Dublin, Georgia. After a year, I applied for a job with the telephone company. The chief operator had gone to school with my father, so I was put ahead of all the other applicants.

At that time, remember, there was a manual board where you said, "Number, please." There was no automatic dialing in Dublin. If you've ever walked into a telephone company, you've seen all these cords being put up. It became a fascinating thing to me to see if I could put up all the cords and then move over to another position, because I was very adept at handling telephone calls. There was one other girl from Dublin who could keep up with me, but only one. This was a challenge to me, to see how fast I could work the switchboard.

In 1946, some people from Macon came to Dublin and signed us up to a union. If you were a female, you paid $0.75 a month to belong to a union, and if you were a male, you paid $1.00. I was an operator and was working eight to five every day, the best shift because of my family's relationship with the chief operator. Suddenly, I was assigned to that horrible tour of one to ten. Someone had come along and taken my privileges away. I was young and carefree, though, 17, 18, and it really didn't make any difference to me, that part of it.

Also, right away in 1946, we obtained our first wage increase. At that time, I was making $15.00 a week as an operator and I got a $10.00 increase. It had a real impact on me that somebody had almost doubled my salary, but I did not understand at that time what it was all about. I had no idea what unionization meant. Pay, it meant more pay. But as for any

other privileges, all it meant was that I went to the bottom of the list, because I was the junior person there.

I remember the first union meeting I ever went to—over in Macon. It was during a strike, and we wanted to see what we were striking for, but we didn't find out. I'm not sure that anyone in Macon knew.

The strike didn't bother me because even though my family were schoolteachers, we had a car. There was only one movie in Dublin, so driving to Macon was something for us to do. I could borrow a quarter to buy a little gas. The Western Electric guys were out on strike also. Everybody would get together at meetings and we'd laugh and talk about the strike, whatever it was about.

Dublin was a pretty small place. We were a close-knit group. I guess that we were friends more because we worked together all day than because we were members of the union. When we returned to work in '47, I remember that we gave the two who had not come out on strike a pretty hard way to travel. I resented them.

It was like being out of school on vacation. In fact, the day we were supposed to return to work, I had a big date that night, what I considered at that time a big date. I called the chief operator and said that I couldn't possibly come to work because I had such a sore throat.

We were so young and naïve that we did not even think of picking up the phone and making calls. You see, with only a manual board there, if we had been militant and known what we were doing, we could have driven Mother Bell nuts. But we did not want to inconvenience in any way. We thought we were a big inconvenience just being out on the street. It was part of this Southern upbringing: we respect authority at all costs. And with Dublin so small, I didn't think of "the company" as huge, nationwide Bell Telephone Company. I thought of the company only as the people I worked with. My grandmother broke her hip during this time, and the chief operator called me at home—my grandmother's home where I was still living—to assure me that she would make sure that any calls from our number went through, even though they were having trouble keeping up on the switchboard because of the strike . . ."

Eloise book

"Follow the Flag"

WABASH

3424

Tonka pickup truck

Value of One Dollar	
Year	Value in 2010 USD
1950	$9.05
1954	$8.11
1955	$8.14
1957	$7.76
1959	$7.47

Values are approximate based upon economic historical data and 2010 U. S. Dollar

1950–1959

As the 1950s began, the average American enjoyed an income 15 times greater than that of the average foreigner. The United States manufactured half the world's products, 57 percent of the steel, 43 percent of the electricity, and 62 percent of the oil. The economies of Europe and Asia lay in ruins, while America's industrial and agricultural structure were untouched and primed to supply the goods needed by a war-weary world. Significantly, in 1954 the Dow Jones Industrial Average regained enough strength to top the highs achieved before the stock market crash of 1929.

In addition, the war years' high employment and optimism spurred the longest sustained period of peacetime prosperity in the nation's history. A decade of full employment and pent-up desire produced demands for all types of consumer goods. Businesses of all sizes prospered. Rapidly swelling families, new suburban homes, televisions, and most of all, big, powerful shiny automobiles symbolized the hopes of the era. During the 1950s an average of seven million cars and trucks were sold annually. By 1952 two-thirds of all families owned a television set; home freezers and high-fidelity stereo phonographs were considered necessities. Specialized markets developed to meet the demand of consumers: amateur photographers, pet lovers, backpackers. At the same time, shopping malls, supermarkets, and credit cards emerged as important economic forces.

Veterans, using the GI Bill of Rights, flung open the doors of colleges nationwide, attending in record numbers. Inflation was the only pressing economic issue, fueled in large part by the Korean War (in which 54,000 American lives were lost) and the federal expenditures for Cold War defense. As the decade opened, federal spending represented 15.6 percent of the nation's gross national product. Thanks largely to the Cold War, by 1957, defense consumed half of the federal government's $165 billion budget.

This economic prosperity also ushered in conservative politics and social conformity. Tidy lawns, bedrooms that were "neat and trim," and suburban homes that were "proper" were certainly "in" throughout the decade as Americans adjusted to the post-war years. Properly buttoned-down attitudes concerning sexual mores brought stern undergarments for women like boned girdles and stiff, pointed, or padded bras to confine the body. The planned community of Levittown, New York, mandated that grass be cut at least once a week and laundry washed on specific days. A virtual revival of Victorian respectability and domesticity reigned; divorce rates and female college attendance fell while birth rates and the sale of Bibles rose. Corporate America promoted the benefits of respectable men in gray flannel suits whose wives remained at home to tend house and raise children. Suburban life included ladies' club memberships, chauffeuring children to piano and ballet classes, and lots of a newly marketed product known as tranquilizers, whose sales were astounding.

The average wage earner benefited more from the booming industrial system than at any time in American history. The 40-hour work week became standard in manufacturing. In offices many workers were becoming accustomed to a 35-hour week. Health benefits for workers became more common and paid vacations were standard in most industries. In 1950, 25 percent of American wives worked outside the home; by the end of the decade the number had risen to 40 percent. Communications technology, expanding roads, inexpensive airline tickets, and a spirit of unboundedness meant that people and commerce were no longer prisoners of distance. Unfortunately, up to one-third of the population lived below the government's poverty level, largely overlooked in the midst of prosperity.

The Civil Rights movement was propelled by two momentous events in the 1950s. The first was a decree on May 17, 1954, when the U.S. Supreme Court ruled "that in the field of public education the doctrine of 'separate but equal' has no place. Separate educational facilities are inherently unequal." The message was electric but the pace was slow. Few schools would be integrated for another decade. The second event established the place of the Civil Rights movement. On December 1, 1955, African-American activist Rosa Parks declined to vacate the White-only front section of the Montgomery, Alabama, bus, leading to her arrest and a citywide bus boycott by Blacks. Their spokesman became Martin Luther King, Jr., the 26-year-old pastor of the Dexter Avenue Baptist Church. The year-long boycott was the first step toward the passage of the Civil Rights Act of 1964.

America's youth were enchanted by the TV adventures of "Leave It to Beaver," westerns, and "Father Knows Best," allowing them to accumulate more time watching television (at least 27 hours) than attending school. TV dinners were invented; pink ties and felt skirts with sequined poodle appliques were worn; Elvis Presley was worshipped and the new phenomena of *Playboy* and Mickey Spillane fiction were created only to be read behind closed doors. The ever-glowing eye of television killed the "March of Time" newsreels after 16 years at the movies. Sexual jargon such as "first base" and "home run" entered the language. Learned-When-Sleeping machines appeared along with Smokey the Bear, Sony tape recorders, adjustable shower heads, Mad Comics, newspaper vending machines, Levi's faded blue denims, pocket-size transistor radios, and transparent plastic bags for clothing. Ultimately the real stars of the era were the Salk and Sabin vaccines, which vanquished the siege of polio.

As the decade drew to a close, Russia fired a rocket heard 'round the world when it launched Sputnik, the first vehicle in space. America's first attempts to counter the Soviet achievement were dismal failures, giving rise to moral self-doubt, and even greater fear that the communist threat would one day conquer America without ever firing a shot or invading American shores.

1950 FAMILY PROFILE

The Duncans, a 50-year-old couple, live in St. Louis, Missouri. Ed works for the telephone company as a lineman, and Gina has never worked outside the home, putting her energy into raising the two children. The couple now has grandchildren and enjoys celebrating their status as being a half a century old along with the nation. Born before airplanes were invented, they now live near one of the nation's busiest airports.

Annual Income: $3,880

Ed is at the top of his payscale after 30 years with the phone company; his wife does not work outside the home, but often babysits her grandchildren.

Annual Budget

Alcoholic Drinks $79.00
Automobile Transportation $410.00
Clothing. $413.00
Education $12.00
Food $1,207.00
Fuel, Light, Refrigeration,
    and Water $154.00
Gifts and Contributions $106.00
Home Furnishing and Equipment. $280.00
Household Operation $140.00
Housing. $401.00
Insurance $180.00
Medical Care. $185.00
Miscellaneous $62.00
Other Transportation $79.00
Personal Care $90.00
Personal Taxes. $302.00
Reading $33.00

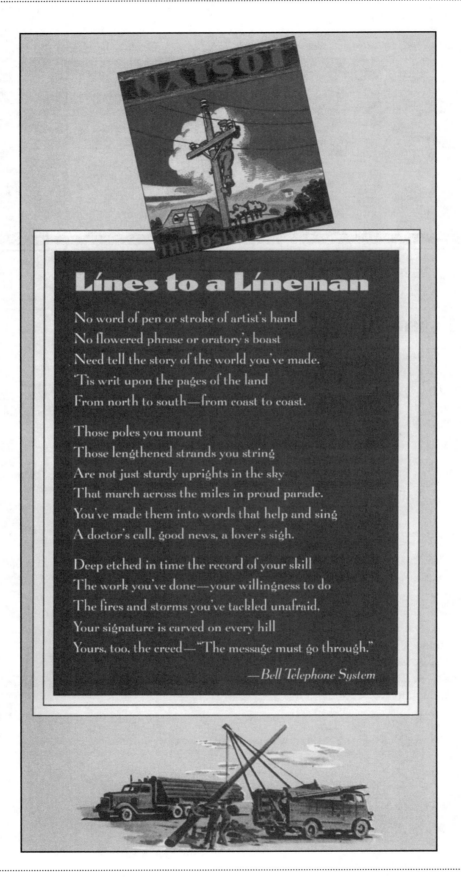

Lines to a Lineman

No word of pen or stroke of artist's hand
No flowered phrase or oratory's boast
Need tell the story of the world you've made.
'Tis writ upon the pages of the land
From north to south—from coast to coast.

Those poles you mount
Those lengthened strands you string
Are not just sturdy uprights in the sky
That march across the miles in proud parade.
You've made them into words that help and sing
A doctor's call, good news, a lover's sigh.

Deep etched in time the record of your skill
The work you've done—your willingness to do
The fires and storms you've tackled unafraid,
Your signature is carved on every hill
Yours, too, the creed—"The message must go through."

—Bell Telephone System

Recreation $173.00
Tobacco $63.00
   Total $4,369.00

Home Furnishing: Total $280.00
Floor Coverings $24.00
Furniture $69.00
Household Textiles $33.00
Kitchen, Cleaning, Laundry
   Equipment $104.00
Miscellaneous $50.00

Clothing: Woman, Total $243.00
Hats, Gloves, Accessories $14.00
Hosiery and Footwear $50.00
Miscellaneous $51.00
Outerwear $102.00
Underwear and Nightwear $26.00

Clothing: Man, Total $155.00
Hats, Gloves, Accessories $14.00
Hosiery and Footwear $31.00
Miscellaneous $15.00
Outerwear $84.00
Underwear and Nightwear $11.00

The couple's grandchildren live nearby.

Life at Home

- The Duncans recently purchased a five-room home in their neighborhood near the airport to control the rapidly rising cost of housing rent.
- Following the war, housing demands are rising quickly as soldiers take advantage of the GI Bill to buy homes, attend college, and start families; veterans' benefits include loans for the purchase or construction of a home or farm at a rate not to exceed four percent.
- The neighborhood includes a mix of young couples with small children and older couples who have lived in the area for 30 years.
- The family's overall cost of housing, including taxes, life insurance, and household expenses has risen 10 percent since 1947; food costs during the same period are up five percent.
- Like many working class families following the war, the proportion of their expenditures available for "sundries" or discretionary spending has risen steadily; for many families expenditures for "luxuries" such as clothing, automobile ownership, recreation, and alcoholic beverages are on the rise.
- Food and shelter, including fuel, light, and refrigeration, require 55 percent of the income of the lowest income group in 1950; but only 40 percent of the highest.
- The family's food costs include two meals outside the home per month, costing approximately $25.00; often this includes a night out with their grandchildren, who live nearby.
- Their two daughters both graduated from high school and married men who fought in World War II; one of the sons-in-law obtained some college training under the GI Bill before going to work at a glass factory.
- Under the GI Bill, the Veteran's Administration pays $500.00 a year toward all tuition and books, plus a monthly subsistence allowance of $85.00 a month.

- The Duncan family has an automobile and two radios, but no television set or air-conditioning; nationwide 10.4 million homes now have television sets.
- The grandchildren do have a Mr. Potato Head to play with at grandmother's house; Mr. Potato Head, an overnight success, proved the power of television, becoming the first toy ever advertised on TV.
- The grandchildren also want grandmother to redo her kitchen in pink like the advertisements in the magazines suggest; pink is the color of the time from prizefighter Sugar Ray Robinson's 1950 pink Cadillac to the pink sports coats worn by young men.
- They now have a telephone with a two-party line; even though he works for the telephone company he did not have a home phone until the early 1940s; like many working class families, an automobile was considered more important than a phone.
- For recreation, this family follows the local professional baseball team, the St. Louis Cardinals; they particularly love baseball player Stan Musial.
- Stan Musial is such a dominant player, Dodger's pitcher Preacher Roe says the best way to get Musial out is "Walk him on four pitches and pick him off first"; another pitcher, Brooklyn's Carl Erskine, says his strategy is, "I just throw him my best stuff, then run over to back up third base."
- Starting in 1941 their "beloved Cardinals" either win the National League pennant or finish second, led by Musial.
- They cannot afford seasons tickets, but go to the ballgame at least a half-dozen times each year; many summer nights are spent on the porch listening to the St. Louis Cardinal's games on the radio.
- They recently went to Chicago on a Greyhound Bus to visit friends; they believe that Chicago is too far to drive, nor have they ever flown in an airplane even though they live near the airport.
- Gina is a great letter writer and often corresponds with friends who have moved from St. Louis; first-class letters cost $0.03 an ounce; airmail is $0.06 an ounce.
- The entire family is very proud that a "man from Missouri" is in the White House; both the man and woman vote for Harry Truman for president in 1948, although the man does not vote for Franklin D. Roosevelt in 1944, saying four terms is too many for any man.

The Duncans loved the St. Louis Cardinals, especially Stan Musial.

Eloise book

Dr. Seuss book

Tonka pickup truck

Erector Set

Mr. Potato Head

Life at Work: The Telephone Company

- In the early days of telephone, telephone poles commonly have eight to 10 cross arms, all holding open telephone wires; storms, common in St. Louis, can tangle and strip the wires.
- Telephone linemen are considered a hardy lot, working through emergencies and bad weather to restore service.
- By reputation linemen have to be rugged, self-reliant types who face danger every day as part of the job.
- Most linemen, like this man, are physically strong, capable of climbing the pole with nothing supporting them but the spurs of the climbing irons dug into the pole and the strength of their arms grasping the pole.
- Once in the desired position on the pole, they have to hang on with one arm while the other unhooks one end of the safety strap from the belt, throws it around the pole, and rehooks it into the ring on the belt—requiring considerable strength and coordination.
- Climbing tall poles at night in a snowstorm can often lead to injury.
- Typically linemen cannot obtain life insurance unless they lie about their occupation.
- Unlike his father, who bought his life insurance on a weekly basis from a local insurance runner, Ed has a life insurance plan at work.
- Routine maintenance includes replacing broken glass insulators on the poles, repairing broken wire, and splicing cables.
- After 30 years on the job, this man often helps train young men in working the poles; he does not hesitate to climb poles himself to demonstrate his skills.
- Ed's compensation benefits include a two-week, paid vacation, which is now standard in most industries in St. Louis for employees with more than one year of service.
- He also receives eight paid holidays a year such as Christmas, New Year's, and Labor Day.
- For the past three years he has also received a Christmas cash bonus.

"The Use and Care of Pole Climbing Equipment: A Field Manual":

"It is hazardous to stand at the foot of a pole while a lineman is working above, ascending or descending. Warn all persons, especially children, to keep away for the following reasons:

1. He may drop tools
2. He may dislodge splinters and chips
3. A lineman's gaff may cut off

A second lineman, preparing to ascend, should always wait until the first has reached the working position and placed his safety strap. In descending, one lineman should remain in his work area until the other has reached the ground. If possible on poles which are wet or on which there is snow or ice, climb with the gaffs engaging the slippery side of the pole in order that the hands may engage the drier side and reduce the hazard of slipping.

Pins, crossarm braces, insulators, and hardware other than pole straps do not furnish a safe support as they may pull loose or break. The gloved hands may be cut on such devices that may be rough or broken. Do not use this equipment for support by the hands or for attachment of the safety strap."

ON THE MISSISSIPPI
SS ADMIRAL AT ST. LOUIS

- St. Louis is becoming more active about creating buried telephone lines in the late 1940s, a move away from open lines.

Life in the Community: St. Louis, Missouri

- The year this man was born, 1900, the population of St. Louis was 575,238; 50 years later, the population of the city is 856,796 but the metropolitan area boasts 1.5 million people.
- The 1904 World's Fair opened in St. Louis; every state and territory but one participated.
- St. Louis was struggling with growth and corruption at the turn of the century also; it earned the title of America's worst-governed city and was the first town to be assailed in Lincoln Steffen's *Shame of the Cities*. It was the only town to be attacked twice by him.

Plans for St. Louis after World War II, December 1942:

"There is no sound reason why St. Louis should become decadent . . . Extensive research would reveal no good reason why St. Louis should not continue to play a most significant role in the development of the nation. Its many natural advantages should enable it to keep in the forefront of large American cities even though local citizens and their leaders fail to make the most of these advantages. Complacency is St. Louis' greatest deficiency."

- In 1916 "Negro segregation ordinances" were passed by heavy majority of the electorate.
- By 1923, the school board of the urban St. Louis announced it would add a pig and a cow to the municipal zoo because so many children had never seen either animal.
- By 1925 a commercial radio station opened and the pride of the city, the St. Louis Cardinals baseball team, was in the World Series.
- In 1931 the mayor ordered construction of the municipal auditorium to provide for unemployment relief.

"Tops Take off Pounds," *Life Magazine,* 1951:

"During the war, when she had a job in a Milwaukee brewery, it was the sensible custom of Mrs. Esther Manz to wear slacks. It was also the pleasant habit of her employer to call a short halt in the mid-morning and mid-afternoon and serve each employee a glass of the company product. Mrs. Manz had always been a bit overweight, and this kind of treatment soon betrayed her. She found she was too fat to get into her slacks.

Then, unlike most U.S. adults who are overweight—as 25 percent of them are—Mrs. Manz did something about it. She quit her job and started TOPS (Take Off Pounds Sensibly") Today, three years later, there are TOPS clubs for some 2,500 overweight women in Wisconsin, Michigan,

California, Massachusetts, Illinois, and South Dakota, and Mrs. Manz is kept busy answering phone calls (she has 5,000) and letters (40 a week) and visiting the 43 clubs in Milwaukee.

TOPS, which has no dues and gives Mrs. Manz no salary, is neither fad nor cult. In some ways, it is modeled after Alcoholics Anonymous, but unlike AA it does not operate in privacy; excess weight, being what it is, is hard to keep secret. At weekly meetings TOPS members gather to weigh in, sing songs ('every mealtime check your eats; count the calories, dodge the sweets') and dance and play games and plan low-calorie meals which are the basis of their reducing method."

- By 1937 the deepening industrial smoke crisis sparked a smoke abatement crusade, resulting in the banning of cheap, impure coal, often brought in from nearby southern Illinois.
- By 1950 the city prides itself on being one of the 10 largest in America, boasting "strategic location, its favorable transportation facilities, the character and diversification of its industries, and its wholesale and retail trade."

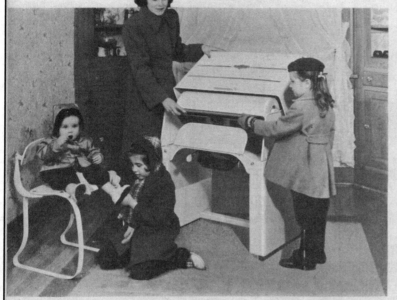

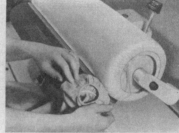

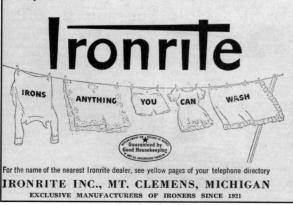

HISTORICAL SNAPSHOT
1950–1951

- The Korean War began
- Congress increased personal and corporate income taxes
- Auto registrations showed one car for every 3.7 Americans
- Blue Cross insurance programs covered 3.7 million Americans
- Five million homes had television sets; 45 million had radios
- President Harry Truman ordered the Atomic Energy Committee to develop the hydrogen bomb
- Boston Red Sox Ted Williams became baseball's highest paid player with a $125,000 contract
- Senator Joseph McCarthy announced in a speech before a women's group in Wheeling, West Virginia, that he had a list containing the names of 205 known Communists in the State Department
- Otis Elevator installed the first passenger elevator with self-opening doors
- Coca-Cola's share of the U.S. cola market was 69 percent; Pepsi-Cola's share was 15 percent
- The FBI issued its first list of the Ten Most Wanted Criminals
- The first transplant of a kidney from one human to another was performed on a 49-year-old woman at a Chicago hospital
- Charles M. Schultz's comic strip, Peanuts, debuted in eight newspapers
- Smokey the Bear, an orphaned cub found after a forest fire in New Mexico, became the living symbol of the U.S. Forestry Service
- *Betty Crocker's Picture Cookbook* was published
- Miss Clairol hair coloring was marketed for the first time
- Minute Rice was marketed
- M&M candy, created in 1940, was stamped with an "M" for the first time to assure customers they were getting the real thing
- The first Xerox copy machine was introduced
- The average cost of four years of college was $1,800, an increase of 400 percent since 1900
- The 22nd Amendment to the Constitution, limiting the term of the president to two terms was adopted
- Univak, the first general-purpose electronic computer, was dedicated in Philadelphia
- CBS introduced color television in a program hosted by Ed Sullivan and Arthur Godfrey
- Lacoste tennis shirts with an alligator symbol were introduced in the U.S. by French manufacturer Izod
- Earl Tupper created the home sale party to market his plastic storage containers directly to householders
- *Jet* news magazine was launched
- Chrysler Corporation introduced Power steering in cars
- More than 75 percent of all U.S. farms were now electrified
- Harvard Law School admitted women

1950 ECONOMIC PROFILE

Income, Standard Jobs

Average of All Industries, Including Farm Labor	$3,180.00
Bituminous Coal Mining	$3,245.00
Building Trades	$3,377.00
Domestics	$1,502.00
Farm Labor	$1,454.00
Federal Civilian	$3,632.00
Federal Military	$2,897.00
Finance, Insurance, Real Estate	$3,217.00
Gas and Electricity Workers	$3,571.00
Manufacturing, Durable Goods	$3,483.00
Manufacturing, Nondurable Goods	$3,154.00
Medical/Health Services Workers	$2,067.00
Miscellaneous Manufacturing	$3,020.00
Motion Picture Services	$3,089.00

"Perfect Wife?" by Naomi Hintze, *Woman's Home Companion*, December 1949:

"On the hot stone terrace outside her cool stone house, Genie Bingham sat cross-legged on a yellow chaise, one finger pressed into her cheek, and smiled. The musical sounds of dishes being washed by somebody else came from the kitchen, but that was not why she smiled. Her legs were a beautiful copper although it was only July, but that was not why she smiled.

Medium pretty, medium tall, she had been a medium good student in school with a B average, but she had just this minute received a one hundred in a quiz entitled, 'How Good a Wife are You?' And so she smiled to herself in delight and satisfaction . . . .

Some of the questions had required no hesitation, those on grooming, cooking, and getting along with her in-laws. Did she nag? Frequent requests for that shelf over the kitchen stove could not be considered nagging. She had needed that shelf ever since they bought the house. Also the extra towel rack in the bathroom. She had asked Tod nicely dozens of times.

She had said, 'Would you, darling please.' No she did not nag but maybe she should.

She had given herself credit for not being extravagant. Eva, the cleaning woman who was responsible for the musical sounds in the kitchen, came only one day a week . . .

The question, 'Are you a little bit jealous?' had required more thought than any of the others. Before writing in her answer Genie had put the magazine down on the flagstones and applied more tanning oil to her legs, then lay back and stared up at the midsummer sky.

There was that secretary of Tod's. That dreamboat. That pastel number with Renoir eyes. Marge Kelly had improbably white-gold hair, which, it was obvious, she washed every night, and a girl who washed her hair every night just for a one-man office was up to no good. She called Tod by his first name. There's such a thing as being too democratic, Genie thought. But when she had told Tod so, he just laughed as if he thought she was funny."

Nonprofit Organization
Workers. $2,578.00
Passenger Transportation. $3,288.00
Personal Services. $2,254.00
Public School Teachers $2,794.00
Radio Broadcasting and
Television Workers $4,698.00
Railroads. $3,778.00
State and Local Government
Workers. $2,758.00
Telephone and Telegraph
Workers. $3,059.00
Wholesale and Retail Trade
Workers. $3,034.00

Selected Prices

1951 Nash Rambler $1,732.00
Admiral Dual-Temp Refrigerator $189.95
Aerowax Floor Wax, Quart. $0.55
Buffalo Bill Costume $2.98
Chapstick Lip Balm $0.25
Charvin Girdle $6.95
Collette Basketball, Official Size $2.98
Columbia Records' Record $4.85
Corning Glass Double Boiler. $3.45
Evenflow Baby Nipple $0.25
Ford Custom Victoria
Automobile. $1,925.00
Goodyear Glide Garden Hose $5.95
Imperial Gas Range, Full Size $99.00
Moran Wee-Walker Shoes $1.19
Mounds Candy Bar $0.06
Noxema Home Facial, Big Jar. $0.59
Oscar Mayer Wieners, per Pound $0.49
Parker Brothers Monopoly Game $4.00
Scott Television, 16 Inch $299.00
Serta Perfect Sleeper Mattress $49.50
Tower Black Carbon Paper, Box $1.19
Tudor Electric Football Game $6.95

She snatched up the shirt and looked at each new button. There was a fleck of lipstick on every thread

But, Genie, they say you *should* be a little bit jealous. . . . It keeps you on your toes . . .

Perfect Wife?

ON THE hot stone terrace outside her cool stone house, Genie Bingham sat cross-legged on a yellow chaise, one finger pressed into her cheek, and smiled. The musical sounds of dishes being washed by somebody else came from the kitchen, but that was not why she smiled. Her legs were a beautiful copper although it was only July, but that was not why she smiled.

Medium pretty, medium tall, she had been a medium-good student in school with a B average, but she had just this minute received a score of one hundred in a quiz entitled "How Good a Wife Are You?" And so

she smiled to herself with delight and satisfaction.

To be sure, she had awarded herself the score—but with meticulous honesty. She had just finished adding it and she was amazed. Now she turned to the front of the magazine to check the questions and make sure she had been absolutely fair.

Some of the questions had required no hesitation, those on grooming, cooking and getting along with her in-laws. Did she nag? Frequent requests for that shelf over the kitchen stove could not be considered nagging. She had needed that shelf ever [continued on page 41]

BY NAOMI HINTZE ILLUSTRATOR: CLYDE ROSS

Woman's Home Companion 17

The Telephone and Telephone Industry

- Shortly after Alexander Graham Bell created the first "dual" lecture in 1877 using telephone lines, St. Louis, Chicago, San Francisco, Albany, and Philadelphia all opened central telephone exchanges; the leasing fee for a phone that year was $100.00.
- Initially the phone company owned all phones and "are rented only to persons of good breeding and refinement," an early advertisement reminded customers.

Clarence Day, *Life with Father*, 1948, on the impact of the telephone on her family:

"Mother agreed with Father—she didn't like telephones either. She distrusted machines of all kinds; they weren't human, they popped or exploded and made her nervous. She never knew what they might do to her. And the telephone seemed to her, and many other people, especially dangerous. They were afraid that if they stood near one in a thunderstorm they might get hit by lightning. Even if there wasn't any storm, the electric wiring might give them a shock. When they saw a telephone in some hotel or office, they stood away from it or picked it up gingerly. It was a freak way to use electricity, and mother wouldn't even touch the queer toy. Besides, she said, she had to see the face of any person she talked to. She didn't want to be answered by a voice coming out of a box on the way." This must be so.

- The yellow pages arrived in 1883 when a printer in Cheyenne, Wyoming, ran out of white paper and simply used the nearest ream of paper, which happened to be yellow; the customers loved it and the phone book evolved.
- Between 1880 and 1893 the number of telephones in the United States grew from 60,000 or roughly one per thousand people to about 260,000 or about one for every 250 people. In 1891 the New York and New Jersey Telephone Company served 7,322 commercial customers, including 937 physicians and hospitals, 401 drug stores, 363 liquor stores,

The 300 Desk Set Series phone designed by Henry Dreyfuss.

Carolyn Reynolds Ortiz, television producer, recalled in a 1993 interview the role of the telephone in her home:

"When I was a little girl in Colorado Springs, the telephone was a formal affair where calls were placed by a live human being while other human beings on the party line were free to listen in. The telephone itself had the stature of a Shinto shrine in our house. As in most forties houses, the Tokonoma corner for the telephone was built in, giving the homeowner no choice for its placement. The telephone had its own kind of anticipatory power. Solid black, slightly warm to the touch like amber, and nice to hold like a well-balanced garden tool, it had four different rings for each party-line member. Two short blasts for us, one for the Halleys down the street and so forth. My mother loved to guess who was calling the other lines, and I suspect that she listened in now and then to see if she was right. We, the children, were subject to strict rules about never answering any but our ring. Because of the party line, the phone was not used to chat for hours or to reveal private matters. When someone on the line picked up the phone, it was a signal to cut the conversations short so others could use it. The telephone had the power of ritual in those days, before it became private and dialed and ubiquitous."

315 livery stables, 162 metalworking plants, 146 lawyers, 126 contractors, 100 printing shops, and only 1,422 residences—mostly the homes of doctors or business owners.

- By 1900, when Alexander Graham Bell's original patent expired, 6,000 new independent telephone companies sprang up nationwide, sometimes in an unused portion of a farmer's barn; several were established in St. Louis—offering a 10-party line to customers for $21.50 a year.
- The working class often shared phones with neighbors and used telephones at the local drug stores; most did not have telephone service in their homes.
- The invention was not universally loved; many businessmen were hesitant to replace the telegraph with the telephone because they valued having a written record.
- Teddy Roosevelt disliked the telephone and used it only in extreme emergencies; Woodrow Wilson hated it and instructed the operators not to ring him; Herbert Hoover was the first president to have a telephone on his desk.
- Dwight Eisenhower was so accustomed to phone service from military and White House operators he did not know how to use a dial phone when he left the White House in 1960.
- From the turn of the century to 1925 the numbers of telephones and automobiles in America were about even; after 1925 automobiles took a commanding lead; more American families were electing to buy cars, electricity, and radios than telephone service.
- By 1930, 60 percent of American families had automobiles, 41 percent had telephones; a connection from one phone to another took six seconds; nationally 36 percent of Bell subscribers shared a two-party line, while 27 percent shared a four-party line.

- Henry Dreyfuss designed the 300 Desk Set Series phone, which appeared in 1937; the 10 finger holes were clearly marked with letters in red and numbers in black to help in dialing, and was available only in black.
- When the 500 series arrived in 1949, it was "the very model of post-war modernity: low-slung and accessible, it hugged the table like a Studebaker hugged the road. Its cord was coiled, its volume adjustable, its classic body an engineering feat."
- By 1954 consumers could not yet buy their own telephones, but they could choose the color they desired—from a limited range.

Post-War America

- In 1950 the United States was completing its transition to a peacetime economy.
- The wealth of America was leveling; by 1950 the percentage of total personal income held by the top five percent in the nation stood at 21.4 percent; in 1930 the top five percent held 30 percent.
- Military spending was pumping millions into the economy; 10 percent of all goods and consumer services in the United States (or about half of the federal budget) went to the armed forces.
- Births were rising sharply after the war, reaching 3.6 million in 1950; the baby boom continued throughout the decade, reaching 4.3 million births in 1960.
- Slightly better than half of all non-farm homes were owned in 1950; a decade later the figure would increase to three-fifths.
- The worker in 1950, who worked 40 hours a week, was considered three times more productive than his grandfather in 1910, who worked 72 hours per week.
- Currently 74 percent of 16-year-olds were in school, up from 43 percent 40 years earlier.

National Airlines premier flight: Star red carpet service between New York, Florida, and Havana, Cuba.

- Unlike in 1918, when working class families sent their teenaged children into the factories, most teenaged children remained in school in the early 1950s; finishing high school was considered a sign of joining the middle class.
- Since 1935 the number of wives in the labor force, especially women 45 to 64, had increased dramatically.
- This group, especially those whose children were grown, became accustomed to working during the war and did not wish to return to full-time homemaking.
- From 1935 to 1950, female participation in the work force increased 12 percent; women were replacing children as subsidiary workers.
- With unemployment low, Black families made substantial economic gains.

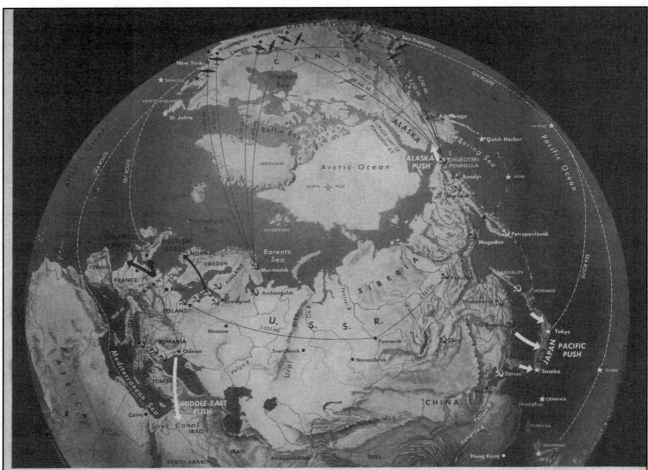

SOVIET BOMBERS COULD REACH U.S. along routes shown on this map, which looks down on Eurasian land mass and across North Pole toward Canada and U.S. The Atlantic and Midwest are within range of Murmansk-based bombers, which would need aerial refueling to get back home. Targets on Pacific coast and as far east as Chicago could be reached from eastern Siberia. Russia's growing two-ocean submarine fleet could harass ship lanes (dotted lines) and might hit U.S. coastal cities with guided missiles.

HOW COULD SOVIET ATTACK COME?

THE REDS, WHOSE WAR PRODUCTION FAR OUTSTRIPS OURS, MIGHT BASE STRATEGY ON A QUICK KNOCKOUT

The danger of war is seen best in one compelling fact: the Soviets are preparing for war (chart, *left*). They are spending tremendous manpower and a quarter of their income to build up a huge military machine. Their satellite armies, including China's, more than double Soviet numerical strength. Their civilian support outside Russia already exceeds Hitler's fifth column. It is led by Communists like Thorez of France and Togliatti of Italy, who openly seek high political office while their party is a potential aid to Soviet military moves.

The chart at left on the opposite page shows how vastly Russian military strength exceeds American, both in "forces in being" and production of weapons. The U.S. Air Force is supplied with 1,200 new planes a year. Russia, with its growing industrial proletariat, is building 7,000 airplanes a year. They include many conventional fighters of the type they used in World War II for ground support but also many modern jets and long-range bombers of the B-29 type—and possibly better. Russia, never a naval power after Japan's navy sank the czar's fleet at Tsushima in 1905, now has a more power-

ful undersea fleet than Germany had at the start of the last war. Its 270 submarines include the latest Schnorkel-equipped U-boats which Germany developed too late in World War II. To oppose these, the U.S. Navy has a far superior surface fleet. But the work horse of antisubmarine warfare, the destroyer, is in short supply. There are only 136 destroyers in commission, plus a rusting and increasingly outmoded moth-ball fleet of 204 more. Americans confidently assume that U.S. industrial capacity would restore dominance in weapons if war came. But meanwhile the Russian advantage increases relentlessly, and the advantage in conventional armaments can be decisive, now that Russia has broken the atomic-bomb monopoly which had made Americans feel secure. Americans at last must realize that, in the era of long-range atomic war, America itself is finally vulnerable to sudden attack.

An opening blow by the Soviets could be a surprise atomic bombing of American cities and industrial targets. Russia today has a striking power not possessed in the last war either by Germany, which sent bombers only as far as Iceland, or Japan, which

as a scare gesture shelled the Oregon and California coasts from submarines and sent bomb-laden balloons floating aimlessly toward the Pacific Coast.

Russia at war presumably would try to knock out the U.S., now without an adequate radar-warning network (*next page*), before a superior force could be mobilized to take the offensive. It might launch a "disaster attack": in which long-range bombers would be thrown against American cities with the suddenness of Pearl Harbor but with far greater force. Cities from Seattle to Boston might be atomized in coordinated raids. The offensive could be sustained better if Soviet land armies first took Western Europe and the Middle East (maps, *left*).

But most U.S. military men believe, despite Soviet preparation and potential, that Russia could not confidently go to war for at least two years, even if her present strategy of trying to gain her expansive ends by threats and pressure proves insufficient. In those two years, by serious effort, the U.S. could make itself strong enough to diminish Russian confidence and reduce the danger to the world.

"Daddy Doesn't Live Here Anymore," *McCall's Magazine*, April 1950:

"There are in this country today hundreds of thousands of young women who are war widows in the most explicit sense, even though their husbands did not meet death in combat. They are widows by decree. Their marriages did not survive the grotesque distortions of wartime living and so ended in divorce.

A husband who has died honorably in the service of his country is not a morbid presence in the thoughts of the woman who loved him. His widow turns herself once more to the realities of living. But the husband who was observed a little furtively last night with a pretty girl on his arm, the husband who comes to see his children and expects all the privileges of their companionship with none of the duties—that man is a more haunting ghost than a man recently dead can ever be.

It is a proud and simple duty to tell the children their father died in the service of his country. It is a difficult moment when the children first ask, 'Mother, what does divorce mean?'

The war widow whose husband died in uniform is cushioned economically, at least to some extent, by the pensions and allowances the government provides and by such life insurance as her husband might have carried. The widow by decree receives none of these benefits. Her only outside source of funds is the alimony granted by the courts. For the rest she is on her own.

Of course, this is not a war problem. We still live in the aftermath of those years of incredible excitements and bewilderments. The notion of divorce, of getting out of a situation that seems hopeless, comes to the heads of half the wives of the land at some time or other . . . .

Pauline Long was born on her father's small farm near Huntington, Ohio, and was graduated from the country high school when she was 18. As in most of the rural districts of the land, teachers were scarce, the formal education required of them was not too elaborate, and so Pauline got a job for the very next school year teaching in the primary grades.

Pauline lived at home and was quite happy with her work for five years. Then, when she was 23, she married Clarence Schroeder, who was 26. He was a machinist, an extremely capable and conscientious workman, who earned good wages. He insisted that Pauline stop working at once. He said that he was able to earn quite enough money for the two of them and that he wanted her to make a nice home and enjoy life.

Even before they were married they decided not to think about children for a while. Both of them were young. It seemed best to have a few carefree years before they took on the responsibilities of a family.

As a matter of fact, six years went by before Judith was born, in 1942. By this time, of course, we were at war. Clarence Schroeder was working at one of the great munition plants in the Cleveland area and had found a home for himself and Pauline and the new baby at Elyria, a pleasant town of about 25,000 some 30 miles from the metropolis. He was engaged in high-precision work, and though he made no effort to avoid the draft he was classified as essential on the home front.

Pauline says, 'He worked terribly hard for long hours every day. Looking back on it, I think he may have worked too hard. But he has always been like that. Ever since I have known him he has worked 12 and 14 hours a day, and even now when he has his own business he does the same thing. The one thing he hates in anybody is laziness . . . .'

Toward the end of the war, in fact, they had almost enough money to do something Clarence Schroeder always had wanted to do—get out of the shop and start a small business of his own. The little town of Wakeman, Ohio, was the crossroads for a whole region of Ohio farm country, and a hardware store there came up for sale. Pauline's mother agreed to lend them enough money, at trifling interest, to stretch out their savings, and they not only bought the business but also a small house to live in.

(continued)

"Daddy Doesn't Live Here . . ." *(continued)*

'That was a happy time for all of us,' Pauline says. 'I wanted to work at the store, but he wouldn't let me. He just could not stand the idea of a woman working outside of her home. So I joined the church clubs and made as many friends as I could.'

In 1945 Pauline found herself pregnant again. Very shortly after V-E Day her son Dennis was born. The baby was exactly three months old when Clarence Schroeder made his announcement to Pauline. He was fed up with bills and responsibilities. Being the head of a family was too much for him. He was through.

There were, of course, other things involved in his decision to call it quits. They have to do with complex human emotions, with the immemorial urge of the male to cast off his encumbrances and look for new adventures, and so they lie with the causes of the divorce, which is not our subject here.

In retrospect, Pauline is of the opinion nowadays that she could have conquered her hot resentments and saved the situation. But the fact is she did not. She was shocked and angered by Schroeder's announcement. And so she went to see a lawyer. She wanted a legal separation rather than a divorce, and she is still a little bitter because the lawyer talked her out of that idea. He told her that such separations never worked, that a clean break was the only thing.

The upshot of it was a divorce granted to Pauline on the grounds of mental cruelty. The court gave her full and unconditional custody of the two children. It also gave her half the proceeds of the sale of the business and house in Wakeman. And in addition the court ordered Schroeder to pay her $60.00 a month toward the upkeep of his children.

So it was that after nine years of marriage, which seemed as happy and satisfying as most marriages, Pauline found herself on her own once more. She was 32 years old. She had $5,000 in

the bank and the court order demanding that her former husband pay her $60.00 a month. She realized at once that her new responsibilities lay beyond the mere feeding and sheltering of her two infants. She had to give them a chance in life . . .

She found a job almost at once in the small town of Columbia, about 10 miles from Elyria, but she couldn't find a place to live there. Pauline's father had died some years before, and her mother had married an elderly farmer. Now her mother bought a pleasant little house on a quiet street in Elyria and rented it to Pauline. Normally the property would bring about $60.00 a month. She gave it to Pauline for $35.00. In the division of the property at Wakeman, Pauline had been awarded the family car, and so her transportation would be taken care of.

'I figured it all out as carefully as I could,' Pauline said. 'My teaching job that first year would pay me about $2,100 and my alimony would come to $720.00—a total of a little more than $2,800. I thought that the only way to get a woman to take care of the house and the children while I was away would be to find someone who needed a home.'

She advertised in the newspapers. It was almost inevitable that the woman who finally came to work for her was herself divorced . . . The woman brought a teenaged daughter to live in the house on Marseilles Avenue. Her own divorce had been an affair of extreme unpleasantness. Her hatred for men—all men—had become ingrained, deep, and relentless. Presently Pauline began to realize that it was her chief subject of conversation . . .

Pauline has another housekeeper now. Perhaps it should be said again that she could not work to earn her living if she did not have a housekeeper. She pays the woman $72.00 a month, plus board and room. In the last four years she has taught her third-grade class of about 30 pupils in Columbia. Pauline's salary

(continued)

DADDY DOESN'T LIVE

A divorced mother says:

"Don't quit your marriage if you can possibly help it. If you do, brace yourself for tough times"

BY MORRIS MARKEY

THERE are in this country today hundreds of thousands of young women who are war widows in the most explicit sense, even though their husbands did not meet death in combat. They are widows by decree. Their marriages did not survive the grotesque distortions of wartime living and so ended in divorce.

A husband who has died honorably in the service of his country is not a morbid presence in the thoughts of the woman who loved him. His widow turns herself once more to the realities of living. But the husband who was observed a little furtively last night with a pretty girl on his arm, the husband who comes to see his children and expects all the privileges of their companionship with none of the duties — that man is a more haunting ghost than a man decently dead can ever be.

It is a proud and simple duty to tell the children their father died in the service of his country. It is a difficult moment when the children first ask: "Mother, what does divorce mean?"

The war widow whose husband died in uniform is cushioned economically, at least to some extent, by the pensions and allowances the government provides and by such life insurance as her husband might have carried. The widow by decree receives none of these benefits. Her only outside source of funds is the alimony granted by the courts. For the rest she is on her own.

Of course, this is not simply a war problem. We still live in the aftermath of those years of incredible excitements and bewilderments. The notion of divorce, of getting out of a situation that seems hopeless, comes into the heads of half the wives of the land at some time or other.

The dream of starting all over again is as old as time — not only with marriage but with life itself — of writing off the losses, wiping out the mistakes, beginning with a clean slate. We know that we cannot climb back into the cradle and look at the world once again with eyes which are innocent and hopeful and expectant. But almost anybody can go into a court of law and wipe out a marriage. Sometimes that [*Turn to page 108*]

The court gave Pauline Schroeder unconditional custody of the children. She says, "I want to keep them as normal as I can. I've seen in other children's faces the marks of the hatred and the quarrels they've listened to. I don't want my children to look like that"

Getting the screens up in the spring is a job for the man of the house—when there is one. Now all the odd jobs are up to Pauline

Teachers who have a college degree can command more money than those who do not. So while she taught she worked for her degree

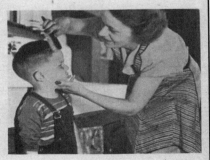

During the school term she leaves her home each morning at seven-thirty and rarely makes it home again before five in the afternoon

"Daddy Doesn't Live Here . . ." *(continued)*

has increased twice, and she now earns $2,450 a year. When her alimony is added this gives her a gross income of $3,170.

Against this income her fixed, overhead expenses for a year amount to $2,388 in a budget that is capitulated like this:

Groceries and Milk	$740
Heat	$120
Light and Water	$94
Rent	$420
Servant	$864
Upkeep of Car	$150

This gives her an apparent surplus of $782.00 over her major costs of living, which would seem to be a fairly comfortable margin, particularly in view of the fact that Schroeder's parents supply the larger part of the clothing for the children.

But every woman knows that the major costs of living are not the whole story by any means. There are doctors and dentists. Even in a small town the schoolteacher must be careful of her dress. And the unexpected extras make a ceaseless assault upon the pocketbook."

1952 News Profile

Union leader Sid Monti was head of the Scovill local when the brass workers of the Naugatuck Valley in western Connecticut struck for a funded pension plan in 1952. The strike was one of hundreds in that year as workers reasserted their rights in a prospering post-war America.

"At one time or another, everyone in Waterbury had at least one member of their family working at Scovill's. They were the largest employer in the town. Such a resentment had been built up against that company.

In negotiations, I used to turn to our guys and say, 'What's the cheapest commodity this company has?' They'd say, 'What do you mean, commodity?' I'd say: 'What's the cheapest thing they have? A piece of machinery? A roof over their head? A piece of equipment to work with? A ton of steel? Copper and brass? The cheapest commodity is you. If you get killed, all they have to do is pick up the phone, call up the employment agency, and say, send me a guy. It doesn't cost them a nickel. But if a piece of equipment goes on the bum, they have to spend money to fix it. So they think more of that piece of equipment than they do of you.'

(In the strike) the issues were manifold. We were probably the lowest-paid brass plant in the country, on any job. Grievances were manifold. They were a very big issue. We also wanted life insurance improvements. Night shift differential was a big thing. The sickness and accident benefit was the lowest in the industry. I think we were getting 25 or 30 bucks a week.

(Before 1952) the contract gave the company the right to re-study the job if they made a change that was five percent or more of the entire cycle. They'd always find a way to get five percent. So they'd make the woman make two steps, for example, and that would take five seconds off the total cycle time, if the total cycle was 22 seconds. They re-studied every job. In fact, we were doing more work for even less money, in spite of a wage increase. One of the major issues at Scovill was a funded pension plan. You want a pension plan that will not be based on payments by the company year out of the cash drawer, so to speak, but will be set up on an actuarially sound, funded basis. That was the strong UAW policy.

The Scovill strike I'm very, very proud of. We didn't have a union shop. We had maybe 600 or 700 dues-paying members and there were 7,000 or 8,000 people in the plant. I was

Sid Monti arrested July 11 during the 1952 Scovill strike.

holding my breath: I didn't know how many people would cross that line. The thing that I liked about the strike was the cohesiveness of the people. They felt that they had to be together, not from a trade union philosophy, but from the standpoint: look, they beat our brains in, now it's our turn to get even.

Everyone was with us. We had no problem getting pickets. If we ever ran short, we'd call up one of the locals and they'd send 100 people down as quickly as you could say 'shift.'

We built a union, and for the next few years they really functioned like a good trade union in all aspects: trade unionism, community activities, political action. On almost every level, we had good guys and good committees going out and doing the work that was necessary.

Immediately following the strike, we had some 21 arbitration cases. We had grievances coming out of our ears—we had 500 or 600 piled up. I think we won 21 or 22 straight arbitration cases. The result was we commanded a lot of respect. We were the first ones to get five-dollar-a month pensions in the brass industry, although they had already gotten them in auto and steel. That was the result of the 1952 strike."

1954 FAMILY PROFILE

The Rochmans, an extended Jewish family in Bangor, Maine, arrived in America in 1943 and joined a well-established Jewish community whose Polish and Russian roots are more than 70 years old. The man works in a clothing store selling men's clothing; his wife works part-time at a shoe store, but spends much of her time caring for their three children and her parents. The children have quickly become American; her grandparents still have not learned to speak English well; none have forgotten the Nazi extermination that drove them out of their home in Poland.

Annual Income: $3,100

The man works for a clothing store on commission. His weekly income varies according to his sales. He supports his wife, three children, and her elderly parents.

Annual Budget

This study focuses on life in this community and provides little personal data concerning expenditures. The consumer expenditures nationally on a per capita basis are:

Auto Parts	$8.01
Auto Usage	$160.72
Clothing	$116.39
Dentists	$8.62
Food	$411.35
Furniture	$23.40
Gas and Oil	$48.03
Health Insurance	$8.62
Housing	$198.30
Intercity Transport	$6.16
Local Transport	$11.70

New Auto Purchase. $66.51
Personal Business $54.19
Personal Care $20.94
Physicians $22.78
Private Education $14.16
Recreation. $83.13
Religious/Welfare Activities $20.83
Telephone and Telegraph $17.24
Tobacco. $30.17
Utilities $57.88
Per Capita Consumption $1,476.86

Life at Home

- This family was forced out of their home in Poland in 1941; after two years of petitions they were granted asylum in the United States.
- The Nazis' policy to exterminate the Jews was carried out extensively in Poland, the country that held the largest concentration of Europe's Jews.
- In December 1942 the Polish Foreign Ministry became the first governmental body publicly to conform to the German authorities' "systematic deliberation at the total extermination of the Jewish population of Poland"; a week later the 11 Allied governments condemned the "bestial policy of cold-blooded extermination."
- They arrived in 1943 and moved immediately to Bangor, Maine, where friends already lived; they knew some English and both they and their children learned quickly; her parents still yearn for Poland and have adopted few American customs.
- Work was readily available when they arrived because of the war effort; in 1948 the man was able to take a job in retailing at a men's clothing store.
- The Jewish Community and Hebrew School are the center of this family's life, especially for the grandparents who still struggle with English.
- Programs at the Community Center include lectures, classes, and cultural and social programs.
- The family now has an automobile, although only the man has learned to drive; regular gasoline for the car costs $0.28 a gallon; bus fare to cross town costs $0.15.
- Recently, her 66-year-old father was hospitalized with chest pains; his ward room cost $10.00 a day; a semiprivate room would have cost $13.00 a day.
- His weekly visits to the doctor now cost $3.50 per visit; if the doctor comes to the house, he typically bills $4.50.
- Haircuts cost $1.50 for the man; a shampoo and wave set for the wife costs $2.00, or a permanent wave runs $11.00.
- Electricity typically costs $3.78 per month for 100 kWh; natural gas costs an additional $1.32 for 10 therms.
- Laundry services are available in Bangor, charging $3.00 for a 20-pound bundle, thrifty washed or fluffed dry.

- Because of his work, dry cleaning expenditures are a necessity; typically dry cleaning and pressing a man's two-piece suit costs $1.40.
- The family regularly goes to a movie, if sales have been good, once a week. The charge is typically $0.70 per person; *From Here to Eternity* and *On the Waterfront* are current hits.
- The Rochmans have purchased a small black and white television set; nationwide 30 million homes have televisions.
- The family has also bought for the children a phonograph turntable capable of playing records at 78, 33 and 45 revolutions per minute; nationwide phonograph and television set ownership are similar: 30 million TVs versus 29.2 million turntables.

- The Rochman family gets the newspaper, including Sunday delivery, which costs $2.20 per month.
- The children like to read, so the man brings home popular magazines when money is available; the most popular magazines that year are *The Saturday Evening Post, Good Housekeeping, McCall's Magazine, Family Circle,* and *Woman's Home Companion.*
- A carton of cigarettes costs $2.20.
- Retail prices of food are stable from 1953 to 1954; retail food prices are fully decontrolled early in 1953 and are virtually the same as food prices in 1951 when price controls were in effect.
- Price-wage controls, in effect during World War II and until late 1946, are re-imposed in January, 1951; the biggest shift in food prices takes place from 1947 to 1949 when food costs increase 12 percent.
- In 1954 apples are $0.15 a pound; lettuce $0.14 a head; eggs $0.58 a dozen; sugar, $0.53 for five pounds.
- The family rarely goes on long trips even though they have a car; cost is one consideration, but many hotels in Maine still do not permit Jewish customers.
- When they travel, they attempt to make arrangements ahead or stay with friends to prevent being refused service and embarrassed.
- The children attend cheders, or Hebrew schools, which maintain the old custom of giving a child a taste of honey when he is beginning to learn—symbolic of the sweetness of study.
- The American Council for Judaism officially opposes schools like cheders that "take children out of the general American environment and train them to lead segregated lives."

Life at Work: Retail

- This man sells men's clothing in a store on Main Street; the shop is owned by a Jewish immigrant whose parents came to Bangor before the First World War.
- Although this man has lived in the United States for 11 years, he still is insecure about his manners.
- Using his hands too much or saying "oy vey" brings disapproving looks from the owner; Bangor Jews do not like to call attention to themselves, priding themselves on being different from New York or Boston Jews.
- The clothing store caters to many of the city's professionals who make seasonal buys; reduced price sales are rarely held.

- He is paid on commission, so his pay varies from week to week.
- Most men wear a suit and hat to church or any public function.
- Since the war ended, times have been good in Bangor; Dow Field brings many military officers into the city and since the war ended, soldiers have been eager to "look sharp."
- The base was closed in 1948 but reopened in 1950 at the start of the Korean War; 4,500 people, including nearly 2,000 civilians, currently work at the base.
- A new wool topcoat of a hard finished fabric sells in his store for $45.25; a two-piece man's suit of new wool with number four tailoring costs $62.00.

- Wool dress slacks for men with a hard finish are sold for $18.50 a pair; rayon/acetate gabardine slacks run $5.80 a piece.
- Broadcloth business shirts, of 128 x 68 combed yard, sell for $3.95; 112 x 60 carded yarn business shirts are available for $2.46.
- Men's Oxford shoes sell for $13.30, while a typical shoe repair runs $3.00.
- He is worried that new department stores will take his customers through sophisticated advertising; American business spends $8 billion in advertising in 1953 to lure customers, four times more than in 1920.
- A new Social Security Act now requires that workers and employers each pay two percent of their total income into the fund; the maximum yearly earnings subject to tax have been raised to $4,200.

Life in the Community: Bangor, Maine

- At the turn of the century, Bangor, Maine, boasted nearly 20,000 people, but many of its brightest and best young people were moving away to greater opportunities.
- Bangor was a city known for its timbering and its wealth, when five shipyards were active in the city carrying wood to Cuba and lumber to South America.
- Bangor businessmen, at that time, controlled 6,000 square miles of forest track, a territory as large as the states of Connecticut and Rhode Island combined.
- Bangor's Russian Jews established themselves near the end of the glory days of timber and shipping in the 1880s and 1890s, taking their place at the bottom of the city's trade in junk, trinkets, clothing, and dry goods.

"Don't Push Children toward Success," by Amy Selwyn, *Coronet*, April 1952:

"If you are like most parents, you are not content just to sit back and daydream of your child's success. You want to do everything possible to improve his chances of attaining it. Before you try harder, however, there is a vital fact you should know: from a certain point on, the harder you strive to insure a fortunate future for your child, the poorer are his chances of achieving it. Recently, a 22-year-old youth sobbed a pathetic tale to an interviewer at a Philadelphia employment agency. 'During the past two years,' he said morosely, 'I have held eight jobs and have been fired from all. The longest I have held any job is four months. I'm desperate for money now, but I don't dare ask my family for help. Ever since I was a child, my parents have drummed it into me that I'd be a big success when I grew up. I have been so scared of disappointing them that I make a mess of everything I do . . .' Such examples are all too common. As Dr. Nina Ridenour, educational director of the National Association for Mental Health, points out: 'Probably far more problems are created by parents out of their desire to improve their children than from negligence, indifference, or just pure cussedness. There are six principal ways to which well-intentioned parents unknowingly push their children toward frustration and failure: they urge them to outshine others; they burden them with too many responsibilities; they praise them too much; they pick their pastimes; they demand perfection and they decide their vocation."

- Most of the Jewish immigrants had been pushed out of Russia and Russia-dominated Poland by violence and poverty.
- Jews in Russia could not own land, were excluded from state schools, and could not be employed in numerous trades.
- Government policy called for Jews to convert to Christianity, emigrate, or be killed.
- From 1891 to 1910 two million Jews emigrated from the area; more than one million came to the United States; between 1899 and 1920, Jews constituted 11 percent of all immigrants, only the Italians boasted more.
- Almost all of the Jews who settled in Bangor in this period originally came from small communities with a few hundred Jewish families; they had lived in cramped, wooden houses with dirt floors, on unlit, unpaved streets surrounded by farms and forests.
- Many arrived in America with limited skills.
- Most Russian Jewish immigrants began American life in the overcrowded sections of New York City, then migrated to other places.
- From 1890 to 1910 only 1,835 Jewish immigrants moved to Maine, compared with 66,023 in Massachusetts and 108,534 in Pennsylvania.
- By 1897 the Jewish community in Bangor was able to build a permanent synagogue; the dedication was attended by 100 people including the mayor and "prominent Gentiles" according to the Bangor Commercial newspaper.
- By 1915 most Orthodox Jews in Bangor, seeking to adapt, shed most of the Orthodox insignia of skullcaps worn by men and wigs by women.
- By 1945, shortly after the Rochmans arrived in Bangor, the Jews of the city learned that the Russian and Polish villages where Bangor's Jewish immigrants had once lived were

now devoid of Jewish life, their histories irretrievably lost to the Nazi campaign against the Jews.

- A special celebration greeted the creation of the state of Israel in 1948; by 1954 the stability of Israel and the threat of war remain.
- By 1951 only a quarter of Bangor's 1,200 Jews still live in the poorer areas, although they remain a self-contained group.
- A census taken by the Jewish Community Council in 1951 shows that Jews own or work in over 200 shoe, clothing, and dry goods stores; more than 300 are self-employed; 51 are professionals.
- The report also shows that 272 men and women are college-educated, 26 have attended graduate schools, and 65 percent of the Jewish Community own their own homes.
- Annually, All Souls Congregational Church and Beth Israel engage in a pulpit exchange as part of an interfaith effort.

The Illustrated Maine Woods, by Henry David Thoreau:

"[Bangor was] like a star on the edge of night, still hewing at the forests of which it is built, already overflowing with the luxuries and refinement of Europe, and sending its vessels to Spain, to England, and to the West Indies for its groceries—and yet only a few axe-men have gone 'up river' into the howling wilderness which feeds it."

"I Have Two Mothers and Two Fathers," by Louise Horner, *Good Housekeeping,* **February 1951:**

"It had always seemed to me that we were an essentially happy family. Divorces happened in other families, not in ours. But the week after I graduated from high school, my two brothers and I were called into our parents' room for one of our infrequent family conferences. We sat in a row on the edge of the big bed and watched the rain beat against the windows. 'Children, please try to understand what we are going to tell you,' Mother said. 'Your father and I—' there was a catch in her voice and she could not go on. Dad looked at a spot on the wall above our heads. Finally his words came in a rush. 'After thinking it over, your mother and I have decided that it would be better for all of us if we lived apart from each other.' He turned his back to us and stared out the window at the rain . . . Eight years have elapsed since then, and because I have gained perspective, I can appreciate the wisdom with which our parents handled the situation. They told us there had been no quarrel. Their life together had to end because they had grown away from each other. They promised that when any problems concerning us arose, they would do their best to solve them together."

- By 1954 only a few families attending Bangor's three synagogues are strictly observant; many no longer follow the rules of kashrut or adhere to Sabbath laws.
- One of the two kosher butcher shops in the city sells non-kosher meat on the side and another gives up selling kosher food and becomes the largest meat market in Bangor.
- In 1954 the Jewish community establishes a funeral chapel so that funeral services no longer need to be held in private homes.
- Guided by a master plan drawn up in 1951, Bangor is beginning to re-orient downtown from the once-bustling docks to handle cars and trucks.
- Efforts are also under way to stop the dumping of sewage directly into the Kenduskeag Stream and the Penobscot River, which also serves as the city's drinking water source.
- After the war ends the women of Bangor—in a daily ritual of sociability—still go downtown to shop, carefully dressed in suits or dresses, gloves, and hats.
- About 8,000 of the city's homes are below national and state standards.
- "Poverty, crime, war, juvenile delinquency, racial discrimination, family disintegration, mental illness, dishonesty in government" are all listed as the social ills of the city that year.

HISTORICAL SNAPSHOT
1954–1955

- The Supreme Court declared racial segregation in public schools illegal
- The first nuclear-powered submarine, *Nautilus,* was launched
- Gasoline averaged $0.29 per gallon
- Texas Instruments introduced the first practical silicon transistor
- Taxpayers with incomes of more than $100,000 paid more than $67,000 each in taxes
- Sales of Viceroy cigarettes leaped as smokers shifted to filter-tipped cigarettes
- Open-heart surgery was introduced by Minneapolis physician C. Walton Lillehe
- RCA introduced the first color television set
- The $13 million, 900-room Fontainebleau Hotel opened at Miami Beach
- *Sports Illustrated Magazine* was introduced
- Swanson & Sons introduced frozen TV dinners
- Births remained above four million per year
- Dr. Jonas E. Salk, U.S. developer of antipolio serum, started inoculating school children in Pittsburgh, Pennsylvania
- The United States boasted 1,768 million newspapers, publishing 59 million copies daily
- 29 million American homes now had television sets
- The U.S. population contained six percent of the world's population, 60 percent of all cars, 58 percent of all telephones, 45 percent of all radio sets, and 34 percent of all railroads
- Marian Anderson was the first Black soloist of the Metropolitan Opera, where she appeared as Ulrica in *Un Ballo* in Maschera
- Blacks in Montgomery, Alabama, boycotted segregated city bus lines; Rosa Parks was arrested for refusing to give up the only seat available, which was in the front of the bus
- The first Chevrolet V-8 engine motorcar was introduced
- The federal minimum wage rose from $0.75 to $1.00 per hour
- AF of L and CIO labor unions merged
- Whirlpool Corporation was created by the merger of three companies
- *National Review* and *Village Voice* began publication
- Crest was introduced by Proctor and Gamble
- Special K breakfast food was introduced by Kellogg Company
- The nation now had 1,800 suburban shopping centers
- The number of millionaires in the United States was reported to be 154
- New television shows introduced that year included *The Adventures of Rin Tin Tin, Father Knows Best, Lassie,* and *Tonight* with Steve Allen.

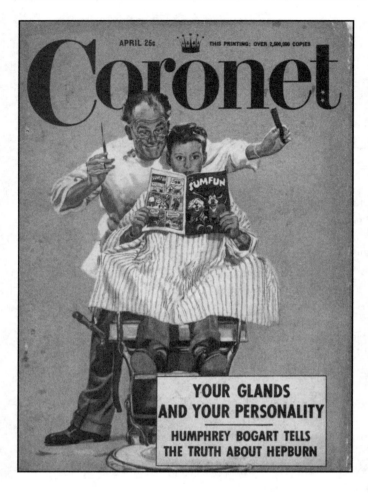

"ARROW" is the most magic word in your shirt-shopping vocabulary. Just say "ARROW" to your salesclerk—and he'll show you the world's finest shirts. Arrow Shirts, famous for their good looks, fine fit and their wonderful Arrow Collars. Arrow shirts that wear and wear and wear!

"DART" is America's most popular shirt. Beautifully tailored in smooth broadcloth, Dart has the fabulous nonwilt, wrinkle-free collar that needs no starch, keeps neat all day. Like every wonderful Arrow shirt, the Dart has gleaming white anchor-stitched buttons that won't break, chip or crack. Price: $3.95.

"MITOGA" means a shirt is specially tailored for appearance and comfort. The shoulders, sleeves and sides taper to follow and flatter a man's contours. Only Arrows are Mitoga-tailored. That's one of the reasons why most men insist on Arrows when they buy shirts for themselves.

"SANFORIZED"! Everyone knows that means the fabric won't shrink more than 1%. All Arrow shirts are "Sanforized"-labeled! And thanks to quality fabrics and exquisite tailoring, Arrow shirts are extra easy to iron. Many women tell us they iron Arrow shirts in half the time it takes to iron others.

1954 ECONOMIC PROFILE

Income, Standard Jobs

Average of All Industries, Including Farm Labor	$4,033.00
Bituminous Coal Mining	$3,959.00
Building Trades	$4,484.00
Domestics	$1,832.00
Farm Labor	$1,498.00
Federal Civilian	$4,507.00
Federal Military	$2,997.00
Gas and Electricity Workers	$4,579.00
Manufacturing, Durable Goods	$4,452.00
Manufacturing, Nondurable Goods	$3,923.00
Medical/Health Services Workers	$2,417.00
Miscellaneous Manufacturing	$3,640.00
Motion Picture Services	$3,929.00
Nonprofit Organization Workers	$3,179.00
Passenger Transportation	$3,914.00
Personal Services	$2,682.00
Public School Teachers	$3,510.00
Radio Broadcasting and Television Workers	$5,957.00
Railroads	$4,544.00
State and Local Government Workers	$3,281.00
Telephone and Telegraph Workers	$3,914.00

Selected Prices

Ann Barton Hair Dryer	$21.50
Automobile Chassis Lubrication	$1.25
Axminster Rug, All Wool	$93.50
Bayer Aspirin, 30 Tablets	$0.30
Betty Crocker Cake Mix, 20-Ounce Package	$0.35
Cotton Jacquard Bedspread	$6.35
Dan River Sheet, Bordered	$10.50
Gas Water Heater, 30 Gallon	$151.90
Goldberger Doll, in Party Dress	$3.98
Hammond Chord Organ	$975.00
Hollob's Supreme Peanut Butter, 12 Ounces	$0.33
Kerrybrooke Wallet	$3.50
Motor Oil, Quart	$0.32
Nylon Hose, per Pair	$0.95
Reardon Laboratories Mouse Seed	$0.25
Table Model Radio	$21.70
Toilet Tissue, per Roll	$0.09

Tooth Extraction $5.50
Upright Vacuum Cleaner. $86.70
Waring Products Blender. $44.50
Zippo Lighter Fluid $0.25

new '55 DODGE flashes ahead in style!

New Dodge Custom Royal V-8 4-Door Sedan in Cameo Red over Sapphire White

It's flair-fashioned . . . and alive with beauty

You will know, from your very first glimpse of its sleek silhouette, that here is a car of a hundred surprises!

A car that gives you a *new outlook* on the world through its swept-back New Horizon windshield.

A car that captures the flair of the future in the taut, eager beauty of its flowing lines.

A car that sweeps you forward at the command of Flite Control, bringing new magic to PowerFlite.

A car of many innovations: Tubeless tires . . . push-button windows and seats . . . an aircraft-type V-8 engine.

You can expect the unexpected in the flair-fashioned '55 Dodge . . . on display now!

Take Command . . . Get the Thrill First Hand!

The Jews in America

- In 1820 approximately 5,000 Jews lived in America; by 1850 the number had grown to 50,000, and by 1880 the number was 10 times larger.
- Although Jews, particularly from Germany, had come to America earlier, after 1880 Jewish immigration became a flood tide.
- More than two million Jews arrived in the United States over three decades, most from eastern Europe where three-quarters of the world's 7.7 million Jews were living.
- In Russia and the Austro-Hungarian empire, the growth of large-scale agriculture squeezed out Jewish middlemen as it destroyed the independent peasantry.
- In some countries savage discrimination and severe restrictions on the jobs they might hold forced them to emigrate.
- By the turn of the century, 700,000 arrived on the shores of the United States; one-quarter were illiterate; many had few skills and almost all were impoverished.

- Often the husband went to America first and by cautious living, he saved enough to fetch his children and wife from the old country.
- The average immigrant arrived in New York with only $20.00 to his or her name.
- The ocean voyage, which cost $34.00 in steerage class, was difficult for all immigrants, but particularly Orthodox Jews, whose religious diet required that they subsist on herring, black bread, and tea—all of which they brought on board with them.
- Upon arrival, according to survey in 1890, 60 percent of the immigrant Jews worked in the needle trades in New York City, typically using primitive machines to sew together cut goods provided by the manufacturer.
- Life in the sweatshops on the Lower East Side was difficult but provided unskilled immigrants with immediate employment opportunities and the chance to earn a weekly wage of $5.00.
- On the Lower East Side, where most of the Jewish families lived, rent was about $10.00 a month, milk was $0.04 a quart, bread was $0.02 a pound, herring was a penny, and a kitchen table could be bought for $1.00.
- Within the tenements, only one room in each four-room apartment received direct air and sunlight; all the families on each floor shared a toilet in the hall.
- Despite the highest population density in the city, the predominantly Jewish Tenth Ward had one of the lowest death rates; this was attributed to the strenuous personal cleanliness of the Jews.
- Tuberculosis, the white plague, did abound, one reason many Jews left the city for farms or other smaller cities such as Bangor to seek their fortune.
- Alcohol use among Jewish immigrants was limited; instead sales of seltzer or soda water to Jewish workers were so high it became known as "worker's champagne."
- Despite their poverty, Jewish families were typically healthy; mothers considered their children woefully underweight unless they were well-cushioned with fat.
- The economic transition of the Jews took place quickly; thanks to an emphasis on education, many began entering white collar and professional jobs.
- Composer Irving Berlin, born in Russia and brought to America as a small child, electrified America with his songs including "Alexander's Ragtime Band" in 1911 and later "Annie Get Your Gun."

Sylvia Alpert Dduze describes the arduous daily routine of her father, Israel Alpert, who worked as a Jewish peddler around 1910 in Maine:

"My father had a team and horse and he went to homes and commercial areas where he bought up scrap metals which he in turn sold to junkyards. Pap got up very early in the morning. In the winter he had to stoke the furnace, add enough coal to last all day, and build up a good fire in the stove. He also shoveled snow and took care of the horse before hitching him to the team, and made sure his family was set for the day before leaving for outlying areas to buy and sell as he went along. In the winter he left before dawn and returned after dark. He was a small, slim man, barely five feet tall, and how he handled all those heavy metal parts by himself, I will never understand. The side of the wagon used by my father in his business had the name of its former owner, 'Bunker,' on it. Not knowing his real name, everyone who did business with him called him Billy or Eddie Bunker."

- Following the First World War and the Russian Revolution of 1917, America closed its doors to immigration.
- In 1917 Congress passed a literacy requirement, over President Wilson's veto, to restrict the flow of immigrants; the 1924 Johnson Bill provided that only two percent of each nationality group be admitted each year, based on the 1890 census; the immigration from southern and eastern Europe virtually stopped.
- Between the wars discrimination was practiced against Jews in housing and employment; many companies made no secret of the fact that they did not hire Jews.
- Certain neighborhoods were restricted to Jews; universities adopted a quota system that limited the number of Jewish students to a certain percentage.
- With Hitler's rise to power in Germany, many Jews—including this family—fled to America to avoid the concentration camps.
- The Nazi "ethnic cleansing" campaign resulted in six million Jews being killed or exterminated in Nazi death camps.
- Under the Displaced Persons Act, thousands of Jews were admitted after the war.

1957 Family Profile

Tom is a 20-year-old skilled journeyman carpenter in Minneapolis, Minnesota, making a little more than $3.00 an hour. He and his 19-year-old wife, Laura, are expecting their first child and are searching for a larger place to live. He is thinking about trading his car for a "family car" and worrying about the seasonal pay of his job.

Annual Income: $6,115

Tom earns $3.10 an hour and works 39 to 40 weeks a year, often picking up overtime on weekends and Sundays. His wife does not work. The family income after taxes is $4,565.

Annual Budget

Alcoholic Beverages	$71.00
Automobile	$900.00
Clothing and Services	$454.00
Education	$53.00
Food at Home	$742.00
Food away from Home	$222.00
Fuel, Light, Refrigeration, Water	$149.00
House Furnishings and Equipment	$253.00
Household Operations	$304.00
Medical Care	$305.00
Other Expenditures	$52.00
Other Travel	$85.00
Personal Care	$131.00
Reading	$30.00
Recreation	$217.00
Rent	$587.00
Tobacco	$73.00

Life at Home

- After high school, this man went immediately to work to support his wife; they were married on his graduation night.
- They rent a small apartment from his uncle, who is also a carpenter, and are looking for a larger place.
- Tom and Laura have looked at several of the suburbs where he is building houses, but don't have the down payment to buy a house and don't want to move downtown where she doesn't feel "safe."
- She is expecting a baby and they want to be settled before the child arrives.
- Through the United Brotherhood of Carpenters and Joiners of America, he has health insurance to cover some of the expense of having a baby.
- She has been reading all the literature to make sure her baby is healthy; if the baby is a boy his life expectancy is 66.64 years; if the baby is a girl her life expectancy is 72.65 years; non-White male children born that year have a life expectancy of 59.13 years.
- They buy from Sears for tools and furniture; like their parents they enjoy reading the catalog, but unlike their parents they go to a local Sears store to buy what they see in the mail order book—a trend across America.
- Although Laura prides herself on being a frugal homemaker, she enjoys drawing and has visited the Walker Art Galleries (cost $0.10), where the collected paintings, jade, and early ceramics of millionaire T. B. Walker are on display; she also enjoys the Institute of Arts (cost $0.25), which has works ranging from Gothic to Renaissance to nineteenth-century French works—her favorite.
- His passion is cars; currently he owns a 1951 two-door Mercury, which he has modified to make it as different as possible from the "Detroit-model"; he enjoys reading *Hot Rod,* and *Car and Custom* to get new ideas.
- They are talking about selling his car and buying a new Nash Rambler Wagon, once the baby comes; the new car will cost $2,410.

M-94—The Narrows, Lake Minnetonka, near Minneapolis, Minn.

7B-H1446

- Street cars are available for a fare of $0.10, as are buses; a taxi ride is $0.25 for the first half-mile, $0.10 for each additional half-mile, while a trip from downtown to the airport in a taxi costs $0.75.
- Most nights they spend together watching television, eating off "TV trays"; *I Love Lucy* and *Gunsmoke* are favorites. During the day she watches *As the World Turns* and *The Edge of Night* which come to be called soap operas because their sponsors are often the makers of soaps and detergents.

Life at Work: Carpentry

- Always good with his hands, Tom is attracted to carpentry by the freedom and the chance to work out-of-doors.
- He has worked for the same contractor for several years, moving from job to job as the contractor changes jobs.
- He is paid by the hour; when there is no work or snow is too heavy, he is not paid that day or week.
- Tom receives no paid holidays or paid vacations; time-and-a-half is paid for work over 40 hours and double-time is paid for Sunday work.
- He became a member of the carpenter's union as soon as possible and now makes $3.10 an hour, often working 50 hours a week; traditionally, the weather allows him to work about 39 weeks a year.
- The 1.2 million carpenters nationwide comprise the largest single group of skilled workers in the country and account for about two-fifths of all building trades craftsmen.
- In general, carpenters saw, fit, and assemble wood, plywood, wallboard, and other materials and fasten these materials by means of glue, nails, bolts, or wood screws to form various structures.

- They use hand tools such as hammers, saws, chisels, and planes as well as power tools such as portable power saws, drills, and rivet guns.
- Initially this man did rough carpentry work, primarily installing flooring in houses and erecting walls; today he does finish carpentry, installing molding around floors and ceilings, wood paneling, cabinets, door frames, and hardware.

- Physically, he is sturdy and well-coordinated; he has grown accustomed to standing for an entire day while installing molding or building a form.
- Tom looks for opportunities to install hardwood floors or hang ceiling molding—both requiring good carpentry skills and often resulting in better pay.
- His work requires extreme accuracy because all his work—including his mistakes—is highly visible.
- He has never had a major injury on the job, although cuts and bruises are an everyday hazard on the job site.
- For the past year he has primarily built houses in the rapidly expanding suburbs of the city; he has also worked on multistory apartments and small office buildings.
- The mid-1950s are a bonanza for builders; new suburban houses are added at an astonishing rate.
- In the California suburb of Lakewood, as many as 100 houses are started each day, and 17,500 are completed in less than three years.
- *House and Garden Magazine* reports that suburbia has become "the national way of life."
- The average suburbanite is earning $6,500 in the mid-1950s and is eager to buy hi-fis, martini glasses, and power lawn mowers with abandon.

Life in the Community: Minneapolis, Minnesota

- Minneapolis boasts a population of 521,718 in 1950, and is the 17th largest city in America; the city has grown from a population of 380,582 in 1920.
- The Twin Cities of Minneapolis and St. Paul are near the geographical center of North America; together they form the nation's eighth largest city and stand at the headwaters of the Mississippi River.
- The appearance of the two cities is different; St. Paul's loop streets are narrow and concentrated, while Minneapolis' center of activity extends many blocks along the broad shopping avenues; St. Paul is hilly, Minneapolis level; the early history of both cities is dominated by French Canadians and Scandinavians.
- French Canadian whisky salesman Pierre Parrant was the first actual settler within the present limits of St. Paul, leading to the popular quip that "while Minneapolis was concerned about water power, St. Paul was born in whisky."
- Thanks to early visionary leadership, thousands of acres of land within Minneapolis was set aside for parks; in the mid-1950s the city boasts 144 parks, embracing 5,253 acres, or one park acre for every 92 people.
- The 32nd state to enter the Union, Minnesota has a population of 3.1 million; only a few square miles of northern

The Face of Minnesota, by John Szarkowski, 1958:

"Farming as a way of life no longer means a frozen pump in wintertime. If the farmer's attitude toward the ideal of farm life has remained constant, his actual style of living has changed enormously. Modern roads and automobiles have made his an increasingly suburban occupation. He has come to rely more and more upon the city—the machine shop, the power plant, laboratory, and supply depot upon which his amazingly complex technical operation depends. And increasingly, the city is also the place from which he and his family get their entertainment, education, mutual life, and news of the world. In the process, the farm family has adopted many of the standards of their urban relations. A professor at the University agricultural school summarized the change by saying that the real problem had become, 'How are you going to keep the girls down on the farm?' Progress toward achieving urban living standards has been amazing. On Minnesota farms in the decade after 1940, the number of mechanical refrigerators increased seven times; by 1950 there were also three times as many modern bathrooms, four times as many running water systems. A survey of the items with which Isanti county farm women reported being most dissatisfied in 1950 were, (in order) children's job prospects, savings, telephone, lawn, sewage disposal system, living room furniture, hours of work, recreational facilities for self, house and public library books."

Minnesota territory produces most of the nation's iron ore and provides the activity for the port of Duluth.

- Minnesota farms produce oats, butter, eggs, milk, corn, wheat, and potatoes; the state boasts 11,000 lakes and great fishing, hunting, and trapping.
- The year this man and woman graduate from high school, the state of Minnesota spends an average of $306.00 per pupil, per year; teachers are paid an average yearly salary of $3,741.
- By comparison, in Mississippi the average expenditure per White pupil is $147.49, $39.93 for African-American students; White teachers are paid $2,025; Black teachers are paid $1,035.

HISTORICAL SNAPSHOT
1957–1958

- President Eisenhower sent paratroopers to Little Rock, Arkansas, to protect nine Black students seeking to attend all-White Central High School
- "Beat" and "beatnik" took hold as new words to describe the "Beat Generation"
- Unemployment in the U.S. reached 5.2 million, a post-war high
- Martin Luther King, Jr., helped organize the Southern Christian Leadership Conference (SCLC) and became its first president
- Evangelist Billy Graham held a five-month-long revival at Madison Square Garden in New York that attracted more than 500,000 people
- After 38 years, *Collier's Magazine* published its final issue
- Tennis player Althea Gibson became the first Black athlete to win at Wimbledon
- *Sputnik I,* the first manmade satellite, was sent into orbit around the earth by the Soviets
- Painkiller Darvon was introduced by Eli Lilly
- A University of Wisconsin study showed that 20 percent of Americans lived in poverty
- New York's first trolley car was retired
- Frisbee was introduced by Wham-O Manufacturing
- Per capita margarine consumption exceeded butter for the first time
- A record 4.3 million babies were born
- The cost of 100,000 computerized multiplication computations fell from $1.26 in 1952 to $0.26.
- Volkswagen sold 200,000 Beetles; Ford introduced the Edsel
- An intensive study of birth control with pills was begun in Puerto Rico
- *Fortune* named Paul Getty America's richest man; his wealth was estimated to be $1 billion
- Average wages for a factory production worker were $2.08 an hour, or $82.00 a week
- Gasoline cost $0.304 cents per gallon
- BankAmericard credit card was introduced
- First-class postal rates climbed to $0.04 per ounce
- The VD rate increased from 122,000 cases to 126,000, the first increase since 1948
- Sweet'n' Low sugarless sweetener was introduced
- The Everly Brothers' song "Wake Up Little Susie" was banned in Boston
- One in three women went regularly to the beauty shop, many for apricot or silver-colored hair

1957 Economic Profile

Income, Standard Jobs

Average of All Industries,
    Including Farm Labor. $4,657.00
Bituminous Coal Mining $5,086.00
Building Trades. $5,120.00
Domestics $2,050.00
Farm Labor. $1,657.00
Federal Civilian. $5,203.00
Federal Military $3,439.00
Gas and Electricity Workers. $5,247.00
Manufacturing, Durable Goods. $5,207.00
Manufacturing, Nondurable Goods . . . $4,540.00
Medical/Health Services Workers $2,612.00
Miscellaneous Manufacturing $4,195.00
Motion Picture Services $4,745.00
Nonprofit Organization Workers. $3,533.00
Passenger Transportation $4,449.00
Personal Services. $2,999.00
Public School Teachers $4,085.00
Radio Broadcasting and
    Television Workers. $6,756.00
Railroads. $5,416.00
State and Local Government
    Workers. $3,747.00
Telephone and Telegraph Workers. $4,471.00
Wholesale and Retail Trade
    Workers. $3,558.00

Selected Prices

Accordion. $189.00
Acoustic Research Loudspeakers,
    Pair $89.00
Arvin Model Electric Heater $12.95
Bulova Royal Clipper Man's Watch $59.50
Colgate Deodorizer, Aerosol Can $0.69
Guitar. $27.50
Harvard Bed Frame $12.95
Hotel Room, Mount-Vue
    Motel $4.00/Night
Man's Arrow Shirt $5.00
Man's Botany 500 Suit. $59.50
Max Factor Hi-Fi Eyeliner. $1.50
Pal Injector Razor Blades, 20 Count $0.79
Perma-Life Brassiere $3.50
Pocket Radio, Zenith Royall 500 . . . . $75.00
Pontiac Bonneville $5,782.00
Sears Iron Jack Plane $6.36

In her spare time, she loved to visit museums.

Stevens Suit $17.95
Sunbeam Rain King Lawn Sprinkler $9.95
Wizard Refrigerator, 80-Pound Freezer . . $259.00
Woman's Brown Paddock Shoes $12.95
Zenith Lafayette Cabinet Model
    Television $550.00

A CHANGING SOCIETY

- America now boasted 71 cities with more than one million residents; in 1914 the number was 16.
- Nationwide the population of the United States increased 13 percent from 1950 to 1957; the gross national product in constant dollars rose 27 percent, while the number of motor vehicles in operation rose 38 percent.
- Since 1900 the death rate in America was cut nearly in half; at the turn of the century the death rate was 17.2 per 1,000 persons, but by the mid-1950s it was 9.2 per 1,000.
- The average lifetime in the country was now about 70 years, or about 30 years more than it had been at the middle of the last century.
- Tuberculosis, which at the turn of the century was the leading cause of death, was no longer among the top 10 causes of death thanks to the widespread use of penicillin and antibiotics.
- Over the same time period, measles, scarlet fever, whooping cough, and diphtheria dropped from 65 deaths per 100,000 to .7 deaths per 100,000.

"Blows against Segregation," *Life Magazine,* **January 1957:**

"The edifice of segregation shook last week and the chips are flying in several southern areas. Montgomery, Alabama, offices have received the U.S. Supreme Court order to let Negroes sit in buses wherever they liked, thus bringing at least a temporary end to the almost total boycott of the city buses which Negroes had maintained for an incredible 381 days. And now, because of the Court's firm stand, new bus desegregation campaigns are gathering momentum in other cities in Alabama, Louisiana, and Florida.

In Montgomery itself the legal triumph still had far to go before it became an accepted fact. Though most Whites adjusted to the new situation and Negroes diligently practiced good manners, sporadic violence flared. Several buses were shot up. In one a Negro woman was wounded in both legs, an incident which caused the jittery city government to halt bus service temporarily.

In Birmingham, Alabama, Negroes defied segregation ordinances and mingled with Whites on city buses after the house of one Negro leader was dynamited. As a result, 22 were arrested. But they obtained a test case to bring before the U.S. District Court.

In Tallahassee, Florida, Negroes, who had been boycotting buses since the end of May, began riding in forbidden seats. When the bus line did not stop it the city council furiously suspended its franchise and drivers were arrested. But the action was unlikely to stand up in court. Said Federal Judge Dozier Devane, as he granted the bus line a temporary injunction, 'Every segregation act . . . is dead as a doornail.'"

Happy New year!

The new television season is just beginning, but the festivities are already in full swing on NBC Television.

MILTON BERLE, BOB HOPE, MARTHA RAYE and DINAH SHORE make Tuesday night a party night. MILTON BERLE is blazing a new trail as Mr. Color Television, with a season of 13 dazzling, full-hour "opening night events" — revues, musical comedies, satires and dramatic shows, all in full color, as well as in black-and-white. On other Tuesday nights you'll enjoy THE BOB HOPE SHOW, with Bob's guest stars, side-splitting routines and big, special traveling shows . . . and THE MARTHA RAYE SHOW, with Martha singing, dancing, acting and clowning. And this year, warm, wonderful DINAH SHORE joins these traditional Tuesday night favorites with her own special full-hour programs.

Sunday night, too, is more exciting than ever. The new COLGATE VARIETY HOUR spotlights the most talked-of personalities in show business — stars of stage, screen and television who are making the world's entertainment headlines. And during the season, DEAN MARTIN and JERRY LEWIS will be touching off their comedy fireworks.

PERRY COMO joins the NBC parade of Saturday night stars with THE PERRY COMO SHOW. It's a glittering, new, star-filled extravaganza, with Perry as singer, star and host of a full hour of high-spirited variety.

And the fun has just begun. All through 1955-1956, you'll find there's a happy new year of TV entertainment on your NBC television station.

 exciting things are happening on
TELEVISION *a service of* RCA

Letter to psychiatrist Fredric Wertham, critical of comic books and their influence on young people:

"Dear Dr. Wertham, We have two boys, 7 and 13, with unusually high intelligence and excellent ability in school and in sports . . . . They have a library of fine books of their own, and read library books almost daily, yet in the presence of comic books they behave as if drugged, and will not lift their eyes or speak when spoken to . . . What we would like to know is, what can be done about it before it is too late? My boys fight with each other in a manner that is unbelievable in a home where both parents are university graduates and perfectly mated. We attribute the so-called 'hatred' they profess for each other to be the harmful influence of these books, plus movies and radio. We consider the situation to be as serious as an invasion of the enemy in wartime, with as far-reaching consequences as the atom bomb. If we cannot stop the wicked men who are poisoning our children's minds, what chance is there for mankind to survive longer than one generation, or half of one?"

- The death rate from diphtheria at the beginning of the century was 50 times as high as the current rate from all four of these communicable childhood diseases combined.
- At the turn of the century, cardiovascular-renal diseases (including diseases of the heart, arteries, and kidneys) and cancer were responsible for 25 percent of the total mortality in the United States; today these diseases accounted for 70 percent of total deaths.
- Accidents took about 90,000 lives a year at this time; only cardiovascular disease and cancer killed more.

"The Age of Psychology in the U.S. Less than a century old, the science of human behavior permeates our whole way of life—at work, in love, in sickness, and in health," *Life Magazine*, January 7, 1957:

"After getting up the other day, John Jones, America, shaved with a razor he had bought on the strength of a magazine ad approved by the head psychologist of an advertising agency. At his breakfast table, in his morning newspaper, he read two columns of psychological fact and advice. One told him that women were absolutely not more intuitive than men, all popular opinions to the contrary notwithstanding. The other invited him to find his 'happiness quotient' by answering a series of 10 questions. He then drove to work, guided by road signs painted yellow and black because a psychologist once discovered that these colors make for easier reading. At the plant he walked past the office of the company psychiatrist, where he would have been free to go in and seek counsel had he felt especially disturbed about anything that morning, and got right to work at his job, to which he had been promoted after taking a series of psychological tests.

Among his other duties this particular morning was a conference with an industrial psychologist who had been retained to advise on the company's spending contract negotiations with the union. At noon, over his lunch, he read two more psychological columns in his afternoon paper, one telling him how to improve his relations with his mother-in-law, the other advising a letter writer that her errant husband probably had a mother fixation. He also read in his favorite gossip column that one of his pet movie actresses, about to go on location in Africa, was taking along her personal psychoanalyst lest she lapse into another of her spells of melancholy . . . .

All these things might have happened to any American last week. They could not have happened to any previous generation and they could not have happened even last week in any other country, for widespread use of psychology as an applied science of everyday living is brand-new and strictly American. The birth of modern psychology took place less than 100 years ago, of psychoanalysis scarcely more than 50. In many parts of the world all knowledge of them is still restricted to the college classroom or the doctor's office. But in the U.S., for better or worse, this is the age of psychology and psychoanalysis as much as it is the age of chemistry or the atom bomb."

- Automobile accidents were responsible for 36,000 deaths each year; of these, 7,900 were pedestrians hit by a motor vehicle. Pedestrian deaths were down from 1928, when 11,420 people died when hit by cars.
- In 1954 injuries around the house claimed 27,500 lives, almost twice as many as were killed in occupational accidents.
- The television set, a novelty as the 1950s began, was now present in 86 percent of the country's homes; the average viewing time was six hours per day.
- Television's impact on Americans included staying up later to watch their favorite shows, forsaking traditional meals in the kitchen or dining room for TV dinners in the living room, and even the timing of their use of the bathroom with commercial and station breaks.

"Pipe-Cleaner Decorations,"
Popular Mechanics Magazine, **June 1958:**

"If pipe smokers are having a difficult time obtaining cleaners for their pipes, it may be because hobbyists and do-it-yourselfers are using these cotton tuft-covered lengths of wire for decorative purposes. Illustrated are many ways in which pipe cleaners may be used to decorate objects. In addition to using standard pipe cleaners, you can decorate with chenille pipe cleaners, which are about twice the length of the former and available in a variety of colors."

Value of One Dollar	
Year	Value in 2010 USD
1961	$7.37
1963	$7.13
1965	$6.92
1966	$6.71
1968	$6.27

Values are approximate based upon economic historical data and 2010 U. S. Dollar

1960–1969

The 1960s was a time of momentous social movements, remarkable space achievements, tragic assassinations, and the longest war in American history. Civil Rights leader Martin Luther King, Jr., would deliver his "I have a dream" speech and President John F. Kennedy would be killed the same year, 1963. King and John Kennedy's influential brother Bobby would both be shot five years later in 1968.

From 1960 to 1964 the economy expanded; unemployment was low. Gross national product and total federal spending increased by nearly 25 percent; inflation was held in check. The power of the United States internationally was immense. Congress gave the young President John F. Kennedy the defense and space-related programs we wanted, but few of the welfare programs he proposed. Then inflation arrived, along with the Vietnam War. From an annual average of less than two percent inflation between 1950 and 1965, suddenly inflation soared, ranging from six percent to 14 percent a year, and averaging a budget-popping 9.5 percent. Investors, once content with the consistency and stability of banks, sought better rates of returns in the stock market or real estate.

The Cold War became hotter during conflicts over Cuba and Berlin in the early 1960s. Fears over the international spread of communism led to America's intervention in a foreign conflict that would become a defining event of the decade: Vietnam. Military involvement in this small Asian country grew from advisory status to full-scale war. By 1968, Vietnam had become a national obsession leading to President Lyndon Johnson's decision not to run for another term and fueling not only debate over our role in Vietnam but more inflation and division nationally. The antiwar movement grew rapidly. Antiwar marches, which had drawn but a few thousand in 1965, grew in size until millions of marchers filled the streets of New York, San Francisco, and Washington only a few years later. By spring 1970 students on 448 college campuses either staged campus strikes or closed down their institutions. Many college campuses made ROTC voluntary or abolished it.

The struggle to bring economic equality to Blacks during the period produced massive spending for school integration. By 1963, the peaceful phase of the Civil Rights movement was ending; street violence, assassinations, and bombings defined the period. In 1967, 41 cities experienced major disturbances. At the same time charismatic labor organizer Cesar Chavez's United Farm Workers led a Civil Rights-style movement for Mexican-Americans, gaining national support which challenged the growers of the West with a five-year agricultural strike.

As a sign of increasing affluence and changing times, American consumers bought 73 percent fewer potatoes but 25 percent more fish, poultry, and meat and 50 percent more citrus and tomatoes than in 1940. California passed New York as the most populous state. Factory workers earned more than $100.00 a week, their highest wages in history. From 1960 to 1965 the amount of money spent for prescription drugs to lose weight doubled while the per capita consumption of processed potato chips rose from 6.3 pounds in 1958 to 14.2 pounds eight years later. In 1960 approximately 40 percent of American adult women had paying jobs; 30 years later the number would grow to 57.5 percent. Their emergence into the work force would transform marriage, child-rearing, and the economy. In 1960 women were also liberated by the FDA's approval of the birth-control pill, giving both women and men a degree of control over their bodies that had never existed before.

This atmosphere of change and challenge had a major impact on public employees, especially those who worked for the 80,000 units of state and local government. Before World War II, public employment meant secure, high-status jobs, often reserved for those with close ties to the city machine or the local good-old-boys network. By the 1960s, civil service employees' wages had fallen well behind those of organized labor. Deteriorating public transit systems, overcrowded classrooms, and welfare offices teeming with new applicants reduced the quality of public employees' work life. Strikes among public employees, for years virtually unknown, were felt throughout the mid-1960s, including teachers and postal workers.

During the decade anti-establishment sentiments grew: men's hair length was longer and wilder, beards and mustaches became popular, women's skirts rose to mid-thigh, and bras were discarded. Hippies advocated alternative lifestyles, drug use increased, especially marijuana and LSD; the Beatles, the Rolling Stones, Jimi Hendrix, and Janis Joplin became popular music figures; college campuses became a major site for demonstrations against the war and for Civil Rights. The Supreme Court prohibited school prayer, assured legal counsel to the poor, limited censorship of sexual material, and increased the rights of the accused.

Extraordinary space achievements also marked the decade. Ten years after President Kennedy announced he would place a man on the moon, 600 million people around the world watched as Neil Armstrong gingerly lowered his left foot into the soft dust of the moon's surface. In a tumultuous time of division and conflict, the landing was one of America's greatest triumphs and an exhilarating demonstration of American genius. Its cost was $25 billion and set the stage for 10 other men to walk on the surface of the moon during the next three years.

The 1960s also saw the birth of Enovid 10, the first oral contraceptive (cost $0.55 each), the start of Berry Gordy's Motown Records, felt-tip pens, Diet-Rite cola, Polaroid color film, Weight Watchers, and Automated Teller Machines. It's the decade when lyrics began appearing on record albums, Jackie and Aristotle Onassis reportedly spent $20 million during their first year together, and the Gay Liberation Front participated in the Hiroshima Day March— the first homosexual participation as a separate constituency in a peace march.

1961 FAMILY PROFILE

The Funakoshi family of four is of Japanese origin, owns one car, but no house. Their children are 16 and 17 years old. The man, Eiji, is a salesman who is currently selling plumbing supplies to large construction projects. His wife, Takaku, does not work outside the home.

Annual Income: $6,550

Eiji is the sole worker, earning a biweekly payment as a salesman; although he brings home $6,550, his income after taxes is $5,450.

Annual Budget

Auto Purchase and Operation $875.00
Clothing, Services $577.00
Food and Beverages $1,909.00
Gifts and Contributions $458.00
Housing $1,729.00
Medical Care $403.00
Other Expenditures $187.00
Other Transportation $253.00
Personal Insurance $545.00
Personal Care $207.00
Reading and Education $212.00
Recreation $306.00
Tobacco $88.00

Life at Home

- The construction boom in Honolulu means that the family income is rising; both of the children are talking about college.
- In the past they had not considered leaving the Islands for school because of the expense; now they are talking about stateside schools.

- The Funakoshi family is also thinking about buying a house; subdivisions with wide, winding streets are being constructed at a torrid pace.
- The family also knows that if a recession hits Hawaii or the building trade, Eiji's income will diminish rapidly; they are afraid of taking on too much debt.
- Earlier in the year, they attended a New Year's Day wedding ceremony for a Japanese couple; weddings are a popular part of the traditional New Year excursions from Japan to Hawaii.
- This family annually makes contributions to charities, including the United Fund, of $458.00.
- To protect his family, Eiji spends $545.00 on life insurance but also a little toward a retirement fund.
- Food and beverages account for 28 percent of this family's budget; shelter requires 16 percent.
- Even though the cost of eggs, dairy products, and fresh produce are very high in Hawaii, fuel costs to heat houses and heavy clothing for the winter are minimal.
- Like most islanders, this family refers to their child as a keiki; they have come to expect to see "kane" and "wahine" on bathroom doors in place of "men" and "women."
- The Funakoshis were very supportive of Hawaiian statehood.
- Statehood, especially for the large population of Japanese living on the island, is a symbol of social acceptance, the chance to be first-class citizens.

Life at Work: Plumbing Retail
- Already an experienced salesman, he finds selling plumbing supplies to major hotels and developments under construction exciting; the money is good, but more important he feels he is part of Honolulu's progress.
- This man is having the most successful year of his life; Honolulu in particular has bought into the idea that "progress is better, more progress is best."

- Following statehood, Hawaii's economy booms, particularly construction.
- Nine-tenths of the construction is on the island of Oahu; its rates of growth and dollar volume exceed even the tourist industry.
- One of the major clients is Roy Kelley, the wizard of Waikiki, who is the largest hotel developer in the state with approximately 2,200 rooms under his control.
- His moderately priced rooms make Waikiki an affordable place for the middle income visitor.
- An island developer for 30 years, today a typical single hotel room built by Kelley costs $8.50 to $12.00 a night.
- The popular joke this year is that Hawaii's new state bird is the Dillingham crane, the long steel tower used for erecting tall buildings.
- Recent high school graduates are fulfilling the need for unskilled labor in the construction industry, but skilled workers are needed to keep pace with the current demand.
- Since 1955 the building industry in Hawaii, especially on Oahu, has experienced the fastest growth factor in the island economy.
- Prior to World War II, private construction averaged six percent growth; in 1961 there is more private construction than in the 16-year period between 1925 to 1941.
- Since World War II, Hawaii has been confronted by a shortage of housing, particularly between 1954 and 1958.

"Admirals Expect Polaris Sub Buildup to Enlarge Pearl Harbor Fleet, Jobs," *Honolulu Advertiser,* March 20, 1961:

"Top naval commanders headquartered in Hawaii agree that President Kennedy's decision to speed up the Polaris program will shortly have a major effect at Pearl Harbor.

They expect: 1) At least 12 Polaris-type nuclear submarines to be assigned to the Pacific Fleet, and all 12 to be home-ported at Pearl Harbor. That would mean an additional 3,000 submariners based here, a 75 percent increase in the present 4,000-man sub force now based at Pearl. 2) That as a result of basing Polaris subs here, there will be an 'appreciable buildup' in overhaul and maintenance at the Pearl Harbor shipyard. The shipyard presently employs 4,000 workers and channels about $12 million annually into Hawaii's economy.

Defense Department plans originally didn't call for Polaris submarines to be stationed in the Pacific until 1965. (The first 19 Polaris subs are tentatively earmarked for the Atlantic Fleet, with five already built and assigned to that fleet.) The reason was 'better target availability' in the Atlantic—in simple language, the nuclear-tipped Polaris missiles were needed to help deter Russia from any idea of launching an atomic attack against the U.S.

Now, however, it is known that President Kennedy believes that more emphasis should be given to the Pacific, with Red China on the verge of acquiring nuclear capability. Although new Defense Department studies ordered by President Kennedy aren't yet complete, it is believed that the Pacific Fleet will now get its first Polaris submarines in 1963—perhaps even sooner, if the Chinese communists get atomic missiles this year. The 12 Polaris submarines to be based here—probably at Ford Island—won't replace any present Pacific subs but will be in addition to them."

Life in the Community: Honolulu, Hawaii

- Hawaii was organized as a territory and carries the motto "Ua Mau Ke Ea O Ka Aina I Ka Pono" or "The Life of the Land Is Preserved by Righteousness."
- The new 390-mile chain of Island State is located 2,100 miles west-southwest of San Francisco.
- Even though Hawaii is composed of a string of islands, 85 percent of the population resides on Oahu, home of the state's capital city, Honolulu.
- In 1960 nearly everyone is talking about a "new Hawaii" that will be the financial, trade, cultural, and educational hub of the Pacific; the resident population is 642,000, but rapid immigration is beginning to strain the resources of the fragile islands.
- Hawaii has turned the economic disadvantage of being in the middle of the Pacific into an advantage; the Islands are now a world travel center, the operational center for the nation's defense in the Pacific and a major center for shipping.
- Hawaii's mild temperature and fertile soil are excellent for growing tropical fruits and vegetables; approximately 75 percent of the world's canned pineapple is produced on the Islands.
- Sugar and pineapples are the leading economic drivers in Hawaii; defense spending on military bases is third and tourism, growing rapidly, is fourth.
- Hawaii leads all domestic sugar producers in wages and yields per acre.
- Hawaii has always been a paradise, but only for the well-to-do; following statehood, thanks to tourism, more workers are feeling the spread of prosperity.
- Statehood also changes Hawaii's image in the tourist market by broadening its appeal from the land of brown-skinned maidens and strange Polynesian food to include American hamburgers and hot showers on American soil.
- The development of a tourism industry is dependent on a major technological breakthrough: regular passenger jet service from the mainland.
- In the 1960s the economy fare from the mainland to Honolulu is $110.00 for pre-arranged groups and conventions.

- When Pan American inaugurated Boeing 707 service to Hawaii in September 1959, the tiresome trip from California was reduced from 15 hours to five hours.
- A super speed deluxe airliner from Hawaii to California costs $79.10 and includes free hot meals, fly now, pay later, and sleeper seats; trips to Wake Island cost $154.40, Guam, $176.00, Okinawa, $200.00, and Tokyo, $284.00.
- Tourism now rivals both sugar and pineapples as the Islands' major industry.

- The number of visitors in 1960 is up 44 percent from 1959; tourism is expected to double in the next five years.
- Unlike the past, tourists come to Hawaii all year 'round now; the tourist "peaks" are disappearing.
- Surveys show that 35 percent of visitors are returnees, who have enjoyed the islands on an earlier visit.

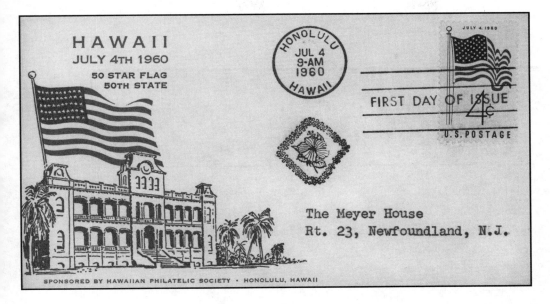

- Waikiki Beach, where 100 hotels are located, is a major tourist destination.
- Reflecting its past, by 1960 one out of every three marriages is racially mixed; the Island population has become one-third Asian, primarily Japanese; one-third partly Hawaiian, Filipino, and Puerto Rican; and about one-third is haole or white.
- Homes in which the head of the household is of Chinese or Japanese ancestry represent the largest annual median incomes on the island.
- A survey of median income by race shows that Caucasians average $5,986 annually; Chinese, $6,730; Filipino, $4,355; Hawaiian, $5,200; and Japanese, $6,842; the average for all groups is $6,055.
- The average wage per hour of field workers in Hawaii is $1.63 plus fringe benefits of $0.48; Louisiana pays $0.71 per hour, Florida, $1.01, and Puerto Rico, $0.51.
- The average weekly wage for all Hawaiian industries in 1960 is $73.19; mining pays $113.62 a week, and the wholesale and retail trade pays $63.32.
- During the past year the cost of living in Hawaii rises three percent; domestic gas rates, shoes, automobile fuel, hospital room rates, and recreation lead the increases.
- During World War II and the Korean War, hundreds of thousands of military personnel trained or traveled through Honolulu, creating a natural thirst to return.
- In 1961 Elvis Presley stars in the culture classic, *Blue Hawaii,* tying his considerable appeal to the Islands.

HISTORICAL SNAPSHOT
1961–1962

- President Kennedy established the Peace Corps two months after his inauguration
- DNA genetic code was broken
- New York's First National Bank offered fixed-term certificates of deposit
- The IBM Selectric typewriter was introduced
- Harper and Row was created through a merger
- The right wing activities of the John Birch Society stirred concerns in Congress
- Black and White "Freedom Riders" tested integration in the South; they were attacked and beaten in Alabama
- Cigarette makers spent $115 million on television advertising
- R.J. Reynolds acquired Pacific Hawaiian Products Company in an attempt to diversify away from tobacco products
- Sprite was introduced by Coca-Cola Company
- A Gallup poll recorded that 74 percent of teens interviewed believed in God; 58 percent planned to go to college. Of the 16- to 21-year-old girls interviewed, almost all expected to be married by age 22 and most wanted four children
- 4,000 servicemen were sent to Vietnam as advisers
- The minimum wage rose from $1.00 to $1.25 per hour
- Canned pet foods were among the top three selling categories in grocery stores
- The Cuban missile crisis pitted the United States against the Soviet Union
- Newly elected President Kennedy reduced tariff duties to stimulate foreign trade
- Electronic Data Systems was founded by H. Ross Perot
- 90 percent of American households had at least one television set
- Of the world's adult population of 1.6 billion, approximately 44 percent were illiterate; total world population was 3.1 billion
- The American Broadcasting Company (ABC) began color telecasts for 3.5 hours per week
- *Silent Spring* by U.S. biologist Rachel Carson was published
- Diet-Rite Cola was introduced as the first sugar-free soft drink
- Tab-opening aluminum drink cans were introduced
- On May 28, 1962, the stock market plunged 34.95 points, the sharpest drop since the 1929 crash

1961 Economic Profile

Income, Standard Jobs

Average of All Industries,
Including Farm Labor $4,961.00
Bituminous Coal Mining $5,357.00
Building Trades $5,938.00
Domestics $2,356.00
Farm Labor $1,929.00
Federal Civilian $6,451.00
Federal Military $3,813.00
Finance, Insurance, and Real Estate . . $5,203.00
Gas, Electricity, Sanitation
Workers $6,390.00
Manufacturing, Durable Goods $6,048.00
Manufacturing, Nondurable
Goods $5,250.00
Medical/Health Services Workers . . . $3,636.00
Miscellaneous Manufacturing $4,753.00
Motion Picture Services $5,871.00
Nonprofit Organization Workers . . . $3,684.00
Passenger Transportation
Workers, Local, and Highway $4,966.00
Personal Services $3,810.00
Public School Teachers $4,991.00
Radio Broadcasting and
Television Workers $7,384.00
Railroads $6,440.00
State and Local Government
Workers $4,721.00
Telephone and Telegraph Workers . . $5,793.00
Wholesale and Retail Trade
Workers $5,932.00

Selected Prices

American Flag Set, 3' x 5'
Flag and Pole $3.95
Barbie Doll Nighty-Negligee $3.00
Bluebrook Margarine, per Pound $0.15
Boy's Life Magazine, monthly $0.25
Chrysler Newport Automobile $2,964.00
Daisey BB Gun $12.98
Ethan Allen Desk, Four-Drawer $85.60
Flintstones Child's Feeding Set $1.99
Jif Peanut Butter, 18 Ounce Jar $0.51
Kelvinator Air Conditioner $169.00
Kodak Brownie Super 27 Camera $22.00
Kraft Miracle Whip Salad
Dressing, Quart $0.43

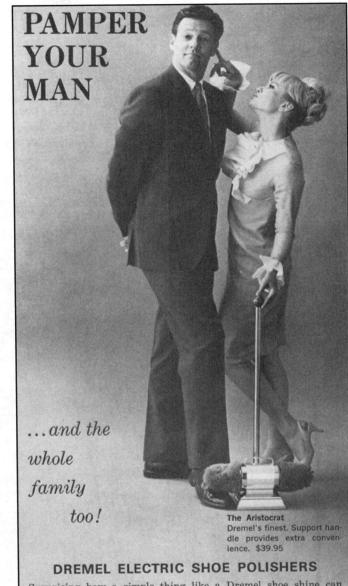
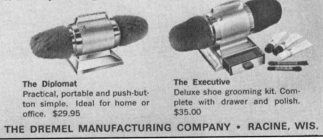

Little Star Dress for Teens $5.00
Magna-Lite Shop Light $6.95
Pakula Necklace $3.00
RCA Victor Tape Recorder,
   Reel to Reel $99.95
Scott Tissues, Two Packages of 400 . . . . . $0.39
Scripto Goldenglo Lighter $5.00
Smarteens Blouse for Girls, Cotton $3.00
Ultra-Sheer Seamless Stockings,
   Box of Six $5.28
Young Men's Caumet Shoes $9.99

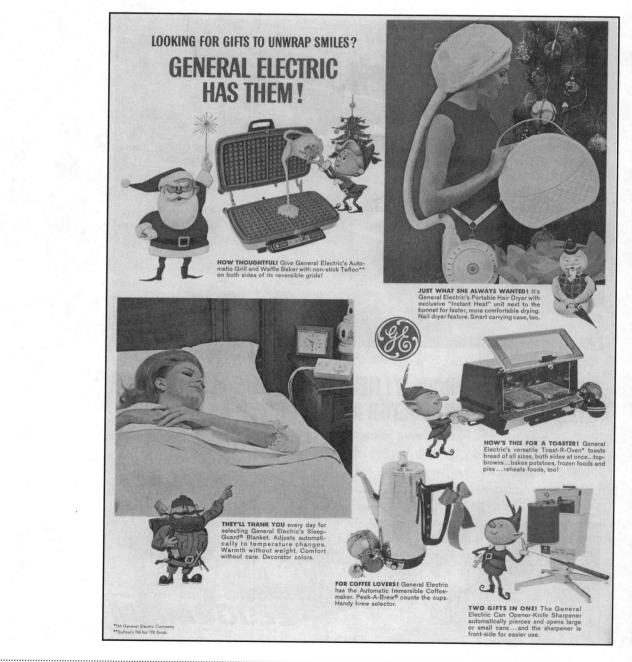

"A Word to Wives, by JFK's Doc," *San Francisco Examiner,* June 16, 1961. "Dr. Janet Travell, President Kennedy's physician, today offered some rules for housewives":

"Scramble your work. Don't spend all of one day cleaning, another day doing laundry, and a third ironing. That way you use some muscles too much, others not enough.

Cultivate a rhythmic pattern. Don't hurry; don't jerk the movements. Just do your housework as if you doing a modern dance.

Take short rests at frequent intervals.

Don't tolerate bad physical and mechanical arrangements in your home. Don't tolerate uncomfortable chairs or too-low sinks.

Counteract housework with an entirely different kind of muscle movement, a variety of exercises."

"Working Girls Beat Living Cost," *San Francisco Examiner,* March 2, 1961:

"The working girl kept a skip and a jump ahead of the rise in the cost of living last year. In fact, she received the equivalent of an extra week's pay—enough to buy one good suit.

John Dana of the Department of Labor disclosed yesterday that the average office girl received a 4.3 percent raise in salary while the cost of living was going up 1.6 percent. This gave her a 1.9 percent increase in real earnings after allowing for high prices and taxes.

Her boyfriend received a somewhat smaller percentage increase, but about the same amount of cash if he worked the year 'round. One analyst remarked that the lower increase for the boyfriend was the more important statistic. The analyst, a woman, explained: 'After all, how is the poor working girl going to get married if her boyfriend can't earn more money?'

Dana, the department's assistant to the Regional Director of Labor Statistics, said local stenographers, with an average weekly salary of $84.00, have received a 47.3 percent boost in wages since January, 1952. In the same period, the cost of living has risen 18.5 percent, giving her a net increase in real spendable earnings of 21.5 percent.

The weekly salaries of women office workers ranged from an average $60.50 for file clerks to $96.50 for secretaries. The report showed that the average woman elevator operator receives $2.05 an hour, $0.22 more than the average male elevator operator, while the average woman janitor or cleaner receives $2.08, $0.07 less than the male janitor. In most skilled occupations studied, men averaged more than $3.10 an hour, with tool and dye makers drawing $3.53, carpenters $3.22, and painters $3.15."

Establishing Statehood

- When Hawaii became an American territory at the turn of the century, the population of the territory was about 150,000, and six out of every 10 people were aliens.
- Fifty years later the population was 500,000, giving Hawaii more inhabitants than four of the existing U.S. states and more than any territory at the time of its admission to the union except Oklahoma.
- The first proposal for statehood was made in 1919; several additional attempts were made in the 1930s.
- Most Hawaiians believed that after the attack on Pearl Harbor in 1941, Hawaii would be named a state for their personal sacrifice.
- Many Americans did not wish to accept a noncontiguous territory as a new state; others were fearful of the large number of Asians living on the island.
- By 1950 nine out of every 10 people in Hawaii were citizens, nearly all of them born on American soil.
- In 1950 Hawaiians elected delegates to a convention to draft a constitution in preparation for statehood; an unprecedented 85 percent of voters turned out for the election.
- Statehood was approved by Congress on March 12, 1959, despite the efforts of Senators Strom Thurmond of South Carolina and James Eastland of Mississippi.
- When statehood was approved, the University of Hawaii emptied and public schools were dismissed for two days so students could celebrate statehood.
- In a show of national unity and pride on Sand Island, a statehood bonfire burned with wood from every state in the union, sent for that special purpose.

Last Among Equals, Hawaiian Statehood and American Politics, by Roger Bell:

"By 1959 an overwhelming majority of congressmen and island citizens accepted that the territory (of Hawaii) was not only legally entitled to statehood, but fully capable of supporting it. Before World War II a joint House-Senate committee had concluded that Hawaii had satisfied all the requirements set for territories up until then. By 1959, Hawaii undisputedly had the requisite populations and resources for the operation of a state government and could contribute its share in support of the federal government. Its population had increased to 620,000, more than three times the population of Alaska in 1958, and larger than the populations of but one territory at the time of admission. Approximately 85 percent of Hawaii's people were United States' citizens. More than 98 percent of all secondary school children were citizens. Its population was larger than that of five existing states: Vermont, Wyoming, Nevada, Delaware, and Alaska. Economically also Hawaii was qualified for immediate statehood. During 1945–59 the Islands' economy underwent unprecedented diversification and growth. Individual per capita income increased from $1,328 in 1945 to $2,274 in 1959. Despite its relatively small population, in the fiscal year 1957–8 Hawaii paid more in federal taxes than 10 states. The 1959 House investigating committee correctly concluded that Hawaii's population was 'sufficiently large' and its 'resources sufficiently developed, beyond question, to support statehood.'"

"Come back to Hawaii"

"Best way to learn the hula is from island girl."

**"You who know Hawaii
only in your dreams...
you who know Hawaii well
...come back to Hawaii."**

There's an island for you in Hawaii, only $100 and a few relaxing jet hours away from Los Angeles and San Francisco. Only United can fly you to Hawaii from so many U.S. cities and show you wide-screen color movies on the way. Just call your Travel Agent or United. And don't forget to return the postcard for your exciting Hawaii Planning Kit, only $1. Come back to Hawaii with United.

UNITED AIR LINES

Welcome aboard the extra care airline

- Admissions Day, on August 21, 1959, came 61 years and nine days after Hawaii's annexation to the United States.
- Once statehood was approved and Hawaii earned the 50th star, the state elected to the U.S. Senate Hiram Fong, a self-made millionaire and the son of a Chinese immigrant.
- Hawaii is among the smallest states in the Union exceeding only Connecticut, Delaware, and Rhode Island in total area.
- Although 47th in size, Hawaii ranks 42nd in personal income, 41st in Internal Revenue collection and seventh among the states in per capita residence consumption of electricity.

"Presley Due Tomorrow; Honolulu Airport Braced," *Honolulu Advertiser*, March 24, 1961:

"Thousands of Elvis Presley fans are expected to jam Honolulu Airport tomorrow when Presley arrives at 12:20 p.m. aboard a Pan American Airways plane for his USS Arizona War Memorial concert benefit. The police department has assigned 75 men to the airport.

All 27 Oahu high schools will send designated representatives to a press conference immediately following Elvis' arrival. Each school has a Presley fan club and most of these fans are expected to be at the airport to greet him. Presley will arrive with a party of 26 from Los Angeles.

At 8:30 p.m. tomorrow he will headline a benefit show at Bloch Arena to raise funds for the Arizona Memorial. There are still tickets available for the show. A telephone campaign was on yesterday in an effort to sell 104 remaining $100.00 tickets. A total of 196 $100.00 tickets already have been sold.

General admission sales have topped 18,000 with $4,500 worth of $10.00 and $5.00 tickets yet to be sold.

Radio station KPOI will cover Presley's arrival live, beginning at 9:00 a.m.

Among those to be on hand to greet the singer will be his manager Col. Tom Parker, who has been here for two weeks making arrangements. Also on hand at the airport will be representatives of the Pacific War Memorial Commission."

"JFK Orders Start of Peace Corps," *San Francisco Examiner*, May 2, 1961:

"President Kennedy today ordered the creation of a peace corps on a temporary basis and asked Congress to make it permanent. And he cautioned those who want to join that their life will not be easy and their pay will be low.

'The volunteer peace corps,' Kennedy said, 'will provide a pool of Americans, mostly young men and women, to go overseas and help a foreign country meet their urgent need for skilled manpower. Applicants will be screened carefully,' he said, 'to make sure that those who are selected can contribute to peace corps programs, and have the personal qualities which will en-

able them to represent the United States abroad with honor and dignity.'

Kennedy said he hopes to send the first members of the corps overseas by late fall and hopes to have 500 to 1,000 in the field by the end of the year. 'Within a few years,' the President said, 'I hope several thousand will be working in foreign lands. Each recruit will receive a training and orientation course varying from six weeks to six months, including instruction in the culture and language of the country to which the corps member is being sent.'"

"The Revolution Nobody Noticed, Timid Taste Turned Bold," *Life Magazine*, December 26, 1960:

"The great revolution in the U.S. household took place so gradually, so close under everybody's nose, that most people did not notice it. The plain pot turned into a colored casserole. Big floral patterns diminished to small elegant patterns. Lace tablecloths gave way to straw mats. When the 25 years of change were added up, the American home had switched from muted to bright, from overstuffed to streamlined, from careful to carefree.

To show the vast difference between the homes of 25 years ago and those of today, a group of home furnishings that Macy's was selling in 1936 was gathered. During the Depression people chose safe, practical colors. Today, with better dyes and easier-to-clean fabrics, light colors are popular. The 1936 furnishings are almost all 18th century reproductions with only a modern chest

and chair. Nineteen-sixty-one's furnishings are international in flavor; the hibachi is from Japan; the black chair with purple seat cushion is Swedish; the colored glasses are Belgian. Technological improvements have brought molded plastic for furniture, foam rubber for upholstery.

Other signs of the new taste of the '60s are easy to spot. A cheery bird has replaced yesterday's glum goldfish and the sansevieria plant is replaced by a big philodendron in a bright stand. Poodles have nosed out cocker spaniels and the master of the house has gone from a lumpy sofa to a cushion. The radio has taken on the appearance of a small book and the block has turned into a star. Bottles, glasses, pans, and even the garbage can have dressed-up-in-parlor splendor which is only fitting since, with servants scarce, the mistress of the house does the work.'"

"The Machines Are Taking Over, Computers Outdo Man at His Work Now and Soon May Outthink Him," *Life Magazine*, March 3, 1961:

"In the peaceful little town of Troy, Ohio, an epic battle was recently fought at the local sausage factory. Once a week for four months top officials of the Braun Brothers Packing Co., each a sausage expert in his own right, gathered in an office to figure furiously with sharp pencils and clicking desk calculators. The experts were pitting their formidable experience against an implacable rival and each time they found they were beaten before they had begun. A robot brain, in the form of an electronic digital computer, was proving that it could give shrewder orders about sausage-making than the most experienced sausage-master could.

Calculating how to blend a variety of slaughterhouse oddments such as beef lips and pork stomachs into a tasty, inexpensive, attractive, nourishing, and cohesive bologna is an intricate art. There are always thousands of possible combinations to consider. Only a very

clever sausage-maker, often an old German who carefully turns his back before consulting a little black book, is normally entrusted with the task.

But Braun Brothers' human sausage maker had magnanimously taught the machine all the tricks he knew. When the computer was informed (by means of coded holes punched into 100 yellow, green, and brown cards) what meat cuts were on hand and their current prices, it hummed softly, its lights flickered, and it riffled the deck of cards over and over again for 36 minutes. Then it automatically punched out the most profitable bologna formula for that particular day. The machine's answer was invariably faster, surer, and cheaper than the answer of the human sausage experts. Braun Brothers now takes it for granted that the computer's decisions are correct, and today all its sausage is mixed by order of the computer."

"A Fresh Look at Honolulu," *Holiday Magazine,* December 1965:

"For the past five years, the largest number of Punahou's graduates have gone to the nearby University of Hawaii, some to finish there and others to transfer to mainland schools at the end of two years. Scorned for years a 'Tokyo College' because of the preponderance among its students of hardworking Japanese-American kids, the University of Hawaii is finally attaining stature under the leadership of Thomas Hale Hamilton, a malihini with abounding energy. It appears to be finally turning into a university for all the people of Hawaii, rather than serving as an 'exit to the mainland' for ambitious boys of Oriental parentage who felt hemmed in by Honolulu's horizons. (It is also relevant to note that it costs about $4,500 for a student from Hawaii to attend a private college in the East for a year, about a third of this figure going toward transportation.)

All of this is preliminary to saying that although the old aristocracy of Honolulu is as clearly defined as the old aristocracy of New York, Philadelphia, or Charleston, and considerably older than the aristocracy of San Francisco, it has a style all its own. It is the only American aristocracy in which racial mixture is a point of pride. It is a world whose conservatism is shown in many small ways. As I was walking down Merchant Street, on the way to the restaurant, it occurred to me that, with the exception of a workman in an aloha shirt and some clerks in shirtsleeves, every man I encountered was wearing a dark gray, or blue suit, a starched white shirt, a dark tie, and black shoes, and all this while the trade winds sighed through the palms and tourists in Waikiki were buying Hawaiian clothes that would make them look like natives."

1966 Family Profile

The Caplan family lives in Portland, Oregon; the 41-year-old man has been a longshoreman on the docks for 20 years and loves his work. He is married and they have two teenage sons.

Annual Income: $8,492

Annual Budget

This study provides little information concerning the annual expenditure of this family; the per capita consumer expenditures nationwide in 1966 are:

Auto Parts	$19.33
Auto Usage	$294.06
Clothing	$158.73
Dentists	$15.26
Food	$555.05
Furniture	$35.61
Gas and Oil	$81.40
Health Insurance	$15.26
Housing	$353.58
Intercity Transport	$11.70
Local Transport	$10.68
New Auto Purchase	$106.84
Personal Care	$117.52
Physicians	$46.29
Private Education	$39.68
Recreation	$156.69
Religion/Welfare Activities	$43.24

Telephone and Telegraph $35.61
Tobacco $43.24
Utilities $93.10
Per Capita Consumption $2,450.14

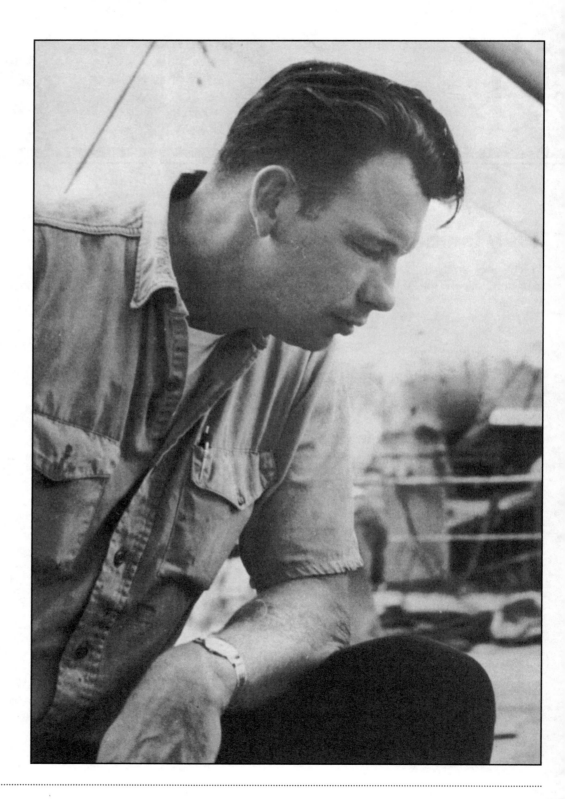

15-562 Sea Lions Sunning on Rocks at Sea Lion Caves - Oregon Coast Hwy.

Life at Home

- Because of the uncertainty of work schedules and weekly paychecks, the Caplans have an uneven cash flow.
- Despite the uneven hours and pay, the yearly income of this longshoreman is very good.
- Each day this man may decide whether to appear in the hiring hall to obtain a job for the day or stay home; this provides an added measure of independence and self-discipline to the job.
- This independence also allows this man to work a very flexible schedule—always realizing that no work or pay may be available in the coming weeks.
- The woman, who does not work, is never sure when her husband will be home or at work.
- To help him bridge the sometimes long periods of inactivity, this family uses its savings and the Longshoremen Credit Union when money is tight.
- Until the creation of the credit unions in the 1950s, loan sharks charged the workers very high interest rates during financially difficult times.
- Like many longshoreman families, the Caplans maintain a large garden—a source of great pride and vegetables for the family table; they live outside Portland to accommodate the garden.
- Nearly all of their friends are longshoremen and nearly all are married; a single man is regarded as a "kid" until he grows up, takes a wife, and begins the highly regarded task of raising children.
- It is not uncommon for this family's brothers and sisters to drop by the house unannounced; entertaining informally—often in the kitchen—is one of the reasons they bought an old farmhouse with a large kitchen.
- But most family matters are private; a man is looked down upon who discusses his wife's faults publicly.
- Women are expected to care for the home and children; rarely would this longshoreman prepare his own breakfast if his wife is around.

- His irregular hours allow him to spend considerable time around his children.
- He also takes time out to help train his sons in sports, including boxing and fistfighting—both family traditions.
- The man gained fighting experience in the marines during the Korean conflict.
- Flexible time also allows him to handle his own remodeling, including installing a new vanity in their home.

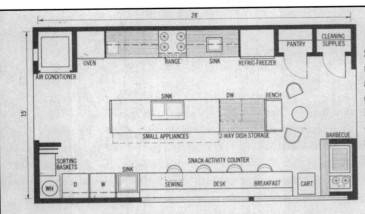

Start with a good kitchen plan. Then take off from there and add your choice of appliances, materials, and accessories. Quality in kitchen planning includes (1) functional use of all the space available and (2) related work areas so that the work flows easily from one area to another. Keep in mind that you need comfortable working heights, adequate and convenient storage facilities, and plenty of counter space to spread out.

CLEAN-UP AREA PLUS. In addition to serving as the clean-up area (with double-bowl sink and cutting board with opening to complement garbage disposer), center island separates that work area from the rest of the room. Dishwasher is raised for easier accessibility. Broken counter heights combine hard maple and glazed ceramic tile counter materials.

Two-way sliding shelves are a great plus feature for storing dinnerware and serving dishes.

Storage space behind dishwasher is compartmented for vases, etc. Raised counter is ideal flower arranging area. Paperware is stored below.

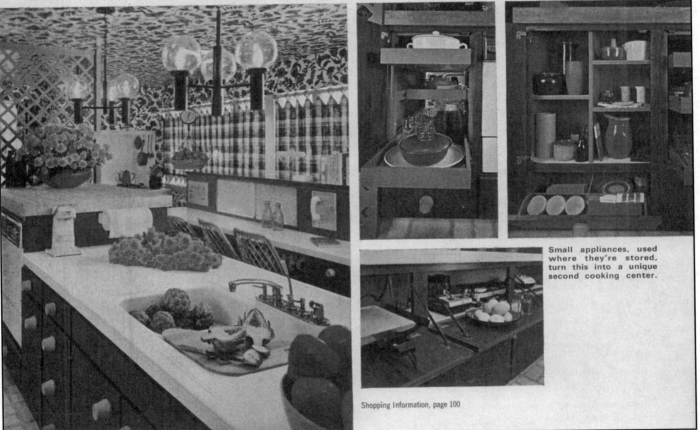

Small appliances, used where they're stored, turn this into a unique second cooking center.

Shopping Information, page 100

- A house with lots of land also allows the Caplans to be "rockhounds," collecting and displaying a large collection of semiprecious stones and fossils they have found.
- They rarely plan major trips or activities for the weekends because pay on Saturday and Sunday is one and a half times the normal pay scale, making it a preferable time to work.

- Fossil hunting trips or visits to her mother's home are more often enjoyed during the week.

Life at Work: The Docks

- Approximately 1,200 longshoremen work in the Portland, Oregon, area, along with their families; they represent a close community of about 5,000 people.
- All are members of The International Longshoreman's and Warehousemen's Union (ILWU); the West Coast-dominated ILWU is not affiliated with the International Longshoremen's Association, which is the largest Longshoreman's union on the East Coast.
- Longshoremen work for themselves, not for a company; most are linked through their Union and their self-image as longshoremen.
- Compensation for Portland longshoremen includes complete coverage for medical care at the Bess Kaiser Hospital and dental care for children.
- Longshoremen are predominantly native-born Americans of northern European ancestry including English, Scandinavian, and German; many of their ancestors first settled in Wisconsin, Minnesota, the Dakotas, or Pennsylvania.
- Longshoremen like to project themselves as rough-and-ready individualists who are part of a very tight-knit community.
- The strike of 1934 is so important in the history of the Union, it is commemorated with the Bloody Thursday Parade, employing the phrase "An injury to one is an injury to all."
- Work schedules are driven by when ships arrive in port and the cargo they carry; the work—and the pay—can be erratic.
- Work is sporadic, some days the docks are overloaded with boats; other days no work can be found for the longshoremen. In addition, weather is always a factor.

The Portland Longshoremen:

An old-time longshoreman explains why he began working around the docks even though he told his mother in 1927 he was saving his money to buy a ranch: "I told my mother, this is a stop-gap, I want to get enough money to buy a ranch. But it seemed as though—oh, we banked our money in the Hibernia Bank on Third and Washington, and we got quite a little bit together. I don't know, twelve or thirteen hundred dollars. And that bank went broke. And it seemed as though one thing after another happened all through the years. And then I will admit the waterfront began to get to me. And I would think to myself, now I've just barely got an eighth grade education. Now where can I work now where I can make $45.00 a week? Because of this crowd I was running with there were kids working in banks, a couple of tailors, this and that, and I had more money than any of them. And I got to thinking—everything was all adding up. There was the freedom. There was the quick pay. You didn't have to wait a month for your pay. When you went up the gangplank, the mate would pay you off in gold. Every job was different. Every ship was different. Every man you worked with, you worked with a different man every day. You meet all kinds, types, every kind of man in the world. You got to see the whole world passing right there in front of your eyes. I guess I fell in love with the waterfront."

- Ships only make money when they are moving goods. Ships do not earn profits when sitting idle or being loaded in port; thus most owners want loading, unloading, and servicing of ships to take place quickly, placing pressure on the longshoremen to work rapidly and on unpredictable time schedules.

- Weather in the Pacific or in the mouth of the Columbia River can dictate how many ships will reach port and how much work can be done.

- This man, as do his fellow longshoremen, often works seven days straight for several weeks in a row, then has no work for three or four days in a row.

- The work itself is physically demanding and can be extremely hazardous; most longshoremen have sustained an injury on the job, and some have been crippled and killed.

- Longshoreman must have confidence in their personal ability to handle a demanding situation in an emergency and expect these same skills among their fellow longshoremen.

- During the course of 1966, he works 1,777 hours or about 34 hours a week on average.

- Yielding to pressure from the International Union, in 1961 the Portland Local 8 allows Blacks to work as casual men, the first step in the traditional recruitment procedure, then as Union members; the younger men now dominating the docks are more open to Black workers than are their elders.

- The hiring hall also serves as a social center for the men where card games and gossip are always in fashion.

OVER WILLAMETTE RIVER, PORTLAND, OREGON

GALLEY — "DAN & LOUIS OYSTER BAR" 208 S. W. ANKENY, PORTLAND, OREGON

The Union: Present Structure and Hiring System, by William W. Pilcher, 1972:

"A man who wished to become a longshoreman needed only to be present in the hiring halls on days of peak activity when the supply of regular longshoremen was exhausted. The paymaster would then issue casual payroll cards to the number of men required to fill the day's needs. These casual men, or 'white cards' as they were called because the payroll card they used was white as compared to a Union permit man's yellow card, could continue to hang around the hiring hall and pick up overflow work on peak days as long as they performed satisfactorily on the job. It was not always necessary for a longshoreman's friend or kinsman to wait until the supply of men already holding casual cards was exhausted before obtaining one for himself. My own case is a good illustration of the differential treatment of longshore kin. When I started on the waterfront, my father took me into the hiring hall and introduced me to the dispatchers. I was then instructed that I would have to wait for a day when the entire labor force was employed and that I had best remain in the hall during all hiring periods until that time. I spent four fruitless days waiting for an opportunity, but during this time there were always white cards that had not been dispatched. On the fifth morning, the dispatcher who was an old friend of my father hid a job slip until the hiring period was completed. He had previously instructed me not to leave the hall after the hiring period as the other men would, so that I would be available immediately afterward. When the hall was empty of other men seeking white cards and longshoremen, I was issued a payroll card and sent to my first longshore job. I was never again shown any favoritism by anyone in the union, nor to my knowledge was anyone else. The other stages of advancement were closely observed and regulated and no abrogation of the procedures was permitted."

- Attempts to change the "hiring hall" system of dispatching longshoremen to their jobs, established in 1934, was resisted in 1948 and again in 1966.
- The Portland hiring hall is located in a converted church; hiring takes place twice a day: 7 a.m. and 5 p.m. for the night shift.
- Gangs are dispatched on strict yearly earnings basis; the gang with the lowest earnings is dispatched first and to the longest job, while the gang with the highest earnings is dispatched last and to the shortest job.
- Board men, who work independently, bid for jobs based on a daily lottery system that determines the order of when each man bids for a job.
- Many longshoremen believe that the nine-to-five routine is too restrictive and insufficiently remunerative.
- Men who are noted fistfighters have prestige among the longshoremen as long as they adhere to the group's standards of fair play and are not bullies.

Life in the Community: Portland, Oregon

- Portland is located at the confluence of the Willamette and Columbia Rivers and owes much of its history and prosperity to its prominence as a seaport.
- Portland, Oregon, is the second largest port on the Pacific Coast in total waterborne commerce; its "city proper" population is 365,000. Including the surrounding five-county metro area, the population is 774,205.

BIRD'S-EYE VIEW.
OREGON CITY. OREGON.

- Oregon has a population of less than two million; nearly a third live in or near the Portland metropolitan area.
- Portland is the largest city in Oregon; no other city exceeds 100,000 residents.
- Ethnically the city was settled by Germans, Scandinavians, and immigrants from New England and the old South; no ethic group has ever dominated or directed the development of the state.
- Ethnic neighborhoods, common in other large cities, are largely unknown in Portland or in Oregon.
- Portland began its history as a seaport with the lumber schooner trade plying the Pacific Coast between the more heavily populated areas of southern California and San Francisco.
- In the early days, Portland was a timber worker's town, and many loggers and sawmill workers easily transitioned to waterfront work; loggers were also familiar with the rigging and gear required on the docks.
- With the lumbermen came their ideas about unions, particularly the liberal, often called radical, ideas of the Industrial Workers of the World.
- Historically, most of Oregon's timber was shipped to the East Coast, Europe, and the Orient.
- Currently Portland ships little to China since the downfall of the Nationalist regime of Chiang Kai-shek.
- Today bulk wheat brought from the inland wheat-growing areas dominates trade through the port; the timber industry and shipping is in decline.
- Other than tourism, two significant industries dominate Oregon: agriculture, east of the Cascade Mountains, and timber to the west.
- According to one researcher, "the predominantly old-line Americans and Scandinavians agree wholeheartedly on the principle of social egalitarianism, and thus reject the concept of social mobility as intrinsically worthless."
- Although a tightly integrated social group, the longshoremen of Portland are scattered throughout the city; no clustering takes place near the docks.

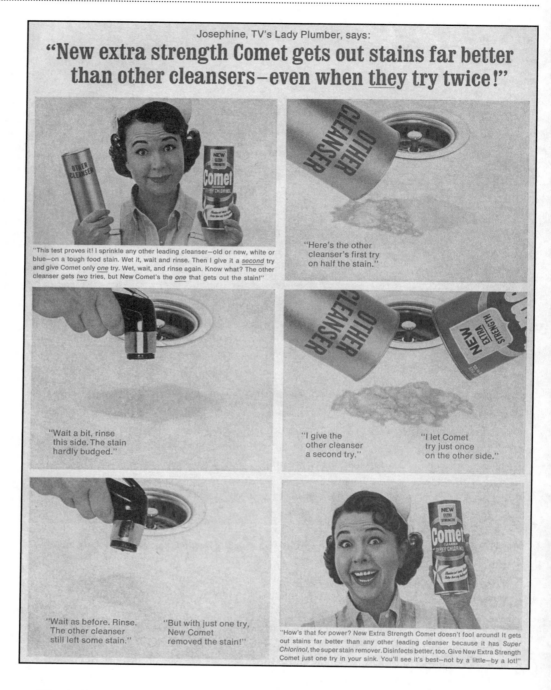

- The docks are stretched out along the Willamette River over a distance of some 10 miles, making it impractical to live near their work since they do not know from day to day on which dock they will be working.

HISTORICAL SNAPSHOT
1966–1967

- Student protests against the Vietnam War began
- Blanket student deferments from the draft are abolished; draft calls reached 50,000 young men a month
- The National Organization for Women (NOW) was founded
- The largest year-to-year rise in the cost of living since 1958 was announced—2.8 percent
- The term "Black Power" was introduced into the Civil Rights movement, signifying the rift between the pacifist followers of Martin Luther King, Jr.'s SCLC and the militants following Stokely Carmichael, SNCC and CORE
- 2,377 corporate mergers took place in 1966
- Per capita consumption of processed potatoes reached 44.2 pounds per year
- Taster's Choice freeze-dried instant coffee was introduced
- 41 percent of non-White families made less than $3,000 annually
- *New York World Journal & Tribute* closed; *Rolling Stone* magazine was founded
- 2.7 million Americans received food stamp assistance
- Nearly 10,000 farmers received more than $20,000 each in subsidies
- Annual per capita beef consumption reached 105.6 pounds
- Burger King Corporation was acquired by Pillsbury Corporation
- Miniskirts, LSD, topless waitresses, and Granny eyeglasses all became popular
- New style dance halls, like the Fillmore in San Francisco, introduced strobe lights, liquid color blobs, glow paint, and psychedelic posters
- The Clean Waters Restoration Act allocated funds for preventing river and air pollution
- The National Association of Broadcasters instructed all disc jockeys to screen all records for hidden references to drugs or obscene meanings
- The U.S. population passed 200 million
- Per capita consumption of processed potato chips rose from 6.3 pounds a year in 1958 to 14.2 pounds a year
- The Rare and Endangered Species list was introduced by the Department of the Interior
- The phrase "Third World" for underdeveloped countries gained currency of usage

1966 ECONOMIC PROFILE

Income, Standard Jobs

Bituminous Coal Mining	$7,398.00
Building Trades	$7,373.00
Domestics	$2,780.00
Farm Labor	$2,923.00
Federal Civilian	$8,170.00
Federal Military	$4,650.00
Finance, Insurance, and Real Estate	$6,239.00
Gas, Electricity, and Sanitation Workers	$7,801.00
Manufacturing, Durable Goods	$7,228.00
Manufacturing, Nondurable Goods	$6,172.00
Medical/Health Services Workers	$4,565.00
Miscellaneous Manufacturing	$5,548.00
Motion Picture Services	$7,397.00
Nonprofit Organization Workers	$4,280.00
Passenger Transportation	$5,737.00
Personal Services	$4,551.00
Private Industries, Including Farm Labor	$6,098.00

"The Grownups' Hour: When Generations Meet," Beefeater Dry Gin Advertisement, *Holiday Magazine*, December 1965:

"The martini could speak volumes if it could tell its own tale—the story of the grownups' hour: a pause where the business of the day drops away and the flow of events moves forward free of trivial concerns. It is a time when adult relationships flourish, and when generation may speak clearly to generation across the span of memories and years. The light, dry martini was born to serve this hour. But it needs a superior gin.

One young householder, newly moved with his growing family to a large apartment learned this when he mixed a martini for the first time in his new establishment. Children were tucked away, dinner was coming along. All was in order. But a gin, a good, ordinary, serviceable gin, produced a dull martini. Simply not up to the job. Kindness prevailed. The father went out to get something better in gin.

Pitcher and glasses went back to the refrigerator, where they acquired the deep chill that preserves the excellent coldness of a great martini. And as soon as the father returned, a great martini was made. The ice smoked as the gin was poured over it, in a pitcher of ample size. Chilled glasses received the new martini. Not another word was spoken on the subject. An excellent gin made all the statement that was needed. The grownups' conversation went on to children and grandchildren and when they were children and other things that matter."

Public School Teachers. $6,142.00
Radio Broadcasting and
    Television Workers. $8,833.00
Railroads $7,708.00
State and Local Government
    Workers $5,834.00
Telephone and Telegraph
    Workers $6,858.00
Wholesale and Retail Trade
    Workers $7,345.00

Selected Prices

Aluminum Lawn Chair $5.99
Black and Decker Drill, Electric $19.95
Child's Magic Grow Slip,
    Package of Three, ... $2.97
Custom 7 Transistor Radio. $12.95
Deluxe Walker-Stroller $18.95
Englander Mattress, Full Size $59.95
Fred Astaire Dance Lessons,
    Eight Lessons, ... $13.95
General Electric Alarm Clock $5.98
Goldblatt's Air Conditioner $498.88
Jarman Shoes. $22.00
Kutmaster, Two-Bladed Knife. $1.00
Polaroid Color Pack Camera $50.00
Schlitz Beer, Six Pack. $0.99
Simonize Car Wax. $0.99
Tru-dent Electric Toothbrush $12.50
Truetone Color Television. $629.95
Viking Chair $11.95
West Bend Coffee Maker $9.95
Wizard Electric Dryer $169.95
Wizard Imperial Manual
    Typewriter. $89.95
Wizard Set 'N' Spray Sprinkler. $9.19

Emerging Consumer America

The new wealth many Americans were experiencing was also resulting in a more scientific look at how consumers shopped and what they wanted. According to the *Milwaukee Journal*'s Consumer Analysis, consumers in 1965 said:

- Friday was their favorite day to grocery shop.
- Most spent between $20.00 and $30.00 on groceries each week.
- 43 percent purchased frozen orange juice during the past month; 23 percent purchased Minute Maid.
- 93 percent purchased white bread; led by Wonder Bread.

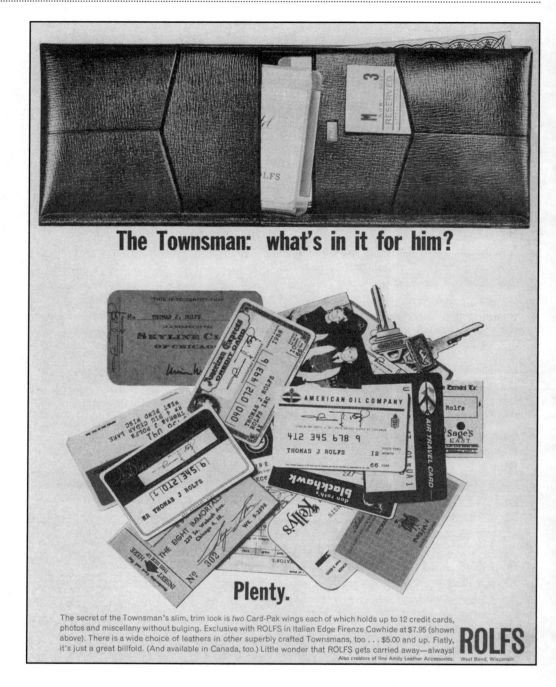

The Townsman: what's in it for him?

Plenty.

The secret of the Townsman's slim, trim look is *two* Card-Pak wings each of which holds up to 12 credit cards, photos and miscellany without bulging. Exclusive with ROLFS in Italian Edge Firenze Cowhide at $7.95 (shown above). There is a wide choice of leathers in other superbly crafted Townsmans, too . . . $5.00 and up. Flatly, it's just a great billfold. (And available in Canada, too.) Little wonder that ROLFS gets carried away—always! Also creators of fine Amity Leather Accessories.

ROLFS
West Bend, Wisconsin

- During the month, 81 percent purchased regular coffee, led by Hills Brothers; 48 percent purchased instant coffee, 24 percent of whom wanted Maxwell House.
- 80 percent of shoppers purchased wieners or frankfurters; 42 percent selected Oscar Mayer.
- 10.6 percent needed strained baby foods; 67 percent selected Gerber.
- Only 35 percent of consumers needed margarine, but 83 percent bought butter; Land O' Lakes was the total butter choice.

"Massillon: The High Price of Prosperity," *Life Magazine*, August 12, 1966:

"Massillon, like many small cities in the country's heartland, is a blend of payroll town and rural trade center, of boosterism and nostalgia for the past, of complacency, generosity, bigotry, progress, and decay. Perhaps best known for its famous high school football team—The Massillon Tigers—the bustling factory town was once an Ohio Canal port and the home of 'General' Coxey, who marched an army of unemployed from Massillon to Washington during the depression of 1894. When Pfc. Herm Wuertz died it suddenly reminded almost everybody in town of a friend or relative who was also in Vietnam and in danger of being killed. Economically, not many localities owe more than Massillon to the Vietnam War. After a series of near-disaster years in which the town's second largest industry moved away and production at its largest—Republic Steel—dropped drastically, the city is prospering once again. Credit is tightening, but loans are available at 6–7 percent; prices are up, but so are wages. At Republic, although the market for automobile steel is off, defense orders have taken up the slack. And the demand for surgical gloves in the hospitals and stations in Vietnam has risen so sharply that Perry Rubber Company is running three shifts six days a week.

Yet the Vietnam war is costing Massillon heavily. Because relatively few of its high school graduates go on to college, the town has contributed its young men to the military in large numbers. More than a half-dozen have been wounded. And so misgivings about Commander-in-Chief Lyndon Johnson's conducting of the war emerged here more quickly than in many other cities. So far as Massillon is concerned, the near-euphoric 'consensus' of Johnson's early months in office has been virtually wiped out by resentment of a war they only dimly understand and disbelief in the reasons given for U.S. involvement."

- Pancake or waffle mix was selected by 51.9 percent of the consumers; 38 percent selected Aunt Jemima.
- During the previous month, 68 percent of consumers needed canned corn; 23 percent wanted Green Giant.
- Only 20.3 percent needed instant tea; 52 percent of those went for Lipton.
- Almost 80 percent of households bought potato chips; Mrs. Drenk's was the top choice, while Red Dot was second.
- 72.9 percent of homes bought peanut butter at least once a month; 55 percent of those bought Skippy.
- Only 14.7 percent of consumers bought from the frozen bakery; 26 percent of those bought Sara Lee.
- 61.4 percent of homes bought candy bars; 47 percent of those picked up Hershey.
- At the liquor store, 6.2 percent of consumers bought scotch; 18 percent of those picked Cutty Sark; Smirnoff was the leading vodka; Fleischmann was the best selling gin.
- Among beer lovers, 61 percent of consumers bought bottled beer over a thirty-day period, led by Blatz; 35 percent of those surveyed purchased canned beer, and Blatz was the winner here also.
- 72.9 percent of households bought bottled soft drinks; Pepsi-Cola was the leader with 27 percent of the market, Graf's had 25 percent, and Coca-Cola claimed 25 percent.

- In 1965, 95 percent of the households surveyed said they had a black and white television and 4.9 percent had a color TV; RCA Victor led both categories.
- 51.8 percent of the consumers surveyed had an FM radio, 27 percent had an electric clothes dryer, and 20.9 percent had a gas clothes dryer; 93 percent of homes had a refrigerator and 26 percent had freezers.
- According to the survey, 7.8 percent of homes had an automatic dishwasher, 33 percent of which were made by General Electric; 44 percent owned a power lawn mower, 83 percent owned cars, and 35 percent had a gasoline credit card.
- Among both men and women, the favorite recreation was bowling; second for both was television, hunting ranked third for men, cards for women.
- The questionnaire designated that "only men" were to answer questions about stock purchases and tires and women were only to answer the sections related to grocery shopping.

"Yeah! Yeah! Yeah! Music's Gold Bugs: The Beatles, They can't read music, their beat is corny and their voices are faint, but England's shaggy-maned exports manage to flip wigs on two continents," *The Saturday Evening Post*, March 21, 1964:

"So far Beatlemania has traveled over two continents. In Stockholm the arrival of the Beatles was greeted with teenage riots. In Paris another congregation held screeching services at the airport and the Beatles' performances at the Olympia Theater were sold out for three weeks. In the Beatles' native Liverpool 60 youngsters collapsed from exposure after standing all night in a mile-long line of 12,000 waiting to buy tickets to the Beatles' performance. When a foreman shut off the radio in the middle of a Beatles record at a textile mill in Lancashire, 200 girls went out on strike.

While the Beatles toured the United States, three of their singles were in the top six and their albums ranked one and two in the record popularity charts. Beatle wigs were selling at $3.00 a piece, high school boys were combing their forelocks forward and hairdressers were advertising Beatle cuts for women. Beatle hats, T-shirts, cookies, eggcups, ice cream, dolls, beach shirts, turtleneck pullovers, nighties, socks, and iridescent blue-and-green collarless suits were on the market, and a Beatle motor scooter for children and a Beatlemobile for adults were being readied for production. American bartenders were confronted by a sudden deluge of orders for scotch and Coke, the Beatles' favorite drink. 'I think everyone has gone *daft*,' says John Lennon. Adds Ringo, 'Anytime you spell beetle with an 'a' in it, we get the money.' In 1964, Beatle-licensed products stand to gross $50 million in America alone. As for the Beatles, their total 1964 income is expected to reach $14 million."

1968 FAMILY PROFILE

The Whitley family lives in Memphis, Tennessee, where she now works at a leading manufacturing plant in the city, one of the first to allow Black workers. They own a single-wide mobile home on property she inherited from her father. He works on farms in the area; they have one child, who is in the third grade.

Annual Income: $9,375

She makes $3.09 per hour or $124.84 a week creating an annual income of $6,375; he makes approximately $3,000 yearly working on farms, fixing tractors, hauling feed, selling fertilizer, and odd jobs. The fruits and vegetables he grows on their own farm and the game animals he hunts supplement their income.

Annual Budget

The study does not provide family expenditures; nationally the per capita expenditures in 1968 are:

Auto Parts	$22.92
Auto Usage	$338.80
Clothing	$178.87
Dentists	$19.93
Food	$605.86
Furniture	$39.36
Gas and Oil	$92.67
Health Insurance	$15.60
Housing	$397.09
Intercity Transport	$15.45
Local Transport	$11.96
New Auto Purchase	$122.07
Personal Business	$141.00
Personal Care	$52.81

Physicians $54.31
Public Education and
    Research $49.33
Recreation $182.85
Religion/Welfare Activities $51.32
Telephone and Telegraph $41.35
Tobacco $46.83
Utilities $100.15
Per Capita Consumption $2,785.67

Life at Home

- The Whitleys live in a single-wide mobile home located on the family farm.
- The man farms the family land and hires out to neighbors, many of them White, in the spring and fall; he also sells fertilizer to earn extra income.
- In addition to growing vegetables for sale and use at home, he prides himself on his hunting skills; deer, squirrel, and turtle are part of the family diet.
- The woman experiences a long drive to work; 40,000 people drive into Memphis to work each morning.
- Developers are buying nearby farms for the expanding suburbs of rapidly growing Memphis; land speculation is rampant. The family is uncertain whether to sell the family farm if asked.
- If they agree to sell the farm, they are uncertain where they will live; most African-Americans in Memphis—even those with money—live in homes in the older section of town that are often substandard, because Memphis has few integrated neighborhoods.
- The approach of suburbs also brings libraries; Memphis now offers nearly 20 library branches. This family's third-grader considers herself a good reader.
- Both parents believe that their third-grade daughter will have a better life with more opportunities than they did, especially if she does well in school.

Life at Work: The Manufacturing Plant

- This nationally-known electronics company began manufacturing operations in Memphis in 1947 with 100 employees producing electronic components such as headphones and condensers.
- Currently the plant employs 1,200 workers, spread evenly over three shifts.
- The bulk of the work force are middle-aged White women who work at machines producing small, delicate components.
- The first Black employee is hired in 1961 during a period of expansion.

The first Black employee of the company, Katie Fuller, described the early days of her employment in 1961:

"I didn't know I was the only colored person. I thought they had hired a bunch of them, you know. And when I got out there—nobody but me and the good Lord knows what I went through. But I just pray. I asked God to help me. I said: 'Help me Jesus, I got to work somewhere . . . .'

And they would have to come down this certain aisle going out. See, they would be getting off, while we would still be working. They'd get off at 3:10, and we'd be working almost to 4:20. And they come through there hollering 'Nigger,' and talking all kind of ugly talk. Cursing. And I would look over to the side, to the space next to me. And I thought these people are crazy. And I'd look at 'em and I would laugh. I'd kinda smile. It took a whole lot out of me, you know. And I never worked with anybody like this before. A whole plant of people in here were—I don't know how to describe it. Devil Action."

- African-American workers are added at the Memphis facility because of corporate pressure and a gradual change in the racial climate in Memphis of such desegregated facilities as cafeterias, drinking fountains, and toilets.
- At the plant racial relationships are considered good by both Black and White workers; in the cafeteria Black workers normally sit together separate from the White workers out of tradition and choice.
- Black leaders believe that changes in hiring practices take place not because of marches or demonstrations, but on the requirements for a non-discriminatory workplace that are placed on government contracts.
- Most African-Americans hired by the company have a high school diploma and one-third have college experience; approximately one-fourth of the White workers do not have a high school diploma and only seven percent attended college.
- By 1968, 50 percent of the new hires are Black women; only 16 Black men are employed among 1,200 workers.
- Typically the jobs require little training; the plant has experienced little unionization.
- The electrical manufacturing industry, dominated by companies such as Westinghouse and General Electric, is growing rapidly.
- From 1923 to 1958 total employment in the electrical manufacturing industry grew by three times; electric power consumption, measured in kilowatt hours, grew by 16 times.
- In 1968 sales for appliances and electronic products increases nine percent and profits, 18.2 percent.

Life in the Community: Memphis, Tennessee

- Memphis, sitting in the extreme southwest corner of Tennessee, sits high on a bluff overlooking the Mississippi River.
- Memphis and the river have long been tied; the city grew as a center where cotton bales were sold, loaded onto riverboats, and shipped down the waterway.
- Firestone, RCA, International Harvester, General Electric, and other well-known industries have settled in the city once known best for the blues, gambling, and catfish.
- Following a national pattern, more neighborhoods near downtown Memphis are becoming Black, while new all-White suburbs have sprung up around the city.
- With a population of nearly 550,000, Memphis is the largest city in not only Tennessee, but the border states of Mississippi and Arkansas.
- About 40 percent, or 200,000 people, are Black.
- Many migrants from the cotton and soybean farms of the Mississippi delta have settled in the city; only 56 percent of the population was born in Tennessee, and more than 25 percent have lived in Memphis less than five years.
- Approximately 57 percent of the African-American families have incomes below the poverty level of $3,000 a year; only 13.8 percent of White families live below the poverty level.
- The median educational level of Memphis Blacks over 25 years old in the 1960 census is 6.7 years; the median White has completed 11.1 years of school.

Memphis, Tennessee, showing Mississippi River and Riverside Drive by Moonlight

- Achievement tests show that Black eighth-graders test two grades behind White eighth-graders.
- The Shelby County school system is not desegregated until 1963; by 1968 the vast majority of the public schools are de facto segregated.
- Three of 13 city councilmen are Black in 1968; five percent of all the school boards are African-American.
- Earlier in 1968, Civil Rights activists encourage the Black garbage workers strike, supported by the American Federation of State, County, and Municipal employees Union and Black ministers in the area; Martin Luther King is to take a leadership role.
- Pay for garbage workers is $70.00 a week; supervisors are all White, while workers are typically African-Americans recruited from farms.
- The mayor feels the strike is unwarranted, declaring "I don't make deals"; King is branded an irresponsible rabble-rouser.
- Memphis' Black ministers use their pulpits to compare the strikers with the Old Testament prophets who crusaded against injustice, take up special collections for the workers, and ask their congregations to join them in daily marches to downtown Memphis.
- In less than a week $15,000 is raised to support the strikers; downtown sales drop by 35 percent.
- On March 14, NAACP Executive Secretary Roy Wilkes speaks to a rally of 9,000; four days later Martin Luther King, Jr., speaks to an even larger audience and calls for a one-day general strike of all workers.
- Riots break out during a downtown march on March 28; one person is killed, 60 injured, 300 arrested.
- The president of the Local Chamber of Commerce blames the violence on activist preachers, saying, "If the Negro ministers would tend to their ministering instead of trying to stir things up, we wouldn't have had this trouble."

WILL NEGRO BLOC VOTE CONTROL SOUTH CAROLINA?

CORE worker carries Communist placard in voter registration march. CORE leader James Farmer said in Columbia that the defeat of Senator Strom Thurmond was one of CORE's main goals.

Martin Luther King shakes hands in Florence, S. C. after a voter registration rally. King said: "We must be an independent force in the Democratic Party in years to come." King predicted this would give Negroes control.

"I believe the Negro vote will have a greater impact this year than any since Reconstruction." said by Rev. I. deQuincy Newman of South Carolina NAACP, March 13, 1966

This year, over 200,000 Negroes are registered to vote in South Carolina. The Negro leaders have made it clear that they will vote as a solid bloc for their Democratic friends who support L. B. J. This means that if the white people remain divided, the Negro vote will decide the election.

It is the oldest story in politics: an elected official must be faithful to those who put him in office. A politician who is elected by the Negro bloc vote will have to answer to the NAACP everytime he casts a vote or makes an appointment. If the bloc vote gains control of OUR STATE GOVERNMENT, OUR SENATORS, AND OUR REPRESENTATIVES, then as surely as night follows day, the Black Revolution which struck Los Angeles, Chicago, Cleveland, and Atlanta will strike South Carolina. THAT MUST NOT HAPPEN!

Stand Up For The Men Who Will Stand Up For You! Support . .
Strom Thurmond — Marshall Parker — Joe Rogers

They Will Represent The People—Not The NAACP Or The Democratic Bosses in Washington.

Lucius Burch, White leader on the Memphis Committee on Community Relations in 1963 to the (MCCR):

"It is now clear beyond argument that no public institution has the right to deny equal facility of use to any citizen because of color. The Negro citizens are naturally restive at being thwarted and delayed in the exercise of their clearly declared rights. Having been successful in establishing their rights through litigation, they now seek to obtain them by 'demonstrations.' These so-called demonstrations are ancient and constitutionally authorized remedies in that all citizens have the right to assemble peaceably, to petition for the redress of their grievances, and to publicize by picketing and other legal means their contentions. There is no legal, moral, or historical basis for condemning the assertion of rights by these methods. Indeed a nation looking with pride at such vigorous precedents as Runnymede, the Boston Tea Party, and Concord Bridge must praise rather than condemn any citizen or group of citizens vigilant and active in the establishment and protection of their liberties. This is straight talk and not calculated to please or flatter or to do other than speak the truth to tough-minded men and women sufficiently concerned to band together to achieve a solution. The trust is that if the White leadership of this community does not actively concern itself with the obtaining of legally declared rights and by its prestige and influence further rather than restrain the exercise of these rights, we must expect the Negroes to exert themselves vigorously to gain these ends which have been judicially declared their legislative due. The Negro leadership in this community is effective and responsible. It is composed of men who have a personal stake in the continued tranquility and future growth of the community. The Negro leaders are ministers, merchants, teachers, bankers, lawyers, etc., and they will suffer even more than their White counterparts from disorder and they have done a magnificent job in preaching responsibility and restrain to those who look to them for leadership. But they first and foremost are members of their race and have a keen sense of injustice. Moreover, they will not remain as leaders of their people without tangible exertion and perceptible progress toward the attainment of their rights. If there is a failure of their leadership, it will be replaced by more radical groups not concerned with long-term and overall community consequences."

- Martin Luther King, Jr., is shot and killed on April 4, 1968, at the Memphis Lorraine Motel while organizing a nonviolent march in support of the garbage workers' strike; Memphis, along with cities across the nation, experiences rioting that night.
- The city eventually agrees to pay the garbage workers an extra $0.10 per hour and to permit union dues check-off if handled through a credit union and then paid to the Union.

HISTORICAL SNAPSHOT
1968–1969

- The U.S. gross national product reached $861 billion
- The Vietnam War and student protests intensified across the nation
- Richard Nixon was elected president
- 4,462 corporate mergers took place
- BankAmericard holders numbered 14 million, up 12 million in two years
- Civil Rights leader Rev. Martin Luther King, Jr., was assassinated at a Memphis, Tennessee, motel; riots occurred in over 199 cities nationwide
- Senator Robert F. Kennedy was assassinated in Los Angeles shortly after winning the California Democratic primary
- In response to the King and Kennedy assassinations, Sears & Roebuck removed toy guns from its Christmas catalog
- Automobile production reached 8.8 million
- Volkswagen captured 57 percent of the U.S. automobile import market
- Television advertising revenues hit $2 billion, twice that of radio
- First-class postage climbed to $0.06
- Inflation was now a worldwide issue
- Yale College admitted women
- The Uniform Monday Holiday Law was enacted by Congress, creating three-day holiday weekends
- Crimes of violence reportedly had increased 57 percent since 1960
- Nationwide 78 million television sets existed
- The average farm subsidy from the government was $1,000
- Neil Armstrong walked on the moon
- The average U.S. automobile wholesaled for $2,280
- Pantyhose production reached 624 million pairs in 1969, up from 200 million in 1968
- The average U.S. farm produced enough food for 47 people
- Blue Cross health insurance covered 68 million Americans
- *Penthouse* magazine began publication; *Saturday Evening Post* folded
- The National Association of Broadcasters began a cigarette advertising phase-out
- The U.S. began the first troop withdrawals from Vietnam; Vietnam casualties now exceeded the total for the Korean War
- Richard Nixon's 43.3 percent victory was the lowest presidential margin since 1912
- Pope Paul VI's ban on contraception was challenged by 800 U.S. theologians
- 20,000 people were added monthly to New York's welfare rolls; one-fourth of the city's budget went to welfare
- The Vietnam War became the longest war in U.S. history

1968 Economic Profile

Income, Standard Jobs

Bituminous Coal Mining $8,169.00
Building Trades $8,332.00
Domestic Industries $6,759.00
Domestics $3,254.00
Farm Labor $3,327.00
Federal Civilian $9,002.00
Federal Military $5,148.00
Finance, Insurance, Real Estate $6,994.00
Gas, Electricity, and Sanitation
   Workers $8,666.00
Manufacturing, Durable Goods $8,002.00
Manufacturing, Nondurable
   Goods $6,849.00
Medical/Health Services
   Workers $5,292.00
Miscellaneous Manufacturing $6,252.00
Motion Picture Services $7,946.00
Nonprofit Organization
   Workers $4,655.00
Passenger Transportation Workers,
   Local and Highway $6,279.00
Personal Services $4,960.00
Private Industries, Including
   Farm Labor $6,772.00
Public School Teachers $7,129.00
Radio Broadcasting and
   Television Workers $9,563.00
Railroads $8,663.00
State and Local Government
   Workers $7,255.00
Telephone and Telegraph
   Workers $7,506.00
Wholesale and Retail Trade
   Workers $8,142.00

Selected Prices

Argus 35-mm Cartridge Camera,
   with Flash $69.95
Black and Decker Drill, Electric $10.99
Child's Fruit of the Loom Briefs,
   Package of Three $2.65
Colgate Toothpaste, 6.75 Ounce Tube . . . $0.55
Custom 7 Transistor Radio $12.95
Cut-Glass Glasses, Includes Six
   Tumblers $2.49
Daisy Golden 750 Rifle $7.50

Davis Super Highway Tire,
    Six-Ply Rating $26.95
DeLong Red Worm Fishing Lure,
    Package of Three $0.49
Delta Airline Fare, Chicago
    to Miami $74.70
Dual-Exhaust Kit for Corvair $18.45
Goldblatt's Air Conditioner,
    Whole House. $498.88
Hunts Catsup, 14-Ounce Bottle $0.22
Jarman Man's Dress Shoes $22.00
Lady Kenmore Electric Shaver $13.97
Mattel Teenage Barbie. $2.29
Pepsi Cola, 10-Ounce Bottles, Six Pack . . $0.59
Seagram's VO Whiskey, 86.8
    Proof, Fifth $5.79
Solid-Oak Nightstand $25.95
Truetone Riviera Television,
    16" B&W $149.95
Western Auto Sunburst Wall Clock $16.25
Wizard Long Life Light Bulbs,
    Four Pack. $1.29
Wizard Washer, 10-Pound Capacity $99.88

Civil Rights in Memphis

- On December 1, 1955, 42-year-old Rosa Parks helped launch a movement by refusing to surrender her bus seat to a White passenger; the federal courts ruled segregation of the Montgomery, Alabama, buses unconstitutional in 1956.
- In response Memphis post office employee O.Z. Evers filed a suit against the Memphis bus company in 1956 to desegregate that city's buses.
- Black banker and NAACP board member Jessie Turner filed a desegregation suit against the Memphis Public Library in 1958.
- John F. Kennedy promised during his 1960 presidential campaign to exercise "moral and persuasive leadership" to enforce the 1954 Supreme Court decision calling for desegregated schools.
- By 1960 a generation of high school Black students had grown up knowing that the Supreme Court had ruled the educational apartheid they were experiencing was against the law of the land.
- Resentment and frustration burst to the surface in the 1960s across the nation.
- Challenges to the official barriers to Blacks seeking public accommodations included sit-in demonstrations at drug stores, freedom rides on public buses across the South, and marches in hundreds of cities across the nation, although principally in the South.
- Student sit-ins began nationwide in 1960; 41 Memphis College students were arrested for entering two segregated libraries.
- The racially mixed Memphis Committee on Community Relations urged voluntary desegregation; the buses were desegrated in the fall of 1960, libraries in October, and the Overton Park Zoo in December of that year.

> ## Reverend Jimmy Grant, who led a voter registration drive in 1961, recalls adjacent Fayette County, Tennessee, in 1940:
>
> "I can remember the lynching of '40. I remember my father saying, 'We don't go out of the house for the next day or two. We don't go downtown. If anyone knocks on the door, let me answer.' And we had his gun behind the door, and he would always peep out before. Because everyone was frightened and leaflets had been circulated saying, 'We got Elbert Williams. Who will be next?' (Williams had organized an NAACP meeting.) And when they found him it was a hideous thing. I didn't know what lynching was, and when I questioned my daddy, he said, 'A man was killed. And you just don't bother, if you don't understand it. I'll tell you later.'"

- To avoid a Black boycott, the Memphis downtown merchants agreed to volunteer desegregation in January 1962—provided that no changes were required during the 1961 Christmas season.
- Thirteen Black students integrated four Memphis schools in the fall of 1961 without incident; officials were so fearful of riots that even the teachers were not informed of the planned integration of their classrooms until the night before.
- In 1962 the movie theaters of the city were integrated secretly. With the cooperation of the theater managers, a Black couple was selected to integrate the Malco Theatre. When nothing happened to the couple, the following week two Black couples were sent to integrate another theater; by April, 1963, 14 theaters had been integrated in this way.
- When publicity about the progressive work of the Memphis Committee on Community Relations appeared in the Memphis newspaper, the White chairman, a respected former Memphis banker, received anonymous letters addressed to the "nigger lover" and stating, "race mixing is communism."
- As part of an agreement to voluntarily integrate the 20 largest restaurants in the city, and thus avoid picketing, the restaurant owners insisted that the *Memphis Appeal* not report that integration of the eating establishments was taking place.
- Until 1965 the Tennessee Department of Employment Security maintained segregated offices; employers who wanted White workers called one office, for Black workers, another separate facility.
- Many Black workers who applied for jobs through the Tennessee Department of Employment Security were told they were too short, too tall, or too young for the jobs; their applications were not taken or processed.
- Reacting to change, the Memphis American Legion raised $10,000 to finance a sustained showing of J. Edgar Hoover's film *Masters of Deceit* in every public school.
- But the South was not singled out for change: race riots in the Watts section of Los Angeles in 1965 resulted in 34 deaths and $40 million in property damage. In 1967 in Newark, New Jersey, 26 people died and 1,500 were injured; in Detroit that same year 40 people died and more than 1,000 were injured in an eruption that required 4,700 U.S. paratroopers and 8,000 National Guardsmen to quell.

"A New Cash Crop for Rural America," advertisement by National Association of Real Estate Board, *Life Magazine*, November 15, 1968:

"The biggest migration of this century has been from America's small towns to the big cities in search of jobs. The Make America Better program of the Realtors salutes Mountain Home, Arkansas, a small community that is successfully reversing this trend. Like most farming communities, Mountain Home was steadily losing its people to the cities. The economy slumped steadily until the town grabbed itself by the bootstraps and began to pull. Though handicapped by limited assets, it succeeded in attracting two industries to locate in the county. As a result, while most rural areas continue to lose population, Mountain Home is gaining steadily. Now that good jobs are available at home, a surprising number of former residents are coming back. And families who otherwise would have emigrated to overpopulated cities are staying at home...Help make America better. Join with the 85,000 Realtors in their Make America Better Program."

1969 News Profile

This 50-year-old Black minister has worked full-time in the Civil Rights movement since 1963. His work is primarily in the area where he was born and spent his early years in the South; he believes there has been little progress.

"Some of the members of my church aren't for freedom. I don't mind telling them about freedom, though, because I feel like I'm working for the Lord. The Lord told me to preach to all the world. If I get out there in a demonstration against injustice, I'm preaching. I figure I can reach more of the world preaching a sermon that way than I could by just isolating myself before people in some hollow of a log somewhere. The Lord is in the business of saving souls, and I'd like to carry Lester Maddox up to heaven with me. I got to join because I'm working for the Lord. I don't think anybody, no agitator between here and hell or nowhere could be more of an agitator than Jesus. I just can't understand people when they think we are far from religion when we are demonstrating. I just don't see it . . .

I believe that religion really helped people in the movement. People had been taught through their religion to have patience. The invisible rewards of the movement didn't discourage them too much because they had been taught their rewards would come later, after death. This served a great purpose: it gave struggling Blacks the patience and the courage they needed, because the victories that have come out of the movement are almost empty, in a way, as the 'pie in the sky.' That isn't to say that 'pie in the sky' doesn't exist, but just that it's not visible. It's about as visible as the rewards of sufferings and jailings. When we started in the movement, many of us thought that we would accomplish first-class citizenship. We thought that the majority of the poor Blacks would taste the fruits of suffering, but there have been no rewards for them. Now the middle-class Blacks are going into office, and Blacks are able to register and vote, but this has not filtered down to the man at the bottom. That man has not tasted the fruit as yet. Until the majority of the poor can taste the fruits of rich America, I don't think we've come close to victory . . .

Giving up money is a great sacrifice. Before the movement, I made $9,000 a year, and I've never made near that much. I had three churches when the movement started; I only have one now. I've worked all my days. I've worked as a skilled laborer, the type of labor that pays well. I have four children who are married now, but back then I had to make a

living for them. If it hadn't been for my wife working, I don't know whether we could have eaten.

A lot of my Blacks who were with us dropped out because of pressure. Many believed in what they were doing, but they were in business and borrowing money was difficult. They were identified with the movement, and for that the Whites penalized them. They couldn't get a loan. The Whites allowed them to go so far and be kind of "Tomish," but when they get to pressing hard and hit some nerve points, they'd be penalized. They might have to pay a higher price for groceries. If someone were trying to run a little store, then the White suppliers might charge him higher prices. People couldn't compete, so they got squeezed out . . .

Some White friends of mine started out with the movement but dropped it. They thought they were going to beg a little; that crumbs would be thrown to us, and that we would then settle back and be quiet. We just kept knocking on the door for public accommodations, and after they gave us that, they thought we would stop. But we wouldn't. So they turned on us and said, 'You have gone too far.' They stopped supporting us. A lot of them had been giving us money, but they never intended for us to reach first-class citizenship.

I know a whole church that had preachers coming in the front door and going out the back door almost in a line. They were firing them very fast during the days of the movement because the ministers spoke out about what was right. One of the ministers of the First Baptist Church went to California for a conference and came back to make a report. He started his report in the church, but he finished it somewhere else because they had him out of there so fast he didn't know what was happening . . .

During the movement, several Blacks were killed in this town over a period of about 10 months. The White man feels that he is god of the earth. When Blacks don't scrape and bow when speaking, he'll shoot them down. Blacks have been getting killed for the last 20 years for a loaf of bread all over the world and all over the United States. Right now they're falling. Whites don't want to cooperate with us. That wouldn't happen if we went to school together. So school is the answer.

    People are saying that Blacks are lazy. Blacks get tired of reaching and coming down with a handful of air for 40 and 50 years. I get tired of telling high school children to stay in school, when they can't get a job when they come out. College graduates can't get a job, and you're telling them to stay in school. Blacks have been beaten and cheated out of their wages for years. Blacks have worked hard, and they don't have anything but a place to sleep! What kind of reward have they gotten for working hard?"

The weather was fair and cold
The weather was fair and cold
Hundreds had promised to come
But only a few were there.

Standing in one place, standing in one place
We could see everyone face to face
With outstretched hand and smiling face
We invited everyone to take their place.

The way out must lead in, the way out must lead in
No matter what's the price, we must pay
We must pay if we shall win.

The police just waited around
As we continued our march downtown
We moved in a single file
They moved around like ushers in an aisle.

We did not know our destination
It must be Highway 82
But the policemen standing there
Would not let us through.

Taking chances to get to the other side
Police just stood there with pistols on their side
They didn't care if we lived or died.

White like you, John, or Black like me.
There was no hesitation in turning the key
If you show the least sign of wanting to be free
A wanting to be free, A wanting to be free.

Jail without bail is a sad story to tell
For day after day we peep through the cell
Day after day we peep through the cell
Peep through the cell, peep through the cell.

Watching others go by, watching others go by
Acting as if there was no bail
And we were the only ones, the only ones in jail.

The way out must lead in, the way out must lead in
No matter what's the price, we must pay
We must pay if we shall win.

Civil Rights protest song created at the time of the march.

425

Value of One Dollar	
Year	Value in 2010 USD
1970	$5.62
1972	$5.22
1974	$4.42
1976	$3.81
1979	$3.00

Values are approximate based upon economic historical data and 2010 U. S. Dollar

1970–1979

The Vietnam War, responsible for deep divisions and raging inflation, finally came to an end during the decade of the 1970s. For more than 10 years the war had been fought on two fronts: at home and abroad. As a result, U.S. policy-makers conducted the war with one eye always focused on national opinion. When it ended, the Vietnam War was the longest war in American history; the total cost was $118 billion, 56,000 dead, and 300,000 wounded, and the loss of American prestige abroad. For the remainder of the century all military conflicts were decided and fought in the shadow of the lessons of Vietnam.

The Vietnam War's spiraling costs not only set off the first of several waves of inflation during the decade, it stripped the United States of its ability to dominate the world economy. In 1971 President Richard Nixon was forced to devalue the U.S. dollar against foreign currencies and allow its previously fixed value to "float" according to changing economic conditions. By year's end the money paid for foreign goods exceeded those for U.S. exporters, for the first time in the century. Two years later, during the "Yom Kippur" War between Israel and its Arab neighbors, Arab oil producers declared an oil embargo on oil shipments to the United States, setting off gas shortages, a dramatic rise in the price of oil, and rationing for the first time in 30 years. The sale of automobiles plummeted, unemployment and inflation nearly doubled, and the buying power of Americans fell rapidly.

The economy, handicapped by the devaluation of the dollar and inflation, did not fully recover for more than a decade, while the fast-growing economies of Japan and western Europe, especially West Germany, mounted direct competitive challenges to American manufacturers. The value of imported manufactured goods skyrocketed from 14 percent of U.S. domestic production in 1970 to 40 percent in 1979. The inflationary cycle and recession returned in 1979 to disrupt markets, throw thousands out of work, and prompt massive downsizing of companies—awakening many once-secure workers to the reality of the changing economic market. A symbol of the era was the pending bankruptcy of Chrysler Corporation, whose cars were so outmoded and plants so inefficient, they could not compete against Japanese imports. The federal government was forced to extend loan guarantees to the company to prevent bankruptcy and the loss of thousands of jobs.

The appointment of Paul Volcker as the chairman of the Federal Reserve Board late in the decade gave the economy the distasteful medicine it needed. To cope with inflation, Volcker slammed on the economic breaks, restricted the growth of the money supply, and curbed inflation. As a result he pushed interest rates to nearly 20—their highest level since the Civil War. Almost immediately the sale of automobiles and expensive items stopped.

The decade was a time of not only movements, but moving. In the 1970s the shift of manufacturing facilities to the South from New England and the Midwest accelerated. The Sunbelt became the new darling of corporate America. By the late 1970s the South, including Texas, had gained more than a million manufacturing jobs, while the Northeast and the Midwest lost nearly two million. Formally, rural North Carolina had the highest percentage of manufacturing of any state in the nation, along with the lowest blue-collar wages and the lowest unionization rate in the country. The Northeast lost more than traditional manufacturing jobs. Computerization of clerical work also made it possible for big firms such as Merrill Lynch, American Express, and Citibank to shift many of their operations to the South and West.

The largest and most striking of all the social actions of the early 1970s was the women's liberation movement; it fundamentally reshaped American society. Since the late 1950s a small group of well-placed American women had attempted to convince Congress and the courts to bring equality between the sexes. By the 1970s, the National Organization for Women (NOW) multiplied in size, the first issue of *Ms. Magazine* sold out in a week, and women began demanding economic equality, the legalization of abortion, and the improvement of women's role in society. "All authority in our society is being challenged," said a Department of Health, Education, and Welfare report. "Professional athletes challenge owners, journalists challenge editors, consumers challenge manufacturers . . . and young blue-collar workers, who have grown up in an environment in which equality is called for in all institutions, are demanding the same rights and expressing the same values as university graduates."

The decade also included the flowering of the National Welfare Rights Organization (NWRO), founded in 1966, which resulted in millions of urban poor demanding additional rights. The environment movement gained recognition and momentum during the decade starting with the first Earth Day celebration in 1970 and the subsequent passage of the federal Clean Air and Clean Water acts. And the growing opposition to the use of nuclear power peaked after the near calamity at Three Mile Island in Pennsylvania in 1979. As the formal barriers to racial equality came down, racist attitudes became unacceptable and the Black middle class began to grow. By 1972 half of all Southern Black children sat in integrated classrooms, and about one-third of all Black families had risen economically into the ranks of the middle class.

The changes recorded for the decade included a doubling in the amount of garbage created per capita from 2.5 pounds in 1920 to 5 pounds. California created a no-fault divorce law, Massachusetts introduced no-fault insurance, and health food sales reached $3 billion. By mid-decade, the so-called typical nuclear family, with working father, housewife, and two children, represented only seven percent of the population and the family size was falling. The average family size was 3.4 persons compared with 4.3 in 1920.

1971 NEWS PROFILE

In 1971 four and a half million Americans work for small manufacturing firms that hire less than 100 people. The first woman works for a company that manufactures and packages ping-pong equipment; the second group of workers work for Bumble Bee in Astoria, Oregon, where they are employed to process tuna fish.

Ping Pong Business: "My job was stocking the Ping-Pong paddles into piles of fifty. Actually I didn't have to count all the way to fifty. To make it a little easier they told me to stack 'em in circles of four with the first handle facing me. When there got to be 13 handles on the second one from the front, then I'd know I had fifty. After a while of stacking I didn't have to count anyway. I could tell fifty just by looking at the pile. I had to work real fast. I had to keep three labelers and three packers supplied all the time. After I stacked 'em, the women would take them off the stacks and put labels on the handles—for whatever brand it was. After that they got packed into table tennis sets, four paddles, two balls, and a net. Sometimes I got ahead building up these barricades of stacks. I would have liked to have finished three full walls all around myself but I never got that far ahead. As soon as I'd stack 'em, they'd unstack 'em. Maybe it wouldn't have been so bad if I could have seen all the piles I stacked at the end of the day. But they were taking them down as fast as I was piling them up. That was the worst part of the job. No, that wasn't the worst part of the job. The worst part was you had to stand up all day doing it…You couldn't talk either. You wouldn't want to anyway because it was too noisy and the way we were all spaced apart, you'd have to lean over and shout. But if you tried to talk Alma would come running over with a lot more paddles or she'd yell, 'Why aren't you finished yet?' So you were alone with your head all day. I once had a job stuffing envelopes and then I didn't mind daydreaming all day. But at the time I was working in the Ping-Pong factory I was having domestic problems with the man I was living with. So I didn't want to be alone with my head all day. And I didn't want to be standing on my feet all day. And I didn't want to be hearing Alma yell at me all day. And at $1.85 an hour, I figured I could afford to quit."

Tuna Fish: "The girls are personally supposed to do so many fish an hour," the line lady explained. "Imports six to eight, local 10 or so, skipjack 12 to 15. Every day we get a line count—how many women on your line—and a fish count, how many fish you did. If their average was low you'd have to make the girls count bones the next day. Only they average by how many girls you had at the beginning of the day," the line lady complained. "You might start with 30 but end up with 24 because some got sick and some got moved to the salmon side. But they figure the average on 30 which I don't think is fair . . ." I asked a skinner and a cleaner which was a better job, skinning or cleaning. "Skinning pays a little higher," the line lady answered for them. "The girls generally prefer skinning. It's a more skilled job."

"Skinning pays $0.04 more per hour," said Irma Utti. Both she and Nan Cappy were skinners. They agreed that skinning was a better job because the women stood elbow to elbow at the head of the line and could have more lively conversation. There are three different jobs in skinning—removing the head and skinning one side, splitting the fish open, and removing the bones and putting the loins on the belt. Everyone agreed that skinning was more interesting because you rotated these three positions.

"The cleaners sometimes work partners," a cleaner interjected. "One can bone and the other will do cat food for a half-hour or so; then you switch. It makes it more interesting and you can stand closer." "We don't let the girls who work partners talk too much," the line lady explained. "But sometimes it speeds up a slow girl if she works with someone. It'll bring your line average up. And then some people are just gifted at digging out bones, and others at scraping off cat food—please call it pet food in the book."

1972 FAMILY PROFILE

Manny Trapelo is an ambulance driver and father of three children. He and his wife, Susan, live outside Chicago, Illinois, where he restores antique cars in his spare time.

Annual Income

He makes $17,225 and is able to spend, after taxes, $14,666.

Annual Budget

Alcoholic Beverages	$120.00
Car Finance Charge	$348.00
Car Purchase—Net Outlay	$991.00
Clothing—Female Child	$476.00
Clothing—Male Children	$748.00
Dry Cleaning	$83.00
Education	$245.00
Electricity and Gas	$407.00
Expenses Not Covered by Insurance	$401.00
Federal Taxes	$2,147.00
Food at Home	$2,059.00
Food away from Home	$489.00
Furniture	$227.00
Gasoline	$528.00
Health Insurance	$220.00
Major Appliances	$155.00
Reading Material	$67.00
Recreation	$885.00
Shelter—Mortgage	$1,281.00
State and Local Taxes	$353.00

Telephone $204.00
Television Purchases $294.00
Tobacco Products $287.00
Water, Trash, Sewage $124.00

Life at Home

- The Trapelos own their own home plus three cars, two they drive and one they restore; currently Manny and his sons are working on a 1948 Buick.
- The suburban Cook County schools these children attend are considered some of the best in the nation.
- One of the family's sons has just entered the army and is currently training at Fort Jackson in South Carolina; the other two children are quietly opposed to the war in Vietnam but rarely say so in front of their parents.
- The presidential race is between incumbent Richard M. Nixon and Democratic challenger, George McGovern, and Manny and Susan are solidly behind Nixon; their children are backing Alfred E. Newman of the popular *Mad Magazine*.
- A new state income tax imposed in 1968 has doubled the amount of money available for local schools and law enforcement, but has reduced the size of this family's weekly paycheck.
- The inflation of the 1970s also has reduced the buying power of this family; under Nixon's inflation-fighting policies, wages are frozen.

Life at Work: Ambulance Driving

- This man has been driving an ambulance for more than a decade; in the past four years the emphasis has been on stabilizing the patient at the scene and attempting some medical care "in the street." When he first began working as an ambulance driver his priority was to get to the scene quickly and return to the hospital even quicker.

- The stress of his job is high; bouts of depression, drug abuse, and suicide are higher among ambulance drivers and paramedics than other professions.

- Hunting for an address in the middle of the night with no real idea of the situation he will face is a constant stress producer.

- Manny's stress is caused by the unusual hours, long hours, and the dramatic fluctuations of adrenaline.

- The job combines long hours of boredom punctuated by moments of terror.

- He loves providing medicine in the street, believing in his instincts for handling tough situations.

- One patient from out-of-town asks to be taken to the hospital closest to her home—two hours away; he declines.

- One of the worst calls for this man is a heart attack; his father died of a heart attack. Forty percent of all heart attack victims die before they reach the hospital.

"Median Income Here $10,242," Chicago Tribune, November 25, 1972:

"Chicago's annual median family income is $10,242 among persons of all races, but only $7,883 among Blacks and $8,366 among Spanish-speaking persons, a United States Bureau of the Census report shows. The figures presented a picture of a city with great wealth and searing poverty, a mobile and richly ethnic population, and a changing profile that resembles that of many other big cities across the nation.

Chicago's population of 3,362,947 includes 2,218,747 Whites (66 percent) and 1,098,569 Blacks (32.7 percent), Spanish-speaking persons comprise the second largest minority group and most of the remaining 1.3 percent of the population. Of Chicago's 1,136,612 households, 1,073,543 have television sets (732,241 UHF-equipped) but only 952,185 have telephones. Here's the breakdown on the number of dwelling units in which other amenities are found: Clothes washing machines, 572,688; clothes dryers, 296,802; dishwashers, 67,146; battery-operated radios, 782,215; and air-conditioning, 407,989. A total of 545,102 households have one automobile, 128,367 have two, and 447,181 have none.

There are 87,915 families, 10.6 percent of the total, below the poverty level, which was $3,700 for a family of four at the time the census sampling was made. Of the 481,842 persons below the poverty line, 56.7 percent were Black."

- Patients often become impatient answering Manny's questions about past medical history; without the information he has no way to help the person.
- Over the Thanksgiving holiday, his first call was a traffic fatality; an 82-year-old man was struck by a car as he crossed North Lamon Avenue. The 24-year-old driver was charged with driving too fast for conditions.
- A typical day working the four-to-midnight shift includes both boredom and high stress. For example, a typical night might run like this:

> The first stop of the night, just after the shift begins, is a doctor's office where the patient complains of heart problems; a 60-year-old salesman, he shows pictures of his grandchildren to the paramedics on the ride to the hospital.
>
> After dropping off the man at the hospital, Manny and his partner cruise the streets, stopping for coffee and reading the newspaper.
>
> At 6 p.m. they are dispatched to help a man lying unconscious on the street; when they arrive he is gone.
>
> Two hours later the dispatcher says a man has collapsed; they determine that the well-dressed man is a seizure victim and take him to the hospital.
>
> At 10 they are summoned to a tiny tenement apartment crowded with furniture and guarded by a large dog; an old man, already diagnosed with cancer, requires oxygen and a trip to the hospital.
>
> That is the last run of the shift.

- When people ask about his work he makes jokes telling them there are only two rules: "all bleeding eventually stops" and "all patients eventually die."
- Since the police, fire, and ambulance drivers work closely together, all are watching closely the six-point program announced by the police chief to improve community relations, particularly in Black communities.
- The police department is plagued with problems ranging from charges of racial persecution to indictments for extortion.
- Responding to competition, Michael Reese Hospital reduces its daily room rates for maternity patients by $46.00 from $166.00 to $120.00; the rate includes room, board, and nursing services for mother and child.
- The total cost of bringing a baby into the world, including the use of the delivery and labor rooms, laboratory fees, and miscellaneous charges for an average four-day visit is about $700.00.

Life in the Community: Chicago, Illinois

- The Trapelo family finds Chicago to be an exciting place to live; they are proud of their city, but glad they live in the suburbs.
- The city of Chicago is losing population and jobs, while the metropolitan region around the city is growing rapidly.
- Since 1950 the suburban population has ballooned from 887,000 to 2.4 million.
- Chicago is the world's largest producer of capital goods.
- Its trucking centers transport 27 million manufactured tons in the last year.
- The port of Chicago docks 683 ocean-going ships each year.
- More than 6.5 million tourists visit the city annually.
- Chicago handles 32 million air passengers a year from O'Hare, the world's busiest airport.
- The city is currently debating whether to build a crosstown expressway, intended to take through traffic away from the central city and reestablish factories on the periphery.

The city was deeply scarred by the rioting during the 1968 Democratic convention.

"How Some Americans Beat Inflation,"
Life Magazine, February 13, 1970:

"It doesn't take an accountant, a computer, or a lot of bar charts to prove that inflation is giving everybody a bad time. But just for the record, last year consumer prices shot up 6.1 percent—the largest jump since the Korean War. The year before they went up 4.7 percent, and, taken together those two years added up to almost as much inflation as we had during the first seven years of the 1960s. The most popular leisure-time activity of 1970 may be moonlighting.

Home Barbering—When Else and Peter Moyer moved to Thousand Oaks, California, four years ago from Germany, they were astonished to find haircuts costing $1.50, and she began to give him his biweekly crewcut in the kitchen. Now an airline copilot, Moyer still gets his hair cut at home. So do sons Lars and his two brothers. The yearly savings: $120.00.

Learning to Sew—Chicago's Ray-Vogue fashion school has added two 13-session evening courses to help teach working girls and mothers how to make clothes at home. Some students want to sew for themselves, others plan on making pin money sewing for friends. Mrs. Evelyn Paige, who is expecting a baby later this month, had to give up her job as a book editor, but hopes to soften the cash loss by making clothing for herself and the baby—particularly if it's a girl. She has already sewn three outfits, and anticipates the first year's savings of about $200.00.

Flea Marketing—Buyers and sellers haggle over prices at Miami's outdoor Flea Market held each weekend on a four-acre drive-in theater lot. The sellers—as many as 500 a day—are usually homeowners who have just cleaned out a basement or attic. 'The tighter money gets,' says the manager, 'the better things get here.' Even on unbroken objects, buyers can save up to 80 percent."

- *The Chicago Tribune*, the city's largest paper, likes to boast that Chicago is "the city that works."
- The city's political life has been tightly controlled by Mayor Richard Daly for two decades.
- Unfortunately, the building boom of the 1960s has resulted in a bust in the early 1970s.
- Panic-stricken apartment owners are running newspaper advertisements offering incentive of three months' free rent, free moving, and choice of premiums such as television sets and dryers to get tenants for the hundreds of brand-new, vacant units.
- Condominiums were introduced into the market in the late 1960s and are also caught in the over supply of housing in the city.
- Shifting populations to the suburbs has reduced total retail sales within the metropolitan area by 50 percent from the 1960s.
- Even many of the suburban office centers, built enthusiastically in the late 1960s, are vacant; new construction is on the wane.
- Efforts are under way by the dominant Democratic organization to modernize local government to maintain the support of the increasingly middle-class constituency.

HISTORICAL SNAPSHOT
1972–1973

- Nearly 30 percent of U.S. petroleum was imported

- Wages, prices, and profits remained controlled by Phase II economic measures

- Dow Jones closed at 1,003.15 on November 14, above 1,000 for the first time

- San Francisco Bay Area Rapid Transit System opened

- *Ms. Magazine* began publication; *Life* magazine suspended publication

- The Polaroid SX-70 system produced color prints

- New York's 110-story World Trade Center opened

- America's birth rate fell to 15.8 per 1,000, the lowest since 1917

- The average farmer produced enough food for 50 people; farm labor represented five percent of the work force

- The median sales price of an existing single-family house reached $28,900

- Vodka outsold whiskey for the first time

- The budget of the Law Enforcement Assistance Administration rose from $63 million to $700 million

- By a five-to-four vote, the Supreme Court ruled that capital punishment was "cruel and unusual punishment" pending further legislation from the states

- The number of fast-food establishments increased to 6,784, up from 1,120 in 1958

- The Massachusetts Supreme Court ruled unconstitutional a law prohibiting the sale of contraceptives to single persons

- Congress passed Title IX, which entitled women to participate equally in all sports

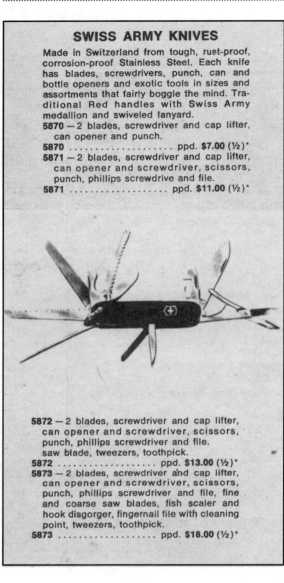

1972 ECONOMIC PROFILE

Income, Standard Jobs

Bituminous Coal Mining.........	$11,323.00
Building Trades	$10,747.00
Domestics.....................	$8,794.00
Farm Labor	$3,900.00
Federal Military	$8,603.00
Finance, Insurance, and Real Estate	$8,861.00
Gas, Electricity, and Sanitation Workers	$11,420.00
Manufacturing, Durable Goods..................	$10,747.00
Manufacturing, Nondurable Goods..................	$8,636.00
Medical/Health Services Workers	$7,499.00
Miscellaneous Manufacturing......	$7,800.00
Motion Picture Services	$8,882.00
Nonprofit Organization Workers	$6,088.00
Passenger Transportation Workers, Local and Highway.....................	$7,496.00
Personal Services	$6,268.00
Public School Teachers...........	$9,284.00
Radio Broadcasting and Television Workers...........	$11,575.00
Railroads	$11,991.00
State and Local Government Workers	$8,898.00
Telephone and Telegraph Workers	$10,518.00

Selected Prices

Adorn Hard to Hold Hairspray, 13-Ounce.......................	$1.09
Ban Roll-On Deodorant, One-Ounce Size..................	$0.49
Calgon Bath Oil Beads, 16-Ounce......................	$0.98
Coloring Book.....................	$0.10
Cougar, 1969 Used Car.............	$2,998
Craftsman Tool Set	$39.99
Dove Liquid Soap, 22-Ounce	$0.57
Downey Fabric Softener, 64-Ounce.......................	$0.99

Advertisement: "The Gas Shortage, What You Can Do about It," *The Christian Science Monitor*, June 28, 1972:

"The national energy crisis is the most serious problem facing America today. Without adequate energy supplies, there is no way to solve most other national problems. The worsening crisis involves all primary fuels: oil, gas, coal, and nuclear together with the electricity dependent on those fuels. National gas, which supplies almost one-third of all U.S. energy needs, is already unable to meet current demands.

Unless the public recognizes the problem and urges government to cooperate with industry for a prompt solution, we would move from crisis to disaster as early as the winter of 1973–74."

Kodak Electric Automatic Movie Camera	$1,000.00
Magna-Lite, Shop Light	$6.95
Man's Leather Jacket	$80.00
Metal Detector	$19.95
Millers Falls Sander	$34.95
Neosynephrine, One-Ounce Drops	$0.66
Pipe, Kirsten	$3.95
Portable Television, 19"	$220.00
Slide Rule, 4"	$2.95
Telephone, Western Electric	$6.95
Visine	$0.99

"The Beat of Life," *Life Magazine*, November 24, 1972:

"Through the day of November 14, curls of excitement washed across the floor of the New York Stock Exchange like precursors of an incoming tide. As skeptics watched, the Dow Jones average swept past the 1,000 mark and stayed there. At the end of trading there was jubilation: the DJ tape wound up at slightly more than 1,003, the first time it had ever crossed over the magic barrier."

The cigarette you can feel comfortable with. Enjoy. And stay with.

THE MODERATE SMOKE

It's not strong. It's not weak. It's blended for the middle.

There are no excesses, except those in quality.

It has premium tasting tobaccos. Two advanced filter systems. And a thoughtful Humidor Pack. To keep your smokes fresher, longer.

Try the Moderate Smoke.

BENSON & HEDGES **MULTIFILTER**

Warning: The Surgeon General Has Determined That Cigarette Smoking Is Dangerous to Your Health.

Regular: 14 mg. "tar", 1.1 mg. nicotine av. per cigarette, FTC Report Apr.

The Vietnam War and the 1972 Presidential Election

- For the first time since 1964, Vietnam was not identified by a Gallup poll as the most important problem facing America in the coming year; the economy captured that spot by a three-to-one margin.
- Polling in 1972 indicated that 61 percent of Americans believed that the "U.S. should withdraw all troops from Vietnam by the end of the year."
- Even though presidential "peace" candidate George McGovern expressed these views, the majority of Americans believed that incumbent president Richard Nixon was better able to handle the economic issues facing the nation.
- Vice President Spiro Agnew was able to characterize the McGovern platform as "amnesty, abortion, and acid," driving a wedge between McGovern and the urban, White ethnic voter who voted for the Nixon-Agnew ticket in droves.
- By the fall of 1972 peace did not seem far away; Secretary of State Henry Kissinger declared that peace is "at hand."
- In 1972 alone, an additional 131 prisoners of war were captured (the largest number since 1967) and the war in southeast Asia escalated.
- At that time American troop presence was down to 50,000 men; ending the war meant little more to America than bringing the POWs home.
- The March on Washington in spring, 1971, included familiar names such as the Student Mobilization Committee and the Black Third World Task Force, but more important was the involvement of organized labor.
- The 1971 March on Washington was the largest of the war; estimates of the crowd size at 750,000 make it the largest demonstration in the history of the country.
- In addition, another 200,000 to 300,000 demonstrators attended a companion rally in San Francisco.
- The marchers encompassed every age group and racial group.
- Following the March it was no longer possible to say that the antiwar protesters included only students or in Vice President Agnew's words an "effete corps of impudent snobs."
- One middle-aged mother and her two young daughters carried a sign reading "The Majority Is Not Silent, The Government Is Deaf."
- The March also included strong participation of the Vietnam Veterans Against the War, now claiming 12,000 members; membership in the VVAW grew from 600 in 1970 to 12,000 thanks to the Winter Soldier hearings conducted by the group and advertising space to recruit memberships donated by *Playboy Magazine*.
- President Nixon revealed on January 25, 1972, that Secretary of State Henry Kissinger had been negotiating secretly with the North Vietnamese to end the war.
- Nixon arrived in China on February 21; North Vietnam launched an offensive across the demilitarized zone on March 30.
- On April 15, Nixon authorized bombing of areas near Hanoi and Haiphong in North Vietnam.
- On May 8, Nixon announced mining of Haiphong harbor and intensification of American bombing of North Vietnam.
- Five men were arrested on June 17 for breaking into the Democratic National Committee offices at the Watergate Complex in Washington, D.C.
- Hanoi radio broadcast details of the agreement in an effort to pressure Kissinger, who was anxious to reassure North Vietnam, declaring, "Peace is at hand."
- Nixon was re-elected November 7, defeating antiwar candidate Senator George McGovern by a landslide.

- Kissinger resumed talks with Le Duc Tho on November 20, presenting him with 69 amendments to the agreement demanded by Thieu.
- Talks between Kissinger and Le Duc Tho began again in December and broke down.
- On December 18, Nixon ordered the bombing of areas around Hanoi and Haiphong; the raids continued for 11 days. North Vietnam agreed to resume diplomatic talks with cessation of the bombing.
- Kissinger and Le Duc Tho resumed talks on January 8; an agreement was initiated on January 23.
- Cease-fire agreements were formally signed in Paris on January 27; Secretary of Defense Melvin Laird announced that the United States draft has ended.
- The majority of the American troops left Vietnam on March 29, 1973.
- American prisoners of war were released in Hanoi, April 1.
- Nixon aides H.R. Haldeman, John Ehrlichman, and John Dean resigned in the wake of the Watergate scandal.
- On November 7, Congress overrode Nixon's veto of a law limiting the president's right to wage war.
- Thieu declared in January, 1974, the war had begun again.
- On May 9, the House Judiciary Committee opened impeachment hearings on Nixon.

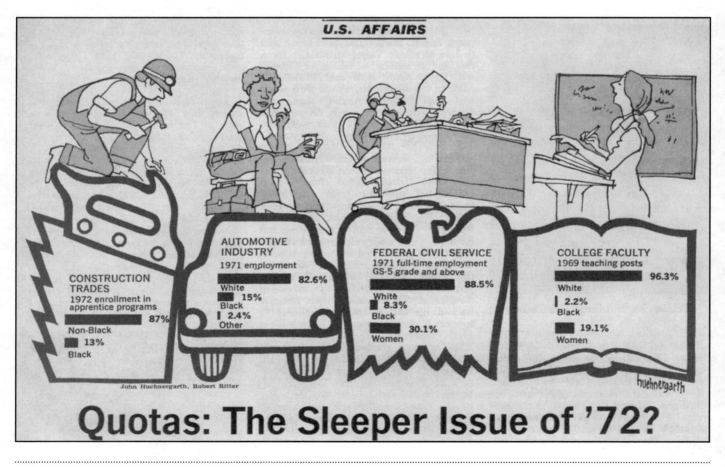

"Quotas: The Sleeper Issue of '72," *Newsweek*, September 18, 1972:

" 'The way to end discrimination against some is not to begin discrimination against others,' said Richard Nixon, Miami Beach, August 23, 1972. Every Presidential campaign, no matter how predictable it may begin, seems inevitably to produce its surprise issue. This year, amid all the expected talk about the war in Indochina and the economy at home, the sleeper has turned out to be quotas, the real or imagined presence of statistical targets for the inclusion of women, Blacks, or some other minority group in American industry, colleges, and professions. Richard Nixon, who took aim at the issue in his acceptance speech, has kept up a steady fire ever since and pounded away at it with special vigor in his Labor Day oratory. And despite George McGovern's nimblest efforts to dissociate himself from the quota cause, the President seemed to be scoring political points.

For the issue appears to have touched raw nerves and prompted what might be called the first respectable backlash since the civil-rights movement began. The impetus toward quotas springs from a decade of effort, both governmental and private, to open up avenues of American society long closed to minorities. And it illuminates the obstacles that still exist particularly for women in professions such as college teaching and for Blacks in such traditionally White-only trades as the construction industry, where apprentice programs are just beginning to break the color bar.

At the root of the controversy is the concept of 'quota' itself, a code word with enormously different meanings for different groups. For many women, Blacks, Latinos, and other minorities, it means simply a guaranteed floor under efforts to achieve reasonable representation in fields previously inhospitable to them. But for many other people the word is a curse. To American Jews, a quota has been historically not a floor but a ceiling or a lock on the door. Only in the last generation have quotas restricting Jews all but disappeared from American life. To ethnic blue-collar workers, 'quota' has come to mean the force-feeding of Blacks at their expense. What's more, many fear that the philosophy of quotas may ultimately be taken to its logical extreme: a system of ethnically proportional representation in the U.S. that is finally unfair to individuals and stultifying to society as a whole."

"New Rules for the Marriage Game? Matrimony experts question 'forever' concept in rapidly changing times," *Ebony Magazine*, October 1972:

"Hanging on till now, old-fashioned wedlock is being attacked as a rather moth-eaten, outdated relic which is still being used as an important social tool. 'Revolutionary' Black sisters, some of whom are middle class and have professional occupations, have begun consciously to seek motherhood without benefit of marriage. Philosophers from the *Playboy* school know sexual exclusivity of the husband-wife relationship, and young people, cutting tradition's umbilical cord, are choosing to live together in an attempt to know each other better before they legalize anything. There are those, of course, who still view marriage as the ultimate of romantic dream worlds, but far fewer people today feel that the traditional march to the altar is the absolute very next step after reaching, say 21.

Even those who are married are increasingly snipping the theoretical lifetime fetters: in California, where social trends usually strike first before hitting the rest of the nation, three out of every four couples are escaping their marriages. In Cook County, Illinois, (it includes Chicago), statistics for the first six months of this year show that for every two couples seeking marriage licenses another couple was seeking divorce. That ratio is identical for the nation as a whole. In 1970, statistics show that while 4,358,000 men and women were tying the knot, another 1,430,000 husbands and wives were breaking the chains. The concept of being married 'til death do you part' is, as psychiatrist Kermit T. Mehlinger puts it, 'gone with the wind.'"

"Dig Warts," the updated last *Whole Earth Catalog*:

I cured my WARTS with a Swiss ARMY KNIFE. A true testimonial by Malaclypse the Younger of San Francisco Plagued with Planters Warts for over a year, and advised by the medical profession that regular medication is generally hopeless, I cured my warts with a Swiss ARMY KNIFE and voodoo. Twice a week for 12 months I cursed the warts and made them feel unwelcome. During that time, I took my stainless steel Swiss ARMY KNIFE and dug at them relentlessly. They have now more or less DISAPPEARED leaving only gaping holes and volcano-like craters in my calluses. I recommend this cure for any person with a cool hand, a knowledge of voodoo, and Swiss ARMY KNIFE. Signed POEE, San Francisco, California.

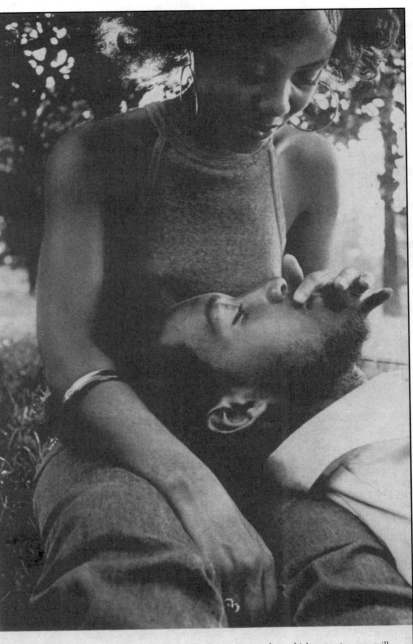

Marriage, in some form or another, has been with us since the beginning of time. In modern times, however, both romanticism and tradition have distorted the real function of wedlock and young love (right) sometimes suffers.

NEW RULES FOR THE MARRIAGE GAME?

Matrimony experts question 'forever' concept in rapidly changing modern times

By Monroe Anderson

Do you promise to honor and obey. . . .

BECAUSE of the nature of human beings— one person's desire for another—various kinds of mating ceremonies and male-female join-togethers have always gone on.

One might imagine a primitive society with a kind of free-floating situation where a man and a woman simply announced their affection for each other and then moved into their very own little cave to live together forever or perhaps for only as long as they fancied each other's loin cloth. But then, as the society grew more complicated, so did the function of mating, until finally not only did people seek love, emotional fulfillment, personal satisfaction and the creation and rearing of children, but mating became a game governed by rules involv-

ing political, civic, social, and economic factors of pretty high stakes.

As time passed, those rules became tradition. And although the society continues to change, the tradition does not.

We call that tradition marriage. And in our society, marriage has become a very peculiar institution. Or as described by Ambrose Bierce, a 19th Century writer whose definition was probably decades ahead of its time, marriage is "a community consisting of a master, a mistress, and two slaves, making in all, two."

As did last century's institution of slavery, marriage as a lifetime bind—for better or for worse—may be slowly crumbling. This modern world is demanding new rules for the function

of marriage—rules which experts say will emancipate master and mistress forever from feeling that marriage is forever.

. . . and do you promise to have and to hold. . . .

Hanging on till now, old-fashioned wedlock is being attacked as a rather moth-eaten outdated relic which is still being used as an important social tool. "Revolutionary" black sisters, some of whom are middle class and have professional occupations, have begun consciously to seek motherhood without benefit of marriage. Philosophers from the Playboy school knock sexual exclusivity of the husband-wife relationship, and young people, cut-

Continued on Next Page
145

The year in pictures **The Bare Look**

Clothes for summer— just barely

In fashion, unlike politics, the least coverage wins the greatest exposure. In the hot summer of '72 women all over the country got the "bare look" message. At Yellowfinger's restaurant in New York (pictures above) the fashion fare was halters and tank tops. But at a Puerto Rican rock festival (right) one couple got by with nothing more than some well-placed leaves.

1974 Family Profile

Pete Rittner is a long-haul, owner-operator trucker who has been on the road five years. He and his wife, Angie, have one small child and live outside New Orleans, Louisiana, where he makes approximately $15,000 a year, rents his home, but has a large mortgage on his truck. They have talked about his "coming off the road," but in an atmosphere of high unemployment they see few alternatives.

Annual Income: $15,000

Annual Budget

Alcoholic Beverages	$83.00
Clothing	$687.00
Food	$1,908.00
Fuel and Electricity	$457.00
Gifts and Contributions	$399.00
Health Care	$529.00
House Furnishing	$437.00
Housing (Rent)	$532.00
Personal Care	$107.00
Personal Insurance	$945.00
Reading Materials	$54.00
Recreation	$686.00
Telephone	$189.00
Tobacco Products	$152.00
Transportation	$1,927.00

Life at Home

- The Rittners' rental home sits in the shadow of their landlord's larger house.
- Most of the furniture are hand-me-downs from Angie's family or the landlord.

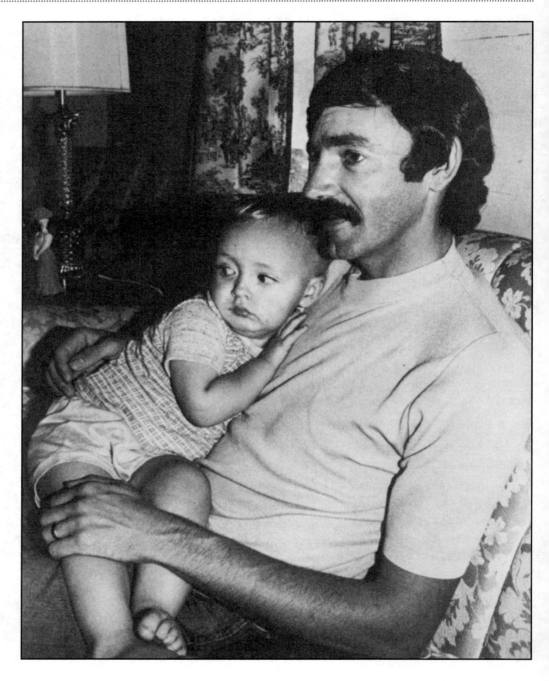

- The house is decorated with trucks: truck pictures, truck toys, truck poems.
- Displayed in the center of the room is a large Bible with colorful illustrations.
- In addition to spending money on food, rent, clothes, and the truck, this family is saving for an occasional trip to a religious retreat.
- The family recently purchases a new television on the installment plan.
- Angie often shows Pete the "want ads" hoping he will get off the road; for him the freedom offered by trucking remains attractive, as is the money.

- She has seen other drivers develop back problems, ulcers, hemorrhoids, and nervous conditions; she wants him off the road before that happens.
- He normally gets home every three weeks.
- When home, he spends most of his time with his family and two friends from high school, neither of whom are truckers. On the road, he only associates with other truckers.
- When he is home on Friday nights, they like to join the Seafood Festival at the Sheraton Motor Inn—all you can eat, including lobster, costing $10.95 a person.
- He calls home every night; recently he missed seeing his son in his school play.
- He is experiencing a toothache but can't match his trucking schedule to a dental appointment.
- During his downtime at home or on the road, he likes to make toy trucks for his son.
- His son loves wearing his Mack Bulldog cap and enjoys riding in the truck, sitting on his father's lap.
- Angie tends a small farm, raising vegetables while he is away.
- Currently, she is very concerned about rising costs; the price of sugar has risen so sharply she is cutting back on baking. A five-pound bag of sugar that cost $0.70 a year ago is now $2.30.
- The Rittners have talked about buying a cattle farm, "when he comes off the road"; currently inflation is driving the cost of fertilizer, fuel, feed, and livestock out of their financial reach.
- The rapidly rising rate of unemployment and personal bankruptcies makes the family believe they have few alternatives for now.
- Both Pete and Angie are high school graduates; neither has any interest in additional schooling.
- He has developed a strong interest in his German heritage and gets angry when people only mention the colonization of New Orleans by the French, Spanish, Cajun, and African-American influences.
- They believe that the "hippie movement" has gone too far and that America is going in a dangerous direction.

Selected Weekly Food Expenditures

Cereals and Bakery Products $3.42
Dairy Products $3.93
Fats and Oils $0.76
Food and Alcoholic Beverages (Total) . . $41.78
Fruits and Vegetables $4.03
Meat, Poultry, Fish, and Eggs $10.74
Soft Drinks and Juices $2.13
Sugar $0.86

Life at Work: Trucking

- As an owner-operator, this truck driver normally works 70 hours during a typical seven-day week; he can be away from his family for as long as three weeks at a time.
- Like many truckers, Pete believes his truck has a distinct personality.
- The truck he drives is a fully equipped, 40-ton 18-wheeler costing approximately $49,000.
- He prides himself on being conservative and careful with his money.
- He put nearly one million miles on his first truck before buying a slightly used Peterbilt.

- He likes to keep his vehicle clean and his logbook up-to-date even though he finds the paperwork one of the least enjoyable parts of his job.
- Nationwide there are approximately 100,000 owner-operator truckers.
- His one vice is playing pinball machines at the various truck stops he visits during a run.
- Many truckers spend much of their earnings on women, drinks, or gambling at pinball machines simply to chase away the boredom.
- He likes his coffee strong, nicknamed "hundred-mile brew," because it will keep him awake for a hundred miles to the cup.
- His diet on the road varies little; coffee, meat, and potatoes are a constant, which he normally eats at "trucker only" restaurants.
- To save money and time he sleeps in the sleeper compartment of his truck.

- He learned to drive from his uncle and on-the-job training; formal truck schools are rare.
- Money worries are constant, as the price of gasoline is rising rapidly and tire prices start at $150.00 each.
- Finding a ready supply of gasoline continues to be a problem.
- President Nixon's decision to raise gas prices and lower the highway speed limit to 55 mph means more time on the road, but rarely more revenues.
- The wide use of the Citizen's Band radio, or CBs, since the early 1970s has helped relieve the loneliness of the road, providing trucker-to-trucker information about road conditions, police activity, gossip, and someone to share thoughts with.
- As an owner-operator, Pete is paid a portion of the amount charged to the shipper under federally approved rates; occasionally he is paid according to miles travelled or hours worked.
- The International Brotherhood of Teamsters promotes the interests of employees of the trucking industry, but generally does not represent independent subcontractors or owner-operators such as this man in wage bargaining.
- In union companies, drivers with seniority normally are allowed to bid first for the best runs.

- His biggest concerns are separation from his family and lack of exercise; he does not mind the long hours or hard work.
- A survey of truck drivers lists their top concerns as road conditions, bad weather, other drivers, unreasonable dispatches, federal and state inspections, and long driving hours.
- During the nationwide truck shutdown in January, Pete stays home, while supermarket shelves and manufacturing inventories dwindle.

Life in the Community: New Orleans, Louisiana

- Living outside New Orleans in the country is the perfect combination for this family, since they can enjoy the city without living there.
- New Orleans is said to be a bit of everything, having been controlled by the French, Spanish, then French again, American, Confederate, and American once again; its unique character stems from the combination of its population—Indians, French, Germans, African-Americans, Spaniards, Acadians, Irish, Italians, and other nationalities.
- New Orleans is also famous for its Creole cuisine ranging from crawfish gumbos to Oysters Rockefeller to jambalaya.
- Sitting on the banks of the Mississippi, New Orleans' early founding, industries, and character have been shaped by the river.
- Although a port city, New Orleans is more than 100 miles from the Gulf of Mexico, so many families prefer to go to the lake to swim and boat on a Saturday afternoon.
- Many residents avoid the French Quarter, which attracts thousands of tourists each year.
- The New Orleans City Council recently raises transit fares $0.10 to $0.25 for regular rides and $0.30 for express because of rising costs; the fares are still below the national average of $0.34.

HISTORICAL SNAPSHOT
1974-1975

- The pocket calculator was marketed for the first time
- President Nixon lowered the highway speed limit to 55 mph to save gasoline
- 110,000 clothing workers staged a nationwide strike
- Unemployment reached 6.5 percent, the highest since 1961
- The universal product code was designed for the supermarket industry
- Year-long daylight savings time was adopted to save fuel
- 3M developed Post-it stock to stick paper to paper
- ITT's Harold Green was the nation's highest paid executive at $791,000 per year
- Time, Inc., issued *People Magazine* devoted to celebrity journalism
- Walgreen's drug chain exceeded $1 billion in sales for the first time
- President Richard M. Nixon resigned in the wake of Watergate; President Gerald Ford granted him a full and absolute pardon
- The first desktop microcomputer became available
- The Equal Opportunity Act forbade discrimination based on sex or marital status
- Pet Rocks went on sale, featuring obedience, loyalty, and low-maintenance costs
- Minnesota became the first state to require businesses, restaurants, and institutions to establish no-smoking areas
- New York City averted bankruptcy with a $2.3 billion federal loan
- The biggest money-making films of the year were disaster films including *Towering Inferno* and *Earthquake;* the supernatural violence of *The Exorcist* also appeared that year
- Beef consumption fell nine percent, while chicken consumption rose nearly 35 percent
- As car sales fell 35 percent from 1973, home construction was down 40 percent
- McDonald's opened its first drive-through restaurants
- AT&T, the world's largest private employer, banned discrimination against homosexuals
- Thousands nationwide stripped to their track shoes as streaking became the biggest fad on college campuses
- Time-sharing of vacation real estate was introduced in the United States
- A record 120,000 Americans declared personal bankruptcy

1974 ECONOMIC PROFILE

Income, Standard Jobs

Bituminous Coal Mining $13,580.00
Building Trades $12,192.00
Domestics $5,260.00
Farm Labor $4,776.00
Federal Civilian $14,080.00
Federal Military $9,594.00
Finance, Insurance, and
    Real Estate $9,853.00
Gas, Electricity, and Sanitation
    Workers $13,031.00
Manufacturing, Durable Goods . . . $12,192.00
Manufacturing, Nondurable
    Goods $9,925.00
Medical/Health Services Workers . . . $8,727.00
Miscellaneous Manufacturing $8,679.00
Motion Picture Services $10,108.00
Nonprofit Organization Workers . . . $7,130.00
Passenger Transportation Workers,
    Local and Highway $8,645.00
Personal Services $7,459.00
Private Industries, Including
    Farm Labor $9,967.00
Public School Teachers $10,249.00
Radio Broadcasting and
    Television Workers $12,779.00
Railroads $14,240.00
State and Local Government
    Workers $10,020.00
Telephone and Telegraph
    Workers $12,503.00

Selected Prices

Ban Roll-On, One-Ounce Size $0.49
Bear Target Archery Set $28.95
Calgon Bath Oil Beads, 16-Ounce
    Package $0.98
Child's Perma-Press Scooby-Doo
    Pajamas $5.99
Craftsman Combination Square $25.99
Dremel Model 572 Saw with
    Attachments $49.95
Electric Iron $19.79
Gorham Pewter Coffee Set $125.00
Gucci Leather Jewel Case $99.00
Lady Wrangler Corduroy Flare
    Pants $15.00

Lifebuoy Soap, Bath Size,
Package of Two $0.40
Man's Lightweight Western-Style
Jacket $65.00
Man's Watch $39.98
Miller Falls Sander $34.95
Sears Bed-Wetting Alarm $19.95
Sears Non-Electric Pressure Cooker $18.99
Smokey the Bear Doll $4.94
The Joy of Sex Book $12.95
Visine Eye Drops $0.99
Wheelbarrow $34.95
Woman's Figure-Hugging Nylon
Body Suit $4.77

Trucking in America

- By 1910 trucks were no longer novelties on America's highways.
- The brand names of the time included Mack, Autocar, White, Reo, Kenworth, and International.
- Repair shops were unknown; a truck driver not only drove the truck, he made all the necessary repairs.
- At first trucks were little more than a car chassis with converted rear ends; conversion kits were sold widely.

Trucker, by Jane Stern:

"The time is now 1975: the town is El Paso (Texas). The long haul trucker is pulling into the Diamond L. truck stop. He has driven practically coast-to-coast in three days, and he hasn't seen his family in more than four weeks. His face is prematurely lined with creases that deepen with the brutal hours of life on the open road. His stomach is rebelling at the diet of greasy pork chops and endless coffee wolfed down in a blurred chain of truck stops. The radiator grill of his truck is muffled against the cold with heavy, quilted blankets, and as he eases it into the long line of parked trucks, its throaty idle joins the chorus of other giant engines. The trucker has just picked up $800.00 for dropping off a load of cattle in some distant town. Once inside the truck stop, he will head for the barber shop, the laundry room, and the gift shop for a shave, a wash, and a pile of souvenirs for his wife and kids. But more than refreshment or trinkets, he wants the comradeship offered by the other truck drivers—men who, like himself, are a long way from home

and help him to forget his loneliness for a time . . . . As he enters the diner, the trucker steps into a world of instant friends—but friends who keep their distance. Around the turn of the century, a cowboy named Andy Downs said, 'The West demands you smile and swallow our personal troubles like your food. Nobody wants to listen to another man's half-digested problems.' Among the truckers, there is a feeling of shared experience in a muted, insulated atmosphere. Eyes seldom meet, and elbows are kept close to the body. In conversation, only certain topics are safe because they're not intrusive. You can talk about your truck, the weather, the food, the road, anything mechanical, and women—as long as it's not your wife. You can ask a trucker where he's headed, or ask him whom he hauls for, but you don't ask what's in the trailer any more than you'd ask a cowboy what's in his saddle bags. That's his business, whether the load is legal or not, valuable or worthless, it's his personal and private responsibility.'"

- By 1915 truck registration reached 160,000 vehicles and continued to climb.
- Heaters were unknown, making leather outfits to fight the cold a necessity; leather gloves were used to prevent frostbite.
- Truck seats consisted of a hard board on the bottom and another board to lean back on; padding was provided by the driver's own anatomy.
- Mack Truck's emblem, the bulldog, was introduced in the 1930s based on the affectionate nickname "the bulldog truck" given by the British for its blunt noise and low growl.
- The diesel engine was invented in the midst of the Depression of the 1930s; the more complicated instrumentation of the new engine required that truck dashboards begin to resemble small planes.
- The Interstate Commerce Commission, which began regulating railroads in 1887, created the Motor Carrier Act of 1935 to control the competitive impact of the merging truckers on the railroads.
- By the 1940s cabs included roll-up glass windows, seats including springs, and hot water heaters were standard.
- The Kenworth introduced the first cab that included a bed behind the seat in the 1940s; it was an immediate success.

- As the number of truckers grew, so did the regulations; by 1935 the Motor Carrier Act was passed to control interstate transport.
- By 1974 the gross revenues of trucking carried by the nation's 21 million men and women truck drivers was $23 billion annually.
- Truck drivers formed one of the largest indirectly supervised work force in the United States.
- Historically, the earnings of this work force, particularly the portion who were members of the International Brotherhood of Teamsters, set the pattern for wage settlements for many other sectors of organized labor.
- Approximately 50 to 60 percent of the industry was regulated by the federal government, divided between contract carriers and common carriers.
- Contract carriers were a special type of regulated, for-hire carrier that were restricted to serving a limited number of specified customers in a well-defined contractual arrangement.
- Common carriers were required to offer their services equally to all shippers and were not permitted to refuse a customer who was prepared to pay the published rate for the service.
- Most freight carried by U.S. motor carriers was handled by drivers who were employees of companies.
- Approximately 25 to 40 percent of the intercity truck transportation in the United States was carried by approximately 100,000 owner-operators nationwide who drove their own trucks.
- Despite an image as rebellious free spirits, drivers tended to stay with the same companies for long periods of time according to studies.

"Aboard the Omnibus," Editor, *Times Picayune*, New Orleans, Louisiana, August 1, 1974:

"Since the nation isn't so hot at inflation fighting and since the old orthodox approaches are now improving conditions much, let's consider what Harvard economist Hendrik S. Houthakker, former member of the Council of Economic Advisors, suggests. Believing there are too many built-in factors that keep prices high, he forwards in a *Wall Street Journal* piece what he calls an omnibus bill to remove these obstacles. It would drop meat import limits, jettison dairy import quotas, subject larger agricultural cooperatives to anti-trust laws, replace food stamps with cash, drop truck routing rules, legalize discount air fares, make approval of reasonable rail rate changes automatic, open coastal shipping to vessels of all nations and largely abolish ship and shipping subsidies.

Then Prof. Houthakker would let banks pay interest on checking accounts, remove ceilings on savings account interest, forbid fair-trade pricing, ban unreasonable membership requirements of unions and abolish union hiring halls, kill some of the federal laws governing wages on federal contracts, exempt juveniles from minimum wage laws and dump the Buy America Act. Too, we would have the Treasury issue cost-of-living bonds geared to the consumer price index to protect investors, and change tax rules to foster industrial expansion. By junking this restriction and dropping that prohibition, competition would be keener and the economy more responsive to efforts to slow down current inflation and make the nation more inflation-resistant."

"The Germans," New Orleans guidebook, by Bethany Ewald Bultman:

"In the 18th century, it became crucial to the survival of the fledgling colony that John Law's Company of the Indies find enough sturdy immigrant farmers to grow something for French settlers to eat. Toward this end, the company inundated southern Germany and Switzerland with handbills promoting Louisiana as a 'paradise.' The first large German-speaking Catholic groups arrived in November, 1719 on the vessel *Les Deux Freres*. The last great 18th century German-speaking migration started out two years later with over 1,000 Germans. No sooner had the four ships left the French port than a cholera epidemic broke out.

Once they arrived they were in for more bad news; they soon realized that New Orleans, the 'Paris of the New World,' was in reality the capital of mildew and malaria, and far from an idyllic place to farm. When John Law's pyramid scheme failed in France, he fled to Italy, leaving the German farmers stranded in the soggy, French-speaking Louisiana colony. Law had promised the Germans money and land, but they were still waiting for both when they learned that their own homeland had been given to the Spanish. The Germans pulled out of New Orleans and found dry land to farm 25 miles upriver in an area that became known as the Côte des Allemands, or the German Coast.

The German farmers did their job well, supplying the city with an abundance of fresh produce. Surnames such as Schexnaider and Hymel (pronounced 'Heemel,' the Francophone version of Himmel) are still prominent in the suburban colonies of Jefferson Parish. Other Germans intermarried with the French or simply found that it was easier to adapt their names to the language of the region. . . . In the middle of the 19th century, at a time when New Orleans still enjoyed a reputation as an Old World European-style city with New World possibilities, a political upheaval in Europe brought yet another wave of Germans to Louisiana. Between 1820 and 1850, more than 50,000 Germans passed into the United States from the port of New Orleans. By 1870, an estimated 17,000 people spoke German as their principal language. This wave of immigrants was proud of its Teutonic heritage. Moving into commerce and banking alongside Americans, these newly arrived Germans seemed to have managed to straddle the fence between the old French social strata and newly moneyed Americans. Many of them settled alongside the Creoles in Faubourg Marigny, which would be nicknamed 'Little Saxony' at the end of the 19th century."

WANTED BY THE FBI

NATIONAL FIREARMS ACT; MATERIAL WITNESS

William Taylor Harris

FBI No. 308,668 L5   Date photographs taken unknown
Aliases: Richard Frank Dennis, William Kinder, Jonathan Maris, Jonathan
      Mark Salamone
Age: 29, born January 22, 1945, Fort Sill, Oklahoma (not supported by birth
                   records)

Height: 5'7"   **Eyes:** Hazel
Weight: 145 pounds   **Complexion:** Medium
Build: Medium   **Race:** White
Hair: Brown, short   **Nationality:** American
Occupation: Postal clerk
Remarks: Reportedly wears Fu Manchu type mustache, may wear glasses,
          upper right center tooth may be chipped, reportedly jogs, swims and
          rides bicycle for exercise, was last seen wearing army type boots
          and dark jacket
Social Security Numbers Used: 315-46-2467; 553-27-8400; 359-48-5467
Fingerprint Classification: 20 L 1 At 12
                           S 1 Ut

Emily Montague Harris

FBI No. 325,804 L2   Date photographs taken unknown
Aliases: Mrs. William Taylor Harris, Anna Lindenberg, Cynthia Sue Mankins,
      Emily Montague Schwartz
Age: 27, born February 11, 1947, Baltimore, Maryland (not supported by birth
                   records)

Height: 5'3"   **Eyes:** Blue
Weight: 115 pounds   **Complexion:** Fair
Build: Small   **Race:** White
Hair: Blonde   **Nationality:** American
Occupations: Secretary, teacher
Remarks: Hair may be worn one inch below ear level, may wear glasses or
          contact lenses; reportedly has partial upper plate, pierced ears,
          is a natural food fadist, exercises by jogging, swimming and
          bicycle riding, usually wears slacks or street length dresses,
          was last seen wearing jeans and waist length shiny black leather
          coat
Social Security Numbers Used: 327-42-2356; 429-42-8003

Patricia Campbell Hearst

FBI No. 325,805 L10   Date photograph taken unknown
Alias: Tania
Age: 20, born February 20, 1954, San Francisco, California
Height: 5'3"   **Eyes:** Brown
Weight: 110 pounds   **Complexion:** Fair
Build: Small   **Race:** White
Hair: Light brown   **Nationality:** American
Scars and Marks: Mole on lower right corner of mouth, scar near right ankle
Remarks: Hair naturally light brown, straight and worn about three inches below shoulders in
          length, however, may wear wigs, including Afro style, dark brown of medium
          length; was last seen wearing black sweater, plaid slacks, brown hiking boots and
          carrying a knife in her belt

CAUTION

THE ABOVE INDIVIDUALS ARE SELF-PROCLAIMED MEMBERS OF THE SYMBIONESE LIBERATION ARMY AND REPORTEDLY HAVE
BEEN IN POSSESSION OF NUMEROUS FIREARMS INCLUDING AUTOMATIC WEAPONS. WILLIAM HARRIS AND PATRICIA HEARST AL-
LEGEDLY HAVE RECENTLY USED GUNS TO AVOID ARREST. ALL THREE SHOULD BE CONSIDERED ARMED AND VERY DANGEROUS.

Federal warrants were issued on May 20, 1974, at Los Angeles, California, charging the Harris' and Hearst with violation of the National
Firearms Act. Hearst was also charged in a Federal complaint on April 15, 1974, at San Francisco, California, as a material witness to a
bank robbery which occurred April 15, 1974.

**IF YOU HAVE ANY INFORMATION CONCERNING THESE PERSONS, PLEASE NOTIFY ME OR CONTACT YOUR
LOCAL FBI OFFICE. TELEPHONE NUMBERS AND ADDRESSES OF ALL FBI OFFICES LISTED ON BACK.**

C M Kelley

DIRECTOR
FEDERAL BUREAU OF INVESTIGATION
UNITED STATES DEPARTMENT OF JUSTICE
WASHINGTON, D. C. 20535
TELEPHONE, NATIONAL 8-7117

Entered NCIC
Wanted Flyer 475
May 20, 1974

If a man does not keep pace
with his companions, perhaps it is because
he hears a different drummer.
Let him step to the music which he hears,
however measured or far away.

Henry David Thoreau

1976 FAMILY PROFILE

Fearing another Korean War, the Lis, a Korean family, immigrated to America during the mid-1960s, settling in New York City. The father, Richard, immigrated first in 1965 and, after gaining citizenship in 1970, sent for his wife Karen, child, and mother-in-law. The family is supported by a corner fruit stand owned by the father. His son works there also to help support the family.

Annual Income: $14,606

Annual Budget

The study does not provide family expenditures; nationally the per capita expenditures in 1976 are:

Auto Parts $52.29
Auto Usage $654.02
Clothing. $300.41
Dentists $42.65
Food $1,082.39
Furniture $64.67
Gas and Oil $197.22
Health Insurance $32.10
Housing. $740.71
Intercity Transport $39.44
Local Transport. $20.18
New Auto Purchase. $175.20
Personal Business $273.81
Physicians $118.33
Private Education and Research $102.74
Recreation $328.28

Religion/Welfare Activities $102.28
Telephone and Telegraph $90.81
Tobacco $77.05
Utilities $222.89
Per Capita Consumption $5,242.74

Life at Home

- The Li family lives in a rapidly developing Korean community in the Flushing community of New York City.
- They rent a small apartment near the fruit stand and often allow guests to stay with them; refusing a fellow Korean a courtesy would be considered rude.
- Karen does not work but keeps the house, though she will help out with the fruit stand when needed.
- The son is expected to help his father before school, make excellent grades in school, and work at the fruit stand after school.
- The son makes As and Bs on his report cards and the father regularly checks his homework; like most Koreans, this family is very supportive of their children's education.

- Once the fruit stand has made enough money, the family is planning to move to the suburbs and start another business; many Koreans consider the greengrocer business a place to start, not end.
- This desire to move to the suburbs once some prosperity is gained is common; it is one of the reasons Koreans have not created communities similar to Chinatown in New York or San Francisco.
- Many Korean families retain the division of labor by gender prevalent in Korea; however, a simple stereotypical view of a male-dominated household with the long-suffering housewife is not the case. Many wives control the household budget and other integral finances.
- Richard believes he has a right to select his son's bride, following the Korean tradition of arranged marriages, although the son, despite his role as eldest male child, avoids discussing the subject with his father.
- The son knows that he is not allowed to date or marry a Caucasian girl, but wishes to choose his own Korean wife.
- The Lis belong to the Presbyterian Church, as do so many other Koreans.
- They tend to be very private, since telling others details of family life is considered very embarrassing to the family.
- The family's grandmother does not know English, nor does she go out much or even watch TV. Her sole social activity is church.

East to America, by Elaine H. Kim:

"Coming to Los Angeles from Seoul at 14 was a shock for me. I started attending Bancroft Junior High School, which was mostly White, with some Latinos and Black kids. My classmates looked like fully grown-up people, at least physically. I just couldn't believe how they all behaved on campus—their makeup, their clothes, their shoes. It just made me sick. When I left Korea, kids were still wearing school uniforms and short, straight haircuts. You could never put on makeup or nail polish; no one even imagined doing those things at that age. Here, the kids wanted to seem like adults by kissing, hugging, and making a lot of gestures. Even the Korean kids in the eighth or ninth grade were already paired in couples. Some of them were dressing like some of the Latino kids, with heavy eyeliner and sexy clothes . . ."

- The club she has joined at the church is called Gyeongnohoe, or the Association of the Respectable Elderly; these clubs tend to be the primary source of socializing available to the elderly parents of Korean immigrants.
- The family is part of a gye which is similar to credit unions except that the gye is controlled by the members and has no formal structure; loans taken out from the gye are generally small, a couple of thousand dollars, because most gyes are modestly funded.
- The gye started in Korea during the Yi Dynasty, which served as a dominant civic and economic institution; the gyes were differentiated along the lines of major life activities such as cattle gye, horse gye, shroud gye.
- The shroud gye pays for the funeral expenses of any member who has a death in the family; the cattle gye pays for the loss of cattle.
- The gye in the United States is an informal association in which members pool some of their resources to create capital to buy home furnishings, create recreational activities, and such; the U.S. gye has shifted its focus from primarily a pool of money for investment to recreational and social activities such as trips.
- Some Koreans, if they have the resources, will buy into a well-funded gye to take out larger loans.
- These gyes are constantly reforming, dropping some members, gaining others, completely disbanding, and reorganizing.
- Children aged four to 12 also attend church a great deal even if their parents do not; parents will take the child to Sunday School, which teaches language lessons, folk singing, folk dancing, and taekwondo.
- Those parents that engage in this activity are normally blue-collar or small shopkeepers; the white-collar workers have enough time to pay special attention to their children's education.
- Church attendance is often dependent on the weather: on cloudy days where outside activity is well-nigh impossible, church attendance is at its peak; on days which are hot and sunny, members of the church tend to go to the beach.

Life at Work: The Fruit Stand

- The Li family raised money to buy the fruit stand by selling wigs and trinkets in Harlem.
- They were able to use the profits to buy a store in the Flushing community of New York City.
- Many Koreans are shop owners because they take little technical expertise and generally less capital than other types of businesses to start.
- Generally a stand can be opened for $5,000.
- The father bought the corner shop from another Korean who was fair, and the father was happy that he was not swindled.
- Other immigrants have been swindled. One couple bought a fruit shop and afterwards, lost all of the customers they had seen, because the seller had cut his prices in half while they scouted the store.
- Richard and his son get up at 4 a.m. to buy fruits and vegetables for the corner shop at Hunt's Point; the day ends when the rush-hour crowd has settled down to their own supper. The father normally puts in 16-hour days.
- They have a lot of competition; many Koreans have opened fruit markets—often the first step in gaining a financial foothold in America.
- Father and son both believe they have a better life in America than they would have enjoyed if they had stayed in Korea even though in Korea the father had a higher status.

Life in the Community: New York City

- Thanks to the reduced restrictions on immigration, 300,000 Koreans live in the United States, 90 percent having arrived since 1965, when the immigration law changed.
- The New York State Advisory Commission on Civil Rights says in 1976 that Koreans will "demonstrate the highest growth rate of all by 1980."
- Estimates today place New York's Korean population between 60,000 and 80,000.
- Four foreign-language newspapers are produced by the Korean community in New York.

Thomas Kessner and Betty Boy Caroli, Today's Immigrants, Their Stories:

"The same men who wear the latest cut in men's Western clothing and follow the newest trends in business continue to believe that a wife should serve her mother-in-law. Housework in Korean is nolda, literally, 'playing.' Custom and its imperfect handmaiden, law, still provide that only a father has total control over the children, including automatic custody after divorce. Moreover, while a woman may legally have been forced to accept as her own the child of her husband's mistress, when the husband dies she receives only a small part of his estate, the greatest share being reserved for the eldest son. Not incidentally many of those emigrating from Korea have been women."

Ovation's but a babe in the wood
Seven years old and lookin' good.

Walnut, spruce, and spanish pine —
Bronze, chrome, and nickel shine.

Fiberglass back and hand-rubbed wood
the sound is true and the seed is good.

Already now the people know
Ovation sound's begun to grow

Ovation Naturally

OVATION® A KAMAN COMPANY

For more detailed information on Ovation products, send 50¢ to
Ovation Instruments, Inc., New Hartford, Conn. 06057.
Poster versions of this ad are also available from Ovation at 50¢ each.

- The charges of influence-peddling by Korean businessman Tong Sun Park and the controversy swirling around Sun Myung Moon's Church have made some Americans suspicious of the Korean immigrants.
- For Koreans the Presbyterian Church is the main source of social activity; ironically Christianity was first introduced into Korea by Catholic missionaries in 1784.
- It was banned soon after by the ruling class because it challenged the Confucian system of loyalties and ancestor worship that laid the foundation for its system.
- Christianity was reintroduced in 1884 when the Presbyterian Board of Missions sent a representative to Korea.
- During the Sino-Japanese War (1894-95), missionaries unselfishly gave their time and efforts to alleviate the suffering of those caught in the conflict. This devotion endeared them to many people, and a number of Koreans converted.
- Though less than 40 percent of Korean immigrants in New York participate in church life, almost all community activities are centered in churches.
- The core constituency of the church is elderly immigrants primarily brought from Korea by their children to administer child care.
- Despite the growing presence of Korean businesses and organizations, little overt 'Koreanness' marks their neighborhoods; the community enjoys being known for its hard work and low profile.
- Koreans are generally nationalistic and therefore tend to identify with the home government. The Korean Consulate General in New York City has emerged as the most influential link between Koreans in America and the Korean Government.
- New links to federal and state governments have formed as Korean immigrants become more concerned about American issues. These links have gotten more powerful as Koreans have realized the need for power in the U.S. after the "Koreagate" scandal, the controversy over the Unification Church, and anti-Koreanism, particularly among Blacks.
- The consulate has gained power in part because many Korean immigrants never renounce their citizenship to Korea. The consulate has administrative jurisdiction over the immigrant Koreans living on the eastern seaboard, except for Maryland and Virginia. It performs many functions normally associated with the government such as issuing passports and other government papers.
- Because of the governmental power the consulate holds it has tended to apply various policies of the South Korean Government onto Korean immigrants in its jurisdiction.
- Korean nationalism is deeply embedded in Korean culture. Thus, many Koreans did not find anything wrong with it and in fact agree with the South Korean Government's assessment that Tong Sun Park's attempted bribery of U.S. congressmen was an attempt to further the home country's policies.

HISTORICAL SNAPSHOT
1976–1977

- The Dow Jones Industrial Average peaked at 1,004; inflation hit 8.7 percent, while unemployment hit 8.3 percent
- Jimmy Carter was elected president
- Bicentennial festivities swept the nation, highlighted by 'Operation Sail' in New York City in which 16 of the world's tallest and oldest windjammers along with thousands of other ships began a tour of the world's major ports
- Congress passed a law to admit women to military academies
- The Supreme Court ruled that employers were not required to give paid maternity leave
- Renowned lawyer F. Lee Bailey defended Patty Hearst, daughter of publisher William Randolph Hearst, against changes of bank robbery claiming she was 'brainwashed'
- President Gerald Ford ordered a major inoculation campaign against a projected swine flu epidemic
- The repeal of the Fair Trade law prevented manufacturers from fixing retail prices
- Colossus Cave, the first computer game, was designed at Princeton
- The arrest rate for women since 1964 rose three times faster than the rate for men
- Sales of bran cereals increased 20 percent and of high fiber bread, 30 percent, as consumers responded to widely published medical studies reporting the health benefits of high-fiber diets
- California legalized the concept of "living wills," giving the terminally ill the right to decree their own deaths
- The Apple computer was developed in a California garage
- 3,420 lobbyists were now registered in Washington, D.C.
- The average SAT scores dropped to 472 in math and 435 in English from 501 and 480 in 1968
- One out of five children now lived in a one-parent home; three out of five marriages ended in divorce
- ABC offered the industry's first $1 million per year contract to Barbara Walters of NBC
- Clothier Abercrombie & Fitch declared bankruptcy
- 100 companies sponsored 76 percent of network TV ads
- Mobil Petroleum bought Montgomery Ward for $1 billion
- Balloon angioplasty was developed for reopening diseased arteries of the heart
- 20,000 shopping malls generated 50 percent of total retail sales nationwide
- American Express became the first service company to top $1 billion in sales

When I was a child, I spake as a child, I understood as a child, I thought as a child: But when I became a man, I put away childish things. ~ *I Corinthians*

SCM SMITH-CORONA

Sure, this stereo cassette system costs all of $400. But after all, you **can** take it with you.

1976 ECONOMIC PROFILE

Income, Standard Jobs

Bituminous Coal Mining	$17,430.00
Building Trades	$14,242.00
Domestics	$6,479.00
Farm Labor	$5,416.00
Federal Civilian	$16,238.00
Federal Military	$10,420.00
Finance, Insurance, and Real Estate	$11,386.00
Gas, Electricity, and Sanitation Workers	$15,653.00
Manufacturing, Durable Goods	$13,622.00
Manufacturing, Nondurable Goods	$11,710.00
Medical/Health Services Workers	$10,465.00
Miscellaneous Manufacturing	$10,148.00
Motion Picture Services	$11,987.00
Nonprofit Organization Workers	$7,701.00
Passenger Transportation Workers, Local and Highway	$10,121.00
Personal Services	$7,943.00
Private Industries Including Farm Labor	$11,430.00
Public School Teachers	$12,038.00
Radio Broadcasting and Television Workers	$14,705.00
Railroads	$17,292.00
State and Local Government Workers	$11,594.00
Telephone and Telegraph Workers	$15,756.00
Wholesale and Retail Trade Workers	$13,684.00

Selected Prices

Bathroom Scale	$17.99
Boy's Bicycle	$79.99
Broadway Theater Ticket (*A Chorus Line*)	$17.50
Child's Corduroy Boxer Pants, Two Per Package	$3.99
Child's Pajamas, One-Piece	$2.79
Drive-In Movie Ticket, Carload	$4.00
Kenmore Dryer	$149.00
Kodak Camera Film, 24 Exposures	$5.49
Kodak TrimLite Instamatic Camera	$129.00
Light Crafters Wonderful Sight Light, Floor Lamp	$78.50
Meal of Broiled African Lobster Tail, with Salad Bar	$6.95

Microwave Oven. $168.00
Quilt with European Goose Down. $109.95
Revlon Ultima II Makeup Crème $8.50
Sears Push Lawn Mower. $79.00
Sears Stereo Headphone Radio. $39.50
Steel Belted Tire. $42.00
Stroh's Beer, Six-Pack $1.49
Upright 16-Cubic Foot Freezer. $219.00

Introducing the Limited Edition
Pick one up. You'll never want to put it down.

See for yourself

The Looks
They look terrific: handset pearl inlay with rich design marquetry. Book matched wood on the sides and back. But even better than their looks is their feel.

The Feel
Hohner's Limited Edition guitars have a special feel because they were shaped by hand. The necks are just right: they give you a smooth wraparound feeling. A feeling that makes it hard to put it down.

The Sound
It's full. It's balanced, and rich. It's a sound that could only come from hand

crafted instruments. Which all Hohner Limited guitars are. All major parts are made and put together by hand: everything from fitting the neck to the body at the proper pitch to sanding the tops for the perfect resonance.

The Price
To get a guitar as good as a Hohner Limited Edition from any of the leading guitar makers, you'll have to spend a lot more.

So the way we see it, with our looks, our feel, our sound and price, there's no way you could put down a Hohner. Once you pick it up.

HOHNER
We also make harmonicas

473

The Korean Migration

- Korea is generally mountainous in terrain with numerous rich valleys; its history, however, has been shaped by its proximity to the superpowers of Russia, China, and Japan.
- Korea and Japan, in particular, have engaged in repeated conflicts for two centuries.
- Only in 1965 could Japan and Korea tolerate each other enough to sign a commercial and diplomatic agreement.
- Korean women have entered this country at twice the rate of Korean men, though most national immigrant movements have been led by men; American couples tended to adopt female children over male children from other countries such as Korea.
- The immigration of Korean war brides by returning soldiers stationed in Korea also contributed to the disproportionate immigration of Korean women.
- Korean immigration to America has occurred in three waves, the first two based around war.
- The first was a result of the Sino-Japanese War which uprooted many Koreans, most of whom went first to the Hawaiian Islands to work on plantations before coming to the United States; these immigrations were limited by the Korean government by limiting emigration.
- As late as 1948, only 46 Koreans were admitted to the United States, and the next year only 40 were admitted.

"The Housing Issue," *New York Times* **editorial, October 21, 1976:**

"The interplay of recession and inflation has had some of its most severe, distorting effects in the housing industry. The nation has lived for so long with the sad reality of big city slums and tar-paper shacks and tumbledown houses in half-hidden rural villages that a housing 'crisis' has come to be regarded as a permanent feature of the social landscape. But the housing problem today is a much wider, more complicated, and more pervasive phenomenon. It touches the lives not only of millions of low-income families but also the whole range of the middle class. Only 15 percent of American families—the top one-sixth of people in this affluent society—can afford a new median-priced home. The price of that median home rose from $23,000 in 1970 to $39,000 in 1975 and is higher today. An estimated 13 million families suffer 'serious housing deprivation.' This includes those who live in the more than five million units that lack adequate indoor plumbing facilities. It includes the families with small children crowded into 'mobile homes.' It includes urban families that occupy one or two rooms in badly converted buildings originally erected as single-family residences.

It would take a high volume of housing production to meet existing and rapidly developing needs. Instead, the number of new housing starts has slumped in the last three years to the lowest levels since World War II. Early in 1973, almost all housing subsidy programs were suspended. By June 1975, the housing industry was in its worst depression since the 1930s . . . ."

- The postwar division of Korea and the hard-fought Korean War prepared more Koreans to leave.
- The second wave began in 1951, at the start of the Korean War, and continued until 1964 as a mixed bag of war brides, war orphans, and students gained permission to enter the United States.
- The third wave, from 1965 to 1975, when this family arrived, was characterized by a high level of education and a tendency to be entrepreneurial in spirit, for most television and movies had prepared them for the environment they would find in America.
- After 1965, more than one-quarter of all Asian immigrants were professional workers; in New York City in 1978, two of every five doctors were graduates from foreign medical schools, many Korean.
- In 1970 over 50 percent of all adult Koreans in New York had four or more years of higher education.
- Koreans in America have formed two large communities, one on each coast; Los Angeles holds the single largest Korean community in the United States, and New York the second.
- Koreans considering a move to America often have their images and expectations shaped by the television images they see; many expect all Americans to be as blond, blue-eyed, and good-looking as Robert Redford.

"Chancellor Failed to Set up Bilingual Education," *New York Times*, October 23, 1976:

"The Board of Education and the school chancellor of New York City were ruled in contempt of court yesterday for having 'failed steadily and repeatedly to exercise their power' to expedite a bilingual education program for Spanish-speaking students. The contempt ruling, by a federal Judge, chastised the school authorities for acting too slowly, but refrained from imposing immediate penalties, which could be ordered later if they fail to carry out the bilingual program. Acting on a complaint by Puerto Rican groups, Judge Marvin E. Frankel made the contempt ruling in Federal District Court in Manhattan."

East to America, by Elaine H. Kim:

"I never won any special awards at school. Students got special awards if their parents handed white envelopes of money to teachers and my parents didn't do that. I was usually one of the top five students in my class, but I always caused trouble, complaining about the special treatment teachers gave certain students. I knew corruption was going on. Teachers would hit me in front of the class for saying things about it. I remember one classmate whose family was very rich. He had a private tutor and was always getting 100 percent on his papers because the teacher gave the tutor all the questions in advance. Once, I got 100 percent and he got only 85 percent on a math test, and the teacher had the whole class retake the test the following day, so that he got 100 percent. Other kids might not have noticed it, but I did. I complained to the other students that it wasn't fair and got hit when the teacher heard about it. I never saw the kids whose parents brought all the white envelopes getting hit. They would even hand out those envelopes right in front of the students. It was not a good example to set. Even today, I don't want to go back and see those teachers when I visit Korea."

"Skateboard Generation Blooms on City and Suburban Concrete," *New York Times,* April 2, 1974, by Warren Hoge:

"Southern California, the source of countless outdoor cults, is now peddling one tied to asphalt and concrete, and the New York metropolitan area, much of which lies under the two substances, is buying. The craze is the skateboard.

Young devotees have suddenly laid claim to steep walkways in the city's parks, to roads and driveways in the immediate suburbs, and to empty pools, drainage ditches, and spillways in the farther reaches of the region. Skateboards have not been complete strangers to the area. Wooden versions with metal wheels ranging in price from $5.95 to $9.95 have been available locally for many years. But that device bears little resemblance to its space age offspring.

Skateboards now come in more than 50 models priced as high as $125.00, with a variety of materials for the board, the wheels, and the axle works, called trucks. Sporting goods retailers in the city, Westchester and Nassau Counties, and New Jersey all reported growing sales, with an average purchase price of $28.00. In addition, a spinoff industry has evolved producing competition uniforms, racing-color tote bags, films, practice runs and tubes, lubricant sprays, posters of skateboard stars, and a magazine that is published every other month called *Skateboard.* It has a circulation of 200,000.

Almost all the outlets for the boards and related equipment are in southern California, with a few in Hawaii and Florida. Sports stores in the metropolitan area have just begun to stock the gear in earnest this year, largely in response to the demands of local youths eager to catch up with the West Coast. Allen Brill, who handles the boards for the Scandinavian Ski Shop at 40 West 57th Street, said: 'We learn about all this from the kids. It's endless. Every week it's something new.'"

"Life on a Treadmill: Financing College for Several Children," *New York Times*, October 21, 1976, by Nadine Brozan:

"A New Orleans rabbi pondered the bills for college tuition on his desk and said, 'My life savings are being tragically depleted and there's no relief in sight. I've had to draw on savings that I thought I'd be able to use for my retirement. I'm feeling pulverized and each year it gets rougher. . . .' Other parents of three or more college-bound students reacted more in anger and frustration than in sorrow over the strain of doling out thousands of dollars in a short span of years.

The total annual charges for a resident undergraduate now average $2,790 at a public university and $4,568 at a private institution. But many of the more prestigious colleges have bro-

ken the $7,000 mark and others are edging up there. So families with three children attending college simultaneously can expect to pay out anywhere from $7,000 to $21,000 after-tax dollars a year, or more if any of the schools are on the graduate level.

For many, the gate to scholarship aid is slammed shut. According to Joe Paul Case, associate director of the College Scholarship Service, which processes aid applications for most of the colleges in the country, a two-parent/three-child family unit with an after-tax income of $12,960 is considered 'to be subsisting at an intermediate standard of living.'"

1976 NEWS PROFILE

This 62-year-old Latin American man has been out of work for three years. He spent 10 years in the coal mines and when the mines gave out he learned the machinist's trade in Houston, Texas; he has also worked on the docks, in construction, as a meat cutter, and as a truck driver. Even though he spends his day outside the unemployment center in Houston, helping others fill out government forms—for a donation—he has little hope of working again.

"The last steady job I had was for this company that made all kinds of accessories for farm equipment. I went there as a machinist and I worked eight years for them. I was head machinist for them, and assistant foreman. But in November, 1973, the plant was closed down completely. First they started laying people off. There was only six of us left of the whole bunch. We was cleaning up and fixing up everything, and then they sold it all and let us go. So I went to collect unemployment, and I collected the first claim. It was 26 weeks, and at that time you could only get three weeks' extension. So they gave me those, and then the lady asked if I had worked during 1973, and I told her that I had made over $8,000. She said, 'Well, you have another claim coming.' So I made another claim. Altogether I got 91 weeks, and then that ran out. So I've been out of work now for about three years.

I started looking for a job right away, but I've got two things against me: my age and the wetbacks. All these companies around here have too many wetbacks working. All they want to pay is $2.00, $2.25 an hour. Even the big companies hire wetbacks. 'Cause the Anglo or the legal immigrant will demand a higher wage, whereas the wetback, if he gets smart, they'll fire him and he can't say nothing. There's 10 or 15 more behind him so they fire him and get another one. See, a lot of wetbacks have fake alien cards . . .

Then there's the companies that tell you you're too old. That makes a guy feel like hell, 'cause you're down already, being out of work. Some companies say, 'Don't you think you'd do better collecting your old-age pension?' They tell you right off. Some companies just say, 'Sorry, ain't got no job for you.'

After a while I just stopped looking so hard. Heck, I knew it was useless for me to keep going the way I was. I was getting my unemployment, and I used to spend around $15.00 or $16.00 on gas a week. Just looking for jobs. And that's not counting what the other guys used to give me. There was a couple of other guys, and they used to give me $6.00 or $7.00 a week. We'd use that gas for my car and just keep going all over. Now I spend most of my time at the unemployment center. I go down there at 7:15 and I stay till about 2:30, 3:00. I help the guys down there fill out their forms. You know all those forms they got. Well, most of the people around here don't know how to fill them out. So I fill out the forms and tell them what to do when they get inside, what window to go to and all that. Then when they go in there, they already know what to do.

I started doing that way back in 1965. I was working for a company that moved away and left me out of a job. I went to claim my unemployment, and when I was filling out my papers over there, there was an old man outside and he was filling out forms for people. Real slow. He was an old man, real slow. So I was filling my forms out and there was a lady next to me. I filled mine out, and she said, 'Will you fill mine out for me?' I said yes, and I filled them out for her. Then she said, 'Here.' I said, 'What?' She says, 'Fifty cents.' I say no. She says, 'Yes, yes, I got charged outside.' So she gave me the $0.50, and then another girl came over and then a guy, and I stayed there and filled out forms and I came out of there with $8.00. They said, 'Are you going to be here tomorrow?' I said, 'Be here tomorrow?' They said, 'A bunch of girls are coming tomorrow. They need somebody to fill out papers.' I said, 'OK, I'll be there.' So the next day I went down at 7:30, and the girls were there. I started filling the papers and I came out with $23.00 that day. So I started going every day and pretty

soon people knew that I filled out papers, so I stayed there. I stayed there about nine months and then I went back to work.

Then when the farm equipment company closed, I was collecting unemployment again, and one day a guy came by and told me, 'You used to fill out papers here before, didn't you?' I said, yes. He said, 'Fill mine out.' I started filling his and then said, what the heck, I might as well start doing this. A lot of people that I knew before were coming back here, so I stayed around to help them out. I used to go out and look for jobs, and then I'd come back and fill out forms. But about two years ago everything went down. It was bad, so bad. It was slow at factories, machine shops, construction work, everything. There was hundreds and hundreds of people at the unemployment office. So I just stayed around there. I didn't go out and look for a job. There was no jobs. And now I just stay there most of the day, every day. I'd rather be working, but since I don't have nothing else to do, I go over there and help them out. They give me a quarter or $0.50, whatever they can afford. I go home with $7.00, $10.00, $12.00, $15.00 sometimes. It depends on how many people come around."

Value of One Dollar	
Year	Value in 2010 USD
1981	$2.40
1984	$2.10
1986	$1.99
1987	$1.92
1989	$1.76

Values are approximate based upon economic historical data and 2010 U. S. Dollar

1980–1989

The decade of the 1980s began with serious problems. Both the interest rates and inflation rates were at a staggering 18 percent. The economy was at a standstill and unemployment was rising. By 1982, America was in its deepest depression since the Great Depression. One in 10 Americans were out of work. Yet, the decade ended on a high economic note with most Americans feeling more prosperous and optimistic.

Convinced that inflation was the primary enemy of long-term economic growth, the Federal Reserve Board brought the economy to a standstill in the early days of the decade. It was a shock treatment that worked. By 1984 the tight money policies of the government, stabilizing world oil prices, and labor's declining bargaining power brought inflation to four percent, the lowest level since 1967. Despite the pain it caused, the plan to strangle inflation succeeded; Americans not only prospered, but many came to believe it was their right to be successful. The decade came to be symbolized by self-indulgence.

At the same time, defense and deficit spending roared into high gear, the economy continued to grow, and the stock market rocketed to record levels (the Dow Jones Industrial Average tripled from 1,000 in 1980 to nearly 3,000 a decade later). In the center of recovery was Mr. Optimism, President Ronald Reagan. During his presidential campaign he promised a "morning in America" and during eight years, his good nature helped transform the national mood. The Reagan era, which spanned most of the 1980s, fostered a new conservative agenda of good feeling. During the presidential election against incumbent President

Jimmy Carter, Reagan joked, "A recession is when your neighbor loses his job. A depression is when you lose yours. And recovery is when Jimmy Carter loses his."

The economic wave of the 1980s was also driven by globalization, improvements in technology, and willingness of consumers to assume higher and higher levels of personal debt. By the 1980s, the two-career family became the norm. Forty-two percent of all American workers were female, and more than half of all married women and 90 percent of female college graduates worked outside the home. Yet, their median wage was 60 percent of that of men. The rapid rise of women in the labor force, which had been accelerating since the 1960s, brought great social change, affecting married life, child rearing, family income, office culture, and the growth of the national economy.

The rising economy brought greater control of personal lives; homeownership accelerated, choices seemed limitless, debt grew, and divorce became commonplace. The collapse of communism at the end of the 1980s brought an end to the old world order and set the stage for a realignment of power. America was regarded as the strongest nation in the world and the only real superpower, thanks to its economic strength. As democracy swept across eastern Europe, the U.S. economy began to feel the impact of a "peace dividend" generated by a reduced military budget and a desire by corporations to participate in global markets—including Russia and China. Globalization was having another impact. At the end of World War II, the U.S. economy accounted for almost 50 percent of the global economic product; by 1987 the U.S. share was less than 25 percent as American companies moved plants offshore and countries such as Japan emerged as major competitors. This need for a global reach inspired several rounds of corporate mergers as companies searched for efficiency, market share, new products, or emerging technology to survive in the rapidly shifting business environment.

The 1980s were the age of the conservative Yuppie. Business schools, investment banks, and Wall Street firms overflowed with eager baby boomers who placed gourmet cuisine, health clubs, supersneakers, suspenders, wine spritzers, high performance autos, and sushi high on their agenda. Low-fat and fiber cereals and Jane Fonda workout books symbolized much of the decade. As self-indulgence rose, concerns about the environment, including nuclear waste, acid rain, and the greenhouse effect declined. Homelessness increased and racial tensions fostered a renewed call for a more caring government. During the decade genetic engineering came of age, including early attempts at transplantation and gene mapping. Personal computers, which were transforming America, were still in their infancy.

The sexual revolution, undaunted by a conservative prescription of chastity, ran head-on into a powerful adversary during the 1980s, with the discovery and spread of AIDS, a frequently fatal, sexually transmitted disease. The right of women to have an abortion, confirmed by the Supreme Court in 1973, was hotly contested during the decade as politicians fought over both the actual moment of conception and the right of a woman to control her body. Cocaine also made its reappearance, bringing drug addiction and a rapid increase in violent crime. The Center on Addiction and Substance Abuse at Columbia University found alcohol and drug abuse implicated in three-fourths of all murders, rapes, child molestations, and deaths of babies suffering from parental neglect.

For the first time in history, the Naval Academy's graduating class included women, digital clocks and cordless telephones appeared, and 24-hour-a-day news coverage captivated television viewers. Compact disks began replacing records, Smurf and E.T. paraphernalia was everywhere, New York became the first state to require seat belts, Pillsbury introduced microwave pizza, and Playtex used live lingerie models in its ads for the "Cross Your Heart" bra. The Supreme Court ruled that states may require all-male private clubs to admit women and 50,000 people gathered at Graceland, in Memphis, Tennessee on the 10th anniversary of Elvis Presley's death.

1981 FAMILY PROFILE

The Sanchez family is composed of Mexican immigrants who have moved to a predominantly Mexican neighborhood outside Los Angeles, California. Juan, Lupé, and their three children are living in the garage of her brother's house; he works in a furniture factory.

Annual Income: $15,250

Annual Budget

The study does not provide family expenditures; nationally the per capita expenditures in 1981 are:

Auto Parts	$66.97
Auto Usage	$1,028.07
Clothing	$424.88
Food	$1,597.77
Furniture	$94.37
Gas and Oil	$425.75
Health Insurance	$63.49
Housing	$1,248.56
Intercity Transport	$76.11
Local Transport	$21.74
New Auto Purchase	$220.49
Personal Business	$471.85
Physicians	$219.18
Private Education and Research	$164.82
Recreation	$567.53
Religion/Welfare Activities	$189.61
Telephone and Telegraph	$134.38

Tobacco $99.15
Utilities $390.09
Per Capita Consumption $8,376.79

Life at Home

- The Sanchez family obtained permission to come to the United States because Lupé's brother was a U.S. citizen and employed in California; 85 percent of legal admissions are granted based on the immigrant having immediate family in the United States.
- They immediately settled in Pacoima in the northern part of Los Angeles County; 93 percent of the residents are also Mexican.
- More than three-fourths of the 36,000 residents are Hispanic; nine out of 10 have a Mexican background.
- Ten percent of the residents of Pacoima came to the United States between 1975 and 1980.
- The family now lives in the garage of her brother's small suburban house until they can afford their own place.
- They place a high value on family ties; the needs of the family often supersede individual needs.
- Juan also dreams of bringing his mother and brother to the United States.
- Like many Mexican families, this one is dominated by the man who is responsible for the economic well-being of the family.
- Parents who cannot discipline their children lose prestige in the eyes of the community; bad behavior by a child can bring shame on the entire family.
- Two of the three children go to a neighborhood elementary school; 90 percent of the children are Hispanic.

THE CHURCH OF CHRISTIAN HOPE

- The third child just started high school; in 1981 the school graduated less than 40 percent of the students who entered four years earlier.
- To reduce overcrowding, caused in part by Mexican immigrants, many schools are now open year-round; these schools are 77 percent Hispanic.
- The children are struggling to keep up in their schoolwork; they are learning to speak English at school; Spanish is primarily spoken at home.
- All schools have a shortage of bilingual teachers.
- Four of five legal Mexican immigrants are former illegal residents who spent on average three years in the United States before applying for permanent residence.

Life at Work: The Furniture Industry

- He is a machine operator in the furniture industry, and has learned to speak English, hoping for a promotion.
- His duties include feeding the planer machine with boards so they can be flattened for cutting.
- He also helps in the sanding area, cleaning up or correcting mistakes made by the machines.
- He has been instructed to wear a breathing mask at all times, though he rarely does so; because the air is filled with sawdust, he goes home covered in tiny wood particles.
- The factory makes furniture for a series of chain stores which sells furniture to the mass market, often at discounted prices.
- He feels lucky to have a job; unemployment among blue-collar workers in southern California is 15 percent.
- Until recently manufacturing jobs in Los Angeles were expanding at twice the national rate, fueled by the less expensive labor available from Mexico and Central America.

- Like most immigrant jobs, the production line position requires little skill; the company is accustomed to workers with limited English skills, so most signs are in English and Spanish.
- Nearly all of the other men working at the furniture factory are Hispanic.

Life in the Community: Los Angeles, California
- Hispanics from Spain and Mexico have played an important role in the development of Los Angeles as a city.
- The name itself comes from that given by Spanish explorers to the Indian village they found, "El Pueblo de Nuestra Senora La Reina de Los Angeles" (The Village of Our Lady Queen of the Angels).
- After Mexico won its independence from Spain in 1822, Los Angeles served as the capital of the Mexican State of California; U.S. forces raised their flag over the city in 1846 during the Mexican War.
- Los Angeles has the largest Hispanic population of any major U.S. city; the majority have Mexican backgrounds.
- In Pacoima, Wilmington, San Pedro, and East Los Angeles signs and billboards in the commercial areas are predominantly in Spanish.
- Historically Mexicans have played a key role in the manufacturing industry of Los Angeles; a 1928 survey of Los Angeles industries showed that 17 percent of all workers were Mexicans.
- Three-quarters of the Mexicans in 1928 were employed in the textile industry; substantial numbers were employed in construction and the railroad yards.
- During the 1970s more than 900,000 Mexicans and other immigrants settled in Los Angeles.

> ## "Fewer Funds But More Traffic," *Los Angeles Times*, February 11, 1981:
>
> "While a predicted, perpetual fuel shortage prompts proposals for an expanded bus system, commuter railroads, people movers, sky shuttles, and subways, the freeways prevail as the Los Angeles region's prime mode of transportation.
>
> The 500-mile asphalt, concrete, and steel web over which an estimated 4.5 million people commute daily is this horizontal city's more dominant man-made form. Indeed for many residents and visitors, the freeways are the city's image.
>
> And like the city and its landscape, the freeways are in constant flux. They are being extended, widened, modified, reconstructed, resurfaced, patched, fenced, walled, decorated, bridged, cleaned, painted, planted, lighted, and metered—to the usual chorus of complaints, by drivers delayed, detoured, or distracted by the construction. But drivers soon may be wishing that there were more familiar flashing yellow arrows warning of construction over which they could grumble. Caltrans is having budget problems that point to a bumpy road ahead for both bureaucrats and drivers."

- The mean household income of Mexican immigrants, who came to California from 1970 to 1980, is $15,000; the mean household income of Mexican-Americans is $17,800; Black households receive $15,900; Asian households average $24,000, and non-Hispanic Whites earn $25,400.

- On a per capita basis, Mexican immigrants, whose households average 4.3 persons, earn $3,538 compared to non-Hispanic Whites, whose average household is 2.3 persons, and who earn $11,165.

- During the 1970s, service sector jobs accounted for 31 percent of the total employment in the county; the health services industry of Los Angeles grew at twice the rate of southern California during the decade.

- Approximately 444,000 immigrants to the United States during the 1970s were employed in Los Angeles County; 210,000 were Mexicans, 74,000 were non-Mexican Hispanics, and 160,000 were non-Hispanics.

- New immigrant workers account for 70 percent of the net employment growth in Los Angeles between 1970 and 1980.

- Mexican workers have practically no impact on white-collar employment during the period.

- Although unskilled blue-collar employment expands by only 71,000, Mexicans hold 116,000 jobs, while other immigrants hold another 52,000.

- Two-thirds of the recent Mexican immigrants in Los Angeles report they have no more than a grade school education.

- Only three percent of Mexican immigrants in Los Angeles County in 1980 have professional or managerial jobs.
- Half of all recently arrived Mexican workers in California are employed in Los Angeles County.
- During the same period, Los Angeles loses approximately 372,000 workers who migrate to other parts of California or the nation.
- Mexican immigrants to Los Angeles tend to cluster in neighborhoods; recent immigrants are related to five other households in their community, while second-generation Mexicans are related to 15 households.
- No other school system in the United States has experienced such a concentrated influx of students from a single foreign country.
- Because the Mexican immigrants tend to settle in the same areas, the impact on some schools is concentrated.
- One out of every 10 workers in Los Angeles County in 1981 is a Mexican immigrant. About half are employed in manufacturing; one-fifth are in employed in service industries.
- Los Angeles County employs more workers in manufacturing than do all the other large western states—Washington, Oregon, Colorado, Arizona, and Idaho—combined.
- Crime is the most serious urban ill facing Los Angeles; the chances of being a victim of a violent crime in the city of Los Angeles are higher than in most other urban areas.
- Statistics show that Mexicans have a low incidence of crime, even though traditionally immigrants—like any newcomers to a community—have been accused of criminal behavior.
- The exception is the violent actions of Mexican youth gangs, which are gaining in size and strength.

Historical Snapshot
1981-1982

- The IBM Personal Computer was marketed for the first time
- 12,000 striking air-traffic controllers were fired by President Ronald Reagan
- Public debt hit $1 trillion
- New York and Miami increased transit fares from $0.60 to $0.75
- Kellogg's introduced Nutri-Grain wheat cereal
- U.S. first-class postal rates went to $0.18, then $0.20
- Sears, Roebuck bought real estate broker Coldwell Banker & Co., and a securities concern, Dean Witter Reynolds
- The U.S. population hit 228 million
- National unemployment rose to eight percent, including 16.8 percent for Blacks and 40 percent for Black teenagers
- A court order broke up the A&T U.S. monopoly into AT&T long-distance and regional telephone companies
- The Japanese marketed a wristwatch-sized television with a 1.2-inch screen
- *USA Today,* the first national general interest daily newspaper, was introduced
- 2.9 million women operated businesses
- Braniff International Airline declared bankruptcy
- United Auto Workers agreed to wage concessions with Ford Motor Company
- U.S. Steel acquired Marathon Oil
- The computer "mouse" was introduced by Apple
- The first successful embryo transfer was performed
- NutraSweet was introduced as a synthetic sugar substitute
- 35.3 million lived below the poverty line
- The 1980 census reported the smallest rate of population growth in the United States since the Depression; women from 15 to 44 averaged 1.9 children compared with 2.5 children 10 years earlier
- Cellular telephones became available to motorists, costing $3,000, plus $150.00 per month for service
- An eight-year study revealed that Vietnam veterans suffered more emotional, social, educational, and job-related problems than veterans of other recent wars
- VCR sales increased 72 percent from the previous year; the U.S. now boasted 3.4 million units in use
- An estimated 750 million people watched the marriage of Prince Charles to kindergarten teacher Lady Diana Spencer in England
- The Rubik's Cube tested the patience of Americans
- Dr. Ruth began her radio sex-talk show

1981 ECONOMIC PROFILE

Income, Standard Jobs

Bituminous Coal Mining	$27,283.00
Building Trades	$20,355.00
Domestics	$9,327.00
Farm Labor	$7,989.00
Federal Civilian	$23,029.00
Federal Military	$15,537.00
Finance, Insurance, and Real Estate	$17,343.00
Gas, Electricity, and Sanitation Workers	$23,959.00
Manufacturing, Durable Goods	$20,810.00
Manufacturing, Nondurable Goods	$17,739.00
Medical/Health Services Workers	$16,288.00
Miscellaneous Manufacturing	$15,169.00

PROTECT YOUR INVESTMENT.

There's no doubt a fine cut of beef really is an investment! And if you're going to invest in top-grade beef don't risk it with an ordinary wine. Serve Egri Bikavér, the rich, robust, red wine imported from Hungary with a classic European taste to stand up to the fullness of beef.

The richness of color and of taste is the reason why, for centuries, the Hungarians have been referring to Egri Bikavér as "BULL'S BLOOD FROM EGER." And as long as there has been a Hungary there has been a bottle of Egri Bikavér next to the beef platter.

See for yourself why Egri Bikavér is the perfect wine with beef. Protect your investment, and discover moderately-priced Egri Bikavér.

$4.89 LB

EGRI BIKAVÉR.
The GREAT Beef Wine.

TABLE WINE IMPORTED BY INTERNATIONAL VINTAGE WINE CO. HARTFORD, CT.

Motion Picture Services $19,856.00
Nonprofit Organization
    Workers $11,153.00
Passenger Transportation
    Workers, Local and Highway . . . $14,446.00
Personal Services $11,195.00
Postal Employees $23,384.00
Public School Teachers $16,606.00
Radio Broadcasting and
    Television Workers $20,813.00
Railroads $27,452.00
State and Local Government
    Workers $16,362.00
Telephone and Telegraph
    Workers $25,090.00
Wholesale and Retail Trade
    Workers $20,324.00

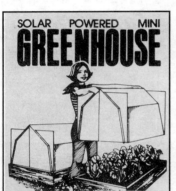

SOLAR POWERED MINI GREENHOUSE

WHY PAY OUTRAGEOUS PRICES for grocery-store vegetables when you can grow your own fresh, rich-tasting vegetables and salad greens almost every month of the year with GUARD 'N GRO mini greenhouses? No artificial light or heat needed. 100% solar-powered. Makes plants grow big and fast . . . even in 22° cold. Works year 'round. Cuts your food bills year 'round. Protects your plants from freezing cold, killing frost, sleet, hail — all this without any artificial light or heat! Measures 40" long x 18" wide x 21" tall. For porch, patio or small-space container gardening. Folds flat for storage. Add-on GUARD 'N GRO units available. Lets you protect your entire garden spring, fall and winter. Mail coupon for startling facts . . . and NO-RISK TRIAL OFFER. Not sold in stores.

MAIL COUPON NOW!

GUARD 'N GRO
Dept. Y10, St. James, NY 11780

Yes! Rush me my FREE GUARD 'N GRO fact kit and details about how I may try GUARD 'N GRO this fall without risking a penny. I understand I'm under no obligation and no salesperson will call.

Name _____
Address _____
City _____ State _____ Zip _____

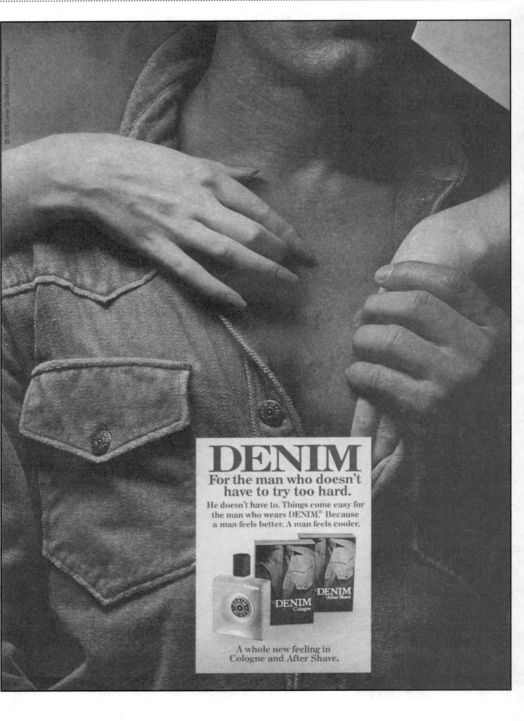

Selected Prices

Bass Tracker One Boat	$3,795.00
Beeman Feinwerkbau 124 Air Rifle	$299.50
Bolla Soave Winem 750 Millimeters	$2.99
Breyers Yogurt, Eight-Ounce Container	$0.89

Cadillac Eldorado
   Automobile, 1981 . . . . $19,700.00

Canvas-Cloth Work Gloves $6.49

Hotpoint Air Conditioner,
   5,950 BTU. $299.00

Lady Wellco The Mesh
   Walking Shoe. $19.99

Laura Lynn Baby Crib. $119.99

Long Distance Telephone Service,
   Chicago to Detroit
   for 10 Minutes. $3.08

Macintosh Computer, 128K $1,788.00

Marples Chisel Set, Set of Six $51.95

Oceanspray Cranapple Juice,
   32-Ounce Bottle $0.93

Pabst Blue Ribbon Beer, 12-Pack $3.19

Pontomac Boat Tours $3.00

Ramada Inn Hotel Room,
   Lake Havasu City, Arizona,
   per Night $27.00

Seiko Ladies' Wristwatch $84.95

Sharp Video Camera $359.50

Turco Saratoga Gas Grill $179.99

Wing-tip, Oxford Men's Shoes $39.99

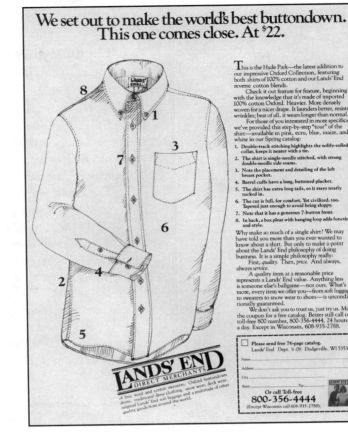

Immigration in California

- Since the gold rush of the late 1840s, California's population growth has been fueled by immigrants from east of the Rocky Mountains.

- Mexicans have been associated with manufacturing in California since the 1920s, when Mexican workers first entered the state in large numbers.

- During the Depression more than a million people went west to California from both the Dust Bowl states and northern industrial centers where jobs had become scarce.

- Unemployment and fears about job security resulted in thousands of Mexicans being "repatriated" to Mexico during the 1930s, often against their will.

- During World War II, millions of people across the nation moved to California to work in defense plants, expanding the state's population by one-third.

- In the late 1960s net migration from other states to California slowed to 370,000 and by the late 1970s had practically disappeared.

- This decline in net migration resulted more from an increase in the number of people leaving California than from a reduction in the number of new immigrants from other states.

"Unemployment of Blacks Hits 28-Year High," *Los Angeles Times*, by Marlene Cimons, September 5, 1981:

"The nation's unemployment rate last month, although rising only slightly for the entire population, reflected the worst job situation for Black Americans in nearly three decades, the Labor Department announced Friday . . . The nation's overall unemployment rate rose slightly in August to 7.2 percent, compared to seven percent in July.

For Black workers, the jobless rate jumped to 15 percent from 13.6 percent in July. It was the highest level of Black unemployment since the Labor Department began compiling statistics 28 years ago. The previous record was in September, 1875. For Black teen-agers, the jobless rate also reached a record, jumping to 50.7 percent last month, a rise of 10 percentage points over July. Unemployment for all minority teenagers was 45.7 percent, another record.

Unemployment reached higher levels during the Great Depression of the 1930s, when record-keeping was not as detailed and accurate as it is today . . . The unemployment rate for the White population was 6.1 percent, including 15.6 percent for teenagers."

- During the decade of the 1970s, 1.86 million foreign-born immigrants arrived in California; this influx represents eight percent of California's total 1980 population of 23.7 million.
- One study suggests that 781,000 of the immigrants are legally in the United States; approximately 1.1 million enter the state in an undocumented—or illegal—status.
- Mexicans are the largest group of foreign-born immigrants to California, non-Mexican Hispanics composing the second largest group; combined they total half of California's immigrants in the 1970. Asians are the next largest group, representing 25 percent of all immigrants.

- Approximately two percent of the Mexican immigrants have a four-year college education, while 11 percent of other Latin American immigrants and 34 percent of Asian immigrants have a college education, while approximately 20 percent of U.S.-born California residents have a college education.
- Four out of five Hispanics who arrived in southern California in the 1970s were of Mexican origin; in the early 1980s this pattern declines as many new non-Mexican immigrants flee the civil strife of Central America.
- Blue-collar employment in California during the 1970s increases at twice the national rate.
- Friction is now developing between Blacks and Hispanics; Black workers are concerned that too many immigrants will depress wage rates and take their jobs.

"Exploding Some Myths about Social Programs," by Vernon E. Jordan, Jr., *Los Angeles Times*, February 16, 1981:

"Federal social programs are under heavy attack. They are widely believed to have failed in their objectives, to be designed to help only Blacks, and to cost more than the economy can afford.

All those beliefs are false.

Federal social programs have worked. Some are among the most successful endeavors of government. Despite an enormous budget, the Pentagon demonstrated that it cannot land helicopters in the Iranian desert, but despite pinched funds, social programs have alleviated hunger, improved the education of the poor, and trained many young people for productive jobs. The food stamp program is an example of how a federal program can make a direct attack on malnutrition and hunger. Before the program was instituted, a congressional investigation found widespread hunger in parts of the country. Recently, a follow-up study found that, thanks to the food stamp program, extreme hunger has largely been eliminated. Sure, the program isn't

cheap. But its rising costs are directly due to the rise in food prices, an inflationary development that makes food stamps even more necessary for the poorest among us.

Head Start is another success. It got bad press in its first few years. But a recent study that followed children from Head Start through young adulthood found that they performed better in school, and were more interested in going to college, and less likely to get into trouble than children with similar backgrounds who did not have the benefit of the program. The lesson of Head Start is that social programs should be seen as investments—by spending on pre-school education, the government saved later and larger expenditures on remedial classes, law enforcement, and training costs. . . . Programs that develop skills, provide basic life supports, and bring hope are indispensable to a civilized society. And anyone who says that these functions can be performed without government intervention is, at best, just plain wrong."

"Lest We Forget, Letters to the Editor," *Playboy Magazine*, January 1980:

"For nearly 20 years, I have lived in this country and worked in many others as an engineer, and I'm now in the process of acquiring U.S. citizenship—more for the purposes of convenience than out of any great emotional or political need. I am neither a Nationalist of any kind nor political in any way, which is why I am writing this letter. I do insist on a degree of personal freedom, including freedom from excessive governmental controls, even when those are benevolent.

What I would like to say is that Americans never cease to amaze me with their constant complaining about injustice, their laws, about the behavior of the police. What U.S. citizens consider intolerable excesses, are accepted as routine, even expected, in most parts of the world. That instances of police brutality or political corruption so disturb Americans always amazes most foreigners, to whom such issues such as civil rights and civil liberties are not even subjects for debate. The fact that Americans are so easily outraged and so willing to fight against governmental authority, in the naïve belief they can do so, is probably the reason the U.S. remains as free a country as it is."

"Irrevocable or Not?" *Sports Illustrated Magazine*, March 3, 1980:

"From the moment President Carter announced it exactly a month earlier, the timing of his February 20 Olympic boycott deadline has caused bafflement. Did Carter settle on so early a date for fear that pro-boycott sentiment might otherwise dissipate? To allow sufficient time to put together an alternative Games? Because the date fell at a time when the world's attention would be riveted on the Winter Olympics? Whatever the explanation, the February 20 deadline passed last week with 70,000 or more Soviet troops still in Afghanistan. Because of Carter's demand that Soviet forces be withdrawn was conspicuously unmet, Administration officials said a U.S. boycott of the Summer Games in Moscow was not irrevocable."

1985 News Profile

Wildly fluctuating farm prices in the 1980s drove many farmers to the point of bankruptcy; most seemed unable to control their economic destiny in a rapidly changing world. This man lives in Gann Valley, South Dakota, and is in the process of losing his farm.

"Look. Jesus, look. Isn't this the most beautiful place? When I was a kid, 25, maybe 30 years ago, I drove down here with my father, saw this land, and said to him, 'I want this to be mine someday.' And now it is mine. Look at it! This is good farmland. Five hundred and eighty acres. And now they're gonna take it all away. How can you figure it? All these years we've worked the land and raised the food, and now Connie and me and the kids have to get food stamps to eat.

The price of cattle is down. The price of wheat is down. Can't get operating costs, can't pay for the machinery. Can't even get insurance. How can you afford insurance? When you've got a steady income, you can do that. But when you don't . . . We even tried breaking more land up to raise some grain. Mother—I call my wife Mother—about had a conniption. This land was native sod, virgin soil. A person lives here all their life, they don't want to see that stuff go under. Once you break the topsoil, it never prairies again. It's not money valuable, just in your heart.

We're $180,000, $160,000 in debt. It's amazing. When I started farming, if someone had said to me I'd owe nearly $200,000 one day, I would have told them they were crazier than hell. I really would have. No way.

It's terrible what they're doing to us farmers. They're just doing it and it ain't ignorance, you can't tell me it's ignorance. 'Cause they're a hell of a lot smarter than that. Nowadays, we live on just about nothing. There's no money coming in. None. Just the food stamps for Connie and me and our youngest daughter, Dawn, and some fuel assistance. Otherwise, we just do without.

We've worked so hard on this place. I'd give anything for this farm, anything. I even lost my arm out there. One night, about nine-thirty, I was driving the hay rack past a pile of old silage and manure and the damn rack got stuck. So I got down—the tractor was still running—reached way under and pulled the pin out. That was as far as I got. The damn thing went whoosh and pulled at me, took my overalls and started wrapping them up at 540 revolutions per minute. That sucker could have flipped me and killed me dead, just killed me

dead. And you know what? That guy above looked down at me and said, 'One more chance.' That damn engine died.

But my arm was still underneath there. I could feel my hand. I reached for my hand. I knew if I could get ahold of that damn hand, I could get the hell out of there, but I couldn't find it. Our pickup was out here in the middle of the yard. I opened the door and the light inside went on. You ever been in a meat locker? You ever see what bone looks like when you scrape the meat off of it?

They buried that arm for me, Connie's dad and the sheriff. I told them to bury it deep, up in the cemetery in a Styrofoam box. So they dug it in and poured cement in it, with a little

marker. The reason I did it that way was I had a friend that lost his leg and they just threw the damn thing in the garbage, and it started to hurt him. So, finally they buried the leg and that was the end of his pain. I don't want no pain, and I don't want some damn animal to come and drag it off. Tough as I am, it'd be liable to die.

Back in 1973, I didn't owe nobody nothing. Period. Then the fall come along and I wanted to buy sheep. But my loan officer down at the bank, he said, 'Naw, you can't buy no sheep. Sheep don't make you no money, no money at all. Buy cattle, you make a lot of money raising cattle.' I said, 'Well, yeah, sure, but they ain't gonna make any money this year.' He wouldn't listen to me. This idiot that don't know nothing. But okay, so hell, I'm gullible. I did what he said. I started buying the damn cattle. On contract. I bought four-hundred-some

head—and I lost that money within six months. We lost every damn thing we had invested in the place, and ended up owing sixty to seventy thousand dollars to the bank besides. We had to take out a second mortgage on the house.

The market was just falling like crazy, and the bank wouldn't stand behind me. They wouldn't give me a guaranteed loan. So I got into FHA, Farmers Home Administration.

They're supposed to be the lenders of last resort. Ha! The problem with these supervisors at FHA, they're young guys, just out of college, never did a damn day's work in their cotton pickin' life. They come out here and tell us farmers what to do . . .

I'll tell you what, I've made my mistakes; Mother reminds me of that. There for awhile, I hardly got to sleep. Because I owed so much money to different people. But I ain't really failed. The system's failed me. There's people in town that says the working class is subsidizing my life-style. The hell they are! I'm subsidizing them because the simple fact is when I grow wheat or corn, this place loses money. You know, back in '73, '74, we were getting about five dollars and something cents for a bushel of wheat. You know what the hell we're getting for our wheat now? Three fifty. And the same thing with beef. When I sell a beef for some fifty, say sixty cents a pound, when the damn thing costs me eighty cents a pound to produce, I'm losing two hundred dollars a head.

Hell, if we ever have to file bankruptcy, a Chapter 7, Connie and me and the family'll lose everything. We asked one lawyer how to figure what our house is worth and he said it's worth what it will bring at an auction sale during the worst blizzard of the year."

1986 Family Profile

The Bellamy family, a meatpacking family of four, is currently without income because of their support of the strike against the Hormel Company in Austin, Minnesota. They believe they are right to stand up to the company, but money is becoming very tight. The family has talked about crossing the picket line, especially if the power company gets serious about cutting off the heat. This man and woman, Rod and Diane, have two boys.

Annual Income

Pre-strike: 1984–85: $22,000
Post-strike: 1985–86: $5,000

Annual Budget

Actual expenditures of this family are not recorded; the per capita expenditures nationwide in 1986 are:

Auto Usage	$1,411.96
Clothing	$576.75
Dentists	$97.65
Food	$1,981.67
Furniture	$130.06
Gas and Oil	$331.18
Health Insurance	$91.83
Housing	$1,752.69
Intercity Transport	$94.32
Local Transport	$32.83
New Auto Purchase	$416.77
Personal Business	$891.31
Personal Care	$180.22
Physicians	$349.46
Private Education and Research	$245.16

Recreation $846.84
Religion/Welfare Activities $292.12
Telephone and Telegraph. $187.40
Tobacco $137.54
Utilities. $487.41
Per Capita Consumption $11,845.00

Life at Home

- The Bellamys, like 75 percent of the working class families in Austin, own their own home.
- Thanks to Rod working 10 years for Hormel, with its reputation for stability, getting a bank loan for the house was easy.
- Since the strike began, the town has been split; this family no longer speaks to some neighbors who support Hormel.
- The Bellamy family no longer shops in stores that support Hormel.
- Their car, which is two years old, sports a "Boycott Hormel" bumper sticker.
- The family has too many assets to be eligible for welfare; the Union strike fund helps pay for a hot water heater that recently needed to be replaced.
- Before the strike, this family was proud they worked for Hormel, the town's flagship company.
- Rod was making nearly $11.00 per hour, one of the highest wages in the plant.
- He agrees with the Union that too many concessions had been made in the past to Hormel; the $2.00 per hour wage cut being demanded by Hormel was too much.
- He does not want to be a strikebreaker, but he also does not want to lose his house, his car, and the chance for his children to go to college.
- They are living on their savings and the $40.00 a week provided through the strike fund.
- Diane is a member of the Austin United Support Group that actively promotes the strike, and is very disappointed that public opinion in Austin is against her, her family, and their way of life.
- She was particularly surprised that the Austin City Council and the local grocery store where she shops is supporting Hormel, not the strikers.
- Her greatest disappointment is saved for her church; in an attempt to remain neutral the church has helped no one, she believes.
- Her sister and brother-in-law have both returned to Hormel as strikebreakers, fearing that they will lose their jobs to the out-of-town replacement workers flooding the city.
- The National Guard recently arrives to control the demonstrations; she has not been arrested in the protests but several of her friends do lie down in front of the plant gates to stop workers from driving into the plant.
- The children's grades are dropping and tension over money and what to do continues to build.

Life at Work: The Hormel Company

- The Hormel Company is the largest employer in Austin; of a total employment of 12,000, approximately 2,400 work for the meat packing plant.
- The second largest employer is the school district.
- The Hormel plant physically dominates the center of town; its presence is so central to the community that at one time it provided electricity to the town.
- Hormel employees are among the best paid packinghouse workers in the country, providing the community with a high standard of living.
- In 1984 one in 10 Austin workers earns more than $30,000 a year.
- Work is generally hard; meat packing has been a way of life so long, few think about the unpleasantness.

Life in the Community: Austin, Minnesota

- Austin is a small community in the rolling prairies of southeastern Minnesota, 100 miles from the Twin Cities; its population peaked at 30,000 around 1960.
- In Austin, "meat means money." According to one report, it is impossible to distinguish the homes of workers from managers.
- During the 1930s, Austin's population increased 49 percent, attributable to the year-round wages and job stability resulting from the one-year layoff notice.
- The Hormel Foundation, founded in 1941, controlled 45 percent of the company's stock and contributed millions to community development projects.
- The Foundation's incorporation documents required that all members of the board be residents of Mower County, whose chief financial interests were in Austin.
- The stability of Hormel's work force encourages long-range investment in the community.
- Banks and businesses tend to extend long-term credit, assured of repayment.
- One study shows that the proportion of purchases made on an installment basis among Hormel employees is greater than in the rest of the state.
- The percentage of homeowners and the frequency of automobile ownership is greater among Hormel employees than among the residents of 29 small cities in four regions of the United States.
- By 1951, three out of four workers in Austin owned their own homes.
- In 1980 the population has declined to 23,000 and will go lower by 1986.
- As a one-industry town, Hormel's generosity also means control.
- At the time of the 1985 strike, the farm economy is in a decline; also local retail businesses are being harmed by national retailers such as Wal-Mart and Target drawing customers.

Timetable of Events

- October, 1984:   Hormel Company announces wage cuts from $10.69 to $8.25 per hour and retroactive benefit cuts
- October, 1984:   First meeting called to form the Austin United Support Group
- January, 1985:   P-9 hires Ray Rogers to organize Corporate Campaign against Hormel
- July, 1985:   Hormel makes contract offer
- August 14, 1985:   P-9 rejects Hormel's offer
- August 17, 1985:   The strike begins
- December 20, 1985:   Civil disobedience begins at plant gates
- January 13, 1986:   Hormel reopens the plant with replacement workers and strike-breakers
- January 20, 1986:   The plant and corporate offices are blockaded and shut down; Governor Rudy Perpich sends in the National Guard
- January 31, 1986:   National Guard leaves; plant is shut down again by protestors
- February 3, 1986:   National Guard returns
- February 15, 1986:   Rally of thousands of supporters in Austin
- February 21, 1986:   National Guard leaves
- March 20, 1986:   More than 100 people arrested in civil disobedience; women spend the night in jail
- April 12, 1986:   Another rally of thousands of supporters
- April 13, 1986:   Jesse Jackson visits Austin
- May 8, 1986:   United Food and Service Workers Union takes over P-9 offices; P-9 ceases to exist; the Austin United Support Group sets up new offices and continues the strike

HISTORICAL SNAPSHOT
1986–1987

- U.S. Protestants numbered 53 million in more than 23,000 churches

- The Supreme Court upheld Affirmative Action hiring quotas

- The U.S. national debt topped $2 billion

- The Dow Jones Industrial Average hit 1,955; the prime rate dropped to seven percent

- Sears celebrated its 100th anniversary

- Office Depot, one of the first office supply warehouse-type stores, opened in Lauderdale Lakes, Florida

- A supercomputer capable of 1,720 billion computations per second went online

- The first bio-insecticides, designed to eliminate insects without harming the environment, were announced

- Elementary and secondary schoolteachers earned an average salary of $26,700

- Approximately 35 percent of high school graduates entered college

- The July Fourth birthday party for the Statue of Liberty included a 40,000-piece fireworks display; the total cost was $30 million

- The Hands Across America chain, stretching from New York City to Long Beach, California, raised $100 million for the poor and homeless

- Eight airlines controlled 90 percent of the domestic market

- The Clean Water Bill passed to address pollution of estuaries and rainwater

- The stock market plunged 508 points in one day (October 19), the largest drop in history

- A New York Stock Exchange seat sold for $1.5 million

- The trade deficit hit a record $16.5 billion

- Harvard University celebrated its 350th birthday

- Fitness foods, which are high in fiber and low in sodium, fat, cholesterol, calories, and caffeine, accounted for 10 percent of the $300 billion retail food market

1986 ECONOMIC PROFILE

Income, Standard Jobs

Bituminous Coal Mining	$34,837.00
Building Trades	$23,590.00
Domestics	$10,061.00
Farm Labor	$10,216.00
Federal Civilian	$27,833.00
Federal Employees, Executive Departments	$24,273.00
Finance, Insurance, and Real Estate	$25,778.00
Gas, Electricity, and Sanitation Workers	$33,222.00
Manufacturing, Durable Goods	$27,147.00
Manufacturing, Nondurable Goods	$23,313.00
Medical/Health Services Workers	$21,652.00
Miscellaneous Manufacturing	$20,145.00
Motion Picture Services	$28,363.00
Nonprofit Organization Workers	$14,350.00
Passenger Transportation Workers, Local and Highway	$16,239.00
Personal Services	$13,403.00
Postal Employees	$26,362.00
Public School Teachers	$21,920.00
Radio Broadcasting and Television Workers	$28,721.00
Railroads	$37,673.00
State and Local Government Workers	$21,949.00
Telephone and Telegraph Workers	$33,705.00
Wholesale and Retail Trade Workers	$26,119.00

Selected Prices

Alpine Car Radio, Removable	$199.00
Apple IIGS Computer	$795.00
Arvin Heater, Fan-Forced Heat	$23.88
Asisc Riger GT Running Shoe	$89.95
Casio Printing Calculator, 12-Digit	$54.95
Coke, Two-Liter Bottle	$1.00
Craftsman Glue Gun	$24.99
Dove Bar Ice Cream	$1.45
Eastman West Sofa, Full Size, Leather	$599.00
Epson Printer	$429.00

INTRODUCING FARBERWARE'S ULTRA CHEF.™ AT $450, IT'S FAST FOOD FOR THE AFFLUENT.

Mussels marinara, beef au jus, cream of asparagus soup. When we say fast food, we don't mean hamburgers and french fries.

Since when have these and a vast array of other wonderful dishes been known as fast food? Since the invention of the Farberware Ultra Chef. Our electronic wonder saves you work, time and clean-up. That's fast food, right? But what food it lets you cook: everything from appetizers through main courses to desserts. It is the logical answer to the modern day problem of how to serve varied and interesting dishes when you don't have time to prepare them.

What does the Ultra Chef do that no other cooker has ever done? It eliminates all the separate steps that complicate cooking: simmering, browning, sautéing. That saves time and several pots. All the ingredients in the recipe go into the glass cylinder *at the same time*. Set the temperature and time for that recipe. Then the miracle begins. The cylinder rotates, the Ultra Chef's electronic heat sensor keeps the temperature exactly right. You don't have to stir or even watch. The Ultra Chef knows when the recipe is cooked just right and turns off automatically.

The Ultra Chef is the perfect addition to a busy schedule, whether you want to cook for your family, yourself or a small dinner party. So now fast food takes on a whole new meaning. Like fast tortellini carbonara, fast chicken curry and fast chocolate mousse pie. Each in under 30 minutes cooking time, without your even having to be there.

If you find all this too good to be true, we suggest you taste the results of the Ultra Chef's labors. Attend a demonstration. To find out where there is one near you, call toll free 1-800-243-3787.*

The Farberware Electronic Ultra Chef. The price may be expensive, but the value is priceless.

COOK INTO THE FUTURE WITH ELECTRONICS FROM FARBERWARE®

1500 Bassett Avenue, Bronx, New York 10461
Subsidiary of Kidde, Inc.
KIDDE

U.S. Pat. No. 4,048,473 4,120,981 4,304,177   *Arizona residents call 957-4923

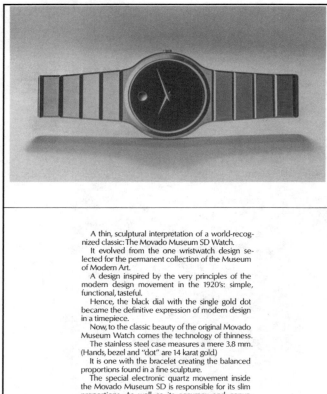

HedBed Pillow $11.00
Kellogg's Corn Flakes, 18-Ounce
    Package $1.59
Mazda RX-Y Roadster
    Automobile $22,000.00
Michelob Beer, 12-Ounce Bottles,
    Case. $9.95
Movie Ticket: *Lady and the Tramp* . . . $2.00
New York Times Fidelity
    Computer Game $149.00
Nylon Hose, Sheer, Three Pairs $8.07
Shop-Vac Mighty Mini-Vac $44.88
Sony Audio Tape, High Power,
    Three-Pack $7.99
Sony Watchman Television,
    Pocket Size $95.00

Labor Relations at Hormel

- The George A. Hormel Company was organized in 1891; owner George Hormel was generally perceived as a benevolent dictator. Efforts to unionize in 1915 fizzled by 1922.
- Most of the early workers were transient packinghouse workers who came to Austin seasonally to kill and pack the meat.
- The workers were social outcasts; few in Austin wanted their daughters to marry a slaughterhouse man.
- In 1931, George Hormel's son Jay attempted to reduce employee turnover and training time by placing the men in one department on an annual wage; the move caused jealousy in the other departments.
- In 1933 the workers organized themselves around the principles promoted by the radical Industrial Workers of the World or Wobblies.
- They advocated a reorganization of the workplace that included non-authoritarian, worker-controlled production, a guaranteed annual wage, and the power to set their own work pace.
- In Austin the Wobblies organized the entire community, including store clerks, cooks, waiters, and even farmers into a single union based on their economic interdependence under the name Independent Union of All Workers (IUAW).
- The resulting sit-down strike was personally settled by the state's governor providing for a year's layoff notice, incentive pay, profit-sharing, and freedom from strikes.
- The workers also gained substantial control over the production process; workloads beyond the normal expecta-

tions were negotiated. Hormel did not experience another strike for 50 years.

- In the early 1960s, the company began demanding wage concessions.
- In 14 of the 20 years between 1963 and 1983, significant concessions were demanded by the company and accepted by the union.
- During the same period, the company frequently raised the specter of relocation from Austin.
- In 1978, in exchange for the company remaining in Austin, the incentive pay of the workers was used as a loan to build a new plan; the union also agreed to no strikes for three years after the completion of the new plant, which opened in 1982.
- In 1980 the previously independent P-9 division merged with the United Food and Service Workers Union (UFSW).
- In the fall of 1984, Hormel announced a 23 percent wage cut from $10.69 to $8.25 per hour "to remain competitive," setting the stage for a strike.
- The company also made cuts, retroactive six months, to health benefits making some workers responsible for the cost of major surgery performed earlier in the year.
- The cutbacks were similar to downsizing efforts by companies nationwide that included lower wages, a reduction in the number of employees, or a complete restructuring to meet economic pressures.

Susan Benson, a member of the Austin United Support Group, on women, community, and the Hormel Strike of 1985–86:

"Austin literally became a one-horse town. Hormel's was the horse that fed it, and it pulled all the strings. We saw it all happen when the strike happened. The loyalties of the town were for Hormel, and the town fathers were standing behind the company. They just wanted those workers to do their job and not moan and groan. They had no idea what the company was doing, and what the company was doing was unbelievable. Hormel counted on that—that people wouldn't believe if the truth were told. And they were right. People said, I can't believe that's happening. So they didn't, and the community didn't support the strike . . . . People were jealous of the Hormel workers. They were the ones that always had the campers, always had the bikes, always had the cars—because it was a good wage. There was almost a sense of vengeance or satisfaction, like meaner, leaner—'Now you're where I've been all these years.'"

"Strikers Huddle with Hormel As 1,500 Apply for Their Jobs," *Chicago Tribune*, January 16, 1986:

"Negotiators representing 1,500 meat packers who have been on strike against the Geo. A. Hormel & Co. plant met with company officials for four hours Wednesday but recessed without reaching a settlement. The strike, the first in more than 50 years at the plant, has torn the city of 22,000 and prompted hundreds of outsiders to apply for the strikers' jobs . . . Hormel vice president David Larson said the company repeated its offer, which he called the most generous in the industry. 'We've gone as far as we can go,' Larson said. 'They're going to take another look . . .'

More than 1,500 people from as far as California and Florida drove into Hormel's Austin complex to the jeers and boos of angry strikers Tuesday and Wednesday to pick up application forms.

But the company said it would not hire any replacements for a couple of weeks, the time needed to process applications. Hormel said the firm hoped enough strikers would return so replacements would not be necessary. The company said about 70 strikers returned this week at its invitation. The union said about 20 went back to work.

The Austin union, meanwhile, laid plans for hundreds of union people to lie down in front of the plant gates to prevent outsiders from entering if they are hired. Local P-9 also plans to send roving pickets to the Hormel plants in Ottumwa, Iowa, and Fremont, Nebraska, if the international union approves, in an effort to close those plants. P-9 officials said they have found food support from the workers in Ottumwa.

Union members were making a base wage of $10.69 an hour when Hormel cut wages by 23 percent to $8.25 an hour in October, 1984, saying the move was needed for the company to stay competitive. Because of the arbitrator's ruling, the base wage had risen to $9.25 an hour when the strike began. P-9 members have twice rejected a federal mediator's proposed contract settlement that would pay $10.00 an hour."

- Other changes included the use of part-time workers, refusal to allow workers the right to sharpen their own knives, and a shifting of the cost of uniforms from the company to the workers.
- Some workers believed the work line was sped up to increase production; injuries at the plant rose.
- On August 17, 1985, 93 percent of the 1,500 members voted to strike.
- It was only the second strike in the company's 50-year history.
- The initial meetings were organized by unionized women workers, who met at a city park, named Todd Park, because the women were not allowed to meet in the union building.
- To gain a national audience for their issues, the union hired Ray Rogers to develop a public relations and fundraising plan for the workers.
- Rogers had successfully coordinated strike campaigns for the Amalgamated Clothing and Textile Workers Union against the J.P. Stevens Company.
- Early strategies, in 1985, included awareness meetings for workers and demonstrations against First Bank, a stockholder in the Hormel Company.
- Strikers, who were demanding a return to $10.00 hourly wages, drew hostile responses from nonstriking, minimum wage workers who were making $3.35 an hour.

- Hog farmers, who had been told for years that Hormel's high union wages prevented the company from paying more for the pigs, were also hostile to the strikers.
- The Chamber of Commerce, which contributed to a strike fund for a meatpacking workers strike in 1948, had taken a strong position against the strikers in 1986.
- The Salvation Army declined to give Christmas baskets to strikers the first year; the second year the strikers received baskets that included Hormel Hams.
- Union support from outside Minnesota provided the striking workers with money and food supplements.
- The utility and phone companies allowed for extended payments from workers while the strike was going on.

"Richard got the BMW and the condo, but at least he didn't get the Kirk Stieff sterling."

◆ KIRK STIEFF
America's Oldest Silversmiths

"Money Managers See Sluggish '86," *Chicago Tribune*, January 17, 1986:

"Two consultants for a major Chicago money management firm predict the nation's economy will limp along at a sluggish growth pace again in 1986 and that the odds of a recession will be increasing by year-end. The economists, who spoke Wednesday at a conference sponsored by Fiduciary Management Associates, also predict that inflation would hold to a moderate pace in 1986.

Gary Shilling, who heads a New York consulting firm bearing his name, said he expects the gross national product "at best" to rise only one to two percent this year after adjustment for inflation, up from an estimated 2.5 percent increase in 1984 and 1985. Shilling said the economy can no longer depend on consumers to spearhead it because they are burdened with a record amount of debt which continues to increase. Consumers, who account for about two-thirds of GNP 'are pretty much at the end of their rope,' Shilling said. He predicted that auto sales will decline while housing sales will remain flat unless mortgage rates drop at least two percentage points during the year."

"Fashion," *American Chronicle*, 1986:

"For young women, the soft, feminine, and casual look remains popular, with even skinnier body-hugging pants and jersey miniskirts and dresses. Denim skirts reach the knee or mid-thigh, and the shorter styles have side or back hem zippers; denim also remains popular in skirts, jackets, and coats . . . Men's shirts are also fashionable, with the shirttails casually knotted in the front. *Out of Africa* safari bush-country styles in twill, khaki, or chino gain in vogue."

1987 NEWS PROFILE

These two workers work for Ford Motor Company, one of the leading automobile manufacturers in the country. In their own words, they present two views of the company.

This Cuban worker was born in 1934, and began working for Ford Motor Company in 1965. He is a check and adjustment person.

"I don't let people at the plant harass me. If they have prejudice, they can keep in their heart. I look for respect, and I give respect. I don't care about nationality, color, or anything. I don't care if you don't like me, as long as you don't tell me to my face. The company pays me to work, not to get harassed. I'm going to do my job, and that's it.

A lot of people in this country don't like it if someone from another country has more than them. But anything you have here, you worked for it. Nobody gave it to you. And I think everyone could have the same if they wanted to.

When I was a kid growing up in Cuba, my dad was in charge of a farm. I went to trade school in the city to learn how to be a mechanic. The mechanics used to argue a lot about what was the best car. I was crazy about Ford. I would say that one day Ford will get ahead of General Motors. That was my dream, and now it has finally happened. I'll always love Ford vehicles. I would rather buy a Toyota than a General Motors car.

After I finished trade school in Cuba, I worked at the Guantanamo naval base. I decided to come to the United States because they were laying off civilians at the base and I was afraid I would get laid off. First I went to Chicago, where my brother works, but I didn't like it there. I moved to the Detroit area and tried to get a job at General Motors' Fisher Body Plant, but they weren't hiring. Finally a friend of mine told my brother he could get me a job at Ford, and he got me an application.

I started at the Michigan Truck Plant in August, 1965, when the plant was just opening up. I was put on the second shift. I had never worked on a line before. It was rough. But I just went to work, and the days started to go by, and then it was no problem. I was a welder in the body shop for seven years before I got into quality control.

My wife works for General Motors, at the Westland Trim Plant. I have a lot of consideration for women who work in the plant. They are working to make a decent living just like us. I respect them just like I respect the men.

If you don't have an education, the only way to make a decent living today is to work in the plant. I made close to $45,000 last year, plus all those fringe benefits. Where can you make that kind of money?

We deserve the money we make. I work hard. I do the best job I can. I'll even miss lunch sometimes if there's a problem. I do that because the quality control manager and the assistant manager give me respect and recognition for what I do. They care a lot about me, and I respect them, too. When I have a problem, I talk to them, and they solve it for me.

It's not like it was 15 years ago. Then, if you went to the plant manager's office for a problem, they would try to get rid of you. Now you can walk into any office and they'll tend to you.

Another example of the new respect in the plant is the program where some hourly employees are given new Bronco trucks to drive home overnight and check for defects. Before, only the supervisors could do that. The hourly employees can discover a lot more problems taking the trucks home because a lot of them have more knowledge than the supervisors. They are the ones fighting the problems every day."

This African-American woman was born in 1952 in Bessmer, Alabama. She came to work for Ford in 1976, hooking up electrical wires on the "final line."

"I wish I didn't have to pay union dues. Ford pays those union people, so they can only do what Ford tells them to do. I don't vote anymore because none of them help you. They're just getting out of running behind those trucks and cars on the line. All they want to do is lay back and smoke their cigarettes and drink their coffee and read their paper and wait for the checks on Friday, while you are out there doing all the damn work.

You don't need a union. What does the union do? Nothing. One time I was sick with the flu, and they wouldn't accept my doctor's excuse. The company-union review board decided they would let it stand on my record. The union people on the review board sit back on their ass and don't do a thing. They never worked on this production line a day in their life and they tell me they can't accept my excuse?

I'm tired of working hard. If I hit the lottery today, I would tell Ford that I appreciate what they did for me, but I don't want to stay there to get 30 years in. If I had to work the rest of my life, I will. But I don't want to.

I have six sisters and four brothers. My mother raised all of us herself. I never met my father until I was 18. We lived in two rooms, a living room and a kitchen. In the kitchen we had a bed, a stove, and an icebox, but no refrigerator. My mother used to pay $0.15 for a big cake of ice from the ice truck. It would last a couple of days. We had a table, but no chairs, so we would stand at the table to eat. There was no bathtub. We had to take baths on the back porch in a tub. In the living room we had a little closet with the toilet in it and a bed on one side and a baby bed. Me, my mother, and my two sisters slept in one bed. Later on my aunt and her boyfriend came to live with us, too.

We didn't even know what a lamp was. We had a socket with an extension cord, and we would screw the bulb in. We would move that socket, and that was our lamp. We used to make a fire when we got up in the morning, all year 'round, that would heat the house, and we'd cook on it.

My family got $150.00 a month from welfare. You weren't allowed to have radio or TV on welfare. But we got surplus cheese, butter, rice, and peanut butter. After my mother started work as a maid and making $20.00 a week, they cut her off welfare. Then it was rough.

Every afternoon, starting in the first grade, I would have to rush home from school. My mother and my two older brothers and one older sister were working, so I would cook dinner. When my mother came home, her kids would be sitting on the porch with their hair combed and clothes clean. Then everyone would eat dinner and clean up. The house was always clean. When my mother had someplace to go at night, I would watch the younger kids.

Food was no problem because my grandmother in Birmingham had a garden and raised chickens. She had pear trees and peach trees. She canned a lot of food. On Saturdays she would go to the grocery store and put groceries for us on the bus, and we would pick them up from the bus driver at the bus stop near our house."

Value of One Dollar	
Year	Value in 2010 USD
1990	$1.67
1992	$1.55
1995	$1.43
1998	$1.34
1999	$1.31
Values are approximate based upon economic historical data and 2010 U. S. Dollar	

1990–1999

The 1990s were called the "Era of Possibilities" by *Fortune* magazine and were dominated by an economic expansion that became the longest in the nation's history. It was characterized by steady growth, low inflation, low unemployment, and dramatic gains in technology-based productivity, especially driven by computers and the emerging Internet.

The decade opened in an economic recession, a ballooning national debt, and the economic hangover of the collapse of much of the savings and loan industry. The automobile industry produced record losses; household names like Bloomingdale's and Pan Am declared bankruptcy. Housing values plummeted and factory orders fell. Media headlines were dominated by issues such as rising drug use, crime in the cities, racial tensions, and the rise of personal bankruptcies. Family values ranked high on the conservative agenda and despite efforts to limit Democrat Bill Clinton to one term as president, the strength of the economy played a critical role in his re-election in 1996.

Guided by Federal Reserve Chair Alan Greenspan's focus on inflation control and Clinton's early efforts to control the federal budget, the U.S. economy soared, producing its best economic indicators in three decades. By 1999 the stock market produced record returns, job creation was at a 10-year high, and the federal deficit was falling. Businesses nationwide hung "Help Wanted" signs outside their doors and even paid signing bonuses to acquire new workers. Crime rates, especially in urban areas, plummeted to levels unseen in three decades, illegitimacy rates fell, and every year business magazines marvelled at the length of the recovery, asking, "can it last another year?"

The stock market set a succession of records throughout the period, attracting thousands of investors to stocks for the first time, including the so-called glamour offerings of high technology companies. From 1990 to the dawn of the 21st century, the Dow Jones Industrial Average rose 318 percent. Growth stocks were the rage; of Standard and Poor's 500 tracked stocks, almost 100 did not pay dividends. This market boom eventually spawned unprecedented new wealth, encouraging early retirement to legions of aging baby boomers. The dramatic change in the cultural structure of corporations continued to threaten the job security of American workers, who had to be more willing to learn new skills, try new jobs, and move from project to project. Profit sharing, which allowed workers to benefit from increased productivity, became more common. Retirement programs and pension plans became more flexible and transferable, serving the needs of a highly mobile work force. The emerging gap of the 1990s was not always between the rich and the poor, but the computer literate and the technically deficient. To symbolize the changing role of women in the work force, cartoon character Blondie, wife of Dagwood Bumstead, opened her own catering business which, like so many small businesses in the 1990s, did extremely well. For the first time, a study of family household income concluded that 55 percent of women provided half or more of the household income.

In a media-obsession decade, the star attraction was the long-running scandal of President Bill Clinton and his affair with a White House intern. At its climax, while American forces were attacking Iraq, the full House of Representatives voted to impeach the president. For only the second time in American history, the Senate conducted an impeachment hearing before voting to acquit the president of perjury and obstruction of justice.

During the decade, America debated limiting abortion, strengthening punishment for criminals, replacing welfare to work, the ending of Affirmative Action, dissolving bilingual education, elevating educational standards, curtailing the rights of legal immigrants, and imposing warnings on unsuitable material for children on the Internet. Nationwide an estimated 15 million people, including smokers, cross-dressers, alcoholics, sexual compulsives, and gamblers attended weekly self-help support groups; dieting becomes a $33 billion industry as Americans struggled with obesity.

The impact of the GI Bill's focus on education, rooted in the decade following World War II, flowered in the generation that followed. The number of adult Americans with a four-year college education rose from 6.2 percent in 1950 to 24 percent in 1997. Despite this impressive rise, the need for a more educated population and the rapidly rising expectations of the technology sector, the century ended with a perception that the decline in public education was one of the most pressing problems of the decade. Throughout the decade school violence escalated, capturing headlines year after year in widely dispersed locations across the nation.

The 90s give birth to $150.00 tennis shoes, condom boutiques, pre-ripped jeans, Motorola 7.7-ounce cellular telephones, rollerblading, TV home shopping, the Java computer language, digital cameras, DVD players, and Internet shopping. And in fashion a revival of the 1960s styling brought back miniskirts, pop art prints, pants suits, and the A-line. Black became a color worn at any time of day and for every purpose. The increasing role of consumer debt in driving the American economy also produced an increase in personal bankruptcy and a reduction in the overall savings rate. At the same time, mortgage interest rates hit 30-year lows during the decade, creating refinancing booms that pumped millions of dollars into the economy, further fueling a decade of consumerism.

1994 News Profile

The single mother emerged in the later part of the 20th century as the new poor, or as one author said, the "feminization of poverty." Marilyn is the divorced mother of two teenagers and a young boy with mental problems. She left school after completing the 10th grade and has worked a variety of jobs ever since.

"I worked for four years in a foundry. They made anything from cast-iron doorstops to manhole covers. It's good money. I made $8.45 an hour and I went from $7.02 to $8.45 in three months. That's good money. Normally I would work from three in the afternoon until midnight. But sometimes you had to work a lot more. It is non-union so you have to do it. Many times we worked from one in the afternoon until three in the morning. And that was six days a week.

I worked on the sorting line. You had to break castings off the molds. Like, if it's a barbell, we made barbells, you pick the weight up, slam on the side of the line to break the mold casting off. You take an air gun, sort of like a dentist's drill with a sander on it, and sand the barbell down smooth. Then you take it over and slide it down a chute. I would do like three or four of these a minute. That would be hard, lifting all night. I got tendinitis in both of my arms.

There are about five people on the sorting line. It's very noisy and very dirty. You have to take a shower before you leave there. It's black sand and oil, pieces of cast-iron metal. You get it in your hair. You are all black. You look like you came out of the coal mine.

They really don't train you. You just put your ear cuffs on, you wear your safety glasses and steel-tip shoes, and go down the stairs. I had a super boss. His boss would come out and yell at him. Then he would come and say, 'Hey, look, you did this wrong but I am supposed to really yell at you, so bear with me.' Then he would scream at the top of his lungs at you, so the big guys would understand that he was yelling at you. Then he would say, 'I'm sorry I had to do that.'

You get two 15-minute breaks and 35 minutes for lunch. They shut down two weeks in the summer. Once you've been there a year, you get paid one week, and the other you don't get paid. After five years you get a whole whopping two weeks. That's still during the shutdown weeks.

I don't know if I could have gone any further. You work there. That's it. That's as far as you go. After five or six months you might get a quarter raise. But I started to get more raises, almost up to $2.80 through my work. I probably would have worked my way up, probably to the weighing scale. They bring the parts over, you weigh them, and that's how they can determine how many parts are in or how many parts are missing."

1995 FAMILY PROFILE

Paula Langone, a single, White schoolteacher from Omaha, Nebraska, lives in New York City, where she teaches in the south Bronx, one of the poorest sections of the city; her life revolves around her students.

Annual Income: $27,000

Annual Budget

Clothing. $600.00
Educational Expenses $4,500.00
Electricity. $288.00
Food $6,200.00
Food away from Home. $600.00
Heat. $0.00
Intercity Transportation. $1,250.00
Personal Care $250.00
Rent $5,780.00
School Supplies $1,000.00
Telephone $960.00
Transportation $1,200.00

Life at Home

- For the past three years, Paula has been living in the Italian Williamsburg section of Brooklyn, New York.
- Her apartment, which sits right on the street, was built at the turn of the century to house immigrant dock workers.
- Later the building became a prosperous bar and brothel.

- Paula's third-floor, 900-square-foot apartment was created by combining two rooms.
- The apartment includes a living room, bedroom, kitchen, and bathroom.
- The bathroom was added in the 1940s when outhouses were removed from the area; the space occupied by the toilet and bathtub was once a closet. There is no room for a sink, so she washes her long hair in the kitchen sink.
- Heat, the cost of which is included in the $480.00 monthly rent, is provided by steam radiators, which can be very noisy.
- Paula lives with her cat and hundreds of books, most concerning teaching, education, or art—her first love.
- The television set is eight years old and stays unplugged.
- Her food expenses include eating at a deli twice a week near Columbia Teacher's College, where she is working on her master's degree in education.
- Her food consists of vegetables from the Korean market, rice, pasta, and chicken; she spends $4.00 a week on cat food.
- Pork, beef, and fish are generally prepared and eaten only on special occasions.
- A pack-a-day smoker, her tobacco bill runs $18.00 a week; she also occasionally buys beer and wine.
- She does not own a car, but she rides the subway to work and home every day and twice a week to night classes at Columbia Teacher's College; she receives some scholarship money to attend the school.
- The subway stop is three blocks from her apartment; she does not hesitate to ride the subway late at night by herself.
- Paula is currently building her teacher wardrobe; a friend in Omaha, Nebraska, who works at a major department store puts away clothing for her all year; she spends $600.00 on clothing that would have cost twice that in New York City.
- During her flight across country to Nebraska to see her parents, she buys the clothes her friend has collected for her; she normally spends a total of $1,200 on trips out West.

- The bulk of her discretionary money goes to buy supplies for her classroom; the $125.00 "teacher's choice" supply allowance covers about one-third of her needs. In addition she buys books and magazines for her use in the classroom.
- School supply buying trips include a visit to the New York City Library where she buys used paperback books for $0.25 and hardbacks for $0.50; friends often donate art supplies and magazines for her use in the classroom.
- Her personal care budget includes perfume and normal toiletries; she does her own hair.
- On major holidays such as Easter, Christmas, and summer she escapes the city by travelling to a monastery in upstate New York where her uncle is a monk.
- On Thanksgiving she often sleeps late and eats Chinese takeout.

Life at Work: Education

- Her fifth grade class in the south Bronx includes 20 children.
- Approximately 40 percent are African-American and 60 percent are Spanish, mostly from Puerto Rico.
- She earnestly believes, "If I can help them, I can save the world."
- She now believes that she has been called to be a teacher of the disadvantaged.
- The parents of more than half the class are on welfare. Most have been in the United States all of their lives, as few new immigrants are moving into the area.
- Three of the 20 children have both a mother and father in the home.

- The school where she teaches was built in 1960 with sleek, modern lines; the janitorial service has worked hard to maintain the facilities despite declining funds.
- Most of her children have serious deficiencies in reading and English, since many speak only Spanish at home.
- Paula often buys with her own money hands-on materials, such as puzzles, to help the children with their reading skills.
- Typically the children are closer to their expected age group in math.
- The school provides both breakfast and lunch; for most of the children in her class these meals are important because they guarantee the children will eat, and are often the biggest meals of the day for them.
- A typical day includes reading, writing exercises, diagramming of sentences, and extensive work with grammar and math through applied science exercises.
- The class also takes a field trip once a month to art museums, zoos, the ballet, and parks.
- In the spring much of the school curriculum revolves around teaching for the annual city and state tests that measure performance and determine funding.
- Test scores are declining; Paula believes it is a "forgotten school."
- Currently, the increasing use of crack is invading her classroom; children come to school exhausted because their parents have gotten and stayed high the night before.
- Some of her best students have the most isolated lives, she says.
- To protect their children from gangs and drugs, parents keep the children inside on weekends, often renting three or four movie videos on Friday afternoon and watching them continuously until Sunday evening.
- Many of the children do attend church on weekends, especially Jehovah's Witness and fundamental Baptist; many of the Spanish families were once Catholic.
- By her own description Paula fell into teaching backwards after two decades in theater and set design.
- Originally from Omaha, Nebraska, while attending an all girl's Catholic high school, her life revolved around the community theater where she both acted and worked in the make-up crew.
- After attending colleges in Nebraska, Florida, and New York, she went to work in theater in 1978.
- She worked primarily in set design and finally left at age 38 to begin substitute teaching in 1991 because "I didn't want to paint scenery anymore."

"Education Transfers and Stops—Public Schools Are Struggling with High Student Turnover," *The New York Times*, March 1995:

"It is March, and Marie Pompeo-Melone, the nurse at Public School 8, is still registering new students—25 in the first eight days of the month alone.

The students keep coming, but the seams of the school do not burst because others are leaving just as fast. In 1993, the school had a mobility rate of 89 percent according to the Education Department, meaning that 89 percent of the children spend part of the year elsewhere. Ms. Pompeo-Melone's file cabinets are crammed with their transfer papers, and her head swims with their faces and names.

'I can't tell you the last time there was a day when I had no transfers,' Ms. Pompeo-Melone said. 'It's just all the time. Words cannot describe how mobile it's become.'

P.S. 8 is not alone. Throughout the county, especially in poor areas, schools are struggling with student turnover rates of 70, 80, and 90 percent. A 1994 report by the General Accounting Office found that nationwide, 17 percent of third graders had attended three or more schools since first grade. At many urban schools, that third-grade percentage is often double.

The consequences can be troubling for both schools and students. Children who move often are more likely to fail a grade and have behavioral problems than those who do not, according to a 1993 study published in *The Journal of the American Medical Association*. 'Even a short move is often stressful,' said David Wood, an author of the study and a pediatrician at Cedars-Sinai Medical Center in Los Angeles.

Lillian Soto was in first grade in Puerto Rico, split the second grade between schools in Hoboken and Jersey City, attended P.S. 8 for third, fourth, and fifth grades, transferred to another Jersey City school for sixth grade and now, as an eighth grader, is back at P.S. 8. Lillian said she did not know why her family had moved so much. But recently, she said, her mother has been thinking about returning to Puerto Rico. Lillian, 13, said her brothers all wanted to go. But she will resist.

'She didn't want to let me finish the eighth grade,' she said. 'I don't want to keep moving to different places. I'm tired already.'

The question, educational experts say, is this: Can any effort to improve public schools succeed if the schoolhouse door is a turnstile?

'Do we really have a prayer of educating these kids?' said L. Scott Miller, author of a study of student mobility, for the Council for Aid to Education. 'I say no.'

Education experts say they have only started examining the problem in recent years, and as a result there are few data, making it difficult to know if the mobility rate is growing worse. But at P.S. 8, the teachers have no doubt.

'Years ago I could see a little kid in the first grade and that kid was here at graduation,' said Linda Herman, who has taught at P.S. 8 for 30 years. 'That was most. Now it's a handful. Everything has just changed so.'

For some families, moving means enhanced fortunes as a parent takes a better job or buys a larger home. But among the nation's most transient families, it is often poverty and its complications that lead to a change in address. A parent loses a job and is evicted. An unemployed mother bounces from the house of one relative to another. An immigrant gives up on his dreams and returns to his homeland.

Poor families move twice as often as those that are not poor, according to a report by the Bureau of the Census. A study by the Council for the Aid to Education linked frequent moving to unemployment, immigrant status, the shortage of low-income housing and problems like drug use, violence, and child neglect.

'Mobility is both a cause and a symptom,' said Mr. Miller, author of the study."

Life in the Community: New York City

- The two most secure institutions in the south Bronx community are the police station and the school; the community includes few banks, grocery stores, or movie houses.
- Most services available within the community are more expensive than those in other sections of New York; many of the families have cars, often nice cars.

HISTORICAL SNAPSHOT
1995–1996

- Chevron settled harassment charges concerning offensive jokes and comments for $2.2 million
- Michael Jordan left baseball, returning to professional basketball
- The longest Major League Baseball strike in history, 234 days, ended
- The Supreme Court ruled that only a constitutional amendment can enforce term limits on Congress
- 40,000 African-American men met in Washington, D.C.
- 25 percent of Americans continued to smoke cigarettes despite health warnings
- The Dow Jones Industrial Average peaked at 5,216; unemployment was at 5.6 percent
- The pushup bra gained enormous popularity
- Casual Fridays were introduced at the workplace
- After 130 years, Mississippi lawmakers ratified the 13th Amendment abolishing slavery
- The nation was divided over the not guilty verdict for O.J. Simpson, accused of killing his wife; polls indicated that 65 percent of Whites believed he was guilty, while 65 percent of Blacks thought he was innocent
- The FBI reported another sharp decline in crime rates
- President Bill Clinton's approval rating surpassed 50 percent for the first time
- About 55 percent of women provided half or more of household income
- The Centers for Disease Control reported a leveling-off of teen sexual activity; 52.8 percent used condoms
- New York became the 38th state to reinstate capital punishment
- For the first time, Ford sold more trucks than cars; demand for light trucks, like minivans and sports utility vehicles, increased in urban and rural areas
- Mars released a blue M&M candy for the first time
- The Minnesota Aid Project for Condoms advertised: "When you give the gift of love, make sure it's wrapped properly."
- The 25th anniversary of Earth Day was celebrated
- Dow Corning declared bankruptcy after failure of its silicone breast device

1995 ECONOMIC PROFILE

Income, Standard Jobs

Bituminous Coal Mining	$42,711.00
Building Trades	$28,465.00
Domestics	$10,854.00
Farm Labor	$15,863.00
Finance, Insurance, and Real Estate	$38,577.00
Gas, Electricity, and Sanitation Workers	$38,936.00
Manufacturing, Durable Goods	$28,507.00
Manufacturing, Nondurable Goods	$24,387.00
Medical/Health Services Workers	$21,234.00
Miscellaneous Manufacturing	$21,798.00
Motion Picture Services	$39,585.00
Nonprofit Organization Workers	$15,016.00
Passenger Transportation Workers, Local and Highway	$18,525.00
Postal Employees	$35,797.00
Public School Teachers	$27,130.00
Radio Broadcasting and Television Workers	$32,223.00
Railroads	$42,175.00
State and Local Government Workers	$29,023.00
Telephone and Telegraph Workers	$35,844.00
Wholesale and Retail Trade Workers	$14,412.00

Selected Prices

Bridgestone High Performance 65 HR Tire	$85.00
Cashmere-Blend Jacket	$69.99
Crest Gel Tartar Control Toothpaste, 6.4 Ounces	$2.00
Disney's *Lion King* Video	$29.97
Everyday Battery, D-Size, Two-Pack	$6.00
Hotel Room at The Talbot Hotel	$160.00
Kirium Chronometer Men's Watch	$1,695.00
Lubriderm Lotion, 16 Ounces	$7.00
Pink/White Lily Flowering Tulip Bulbs, 100	$43.00
Rand Barbie 12" Girl's Bicycle	$49.97

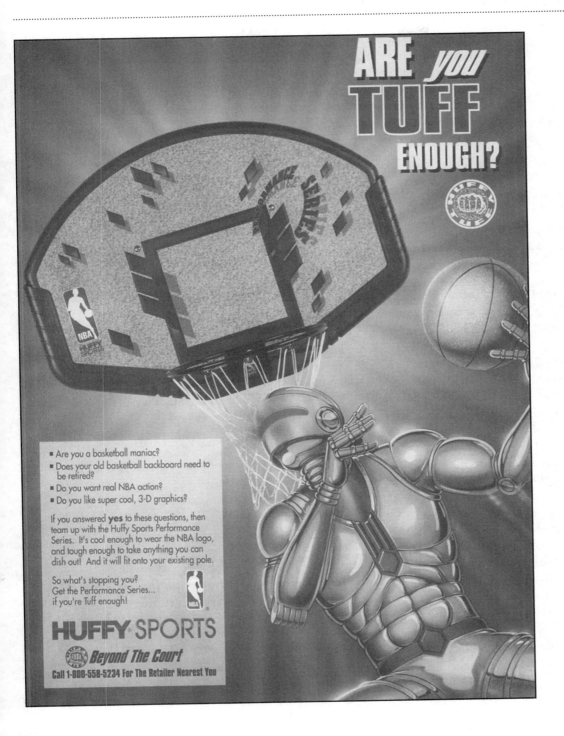

Robitussin DM Cough
Suppressant, Four Ounces. $3.00
Secret Deodorant, 1.7 Ounces $1.50
Sierra Four-Piece Setting; Bakelite
Handles $40.00
Sofa, Green Stripe Cover. $999.00

SOLO Radar and Laser
    Cordless Detector $199.00
Ultra-Downy, 20 Ounces $2.00
Variflex Rollerblades $34.97
Wing Chair, Floral Cover $699.00
Zenith 19" Color Television $139.00
Zinsser's Blend & Glaze
    Decorative Paint, Gallon $25.00

"Despite Higher Rates, Miles Wear on Trucker," *The New York Times:*

"Charles Holman had no time to clean out the mud and the dung from his livestock trailer because he had to drive 760 miles after delivering a truckload of cattle in Colorado the day before.

Now, on a west Texas ranch, he was coaxing and prodding 111 terrified calves into the trailer, a double-decker aluminum labyrinth of cramped compartments.

They kicked, they scrambled, they bellowed. They added to the malodorous mess and they splattered it on his jeans, his shirt, and his face.

To stomp around in this slop day after day 'you've got to have diesel fuel for blood,' Mr. Holman said, 'and manure for brains.'

An an independent trucker with his own rig, he also has to have the financial savvy of a corporate treasurer to turn a profit when the industry he depends on—ranching—is in a slump.

Judged by one important number, his business is picking up. Mr. Holman managed to negotiate a nine percent increase in his rates this year, to $2.40 a loaded mile from $2.20. That's three times the three percent consumer price inflation rate that most economists are predicting for the United States for all of 1995.

But Mr. Holman is not celebrating. For one thing, his bottom line still looks pretty weak. He says his income this year—after expenses but before taxes—from the truck he operates and a second trailer that he rents out will total

$18,000 at most. And if ranchers keep cutting back their herds, he adds, he might have to go out hustling for business again. 'I read where the economy is getting better every day,' he said. 'But live in a farming and ranch area. It doesn't look like it's getting better here.'

The biggest threat to his prosperity at the moment, though, probably isn't economic uncertainty. It is his age. At 56, he can still bound up into his cab without a grunt and, brandishing his yellow electric prod, can still let the cattle know who's boss. But his beard has turned white and he is less willing to sleep in an upholstered sleeping compartment instead of at home with his wife in Childress, in the Texas panhandle. After almost four decades of driving, he said, 'The old miles just kind of wear me down.'

As he drives less, with the gross income from his truck falling to a projected $70,000 this year, from $102,000 in 1994, Mr. Holman is taking no chances. Instead of buying a shiny new rig, he has stayed with a 1985 Autocar that he found for $30,000 in 1990, less than half the original price. It has now been driven 1.2 million miles.

His son got a nearly new truck last year just by agreeing to assume someone else's payments. After five months, Mr. Holman recounts, the bank had the truck and his son was calling him for leads on a new job."

Time Magazine, December 21, 1998:

"The story was a headshaker. Ruth Sherman, a White Brooklyn, New York, elementary school teacher, assigned her class a book called *Nappy Hair*, about a little girl's proud acceptance of her coily mane, in order to bolster the self-esteem of her Black and Latino charges. But some parents, after seeing only a few photocopied pages, assumed the book was a racist put-down and essentially ran Sherman out of the school. Most New Yorkers were torn between amazement at the brouhaha and pity for the children, who have lost a good teacher. But for Trevelyn Jones, book-review editor of the *School Library Journal*, the real surprise was that the book made it into Sherman's classroom at all. 'Many teachers find it easier to stick with the tried and true,' she says. 'That Sherman even knew about this book is unusual.'

Reading, so we're told, is fundamental to a child's education. But trying to get good books—not just the classics but also worthy contemporary works—into young hands is increasingly providing a pit of problems. Spotty teacher training, lack of library assistance (if not lack of libraries themselves), and fear of controversy all help push teachers toward outdated or bland book choices. Those who fight back with verve risk being drummed out of a job or even chased into court . . .

. . . According to the National Children's Book and Literacy Alliance (N.C.B.L.A.), 48 states don't require children's literature training for state certification. What's more, the budget cuts of the 1980s left a quarter of all American schools without libraries and many of those remaining are manned by untrained volunteers."

Economics and Education

- Income is not the sole determinant of how children turn out, but many believe parental income is the single most important influence on a child's chances.
- Poor children weigh less than rich children at birth and die more often in their first year of life.
- When they enter school, poor children score lower on standardized tests.
- Poor children are absent more often from school and have more behavior problems.
- Poor teenagers are more likely than teenagers of affluent families to have a baby, drop out of school, and get in trouble with the law.
- Children raised in poverty are more likely to end up poor and in need of public assistance.
- From the Great Depression to the 1970s, U.S. policy was dominated by the theory that income support can cure many of the problems of poor children.
- Prior to the Great Depression, poverty was viewed as a sign of weak character.
- Aid to families with dependent children grew from 3.1 million families in 1960 to 6.1 million in 1969.

"To End Pog Fights, Schools Ban Game," *The New York Times,* **March 22, 1995:**

"Schools around the country are finding that it is easier to ban Pogs, the Hawaiian disk game that is supplanting children's pastimes like marbles, than to spend hours straightening out school-yard fights.

In Wormleysburg, Pennsylvania, the raucous recess game is no longer permitted. 'We have to put them away or we get sent to the principal's office,' said Laura Arter, 10.

'Pogs is often played for keeps, with the winners taking home the pog disks as spoils, a situation ripe for conflicts,' said Mary Larcome, a fourth-grade teacher in Haverhill, Massachusetts. 'It takes away from your teaching time when you're trying to settle the problems,' she said.

The game has also been discouraged or banned in schools from Windham, New Hampshire, to Spokane, Washington.

There are various ways to play Pogs, also known as 'milk caps,' but generally each player has some of the waferlike cardboard disks and a heavier disk, usually made of plastic, called a 'slammer.' The disks are stacked and a player throws the slammer on them; in one version of the game, he keeps all the ones that flip over.

Pogs started taking off in Hawaii in 1992. The name comes from the abbreviation on the caps of a popular Hawaiian drink containing passion fruit, orange, and guava juice.

The game is now a multimillion-dollar industry, with fancier caps that carry designs like cartoon and movie characters. The disks cost from a few pennies to about $7.00.

At Thompson Middle School in St. Charles, Illinois, 'they became a pretty hot item to steal as well as the cause of arguments,' said Kurt Anderson, the principal. 'We just ask the kids not to bring them.'"

AMANDA BURNS

MANDA BURNS HOLDS A MARBLE called a shooter in the curl of her right index finger. She "knuckles down" by placing the knuckles of her right hand just outside a 10-foot circle. In the middle of the circle are 13 marbles set in the shape of a cross.

"The idea is to knock a marble out of the circle," says Amanda, the 1993 girls' national marbles champion. "If you knock a marble out and your shooter stays in, you get another shot."

Amanda flicks her shooter into the circle. *Whack!* A marble skips out of the ring.

Amanda is playing "ringer." The first person to knock seven marbles out of the ring wins.

Amanda has played marbles since age 10.

"I don't know if I'm going to play in any more tournaments," she says. "I'm sort of afraid to play. I'm the champion now, but if somebody beats me, then I'm not the champ anymore."

AGE: 13 **GRADE:** 7th
HOMETOWN: Moss, Tennessee
OTHER SPORT: Basketball
FAVORITE TEAM: Dallas Cowboys
PETS: "I have 10 cows and five goats. I'm lookin' to get me another goat."
SOMEDAY: "I want to go to college and then live on a farm in Tennessee."

AMANDA "KNUCKLED DOWN" TO WIN THE NATIONAL CHAMPIONSHIP IN MARBLES

What Money Can't Buy, Family Income and Children's Life Changes:

"An assistant principal in a school in which nearly all the students are economically disadvantaged described it this way: 'A lot of time the parents want to have expectations for their kids. But they think it doesn't do any good to have expectations if you don't think it's ever going to be in the reach of the child. So they don't follow through. Lack of hope. That is one of the most profound things. Simply the lack of hope. You take most of the parents that we work with and they would like to hope that their child will go to college, but they don't really see a way that they are going to make that happen.'"

"A Happier Twist on Housing:
From Bad Landlords to Co-ops,"
The New York Times, September 17, 1995:

"When Robert Santiago moved into his apartment on Division Avenue in Williamsburg 20 years ago, it had no boiler, no heat, and few tenants, and the landlord did not pay property taxes. The city took over the building in the mid-1980s.

Now, Mr. Santiago and the other tenants won the building: They bought it four years ago from the city for $250.00 an apartment to form a co-op. Every month, they meet to pay bills and discuss repairs. 'When I came here, it was the *Twilight Zone*,' said Mr. Santiago, 38. 'I can sleep now. I couldn't sleep before.'

Weighed down by the costs of maintaining buildings it has seized, the city has increased its efforts to sell them—to private landlords, non-profit groups, and tenant co-ops. And a survey released last week indicates that, among Brooklyn residents in current and former city-owned housing, tenant co-ops are by far the most popular. The co-ops scored highest in terms of services like heat and hot water, management, and safety; city-owned units came out last. The city owns 2,885 occupied buildings seized for tax delinquency, 1,054 of them in Brooklyn.

The survey, sponsored by a group of housing organizations, polled 3,000 residents in 500 Brooklyn buildings.

Deborah C. Wright, Commissioner of the Department of Housing Preservation and Development, which oversees city-owned housing, said that when the city sells a building, tenants are given the option to form co-ops. But 60 percent of the residents must agree to do so and must take classes in management, budgets, and repairs. 'Some people are highly motivated and want to own and take responsibility for every aspect of their buildings,' she said. 'Other people just want to rent.'

Ms. Wright said that she thought the survey's conclusions did not reflect recent changes in housing programs under the Giuliani administration. 'The one thing we agree on 100 percent is that the city is the worst landlord in the city,' she said.

Standing in a newly painted hallway of his tenant co-op on Division Avenue, Santana Rosendo said taking on the responsibility was worth the effort. 'Everyone owns their apartment,' said Mr. Rosendo, 74. 'Everything is better because it is our own.'"

1998 Family Profile

The lives of Mike and Helen Howard, who are in their late 50s, changed seven years ago when she was in a serious automobile accident two weeks before Christmas. She has been an invalid ever since. For 35 years he had been a printer and was forced to decide between caring for his wife or continuing to work. The cost of her care is rapidly eating into their savings.

Annual Income: $75,000

Mike makes $15,000 a year working for a Boy's Home near his house; the remainder of the income is produced by investments from Helen's retirement funds, their savings, and the proceeds of a legal settlement against the automobile manufacturer.

Annual Budget

Automobile	$9,600.00
Electricity	$2,200.00
Food at Home	$6,500.00
Food away from Home	$3,600.00
Housing	$8,400.00
Medical Care	$47,000.00
Medicine	$6,100.00
Personal Care	$2,800.00

Life at Home

- They live in an attractive, compact 1,200-square-foot house they designed themselves outside Rock Hill, South Carolina; the entire house has been renovated to accommodate a wheelchair.
- They live seven miles from town on four acres of property, which she inherited from her mother.

- Both were married before, and each have two sons.
- Six years ago, while on the way to work, she was severely injured when her car skidded on a wet road only one mile from their house.
- Following the accident she was in a coma for seven months in another city; Mike visited her seven days a week, twice a day, travelling one hour each way even though she did not recognize him.
- Helen's 24-hour care is provided by two nurses and her husband; the cost of nursing care is normally $800.00 a week—more if he leaves town for the weekend.
- Today she is unable to feed or dress herself; intermittently she will engage in witty conversation for short periods, but most of the time she sleeps or declines to communicate.
- Her ability to communicate and recognize her surroundings varies widely from day to day; even on good days her speech is difficult to understand.

- Friends often come to the lake on Sunday afternoons to fish, drink beer, and socialize; one of the friends supplied most of the metal foundation for the dock, while another did the electrical wiring so that lights would be available.
- The special diet required by her condition elevates the food bill to more than $100 a week.
- Her diapers cost $17.00 a pack; typically she requires three packs a week.
- Her routine medication costs approximately $100.00 a month even though they have excellent insurance coverage.
- Her company's insurance has covered many of the medical bills, but money is often tight.
- The cost of around-the-clock nursing care equals three times his annual pay.

- She sees a doctor at least once a month and has been in and out of the hospital throughout the past six years for severe headaches, infections, and bladder disorders.
- Insurance and the proceeds of a legal settlement with the automobile manufacturer have allowed them to provide her with excellent care and to avoid bankruptcy.
- Because his wife often sleeps for long periods, Mike works on projects around the property; he is now restoring a 1926 farm tractor he bought for $300.00, and has also built a dock on the small lake on their property so Helen can sit by the water.

- He has also planted large numbers of roses on the side of the house facing her bedroom window.
- For more than a year, he spent all of his time caring for his wife and redoing their home, including installing a bathroom capable of accepting a wheelchair.
- He is finally realizing that she will never be better.
- They have purchased a special van, which is specially fitted for her disabilities, so she can travel around the community comfortably; it cost $40,000 to equip.
- Before the accident they spent weekends travelling to antique shows and markets; he bought and sold old bottles, while she looked for decorative pottery.
- Mike's collecting interests include 150-year-old bitters bottles made in the shape of Indian squaws, an ear of corn, or log cabins.
- Occasionally he still attends antique shows but rarely buys anything; he has lost much of his interest in fine antique bottles.

Life at Work: Printing and the Boy's Home

- Before the accident, he had worked as a printer for 35 years, operating sophisticated, four-color printing presses, as well as supervising regular black and white print runs.

He collects 150-year-old bitters bottles.

- He often went to work at 4 a.m. to meet deadlines or worked late at night; he was allowed to set his own schedule as long as deadlines were met.
- Three years ago, the company consolidated its operations in another city, and he was offered a job in the new location but declined.
- To fill his time, he now works as a facilities supervisor at a Boy's Home near his house doing maintenance and helping the boys; the hours are flexible and management is supportive of his situation.
- He sees himself in many of the unfocused young men who are sent to the home; most repairs and construction projects are designed to include assistance from the boys.
- The 14 boys living in the home have all been expelled from school at least once before coming here and most were sentenced by the courts to a home; most of the boys believe they have no future and act accordingly.
- The Boy's Home is now making plans to create a regular school for the boys in the home; most find themselves expelled from the Rock Hill schools shortly after coming to the home.
- Thanks to friends willing to serve as volunteer teachers, Mike is now conducting classes in refrigerator repair and auto mechanics.

Life in the Community: Rock Hill, South Carolina

- Mike has lived in Rock Hill his entire life, accumulating many friends.
- His mother still lives nearby, although she is not in good health.
- The members of the American Veterans of Foreign Wars have been very supportive; this family has attended several dances at the VFW and danced despite the limited use of Helen's legs.
- He served in the navy when only 17 years old, earning his place in the VFW while in a combat zone near Lebanon in the 1950s; he was stationed on a mine sweeper.
- Historically, Rock Hill was a textile town dominated by a few industries; textile villages, composed of hundreds of small houses, dominated the community.

What's it take to be a millionaire in the year 2000?

"According to *Millionaire Magazine*, a million dollars in pre-Depression 1920 was worth the equivalent of $8.3 million today; $1 million during the postwar boom in 1950 was worth $6.9 million and even in 1970, $1 million was worth 4.3 times what it is now. In 1996, the last year for which figures are available, the Internal Revenue Service handled 110,912 tax forms for people who made more than $1 million that year."

- The city is proud of Winthrop University, originally established as a teacher's college, which is in the center of town.
- The largest garden in Rock Hill is the Glencairn Garden, opened by its owner, who donated the six-acre park after planting hundreds of azaleas, camellias, and other southern favorites.
- The city of Rock Hill is fast becoming a suburb of the rapidly growing city of Charlotte, North Carolina.

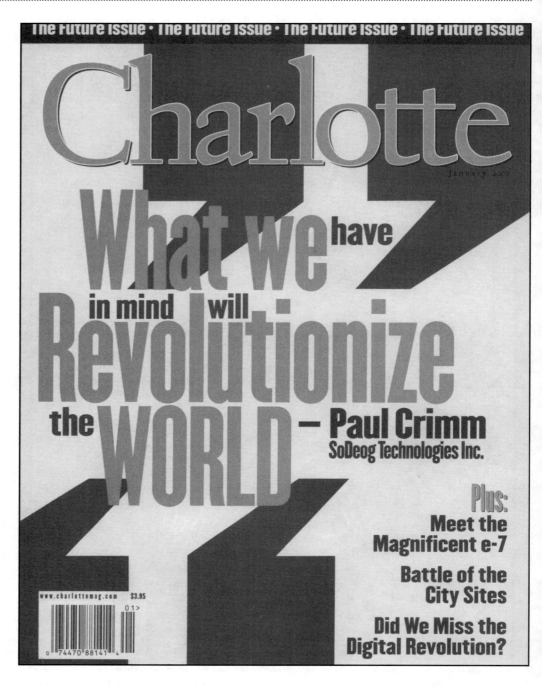

- Through a series of mergers, two of the banks headquartered in Charlotte are now among the 10 largest in the nation; between them they employ 20,000 people in Charlotte.
- IBM, Microsoft, and other major corporations have established facilities in Charlotte, drawing workers from a 10-county region, including Rock Hill.
- Every morning more than 22,000 Rock Hill residents travel north on Interstate 77 for jobs in Charlotte; the roads are often jammed.

HISTORICAL SNAPSHOT
1998

- The Dow Jones reached 9,374, inflation only 1.6 percent

- The undergraduate tuition/room and board at Harvard reached $22,802/$7,278

- President Bill Clinton was impeached

- *Gotham: A History of New York to 1898* by Edwin G. Burrows won the Pulitzer Prize for U.S. History

- The number of welfare recipients dropped below four percent, the lowest in 25 years; unemployment, interest rates, murders, juvenile arrests, births to unwed mothers, infant mortality, and gas prices fell to 25 to 35 year lows

- Government-measured rates of obesity targeted 50 percent of the population

- Biotechnological stocks showed long anticipated potential, increasing 44 percent for the year

- Professional basketball players were locked out by owners

- Major efforts were begun to avert a catastrophic "Y2K" blackout when computers may misread the year 2000 as 1900

- The South Carolina legislature approved a constitutional amendment to remove from the state constitution a 103-year-old paragraph that made marriages between Blacks and Whites illegal

- The IRS Reform Bill shifted the burden of proof from the taxpayer to the IRS

- 17 major newspapers called for President Bill Clinton's resignation after he admitted a sexual relationship with a White House intern

- *Titanic* was the highest grossing film in history at $850 million

- Tobacco companies made a $260 billion settlement with states for smoking-related illnesses

1998 ECONOMIC PROFILE

Selected Prices

Amaretti Soft Almond Cookies
in Tin $18.00
Answering Machine, Bank &
Olufsen Beotalk 1100 . . . . $250.00
Bath Towel, 100 Percent Cotton
Long Terry Loop $24.00
Belt, Fine-Grained Italian
Leather $42.00
Canon Camera, 35 mm with
Eye Control $1,900.00
Epson Stylus Color Printer $279.00
Field Jacket, Cotton Canvas with
Corduroy Collar $69.50
Flannel Pants by Diane Richard $28.00
Geometrics from Pakistan Rug,
9'1" x 12'1" $2,458.00
Ladderback Chair, Walnut
Construction $195.00
Leather Chart Case,
Willis & Geiger $470.00
Loafers of Flexible Nappa Leather $68.00
Mr. Potato Head Coin Bank $19.95
Olive Oil in a Hand-Etched
Glass Decanter, 23 Ounces. $32.00
Palm III Electronic Organizer $369.00
Pulsar Solar Watch, Man's $215.00
Sterling Silver Ring with Cubic
Zieconia, Woman's $40.00
Turtleneck Underwear, Pure Silk. $32.50
Viansa, 1997 Sauvignon Blanc $12.00
Volvo S70 Sedan, New. $26,895.00

The Price of Living

Pound of Bananas
1980 . . . . $0.38
1990 . . . . $0.61
1997 . . . . $0.54

Carton of Cigarettes
1980 . . . . $4.01
1990 . . . . $11.09
1997 . . . . $14.04

Monthly Mortgage
(for 1,800-Square-Foot Home)
1980 . . . . $527.00

"Good Times Mask Concerns about Financing Retirement, College," *The Charlotte Observer*, March 7, 1998:

"David Wheat is only 13 months old. But already his parents, Steve and Mary, worry about how they'll be able to send him to college. It's a common concern. College costs seem so high that many parents don't attempt to save for college, experts say. The average for a year's tuition and fees at public universities is $3,111, and $13,664 at private schools. By the time David Wheat is college-age, that's expected to more than double, according to the American Association of State Colleges and Universities. In a recent poll, *Money* magazine found that 47 percent of parents who expect to attempt college said they hadn't saved any money to cover the costs. Six months before David was born, the Wheats set up a college savings fund. But they want to buy a house. David was born three months premature, so there are still hospital bills. There are also payments for the new car. 'Paying for college is always in the back of my mind,' Steve Wheat says. 'We're not going to be able to afford Harvard or nothing . . . I'd like for him to go to the best place he could, but it will probably be the best place we can afford.'"

"How to Clone a Herd," *Time Magazine*, December 21, 1998:

"First there was Dolly the Scottish sheep. Then, last July, came several litters of cloned mice. Now scientists at Japan's Kinki University have produced something even bigger and a good deal tastier: eight identical calves cloned from a single cow.

Writing in last week's issue of *Science*, the Japanese researchers report that they achieved this feat of bovine photocopying using two different types of cells, taken from a single cow's ovaries and fallopian tubes. Those cells—all carrying the same genetic payload—were introduced into cow ova whose genes had been scooped away. Ten such identical embryos were then implanted in the wombs of surrogate cow mothers, and all but two came to term.

No one knows why the Kinki team managed to bat .800 (while Dolly's creators needed 29 embryos to get one hit). Japanese scientists hope to learn more when other calves—cloned from liver, kidney, and heart cells—are born next spring. The beef industry is anxiously awaiting the answer: the clones come from a line of prize cows whose meat sells for $100.00 a pound."

1990 . . . . $789.00
1997 . . . . $735.00

Man's Haircut
1980. . . . . $4.08
1990 . . . . $7.80
1997. . . . . $8.00

Hospital Room
(Semiprivate Room per Day)
1980. . . . . $96.75
1990 . . . . $220.00
1997 . . . . $367.00

College Tuition

	1998 Costs	2016 Projected
Public	$3,111.00	$8,017.00
Private	$13,664.00	$32,884.00

U.S. Consumer Debt
(Per Person)
1967 . . . . $633.00
1984 . . . . $2,299.00
1997 . . . . $5,446.00

"Low Long-Distance Rates Go to Web Users," *The Charlotte Observer*, February 16, 1998:

"Consumers looking for the cheapest long-distance telephone rates need only log on to the Internet, the newest arena of intense competition, where companies are offering special prices from $0.05 to $0.10 a minute. This week, AT&T Corp. is expected to start offering its Internet customers long-distance calls at just $0.09 a minute, matching new rates introduced recently by MCI Communication.

Both giants are scrambling to respond to the initiative of a little player that had a big idea: Tel-Save Holdings, a long-distance provider in New Hope, Pennsylvania, that caters primarily to small- and medium-sized businesses. Since December 18, it has contracted with America Online to offer the $0.09-a-minute rate to the online services' 11 million subscribers. America Online has signed up almost 400,000 customers so far, and expects to have a million by the end of June."

Nostalgic Metal Signs

This fabulous collection of yesterday's historical signs and famous trademarks takes you back to a more simple time. Turn your office or den into a nostalgia-filled gallery of yesteryear with these unique metal signs displaying yesterday's popular personalities and manufacturers. Because these signs are reproductions of the originals, they may contain flaws or imperfections, which add to their authentic look. Each sign features mounting eyelets.

I Love Lucy
179 Episodes of Television History. 16"x 12 3/4".
128216N $12.95

Coca-Cola
Stop for a Pause - Go Refreshed. 16 3/4"x 7 3/4".
128212N $12.95

Felix
The Cat, 75 Years as Top Cat. 13"x 16".
128213N $12.95

His Master's Voice RCA
16"x 11".
127648N $12.95

Smokey the Bear
Our Most Shameful Waste! Remember - Only You Can Prevent Forest Fires! 11 1/2"x 15 3/4".
128214N $12.95

"I Love Lucy" 16"x 12 1/4".
127647N $12.95

Popeye
Popeye says "No Smoking!" 12"x 15 7/8".
126955N $12.95

Hershey Syrup
Hershey Syrup, Stepping Stones to Health. Genuine Chocolate Flavor. 12 1/4"x 16".
128211N $12.95

Pepsi: Cola
Good! Good! Good! Pepsi-Cola 5¢. 11"x 15".
126958N $12.95

Lucille Ball
"RC tastes best!" says Lucille Ball. 16"x 10 1/2".
126953N $12.95

Order Toll-Free 1-800-826-6600

"Jobless Rate Hits Low Again,"
The Charlotte Observer, March 7, 1998:

"Surprisingly robust job growth pushed the nation's unemployment rate to a 24-year low of 4.6 percent in February, renewing concerns that the United States is running short of skilled workers . . . Two temporary factors—unseasonably mild winter weather and historically low mortgage rates, which have risen a bit since—account for some of the job growth. But analysts attributed much of the advance to the strength of the U.S. economy, which at least so far is showing only modest signs of spillover from Asian financial turmoil. Economist Mark Zandi of Regional Financial Associates in West Chester, Pennsylvania, said the unemployment rate could sink to four percent by late summer, a level unseen since the 1960s."

"Bowater's Buy Is Big News,"
The Charlotte Observer, March 10, 1998:

"By early summer York County can expect to have a new marketing plug to help attract new business: home to a plant of the second-largest newsprint company in the world. Greenville, South Carolina-based Bowater, Inc., said Monday it will buy Canadian papermaker Avenor Inc. for $2.5 billion in cash, stock, and assumed debt, substantially increasing its clout in the paper industry . . . Analysts and local business leaders—who were surprised at Monday's announcement—predict the merger will mean good things for York County. 'It will only help the area,' said Clay Andrews, executive director of the Rock Hill Economic Development Corp."

1999 News Profile

New York Times, August 1, 1999
The New York Times profiled families as the century came to a close, discovering that families making $50,000 were often "budget constrained." "Clearly, middle-income families in America have acquired more possessions than their parents and grandparents had. But the middle-class comforts of an earlier day were accessible to families with just one earner; today, middle-income families find that they must combine at least two incomes, and often three, in pursuit of a lifestyle that seems always out of reach."

"The Fraziers: When the Fraziers—Carl 65, and his wife Geraldine, 54—imagine the good life, they think of the vacation they take almost every year in a $400.00-a-week condo in Fort Myers, Florida. 'The sand is so white,' Mr. Frazier said. 'You are sitting on the porch, looking out over the bay. All you have to do is change your bathing suit once in a while.'

The Fraziers have a slightly greater annual income than the typical family—more than $50,000 a year—yet in their own perception, life has been hard. They are the only couple of the four profiled (by the *New York Times*) still living in their original home—a single-story, three-bedroom brick house in the northwestern part of Cincinnati, Ohio. They bought it for $19,500 in 1971, the year they were married. The long stay was not Mr. Frazier's intention.

'My original plan was to use this house as a stepping stone,' he said. 'I was a real estate broker then, and I got this house on a repossession. Segregation, as far as home-buying was concerned, was winding down, and there were good houses available. I was going to upgrade my neighborhood.'

The civil rights movement, however, diverted him. Mr. Frazier worked at General Electric's big jet aircraft engine plant here. After service in the Navy, he went to night school for four years, earning a degree as a specialist in electrical power. And G.E. picked him as the first Black to work in technical publications, writing manuals and other material about the engineers.

But some of his new office colleagues resisted his presence, Mr. Frazier said, refusing for a while to break him in on the job. Dealing with that absorbed his energy and blunted his progress. Racial tension at a public school affected one of the four children in the Frazier household, eating up their attention and energy. 'I was spreading myself too thin,' Mr. Frazier said. 'I lost my focus on my plan.'

The Fraziers today contribute roughly equal amounts to the family income. Mrs. Frazier, a secretary at the University of Cincinnati, brings home $28,500 a year in a job that also offers group health insurance. Mr. Frazier found himself forced into retirement in 1995 as G.E. downsized. His Social Security and company pension total $12,000 a year, and he works a few hours a day at a YMCA for $11,000 more. And Mrs. Frazier signed on for night work with H&R Block during the tax season earning $800.00, so their income this year will be just over $52,000.

But there are debts—and desires. Years ago, the Fraziers got in over their heads in credit card spending, and when Mr. Frazier retired they still owed more than $6,000. His severance package and a $35,000 home equity loan, at seven percent, got their finances in order and allowed the purchase of a minivan and central air-conditioning, along with a dining room table, a living room sofa, and stereo equipment (bought at a garage sale).

Mr. Frazier has discovered the interest-free 90-day payment plan and has used it for several recent purchases, including a dining room sideboard and an elaborate outdoor grill. But there are more needs, including a car for Mrs. Frazier to drive to work and various home repairs that Mr. Frazier is resisting. Having avoided new credit card debt, except for a small balance from this year's vacation, he wants to wait until the home equity loan is paid off, at $700.00 a month for three more years.

That is hard on Mrs. Frazier. 'I want my house set, so that when I come to it I have it the way I want it,' she said. 'But if we make a wrong move, the pressure we had from the bills will come back, and that is painful.'"

Value of One Dollar	
Year	Value in 2010 USD
2000	$1.27
2002	$1.21
2005	$1.12

Values are approximate based upon economic historical data and 2010 U. S. Dollar

2000–2006

History will record that the new century began in the United States on September, 11, 2001, when four American commercial airliners were hijacked and used as weapons of terror. After the tragedies at the World Trade Center in New York, NY; Shanksville, PA; and the Pentagon in Washington, DC, Americans felt vulnerable to a foreign invasion for the first time in decades. America's response to the attacks was to dispatch U.S. forces around the world in a "War on Terror." The first stop was Afghanistan, where a new brand of terrorist group known as al-Qaeda had formed. Finding its leader Osama bin Laden and stabilizing a new government, however, proved challenging.. With the shell-shocked economy in overall decline and the national debt increasing at a record pace, the United States shifted its focus from Afghanistan to Iraq. President George W. Bush launched Operation Iraqi Freedom with the goal of eliminating the regime of Saddam Hussein and his cache of weapons of mass destruction, despite vocal opposition from traditional allies such as Germany and France. The invasion resulted in worldwide demonstrations, including some of America's largest protest marches since the Vietnam War. As in the invasion of Afghanistan, the U.S. achieved a rapid military victory, but struggled to secure the peace. When no weapons of mass destruction were found, soldiers continued fighting while an internal, religious civil war erupted. American support for the war waned and vocal protest increased.

Despite the cost of the war in Iraq, the falling value of the dollar and record high oil prices the American economy began to recover by 2004. Unemployment declined, new home purchases continued to surge, and the full potential of previous computer innovation and investment impacted businesses large and small. Men and women of all ages began to buy and sell their products on the Internet. eBay created the world's largest yard sale; Amazon demonstrated, despite sneering critics, that it could be the bookstore to the world; and we all learned to Google, whether to find the exact wording of a Shakespearian sonnet or the menu at Sarah's Pizza Parlor two blocks away. At the same time, globalization took on a new meaning and political importance as jobs, thanks to computerization, moved to India, China or the Philippines, where college-educated workers were both cheap and eager. American manufacturing companies that once were the centerpiece of their community's economy closed their U.S. factories to become distributors of furniture made in China, lawn mowers made in Mexico and sheep skins from Peru. The resulting structural change that pitted global profits and innovation against aging workers unable to support their families resulted in a renewed emphasis in America on education and innovation. If the U.S. was to maintain its economic dominance, the pundits said, innovative ideas and research would have to lead the way.

Sports during the first decade of the twenty-first century became a 24/7 obsession for many. With the dramatic expansion of the Internet, cell phones, the addition of new cable channels and a plethora of new sporting events, America was clearly addicted to sports, including many whose lure was tinged with danger. NASCAR expanded its geographic reach and began challenging football for most viewers, the Williams sisters brought new life to professional tennis and Tiger Woods continued his winning ways on the golf course. Despite a decade of falling television ratings, NBC paid an astonishing $2.3 billion for the combined rights to the 2004 and 2008 Summer Games and the 2006 Winter Games.

Cyclist Lance Armstrong captivated racing and non-racing fans alike as he won the Tour de France an unprecedented seven consecutive times. Baseball's Boston Red Sox finally shook the "Curse of the Bambino" to win a World Series, and Barry Bonds slugged 73 home runs for the San Francisco Giants in 2003, only to be accused of improper drug use as the decade came to an end.

Professional women, who for decades had struggled to rise past the glass ceiling in their companies, began to find bigger opportunities in the 2000s. Significantly, the promotion of a woman to a top slot in a Fortune 500 company ceased to make headlines. Some top female CEOs even began to boldly discuss the need for more balance in the workplace. Yet surveys done at mid-decade showed that more Americans were working longer hours than ever before to satisfy the increasing demands of the marketplace and their own desire for more plentiful material goods. In some urban markets the average home price passed $400,000; average credit card debt continued to rise; and the price of an average new car, with typical extras, passed $20,000.

2001 PROFILE

Lana Evergood had eked out a living as a poorly paid waitress for years when the United States was attacked by terrorists on September 11.

Annual Income: $34,800 (Husband -- $18,000; Wife -- $16,800)
Annual Budget

Housing	$5,136
Food	$7,044
Child Care	$7,040
Transportation	$3,500
Health Care	$4,056
Other	$4,600
Taxes	$2,400
Total	$33,776

Life at Home

- At 42 years old, Lana Evergood thought she looked like an agitated, overweight, pink bumble bee in her waitress uniform that had been designed by the restaurant owner's wife.
- After dozens of restaurant jobs, Lana just chalked up the uniform to "getting by" and didn't worry about it unless an attractive single guy with money came in for a meal.
- Born Lana Louise Lovelace in 1960, Lana's early childhood education was mostly in geography: before she started the first grade, the family moved a dozen times—following work up and down the Eastern seaboard, especially where Wal-Marts were being constructed.
- "Any man who works for Wal-Mart will not want for work," her father liked to say.
- Her mother took in laundry and did daycare until she died when Lana was 13; the cause of death listed as "undetermined," but her father was convinced asbestos played a role.
- Lana's mother had grown up in houses built around Georgia's textile mills, many notorious for using discredited fiber once viewed as the low-cost answer to residential construction.
- Most of the houses' interiors also were painted with multiple coats of various lead-based paints.

Lana Evergood's struggle as a waitress seemed to get worse after 9/11.

- Lana liked school even when it was hard, but when she reached middle school, she realized that the teachers expected little from her except backtalk, so she grew dutifully uninvolved.
- By the time she was 16, Lana was pregnant; when she was 18, the father's parents sued for custody and won, allowing her only supervised visits every other weekend with her own child.
- A yearlong trip to Texas and a short stay in a Pennsylvania jail did little to enhance her position in the custody battle, or her relationship with her ex-boyfriend and his parents.
- Lana went back to school at 21 to get her GED; she waitressed nights and made at least two Alcoholic's Anonymous meetings each week.
- The meetings helped put her life back in perspective, kept her sober, and resulted in more than a few invitations to dinner and dessert.

Lana hated her uniform, which was designed for perky young women.

- By the time she was 31, she had remarried, had another child, and regained her visitation rights.
- A decade later, Lana was married to a man who never came home, but she was enormously proud of her 11-year-old daughter and delighted that she herself was about to be a grandmother—even though she hated thinking of herself in that way.
- Her first child graduated high school, attended two years of community college, and then married a man who had gotten an engineering degree from Georgia Tech.
- Their baby was due in September 2001.

Life at Work

- Lana Evergood had planned to sleep late that Tuesday morning; she had worked the night shift, and once Laura was off to school, she planned to return to bed.
- On a whim, she turned on the TV and watched the television commentators ineptly attempt to make sense of an airplane hitting the World Trade Center in New York City.
- Transfixed, she watched, horrified, as a second plane appeared and also crashed into the famous Twin Towers, scattering debris for blocks.

After the Twin Towers were attacked on 9/11, Lana's money troubles got worse.

- America was under attack and Lana was terrified; her first call was to Laura's school.
- When she realized that the phone lines were impossibly jammed, she drove to the school to rescue her child; Lana was convinced from past conversations that Atlanta would be a prime target when war broke out.
- She even realized that if Laura were to die, then she would consume the first bottle of alcohol she encountered—despite 20 years of sobriety.
- Her next call was to the cell phone of her pregnant older daughter; the stress of the morning's events had triggered labor pains—they were on the way to the hospital.
- One of the reasons Lana had migrated to restaurants like Doug's Country Kitchen, where the tips were poor and the other waitresses mean, was alcohol.
- A few drinks with dinner not only enhanced the potential profitability of that customer, but also dramatically raised the amount of the tips Lana could receive.
- Restaurants like Doug's based their profitability on serving large numbers of people a fairly simple, nutritious menu that could largely be prepared ahead of time and easily stored for the next day.
- A typical menu offered customers a choice of four meats and twelve sides including cold slaw, green beans or sweet potatoes.
- Service was fast—very fast.
- Each table needed to turn over three times at lunch and five times at dinner to be profitable; dozens of customers sitting around savoring a glass of Chablis was not part of the formula.
- And for Lana, a Country Kitchen-type restaurant reduced the temptation to drink and the tendency of men to proposition her.
- When she worked nights at the Dutch Inn, the tips were excellent but the invitations to meet men after work became too frequent for her to feel comfortable; one night when her husband showed up at midnight, drunk and convinced she was cheating, she knew then she needed another job.
- Doug's Country Kitchen was the answer, even though her tips fell from $125 a day to $40.
- At Doug's, all the tips were shared; the hardest-working and the laziest waitresses were rewarded equally.
- Lana hated sharing her tips, and she hated the other women for talking about her behind her back.
- She worked hard and deserved their respect, not their jealousy.
- Her boss operated a dozen restaurants throughout the Atlanta region, each based on the same formula—one that emphasized promptness; she was once laid off for three days for reporting to work five minutes late.
- By 2:30 in the afternoon, Laura was home and huddled around the television set with two friends watching videotaped replays of the Twin Towers collapsing over and over.
- Lana's older daughter was still in labor, and Lana had to go to work.
- People like to eat in good times and bad, she rationalized.
- But she was wrong.

- That day, the restaurant saw only a handful of customers.
- Her total tips for the night were $5.90—barely enough to cover her gas.
- The next night was just as still; even Atlanta's perennially clogged highways were quiet.
- America was hunkered down watching the TV version of Terror in America play out.
- Meanwhile, young men lined up at military recruiting offices, thousands volunteered to give blood, and many more vowed vengeance on Osama bin Laden and his terrorist army.
- As the weeks passed, Americans became unglued from their television sets, home-centered projects like gardening gained momentum, and the country slowly returned to a disquieted mourning.

Lana was enormously proud of her 11-year-old daughter, Laura.

- Lana did not have her first $75-tip day until mid-December.
- By then, a car payment had been missed, she was behind in the rent, and gifts for her first grandbaby—a girl—were slim.
- But Lana figured she could always give love; three mornings a week she dropped Laura at school and picked baby Elizabeth up for a morning of grandmother time.
- The arrangement worked so well she also took in a neighbor's child—an October-born boy—and thought that she had found a way to make Christmas a celebration of birth and giving.
- Then she was notified that her Doug's Country Kitchen would be closing February 1.
- She was given a choice of working at a restaurant 40 miles away or finding another job.
- When she told baby Elizabeth about her troubles, the newborn simply wriggled.

Life in the Community: Atlanta, Georgia

- Atlanta, which began as a settlement located at the intersection of two railroad lines, was incorporated in 1845 and quickly grew to become a major business city and transportation hub by 2001.
- Hartsfield–Jackson Atlanta International Airport had been the world's busiest airport since 1998; the city of Atlanta boasted the country's third-largest concentration of Fortune 500 companies.
- In addition, more than 75 percent of Fortune 1000 companies had business operations in the metropolitan area, including the world headquarters of The Coca-Cola Company, Turner Broadcasting, The Home Depot, AT&T Mobility, UPS, Arby's, Havertys Furniture, Cumulus Media, The Weather Channel, Chick-fil-A, Waffle House, and Delta Air Lines.
- Renowned for its robust cultural institutions, mild weather and dense tree coverage, Atlanta attracted an international community, with foreign-born people accounting for 13 percent of Atlanta's population.

- The city's population of 420,000 within its metropolitan area, comprising 5.3 million, made it the ninth-largest metropolitan area in the U.S.
- Atlanta got its start in 1836, when the Georgia General Assembly voted to build the Western and Atlantic Railroad to link the port of Savannah and the Midwest.
- The initial route was to run from Chattanooga to a spot called simply "Terminus," located east of the Chattahoochee River, which would eventually be linked to the Georgia Railroad from Augusta and the Macon and Western Railroad.
- The engineer chosen to recommend the location of the terminus drove a stake into the ground in what is now Five Points.
- A year later, the area around the railroad terminus had developed into a settlement, called Thrasherville, for John Thrasher, a local merchant who built homes and a general store in the settlement.

Downtown Atlanta, Georgia.

- The chief engineer of the Georgia Railroad, J. Edgar Thomson, suggested renaming the area "Atlantica-Pacifica" to highlight the rail connection westward, shortened to "Atlanta."
- The residents approved, and the town was incorporated as Atlanta on December 29, 1847.
- During the Civil War, the nexus of multiple railroads in Atlanta made the city a hub for the distribution of military supplies.
- On September 1, 1864, following a four-month-long siege of the city by the Union Army under the command of General William Tecumseh Sherman, Confederate General John Bell Hood made the decision to retreat from Atlanta.
- General Hood ordered that all public buildings and possible assets to the Union Army be destroyed; on November 11, 1864, Sherman ordered for Atlanta to be burned to the ground, sparing only the city's churches and hospitals.
- From 1867 until 1888, U.S. Army soldiers occupied the McPherson Barracks in southern Atlanta to ensure that the Reconstruction Era reforms were carried out.
- To train Georgians to develop new industries, the state established the Georgia School of Technology—today's Georgia Tech—in Atlanta in 1885.
- The Cotton States and International Exposition in 1895 successfully promoted the New South's development to the world, and was the site of Booker T. Washington's landmark speech encouraging racial cooperation.
- On May 21, 1917, the Great Atlanta Fire destroyed 1,938 buildings, mostly wooden, resulting in 10,000 people becoming homeless.

- On December 15, 1939, Atlanta hosted the film premiere of *Gone with the Wind*, the epic film based on the bestselling novel by Atlanta's Margaret Mitchell.
- Several stars of the film, including Clark Gable, Vivien Leigh, Olivia de Havilland, and its legendary producer, David O. Selznick, attended the gala event, which was held at Loew's Grand Theatre; African-American Hattie McDaniel, who had played Mammy in the film, was not invited.
- During World War II, Atlanta dramatically expanded, thanks to manufacturing industries such as the Bell Aircraft Company and the manufacture of railroad cars.
- Shortly after the war, the federal Centers for Disease Control and Prevention was founded in Atlanta.
- In the 1950s, the city's newly constructed freeway system enabled middle class Atlantans to relocate from the city to the suburbs.
- During the 1960s, Atlanta was a major organizing center of the Civil Rights Movement, with Dr. Martin Luther King, Jr., Ralph David Abernathy, and students from Atlanta's historically Black colleges and universities playing major roles in the movement's leadership.
- In 1961, Atlanta Mayor Ivan Allen Jr. became one of the few Southern white mayors to support desegregation of his city's public schools.
- African-Americans became a majority in the city by 1970, and exercised their new-found political influence by electing Atlanta's first black mayor, Maynard Jackson, in 1973.
- By 2001, Atlanta had transformed into a cosmopolitan city, becoming well known for its cultural offerings, driven by young, college-educated professionals who had moved into Atlanta by the thousands, seeking a lifestyle rich in cultural variety, diversity, and excitement.

HISTORICAL SNAPSHOT
2001

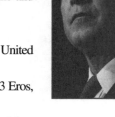

- A black monolith measuring approximately nine feet tall appeared in Seattle, Washington's Magnuson Park, placed by an anonymous artist in reference to the movie *2001: A Space Odyssey*
- The U.S. Federal Trade Commission approved the merger of America Online and Time Warner to form AOL Time Warner
- Wikipedia, The Free Encyclopedia, was launched on the Internet
  George W. Bush succeeded Bill Clinton as the forty-third president of the United States
- The *NEAR Shoemaker* spacecraft touched down in the "saddle" region of 433 Eros, becoming the first spacecraft to land on an asteroid
- FBI agent Robert Hanssen was arrested and charged with spying for Russia for 15 years
- Seven-time NASCAR Winston Cup champion Dale Earnhardt died as a consequence of an accident in the last turn of the 2001 Daytona 500
- The Russian space station Mir re-entered the atmosphere near Nadi, Fiji, and fell into the Pacific Ocean
- *Soyuz TM-32* lifted off from the Baikonur Cosmodrome, carrying the first space tourist, American Dennis Tito
- In Terre Haute, Indiana, Timothy McVeigh was executed for the Oklahoma City bombing
- The world's first self-contained artificial heart was implanted in patent Robert Tools
- President George W. Bush restricted support for federal funding of research on embryonic stem cells
- After years of litigation, the U.S. Justice Department announced that it no longer wished to break up software maker Microsoft, and would instead seek a lesser antitrust penalty
- Nearly 3,000 were killed in the September 11 attack when American Airlines Flight 11 and United Airlines Flight 175 crashed into the World Trade Center's Twin Towers, American Airlines Flight 77 crashed into the Pentagon, and United Airlines Flight 93 crashed onto grassland in Shanksville, PA
- The 2001 anthrax attack commenced as letters containing anthrax spores were mailed from Princeton, New Jersey, to ABC News, CBS News, NBC News, the *New York Post*, and the *National Enquirer*; 22 people in total were exposed and five of them died
- In the first such act since World War II, President George W. Bush signed an executive order allowing military tribunals against any foreigners suspected of having connections to terrorist acts or planned acts against the United States
- *Harry Potter and the Sorcerer's Stone* was released in theaters, starting a series of successful films until 2011
- George Harrison, former lead guitarist of the Beatles, died of lung cancer at the age of 58
- Enron filed for Chapter 11 bankruptcy protection—the largest bankruptcy in U.S. history—five days after Dynegy canceled an $8.4 billion buyout bid
- Officials announced that one of the Taliban prisoners captured after the prison uprising at Mazari Sharif, Afghanistan, was John Walker Lindh, an American citizen
- The U.S. Government indicted Zacarias Moussaoui for involvement in the September 11 attacks
- President Bush announced the United States' withdrawal from the 1972 Anti-Ballistic Missile Treaty

Selected Prices

Automobile, Volvo Sedan	$26,895
Bath Towel	$24.00
Breadmaker	$129.99
Cell Phone	$49.99
Computer, Apple MAC Performa	$2,699.00
Digital Camera	$800.00
Man's Belt, Italian Leather	$42.00
Palm Pilot	$369.00
Wine Bottle Holder	$150.00
Woman's Purse, Kenneth Cole	$148.50

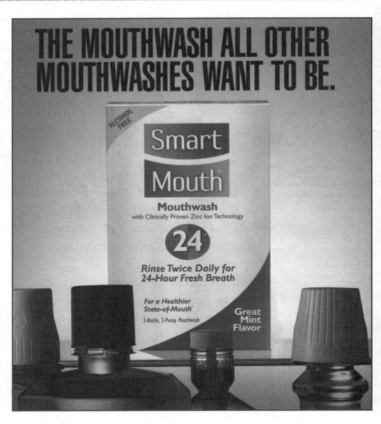

"Tired of It," *I Am a Waitress,*
www.Personalexperiece.com, March 11, 2009:

i am so tired of being a waitress. yes, already. i am tired of rolling silverware everynight for 2.13 aN hour after making only 30 dollars allllllllllllllllll saturday. last weekend i made freaking 60$ all weekend. 60 dollars. that is pathetic. the waitresses at my job and i am sure everywhere else put up with too much ****, and dont make enough money. it is awful. i hate it. now that my husband is home from afghanistan, i no longer want to work every friday satruday and sunday because as other army wives know, that is the only time you really have to enjoy your husband. i want to quit but my husband wont let me. he said once i find another job i can quit but i already had a hard enough time finding this job. there are no jobs here and i am stuck. i kind of want to do something to get my *** fired thats how pissed off i am.

"Waitress Hero," *I Am a Waitress,*
www.personalexperience.com, October 21, 2009:

I find myself going to work every day wishing i was going to another occupation. but, once i get there i am reminded why i stay. i love to work with people and sometimes all a person needs is a good meal and a friendly smile to make on off day on. i am currently seeking another occupation but plan to still pick up shifts every now and then for some extra money. i am 22 years old with a 3 year old daughter. the economy has been down so tips seem to have gone down too. just yesterday i was reminded why i loved waitressing to begin with....

....a women probably in her mid 60s came in, she is a victim of cancer (my mother having bone cancer really made me relate with her) she was so week and brittle but kept on smiling. all she wanted was some hot tea. at my restaurant the hot tea we serve is out of individual tea bags you serve with hot water in a coffee cup. so i also put a few packs of honey on the saucer beside the tea bag. when i came back to check on her she was just so thankful for the honey! she said she had never tried it before and she loved it. it made my day to see how something so simple could make someone who had every right to be bitter just so happy. i ended up giving her about ten packs of tea and honey to take home with her. i figure if it makes her happy she can have it she is probably one of about 4 other people that ever order hot tea so i knew it wouldnt brake us. and if it was my mom i would want somone to treat her the same way.

my conclusion to this is to remember we are heroes in our own right. we have the power to make somones day better at just a tone in our voice and a smile on our face. a kind gesture, or an extra effort made. it takes a special type of person to wait on tables, i commend every wait staff/ servers out there.!

"Some Skimp on Tinsel as Others Splurge," Melinda Ligos, *The New York Times*, December 5, 2001:

This year, many managers are cutting back or canceling office parties, but Alfred Portale is not one of them.

Mr. Portale, chef and co-owner of Gotham Bar and Grill in New York, plans to close his Greenwich Village restaurant on Super Bowl Sunday for a post-holiday gathering that will include more than 400 employees and their family members.

Santa will be there. As will Winnie-the-Pooh, some characters from *Toy Story*, a host of Pac-Man and air-hockey machines, five large-screen televisions, gift bags for the children, and an open bar and lavish spread for the adults. The annual event is the only time that many employees, from dishwashers to food servers, feel comfortable coming into the restaurant as patrons, Mr. Portale says.

"The show must go on," he said, adding that he "wouldn't dream in a million years" of abandoning a tradition he began 16 years ago.

Around half of all companies are pooh-poohing the idea of skimping on holiday gatherings this year. A survey last month by Battalia Winston International, an executive search firm, found companies split on the issue. Of those changing their plans, 82 percent said their holiday parties would be smaller or less expensive than in years past, and the remaining 18 percent will have no parties. Many gave the weak economy and the war on terrorism as rationales.

But for Mr. Portale and others like him, it is more important than ever to hold holiday parties, both to bolster employees' spirits and to defy the terrorists.

"We have all been through a lot of bad stuff this year," he said. "We need this party more now than we ever have before." The event will set him back more than $8,000, not counting the thousands in lost revenue from closing the restaurant for the day.

Michael Silver, president of Equis, a commercial real estate firm in Chicago, shares that sentiment. Not only is the Equis Chicago branch holding its regular holiday dinner at one of the city's most expensive restaurants, Naha, but for the first time it is inviting its 150 employees to bring along spouses. The five-hour party will include live entertainment and top-shelf liquor, even though profits are down 8 percent.

"I don't care if the economy's bad," Mr. Silver said. "I want our employees to feel a sense of community right about now." He derided managers who have canceled holiday parties this year as Scrooges.

Companies going ahead with elaborate celebrations are often tapping into nationalism awakened by Sept. 11.

(continued)

"Some Skimp on Tinsel as Others . . ." *(continued)*

"We're seeing a huge pro-America sentiment in the corporate parties we're planning," said Carey Smolensky, chief executive of Carey Smolensky Productions, an event-planning and promotions company in Wheeling, Ill. Mr. Smolensky said he had had an "unusually high number of requests" for items like flag pins and Christmas trees painted red, white and blue. At a party for a jewelry company, he had a large group of vocalists light candles and sing "God Bless America," he said.

"Everyone's looking not just to party, but to send employees a message that's more poignant and heartfelt," he said.

The HomeBanc Mortgage Corporation in Atlanta briefly considered canceling its festivities but decided to go ahead to bolster employee morale. The party in Atlanta, held on Monday, had 1,800 guests. HomeBanc also scheduled parties in late November and early December in Tampa, Orlando, Palm Beach,

and Davie, Fla., in some cases expanding the guest lists by more than 40 percent from last year, according to Andrea Back, vice president for marketing.

"We have an awful lot to celebrate this year," Ms. Back said, noting that the company surpassed $4 billion in sales for the first time. "And many of our competitors are canceling their events, so this is our time to really shine." The theme was "home for the holidays," she said, and 18-wheeler trucks were commissioned to ship components of a life-size house to each event to serve as décor. Live bands played underneath a fake fireplace, and enormous windows and columns lined each ballroom.

In between feasting on chocolate fondue and made-to-order pasta, guests in floor-length gowns and tuxedos were asked to contribute to Habitat for Humanity, one charity the company supports. "Even though the events are huge, they're very touchy-feely this year," Ms. Back said.

"Angry Americans Flock to Enlistment Centers," *Doylestown Intelligencer* (Pennsylvania), September 13, 2001:

Josh Gipe had been considering joining the Army to pay for college. The two recent attacks against the very symbols of American power steeled his resolve.

He went straight to an Army office Wednesday morning, filling out paperwork and answering recruiters' questions. The 24-year-old hopes to be in basic training in two weeks.

"As an American, I feel like I owe something to my country," Gipe said. "Our freedom has been put in jeopardy, and I want to be someone who helps defend that."

Across the country, military recruitment offices reported a jump in visitors and phone calls in the hours of the New York and Washington attacks. Recruiters heard from angry teenagers as well as sober veterans just calling to know how they could help.

An Army major in Florida called it a "patriotic swell" among Americans whose first reaction, after the horror wore off, was an urge to enlist to defend their country.

In Bakersfield, California, the Army recruitment office took dozens of calls and walk-ins Tuesday and Wednesday three to four times the normal activity, station commander William K. Hurley said.

2003 PROFILE

After years of struggle and hard work, Ben Barber had gained a reputation as a dependable, heavy-equipment operator who could handle complicated circumstances.

Annual Income: $19,200
Annual Budget

Housing	$2,136
Food	$7,044
Child Care	$1,040
Transportation	$5,500
Health Care	$2,056
Other	$4,600
Taxes	$1,400
Total	$23,776

Life at Home

Ben Barber transitioned from cattle farmer to successful heavy machinery operator.

- When the twenty-first century arrived, Ben Barber was convinced this was his time; pay was good, his marriage was going well, and he loved fishing with his teenage son.
- Born on July 4, 1961, Ben grew up pleased that the city of Olive Hill, Kentucky, staged an annual celebration on his birthday and shot up so many fireworks.
- As a boy, Ben worked alongside his father in the cattle and tobacco business; his mother managed to build a successful florist business.
- Family stories included the tale of fighting off Indians.
- Ben often found arrowheads and spear points during spring plowing and planting, evidence of the Native American tribes who once hunted the lush land.
- He respected his mother's German heritage and his father's Scotch-Irish ancestry.
- The state that was known for bourbon and whiskey distilling, tobacco, horse racing, and college basketball was also influenced by the substantial migration of Germans.

- In all, the farm encompassed 300 head of cattle and two large patches of tobacco.
- Ben had dreams of farming his entire life: He loved the problems, the solutions and the work; as far as he could see, his future was in agriculture.
- Then, Ben's parents divorced when he was 14, just as the cattle market crashed; Ben was needed on the farm if the land was to stay in the family.
- He dropped out of school in the ninth grade to help his father on the farm; he was accustomed to hard work and long hours and never returned to school.
- He also spent some of his teenage years running wild; "After the divorce, I was like a herd of cattle that has been penned up too long; when the gate opened, I ran, bucked, jumped and enjoyed my freedom."
- The mid-1970s were hard times for the average farmer, and Ben's father had compounded the problem by going into debt to install a cattle feeding system just as the bottom fell out.
- Then the gas crisis and the price increases changed the economics of beef farming; the prices of feed and supplies were exaggerated by rampant inflation just as the government's campaign against tobacco smoking got underway.
- The family managed to keep the farm, thanks to Ben's willingness to drop out of school; his brothers and three sisters were grown and gone.
- It was left to the baby boy to help his dad; "I was the hind teat boy who had to work for his supper. Didn't have money for clothes, but I always had plenty of work to do."
- Ben loved farming: the seasonal rhythms, the sense of accomplishment that came so often on a farm, the smells and the way his muscles felt after a difficult day of harvesting or rebuilding tractor engines in the shop.
- All the while, there were those who predicted failure: "Just a bunch of vultures flying over you waiting for you to go belly up. They are always around."
- By the time he turned 19 in 1980, his father decided to push Ben out of the nest.
- After five years of working full time beside his father, Ben was told his services were no longer needed.
- His father was bored with farming, resentful of the continually rising cost of cattle feed and the stagnating market price of beef, and ready to convert his most level fields into grass runways for airplanes.

When Ben's father turned his farmland into airplane runways, Ben moved to Kansas.

- He wanted to use his energy to operate a private airport, where pilots could come for fuel, maintenance and repainting of their planes.
- It was time for his father's avocation to become his occupation; he had no patience for any conversation that did not involve flying.
- Even the death of his brother in a dramatic crop dusting accident had not tempered his joy of flying small aircraft—including several he had built himself.
- Ben, who shared his father's enthusiasm for flying, felt betrayed and abandoned.
- His father sold 100 acres to finance the aircraft operation and his retirement.
- "He just shooed me off like an unwanted weed—took me a long time to get over that," Ben said.
- So Ben left Kentucky and traveled west to find himself—until he ran out of money in Wichita, Kansas, where he took a job as a pump jockey and auto mechanic.
- By day he pumped gasoline and washed windshields at one full-service gas station, then spent his evenings repairing cars at a second service station just down the street.
- When his earnings at the part-time night job began to exceed his full-time day job, he quit pumping gas to be a mechanic full time.
- There he discovered, outside the shadow of his father, that he had valuable skills, and was appreciated for his magical ability to bring cars back to life.
- At the same time, the Federal Reserve was beginning to wage war against the persistent inflation within the United States by clamping down hard on the money supply.
- By refusing to supply all the money an inflation-ravaged economy wanted, the Fed caused interest rates to rise even further.
- As a result, consumer spending and business borrowing slowed in the late 1970s and early 1980s, the economy fell into a deep recession, and unemployment began to rise just as Ben grew restless of being a grease monkey.
- He didn't like punching a clock or taking orders; he was highly suspicious of deals that appeared too good to be true.
- In 1982, business bankruptcies rose 50 percent over the previous year, and farmers suffered as agricultural exports declined, crop prices fell, and interest rates rose.
- But the aggressive, government-sponsored slowdown did break the destructive cycle in which the economy had been caught.
- By 1983, inflation had eased, the economy had rebounded, and the United States began a sustained period of economic growth.
- Ben returned to Kentucky and made a fragile peace with his dad.
- Soon after, Ben married a local girl and helped pay her way through cosmetology school.
- He and his young family moved into an 800-square-foot starter house that his stepfather had bought and fixed up.
- Originally, the house had been built as a worker's home for a clock-making factory nearby.
- Ben personally expanded the house over the next decade, until their home contained 2,400 square feet and a little baby.

Ben expanded a small house for his wife and baby.

Life at Work

- With the confidence he had earned in Kansas, Ben Barber returned to Kentucky in the early 1980s and started working as a motor grader, developing major construction projects.
- He learned to prepare a sprawling woodland site for the largest shopping mall in the area; for a residential subdivision, he learned scraping, how to form the crown in the road, the slope of the ditch, and the most economical ways to move dirt from one place to another.

Ben developed major construction projects.

- Throughout Kentucky, West Virginia, and North Carolina, subdivisions were being built on abandoned farmland, where the land was cheaper and carried fewer zoning restrictions.
- Ben was often left to work on his own because of his ability to work independently, economically, and honestly.
- Developers knew he would deliver an honest day's pay and not fall prey to the emerging culture of drug use.
- His skills were in such demand that by the late 1980s, he was running crews with 10 men or more clearing huge tracts of land.
- In the beginning he was paid $12 an hour, but by the 1990s, his pay had more than doubled to $25 per hour.
- From walking through the woods putting ribbons on trees that needed to be plowed to grading the final project for the whole crew of men, he could do it all.
- Some weeks he would show up at 6 a.m. and work until 6 p.m., six days a week, and often drove more than an hour to get to the development site.
- Heavy construction jobs were plentiful.
- Since the end of World War II, the hours worked by Americans had been increasing.
- In the late nineteenth century, workers had fought vigorously for the right to work only 10 hours a day, while the Progressive Movement of the teens and early 1920s had bargained for the eight-hour day.
- By the 1980s, American workers and unions were more often negotiating for income and benefits—including company-supported health care and paid vacation time.
- As an independent contractor, Ben received no insurance benefits, paid vacations or regular holiday pay.
- What he got instead was independence, including the freedom to move from job to job.
- Ben loved problem solving; he liked for each job to be different.
- In low-lying areas, a 96-inch pipe might be required to divert the water so the property could be developed; on other projects, the issue might be cost containment when scraping a storm drain or building a road.

- After all, potential buyers would judge the quality of the subdivision based on roadwork long before they viewed a house for sale; plus, the more efficiently Ben and his crew did their work, the lower the lot price.
- The costs of developing a subdivision's roads and ditches were directly reflected in the price of a house.

- But finding quality help for his work crews was becoming harder; many of the workers showing up claiming to possess the necessary skills to drive a motor grader, front-end loader, or excavator were on drugs.
- "Sometimes we were scraping the bottom of the barrel," Ben said. "If they weren't high on drugs when they arrived for work, then they needed time off to report to their probation officer."
- And when the equipment was not running on a job, the contractor was losing money; everything had its cost.
- By the late 1990s, meth and marijuana were becoming cheaper and more widespread; many of the potential employees appeared to consider dope smoking the "breakfast of champions."
- Ben also came to believe that President Ronald Reagan was right when he said, "Government is not the solution to our problem. Government is the problem," and supported slashing taxes for the rich, outlays on public services, and investments as a share of national income.
- At the same time, Ben witnessed the impact of the rise of global competition in the information age as dozens of local businesses and thousands of jobs decamped the region for Mexico, China or the Philippines.
- Factories closed, grocery stores disappeared, "For Sale" signs popped up like dandelion weeds, and neighbors declared bankruptcy.
- Then, 2003 arrived, and many building projects came to halt; Ben intentionally took a layoff and collected unemployment benefits while he cared for his father, who was sick with lung cancer.
- It was time to be close to home and family.
- Besides, his son was now playing high school football, and Ben never missed a game.
- His son looked like a football player and played like a demon; the newspapers referred to him as the "iron man" because he played on both the offensive and defensive lines.
- One opposing player confessed to his coach that he had faked an injury "so I wouldn't get hit by him anymore."
- Several colleges expressed interest in Ben's son, thanks to his ability to block and tackle, but more school was not a high priority.
- During breaks in the school year, the entire family headed east to North Carolina's beaches, where they surfed and fished for red drum, spots and sharks.
- Ben's wife continued to style women's hair—a business that remained steady; hair continued to grow in good times and bad.
- The crash of Air Midwest Flight 5481, a Beechcraft 1900D operating as a US Airways Express flight, crashed into a US Airways hangar on takeoff from Charlotte/Douglas International Airport at Charlotte, North Carolina, killing all 22 people.
- The accident investigation determined that the crash resulted from improper maintenance and because the aircraft was overweight, even though Air Midwest used Federal Aviation Administration-approved estimated passenger weight tables.

- The problem was that these tables had not been updated since 1936, when the average weight of an American passenger was 20 pounds lighter than in 2003.
- Still, the crash frightened many.
- As the business began to dry up, Ben made calls to the region's biggest developers to see what dirt needed moving—just in case he needed to climb back into the cab of a giant earth-moving machine.

Life in the Community: Olive Hill, Kentucky

- Early in its history, Kentucky gained recognition for its excellent farming conditions, and was the site of the first commercial winery in the United States in 1799.
- Because of the high calcium content of the soil, the Bluegrass region quickly became a major horse-breeding area.
- By 2003, Kentucky ranked fifth nationally in goat farming, eighth in beef cattle production, and fourteenth in corn production.
- The state's economy expanded to include auto manufacturing, energy fuel production, and medical expertise.

Kentucky was a significant horse-breeding area.

- Kentucky ranked fourth among U.S. states in the number of automobiles and trucks assembled, to include the Chevrolet Corvette, Cadillac XLR , Ford Explorer, Ford Super Duty trucks, Ford Excursion, Toyota Camry, Toyota Avalon, Toyota Solara, and Toyota Venza.
- Located in eastern Kentucky, the town of Olive Hill began as a rural trading post established by the Henderson brothers in the early nineteenth century.
- In 1881, the town was moved from a hillside location to its current one in the Tygarts Creek Valley, where the Elizabethtown, Lexington and Big Sandy Railroad had laid tracks.
- The hillside location become known as Old Olive Hill and served as the city's residential area.
- On March 24, 1884, Olive Hill was incorporated as a city and served as the county seat of the short-lived Beckham County from February 9 to April 29, 1904.
- According to the 2000 Census, Olive Hill had a population of 1,813, composed of 98.73 percent whites, 0.17 percent African-Americans, 0.50 percent Native Americans, and 0.6 percent other races.
- The median income for a household in the city was $22,958, compared to $28,513 in the state as a whole—forty-third in the nation.

Toyota was a major employer in Kentucky.

HISTORICAL SNAPSHOT
2003

- The Space Shuttle *Columbia* disintegrated during re-entry over Texas, killing all seven astronauts on board
- More than 10 million people in over 600 cities worldwide protested the planned invasion of Iraq by the United States
- An American businessman was admitted to the Vietnam France Hospital in Hanoi, Vietnam, with the first identified case of SARS; both the businessman and his doctor later died of the disease
- The journal *Nature* reported that 350,000-year-old upright-walking human footprints had been found in Italy
- FBI agents raided the corporate headquarters of HealthSouth Corporation in Birmingham, Alabama, on suspicion of massive corporate fraud led by the company's top executives
- The Iraq War began with the invasion of Iraq by the U.S.; within days U.S. forces seized control of Baghdad, ending the regime of Saddam Hussein
- Syracuse won the college basketball National Championship
- The Human Genome Project was completed, with 99 percent of the human genome sequenced to 99.99 percent accuracy
- Pen Hadow became the first person to walk alone, without any outside help, from Canada to the North Pole
- Eric Rudolph, the suspect in the Centennial Olympic Park bombing in 1996, was captured in Murphy, North Carolina
- Martha Stewart and her broker were indicted for using privileged investment information and then obstructing a federal investigation; Stewart also resigned as chairperson and chief executive officer of *Martha Stewart Living*
- *The Spirit of Butts Farm* completed the first flight across the Atlantic by a computer-controlled model aircraft; the flight set two world records for a model aircraft—for duration (38 hours, 53 minutes) and for non-stop distance (1,883 statute miles)
- The Concorde made its last scheduled commercial flight
- The U.S. Supreme Court upheld Affirmative Action in university admissions and declared sodomy laws unconstitutional
- Using information leaked by George W. Bush's Administration, *Washington Post* columnist Robert Novak published the name of Valerie Plame, blowing her cover as a CIA operative
- The electorate of the Cherokee Nation of Oklahoma approved a new constitution re-designating the tribe "Cherokee Nation" without "of Oklahoma" and specifically disenfranchising the Cherokee Freedmen
- Facing an investigation surrounding allegations of illegal drug use, right-wing radio host Rush Limbaugh publicly admitted that he was addicted to prescription painkillers and would seek treatment
- The Florida Marlins defeated the New York Yankees to win their second World Series title

Selected Prices

Airplane, Hawker 400XP $387,500
Backup Hard Drive $44.71
Book, Paperback $10.20
Business Cards, 250 Count $19.99
Coffeemaker, Krups $90.00
Combination Router/Modem $160.00
GPS Navigation System, In-Car $1,000
Phone Service, Land Line, Monthly $70.00
Printer Ink, Three-Pack $71.00
Trimline Corded Telephone $14.72

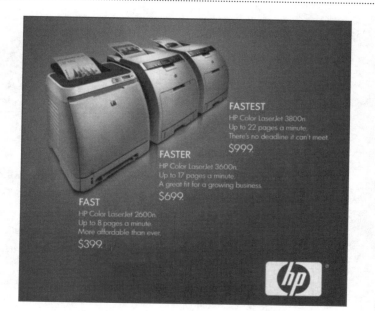

"New Housing Development Could Tighten,"
C. R. Ely Bond, *Cedar Rapids Gazette*, October 24, 2002:

In something for pioneering venture, housing development in far southern Cedar Rapids is coming to a spot where city housing has never been—C Street, southwest of Hwy. 30 on Ely Road....

Local realtor Scott Olsen says the Wheatland Park addition, being planned by High Development Corp. of Cedar Rapids, is the start of the landscape change.

In 20 years, houses will stretch from this new development all the way to Ely, Olson predicted....

Housing development plans are slated for 50 acres recently annexed into the city.

The "mixed-use" development calls for a neighborhood of 67 single-family homes in the $150,000-$200,000 price range.

Closer to C Street will be a dozen 12-unit luxury apartment buildings and 80 townhouses, to be priced from the low 90,000s to about $110,000.

Darryl High, president of the development company told the City Planning Commission this week that he intends to create a place with "a real neighborhood feel."

High said the development would be a mix of "high class and affordability."

"End of Noise Is Music to Students' Ears," *Chicago Daily Herald*, April 8, 2002:

After months of living in a construction zone, you learn to adjust to your surroundings.

And if you're like Leslie High School band conductor Steve Green, you incorporate the distractions into your daily routine.

"That bulldozer outside a little flat," Green told the class of freshmen on Friday.

Despite that bulldozer, members of the Music Department last week experienced the first physical proof that all the disruption of the school's $15.1 million renovation project wasn't in vain.

The students finally got to rehearse in their recently completed band room.

The space has well-proportioned, lofty and has windows—a significant difference from the cramped room students and teachers were accustomed to.

"When we did our sectionals for grading, we had to use a stage of the lunchroom," Green said. "We were teaching in the storeroom."

Now the horn section no longer bumps into the woodwinds, and percussionists have room to swing a cymbal. Green and teachers Scott Gumina have separate offices instead of trying to squeeze into one closet-sized room.

"Overall, the increase in square footage and number of music rooms lets us have flexibility with our scheduling," Green said.

Teachers hope the increased space will eventually clear the way for some new courses and start another band or chorus.

The band room is the first section to be completed as part of a 15-month renovation project to bring the school, which was built in 1974, into the new century.

Economic Hope Fades," *Madison Capital Times*, February 26, 2003:

Wisconsin residents are slightly less optimistic about state and local economies in the year ahead than they were five months ago, according to the latest Badger Poll.

Their views on the direction of the national economy remain stable from last month but are still less optimistic than they were in September, the Poll also found.

The survey of 500 state residents, conducted February 11-19, found that 42 percent believe the national economy will stay "about the same" over the next nine months.

A third of those polled said they expect the national economy to get better, while 23 percent said it would get worse.

These figures represent a substantial change from the first Badger Poll in March 2000, when 56 percent of those polled said the economy would get better and 12 percent said it would get worse.

At the state level, 47 percent said Wisconsin's economy will stay about the same in the coming year, roughly equivalent to 49 percent who gave the same answer last September.

There was no change in the percentage who said the economy would get better, but 28 percent of those who said it will get worse rose from 18 percent to 23 percent.

This was a similar decline in optimism at the local level, said Poll director G. Donald Ferree, Jr. The percentage of those who expected the economy to get worse rose from 18 percent in September to 21 percent this month.

Ferree has noted a sharp difference in optimism between men and women. Men were more likely to be optimistic about the national economy and women less so. Republicans were also more likely to be optimistic about the economy than Democrats and Independents.

2003 News Feature

"Commercial Property Fallout From War; Hotel Use Declines; Office Sector Faces Uncertainty," John Holuha, *The New York Times*, March 30, 2003:

The war in Iraq is hurting the hotel industry in the New York metropolitan region, as airlines scale back their flight schedules and the threat of terrorist attacks makes people reluctant to visit the region, real estate executives say.

The effect on the office leasing and investment sales markets is not as easy to measure. Some executives say uncertainty about the conflict's duration and economic effects is causing companies to put off making decisions to buy or lease. Others, though, say it is a good time for bargain shopping, particularly for tenants who want to lock in a good deal.

Bookings at hotels started to drop even before the war broke out, said Thomas P. McConnell, senior managing director of the hotel group at Insignia/ESG, the brokerage and services company. "The impact on travel took hold at the beginning of the year," he said, with hotel revenues down 5 to 10 percent from last year's level. "A lot of people blamed it on the weather, but a lot of travel was curtailed in anticipation of the war."

Hotels, he noted, are the most vulnerable of real estate sectors to shifts in public moods, because rooms are rented on a night-to-night basis. "Lodging is the most likely to be affected," Mr. McConnell said. "It is the first to go up and the first to go down."

Nicholas Buss, vice president of research for PNC Real Estate Finance Group, said: "The hotel sector is most at risk. It has been reeling since 9/11, and if travel continues to decline, we could see some distressed hotel owners."

The war is likely to delay, but probably not prevent, an expected upturn in occupancy rates and revenues, said Daniel H. Lesser, managing director of the hospitality industry group at Cushman & Wakefield, another major brokerage and services company. He said hotels have adjusted their marketing strategies to appeal to domestic travelers rather than the international tourists that previously sustained the local industry.

"The fly-to markets are softer than the drive-to markets, so hotels are reorienting toward the drive-to markets," he said. "In New York, hotels are marketing to people who live within 500 miles of the city, rather than the international travelers, who are not coming anyway."

He said the industry has been depressed for so long that a cyclical recovery can be expected. "It is not a matter of if, but when," he said. But, he conceded, the war could push back the time of the recovery.

"If we have a quick war and do not experience a terrorist attack, there will not be much impact on the industry in New York," he said, noting that outside investors are still interested in buying hotels in the city.

Nationally, PricewaterhouseCoopers, the accounting and consulting company, said a brief war—defined as one lasting 30 to 45 days—would depress hotel revenues during the first half of this year, with normal growth resuming in the second half. Under this chain of events, the revenue per available room, a standard industry measurement, would increase only 0.5 percent in the first half of the year, compared with what had been anticipated as a growth of 2.1 percent. A war lasting more than a month and a half, however, would reduce first-half revenues to 0.1 percent and shrink them 3.6 percent in the second half, according to the study.

In other sectors of the market, the economic uncertainties produced by the war are seen as an opportunity for the determined to lock in deals when landlords are willing to make concessions to fill office space.

Quoting a saying that she attributed to an early Rothschild, "Buy when there is blood in the streets," Ruth Colp-Haber, a partner in Wharton Property Advisors, a tenants' broker, said, "There are good deals out there, and now is the time to lock in good long-term leases."

She said some of the best deals are to be found in sublease space that was expensively bought out for dot-com and telecommunications companies and then returned to the market. "They can be complicated deals, but they are among the best available," she said. "The space is built and the phones are installed, so a tenant can move in two weeks rather than waiting nine months if you are starting with raw space."

2005 Profile

Anna Reynolds quickly realized that telemarketing could be extremely lucrative, depending upon the products sold and the ways the fees were split.

Annual Income: $24,600
Annual Budget

Housing	$8,621
Food	$4,044
Child Care	$3,000
Transportation	$4,500
Health Care	$2,056
Other	$2,600
Taxes	$1,400
Total	$26,221

Life at Home

- The craigslist advertisement Anna answered described the job as "sales," but failed to say the position required non-stop outbound telemarketing.
- The woman who interviewed Anna told her she had a lovely voice; the women at the phone station where she was assigned told her she was the third person that year to occupy that seat.
- Growing up in Seattle, Washington, Anna had dreamed of being a nurse—even a doctor.
- But that was all before she met charming Alexander her junior year in high school.
- For the first time in her life, she cut school and declared homework to be unimportant.
- Her father, a postal service worker on disability, pleaded with her to keep her grades up; her mother tried to lock her in her bedroom.
- All she wanted was more time with Alexander, who dumped her and moved on.
- Anna's resulting depression made her rebellious and apathetic.
- As her senior year in high school came to an end, Anna left home on a bus bound for San Francisco on the day her parents expected her to graduate.
- She would not return to Seattle for two years.

Anna Reynolds thrived in the fast paced, competitive field of telemarketing.

- Anna's parents welcomed her home: her bedroom was exactly as she had left it.
- But she quickly chaffed under the glare of anxious parents.
- It was not their business where she was going or when she would be back.
- They didn't approve of her "more expressive" vocabulary, they hated her tattoo, and they wanted to hover.
- She just wanted a place to crash that didn't require sex in exchange.
- Quickly it became clear that having her own cash would reduce parental control; cash was king in Seattle—a city still influenced by the dot-com stock market meltdown of 2000.
- Anna didn't actually own any stock, but since she wanted to, it was only natural for her to feel connected to the roller coaster ride now being experienced by investors.

As a young girl, Anna loved school and got perfect grades.

- Nearly everyone secretly dreamed of becoming an overnight dot-com millionaire.
- Almost a decade earlier, venture capitalists who were investing in dot-com companies experienced meteoric rises in their stock prices, driven by the potential of the emerging Internet, low interest rates in 1998–1999 for startup capital, and thousands of fascinating ideas.
- A typical dot-com company's business model relied on harnessing network effects by operating at a sustained net loss to build market share; the mantra "get big fast" reflected this strategy.
- Many dot-coms named themselves with onomatopoeic nonsense words that they hoped would be memorable, and 17 dot-com companies each paid more than $2 million for Super Bowl XXXIV ads in January 2000.
- By contrast, in January 2001, just three dot-coms bought advertising spots during Super Bowl XXXV.
- Dozens of American cities competed to become the "next Silicon Valley" by building network-enabled office space to attract Internet entrepreneurs.
- Communication providers, convinced that the future economy would require ubiquitous broadband access, went deeply into debt to improve their networks with high-speed equipment and fiber optic cables.

When her boyfriend, Alexander, dumped her during high school, Anna rebelled.

- Then, in 2000, the U.S. Federal Reserve increased interest rates six times, and the economy began to lose speed.
- The dot-com bubble peaked on Friday, March 10, 2000, when the technology-heavy NASDAQ Composite index peaked at 5,048.62—more than double its value just a year before.
- The stock market crash of 2000–2002 caused the loss of $5 trillion in the market value of companies from March 2000 to October 2002; the 9/11 terrorist attacks on America in 2001 further disrupted the well-being of the U.S. and its financial markets.

Life at Work

- When Anna Reynolds took the new job, few would dispute that telemarketing and teleservices needed an image makeover.
- Telemarketers regularly ranked last in polls concerning business ethics.
- Millions of Americans had rushed to join the National Do Not Call Registry in hopes of eliminating the intrusive calls.
- And some financial advisors told their clients to hang up on anyone they didn't personally know.
- On Anna's first day on the job selling diabetic supplies which she barely understood, she was yelled at, cursed, and hung up on.
- She quickly developed "phone fear" and was caught by her supervisor pretending to make sales calls so she would not be told "no" again.
- It was especially painful to call the homes of individuals who had signed up to be on the Do Not Call Registry.
- Unfortunately for Anna, the Do Not Call Registry was less effective than advertised; exclusions to the program were not well understood.
- Companies like TTR Networking used pre-established relationship and partner programs, surveys, and political and charity exceptions to get around the legislation.
- Consumers still got calls they didn't want, only now they thought Anna was breaking the law when she called.
- Then it happened: Anna made a sale to an elderly lady who was extremely pleased that someone had called at all.
- The customer was also ecstatic that "a real American" was calling, not "some foreigner."
- For many Americans, the evolving world of globalization was symbolized by the accented voice on a telemarketing call.
- The very legislation created to govern and police the industry's ethics and practices had only tarnished telemarketing even further.
- And Anna loved it; the verbal duels with unseen customers brought a particular joy.
- The interplay reminded her of dating and the musky intrigue that it engendered; the buyer had all the power but she had all the tools.
- They had the power to hang up and end the verbal arm wrestling; she had the motivation to keep them talking until they said yes to something.
- After all, Americans really did buy over the telephone, despite what they told their friends.
- A 2003 survey by the Direct Marketing Association showed that one-third of adult Americans (66 million) bought products or services by phone as a result of an outbound telemarketing campaign.
- These customers, equally comprising men and women, spent $9 billion on products averaging about $135.
- Nearly 60 percent said their purchase specifically suited their needs.
- Nearly 40 percent felt the savings and trial offers they received over the phone were a strong reason they made the purchase.

- Anna's training sessions included the psychology of selling over the phone to help her prevail over rejection and to uncover a physical stamina to handle a minimum of eight hours of quality phone calls a day.
- Burnout was discussed and closely monitored, along with phonetics and her mastery of a long checklist of skills necessary for success: the tone, rate, pitch, duration, pause, pregnant pause, delivery and timing of open- and close-ended questions.

Anna enjoyed working with her fellow telemarketers.

- She also learned how body posture, facial expressions, hands as an illustrator and motion can dramatically improve a voice and projection—even if it goes unseen over the phone.
- Her new job also taught her about accepting criticism as well as self-monitoring and reflection.
- Within months, Anna was given a raise to $9.90 an hour, a spot bonus of $150, and the right to compete in the daily music rodeo.
- As a motivational tool, TTR Networking permitted each day's winning team to select the music that would be played in the background.
- Before Anna arrived, the Red team had dominated the sales each day, and they always selected urban rap.
- Anna and her Blue team were determined to alter that trend; they even decided they wanted an entire day featuring Garth Brooks.
- The pace was brutal but rewarding; the Red team was astonished that it had been defeated.
- For Anna, winning was sweet—she had put a lot of distance between her victories.
- She also discovered that she liked hanging out with her fellow telemarketers.
- Nationwide, African-American women made up half the total number of employees.
- Working mothers were more than 60 percent, and more than one-quarter were single working mothers.
- Only five percent had a college degree.
- And nearly one-third reported being "recently" on public assistance or welfare.
- The industry estimated that six million people worked in telemarketing, many of whom were unemployable.
- After a year, Anna changed jobs to handle in-bound calls for a bank whose center in a suburb of western Seattle was the area's second-largest employer.

Life in the Community: Seattle, Washington

- The seaport city of Seattle, with 608,000 residents, was the largest city in the Northwestern United States; its metropolitan area of about 3.4 million inhabitants was the fifteenth-largest metropolitan area in the country.
- The Seattle area was inhabited by Native Americans for at least 4,000 years before the first permanent white settlers arrived.

- The settlement was named "Seattle" in 1853, after Chief Seattle of the local Duwamish and Squamish tribes.
- Logging was Seattle's first major industry, but by the late nineteenth century the city had become a commercial and shipbuilding center as a gateway to Alaska during the Klondike Gold Rush.
- By 1910, Seattle was one of the 25 largest cities in the country, but a combination of strikes and the Great Depression severely damaged the city's economy.
- Growth returned during and after World War II when the local Boeing Company established Seattle as a center for aircraft manufacturing.
- Seattle developed as a technology center in the 1980s.
- The stream of new software, biotechnology, and Internet companies led to an economic revival, which increased the city's population by 50,000 between 1990 and 2000.
- More recently, Seattle has become a hub for "green" industry and a model for sustainable development.
- The birthplace of rock legend Jimi Hendrix and the rock music style known as "grunge," Seattle birthed Nirvana, Soundgarden, Alice in Chains, and Pearl Jam.
- Beginning with Microsoft's 1979 move from Albuquerque, New Mexico, to nearby Bellevue, Washington, Seattle and its suburbs became home to a number of technology companies including Amazon.com, RealNetworks, McCaw Cellular and biomedical corporations such as HeartStream (later purchased by Philips), Heart Technologies (later purchased by Boston Scientific), Physio-Control (later purchased by Medtronic), ZymoGenetics, ICOS (later purchased by Eli Lilly and Company) and Immunex (later purchased by Amgen).
- This success brought an influx of new inhabitants and saw Seattle's real estate become some of the most expensive in the country.

Microsoft is one of many technology companies who moved to Seattle and its suburbs.

HISTORICAL SNAPSHOT
2005

- *Deep Impact* was launched from Cape Canaveral by a Delta 2 rocket
- The Huygens probe landed on Titan, the largest moon of Saturn
- George W. Bush was inaugurated in Washington, DC, for his second term as the forty-third president of the United States
- The Kyoto Protocol went into effect, without the support of the U.S. and Australia
- The People's Republic of China ratified an anti-secession law, aimed at preventing Taiwan from declaring independence
- Pope John Paul II died, prompting over four million people to travel to the Vatican to mourn
- The first thirteenth root calculation of a 200-digit number was computed mentally by Frenchman Alexis Lemaire
- Demonstrators marched through Baghdad denouncing the U.S. occupation of Iraq, two years after the fall of Saddam Hussein, and rallied in the square where his statue had been toppled in 2003
- Pope Benedict XVI succeeded Pope John Paul II, becoming the 265th pope
- The Superjumbo jet aircraft Airbus A380 made its first flight from Toulouse
- The Provisional IRA issued a statement formally ordering an end to the armed campaign it had pursued since 1969, and ordering all its units to dump their arms
- The largest UN World Summit in history was held in New York City
- Cartoons that included depictions of Muhammad printed in the Danish newspaper *Jyllands-Posten* triggered Islamic protests and death threats
- The second Chinese spacecraft, *Shenzhou 6*, was launched, carrying Fei Junlong and Nie Haisheng for five days in orbit
- Scientists announced that they had created mice with small amounts of human brain cells in an effort to make realistic models of neurological disorders
- Another second was added, 23:59:60, called a leap second, to end the year 2005; the last time this occurred was on June 30, 1998

Selected Prices

Bathroom Scale, Digital $49.99
BlackBerry Phone $649.99
Bluetooth Headset $99.99
Computer, Toshiba Laptop $499.99
GPS Navigator, Garmin $219.99
La-Z-Boy Recliner $499.99
Pampers, 176 Count $48.99
Refrigerator/Freezer, Whirlpool $471.72
Sole F80 Treadmill $1,999.99
Vacuum, Hoover WindTunnel $129.99

"Financial Firms Hasten Their Move to Outsourcing," Saritha Rai, *The New York Times*, August 18, 2004:

BANGALORE, India—Last February, when the online lending company E-Loan wanted to provide its customers faster and more affordable loans, it began a program in India. Since then, 87 percent of E-Loan's customers have chosen to have their loans financed two days faster by having their applications processed in India.

"Offshoring is not just a fad, but the reality of doing business today," said Chris Larsen, chairman and chief executive of E-Loan, "and this is really just the beginning."

Indeed, seemingly a myriad of financial institutions including banks, mutual funds, insurance companies, investment firms and credit-card companies are sending work to overseas locations, at a scorching speed.

From 2003 to 2004, Deloitte Research found in a survey of 43 financial institutions in seven countries, including 13 of the top 25 by market capitalization, financial institutions in North America and Europe increased jobs offshore to an average of 1,500 each from an average of 300. The Deloitte study said that about 80 percent of this went to India.

Deloitte said the unexpectedly rapid growth rate for offshore outsourcing showed no signs of abating, despite negative publicity about job losses. Although information technology remains the dominant service, financial firms are expanding into other areas like insurance claims processing, mortgage applications, equity research and accounting.

"Offshoring has created a truly global operating model for financial services, unleashing a new and potent competitive dynamic that is changing the rules of the game for the entire industry," the report said.

Michael Haney, a senior analyst at research firm Celent Communications, said: "With its vast English-speaking, technically well-trained labor pool and its low-cost advantages, India is one of the few countries that can handle the level of offshoring that U.S. financial companies want to scale to."

In a recent report, "Offshoring, A Detour Along the Automation Highway," Mr. Haney estimated that potentially 2.3 million American jobs in the banking and securities industries could be lost to outsourcing abroad.

Girish S. Paranjpe, president for financial solutions at Wipro, a large outsourcing company in India, said, "Pent-up demand, recent regulatory changes and technology upgrade requirements are all making global financial institutions increase their outsourcing budgets." His company's customers include J.P. Morgan Chase, for which it is building systems for measuring operational risk, and Aviva and Prudential, the British insurers.

Several recent studies concur that there has been an unexpected and large shift of work since the outsourcing pioneer Citigroup set up a company in India two decades ago. They cite cost advantages as the primary reason. According to Celent, in 2003 the average M.B.A. working in the financial services industry in India, where the cost of living is about 30 percent less than in the United States, earned 14 percent of his American counterpart's wages. Information technology professionals earned 13 percent, while call center workers who provide customer support and telemarketing services earned seven percent of their American counterparts' salaries.

Experts say that with China, India, the former Soviet Union and other nations embracing free trade and capitalism, there is a population 10 times that of the United States with average wage advantages of 85 percent to 95 percent.

"There has never been an economic discontinuity of this magnitude in the history of the world," said Mark Gottfredson, co-head of the consulting firm Bain & Company's global capability sourcing practice. "These powerful forces are allowing companies to rethink their sourcing strategies across the entire value chain."

A study by India's software industry trade body, the National Association of Software and Services Companies, or Nasscom, estimated that United States banks, financial services and insurance companies have saved $6 billion in the last four years by offshoring to India.

(continued)

"Financial Firms Hasten . . ." *(continued)*

But cheap labor is not the only reason for outsourcing. Global financial institutions are moving work overseas to spread risks and to offer their customers service 24 hours a day. "Financial institutions are achieving accelerated speed to market, and quality and productivity gains in outsourcing to India," said Anil Kumar, senior vice president for banking and financial services at Satyam Computer Services, a software and services firm. Satyam works with 10 of the top global capital markets firms on Wall Street.

Mastek, an outsourcing company based in Mumbai, is another example. Two years ago, Mastek turned from doing diverse types of offshore work to specializing in financial services. The results are already showing. In the year ended in June, 42 percent of Mastek's revenues, $89.28 million, came from offering software and back-office services to financial services firms, up from 22 percent last June.

Fidelity Investments, the world's largest mutual fund manager, started outsourcing to Mastek 18 months ago and is now among the top five clients in its roster.

Sudhakar Ram, chief executive of Mastek, said, "It is rare that within a year a new customer turns a top customer; this illustrates the momentum in the market."

Another Mastek customer, the CUNA Mutual Group, which is based in Madison, Wis., and is part of the Credit Union National Association, started a project billed at less than $100,000 two years ago. Now the applications that Mastek is building for CUNA, to handle disability claims, amount to a multimillion-dollar deal.

In the transaction-intensive financial services industry, offshoring of high-labor back-office tasks is becoming the norm.

ICICI OneSource, based in Mumbai, has added 2,100 employees in six months and signed on four new financial services clients, including the London-based bank Lloyd's TSB, for which it provides customer service.

In one year, from March 2003 to March 2004, ICICI OneSource grew to $42 million in revenues from $17 million. Today, more than 70 percent of its revenues come from the financial services industry, up from 40 percent two years ago.

For India's outsourcing firms, growth has not been without hiccups. Earlier this year, Capital One canceled a telemarketing contract with India's biggest call center company, Spectramind, owned by Wipro, after some workers were charged with enticing the credit-card company's customers with unauthorized free gifts. Weeks earlier, the investment bank Lehman Brothers canceled a contract with Wipro, saying it was dissatisfied with its workers' training.

In response, outsourcing companies are improving their offerings. Leading companies are investing in privacy and security due diligence as they handle sensitive customer data, doing reference checks on employees, providing secure physical environments with cameras, and banning employees from using cell phones and other gadgetry on the work floor.

Deloitte forecasts that by the year 2010, the 100 largest global financial institutions will move $400 billion of their work offshore for $150 billion in annual savings. Its survey forecasts that more than 20 percent of the financial industry's global cost base will have gone offshore in that period.

With competence levels rising, Indian companies are tackling more complex tasks. DSL Software, a joint venture of Deutsche Bank and HCL Technologies, a software company, is handling intricate jobs for the securities processing industry. "Indian firms are taking offshoring to the next level; in the banking industry, for instance, they are getting into wholesale banking, trade finance and larger loan processing type tasks," said Mr. Haney, the analyst from Celent.

But the relentless demand for skilled workers is putting pressure on wage rates, narrowing the wage gap with the United States and other Western economies. Simultaneously, companies are plagued by higher attrition rates that may lead to quality and deadline pressures.

For the moment, however, there is no indication the industry cannot cope with the unflagging demand to send work offshore. "If India can continuously pull less paid, less educated people into the labor pool," Mr. Haney said, "a substantial wage gap will continue to exist."

"Take a Pay Cut to Telecommute?" Margaret Price, *The Christian Science Monitor*, July 22, 2011:

Several years ago, Lisa Hammond quit her job as an assistant manager at the Wal-Mart in Wichita, Kansas, took a 60 percent pay cut to work for a call center, and came out ahead.

How? She worked from home.

This way, she saved on commuting and day-care costs, which had swallowed about half of her approximately $2,000-a-month take-home pay from Wal-Mart. Today, and two work-at-home jobs later, she earns more as a work-at-home field representative to the United States Census Bureau than she did at Wal-Mart while still avoiding commuting and day-care costs.

"I'm spoiled now. I wouldn't want to go back to working in an office," said Ms. Hammond, a married mother of three.

Amid traffic jams, high gas prices, family needs, and a yen for more flexibility, what twenty-first-century worker hasn't thought about skipping the office scene and telecommuting instead? But taking a pay cut to do it? To some, the benefits outweigh the lost income. A survey by New York-based Dice Holdings released earlier this year found that 35 percent of technology professionals would take up to 10 percent less pay to telecommute full-time.

"This is what people really want so much so that some of them would be willing to give up salary for it," says Jennifer Bewley, a spokeswoman for Dice Holdings, a career website for technology professionals.

For the past two years, Monica Cheick-Luoma has been working from home as a publicist for PublicCity PR, a public relations firm in the Detroit area. Her two other colleagues also work remotely.

"While my salary is lower than at my previous position, and I don't have health benefits or a 401(k), working from home has been something I've always wanted to do," she says.

"I've been offered other positions since taking the current job. But the perk of working from home and not dealing with the cost of commuting, gas prices, lunches, and office wardrobe seems to keep me put." Moreover, she's now better able to care for her aging parents, she says.

How much can workers save? Employees working at home for half the work week (versus every work day) save an average of $362 per person per year on gas costs, according to analysis by Telework Research Network. Among other possible savings: an average $7.37 a day on meals and $2.41 a day on professional clothes, calculates TRN, a San Diego-based consulting and research firm specializing in the benefits of telework.

Overall, workers can save as much as $6,800 a year by being home for half of every work week. "It offers good balance between teleworking's advantages and disadvantages," says TRN president Kate Lister.

Value of One Dollar	
Year	Value in 2010 USD
2007	$1.05
2009	$1.02

2007-2012

Economically, the opening decade of the twenty-first century was the worst for the U.S. economy in modern times, resulting in a lost decade for American workers. After eight years of the presidency of George W. Bush, America's economy was in recession—the victim of its own excesses: too much consumer borrowing; extensive speculation in the housing market; and widespread use of "exotic" financial instruments that failed to reduce risk as advertised. It was a sharp reversal from a long period of prosperity during the past 70 years, when the U.S. economy grew at a steady clip, generating perpetually higher incomes and wealth for American households. But in the 2000s, the story was starkly different—a trend accentuated by the housing meltdown of 2008, which kicked off a cavalcade of foreclosures, bankruptcies and job losses. America experienced zero net job creation. No previous decade since the 1940s had job growth of less than 20 percent. The result was national unemployment at the 10 percent level that refused to significantly budge. Nationwide, 140 banks failed in 2010 alone, up from three in 2007. Middle-income households made less money in 2011, when adjusted for inflation, than they had in 1999, and the net worth of American households—the value of their houses, retirement funds and other assets minus debts—also declined. Banks sharply reduced their loan activity to many viable large and small companies, starving American businesses of needed capital. Federal efforts to stimulate the anemic economy prevented it from getting worse, but failed to produce job growth or a political consensus on the best ways to break the back of the recession. Already burdened with America's $13 trillion debt, largely accumulated during the 2000s, recovery was slow even though other governments such as China and Japan showed a willingness to buy this debt.

The American population, which had more than tripled during the twentieth century from about 76 million in 1900 to 281 million in 2000, reached the 300 million mark on October 17, 2006. As of 2012, the United States had a total resident population of 312,901,000, making it the third most populous country in the world. The Census Bureau projected a U.S. population of 439 million in 2050, a 46 percent increase from 2007, unlike most European countries, especially Germany, Russia, and Greece, or Asian countries such as Japan or South Korea, whose populations are slowly declining. Immigration, a traditional growth factor in America, was adding 1.2 million residents per year in the early days of the decade, a pace that had slowed by 2012. Nevertheless, the fastest-growing segment of the American population was the children of immigrants.

Industrial trends toward globalization accelerated during the second half of the decade, as both working class and middle class jobs were exported. Sprawling telemarketing centers were established in India, furniture factories in China and Vietnam, and software development in the Philippines. Rising fuel costs, communications difficulties and manufacturing lag times caused some companies to rethink their globalization strategies, slowing the trend by 2012. Yet rising costs and a recession had little impact on American commuting patterns. Even as the gasoline cost at the pump rose from $1.50 in 2000 to more than $3.00 in 2012, 76 percent of the American workforce drove alone to work.

No industry was rocked more by the Internet than the music industry. The online music decade started with Napster, a free music file-sharing service that eventually morphed into Apple's iTunes, which offered songs for $0.99. MySpace and Facebook became popular hangouts for local bands, especially indie rockers. Bloggers pushed their way to the front with the unsanctioned message: the music industry heads were no longer in control of the manufacturing or distribution of music. Nearly 20 years after record stores dumped their records and replaced them with the bright, shiny compact discs, the CD itself was replaced by digital music. Fans could virtually make their own albums. The TV show *American Idol* turned the nation into talent scouts and music judges, producing pop culture phenomena Kelly Clarkson, country heavyweight Carrie Underwood, rocker Chris Daughtry and fan favorite Clay Aiken. The decade was extraordinarily rough on soap operas. *As the World Turns* and *The Guiding Light* both ended half-century runs as the number of entertainment devices, cable channels and DVRs exploded.

In science, the promise of new cures arising from the decoding of the human genome in 2000 were just beginning to show results, while NASA was de-emphasizing the International Space Station and closing down plans for a permanent moon base to focus on unmanned deep exploration of the solar system and manned missions to Mars.

2007 NEWS FEATURE

"Freed From Debt, a Hair Stylist Looks to a Brighter Future," Kari Haskell, *The New York Times*, November 20, 2007:

The Jolie Femme hair salon is carved out of a barbershop in Harlem. Past the black combs soaking in blue Barbicide and the buzzing clippers, Aurea Casellas, 33, tends to her clients. She twists women's hair into up-dos, or irons spiral locks pin-straight. Her specialty, however, is weaves.

And like the hair she so skillfully interlaces with new tresses, Ms. Casellas, a mother of two, is slowly piecing together a brighter future with the help of a nonprofit organization, the Children's Aid Society.

"Children's Aid helped me realize my potential," Ms. Casellas said on a recent Friday morning at her home in Upper Manhattan. The Children's Aid Society is one of seven agencies supported by The New York Times Neediest Cases Fund.

Before she took part in the Children's Aid Society's Families With a Future program this year, Ms. Casellas said, insecurity had kept her from leaving a dead-end job as an assistant at a hair salon downtown.

"I wasn't challenging myself—it was limited, what I could do there," she said.

As an assistant, she washed hair and swept trimmings from the floor, earning $200 a week, without benefits. Though rent subsidies covered all but $70.40 a month on her one-bedroom apartment, it was difficult to pay for utilities every month and to keep her daughters, Brazil, 4, and Shauna, 18, clothed and fed. When tips were good, she managed. When they weren't, she prayed.

Then in March, the $270 a month the family received in food stamps was cut off. "They said it was because Shauna wasn't attending her G.E.D. classes," said Ms. Casellas. That was enough to break her tenuous budget. "That was not a good time," Ms. Casellas said over the rattling of a passing subway train outside. "I didn't think I was going to get kicked out here," she said, sliding a barred window shut, "but I didn't have $100 for food."

By June, she owed two months' rent, $227.14 on an outstanding beauty school loan and $1,016.90 for dental work the previous year, when two teeth had to be replaced with implants because of gum disease. Her sisters and her mother, who live nearby, donated food stamps when they could, Ms. Casellas said.

"Fortunately, I am not the type to take it out on my children, but I know I wear sadness on my sleeve," she said. Her voice trailed off.

"I lost myself long ago," she continued. "I was smart. I wanted to be a lawyer, but growing up I had no restrictions." At 15, pregnant with Shauna, she dropped out of school. Shauna's father had his own wild streak, which led to trouble with the law, she said.

What followed were years of lost opportunities, struggle and hardship. "I am dealing with what I am dealing with now because of the mistakes I've made," she said, then added, "I was too young with Shauna, but now I really understand how hard it is."

Coming to terms with her misspent past was one of the things she worked on during weekly visits with Rebeka Penberg, a life coach at the Families With a Future program. She also took part in a monthly support group. "It's good to be around a group of people speaking in a positive direction—it's not just my problems, my problems; it's about moving forward," she said.

During a session with Ms. Penberg, she mentioned her stifling debt. Ms. Penberg encouraged her to apply for a grant through the Children's Aid Society from the Neediest Cases Fund and guided her through the steps to have her food stamps reinstated. The grant was approved in July. "That was a good day," said Ms. Casellas. "It was a relief. I was very grateful."

The boost gave her the confidence to pursue the stylist position at Jolie Femme. She started in July, and little by little, her clientele is growing.

"Certain things just take time and patience," she said. "It will happen. I just have to stay focused."

2009 PROFILE

Jesus Mendez was a third-generation Mexican-American who had stayed in the construction trade his entire life simply because he enjoyed being a roofer.

Annual Income: $18,400
Annual Budget

Housing	$2,136
Food	$ 6,985
Child Care	$500
Transportation	$5,500
Health Care	$3,056
Other	$2,600
Taxes	$1,200
Total	$21,841

Life at Home

- Jesus Mendez's first real job, almost 30 years earlier, was building houses; his most recent construction job, lost eight months ago, was roofing houses in affluent neighborhoods.
- His current job was carrying a sign in front of a strip mall outside St. Louis, Missouri that read "We Buy Gold."
- Six days a week, six hours a day, Jesus carried the cardboard laminated sign along the narrow strip of grass in front of the shopping mall, easy but monotonous work.
- For three decades, Jesus had risen before dawn to tackle the steepest roofs in St. Louis; the jobs required skill, careful planning, and a certain level of tenacity.
- Only three years earlier, he was on top of the world, financially, emotionally and physically.
- As the housing collapse progressed, housing construction came to a standstill.
- Jesus was born April 21, 1961, in Belleville, Illinois.
- His grandparents had emigrated from Mexico after the Second World War, believing that their two teenage daughters would find greater opportunity in United States.

Jesus Mendez enjoyed being a roofer.

- The marriage ceremony was performed for both couples at the same time; they even took the same train to Chicago for their honeymoon.
- Jesus' mother was the younger of the two; he was a second child born to Pedro and Elizabeth Mendez, and the first boy.
- Ironically, the white flight from the city to the suburbs in the 1950s and 1960s provided Jesus' father with a steady stream of construction jobs and an opportunity for Jesus to learn his father's craft.
- Jesus could drive a 10-penny nail with three blows before he was six and was familiar with most common power tools before he was 10,
- At 12, he laid his first roof, and at 14 he ran his own crew—mostly Mexican immigrants older than Jesus.
- His father's one rule was school before work.
- He fully understood that a high school education was the ticket to success in America.

Life at Work

- Jesus Mendez left St. Louis the day after he graduated from high school, because he wanted to see the world starting with the ocean.
- When he arrived in Miami two days later, he was exhausted.
- After two weeks, he found the beaches too bright, the sun too hot, and the Spanish-speaking girls cold.
- The attractive women of Miami—most with a Cuban background—had little time for an American-born construction worker suffering from a major sunburn.
- Jesus tried working on a shrimp boat, serving food, and cutting sugar cane.
- After six months he was ready to return to St. Louis.
- During the next two decades, he worked heavy construction, helped build several of the city's tallest buildings and handled renovations.
- By the time the twenty-first century dawned, Jesus had a wife, a small house, a boat and four children.

- Then cancer struck his youngest daughter, ending her life at 11 years old and putting the family $180,000 into debt.
- Jesus worked double shifts, got help from the Catholic Church and sold his boat, but could not make headway against the debt.
- His father suggested that Jesus run his own crew and specialize in roofing houses with complicated designs.

When cancer struck Jesus' 11-year old daughter, it depleted their savings and put the family in debt.

- The demand was great and the expertise rare.
- For three years, Jesus worked from 6 a.m. to 6 p.m. supervising three or four jobs at a time.

- At one point, he had 42 roofers employed—not counting office staff—and was building a reputation as the "go-to guy" for builders who had complex jobs.

THE IMMIGRATION DEBATE

- In 2006, Jesus reported an income to the IRS of $76,000—which did not include the jobs for which he was paid partially or fully in cash.

- His oldest son was attending an upstate Illinois community college, determined to use his hands for holding books, not sun-heated shingles.

- Jesus felt so good about the direction of his life, he purchased a house in the upscale neighborhood where his crews typically worked.

- The year 2007 was even more successful.

- American homeowners could not do renovations fast enough; Jesus was told by one homeowner, "if you move me to the head of your list, you can double your bid."

- Increasingly, Jesus and his crews took only the most difficult, high-end projects that promised the highest margin.

- Jesus even felt secure enough to become politically active and advocate for immigration policies that would allow Mexican workers with jobs to freely move back and forth between Mexico and the U.S.

- A guest worker program, he believed, would provide more stability to the worker's family by reassuring workers they could return home after a job.

- At the turn of the previous century, when more than a million immigrants a year were coming to America for economic opportunity, many Italians, Greeks and Irish periodically returned to their homeland, often to visit the family they had left behind.

- His political leanings cost him a few jobs and drew lots of unsigned hate mail.

- Despite having lived in St. Louis most of his life and having an ancestry going back 60 years, he was told "Go back to where you came from."

- The Census placed the Latino population of St. Louis at 3.5 percent.

- Business in 2008 was strong in the beginning, even though he was finding it harder to get final payment on some jobs.

- Then, overnight, the bottom fell out; the housing bubble had burst.

- Renovations were suddenly canceled, developers stopped calling, and customers quit paying.

- Two banks that had been courting Jesus for his business no longer had time to talk.

- A supplier sued Jesus for non-payment of specialized roofing materials, his new truck was repossessed, and he fell behind on the mortgage.

- By the end of 2009, Jesus' company was out of business, his house in foreclosure, his son bitter that he was unable to afford college, and the hospitals were calling to collect the remaining debt on his daughter's medical bills.

- The only job the 50-year-old father of four could find at Christmas was carrying a placard up and down the street reading "We Buy Gold."

Life in the Community: St Louis, Missouri

- Over its long history, St. Louis had seen itself as a city welcoming to newcomers.
- The French who had founded the city in 1764 mingled freely with the Irish, Scots and Anglo-Americans who came West in the early 1800s.
- Irish immigrants, scorned in many places, found St. Louis hospitable, so they established themselves in business, education, and state government.
- When the failure of Ireland's potato crop and repressive British policies in the late 1840s brought starvation to Ireland, thousands of Irish immigrants came to St. Louis.
- German immigrants came in large numbers between 1830 and 1850, spurred by the widely published letters of Gottfried Duden, who lived along the lower Mississippi River between 1824 and 1827.

St. Louis, Missouri.

- He extolled the glories of the region because it reminded him of the Rhine Valley.
- They were followed by the Bohemians, Slovaks and Croatians, who established native-language churches and cultural centers.
- The Italians came to the city after the Civil War, Jews arrived around the turn of the century, Southern African-Americans arrived in large numbers during World War I, and Mexicans found St. Louis after World War II.
- Discrimination in housing and employment were common in St. Louis, and starting in the 1910s, many property deeds included racial or religious restrictive covenants.
- During World War II, the NAACP campaigned to integrate war factories, and restrictive covenants were prohibited in 1948 by the *Shelley v. Kraemer* Supreme Court decision, which had originated as a lawsuit in St. Louis.
- De jure educational segregation continued into the 1950s, and de facto segregation continued into the 1970s, leading to a court challenge and interdistrict desegregation agreement.
- St. Louis, like many Midwestern cities, expanded in the early twentieth century due to the formation of many industrial companies and wartime housing shortages.
- It reached its peak population of 856,796 at the 1950 Census.
- Suburbanization from the 1950s through the 1990s dramatically reduced the city's population, and although small increases in population were seen in the early 2000s, the city of St. Louis lost population from 2000 to 2010.
- By 2009, Greater St. Louis was ranked 18th-largest metropolitan area in the country and the fourth-largest in the Midwest.
- During most of the twentieth century, the economy of St. Louis was dependent on manufacturing, trade, transportation of goods, and tourism.
- The city was home to several major corporations, including Cassidy Turley, Express Scripts, Enterprise Rent-A-Car, Graybar Electric, Scottrade, Anheuser-Busch, Edward Jones Investments, Emerson Electric, Energizer, and Monsanto.
- St. Louis was also home to three professional sports teams, including the St. Louis Cardinals, one of the most successful Major League Baseball clubs.

HISTORICAL SNAPSHOT
2009

- In the Super Bowl XLIII, the Pittsburgh Steelers defeated the Arizona Cardinals 27-23
- The Icelandic government and banking system collapsed as a result of the home mortgage crisis in America
- The Taliban released a video of Polish geologist Piotr Stańczak, whom they had abducted a few months earlier, being beheaded
- A Russian and an American satellite collided over Siberia, creating a large amount of space debris
- The International Criminal Court (ICC) issued an arrest warrant for Sudanese President Omar Hassan al-Bashir for war crimes and crimes against humanity in Darfur
- The Florida Gators defeated the Oklahoma Sooners 24-14 in front of a record crowd of 78,468 to win the 2009 BCS National Championship Game
- NASA's Kepler Mission, a space photometer which will search for extrasolar planets in the Milky Way Galaxy, was launched
- Lady Gaga's debut single "Just Dance" hit number one on the Billboard Hot 100 after 22 weeks—the second-longest climb to number one, since Creed "With Arms Wide Open" in November 2000
- Kelly Clarkson broke records for the biggest jump to number one on the Billboard Hot 100 when her single "My Life Would Suck Without You" soared from number 97 to number one, fueled by 280,000 digital downloads on the first week of release
- At the 51st Grammy Awards, Alison Krauss and Robert Plant won five Grammys for their duet album *Raising Sand*, which also won Album of the Year
- Entertainer Michael Jackson died at 50 years old in the midst of planning a comeback/farewell tour
- An outbreak of the H1N1 influenza strain, commonly referred to as "swine flu," was deemed a global pandemic, a designation that had not been used since 1967-68
- The longest total solar eclipse of the twenty-first century, lasting up to six minutes and 38.8 seconds, occured over parts of Asia and the Pacific Ocean
- Bolivia became the first South American country to declare the right of indigenous people to govern themselves
- Paleontologists announced the discovery of an *Ardipithecus ramidus* fossil skeleton, deeming it the oldest remains of a human ancestor yet found

Selected Prices

Bookcase	$119.00
Bottled Water	$1.50
Coffee Grinder	$60.53
Concert Ticket, Allman Brothers	$159.00
Digital Cordless Phone	$119.99
Kindle, 3G + Wi-Fi	$189.00
Phone, Camera Flip Phone	$99.00
Printer, HP All-in-One	$548.88
Sofa	$899.00
Toolset, 137 Pieces	$99.99

"Should Unemployed People Work for Free," *Parade, Komono Tribune* (Indiana), October 11, 2009:

More than half a million Americans file new unemployment claims each week, relying on state benefits to keep them afloat as they spend their days looking for jobs. But in Georgia, thousands of unemployed people are working without a salary in "auditions" for paying gigs.

Under the Georgia Works Program, jobless citizens work part-time for up to six weeks at businesses with job openings. They earn no salary, but the state pays unemployment benefits along with a weekly stipend for transportation, childcare, and other expenses. And while the businesses don't issue paychecks, they do provide valuable on-the-job training, according to Michael Thurmond, the state's labor Commissioner. So far, some 3,000 Georgians (58 percent of participants) have been hired at the places where they started working for free. Thurmond calls it a "win, win, win" program that has helped the unemployed find work; saved employers nearly $15 million in labor, hiring, and training costs; and saved the state $5.3 million in benefits that would have been paid to the people who remained unemployed. At least 17 other states have asked about starting similar programs.

Still, there are critics. Andrew Stettner of the National Employment Law Project says that unemployed workers should spend their time looking for the right job. He fears the Georgia program could lead to mandatory unpaid work for the unemployed if it were replicated in other states. "The purpose of unemployment had to be to enable people to search for suitable work, not give employers free labor," he says.

"Unemployment by the Numbers," Christopher Leonard, *The Hawk Eye*, Burlington, Iowa, October 3, 2009:

If the recession is really ending, someone forgot to tell the nation's employers. A net total of 263,000 jobs vanished from the economy last month, much worse than economists' expectations of 180,000 job losses.

The Labor Department figures set the stage for a scenario that labor analysts expect: joblessness will continue to rise after the economy starts to rebound.

The unemployment rate stands at 9.8 percent, a 26-year high. The rate would have been higher if 571,000 people had dropped out of the labor force, which many did in frustration over failing to find jobs.

That leaves 15.1 million Americans out of work, a huge pool of people. That's why the overall unemployment rate measuring people searching for work and who can't find it can continue to rise even after employers start creating thousands of jobs each month.

Even though economists think the economy has begun to grow, it could be well into 2010 before job creation ramps up. Here are some details by the numbers.

Slack in the workforce

33: the number of hours in the workweek. This figure fell back to the record low earlier this year. It indicates many companies are not operating near full capacity, and they may boost the hours of their part-time workers before hiring more full-time staff.

103,000: the increase in people who hold a part-time job because they can't find full-time work. That number has climbed steadily this year, reaching 9.1 million in September.

$616.11: the average weekly earnings of prior private sector workers. This figure has fallen 1.3 percent since January, in part because employers are cutting hours.

$18.67: the average hourly wage. Up a penny from August.

Dismal prospects

26.2 weeks: the average duration that unemployed workers are out of a job, a record high since the Labor Department started tracking the figure in 1948. The figure is up from 19.8 weeks in January.

5.4 million: The number of people unemployed longer than 27 weeks, also a post-World War II peak, though today's larger labor market is a contributing factor.

17 percent: the unemployment rate that includes frustrated workers who have dropped out of the labor market, people forced into part-time work, or those who want a job but haven't looked recently.

263,000: the number of jobs lost in September.

Leading in job losses

64,000: the number of construction jobs lost in September, mostly in nonresidential and heavy construction. This sector has lost 1.5 million jobs since the recession began.

51,000: the number of manufacturing jobs lost in September. This sector has lost 2.1 million jobs since the recession began.

One healthy sector

19,000: the number of healthcare jobs added in September.

559,000: the number of healthcare jobs added since the recession began.

22,000: the average monthly job gains in the healthcare sector this year.

30,000: the average monthly job gains in the healthcare sector last year.

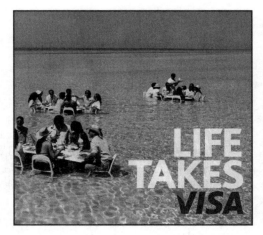

"I Was a Roofer With a Fear of Heights," Knowlton Thomas, *Globe and Mail*, Toronto, Canada, June 22, 2010:

I bear no shame in admitting that I once feared heights. I refused to ride roller coasters or climb ladders. I hadn't flown in a plane since I was too young to grasp the notion that I was literally above the sky.

When I was 13, I rode my first roller coaster. My friend's peer pressure got me on the ride but it couldn't pry my eyes open. As I heard the slow clank-clank-clank of the coaster cart pulling itself up that initial ascent, I was near tears. My heart leapt from my throat on the rush down and I didn't find it again for some time after.

I hoped this might have cured me of my phobia. Alas, it did not. Eventually, I was able to accept airplanes and roller coasters because there is a certain level of assurance embedded into those. I can put my trust in human engineering and the safety of the mechanics and manage to enjoy—or at least tolerate—the experience. The only things that still gave me the shakes were ladders.

And then I became a roofer.

Roofing was the last thing I would have preferred to do for money. Yet my job hunting had been sour for months and I was itching for extra cash. So when I was offered a roofing position, I had a two-second battle between caution and lust.

"I can start Monday," I replied with dollar signs in my eyes and caution curled up, bloodied and beaten in some dark alley corner.

"Aren't you afraid of heights?" my mother asked with a raised eyebrow when I told her the news.

"Yeah," I replied with a shrug. "I'll deal with that on Monday."

The first day was easy. We worked on a one-storey house with a flat roof, and I found the courage to ascend nine feet of ladder rungs.

The second day was a stark contrast to the first. The house was two storeys with an attic and an impossibly steep roof. I watched with growing terror as the ladder clanked up against the side of the house, stretching higher and higher until it reached the top. To achieve such height, the ladder had to be set at nearly 90 degrees. I stared at the crew ascending, rung by solemn rung, cringing with every shake and clatter of that terrible steel beast.

Naturally, I had positioned myself to be the last climber and had let those who came before me carry the tools up. I figured I would need at least two hands to survive. Grabbing onto eye-level rungs with fearful intensity, I made the slow ascent, tuning out the ladder's metallic groans as best I could.

In what felt like both an eternity and a fleeting moment, I reached the top. Alive. I dug my spiked shoes into the old wood roof and carefully made my way to the peak. I had conquered what felt impossible only a minute ago and it felt good.

But I was still scared of heights. I was scared when I was on the roof, and almost every other roof I climbed

(continued)

"I Was a Roofer . . ." *(continued)*

from that day on. The fear never quite went away. But I learned to deal with it enough to keep working.

Then, three months later, it happened. I fell.

It was a crisp autumn morning, and we headed east to tear the raggedy wooden roof off a farmhouse. A light fog drifted across the field as we pulled up, and I could relate: My own mind was a bit foggy. I had slept poorly and fatigue was still weighing down my eyelids.

The farmhouse was a storey-and-a-half high with an easy incline on the roof. Aside from tearing off the old cedar shingles, which would be tedious, the day was looking like a gravy train.

The boss climbed up first to survey, followed closely by another worker, then me. I grabbed the toolbox. A great big heavy thing it was, but easy enough to drag up 15 feet.

I reached the top almost lazily, still groggy, and put out a foot. By habit, I had always stepped off the right side of the ladder. But it had rained the night before, leaving the cedar slick as oil. On the left side was a dry wooden plank.

Habit and a fuzzy mind bested the notion of looking at my footing—I'd done this hundreds of times by now. I put all my weight into the step to heave myself onto the roof, and my foot slipped in immediate response. I flew backward off the ladder.

I let go of the toolbox. Blue sky was above, and for one swift second, nothing was below.

Then my back thundered into hard-packed dirt. The toolbox chased me down, its steel lock breaking on contact with my forehead. Through blackness, I heard voices shouting. I writhed on the ground feebly. Then I arose, my head throbbing and my back shooting with pain, and muttered, "Let's get this day going. What do you want me to do, boss?"

I ended up getting a ride home at lunch and missed another day's work with a concussion and whiplash.

The roofing company shut down shortly afterward for winter and I didn't return in the spring. But what should have caused a permanent phobia instead erased my fears. The fall was probably the worst that could happen to me, and it made me indifferent to heights. I just hope my next fear can be conquered without a concussion.

2011 PROFILE

When Adam Reynolds lost his job hauling waste coal ash for Duke Energy Company, he decided to start his own business.

Annual Income: $16,400

Annual Budget

Housing $2,000
Food $3,000
Education $2,500
Transportation $5,500
Health Care $3,056
Other $2,600
Taxes $1,200
Total $18,856

Life at Home

- Raised in the rural southwestern Virginia hills, Adam Reynolds grew up running a chainsaw.
- As a youngster he could identify trees by its bark or its leaves.
- With the country in a recession that looked a lot like a depression from Adam's front porch, he decided to go into business with his father.
- Together they purchased a portable sawmill and printed a boxful of business cards.
- Then, all they needed was a product, a plan, a little more capital and some customers.
- Born May 26, 1986, Adam grew up playing baseball and football, excelling at both.
- A powerful hitter, Adam played multiple positions on the baseball diamond; in football, he was a hard-hitting lineman who could hold his own on offense or defense.
- In the wintertime, he became a master at splitting firewood and handling the chainsaw like a pro; summers were spent mowing lawns.
- "I was always tearing something apart; I'd use three bikes to make one that was perfect."
- In the seventh grade he learned how to judge timber and cattle; shortly thereafter, he fell in love with his high school sweetheart and the smell of wood.

When Adam Reynolds lost his job hauling waste coal ash, he realized his dream of being a woodworker.

- After high school, he took technical drawing courses and AutoCAD at a local community college.
- He also married his high school sweetheart in 2007 and soon after moved into the house where he had grown up, now vacant and available.
- But times were tough—the local economy had been in a steep decline for nearly a decade.
- Throughout the region, the closing of furniture and textile plants made job hunting difficult.
- Adam thought he was ill suited to the telemarketing jobs coming to the area; spending his day inside, selling products he didn't respect, to someone he had never met seemed like a colossal waste of time.
- Besides, once the state and county incentives matured, the telemarketing companies seemed to move to another location—where a fresh set of tax breaks and cash incentives were being dangled.
- Adam liked to work, loved his wife and needed a job.
- Teaming with his father, Adam took a job executing the waste pond fly ash from a power plant in nearby Greensboro, North Carolina.
- His wife took a job as a waitress and then at a local bank.
- Then, the pond ash project ended, he went on unemployment, was the victim of a motorcycle accident and the recipient of an insurance check.
- Out of work for a year, Adam was prepared to invest $17,000 in his own future.
- He told his father he wanted to use the money to buy a sawmill and go into business together.

Adam and his father bought a sawmill.

Life at Work

- Adam Reynolds and his father found the portable sawmill they needed in Louisiana; a used log skidder was located in North Carolina and a log trailer was obtained in a swap.
- Adam's first major job was building storage barns, then he tackled a logging project creating cross ties, followed by processing surplus logs into firewood.
- The work was more satisfying than the financial rewards.
- But times were hard everywhere in 2009; official unemployment in the area topped 19.5 percent and most business owners acknowledged that the real unemployment was closer to 25 percent.
- Adam worked on several barn designs to make the building process more efficient and profitable.
- Then, the barn building business dried up as the mortgage crisis worsened, bank lending disappeared, and homeowners became cautious about home improvements or expansions.
- "Things were bad when we got started," Adam said.
- His goal was to make $100 a day, or $600 a week; $350 went home and $250 stayed in the business.
- He also learned that his wife was pregnant.

- He started contracting with horse farm operations to clean their barns so he could earn cash for the cleaning and the sale of the manure as mulch.
- And he cut firewood for sale in small batches, which he sold to area residents who could not afford a $300 load all at once, but still needed to stay warm.
- Always a little shy around new people, Adam learned how to talk with customers, discover their needs and make them feel good about the interaction.
- The business took another step in 2010 when Adam and his father leased a two-acre tract that included a 5,000-square-foot metal building and excellent visibility to the most heavily traveled road in their region.
- On that site, the sawmill could be used to saw trees to the customer's specifications, or simply create lumber suitable to the building trades.
- When a massive windstorm leveled a 100-year-old oak tree, a local doctor paid Adam to remove the multi-ton tree and then slice it into six-inch slabs that could be used as tabletops.
- When the local woodturning club expressed interest in local woods, Adam devised a way to quickly create cherry, poplar and walnut bowl blanks on a bandsaw.
- This led to the creation of a picture-saturated website to sell the blanks nationwide—where Adam was confronted with dozens of wood suppliers better capitalized to handle mail-order business.
- Next came handmade picnic tables constructed of white and red oak.
- The tables sold okay at first, but the summertime sun created severe cracks in the table and seats, making them less desirable.
- Adam and his father each drew a salary based on the minimum wage or about $320 a week.
- That's when Adam hit upon an idea that met his needs for cash flow, creativity and salability—outdoor furniture constructed with Eastern cedar.
- Its rich red color was creamy to the touch, delightful to smell and easy to saw and nail.
- "I built a few pieces out of cedar and people liked it and were willing to pay extra for the cedar look."

Adam experimented with different woods and designs; above are bowls from cherry, poplar and walnut, and below is an oak table.

- Using the Internet, Adam looked at various furniture designs, borrowed dozens of woodworking books and experimented with various types of furniture—from beach chairs to natural-edge benches—and tried out numerous ways to spray finish on the wood.
- "Whatever I think I can do—I'll try."
- After months of work and the sale of more than 50 pieces of furniture, he and his father decided to display the work in a coastal home show.

- Immediately they began debating how much space they needed, what furniture to emphasize, and whether their product was "good enough."
- For Adam, these questions set off another round of designing, reading books about the history of furniture, and rethinking how to sand each piece.
- Some chairs were judged to be uncomfortable and were reconfigured, so the blades on some tools were readjusted to produce a smoother cut and reduce sanding time.
- All the while, Adam was developing his own style that emphasized the natural flow of the wood figure.
- To improve profitability, the cedar sawdust was bagged and sold for animal bedding, cedar scraps were made into birdhouses, and extra care was taken to construct an entire table from the wood of a single tree to improve the color matching.
- While Adam created and built in the shop, his father met with customers, located large stands of cedar to harvest, and paid the bills.
- At the end of the day, Adam was always amazed that his cedar furniture was evolving to be the center of a new business.
- While stacks of walnut, cherry and oak boards were slow movers, cedar had risen from its humble status to a cherished wood

Outdoor cedar furniture became the focus of Adam's business.

Life in the Community: Ridgeway, Virginia

- With a population of 775 people, Ridgeway, Virginia, was a town best known as the home of NASCAR's Martinsville Speedway.

- The paper clip-shaped Martinsville Speedway, the shortest track in NASCAR stock car racing at 0.526 miles, was also one of the first paved "speedways" being built in 1947.

- Located only a few miles from the North Carolina line, Ridgeway claims a total area of 0.9 square miles and resides in Henry County, named for revolutionary patriot Patrick Henry, who briefly lived in the area.

- The area's chief industry for many early years was the manufacture of plug chewing tobacco; the Henry County area became known as the "plug tobacco capital of the world."

Ridgeway, Virginia was the home of Martinsville Speedway.

- Beginning in the nineteenth century, several local plug firms successfully sold their merchandise nationwide.

- Local families were heavily involved in these companies, bestowing their names on them and reaping sizeable profits until the early twentieth century, when the tobacco monopolies created by R.J. Reynolds and James Buchanan Duke bought out dozens of small competitors so they could be shut down.

- For most of the twentieth century, the region's economy was dictated by furniture construction.

- Shortly after World War II, DuPont built a chemical manufacturing plant, and later a large manufacturing plant for producing nylon, a vital war material, which made the city a target for strategic bombing during the war and afterwards in the Cold War.

- This nylon production jumpstarted the growth of the textiles industry in the area; for several years Martinsville was known as the "Sweatshirt Capital of the World."

- In the early 1990s, changing global economic conditions and national trade treaties made textiles and furniture manufacturing economically unsustainable.

- As many firms closed and moved their manufacturing facilities to China, thousands of workers were laid off.

- Martinsville was also home to the Virginia Museum of Natural History, an affiliate of the Smithsonian Institution.

HISTORICAL SNAPSHOT
2011

- Southern Sudan held a referendum on independence, paving the way for the creation of the new state
- The Arab spring resulted in the Tunisian government falling after a month of increasingly violent protests; Egyptian President Hosni Mubarak resigned, leaving control of Egypt in the hands of the military, while in Libya, former Libyan leader Muammar Gaddafi was killed in Sirte, ending the civil war
- An estimated two billion people watched the wedding of Prince William, Duke of Cambridge, and Catherine Middleton at Westminster Abbey in London
- Osama bin Laden, the founder and leader of the militant group Al-Qaeda, was killed during an American military operation in Pakistan
- The Green Bay Packers' 31-25 defeat of the Pittsburgh Steelers in Super Bowl XLV attracted 111 million viewers, making the Fox broadcast the most watched program in American TV history, surpassing the previous record of 106.5 million viewers for Super Bowl XLIV one year earlier
- Sony, IMAX, and Discovery Communications launched 3net, a new 3D TV channel
- The world's first artificial organ transplant was achieved, using an artificial windpipe coated with stem cells
- Space Shuttle *Atlantis* landed successfully at Kennedy Space Center, concluding NASA's space shuttle program
- NASA announced that its Mars Reconnaissance Orbiter captured photographic evidence of possible liquid water on Mars during warm seasons
- The movie *Pirates of the Caribbean: On Stranger Tides* grossed $1,043,871,802 to become only the eighth film to have surpassed the billion dollar mark
- ABC cancelled of two of its long-running daytime dramas—*All My Children*, which ended its 41-year run, and *One Life to Live*, after 43 years
- Cellular phone company Verizon Wireless announced it would phase out its famous "Can You Hear Me Now?" campaign; the catchphrase had been uttered on Verizon commercials since 2002 by the "Verizon Test Guy"
- The global population reached seven billion people

Selected Prices

Bathroom Scale, Digital.................................$49.99
BlackBerry Phone $649.99
Bluetooth Headset..$99.99
Computer, Toshiba Laptop............................$499.99
GPS Navigator, Garmin $219.99
La-Z-Boy Recliner $499.99
Pampers, 176 Count......................................$48.99
Refrigerator/Freezer, Whirlpool....................$471.72
Sole F80 Treadmill.....................................$1,999.99
Vacuum, Hoover WindTunnel.......................$129.99

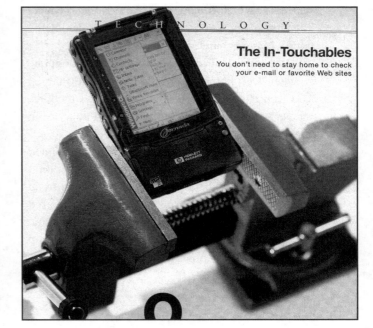

"Recliner No Decliner, Easy Chair Sales a Bright Spot for Furniture Industry," Emory Dalesio, *Arlington Heights Daily Herald* (Illinois), October 21, 2009:

Ah, the recliner. The American invention that linked lazing in the living room to television and frozen dinners is one of the few bright spots in a well-worn U.S. household furniture industry.

Sales from planning shares are getting a lift from the growing popularity of high-tech TVs, home theater equipment, and video games, as well as an aging population that is less active. Even the recession, which forced many Americans to cancel vacation plans, seems to have helped sales of the comfy lounge chairs.

"People think 'I'm not going to travel. Doggone it, when I go home I'm going to be comfortable,' said Don Hunter, who heads Catnapper, a recliner-focused division of Jackson Furniture Industries in Cleveland, Tennessee.

Sales for reclining chairs and sofas totaled $3.5 billion last year and are expected to climb to $4 billion within five years, according to trade magazine *Furniture/Today* and New York-based Easy Analytic Software Inc. Nevada and Arizona, both popular states for retirees, will see sales jump 25 percent.

That's a stark contrast to the nearly 13 percent drop in sales that furniture stores saw through September this year, compared with the same nine-month period last year, according to Census data. That bad news included a slight 1.4 percent rise in retail sales from August to September, the government reported this week.

On Saturday, as the household furniture industry assembles in High Point, North Carolina, for the start of its twice-a-year international tradeshow, several manufacturers will be showcasing recliners with more gizmos.

Berkline has introduced a recliner line starting at $699 with installed stereo speakers, a subwoofer, and a plug for an iPod. The company has an existing model that can be hooked up to a special amplifier that delivers the shakes and vibrations of the action in your home theater system.

Also new this year is a top end to the line of massage chair retailing for about $1,200-$2,400. The deluxe version offered this year cost $2,599, conforms to the shape of the user's body, and includes a system of pressurized air bags for a massage that mimics human hands.

"Administration Eyes Ways to Help Jobless," *The Bakersfield Californian*, October 4, 2009:

The Obama administration is considering steps to ease the burdens of laid-off workers, including possible extensions of unemployment and health benefits, officials said Saturday.

The administration has stopped short of calling for a second economic stimulus package to augment the $787 billion measure approved this year. But with the jobless rate continuing to climb, President Barack Obama said Saturday he is exploring the "additional options to promote job creation."

Administration aides said possibilities include:

Extending the enhanced employment insurance benefits beyond December 31, when they are set to expire.

Extending the tax credit for laid-off workers who buy health insurance through the COBRA program. That program allows workers to keep their company's health insurance plan for 18 months after they leave their job, if they pay the premiums.

Extending a tax credit for first-time home buyers. This credit also is set to expire soon.

The administration has discussed these possibilities with congressional leaders, officials said, but no decisions have been made.

White House economic advisor Lawrence Summers expressed interest in these ideas in an online interview with the *Atlantic* magazine. "I don't know what the term 'second stimulus package' exactly means," Summers said. "We certainly need to continue to support people who are in need, whether it's unemployment insurance, or a COBRA program that for the first time provides that people who are laid off get supported in being able to maintain their health insurance."

In his weekly radio and Internet video address Saturday, Obama said his proposed healthcare overhaul would create jobs by making small business startups more affordable. If aspiring entrepreneurs believe that they can stay insured while switching jobs, he said, they will start new businesses that hire workers.

Dismissive Republicans blamed the continuing job losses on Democratic policies and said the president's health proposals won't help.

The unemployment rate rose to 9.8 percent in September, the highest since June 1983, as employers cut far more jobs than expected.

2012 Profile

Patty Harrison didn't need to read the newspapers to know that the manufacturing sector was undergoing change.

Annual Income: $55,000 (Husband -- $28,000; Wife -- $27,000)

Annual Budget

Housing	$12,136
Food	$7,900
Transportation	$14,500
Health Care	$5,056
Other	$6,600
Taxes	$7,200
Total	$52,392

Life at Home

- When Patty Harrison opened her eyes on New Year's morning, her first thought was upsetting: "I'm starting 2012 unemployed."
- Two weeks earlier she was laid off from her manufacturing job in Princeton, West Virginia, where she made shipping boxes for companies like Federal Express—the fourth time she'd been laid off.
- Jobs were disappearing as machines grew more sophisticated and automated; jobs were migrating to cheaper labor overseas and factory jobs were evaporating through industry mergers.
- Her latest job loss occurred thanks to an aggressive consolidation within the box-making industry that cut the number of factories by a third.
- Born in Portland Oregon, in 1953, Patty grew up around Los Angeles where her father drove a delivery truck and her mother kept the books.
- When Patty was eight years old, her parents divorced, igniting a cycle of instability.
- During these years, Patty and her brother were sent to a foster home, kidnapped by their mother, abandoned by their father, made wards of the state, placed with a couple who forced Patty to miss 31 days of school, and—eventually—reunited with their mother.

After being laid off in December, Patty Harrison's 2012 New Year's resolution was to find a new job.

- When she was 12, her father moved in with a woman who had four children, several of whom had started to call him "daddy."
- "I said, 'he's not your daddy and he's not even divorced.'"
- It was the last time she was invited back and rarely saw her father while she was growing up.
- In all, Patty attended 18 schools, including two different junior high schools and four high schools.
- "We were poor and moved around a lot."
- Patty helped support the family by babysitting for a neighbor's five children for $1.00 a night.
- In the early 1970s, her mother married a man she had known for 10 days and moved the family across the country to Princeton, West Virginia.
- After a childhood of West Coast urban noises and city sights, Patty was confronted with a farmhouse that still employed an outhouse and sometimes lost electricity.
- Newcomer Patty stuck out like a sore thumb; everything about her shouted, "Not from here!"
- Although she did well in school, she does not remember her high school counselor ever mentioning the possibility of Patty attending college.
- She did not attend her high school graduation ceremony because her family did not have the money to pay for a cap and gown.
- After finishing high school, her first job was in Chesapeake, Virginia, where she worked for General Electric operating the machine that put terminals on the ends of wires inside television sets.
- She made $2.47 per hour.
- When layoffs loomed, she quit and moved back to Princeton, where she got a job at Burger King.
- Shortly thereafter, at 19 years old, she met her future husband.
- They were married in the minister's living room.

Life at Work

- Patty Harrison's third job was handling gluing, stuffing and inspection in the upholstery department of a furniture company.
- She made $2.09 and never got a raise.
- Next, she worked in the deli section of a grocery store for a short time, but lost that job, she was told, because she was left handed and could not properly operate the meat-slicing equipment.

Patty set high standards for herself at the box-making factory.

- That's when she began to realize that employees needed to understand their rights.
- Meanwhile, her husband was finding success as the driver of an asphalt pouring truck.
- Her next job was as a cashier at a variety store, followed by waitressing at the Holiday Inn, and then five years handling food service at a manufacturing plant.

- In 1981, when she became pregnant, Patty combined all of her sick leave and maternity leave so she could have the maximum time with her new baby.
- Then, when she became dissatisfied with the quality of daycare that was available, she quit and stayed home to raise her child.
- When her son was one year old, she went to work part-time as a hostess and kitchen cashier.
- But when the coal miners nearby went on strike, business dried up; "No one was spending money and they wanted me to just work a couple of hours a day."
- Many people, including Patty, believed NAFTA as well as other corporate and political maneuvering were responsible for the majority of jobs lost in the U.S., so she quit and in 1984 went to work for a furniture company where she stayed for 16 years.
- She started at $3.35 an hour, and when she left in 2000 she was making $8.75 per hour for her work on the assembly line.
- Using air power tools and brad guns, she built curio cabinets, desks and hall trees.
- To improve the quality of her work and reduce the time required for measuring, Patty set up measuring devices on her table so that the placement hinges on doors could be handled quickly.
- Over time, she trained several people, including men, who were soon making more than she.
- "The majority of the time, women got a $0.10 an hour raise, while the men got $0.15 to $0.20 more each."
- "Some days I would've loved to have stayed home full-time with my son, but I realized it took two working wages to make a living."
- Her husband had moved into long-haul trucking and would come home on Sundays and leave on Tuesdays.
- He was on the road in Ohio when he had a heart attack.
- A fellow trucker's wife Patty barely knew volunteered to ride with her to Ohio; "She was the angel God provided."
- He survived, but recovery was slow.
- She wishes someone had explained to her about unemployment insurance; the knowledge would have given her the opportunity to make better choices.
- After the furniture factory closed in 2000, Patty attended a job fair in which hundreds of recently riffed workers were competing for a handful of jobs.
- When it was Patty's turn to meet with the plant manager, her husband suggested that she "cut up and have fun" as a way of standing out from the rest.
- The company created sheets of corrugated board that were fashioned in specialized boxes for major corporations across the nation.
- She had a wonderful time at the interview and made the plant manager laugh; as she was going out the door, she heard him say "find this woman a job."

Sheets of corrugated board were made into specialized boxes.

- A few weeks later, the Human Resources department called for a second interview and drug test.
- Patty passed both and was employed at the plant for six years.
- During those years, she developed carpal tunnel syndrome in both hands and had just undergone surgery for a tumor on her right middle finger when a plant-wide meeting was held.
- The factory, the man said, was closing and everyone needed to go clean out their locker—"That's it."
- Patty was still under a doctor's care and was not eligible for unemployment benefits until she was released.
- She needed a job, surgery on both hands, and a new opportunity.
- She decided to seek additional education—something she had dreamed about for decades—thanks to an offer from a local for-profit college to help her find funding.
- So for the next two years, Patty took classes and relied on her husband to support the family.
- "I was scared about going to college at 55 years old."
- She made two B's and the rest were A's.
- Her goal was to enter the medical field—and based on her scores, she was well qualified—but when she completed her Associate of Science degree with a 3.92 GPA in the fall of 2009, hospitals and doctors' offices in the area said she lacked sufficient experience and training in computer coding and billing.
- "There were no jobs to go to; additional education was not what they made it out to be."
- She spent most of 2010 looking for a job, but very few were offering insurance benefits or approached the wages she had been earning.
- In 2011 she picked up a lead on the Internet; despite her newly acquired education, it was her skills and operating an automated box-folding machine that brought her employment.
- Officially, the recession ended, according to government statistics, but few people within Patty's network of friends felt a recovery from their personal lives, and most were concerned that the economy was getting worse, not better.
- To complicate the economic picture, America's national political leadership was locked in a power battle and could not agree on how to improve the economic outlook for America's workers.
- "When the elephants fight, only the mice get hurt," Patty observed.
- Many of American workers still feel disconnected and abandoned by their political leadership in Washington.
- It appeared to Patty that it was more important for the politicians to make the other side look bad than to get anything done.
- After she had spent a year looking for a job, her break came just as 2011 was beginning.
- She was hired because of her experience on a flexo-folder machine.

Republican Mitt Romney, left, hopes to challenge Barack Obama in the 2012 presidential election.

- At work, Patty set a high standard for productivity, challenging herself to process 9,000 boxes per hour during the early part of the shift so that when breakdowns, smoking breaks and mistakes happened later in her shift, her daily quota was covered.
- Several of her fellow workers were upset by her efficiency and sneeringly told her, "You are messing up a good thing for everyone else."
- Her machine could establish a cardboard layout, print on the cardboard, set up pre-cuts, apply glue, fold and then stack.
- But after 10 months on the job, the plant closed; three plants were being combined into one.
- So Patty started 2012 the same way she started 2011 and 2010—looking for a job.
- "It's okay; I'm a survivor."

Life in the Community: Princeton, West Virginia

- Southern West Virginia had long been identified with coal mining and railroads, with both forming the backbone of the regional economy.
- Early on, much of the region's bituminous coal was sent west to the Great Lakes, east to the Baltimore and Ohio Railroad's coal piers at Baltimore, or to the ice-free port of Hampton Roads in eastern Virginia.
- The eastern-bound coal transported by the Chesapeake and Ohio Railroad was highly valued for steam-powered ships, notably those of the U.S. Navy.

Princeton, West Virginia.

- Loaded into large ships called colliers, the West Virginia "smokeless coal" was highly prized.
- Princeton's location was east of the primary coalfields, and most of the coal mining and railroad activity was initially elsewhere.
- In the early 1870s, civil engineer William Nelson Page came to West Virginia to help survey and build Collis P. Huntington's C&O railroad through the valleys of the New River and the Kanawha River to link Virginia with the Ohio River.
- Princeton currently boasts a population of 7,562.
- The city served as a hub of the Four Seasons country area of Southern West Virginia and Southwest Virginia, and a number of hotels, restaurants and shopping areas were developed near the intersection of the West Virginia Turnpike and U.S. Highway 460.
- Cultural events were found at the Chuck Mathena Center, which opened its doors in July 2008, and to date has welcomed visitors from 38 states and nine countries.
- The 1,000-seat theater hosts plays, concerts, and community gatherings, and also contains a number of meeting rooms for civic groups, receptions and weddings.
- The goal of the Center is to enhance the cultural life of the region and foster an appreciation of the arts in this area.
- In recent years, an arts movement has shaped the downtown area of Princeton on its main thoroughfare, Mercer Street.
- The RiffRaff Arts Collective, along with other creative endeavors, are fueling a revitalization marked by progressive thinking and a positive outlook.
- The remodeled Princeton Public Library and the new Railroad Museum have been called "bookends" to a downtown that is seeing significant growth.

International worries – from the fragility of financial markets to the threat of nuclear war – continued into 2012.

Smart phones and shipping options abound in 2012.

"For Jobless, Little Hope of Restoring Better Days," Motoko Rich, *The New York Times*, December 1, 2011:

People across the working spectrum suffered job losses in recent years: bricklayers and bookkeepers as well as workers in manufacturing and marketing.

But only a select few workers have fully regained their footing during the slow recovery.

Katie O'Brien Mowery is one of the lucky ones. After losing her job in the marketing department of a luxury resort in Santa Barbara, Calif., in early 2010, she eventually found a position with better benefits and the promise of a brighter future.

"I wished that it happened sooner than it did," said Ms. Mowery, who is in her mid-thirties, referring to her nearly yearlong job search. "But looking back, my new position wouldn't have been available when I was laid off, and now I'm very happy."

Even though the Labor Department is expected to report on Friday that employers added more than 100,000 jobs in November, a new study shows just how rare people like Ms. Mowery are. According to the study, to be released Friday by the John J. Heldrich Center for Workforce Development at Rutgers, just 7 percent of those who lost jobs after the financial crisis have returned to or exceeded their previous financial position and maintained their lifestyles.

The vast majority say they have diminished lifestyles, and about 15 percent say the reduction in their incomes has been drastic and will probably be permanent.

Bill Loftis is one of the unfortunate ones. He is without a college degree or specialized skills, and also worked in an industry, manufacturing, that has added back only about 13 percent of the jobs that it lost during the recession.

After 22 years on the job, Mr. Loftis, 44, was laid off from a company that produces air filters and valves in Sterling Heights, Mich., three years ago. Managers "looked me dead in the eye," he recalled, "and said, 'We're laying you off, but don't worry, we're calling you back.'"

He has heard nothing since. Despite applying for more than 100 jobs, he has been unable to find work. He has drained most of his 401(k) retirement fund, amassed credit card debt, and is about to sell his car, a 2006 Dodge Charger. "It's looking hopeless," he said.

According to the Rutgers study, those with less education were the most ravaged by job loss during the recession. Even among those who found work, many made much less than before the downturn.

"The news is strikingly bad," said Cliff Zukin, a professor of public policy and political science at Rutgers who compiled the study, which was based on surveys of a random sample of Americans who were unemployed at some point from August 2008 to August 2009. The numbers represent "a tremendous impression of dislocation and pain and wasted talent," he said.

More than two years after the recovery officially began, American employers have reinstated less than a quarter of the jobs lost during the downturn, according to Labor Department figures. Of the 13.1 million people still searching for work, more than 42 percent have been unemployed for six months or longer. About 8.9 million more are working part-time because they cannot find full-time work.

While health care and some energy-related jobs have boomed throughout recent years, the other winners have mostly been in skilled professions like computer systems design, management consulting and accounting, where employers have added back as many or more jobs than were cut during the downturn.

(continued)

"For Jobless, Little Hope . . ." *(continued)*

Companies like Ernst & Young, KPMG and PricewaterhouseCoopers, which offer accounting and other business advisory services, as well as management consulting firms like Bain & Company, have returned to peak hiring levels. Many Silicon Valley firms are aggressively recruiting. Google, for example, announced that it has hired more people in 2011 than in any previous year.

Other employers are adding back jobs that were cut, though not yet enough to reach pre-recession peaks. What is more, these jobs are in areas like retail, hospitality and home health care, categories that pay low wages and are unlikely to give workers much economic security.

The sectors that have been slowest to recover are those that endured the most acute job losses, like construction and state and local government. Construction workers are among the biggest sufferers, stung by a housing collapse that led to the loss of two million jobs. Since the recovery began, the industry has added just 47,000 jobs.

Even manufacturing, which has shown a relatively healthy pace of job creation during the recovery, has added just over a tenth of the 2.3 million jobs that disappeared in the downturn.

The hard truth about income inequality
BY RANA FOROOHAR

Either fix our schools or get used to failure
BY FAREED ZAKARIA

Pew poll: iPhones vs. IRAs
BY MICHAEL CROWLEY

TIME

CAN YOU STILL MOVE UP IN AMERICA?

SOURCES

880–1899

Thomas J. Archdeacon, *Becoming American, An Ethnic History,* (The Free Press, New York, 1983)

Susan Porter Benson, *Counter Culture,* (University of Illinois Press, Urbana, Illinois, 1986)

Scott Derks, *The Value of a Dollar, 1860–1999,* (Grey House Publishing, Lakeville, Connecticut, 1999)

John Samuel Ezell, *The South Since 1865,* (The Macmillan Company, New York, 1963)

Neil Harris, ed., *The Land of Contrasts, 1880–1901,* (George Braziller, New York, 1970)

Dorothy and Thomas Hoobler, *The Irish American Family Album,* (Oxford University Press, New York, 1995)

Laurence M. Larson, *The Log Book of a Young Immigrant,* (Norwegian-American Historical Association, Northfield Minnesota, 1939)

Frank B. Latham, *1872 to 1972 A Century of Serving Customers, the Story of Montgomery Ward,* (Montgomery Ward & Co., Chicago, 1972)

James P. Mitchell, *How American Buying Habits Change,* Secretary of Labor, U.S. Department of Labor, Washington, D.C., 1959.

Daniel Nelson, *Managers and Workers, Origins of the New Factory System in the United States, 1880–1920,* (University of Wisconsin Press, Madison, Wisconsin, 1975)

James Michael Russell, *Atlanta, 1847–1890,* (Louisiana State University Press, Baton Rouge, Louisiana, 1988)

Elmer L. Smith, *Early American Home Remedies,* (Applied Arts Publishers, Lebanon, Pennsylvania, 1975)

Susan Tucker, *Telling Memories Among Southern Women, Domestic Workers and Their Employers in the Segregated South,* (Louisiana State University Press, Baton Rouge, Louisiana, 1988)

Negroes of Farmville, Virginia, Bulletin of the Department of Labor, No. 14, January, Washington D.C., 1898

1900–1909

Susan Porter Benson, *Counter Cultures,* (University of Illinois Press, Urbana, Illinois, 1986)

Ray Broekel, *Land of the Candy Bar,* (American Heritage, November/December, 1986)

Elizabeth Beardsley Butler, *Women and the Trades,* Pittsburgh, 1907–1908, The Pittsburgh Survey, (Russell Sage Foundation, Charities Publication Committee, New York, 1911)

Allen Churchill, *Remember When, A loving look at days gone by 1900–1942,* A Ridge Press Book, (Golden Press, New York, 1967)

Peter d'A Jones and Melvin G. Holli, *Ethnic Chicago,* (William B. Eerdmans Publishing Company, Grand Rapids, Michigan, 1981)

Scott Derks, *The Value of a Dollar, 1860–1999,* (Grey House Publishing, Lakeville, Connecticut, 1999)

Lee K. Frankel, *The Cost of Living In New York,* (Charities and the Commons, New York, 1907)

Karen Greenspan, *The Timetables of Women's History,* (A Touchstone Book published by Simon and Schuster, New York, 1996)

Stephen Hardy, *How Boston Played, Sport Recreation and Community, 1865 to 1915,* (Northeastern University Press, 1892)

Dorothy and Thomas Hoobler, *The Irish American Family Album,* (Oxford University Press, New York, 1995)

Hartmut Keil and John B. Jentz, *German Workers in Chicago, A Documentary History of Working-Class Culture from 1850 to World War I* (University of Illinois Press, Urbana and Chicago, Illinois, 1988)

David M. Kennedy and Thomas A. Bailey, *The American Pageant*

John M. Kochiss, *Oystering from New York to Boston*, (Wesleyan University Press, Middletown, Connecticut)

George J. Lankevich, *American Metropolis, A History of New York City*, (New York University Press, New York, 1998)

James P. Mitchell, *How American Buying Habits Change*, Secretary of Labor, U.S. Department of Labor, Washington, D.C., 1959.

Louise Bolard More, *Wage-Earners' Budgets, a Study of Standards and Cost of Living In New York City*, (Henry Holt and Company, New York, 1907)

Marie Obenauer, *Working Hours of Wage-Earning Women in Selected Industries in Chicago*, Bulletin of the Bureau of Labor, Bulletin Number 91, Washington, D.C., November, 1910

Carl Seaburg, *Boston Observed* (Beacon Press, Boston, 1971)

Peter R. Shergold, *Working-Class Life, The American Standard in Comparative Perspective, 1899–1913* (University of Pittsburgh Press, 1982)

Grace Shirley, *Women's Secrets or How to be Beautiful*: Diamond Hand-Book Series No. 3 (Street and Smith, New York.)

Robert Sklar, *Movie-Made America, A Cultural History of American Movies*, (Vintage Books, New York, 1975)

Leon Stein, *Out of the Sweatshop, the Struggle for Industrial Democracy*, (Quadrangle/The New York Times Book Company, 1977)

Vincent Tompkins, *American Decades, 1910–1919*, (A Manly, Inc. Book, Gale Research, Detroit, Michigan, 1996)

Horace G. Wadlin, Chief of the Bureau of Statistics of Labor; (*Prices and the Cost of Living: 1902*, Boston: Wright & Potter Printing Co. State Printers)

Short Talks about Working Women, United States Department of Labor, Bulletin of the Women's Bureau, No. 59, Washington, D.C., 1927

Women in the Candy Industry in Chicago and St. Louis: A Study of Hours, Wages and Working Conditions in 1920–1921, Bulletin of the Women's Bureau.

1910–1919

Frederick Lewis Allen, *Only Yesterday, An Informal History of the Nineteen-Twenties*, (Perennial Library, Harper and Row, New York, 1931)

John Bodnar, *Immigration and Industrialization, Ethnicity in an American Mill Town, 1870–1940*, (University of Pittsburgh Press, 1977)

David Brody, *Steelworkers in America, The Nonunion Era*, (Harper & Row, New York, 1960)

Patricia A. Cooper, *Once a Cigar Maker, Men, Women and Work Culture in American Cigar Factories, 1900–1919*, (University of Illinois Press, Urbana, Illinois, 1992)

Encyclopedia of American Business History and Biography, The Iron and Steel Industry in the Nineteenth Century (Facts on File, New York, 1989)

Karl H. Grismer, *Tampa, A History of the City of Tampa and the Tampa Bay Region of Florida*, (St. Petersburg Printing Company, Inc. 1950)

A.E. Hamilton, *This Smoking World*, (The Century Co. New York, 1927)

Albert Bushnell Hart, ed., *American History Told by Contemporaries, Twentieth Century United States, Volume V 1900–1929*, (The MacMillan Company, New York, 1919)

Walter Renton Ingalls, *Wealth and Income of the American People, A Survey of the Economic Consequences of the War*, (G.H. Merlin Company, York, Pennsylvania, 1922)

Paul Underwood Kellogg, ed., *Wage-Earning Pittsburgh, The Pittsburgh Survey*, (New York, 1914)

Arthur S. Link, William A. Link and William B. Catton, *American Epoch: A History of the United States Since 1900*, Volume I: 1900–1945, Sixth Edition, 1987

Arthur S. Link, William A. Link and William B. Catton, Alfred A. Knopf, *American Epoch: A History of the United States since 1900*, New York, 1987

Samuel Eliot Morison, *The Oxford History of the American People, 1869 Through the Death of John F. Kennedy Volume Three*, 1963

Gary R. Mormino and George E. Pozzetta, *The Immigrant World of Ybor City*, University of Illinois Press, 1987

June Namias, First Generation, *In the Words of the Twentieth-Century American Immigrants*, (Beacon Press Boston, 1978)

Charles P. Neill, *Conditions of Employment in the Iron and Steel Industry in the United States, Volume III: Working Conditions and the Relations of Employers and Employees*, Commissioner of Labor, 1913.

Peter R. Shergold, *Working-Class Life 1899–1913*, (University of Pittsburgh Press, 1982)

L. Glenn Westfall, *Tobacco, Steam and Stone South Florida History Magazine*, Winter, 1996

Retail Prices 1913 to December, 1919, U.S. Department of Labor, Bureau of Labor Statistics, Bulletin No. 270, Washington, D.C., 1921

The Cost of Living Among Wage-Earners, Lawrence, Massachusetts, Nov. 1919, Research Report Number 24, December 1919, National Industrial Conference Board, Boston Massachusetts

Wages and Hours of Labor in the Cigar and Clothing Industries 1911 and 1912, U.S. Department of Labor, Bureau of Labor Statistics, Washington, D.C., 1913

1920–1929

Loren Baritz, ed., The Culture of the Twenties, (The Bobbs-Merrill Company, New York, 1970)

Alexander Ramsey Batchelor, *A Textile Community*, Thesis, Department of Psychology and Philosophy of the University of South Carolina, Columbia, 1926.

Patrick J. Blessing, *The British and Irish in Oklahoma*, (University of Oklahoma Press, Oklahoma City, 1980)

Stuart Chase and F.J. Schlink, *Your Money's Worth, A Study in the Waste of the Consumer's Dollar*, (The MacMillan Company, 1928)

Virginius Dabney, Richmond, *The Story of A City*, (Doubleday & Company, Garden City, New York, 1976)

Wilson Gee and William Henry Stauffer, *Rural and Urban Living Standards in Virginia*, the Institute of Research in the Social Sciences University, Virginia, 1929

David P. Harry, Jr., Ph.D., *Cost of Living of Teachers in the State of New York*, Teachers College, Columbia, University, (Bureau of Publications, Teachers College, Columbia University, New York City, 1928)

Albert Bushnell Hart, ed., *American History told by Contemporaries, Volume V, Twentieth Century United States, 1900–1929*, (The MacMillan Company, New York, 1929)

Walter Renton Ingalls, *Wealth and Income of the American People, a Survey of the Economic Consequences of the War*, (G.H. Merlin Company, York, Pennsylvania 1922)

George E. Mowry, ed., *The Twenties, Fords, Flappers and Fanatics*, (Prentice-Hall, Inc. Englewood Cliffs, New Jersey, 1963)

Marjorie A. Potwin, Ph.D., *Cotton Mill People of the Piedmont, A study in Social Change*, (Columbia University Press, New York, 1927)

Betty Spears and Richard Swanson, *History of Sport and Physical Activity in the United States*, (Wm. C. Brown Company Publishers, Dubuque, Iowa, 1978)

Bertrand M. Wainer and Edith Brooks Oagley, *Exploring New York State*, Harcourt, (Brace and Company, New York, 1948)

Handbook of Labor Statistics, 1929 Edition, U.S. Department of Labor, Bulletin 491

1930–1939

Roger Butterfield, *The American Past*, (A Fireside Book, Published by Simon and Schuster, 1976)

Paul D. Casdorph, *Let the Good Times Roll*, (Paragon House, New York, 1989)

Scott Derks, *The Value of a Dollar: 1860–1999*, (Grey House Publishing, Lakeville, Connecticut, 1999)

Andrew J. Duncbar and Dennis McBride, *Building Hoover Dam, An Oral History of the Great Depression*, (Twayne Publishers, New York, 1993)

Frank Freidel, *The New Deal and The American People*, (Prentice-Hall, Inc. Englewood Cliffs, New Jersey 1964)

Sherna Berger Gluck, *Rosie the Riveter Revisited, Women, the War and Social Change* by Sherna Berger Gluck, (Twayne Publishers, Boston, 1987)

David M. Kennedy, *Freedom From Fear: The American People in Depression and War, 1929–1945*, (Oxford University Press, New York; 1999)

Alice Kessler-Harris, *Out to Work, A History of Wage-Earning Women in the United States*, (Oxford University Press, New York, 1982)

William K. Klingaman, *The Year of the Great Crash: 1929*, (Harper & Row; New York; 1989)

Hazel Kyrk, *Economic Problems of the Family*, (Harper & Brothers Publishers, New York, 1933)

Robert Lacey, Ford, *The Men and the Machine*, (Little, Brown and Company, Boston, 1986)

George J. Lankevich, *"American Metropolis: A History of New York City"*

Arthur S. Link, William A. Link, William B. Catton, *American Epoch, A History of the United States since 1900, Volume I 1900–1945*, (Alfred A. Knopf, New York, 1987)

Arthur E. Morgan, *The Making of the TVA*, (Prometheus Books, Buffalo, New York, 1974)

Winona L. Morgan, *The Family Meets the Depression*, (Greenwood Press, Westport, Connecticut, 1939)

Joyce Shaw Peterson, *American Automobile Workers: 1900–1933*, (State University of New York Press, Albany, New York, 1987)

David A. Shannon, *Between the Wars, America, 1919–1941*, (Houghton Mifflin Company, Boston, 1979)

Marshall W. Stearns, *The Story of Jazz*, (Oxford University Press, New York, 1958)

Susan Tucker, *Telling Memories Among Southern Women, Domestic Workers and their Employers in the Segregated South*, (Louisiana State University Press, Baton Rouge, Louisiana, 1988)

John N. Webb, Coordinator of Urban Research, *The Migratory-Casual Worker*, Works Progress Administration, Research Monograph VII, United States Printing Office, Washington, 1937

Willson Whitman, *God's Valley, People and Power along the Tennessee River*, (The Viking Press, New York, 1939)

A History of the Tennessee Valley Authority, (Tennessee Valley Authority, Knoxville, Tennessee, 1984)

An International Enquiry into Costs of Living. Studies and Reports Series N (Statistics) No.17 Geneva 1931 Published in United Kingdom for International Labour office (League of Nations) By P.S. King & Son. Ltd

Employment Handbook in Railroad Occupations, United States Department of Labor, Bulletin No 961, 1949

The United States Bureau of Labor Statistics Bulletin No. 643 (Vol. II).

1940–1949

Ronald H. Bailey, *The Home Front: U.S.A.,* (Time-Life Books, 1977)

Scott Derks, *Value of a Dollar,* (Grey House Publishing, Lakeville, Connecticut, 1999)

Lenore A. Epstein, *Wartime Earnings and Spending in Honolulu, 1943,* Cost of Living Division, Bulletin N. 788, Monthly Labor Review, April 1944

Ross Gregory, *America 1941, A Nation at the Crossroads* (The Free Press, a Division of Macmillan, Inc. New York, 1989)

Robert Heide and John Gilman, *Home Front America, Popular Culture of the World War II Era,* (Chronicle Books, San Francisco, 1995)

Roy Hoopes, *Americans Remember the Home Front, an Oral Narrative,* (Hawthorn Books, New York, 1973)

Arthur S. Link, William A. Link and William B. Catton, *American Epoch, A History of the United States since 1900, Sixth Edition,* (Alfred A. Knopf, New York, 1987)

Jay Lovinger, *Life Celebrates 1945,* (Time-Life, 1995)

Marc S. Miller, *Working Lives, the Southern Exposure History of Labor in the South,* Pantheon Books, New York

Clyde A. Milner II, Carol A. O'Connor, Martha A. Sandweiss, *The Oxford History of the American West,* (Oxford University Press, 1996)

Robert Sklar, *Movie-Made America, A Cultural History of American Movies,* Vintage Books, New York, 1975

Kyoko Oshima Takayanagi, *Nisei Daughter First Generation, In the Words of Twentieth-Century American Immigrants,* by June Namias, Beacon Press, Boston, 1978

Cost of Clothing for Moderate-Income Families, 1935–1944, Department of Labor, Bulletin No. 789

Family Spending and Saving in Wartime, United States Department of Labor, Bureau of Labor Statistics, Bulletin No. 822

Retail Prices of Food 1944 and 1945, U.S. Bulletin of Labor Statistics, No. 899

1950–1959

Jeremy Brecher, Jerry Lombardi, Jan Stackhouse, Brass Valley, *The Story of Working People's Lives and Struggles in an American Industrial Region,* (Temple University Press, Philadelphia, Pennsylvania, 1982)

Clair Brown, *American Standards of Living,* Blackwell, Cambridge, Massachusetts, 1994

Frances Butwin, *The Jews of America,* (Behrman House, New York, 1969)

Lewis Coe, *The Telephone and Its Several Inventors,* (McFarland & Company, Inc. Jefferson, North Carolina, 1995)

Scott Derks, *The Value of a Dollar 1860 to 1999,* (Grey House Publishing, Lakeville, Connecticut, 1999)

David Engel, *Facing a Holocaust, The Polish Government-in-Exile and the Jews, 1943–1945,* (The University of North Carolina Press, Chapel Hill, North Carolina, 1993)

Claude S. Fischer, *America Calling, A Social History of the Telephone to 1940,* (University of California Press, Berkeley, California, 1992)

Judith S. Goldstein, *Crossing Lines, Histories of Jews and Gentiles in Three Communities,* (William Morrow and Company, Inc. New York, 1992)

Karen Greenspan, *The Timetables of Women's History,* A Touchstone Book, New York, 1996

Fabian Linden, *Expenditure Patterns of the American Family,* National Industrial Conference Board, 1961

Rob Rains, *The St. Louis Cardinals,* (St. Martin's Press, New York, 1992)

Ellen Stern and Emily Gwathmey, *Once Upon A Telephone, An Illustrated Social History,* (Harcourt Brace & Company, 1994)

John Szarkowski, *The Face of Minnesota,* (University of Minnesota Press, Minneapolis, Minnesota, 1958)

Frederick J. Tietze and James E. McKeown, *The Changing Metropolis,* (Houghton Mifflin Research Series Number 10, Boston, 1964)

Gary M. Walton and Ross M. Robertson, *History of the American Economy,* Harcourt Brace Jovanovich, New York, 1983

Average Retail Prices, 1955, Bulletin No. 1197, United States Department of Labor, Bulletin No.1197, June, 1956.

Family Budget of City Worker, October 1950, United States Department of Labor, Bulletin 1021.

Family Income, Expenditures and Savings in 1950, Bulletin No. 1097 United States Department of Labor

Information Please, Almanac 1956, (Dan Golenpaul Associates, New York, 1955)

Minnesota, A State Guide, Compiled and Written by the Federal Writers' Project of the Works Progress Administration, (Hastings House, New York, 1954)

Occupational Outlook Handbook, 1957 Edition, Employment information on major occupations for use in guidance, United States Department of Labor, Bulletin No. 1215

Officer Workers, Salaries, Hours of Work, Supplementary Benefits, United States Department of Labor, Bulletin No. 992, Boston, January, 1950.

Retail Prices of Food, 1953–54, Bulletin 1183, United States Department of Labor, June 1955

The American Dream: The 50s, Time-Life Books, Alexandria, Virginia, 1998

Who Built America, Working People & The Nation's Economy, Politics, Culture & Society, Volume Two, (Pantheon Books, New York, 1992)

1960–1969

Roger Bell, *Last Among Equals, Hawaiian Statehood and American Politics,* (University of Hawaii Press), Honolulu, Hawaii, 1984

Gavan Daws, *Shoal of Time, A History of the Hawaiian Islands,* (University of Hawaii Press, Honolulu, Hawaii, 1974)

Scott Derks, *The Value of a Dollar, 1860–1999,* (Grey House Publishing, Lakeville, Connecticut, 1999)

Bernard Grun, *The Timetables of History, a Horizontal Linkage of People and Events,* A Touchstone Book, (Published by Simon and Schuster, New York, 1982)

William W. Pilcher, *The Portland Longshoremen, A Dispersed Urban Community,* (Holt, Rinehart and Winston, New York, 1972)

Theodore V. Purcell and Gerald F. Cavanaugh, *Blacks in the Industrial World, Issues for the Manager,* (The Free Press, New York 1972)

Robert A. Sigafoos, *Cotton Row to Beale Street, A Business History of Memphis,* (Memphis State University Press, 1979)

Ruth M. Tabrah, Hawaii, *A Bicentennial History,* (W.W. Norton & Company, Inc., New York, 1980)

David M. Tucker, *Memphis Since Crump, Bossism, Blacks and Civic Reformers 1948–1968,* The University of Tennessee Press, Knoxville, Tennessee, 1980.)

A Special Study of Household Income and Expenditures and the Extent of Newspaper Penetration on Oahu; The Honolulu Star-Bulletin 1960 Consumer Analysis Survey

LIFE The '60s, (A Bulfinch Press Book: Little, Brown and Company, Boston, 1989)

The Milwaukee Journal 1965 Consumer Analysis, 42nd Annual Edition

Survey of Consumer Expenditures, 1960–1, Honolulu Hawaii, United States Department of Labor, BLs Report 237–78, November, 1963

1970–1979

Bethany Ewald Bultman, *New Orleans,* (Compass American Guides, Fodor's Travel Publications, Inc.) Oakland, California, 1998

Bong-youn Choy, *Koreans in America* (Nelsons-Hall Inc., Chicago, 1979)

Scott Derks, *The Value of a Dollar, 1860–1999,* (Grey House Publishing), Lakeville, Connecticut, 1999

Charlie Dufour, *New Orleans,* (Louisiana Press, New Orleans, Louisiana, 1980)

Barbara Garson, *All the Livelong Day, The Meaning and Demeaning of Routine Work* (Doubleday & Company, Inc., Garden City, New Jersey, 1975)

Pat Ivey, *EMT: Beyond the Lights and Sirens,* (Diamond Books, Austin, Texas, 1989)

Richard J. Jensen, Illinois, *A Bicentennial History,* (W.W. Norton & Company, Inc., New York, 1978)

Thomas Kessner and Betty Boyd Caroli, *Today's Immigrants, Their Stories,* (Oxford University Press, New York, 1982)

Illsoo Kim, *New Urban Immigrants, The Korean Community in New York,* (Princeton University Press, Princeton, New Jersey, 1981)

Harry H.L. Kitano and Roger Daniels, *Asian Americans, Emerging Minorities,* (Prentice Hall, Englewood Cliffs, New Jersey, 1988)

Ho-Youn Kwon, *Korean Cultural Roots, Religion and Social Thoughts,* (North Park College and Theological Seminary, Chicago, 1995)

Stephen G. Lynn, M.D. with Pamela Weintraub, *Medical Emergency,* (Hearst Books, New York, 1996)

Harry Maurer, *Not Working, An Oral History of the Unemployed,* (Holt, Rinehart and Winston, New York, 1979)

Ng, Franklin, *Asians In America, Asian American Issues Relating to Labor, Economics, and Socioeconomic Status,* (Garland Publishing, Inc., New York, 1998)

David Palumbo-Liu, *Asian / American, Historical Crossings of a Racial Frontier,* (Stanford University Press, Stanford, California. 1999)

Jane Stern, *Trucker, A Portrait of the Last American Cowboy,* (McGraw-Hill, New York, 1975)

Lloyd Wendt, *Chicago Tribute, The rise of a great American newspaper,* (Rand McNally & Company, Chicago, 1979)

D. Daryl Wyckoff, *Truck Drivers in America,* (Lexington Books, Lexington, Mass, 1979)

In-Jin Yoon, *On My Own, Korean Businesses and Race Relations in America,* (The University of Chicago Press, Chicago, 1997)

Consumer Expenditure Survey Series: Interview Survey 1972–73, Annual Expenditures and Sources of Income Cross-Classified by Family Characteristics, U.S. Department Of Labor Bureau of Labor Statistics, 1978, Bulletin, 1985.

County Business Patterns 1976, New York, U.S. Department of Commerce

1980–1989

Scott Derks, *The Value of a Dollar, 1860–1999,* (Grey House Publishing, Lakeville, Connecticut, 1999)

Edited by Richard Feldman and Michael Betzold, *End of the Line, Autoworkers and the American Dream,* (Weidenfeld & Nicolson, New York, 1988)

Lois Gordon and Alan Gordon, *American Chronicle,* (Yale University Press, New Haven, Connecticut, 1999)

Hardy Green, *On Strike at Hormel,* (Temple University Press, Philadelphia, Pennsylvania, 1990)

Thomas Muller, Thomas J. Espenshade, *The Fourth Wave, California's Newest Immigrants* (The Urban Institute Press, Washington, D.C. 1985)

Eugene Richards, *Below the Line, Living Poor in America,* (Consumers Union, Mount Vernon, New York, 1987)

Roy Rosenzweig, Consulting Editor, *Who Built America, Working People and the Nation's Economy, Politics, Culture and Society*, (Pantheon Books, New York, 1992)

1990–1999

Scott Derks, *The Value of a Dollar, 1860-1999*, (Grey House Publishing, Lakeville, Connecticut, 1999)

Lois Gordon and Alan Gordon, *American Chronicle*, (Yale University Press, New Haven, Connecticut, 1999)

Marcia Millman, *Warm Hearts and Cold Cash*, (The Free Press, New York, 1999)

Virginia E. Schein, *Working from the Margins, Voices of Mothers in Poverty*, (ILR Press, Ithaca, New York, 1995)

2000–2012

Marc S. Miller, *Working Lives, The Southern Exposure History of Labor in the South* (Pantheon Books, New York, 1980)

Les Krantz and Jim McCormick, *Peoplepedia, The Ultimate Reference on American People*, (A Henry Holt Reference Book, New York 1996)

Barbara Ehrenreich, *Nickeled and Dimed on (NOT) Getting By in America*, (A Metropolitan/Owl Book, Henry Holt and Company, New York, 2001)

John Egerton and Bill Weems, *South*, (Graphic Arts Center Publishing Company, Portland, Oregon, 1987)

Robert E. Hannon, *St. Louis: Its Neighborhoods and Neighbors, Landmarks and Milestones*, (St. Louis Regional Commerce and Growth Association, St. Louis, Missouri, 1987)

Deborah G. Felder, *A Century of Women, The Most Influential Events in 20th Century Women's History*, (A Birch Lane Press Book, Carol Publishing Group, Secaucus, NJ 1999)

INDEX